THE YALE EDITIONS OF

The Private Papers of James Boswell

(Research Edition)

Volume 1 THE CORRESPONDENCE OF JAMES BOSWELL AND JOHN JOHNSTON OF GRANGE, edited by Ralph S. Walker, 1966

Volume 2 THE CORRESPONDENCE AND OTHER PAPERS OF JAMES BOSWELL RELATING TO THE MAKING OF THE "LIFE OF JOHNSON", edited by Marshall Waingrow, 1969

Volume 3 THE CORRESPONDENCE OF JAMES BOSWELL WITH CERTAIN MEMBERS OF THE CLUB, edited by Charles N. Fifer, 1976

Volume 4 THE CORRESPONDENCE OF JAMES BOSWELL WITH DAVID GARRICK, EDMUND BURKE, AND EDMOND MALONE, edited by Peter S. Baker, Thomas W. Copeland, George M. Kahrl, Rachel McClellan, and James M. Osborn, with the assistance of Robert Mankin and Mark Wollaeger, 1986

FRANK BRADY (1924-1986)

This volume is dedicated to the memory of Frank Brady, who died suddenly while it was in press. It shows his care in every part. His accurate and extensive learning, his sharp critical intelligence, his cheerful wit, even at times his bemused resignation, contributed to the pleasure his colleagues found in working with him. For those who knew him best, his warmth and generosity and sense of festivity created moments which were, in Boswell's words, ″as much as can be made of life″.

THE CORRESPONDENCE OF *James Boswell* WITH DAVID GARRICK, EDMUND BURKE, AND EDMOND MALONE

DAVID GARRICK

edited by

GEORGE M. KAHRL
Professor of English Emeritus
Elmira College

RACHEL McCLELLAN
Associate Research Editor
Yale University

EDMUND BURKE

edited by

THOMAS W. COPELAND
Late Commonwealth Professor of English
University of Massachusetts

with the assistance of

PETER S. BAKER, RACHEL McCLELLAN, ROBERT MANKIN, and MARK WOLLAEGER

EDMOND MALONE

edited by

JAMES M. OSBORN
Late Senior Research Associate
in English
Yale University

PETER S. BAKER
Assistant Professor
of English
Emory University

HEINEMANN · LONDON

First published in 1986

William Heinemann Ltd
10 Upper Grosvenor Street, London W1X 9PA
LONDON MELBOURNE
JOHANNESBURG AUCKLAND

0–434–83702–4

Filmset by Deltatype, Ellesmere Port
Printed in Great Britain by
St Edmundsbury Press
Bury St Edmunds, Suffolk

Boswell's Correspondence, Volume 4
General Editor: Frank Brady

THE CORRESPONDENCE OF JAMES BOSWELL WITH DAVID GARRICK, EDMUND BURKE, AND EDMOND MALONE

EDITORIAL COMMITTEE

ADVISORY COMMITTEE

GENERAL EDITORIAL NOTE

The research edition of the Private Papers of James Boswell will consist of three co-ordinated series: Boswell's journal in all its varieties, his correspondence, and the *Life of Johnson*. The undertaking is a co-operative one involving many scholars, and publication is proceeding in the order in which the volumes are completed for the press. It is expected that the whole edition will consist of at least thirty volumes.

The journal and its related notes and memoranda will be presented in one chronological sequence, but the correspondence is appearing in three kinds of volumes: *subject* volumes of letters relatable to a topic or theme, *single-correspondence* volumes (published in one-volume collections, as here, or individually, as was Boswell's correspondence with John Johnston of Grange); and *miscellaneous-correspondence* volumes of the remaining letters in chronological sequence. The *Life of Johnson* will be presented in an arrangement which will show the method and progress of its composition.

In the parallel "reading" or "trade" edition, which began publication in 1950 and has now reached its thirteenth volume, those portions of the papers have been selected which appeared likely to interest the general reading public, and the object of the annotation in that series has been to turn in towards the text.

The annotation of the research edition is turned out from the text and is intended to relate the documents to the various areas of scholarship which they are capable of illuminating: history (literary, linguistic, legal, medical, political, social, local), biography, bibliography, and genealogy. The comprehensiveness and coherence of the papers that Boswell chose to preserve make them highly useful for such exploitation.

ACKNOWLEDGEMENTS

It is unfortunately impossible to acknowledge the assistance of everyone who has helped us to prepare this edition or to indicate specifically the nature of their contributions. We can, however, list the names of those, not always mentioned in the notes, to whom we are particularly indebted for their co-operation and generosity. We are especially grateful to members of the Boswell Office staff, past and present: Irene Adams, Harriet Chidester, Tulin Duda, Ian Duncan, Elizabeth Gregory, Caterina Kazemzadeh, Marcia W. Levinson, and Marion S. Pottle. Alvaro Ribeiro also made a special contribution. H. W. Liebert, Martin Price, and Marshall Waingrow of the Editorial Committee, and Sheila Lambert and Roger Lonsdale of the Advisory Committee, read proof and returned valuable suggestions.

For other acts of literary kindness we are greatly obliged to J. C. Andrews, Stephen Astley, Clare Austin, E. G. W. Bill, W. H. Bond, D. A. Burr, C. K. Cathrow, F. C. Coulter, Tom Davis, A. Dawson, Andrea Duncan, Viscountess Eccles, John Edgcumbe, Joseph Foladare, Levi Fox, Liliane Greene, Edward Halliday, P. H. Highfill, Jr., F. W. Hilles, C. B. Hogan, A. A. Houghton, Jr., Monica Humphries, R. D. Ireland, M. E. Knapp, Andrew McClellan, Maynard Mack, Sir Robin Mackworth-Young, M. R. Mahard, Sarah Markham, Jean Munro, J. S. Owaroff, S. R. Parks, J. M. Pinkerton, David Postles, J. C. Riely, Emma Robinson, L.-P. Roy, Ben Schneider, Jr., Francis Sheppard, A. C. Short, D. M. Smith, E. M. Waith, Lucyle Werkmeister, J. I. Whalley, G. W. Williams, Laetitia Yeandle; the British Library; the Forster Collection, Victoria and Albert Museum; the Hyde Collection, Somerville, New Jersey; the James Marshall and Marie-Louise Osborn Collection, Yale University; the Pierpont Morgan Library; and Olive, Countess Fitzwilliam's Wentworth Settlement Trustees and the Director of Libraries and Information Services, Sheffield City Libraries.

Finally, we thank the staffs of Beinecke and Sterling Libraries at Yale.

F. B.

CONTENTS

LIST OF CORRESPONDENCES

[1] Letters marked with a dagger are known from various sources to have existed, but the manuscripts are not reported and no printed texts of them have been found.

LIST OF CORRESPONDENCES

PREFACE

This volume contains the known correspondence between James Boswell and three members of The Club: David Garrick, Edmund Burke, and Edmond Malone. The letters published in the present volume were set apart for considerations of space and significance and form a companion volume to *The Correspondence of James Boswell with Certain Members of The Club*, ed. C. N. Fifer, 1976. We print the texts of 150 letters, 82 from Boswell and 68 to Boswell. Thirteen of these letters are to Garrick and 16 from him; 26 are to Burke and 11 from him; and 43 are to Malone and 41 from him. Sixteen additional letters (10 to Boswell and 6 from him) of which no texts are known to be extant, receive notice under their proper dates, with as much information about their contents as could be gathered. Also included are 2 letters enclosed in Burke's correspondence with Boswell: 1 to and 1 from Henry Seymour Conway.

The editing history of this volume is complex. The Garrick section is based on a draft by G. M. Kahrl, fully revised by Rachel McClellan. The Burke section is based on a draft by the late T. W. Copeland, which has been fully revised, under the supervision of the General Editor, by P. S. Baker, Rachel McClellan, Robert Mankin, and Mark Wollaeger. The Malone section is based on a draft by the late J. M. Osborn, fully revised by P. S. Baker. The General Editor wrote the Introductions to the Garrick and Burke sections, and P. S. Baker wrote the Introduction to the Malone section.

FRANK BRADY
Chairman

JAMES BOSWELL—CURRICULUM VITAE TO 1767

1740 29 October: Born.
1753 Autumn: Matriculated at University of Edinburgh.
1759 Autumn: Matriculated at University of Glasgow.
1760 Spring: Ran away to London with intention of becoming a Roman Catholic.
Published *A View of the Edinburgh Theatre . . . Summer Season 1759.*
Published *Observations . . . on . . . "The Minor".*
1761 Published *An Elegy on the Death of an Amiable Young Lady.*
Published *An Ode to Tragedy.*
1762 Published poems in *A Collection of Original Poems by Scotch Gentlemen.*
7 March: Signed a deed in which he consented to be put under trustees of his father's choosing in case he succeeded to Auchinleck.
Published *The Cub at Newmarket.*
30 July: Passed his trials in Civil Law and received permission to go to London to try to obtain a commission in the Foot Guards.
15 November: Left for London.
1763 Published *Critical Strictures on the New Tragedy of "Elvira".*
Published *Letters between The Honourable Andrew Erskine and James Boswell, Esq.*
16 May: Introduced to Samuel Johnson.
August: Travelled to Utrecht for further study of law.
1764 June: Left Utrecht for tour through Germany, Switzerland, Italy, Corsica, and France.
1766 11 January: His mother died while he was in Paris.
12 February: Returned to London from the Continent.
11 July: Passed examination in Scots Law.
26 July: Passed advocate, printed thesis *De Supellectile Legata.*
1767 Volunteer in the Douglas Cause, about which he published a number of works: *The Douglas Cause, Dorando, The Essence of the Douglas Cause, Letters of Lady Jane Douglas.*
Published *Prologue for the Opening of the Theatre Royal.*

EDITORIAL PROCEDURES

THE TEXTS

Choice and Arrangement of Letters

The copy-text has been the MSS. of letters sent, whenever such MSS. were available; failing letters sent, we have used MS. drafts and copies.

"Not reported" in the head-notes means that, though there is evidence that the letter in question was sent, we have no evidence that any kind of MS. of it survived the sender and the recipient. "Missing" bears the ordinary narrow sense "not in the place where one would expect it to be", as "the lower half of the second leaf is missing".

Transcription

In conformity with the plan of the research edition as a whole, the manuscript documents in this edition have been printed to correspond to the originals as closely as is feasible in the medium of type. A certain amount of compromise and apparent inconsistency seems unavoidable, but change has been kept within the limits of stated conventions. A few clear inadvertencies have been set right without notice, but no change that could affect the sense has been made silently.

The editorial conventions governing the presentation of text and annotation are many, complex, and minute; only the most important of them have been stated here. Since the three correspondences included in this volume were edited separately, a few minor variations in their conventions occur and have been allowed to stand. The presentation of the Boswell-Malone correspondence of 1785 is governed by special rules (see pp. 185–88). The writers' paragraphing and capitalization is retained, as is spelling, except for certain inadvertencies which are corrected in the text and recorded in the notes.

Editorial intervention has been more active in formulary and mechanical elements than elsewhere. The following editorial conventions are imposed in the volume as a whole without notice:

Addresses. Elements appearing on separate lines in the MS. are run together and punctuated according to modern practice. Handwriting is that of the sender unless otherwise specified.

Headings. Headings are in the hand of the writer or, in the case of copies, that of the copier, unless otherwise specified.

Datelines. Places and dates are joined at the head of the letter regardless of their position in the MS., and the punctuation regularized.

Salutations. Abbreviations are expanded. Commas and colons after salutations are retained; when the manuscripts show other punctuation, colons are substituted. The first word following the salutation is capitalized.

Complimentary closes. The punctuation of complimentary closes and signatures is regularized. Elements appearing on separate lines in the MS. are run together. Complimentary closes separately paragraphed in the MS. are printed as continuations of the last line of text. Abbreviations are expanded.

Postscripts. The punctuation of the symbol P.S. is regularized, and the postscript is treated as a separate paragraph of the text.

Endorsements. Unless otherwise specified, handwriting in the case of originals is that of the recipients, in the case of drafts or copies that of the writer.

Punctuation. Periods are supplied at the end of sentences, unless sentences are concluded with a dash. Following a period, a sentence always begins with a capital. Some nonsensical periods have been read as commas, and vice versa. Where the end of a line stands in place of punctuation in the MS., commas or other punctuation have occasionally been supplied to clarify meaning. Periods following cardinals have been removed, as have periods following ordinals except in datelines, where they serve as punctuation separating elements of the date. Punctuation in lists is regularized. Question marks are read as exclamation points when required by sense.

Interlineations and marginalia. The insertion of interlineations and marginalia is explicitly indicated only in unusual cases.

Changes. Substantive additions and deletions are recorded in the notes in all cases for originals, and for drafts or copies when originals are unavailable. They are recorded only if significant in drafts or copies when originals are available.

Lacunae. Words and letters missing through a tear or obscured by a blot are supplied within angular brackets. Inadvertent omissions by the writer are supplied within square brackets.

Abbreviations, contractions, and symbols. The following abbreviations, contractions, and symbols, and their variant forms, are expanded: abt (about), acct (account), affecly (affectionately), agst (against), Bp (Bishop), cd (could), compts (compliments), Dr (Dear), evng (evening), ed (editor), edn (edition), humb (humble), Ld (Lord), Lop (Lordship), Ly (Lady), Lyship (Ladyship), obt (obedient), p (per), Q (query), r (read), recd (received), sd (should), sert (servant), Sr (Sir), wc (which), wd (would), wt (with), witht (without), ye (the), yr (your), yt (that), & (and), &c (etc). All retained abbreviations and contractions are followed by a period.

Superior letters. Superior letters are lowered, except in foreign postmarks.

Quotations. Primary quotation is indicated by double quotation marks, secondary by single. Quotation marks repeated at the beginning of each line of a paragraph are deleted, as are quotations marks around wholly italicized passages. Omitted quotation marks are supplied where one is indicated and the other missing at the beginning or end of a passage.

Brackets. Parentheses replace square brackets in the text, brackets being reserved for editorial use.

Devices of emphasis. Underlinings for purposes of emphasis are printed in italics. Words written in particularly large letters or those doubly underlined are printed in small capitals. Underlinings which seem to be meaningless flourishes are ignored.

THE ANNOTATION

Headnotes. Where more than one text is cited, the first mentioned is the one reproduced. Former printings are mentioned only if the original remains untraced. Where an address is not given, usually the letter was sent "under cover".

Footnotes. Reference titles in the footnotes are sufficiently complete for ready identification. Except where the works have been directly quoted, no source is given when the information is available in the DNB, an encyclopaedia, or other general reference works, such as gazetteers, the *British Library Catalogue of Printed Books*, Joseph Haydn and Horace Ockerby's *Book of Dignities*, and H. B. Wheatley and Peter Cunningham's *London Past and Present.* When an abbreviated source is given, the full citation either appears in a preceding note or is found in the list of cue titles which follows.

CUE TITLES AND ABBREVIATIONS

This list omits familiar abbreviations of such standard works of reference and periodicals as DNB, OED, and N & Q.

Note: All manuscripts referred to in the footnotes without mention of a repository are in the Yale Collection. Catalogue numbers are supplied in some instances to facilitate identification.

Alum. Cant. I: John and J. A. Venn, *Alumni Cantabrigienses*, Part I (to 1751), 4 vols., 1922–27.

Alum. Cant. II: J. A. Venn, *Alumni Cantabrigienses*, Part II (1752–1900), 6 vols., 1940–54.

Alum. Oxon.: Joseph Foster, *Alumni Oxonienses . . . 1715–1886*, 4 vols., 1887–88.

Annals: *Annals of The Club*, 1914.

Ann. Reg.: *The Annual Register*, 1758–1862.

Applause: *Boswell: The Applause of the Jury, 1782–1785*, ed. I. S. Lustig and F. A. Pottle, 1981.

Army List: *A List of the Officers of the Army*, 1756—.

Ayrshire: *Ayrshire at the Time of Burns*, Ayrshire Archaeological and Natural History Society, vol. v., 1959.

Bailey: James Boswell, *The Hypochondriack*, ed. Margery Bailey, 2 vols., 1928.

Bell: Robert Bell, *A Dictionary of the Law of Scotland*, 2 vols., 1807.

Binney: J. E. D. Binney, *British Public Finance and Administration, 1774–92*, 1958.

Biog. Dict.: *A Biographical Dictionary of Actors, Actresses, Musicians, Dancers, Managers & Other Stage Personnel in London, 1660–1800*, ed P. H. Highfill, Jr., K. A. Burnim, and E. A. Langhans, 1973—.

Boaden: *The Private Correspondence of David Garrick with the Most Celebrated Persons of His Time*, [ed. James Boaden], 2 vols., 1831–32.

Book of Company: Records kept by JB from 18 Sept. 1782 to 10 Jan. 1795 of his guests at Auchinleck (Hyde Collection).

Boswelliana: *Boswelliana. The Commonplace Book of James Boswell*, ed. Charles Rogers, 1874. The greater part of the manuscripts Boswell himself labelled "Boswelliana" was published in Rogers's book and is now in the Hyde Collection. The Yale Collection also contains some "Boswelliana" papers, which are cited here by catalogue number.

BP: *Private Papers of James Boswell from Malahide Castle in the Collection of Lt.-Colonel Ralph Heyward Isham*, ed. Geoffrey Scott and F. A. Pottle, 18 vols., 1928–34.

Burke's Landed Gentry: Sir Bernard Burke, *Burke's Genealogical and Heraldic History of the Landed Gentry*, various years.

Burke's Peerage: Sir Bernard Burke, *Burke's Genealogical and Heraldic History of the Peerage, Baronetage, and Knightage*, various years.

Burney Diary: *Diary . . . of Madame d'Arblay*, ed. Charlotte Barrett and Austin Dobson, 6 vols., 1904–05.

Cal. Merc.: *The Caledonian Mercury*, 1720–1867.

CG: Covent Garden Theatre.

Chapman: See *Tour*.

Charlemont Papers: *The Manuscripts and Correspondence of James, First Earl of Charlemont*, ed. J. T. Gilbert, Historical Manuscripts Commission, 12th Report, App. pt. 10; 13th Report, App. pt. 8, 1891–94.

Clifford: J. L. Clifford, *Hester Lynch Piozzi (Mrs Thrale)*, 2nd ed., 1952.

CUE TITLES AND ABBREVIATIONS

The Club: *The Club: The Founders' Era*, ed. James M. Osborn and Ardelle Short, forthcoming.

Comp. Bar.: G. E. C[okayne], *Complete Baronetage*, 5 vols., 1900–06.

Comp. Peer.: G. E. C[okayne], *Complete Peerage*, rev. Vicary Gibbs, H. A. Doubleday, and others, 13 vols., 1910–59.

Cone: C. B. Cone, *Burke and the Nature of Politics*, 2 vols., 1957–62.

Corres. EB: *The Correspondence of Edmund Burke*, ed. T. W. Copeland and others, 10 vols., 1958–78.

Corres. HW: *The Yale Edition of Horace Walpole's Correspondence*, ed. W. S. Lewis and others, 48 vols., 1937–83.

Crit. Rev.: *The Critical Review*, 1756–1817.

Croker: James Boswell, *Life of Samuel Johnson, LL.D.*, ed. J. W. Croker, 5 vols., 1831.

Davies: Thomas Davies, *Memoirs of the Life of David Garrick, Esq.*, 2 vols., 3rd ed., 1781.

Defence: *Boswell for the Defence, 1769–1774*, ed. W. K. Wimsatt and F. A. Pottle, 1959.

DG: David Garrick.

Dibdin: J. C. Dibdin, *Annals of the Edinburgh Stage*, 1888.

DL: Drury Lane Theatre.

Earlier Years: F. A. Pottle, *James Boswell: The Earlier Years, 1740–1769*, 1966.

EB: Edmund Burke.

Edin. Adv.: *The Edinburgh Advertiser*, 1764–1824.

Edin. Eve. Cour.: *The Edinburgh Evening Courant*, 1718–1859.

Ellis: Kenneth Ellis, *The Post Office in the Eighteenth Century*, 1958.

EM: Edmond Malone.

Eminent Friend: T. W. Copeland, *Our Eminent Friend Edmund Burke*, 1949.

Eur. Mag.: *The European Magazine*, 1782–1826.

Extremes: *Boswell in Extremes, 1776–1778*, ed. C. McC. Weis and F. A. Pottle, 1970.

Fac. Adv.: *The Faculty of Advocates in Scotland, 1532–1943*, ed. Sir Francis J. Grant, 1944.

Fifer: *The Correspondence of James Boswell with Certain Members of The Club*, ed. C. N. Fifer, 1976.

Gazetteer: *The Gazetteer and New Daily Advertiser*, 1735–97.

Gen. Eve. Post: *The General Evening Post*, 1733–1822.

Gent. Mag.: *The Gentleman's Magazine*, 1731–1907.

Hebrides: *Boswell's Journal of a Tour to the Hebrides with Samuel Johnson, LL.D., 1773*, ed. from the original MS. by F. A. Pottle and C. H. Bennett, new ed., 1961.

Hyde Collection: The Hyde Collection, Somerville, New Jersey.

Inner Temple: *A Calendar of the Inner Temple Records*, ed. R. A. Roberts, 5 vols., 1896–1936.

Jackson: John Jackson, *A History of the Scottish Stage*, 1793.

JB: James Boswell.

JHC: *Journals of the House of Commons*.

Johns. Misc.: *Johnsonian Miscellanies*, ed. G. B. Hill, 2 vols., 1897.

Journ.: JB's journal, Yale. Transcribed conservatively from the MS.

Journey: Samuel Johnson, *A Journey to the Western Islands of Scotland*, 1775 (*Works SJ* ix).

Knapp: M. E. Knapp, *A Checklist of Verse by David Garrick*, 1955.

Laird: *Boswell, Laird of Auchinleck, 1778–1782*, ed. J. W. Reed and F. A. Pottle, 1977.

Later Years: Frank Brady, *James Boswell: The Later Years, 1769–1795*, 1984.

Letters DG: *The Letters of David Garrick*, ed. D. M. Little and G. M. Kahrl, 3 vols., 1963.

CUE TITLES AND ABBREVIATIONS

Letters JB: *Letters of James Boswell*, ed. C. B. Tinker, 2 vols. 1924.

Letters Reynolds: *Letters of Sir Joshua Reynolds*, ed. F. W. Hilles, 1929.

Letters SJ: *The Letters of Samuel Johnson*, ed. R. W. Chapman, 3 vols., 1952.

Life: *Boswell's Life of Johnson, Together with Boswell's Journal of a Tour to the Hebrides and Johnson's Diary of a Journey into North Wales*, ed. G. B. Hill, rev. L. F. Powell, 6 vols., 1934–50; vols. v and vi, 2nd ed., 1964.

Lit. Anec.: John Nichols, *Literary Anecdotes of the Eighteenth Century*, 9 vols., 1812–15.

Lit. Car.: F. A. Pottle, *The Literary Career of James Boswell, Esq.*, 1929.

Lit. Illust.: John Nichols and J. B. Nichols, *Illustrations of the Literary History of the Eighteenth Century*, 8 vols., 1817–58.

Lond. Chron.: *The London Chronicle*, 1757–1823.

London Journal: *Boswell's London Journal, 1762–1763*, ed. F. A. Pottle, 1950.

Lond. Mag.: *The London Magazine*, 1732–85.

Lond. Stage: *The London Stage*, Part III (1729–47), ed. A. H. Scouten, 1961; Part IV (1747–76), ed. G.W. Stone, Jr., 1962; Part V (1776–1800), ed. C. B. Hogan, 1968.

LPS 83: James Boswell, *A Letter to the People of Scotland on the Present State of the Nation*, 1783.

LPS 85: James Boswell, *A Letter to the People of Scotland on . . . Diminishing the Number of the Lords of Session*, 1785.

Maxted: Ian Maxted, *The London Book Trades, 1775–1800*, 1977.

Mem.: JB's memoranda, Yale. Transcribed conservatively from the MS.

Minute Book: Minute Book of The Club (on permanent loan to the British Library).

Monthly Rev.: *The Monthly Review*, 1749–1844.

Morn. Chron.: *The Morning Chronicle*, 1769–1865.

Morn. Her.: *The Morning Herald*, 1780–1869.

Morn. Post: *The Morning Post*, 1772–1937.

Murray: John Murray, "James Boswell in Edinburgh", Diss. Yale, 1939.

Murray, *Burke*: R. H. Murray, *Edmund Burke*, 1931.

Namier and Brooke: Sir Lewis Namier and John Brooke, *The House of Commons, 1754–1790*, 3 vols., 1964.

NCBEL: *The New Cambridge Bibliography of English Literature*, ed. G. Watson, I. R. Willison, and J. D. Pickles, 5 vols., 1969–77.

NLS: National Library of Scotland.

Notes: JB's condensed journal, Yale. Transcribed conservatively from the MS.

Oman: Carola Oman, *David Garrick*, 1958.

Ominous Years: *Boswell: The Ominous Years, 1774–1776*, ed. Charles Ryskamp and F. A. Pottle, 1963.

Osborn Collection: The James Marshall and Marie-Louise Osborn Collection, Beinecke Rare Book and Manuscript Library, Yale.

Parl. Hist.: *The Parliamentary History of England from the Earliest Period to the Year 1803*, 36 vols., 1806–20.

Percy Corres.: *The Correspondence of Thomas Percy and Edmond Malone*, ed. Arthur Tillotson, 1944.

Percy's diary: Thomas Percy's MS. diary, BL Add. MSS. 32336, 32337.

Pierpont Morgan: The Pierpont Morgan Library, New York.

Poetical Review: John Courtenay, *A Poetical Review of the Literary and Moral Character of the Late Samuel Johnson, L.L.D.*, 1786.

CUE TITLES AND ABBREVIATIONS

Pol. Car.: Frank Brady, *Boswell's Political Career*, 1965.

Portraits: *Portraits by Sir Joshua Reynolds*, ed. F. W. Hilles, 1952.

Prior, *Burke*: Sir James Prior, *Memoir of the Life . . . of Edmund Burke*, 2nd ed., 2 vols. 1826.

Prior, *Malone*: Sir James Prior, *Life of Edmond Malone*, 1860.

Pub. Adv.: *The Oracle and Public Advertiser*, 1752–94.

Reg. Let.: JB's register of letters sent and received, Yale.

Roberts: William Roberts, *Memoirs of the Life and Correspondence of Mrs. Hannah More*, 4 vols., 1834.

Roy. Kal.: *Royal Kalendar*, 1767–?1893.

St. James's Chron.: *The St. James's Chronicle; or, British Evening-Post*, 1761–1866.

Scot. Nat. Dict.: *The Scottish National Dictionary*, ed. W. Grant and D. D. Murison, 1931–76.

Scots Mag.: *The Scots Magazine*, 1739–1817.

Scots Peer.: Sir James Balfour Paul, *The Scots Peerage*, 9 vols., 1904–14.

Sim: *The Poetical Works of William Julius Mickle*, ed. John Sim, 1806.

SJ: Samuel Johnson.

Somervell: Papers in the Collection of Mrs. Peter Somervell, on deposit at the NLS.

Stone and Kahrl: G. W. Stone, Jr. and G. M. Kahrl, *David Garrick: A Critical Biography*, 1979.

Tierney: J. E. Tierney, "Unpublished Garrick Letters to Robertson and Millar" in *Yearbook of English Studies*, 1975.

Todd: William B. Todd, *A Bibliography of Edmund Burke*, 1964.

Tour: In the Boswell-Malone correspondence, *Tour* is a cue title for any edition of JB's *Journal of a Tour to the Hebrides*, except for *Hebrides* (see *ante*). The following editions are cited individually: 1st ed., 1785.; 2nd ed., 1785.; 3rd ed., 1786; *Life* v (reprints 3rd ed.). Chapman: *Johnson's Journey to the Western Islands of Scotland and Boswell's Journal of a Tour to the Hebrides with Samuel Johnson, LL.D.*, ed. R. W. Chapman, 1924.

"Tour" MS.: Printer's copy for *Tour*: MSS. Yale J 33, M 132, M 133.

Univ. Brit. Directory: *Universal British Directory of Trade*, 1791–[?98].

Univ. Mag.: *The Universal Magazine*, 1789–93.

Waingrow: *The Correspondence and Other Papers of James Boswell Relating to the Making of the "Life of Johnson"*, ed. Marshall Waingrow, 1969.

West. Mag.: *The Westminster Magazine*, 1772–85.

Wheatley and Cunningham: H. B. Wheatley and Peter Cunningham, *London Past and Present*, 3 vols., 1891.

Windham Papers: *The Windham Papers: The Life and Correspondence of the Rt. Hon. William Windham*, ed. the Earl of Rosebery, 2 vols., 1913.

Works EB: *The Works of the Right Honourable Edmund Burke*, 4th ed., 12 vols., Boston, 1871.

Works SJ: *The Yale Edition of the Works of Samuel Johnson*, ed. A. T. Hazen, J. H. Middendorf, and others, 1958—.

World: *The World*, 1787–94.

INTRODUCTION TO THE BOSWELL-GARRICK CORRESPONDENCE

I

DAVID Garrick and James Boswell were two of a kind, but because of the wide difference in age and position, their similarity could hardly have been apparent when they first met in 1760. Garrick (1717–79) was near the height of his career as dramatist, co-manager of Drury Lane Theatre, and of course the most celebrated actor of his time. He had made himself rich and his profession respectable. Next to William Pitt and the King himself, he was the best-known man in Great Britain.

Boswell (1740–95) was little more than a teen-ager who, a few years earlier in provincial Edinburgh, had awakened to the pleasures of the theatre. "I used to walk down the Cannongate and think of Players", he remarked later, "with a mixture of narrow-minded horror, and lively-minded pleasure: and used to wonder at painted equipages and powdered Ladies" (Journ. 14 Dec. 1762). Here was the alternate world he was seeking to the humdrum respectability of local society, with actors as friends and models, and actresses as longed-for and, later, actual mistresses. The stage inspired his first pamphlet, *A View of the Edinburgh Theatre during the Summer Season, 1759* (1760), and he tried his hand at a Prologue for a comedy, *The Coquettes*, by his cousin Lady Houston.

When Lord Auchinleck, alarmed by his son's stage-struck progress, transferred the scene of his activities in autumn 1759 to the University of Glasgow, Boswell responded the following March by running away to London. And for three delightful months, until his father fetched him home, London lived up to every expectation, among them the opportunity to watch Garrick on stage, whom from a boy he "used to adore and look upon as a Heathen God" (Journ. 20 Jan. 1763). Unluckily, the only specific part Boswell mentions having seen Garrick play was that of Aemilius in John Home's ephemeral historical tragedy, *The Siege of Aquileia*—no extraordinary theatrical success, Boswell thought, though the principal roles were "exquisitely performed by Mr.

Garrick and Mrs. Cibber".[1] But that spring Garrick acted a wide range of his most noted parts: Ranger, Bayes, Don Felix, Lusignan, Archer, Lothario, Chamont, Sir John Brute, and Abel Drugger, as well as two of his greatest Shakespearian roles: Richard III and Benedick. And surely Boswell attended the theatre often.

Nor, typically, was Boswell content to gaze at a god from afar. Where or when he met Garrick is uncertain, but we know who introduced them: Samuel Derrick, a very small writer. Derrick's main role in Boswell's life was to initiate him "in the knowledge of the *town* in all its varieties of wits, players, ladies to which he could attain",[2] and though on his next visit to London Boswell ungratefully avoided him as "a little blackguard pimping dog" (Journ. 28 Mar. 1763), Derrick had been able to attain to Garrick (*Life* iii. 371).

When they met again in 1763, Garrick's first question was whether Lord Auchinleck had "got over the pangs" of Boswell's forsaking the law for the Guards (Journ. 13 Jan. 1763). This question and Boswell's later expression of "warm gratitude" for Garrick's "kind attention . . . from the first hour" of their acquaintance (To Garrick, 25 Dec. 1772) suggest that Garrick had been immediately assigned and had accepted the role of personal adviser.

Immured in Edinburgh the next year (1761), Boswell recalled the theatre in his *Ode to Tragedy*, in which he gave four lines to Garrick as Lear, an effort of the imagination rather than memory since Garrick had not played Lear in the spring of 1760. But as Boswell told Andrew Erskine, on the first day of his return to London (19 November 1762) he tried unsuccessfully to give substance to his vision:

> I was too late for getting into Drury-Lane, where Garrick played King Lear. That inimitable actor is in as full glory as ever; like genuine wine, he improves by age, and possesses the steady and continued admiration even of the inconstant English.[3]

[1] To Sir David Dalrymple, 22 Mar. 1760 (A. G. Hoover, "Boswell's First London Visit", *Virginia Quarterly Review*, 1953, xxix. 246).

[2] *Hebrides*, p. 416; an alternate formulation appears in *Life* i. 456.

[3] *Letters between The Honourable Andrew Erskine and James Boswell, Esq.*, 1763, p. 155.

And what did Garrick make of his young admirer? When Boswell caught up with him that winter, Garrick was not only complimentary but discerning:

> "Sir", said he, "you will be a very great man. And when you are so, remember the year 1763. I want to contribute my part towards saving you. And pray will you fix a day when I shall have the pleasure of treating you with tea." I fixed next day. "Then Sir" said he "the cups shall dance, and the saucers skip."

Naturally Boswell was overwhelmed, but he retained sufficient self-possession to return the compliment:

> I was quite in raptures with Garrick's kindness . . . [and] to find him paying me so much respect. . . . I was this day with him, what the French call *un Etourdie*. I gave free vent to my feelings. Love was by, to whom I cried, "This Sir is the real scene." And taking Mr. Garrick cordialy by the hand, "Thou greatest of men" said I, "I cannot express how happy you make me." This, upon my soul was no flattery.[4] He saw it was not. And the dear great man was truly pleased with it.[5]

But mostly that year Boswell saw Garrick in public: as Scrub in *The Beaux' Stratagem*; King Henry in *2 Henry IV*; and Alonzo in Mallet's ill-begotten *Elvira*, which so displeased Boswell and his companions, Erskine and George Dempster, that they clubbed together a sixpenny pamphlet, *Critical Strictures on "Elvira"*, in which Garrick, unlike any other reader, discerned a half-dozen "clever things" (Journ. 22 Mar. 1763). Then there was the mortification of hearing Garrick read Mrs. Sheridan's Prologue to her comedy *The Discovery* after Boswell had written one on request, only to have her husband reject it.[6] The climax of Boswell's playgoing season came when he finally saw Garrick as Lear (12 May 1763):

> So very high is his reputation even after playing so long, that the Pit was full in ten minutes after four, altho' the Play did not begin till half an hour after six. I kept myself at a distance from

[4] It must be remembered that Boswell was sending this journal to John Johnston as he wrote it.

[5] Journ. 20 Jan. 1763. James Love, who had once been Boswell's second-best friend (To W. J. Temple, 16 Dec. 1758—MS. Pierpont Morgan), was a famous Falstaff.

[6] Journ. 18 Jan., 3 Feb. 1763.

> all acquaintances, and got into a proper frame. Mr. Garrick gave me the most perfect satisfaction. I was fully moved and I shed abundance of tears.

The next morning they had breakfast, and Garrick said "he would undoubtedly go to Scotland some one summer, and play a night for each of the charitys at Edinburgh. I told him that he would be adored as something above humanity" (Journ. 12, 13 May 1763).

Boswell planned one last meeting that spring: ". . . Then go to Garrick's. Be lively and easy yet retenue and fix a night before he leaves the town" (Mem. 28 May 1763). But Garrick had vanished. It made no difference; with his "happy facility of manners",[7] Boswell had already consolidated his acquaintance with an even more finished master of the art of pleasing.

Four years were to pass before the extant correspondence between Boswell and Garrick opens. Both had spent some of this period on the Continent. Garrick returned to reclaim that ascendancy on the stage which he was to maintain until he retired in 1776. Boswell, as he said about himself, got upon a rock in Corsica and jumped into the middle of life. He re-established contact shortly before the publication of his *Account of Corsica* (1768) to report his having been pressed into the law. For a moment their relationship resumed its old tone. Garrick wrote:

> I most cordially wish You joy of having fix'd at last to the *Law*, and that You have drop'd Your Military Spirit—Be assur'd dear Mr. Boswell, when Your Youth and extraordinary Vivacity subside a little, And thought and prudence take their turns, You will be happy in your most comfortable, and honourable Establishment, and have an additional Satisfaction that You have made Your Father happy by the Choice—But my Moralizing is impertinent—I am not to talk to You *now*, as I did formerly, so You will excuse me and my honest intentions (From Garrick, 25 Nov. 1767).

When Garrick offered this exercise in conventional wisdom, did he forget that his own career defied family disapproval? In any case, the *Account of Corsica* marked Boswell's coming of age, and Garrick, who like the rest of the world found it delightful, paid due

[7] Adam Smith's compliment (see *Earlier Years*, p. 43).

praise: "Your Book is well spoken of Everywhere" (From Garrick, 8 Mar. 1768).

Youth and extraordinary vivacity were still very much evident in their next notable encounter, at the Stratford Jubilee of 1769. Boswell arrived, as he says,

> exceedingly dirty; my hair hung wet about my ears, my black suit and the Postilions grey duffle above it several inches too short every way, made a very strange appearance. I could observe people getting together, and whispering about me; for the church was full of well-drest people. At last Mr. Garrick observed me. We first made an attitude to each other and then cordially shook hands. I gave him a line I had written, to let him know I was *Incognito*, as I wished to appear in the Corsican dress for the first time they should know me. Many of those who had stared, seeing that I was intimate with the Steward of the Jubilee, came up to him, and asked who I was. He answered, "a Clergyman in disguise".

The entire occasion was an exercise in artificiality, including a masquerade ball at which Boswell appeared, much to his satisfaction, as an armed Corsican chief. He also wrote some *Verses* in that character which included the inevitable conjunction of supreme dramatist and supreme actor:

> Had Garrick who Dame Nature's pencil stole
> Just where old Shakespeare dropt it,

etc. Pleased with the compliment, Garrick read the *Verses* aloud to their elated author; he also lent Boswell five guineas to finance his return to London (Journ. 6–8 Sept. 1769). And with the identifying legend "Corsica Boswell" on his hat, an actor duly impersonated Boswell in the Jubilee pageant on the London stage, performed to satisfy those who had missed the original production (*Earlier Years*, pp. 427, 561–62).

Boswell had now turned patron. On his way to and from the Jubilee he stopped at Oxford to interview his new protégé, William Julius Mickle, who implored his intercession with Garrick for an historical tragedy, "Chateaubriant". The story of this venture appears in detail in the Boswell-Garrick correspondence, but it may help to summarize it here. Garrick's long and unpleasant experience with aspiring playwrights and their patrons had taught him to be adamant on one point: he would not put on a play he thought would fail. So in spite of Boswell's warm recommendation, he refused the play on first reading.

What Mickle lacked in talent he made up for in persistence. In rejecting "Chateaubriant", Garrick had suggested that Mickle ask his Oxford friend, Thomas Warton, to point out its defects. Mickle seized on this hint, and on 30 March 1771 Boswell was able to convey some good news to Garrick: "Mr. Mickle of oxford writes me that under the auspices of Mr. Thomas Warton and by your direction he is new-Modelling his Tragedy. I would fain hope that he May be able to Make it fit for the Stage. He Certainly is a Man of genius." In his reply Garrick ignored Mickle,[8] but Boswell returned to the charge. Mickle's play had "passed through the hands of both the Wartons" (literally true: Joseph Warton had had the play in his possession without reading it);[9] as an added, if irrelevant, inducement Boswell emphasized that Garrick had no warmer, more constant, or bolder admirer and friend than himself: "All these things considered, I would hope that Mr. Mickle who has waited long in the Antichamber, will soon be introduced, and not be shoved back by others who are more bustling and forward" (To Garrick, 18 Sept. 1771).

But Garrick was too experienced a manager to be easily manoeuvred, and when Boswell, learning that the letter just cited had been mislaid, repeated its substance (To Garrick, 27 February 1772), he got an immediate and explicit reply. Mickle was a rising poetic genius, but he showed no dramatic talent at all. Garrick had not seen the revised play and, perhaps, he added hopefully, "he has chang'd his Mind, or perhaps he has offer'd it to the Other house" (From Garrick, 2 Mar. 1772).

No such "perhaps". "Chateaubriant" had metamorphosed into *The Siege of Marseilles*, and Boswell, on his jaunt to London in spring 1772, was much taken with it in its revised form (To Mickle, 24 Apr. 1772). Garrick, however, remained as firm in conversation as in writing. He had not seen the new version but he could not be encouraging in any case (Journ. 16 Apr. 1772), and when at the end of the year he rejected it once more, Boswell acquiesced in his decision:

[8] To Garrick, 30 Mar. 1771; From Garrick, 18 Apr. 1771.

[9] Joseph Warton to Mickle, 10 June 1771 (MS. Osborn Collection), printed in part in Sim, p. xlv n.

> Mickle has announced to me your refusal of his play. You know the confidence which I have always had in your candour, and how earnestly I have inculcated it on him. I have written a letter of friendly admonition to him. Perhaps he may produce a more perfect Play (To Garrick, 25 Dec. 1772).

It was true that for some time Boswell had been trying to prepare Mickle for disappointment and had warned against a resentful reaction.[1] But Mickle was prickly by nature, and to have his long labour absolutely rejected enraged him. He would publish *Marseilles* and show the poverty of Garrick's taste and the arbitrariness of his choice of plays for Drury Lane. In his fury, Mickle advanced the curious analogy that since he had spent so much time writing and revising *Marseilles*, he was as much entitled to having his work performed as a farmer is to sell his corn in the market without hindrance from the magistrate. He proceeded, in fact, to send Garrick a proof-sheet of the Preface to *Marseilles*, which attacked him, but went no further with the printing when his new patron, Gov. George Johnstone, told him to desist. Nor did he write, as portended, a new *Dunciad* with Garrick as its hero.[2] Vengeance dwindled to a disparaging comment about Garrick in a footnote buried in his translation of the *Lusiad* (1776), and even that disappeared in the second edition.

Garrick, who admitted to a "little Gun powder" in his own disposition,[3] and whose sensitivity to criticism was notorious, reacted in anger and contempt. He wrote to Boswell:

> Your friend Mickle threatens me much. I only Wish that he would put his threats in Execution, and if he prints his play, I will forgive him. . . . I despise all that he can do, and am glad that I can so Easily get rid of him, and his ingratitude[4]—I am harden'd both to abuse, and ingratitude.
>
> You, I am sure, will no more recommend Your Poetasters to my civility and Good Offices (From Garrick, 14 Sept. 1773).

[1] To Mickle, 24 Sept., 1–25 Dec. 1772.

[2] From Mickle, 18 Nov. 1772, [between 16 Sept. and 5 Nov. 1773]; Mickle to John Hoole, 15 Nov. 1773 (W. J. Mickle, *Poems and a Tragedy* [ed. John Ireland] 1794, pp. xlii[i]–xliv); William Ballantyne to Mickle, 27 Dec. 1773 (MS. Osborn Collection).

[3] Garrick to ?Richard Cox [?May 1767] (*Letters DG* ii. 576).

[4] Garrick had taken twenty subscriptions to Mickle's *Lusiad* at twelve shillings apiece.

Boswell provoked one final reverberation of the Mickle-Garrick quarrel when he printed this last letter of Garrick's in his *Journal of a Tour to the Hebrides* (1785). Mickle's name, it is true, had been replaced by dashes, but the victim was convinced the whole world knew who was meant, and though Garrick had been dead for several years Mickle wanted to rip up all his grievances in the review of the *Tour* he was writing for the *European Magazine*. Isaac Reed, who had commissioned the review, had a good deal of difficulty in persuading him that the public would care nothing about this trivial long-past dispute.[5]

Boswell's attempt to play patron is an extreme example of the pattern of action and reaction which runs through his correspondence with Garrick. Mainly, Boswell initiates and Garrick responds: besides the unlucky Mickle, Boswell's topics include his forthcoming visits to London; reports on the Edinburgh theatre; new plays, especially by Garrick; book auctions; Johnson and his works; entreaties to Garrick to visit Scotland and to play Macbeth. Boswell is ingratiating, and Garrick genial but brief.

In spite of their disagreement over Mickle, they were at their closest during Boswell's London visit of 1772. Boswell called on, breakfasted, and supped with a "most frendly" Garrick (Notes, 10 May 1772); in turn, Garrick came to hear Boswell's maiden speech at the bar of the House of Lords, telling him that he "had done very well . . . only might have been a little more animated" (Journ. 15 Apr. 1772). As a mark of special favour, Garrick appeared early one morning at Boswell's lodgings, announcing himself as "Rantum Scantum" (harum-scarum). While they walked through St. James's Park, Garrick took off Johnson on Garrick: "Davy has some convivial pleasantry about him, but 'tis a futile fellow." Then, on the banks of the Thames, Garrick recited Macbeth's "Canst thou not minister to a mind diseas'd?", an experience that Boswell cherished.[6]

All their friends realized that Johnson's jealousy of Garrick's success made him belittle acting as a profession, and Garrick's merit in particular; Garrick, in turn, was hurt that his old teacher and friend, whom he admired so greatly, refused to give him the

[5] Isaac Reed to Mickle, 30 Nov. 1785, 2 Feb. 1786 (both MSS.—Osborn Collection). This episode is discussed in Frank Brady's "Mickle, Boswell, Garrick, and *The Siege of Marseilles*" forthcoming in the *Transactions* of the Connecticut Academy of Arts and Sciences.

[6] Notes, 8 May 1772; *Life* ii. 326; To Garrick, 29 Mar. 1773.

praise which he had earned, and which the rest of the world offered in abundance.[7] Langton asserted that there had never been so much intercourse between them as Garrick "used to profess an anxious wish that there should be"; and Percy claimed that, "as Johnson kept Garrick much in awe when present, David, when his back was turned, repaid the restraint with ridicule of him and his dulcinea [Mrs. Johnson], which should be read with great abatement."[8] But their relationship was complicated: beneath a mutual resentment there was a strong tie, like that between members of a family.

Boswell failed to grasp the nature and strength of this tie when he wrote to Garrick in autumn 1772:

> I know you will give me your kind assistance in collecting every thing that may be had with regard to your old Preceptour, of whom you allways entertain a high idea, notwithstanding the *hiatus valde deflendus* in the Preface to his Shakespeare,[9] for which I have often sincerely felt. If I survive Mr. Johnson, I shall publish a Life of him, for which I have a store of materials. I can with pleasure record many of his expressions to your honour; and I think I can explain with truth, and at the same time with delicacy, the coldness with which he has treated your Publick Merit (To Garrick, 10 Sept. 1772).

Doubtless Boswell had the best of intentions, but Garrick trusted no one but himself to treat his thin-skinned person with delicacy. He must have greeted this promise to interpret Johnson's attitude towards him with the same resentment at interference Johnson had shown when Boswell, at their first meeting, asserted that Garrick would not refuse Johnson a ticket for Drury Lane (*Life* i. 392). In his reply, Garrick ignored Boswell's officiousness.

It seems a mistake to make very much of this particular offence but, for whatever reason, Garrick now began from time to time to disparage Boswell as he had never done earlier. Both were elected to The Club in spring 1773, an acknowledgement of their status as men of letters which also created a formal bond between them. It

[7] Journ. 15 Apr. 1772; Notes, 9 May 1772; *Life* ii. 192.

[8] *Life* iv. 7, i. 99 n. 1.

[9] "Omission greatly to be regretted", i.e. Johnson's failure to mention Garrick, compounded by his complaint that collectors of old editions (of whom Garrick was by far the most noted) were not very willing to lend them for collation.

put them, however, on an equal footing, which may have been less to Garrick's taste.

Still, Boswell and Johnson's Hebridean jaunt that autumn produced the only exchange in this correspondence of much vitality. Inspired by Johnson's recitation from *Macbeth* as they crossed the blasted heath at Forres, and by the ruins of Macbeth's castle at Inverness—no matter that both were inaccurately identified—Boswell wrote:

> Look back, *Davy*, to Lichfield,—run up through the time that has elapsed since you first knew Mr. Johnson,—and enjoy with me his present extraordinary Tour. I could not resist the impulse of writing to you from this place. The situation of the old Castle corresponds exactly to Shakespeare's description. When we were there to-day, it happened oddly, that a Raven perched upon one of the Chimney tops, and croaked. Then, I in my turn repeated. . . .

(It is possible to believe, without much cynicism, that a crow would have served just as well.) Garrick wrote back with real friendliness: "Your Account of Your Journey to *Forres*, *the Raven old Castles* etc. etc. made me half Mad." He then demolished Mickle and provided an epitaph by Johnson that Boswell had asked for; he signed himself for the only time in their correspondence, "Yours Ever".[1] This letter reached Boswell at Inveraray, and he relished it as "a Pine-Apple of the finest flavour, which had a high zest indeed amongst the heath-covered mountains of Scotia" (To Garrick, 11 Apr. 1774).

And his good feelings about Garrick persisted. Writing to him in December 1775, Boswell "felt particles of vivacity rise by a sort of contagion" (Journ. 21 Dec. 1775). When he called comfortably at Garrick's house in the Adelphi one evening the following March, he found Garrick with his wife and their protégée, Hannah More, "and stayed with him till near twelve drinking port and water, and eating bread and a hampton Nonpareil. He was quite easy and gay as usual".[2]

But if Garrick could be easy and gay, he could also be very

[1] To Garrick, 29 Aug. 1773; From Garrick, 14 Sept. 1773.

[2] Journ. 19 Mar. 1776. A nonpareil is a kind of apple. Speaking of this occasion, Hannah More described "Corsican Boswell" as "a very agreeable and good-natured man" (Hannah More, *Letters*, ed. R. B. Johnson, 1925, p. 36).

critical. After Boswell, rather drunk, vigorously encored an actress during one of his performances, Garrick (Boswell wrote) "attacked me for making uproar in pit in his rhodomontade style" (Notes, 27 Apr. 1773). Garrick also scolded him for carrying tales, though Boswell promised better behaviour:

> "I'm cured of repeating to people any thing said of them which they would dislike." "I am glad of it" said he. "You had once like to have made sad mischief by that. I will not tell you between whom, as I have it in confidence." Garrick some years ago spoke to me very seriously on this subject, and I think with good effect (Journ. 11 Apr. 1776).

And leopards change their spots.

On another occasion, Garrick told Boswell he was "as drunk as *muck*";[3] then, contradictorily, a year later he "plagued" Boswell about a recent resolve to stick to water, announcing at dinner: "You shall not have the wine of our conversation. I know it will hurt my health a little. But I drink to be good companion, to be on a level with my friends. The Crows will follow you, you look so ill." Boswell was so disconcerted that he got a dispensation from his mentor, General Paoli, from water-drinking.

Garrick's sniping may have had something to do with a contest that had taken place that morning (10 May 1776) at his house, he and Boswell competing as mimics of Johnson. Hannah More gave the prize to Garrick in reciting poetry and to Boswell in familiar conversation, a fine testimonial to his ability to catch Johnson's voice, phrasing, and manner.[4] Garrick never liked rivals of any sort. And, as an undated fragment of conversation illustrates, Boswell spoke to him with a familiarity and insight that Garrick may also have resented:

> For Johnson's Life or perhaps that of Garrick Introduce Garricks love of flattery. . . . That Colman said another man has his dram and is satisfied but Garrick must have a sip every quarter of an hour. I owned to him [Garrick] that I was pleased with the flattery of a hackney Coachman. I like it so much I can drink it out of a wooden dish or a brown can. He denied. Indeed

[3] Journ. 27 Mar. 1775. "Drunk as muck" means thoroughly and disgustingly drunk.

[4] Notes, 10 May 1776; Hannah More, *Memoirs*, ed. William Roberts, 1834, i. 213. Here and elsewhere, Boswell's abbreviated words are expanded silently.

he had it in golden goblets. Lord Mansfield Lord Chatham—
Rich and exquisite flattery.[4a]

Boswell did not visit London in 1777, and his interchange with Garrick was limited to the usual pleasant letters. But their encounters in the spring of 1778 were the sharpest yet. Among a brilliant company at Sir Joshua Reynolds's after dinner (9 April), Garrick remarked to Johnson, " 'Here Sir is the great *Boswell* from *Scotland* as sublime as ever' (ridiculously)." Then they recurred to Boswell's water-drinking, and Garrick said, " 'Let it be a law of the Club either drink or we[']ll search him that he maynt have book. If he wont let wine search him, we will.' " "Nonsence", Boswell commented irritably in his journal, "As if I had book and wrote in company and could not carry in my *head*."[5] Nonsense, but Garrick seemed to have been nervous about what Boswell was recording in his journal.

Their most dramatic meeting (Journ. 24 April 1778) was also to be their last and needs to be quoted in detail, since it epitomizes the strains and resolutions of the relationship. Boswell writes:

> I went to Garrick's. Servant said "He's just going out." I said I'd see him for a little. Was shewn into his library. He had a little table and breakfast upon it. He was standing with a dish of tea in his hand. And with his instantaneous attitudinal position and smartness He without bowing or "how d ye do" Or any thing called out "I have not a minute to stop." He no doubt meant that I should lament this; and make some fawning or courting speech. . . . But (what happens to me rarely) I was prompt—and flashed upon him—"I am very glad." Then, strutting up close to the little Man and I think putting my hands on his shoulders and looking with his own tragicomick dubious cast "Don't give yourself airs." This did with him and in reply to my "Im very glad" He smartly took himself "But I'm vexed."

Next, after agreeing to stay in town an extra day to give Boswell breakfast, Garrick said, " 'Every body I find speaks well of you. But I don't.'—Said I 'Pray dont talk so. Do you know you fretted me a little at Sir Joshua Reynolds's by saying Mrs. Garrick liked me better than you did.' " But then Boswell read to Garrick

[4a] Boswelliana—M 58. See Journ. 15 Apr. 1772.

[5] Journ. 9 Apr. 1778. Parentheses added.

(presumably from a loose sheet of journal) the "high character" Johnson had recently given of him. They walked out.

> I told him "My good humour is but a sweet sauce to a pretty bitter dish. I have a good deal of *amertume.* I am as proud as Lucifer. I am an old Scot proud of being descended of Ancestors who have had an estate for some hundreds of years."

Garrick remarked that though Principal Robertson thought Boswell was a little eccentric, the Scots

> "allowed you had a good heart and talents. This he said or may I be damned. Had he spoken ill of you I should not have told you. But I thought it right to tell you this." BOSWELL. "It is benevolent to tell people such things." GARRICK. "It has been my way allways amongst freinds to *heal.*". . . He was very pleasant as we walked down the Strand arm in arm (Journ. 24 Apr. 1778).

This last image is a faithful reflection of their lively acquaintance at its best.

A few weeks after Garrick's death on 20 January 1779, Boswell wrote to Johnson: "I received many civilities from him. . . . I shall always remember him with affection as well as admiration."[6] "Civilities" does not suggest feelings of close friendship, but the affection and admiration were genuine.

In the conversational post-mortem that took place during Boswell's next visit to London, Johnson pronounced an impartial epitaph: Garrick was "diffused", a man who did not need particular friends. Yet he "was a very good man, the cheerfullest man of his age; a decent liver in a profession which is supposed to give indulgence to licentiousness", and a generous man. When Boswell, playing the sophist, questioned Johnson's eulogy of him in the *Lives of the Poets*, Johnson defended it vigorously: Garrick's death had indeed "eclipsed the gaiety of nations and impoverished the publick stock of harmless pleasure".[7]

Garrick played his final scene in Boswell's life two years later (20 April 1781) when Boswell manoeuvred himself an invitation to Mrs. Garrick's first dinner-party since her husband's death; the company included Johnson, Dr. Burney, Reynolds, Mrs.

[6] To SJ, 2 Feb. 1779 (*Life* iii. 371).

[7] *Life* iii. 386–87; *Lives of the English Poets*, ed. G. B. Hill, 1905, ii. 21.

Boscawen, Mrs. Carter, and the inescapable Hannah More. The entertainment was elegant, the conversation agreeable, "the very semblance of David Garrick" (his portrait over the chimney-piece) "was cheering". The many pleasant hours Boswell recalled with him "who gladdened life" provided a warm background to his present enjoyment, and he whispered to Mrs. Boscawen, "I believe this is as much as can be made of life."[8]

II

The correspondence between Boswell and Garrick offers a few incidental revelations, but mainly it records how they kept in touch between those meetings which Boswell sometimes preserves in sharp detail. The deeper interest in their relationship inheres in what Boswell made of Garrick as a person—to Garrick, Boswell was simply a good-humoured if occasionally irritating friend—and Boswell's portrayal of him in the *Life of Johnson*.

As a young man, Boswell had three faraway idols: Johnson, Burke, and Garrick. Johnson was to become the revered sage, spiritual father, guide, philosopher, and friend. Burke was the admired combination of intellectual, orator, and statesman. Garrick was the envied public figure, the observed of all observers; he had secured that never-wavering place in the limelight that Boswell always aspired to. But Garrick was also the paradigm of the actor, and actors fascinated Boswell. To begin with, they were a social anomaly, often celebrated and well-rewarded but not quite acceptable in society, and lax in observing its financial and sexual rules. This aspect of the profession was what aroused Boswell's eager interest as a young man. Here Garrick was an exception. Part of his reputation for respectability derived from his care to separate his public from his private life; Hannah More said she only once saw a person "of his own profession at his table".[9]

A far more mysterious and intriguing aspect of the actor's career is that he plays parts; he is someone other than himself. Early in life, Boswell learned not only that social relations

[8] See *Portraits*, p. 166; *Life* iv. 96–97.

[9] *Memoirs* i. 149. But Miss More did not meet Garrick until late in his career. Cf. Oman, p. 376.

demanded adaptation to others, a compromise of the self, but that he was more able than most to attune himself to others' feelings and attitudes (see *Earlier Years*, p. 191); the price of this flexibility was that divided perception which results from playing a part. Like most young people, Boswell tried on various roles, to enjoy an experiment, or consciously to stabilize and improve his character, or just to discover what character suited him best—identity for anyone being much a matter of imitation and learned behaviour. But even after Boswell achieved a settled identity,[1] he continued to wonder at an actor's ability to be himself and someone else at the same time.

This ability is a central topic, and Garrick the prime example, in Boswell's three essays, "Remarks on the Profession of a Player",[2] his most extended questioning of the relation of the private to the social self. "A good player", he wrote,

> is indeed in a certain sense the character that he represents, during the time of his performance; and that this is truly the case, I have been assured by that great ornament of the stage, whom I have had occasion to mention several times in the course of these reflexions.

But, according to Boswell, Johnson disagreed: " 'If, sir', said he, 'Garrick believes himself to be every character that he represents, he is a madman and ought to be confined.' " Boswell appeals to Garrick to write an essay on the subject: "as he is so fully master of it, and writes with precision and vivacity, such a performance by him would be a curious and entertaining present to the public."

A deeper and more disturbing problem now appears: an actor, like a barrister (according to Boswell), must cope with double feelings, but professional necessity is only a special instance of the dissimulation necessary in society. There is hardly a scene of social life, Boswell comments, where one does not have to work himself into the proper mood to participate. Further, "the greater degree a man is accustomed to assume of artificial feeling, the more probability is there that he has no character of his own on which we can depend, unless indeed he be born of an uncommon degree of firmness." Only a great man can assume an external

[1] See, for example, Journ. 19 Jan. 1768: "felt myself *Mr. James Boswell*, comfortable and secure".

[2] *London Magazine* (1770) xxxix. 397–98, 468–71, 513–17.

character without hurting his own. Then, too, we are transmuted into various characters according to times and circumstances. This line of thought reminds Boswell of Hume's view that men "are nothing but a bundle of perceptions". Questions about identity tended to make Boswell very uneasy, and now, having puzzled himself into a corner, he is reduced to restating firmly that the "art of a player is not dissimulation but a mysterious power of being to a certain degree the character which he represents". Garrick is the prime example, but he provides no answer to the mystery or significance of this power.

Boswell now shifts to the final important point of these essays. Dramatic performance cannot be fixed:

> There are many minute circumstances in the exhibition of a character upon the stage, which do not appear from reading the poet, but must be supplied by the player from his observation of human life. These minute circumstances may be preserved in a theatrical review.

Here Boswell echoes his constant frustration as a diarist that words express images so imperfectly:

> In description we omit insensibly many little touches which give life to objects. With how small a speck does a Painter give life to an eye. The vivid glances of Garrick's features which cannot be copied in words will illuminate an extent of sensation if that term may be used—as a spark from a flint will throw a lustre in a dark night for a considerable space arround it (Journ. 16 Sept. 1769).

The play of the human face is equally expressive and fleeting, and Garrick's, in Johnson's phrase, had "double the business of any other man's" (*Burney Diary* i. 57). More often in his writings, Boswell tries to catch Garrick's habits of speech. He picks up what he can from others. In his journal, for example, he cites Samuel Foote, a close and hostile observer, on Garrick's artificial voice, "his *aw-aw-aw*—hesitating way of speaking, which", Boswell interjects, "is indeed strange", and then adds Foote's description of him as "a man born never to finish a sentence" (Journ. 30 Mar. 1772).

But Boswell himself provides our most telling examples of Garrick's way of talking: "What! eh! is Strahan a good judge of an

Epigram? Is not he rather an *obtuse* man, eh?" (*Life* iii. 258–59). Even in a footnote Boswell is careful to recall Garrick's manner:

> Beauclerk had for a short time a pretty high opinion of [Adam] Smith's conversation. Garrick after listening to him for a while, as to one of whom his expectations had been raised, turned slyly to a friend, and whispered him, "What say you to this?—eh? *flabby*, I think" (*Life* iv. 24 n. 2).

Nor does Boswell hesitate to alter his original material if he can bring it closer to his mental image of Garrick. An impressive instance occurs in his *Journal of a Tour to the Hebrides* where he is discussing Johnson's ability to laugh at little things. He writes in his journal (23 Sept. 1773):

> I have seen him do so at a small matter that struck him, and was a sport to no one else. Langton told me that one night at the Club he did so while the company were all grave arround him; only Garrick, in his smart manner addressed him, "Mighty pleasant Sir, mighty pleasant Sir".

When Boswell was adapting the journal for publication, he took exceptional pains with this passage. First he made changes in the manuscript which passed in the first proof,[3] but then altered it again so that the published passage reads: "only Garrick, in his significant smart manner, darting his eyes around, exclaimed, '*Very* jocose, to be sure!' " Boswell is not even reaching back in his own memory to rework the phrasing; Langton told him this story. But he could see and hear Garrick in his mind; he *knew* Garrick.

The story of Garrick's long and difficult relationship with Johnson was a notorious piece of literary folklore that Boswell found highly useful in the *Life of Johnson*, where Garrick fits in easily as one of the most important foils to the hero. They had been master and pupil; they were each other's oldest friend in London; each had achieved great eminence. And, as remarked earlier, they were fond of and mistrusted each other. Their story was simple to retrace: the *Prologue at the Opening of Drury-Lane*, the production of *Irene*, the Rambler's characterization of Prospero, the falling out over Johnson's edition of Shakespeare. When irritated, Johnson might attack Garrick as an actor: "What, Sir, a

[3] "Tour" MS. p. 348; proof-sheets of the *Tour*, pp. 304–05. The intervening stages will be shown in the Yale research edition of the *Tour*.

fellow who claps a hump on his back, and a lump on his leg, and cries '*I am Richard the Third*'?" Garrick resorted to direct mimicry, "squeezing a lemon into a punch-bowl, with uncouth gesticulations, looking round the company, and calling out, 'Who's for *poonsh*?' "[4] Yet their praise of each other could be whole-hearted. Garrick, said Johnson, "is the first man in the world for sprightly conversation". Johnson, said Garrick, in wit surpasses Rabelais and all others: "You may be diverted by them; but Johnson gives you a forcible hug, and shakes laughter out of you, whether you will or no."[5]

Boswell sometimes quotes Garrick directly on Johnson: "Now . . . he is thinking which side he shall take" (*Life* iii. 24), but more often uses Garrick as a topic—"I then slily introduced Mr. Garrick's fame, and his assuming the airs of a great man"—not only to elicit Johnson's opinion of Garrick, but also to bring out Johnson's vigour of mind, the independence of his opinions, his ability to make clear discriminations, and his forcefulness and clarity of expression:

> JOHNSON. "Sir, it is wonderful how *little* Garrick assumes. No, Sir, Garrick *fortunam reverenter habet*.[6] Consider, Sir: celebrated men, such as you have mentioned,[7] have had their applause at a distance; but Garrick had it dashed in his face, sounded in his ears, and went home every night with the plaudits of a thousand in his *cranium*. Then, Sir, Garrick did not *find*, but *made* his way to the tables, the levees, and almost the bed-chambers of the great. Then, Sir, Garrick had under him a numerous body of people; who, from fear of his power, and hopes of his favour, and admiration of his talents, were constantly submissive to him. And here is a man who has advanced the dignity of his profession. Garrick has made a player a higher character" (*Life* iii. 263).

Unfortunately few meetings between Garrick and Johnson are described in the *Life*, but one deserves comment. Boswell had invited a company to dine with him at his lodgings (16 October 1769); and as they waited for a fellow guest,

[4] *Life* iii. 184, ii. 464.

[5] *Life* i. 398, ii. 231. Garrick seems to be reshuffling Pope's line: "Or laugh and shake in Rab'lais' easy Chair" (*Dunciad* i. 20).

[6] "Has respect for fortune."

[7] Shakespeare and Voltaire.

> Garrick played round him [Johnson] with a fond vivacity, taking hold of the breasts of his coat, and, looking up in his face with a lively archness, complimented him on the good health which he seemed then to enjoy; while the sage, shaking his head, beheld him with a gentle complacency (*Life* ii. 82–83).

The physical movement makes its own point, the playing around Johnson, taking hold of the breasts of his coat, as the small Garrick looks up at the gigantic Johnson. Details that suggest their long intimacy—who else would have dared to take Johnson by the lapels?—are shaded by phrases, "fond vivacity" and "lively archness", that bring out Garrick's mixture of attitudes: polite congratulation, fondness, his notorious play-acting; and the overtones of fundamental characteristics: detachment, self-consciousness, even a touch of irony.

In contrast, Johnson, abstracted into "the sage", stands virtually immobile—the fox plays round the hedgehog—but his reaction is ambiguous: is the shaking of the head a disclaimer of health or a sign that he is not deceived by Garrick's act? "Gentle complacency" at least suggests a benevolent, perhaps wary, mood. This tiny scene, which takes up only a sentence, vibrates with the past of their complex relationship while adding one more line to it. And equally it demonstrates Boswell's ability to condense complicated situations into clear, plain phrases.

In the end comes simplicity. After leaving Mrs. Garrick's on the happy occasion mentioned earlier, Boswell and Johnson looked out on the Thames from the rails of the Adelphi. Boswell recalls: "I said to him with some emotion that I was now thinking of two friends we had lost, who once lived in the buildings behind us, Beauclerk and Garrick. 'Ay, Sir,' (said he, tenderly) 'and two such friends as cannot be supplied' " (*Life* iv. 99).

What Boswell and Garrick had in common caused the friction noticeable in their later meetings. Both were intensely social beings, sharp observers and excellent mimics, actors who needed to entertain their audiences, and self-conscious individuals who were quick to criticize themselves before others criticized them. They saw life dramatically, in scenes; they were hungry for fame and fed on applause. But each as an artist was unyielding. Garrick ran Drury Lane according to his lights; he never hesitated to confront an actor, a playwright, or a patron. Boswell would compromise on almost any matter but his writing; he was grateful for help, but he made his own decisions. In one major respect they were different: Garrick tended to impose his personality on others, to attack sharply; Boswell, most obviously in the case of Johnson, let others "sink in" on him. Each achieved his goal: Garrick in the recurrent moments of theatrical triumph that consolidated his fame; Boswell in the books that not only present a hero but vivify a world.

F.B.

To Garrick,
late 1767

Not reported. Known only from DG's acknowledgement in his letter to JB, *post* 25 Nov. DG addressed his reply to JB at Auchinleck, which suggests that JB's letter to him had been written from there. JB went to Auchinleck on 13 Oct. (To John Johnston, 9 Oct.), returning to Edinburgh for the beginning of the Winter Session of the Court of Session on 12 Nov.

From Garrick,
Wednesday 25 November 1767

MS. Yale (C 1336).
ADDRESS: To James Boswell Esqr., at Auchinlech, Ayrshire.
POSTMARK: 28 NO.

Novr. 25th 1767, Hampton[1]

DEAR SIR: Tho I have been ill for some time, and busy from Morning to Night,[2] yet I cannot so far give up my Pleasures, as not to pay my Acknowledgments to You, for Your most agreeable letter[3]—I have heard often of Your Exploits abroad, and in particular, Your visit and Attachment to the great defender of his Country's Liberties, the great PAOLI![4]—I admir'd Your Curi-

[1] Hampton House, in the village of Hampton-on-Thames, some thirteen miles from London; DG purchased the house as a summer residence in 1754 (*Letters DG* i. 205 n. 4).

[2] DG also gives business and illness as excuses for not writing in letters to Marie-Jeanne Riccoboni, 6 Oct., and to the Earl of Pomfret, 7 Dec. (*Letters DG* ii. 584–85, 590). The nature of the illness is unspecified; it did not, at any rate, prevent him from acting at DL 28 Oct., 7, 11, 14, 23 Nov., 1, 3, and 14 Dec., though his performance scheduled for 18 Nov. was cancelled because DG was "suddenly taken ill" (*Lond. Stage* pt. 4, iii. 1287–99). For a record of DG's health from 1742 to 1776, see Stone and Kahrl, pp. 672–73.

[3] Although DG first met JB in 1760 and was often in his company in London in 1762–63, JB's letter is the first evidence of his having initiated a correspondence with DG. In DG's style, dashes often stand for periods; they are usually followed by initial capitals here.

[4] JB had visited Pasquale Paoli (1725–1807), leader of the Corsican rebellion against Genoa and France, at Sollacarò, Corsica, from about 21 to 29 Oct. 1765 (Joseph Foladare, *Boswell's Paoli*, 1979, pp. 28–29). On his return to the mainland shortly afterwards, JB started an elaborate

osity, and Your Spirit; and I was told at Court this day, (where I din'd with some of Your friends),[5] that[6] You would soon give Us Some Account of Corsica and It's Hero:[7] the Subject is well worthy of Your Pen and Spirit, and I shall wait with great expectation and impatience for the Production. Had I been happy enough to have Met You in my ramble abroad,[8] I shuld have had, I speak sincerely, a[9] great addition to my pleasure there: I wanted now and then a Man of fire, to kindle up my fancy, and set my Electrical Matter afloat;[10] I have often been rais'd to rapture at the remains of Antiquity, but the continuance of the fit, can only be supported by social intercourse, and, as our friend Johnson would call it, by an *animated reciprocation of Ideas*.[11]

You flatter me much by thinking my triffle at Strasburgh worth the answering[12]—You have (like a good Lawyer) made a fine plea for a bad Cause—If You Entertain'd our friend Monsr. Gayot Your time was Spent, and your Muse well Employ'd; he is a most agreeable Man, and I wish I could present my gratefull Services to him[13]—The Prince of Baden Durlach did me great honour by

propaganda campaign intended to secure British support for the Corsicans (ibid. pp. 41–43 and passim).

[5] DG was at Court perhaps at the invitation of Richard Berenger or Nicholas Ramus, old acquaintances who were both members of the Royal Household. Berenger was a Gentleman of the Horse; Ramus, as Senior Page of the Back Stairs, was in charge of theatrical productions at St. James's (*Letters DG* ii. 477, 507–08, 629; *Roy. Kal.* 1767, pp. 72, 84). He may have heard news of JB either from Alexander, tenth Earl of Eglinton, a Lord of the Bedchamber, or Sir John Pringle, Physician Extraordinary in the Queen's household (*Roy. Kal.* 1767, pp. 71, 88).

[6] MS. "and They told Me" deleted before "that"

[7] *An Account of Corsica, the Journal of a Tour to That Island; and Memoirs of Pascal Paoli* was advertised for sale in London on 12 Feb. 1768 (*Pub. Adv.* 12 Feb. p. [3]) and entered in the Stationers' Register on 15 Feb. 1768 (*Lit. Car.* p. 61).

[8] Sept. 1763 to Apr. 1765 (Stone and Kahrl, pp. 159–64).

[9] MS. "a a"

[10] Perhaps a reference to the notion—widely held in the mid-eighteenth century—that electric "fire" or "matter" (something akin to Newton's *subtil spirit*) could be "collected" by electrification and transferred to the human body, to penetrate it through the pores as some supposed or, at least, to pass over its surface (*Gent. Mag.* Nov., Dec. 1750, xx. 508–10, 537). Still others believed that "electric fire" already existed within the human body and could be kindled (thereby quickening the circulation) or expelled by electrification (Park Benjamin, *The Intellectual Rise in Electricity*, 1895, p. 503). In 1769 DG commented to H. P. Sturz that the "Heart" of the actress Mlle. Clairon "has none of those instantaneous feelings, that Life blood, that keen Sensibility, that bursts at once from Genius, and like Electric fire shoots thro' the Veins, Marrow, Bones and all, of every Spectator" (*Letters DG* ii. 635).

[11] The source of this remark has not been located; the conditional tense perhaps indicates that DG is approximating SJ's style.

[12] See Appendix 1 below.

[13] Félix-Louis Gayot (c. 1735–69)—

his Judgment, but had *I* been the Judge, I should most certainly have given the Cause against Myself[14]—

You do me great honour in desiring to hear from me now and then—I shall with pleasure Obey your Commands, and follow my own Inclinations—I most cordially wish You joy of having fix'd at last to the *Law*, and that You have drop'd Your Military Spirit—Be assur'd dear Mr. Boswell, when Your Youth and extraordinary Vivacity subside a little, And[15] thought and prudence take their turns, You[16] will be happy in your most comfortable, and honourable Establishment, and have an additional Satisfaction that You have made Your Father happy by the Choice[17]—But my Moralizing is impertinent—I am not to talk to You *now*, as I did formerly,[18] so You will excuse me and my honest intentions; and be Assur'd no One takes more delight in Your Wellfare than, Dear Sir, Your most Obedient, humble Servant,

D. Garrick

whom DG "had been much with" in Strasbourg in early autumn 1764 (Journ. 21 Nov. 1764)—served as one of six "sénateurs nobles" of Strasbourg from 1762–65 (Jacques Hatt, *Liste des membres du grand sénat de Strasbourg . . . du XIIIe siècle à 1789*, 1963, pp. 368–70, 436). "Ein damals 33jähriger vielversprechender Mann", he succeeded his father, François-Marie Gayot, as Royal Praetor in 1768 (Ingeborg Streitberger, *Der Königliche Prätor von Strassburg, 1685–1789*, 1961, p. 204). He died of consumption in March of the following year (ibid. pp. 205, 380 n. 18). JB found him "a genteel black little man, much of the Gentleman and the man of the World", who "spoke good english, tho' his accent was foreign . . . a noble fellow" (Journ. 21, 22 Nov. 1764). Gayot is mentioned in two anecdotes in *Boswelliana* (p. 234).

[14] Karl Friedrich (1728–1811), Margrave of Baden-Durlach, whom JB had met at Karlsruhe in Nov. 1764 (Journ.). The Margrave's reply of 9 Dec. 1764—the only letter JB received from him (*Earlier Years*, pp. 222–23, 279–80)—says nothing about the merit of DG's verses, but shows that he shared DG's opinion of the shops around the cathedral.

[15] MS. "And" superimposed upon "into"

[16] MS. One or two illegible words deleted before "You"

[17] JB's father, Alexander Boswell (1707–82), styled Lord Auchinleck from his position as a judge of the Courts of Session and Justiciary, wished him to become an advocate. The last time DG had seen JB was in London in 1763, when JB was pursuing a commission in the Guards (Journ. 13 Jan. 1763), but eventually JB acceded to his father's wishes and, after making the Grand Tour, "passed advocate" on 26 July 1766. JB's favourite comment on his situation, which he even repeated to George III as late as 1781, was, "I am prest into the service. . . . But I have observed that a Prest Man either by Sea or Land after a little time does just as well as a Volunteer" (Boswelliana MS. p.[90]—Hyde Collection; see also *Boswelliana*, p. 242; Journ. 27 May 1781).

[18] No doubt JB asked for DG's advice about his alternatives, the Guards and the law, more than once, but the only occasion he records is on 13 Jan. 1763. DG said that being a soldier was preferable but asked whether Lord Auchinleck was reconciled to his choice (Journ.).

To Garrick,
February 1768

Not reported. From Edinburgh. DG's letter, *post* 8 Mar., makes it clear that JB had written to DG some time after the publication of *An Account of Corsica* on 12 Feb. saying that he would present him with a copy of his book when he got to London that spring.

From Garrick,
Tuesday 8 March 1768

MS. Yale (C 1337).
ADDRESS: To James Boswell Esqr., at Edinburgh.
POSTMARK: [London] 10 MR.

March 8th 1768

DEAR SIR: Did You imagine that I could Stay till I receiv'd your most agreeable performance from Your own hand?[1]—No indeed Sir, I have more literary impatience, and regard for the Author and Friend of Paoli, than to bridle my Curiosity for a long Month! In Short I have read the *History of Corsica* with much delight, and You have done Your Friend great honor by Your Account of him—He is already rais'd Cent p. Cent in the Minds of the People, and I assure you, (for I hate Flattery upon these Occasions) that Your Book is well spoken of Everywhere. You little think that You have paid Me a great Compliment in Your Work–I will assure You, tho I have often talked of the Sweets of Panegyrick, yet I never was more flatter'd in my Life—That You should chuse my hurly burly Song of *Hearts of Oak*,[2] to spirit up the

[1] JB's presentation copy of *An Account of Corsica*, "map, calf extra", second edition, 1768, was listed, No. 296, in the *Catalogue of the Library of David Garrick . . . Sold by Auction . . . by Mr. Saunders*, 1823. It was sold by Parke-Bernet in Oct.–Nov. 1940 for $150 (Gribbel sale, pt. 1, lot 64). JB had written to DG saying that he would present him with a copy personally on his arrival in London (*ante* To DG, Feb. 1768).

[2] DG appears to have written the song *Heart of Oak* for his pantomime *Harlequin's Invasion* (Knapp, no. 449), which was first performed on 31 Dec. 1759, at DL (*Lond. Stage* pt. 4, ii. 765), though the only evidence that it was written for this pantomime comes from *Univ. Mag.* (Mar. 1760) xxvi. 152–53, where the song (with music by William Boyce) was published with the heading: "A New Song, sung by Mr.

Corsicans gave me great Pleasure! and tho I have heard it sung from North to South and East to West in England, yet I never dreamt that it would reach Corsica.[3]

Sublimi feriam Sydera vertice![4]

I saw the first copy that was printed of your Prologue, and was hurt at the shamefull inaccuracies, but rejoic'd when I saw it come forth as it should do[5]—You did my Friend Ross great honour—I hope he goes on well—He must Succeed if he will not be too lazy.[6]

Champness in Harlequin's Invasion". It does not appear in the Barton-Ticknor MS. of *Harlequin's Invasion* in the Boston Public Library (Knapp, no. 449 n.).

[3] "My good friends [the Corsicans] insisted also to have an English song from me. I endeavoured to please them in this too, and was very lucky in that which occurred to me. I sung them 'Hearts of oak are our ships, Hearts of oak are our men.' I translated it into Italian for them, and never did I see men so delighted with a song as the Corsicans were with Hearts of oak. 'Cuore di querco, cried they, bravo Inglese.' It was quite a joyous riot. I fancied myself to be a recruiting sea-officer. I fancied all my chorus of Corsicans aboard the British fleet" (*An Account of Corsica*, 1768, p. 319). "Querco" was corrected to "quercia" in the 3rd ed.

[4] "I shall touch the stars with my exalted head" (Horace, *Odes* I. i. 36, trans. C. E. Bennett, Loeb ed.).

[5] The *Prologue* was written for the reopening of the Canongate theatre (now styled the Theatre Royal), Edinburgh, on 9 Dec. 1767 under the management of David Ross, after the theatre had been granted a royal patent on 2 Sept. 1767 (Jackson, p. 72). Spoken by Ross, it introduced the first legal performance of a play in Scotland. The playgoing public offered strong opposition to Ross, who was unknown in Edinburgh, when it was discovered that the proprietors of the theatre had, contrary to their promises, hired him as manager without the public's knowledge or approval (Dibdin, pp. 144–48). Ross, though he did not know JB personally, solicited the *Prologue* because he thought JB would be sympathetic to him; and apparently it played a conciliatory role in making the reopening of the theatre a success. The *Prologue* was imperfectly printed in *Lond. Chron.* (17–19 Dec. 1767) xxii. 591; a different version appeared in *Lond. Mag.* (Dec. 1767) xxxvi. 646–47 (*Lit. Car.* pp. xxxvi–xxxvii, 222, 241).

[6] Except for his venture into management (see preceding note), David Ross (1728–90) spent most of his life as an actor. He began his career in Dublin in 1749; DG hired him in 1751 for DL, where he was an immediate success, excelling particularly in tragedy and in roles in which he played the "real fine gentleman" (Davies i. 169–70), though "laziness and intemperance" were even then beginning to limit his usefulness (Margaret Barton, *Garrick*, 1949, p. 122). In 1757 he moved to CG, where, with the exception of the three years he spent in Edinburgh, he was to remain until his acting career was brought to an end by a broken leg in 1778. It was during his stay in Edinburgh that, through Ross's initiative, the new Theatre Royal was built, by subscription, in 1768/69 (Dibdin, pp. 151–52); but the first season, 1769/70, was a failure—Dibdin (p. 152) suggests that Ross lacked the capital to hire a good company—and he returned to CG, leasing the Theatre Royal to Samuel Foote for the 1770/71 season (*post* To DG, 30 Mar. 1771, n. 6). JB, who sometimes calls him "Royal" Ross (Journ. 27 Apr. 1773, 22 Jan. 1779, 14–15 July 1785), remained on friendly terms with him after their initial meeting in 1767. He wrote to W. J. Temple, 15 Sept. 1790: "My old friend Ross the Player died suddenly yesterday morning. I was sent for

I shall with great Pleasure expect the favour of a Visit,[7] and shall reserve the best Nich in my Library for the *History of Corsica*.[8] I am, Dear Sir, most Sincerely, Your humble Servant,

D. Garrick

From Garrick,
Friday 6 May 1768

MS. Yale (C 1338).
ADDRESS: To James Boswell Esqr.

May 6th 1768

Dear Sir: Had You left me Your direction When You did me the honour of calling upon me,[1] I should have instantly paid my respects to You—And indeed I have been hurt, that I did not know what was become of You—

I am very sorry that You have been ill—I am oblig'd to go into the Country to Morrow,[2] I shall return to play the fool on Saturday Sennight.[3] You may depend, that very soon after I

as his most particular friend in town, and have been . . . busy in arranging his funeral at which I am to be chief mourner. . . . Poor Ross. He was an unfortunate man in some respects. But he was a true *bon vivant*, a most social man, and never was without good eating and drinking, and hearty companions. He had schoolfellows and friends too who stood by him wonderfully. I have discovered that Admiral Barrington once sent him £100, and allowed him an annuity of £60 a year" (MS. Pierpont Morgan). Presumably JB wrote the obituary of Ross which appears in *Lond. Chron.* (21 Sept. 1790), lxviii. 283 and in *Gent. Mag.* (Sept. 1790), lx. 864–65 (see *Lit. Car.* pp. 232, 250).

[7] JB arrived in London on 22 Mar., but no record survives of his meeting DG until the week of 15 May (*post* From DG, 6 May, n. 1; 18 May, n. 4).

[8] JB wrote to W. J. Temple on 24 Mar.: "My Book has amazing celebrity. Lord Lyttelton Mr. Walpole Mrs. Macaulay Mr. Garrick have all written me noble letters about it" (MS. Pierpont Morgan).

[1] The date of JB's call is unknown, but presumably it was before he was confined to his rooms with venereal disease about 6 Apr. (To W. J. Temple, 16 Apr.—MS. Pierpont Morgan). He remained confined until the latter half of May (Journ. 21 Apr.–16 May).

[2] DG returned to London from Hampton late in the evening of the 10th (*Letters DG* ii. 608).

[3] Princess Louisa Anne, the King's sister, died on 13 May; as a result the theatres were closed from that date until 23 May. On 9 and 10 May, *Pub. Adv.* (pp. [3, 2]) had carried an announcement that on Saturday 14 May DG would perform the part of Ranger in Benjamin Hoadly's *Suspicious Husband* by "desire of several Foreigners of Distinction" (*post* From DG, 18 May).

shall wait upon You; I have as keen inclinations as Your honor, and shall lose no time at my return to convince You of my readiness to Obey Your Commands.[4] I am, Dear Sir, Your most obedient, humble Servant,

D. GARRICK

I hope You received my last letter directed to Edinburgh.[5]

From Garrick,
Wednesday 18 May 1768[1]

MS. Yale (C 1339).

ADDRESS: To ——— Boswell Esqr., in half Moon Street, Piccadilly, London.[2]

POSTMARK: ISLEWORTH, 19 MA.

Hampton, May the 18

DEAR SIR: An Accident happen'd which Oblig'd Me to return into the Country as soon as I heard of the Princess's Death, and before I could pay my Respects to You—I shall be in London in a day or two and will certainly call upon You[3]—It is not in my Power to fix a day for the Pleasure of dining with You,[4] I am yet upon Duty in Drury Lane, and must do some Stage-honours for the Prince of Monaco etc.[5] I have a Bill in Chancery depending which takes up

[4] *Post* From DG, 18 May.

[5] *Ante* From DG, 8 Mar. Presumably JB received this letter before he left Edinburgh on 16 Mar. (Journ.).

---

[1] The year is indicated by the allusion to the death of Princess Louisa Anne and the visit to England of the Prince of Monaco.

[2] Immediately upon his arrival in London, JB put up at the Star and Garter in Bond St.; there he found his friend John Dick, British Consul at Leghorn, who secured him lodgings at Mr. Russel's, upholsterer, in Half Moon St. (Journ. 22 Mar.; To W. J. Temple, 24 Mar.—MS. Pierpont Morgan.)

[3] He was back in London by 22 May (*post* From DG, 24 May).

[4] In a letter to W. J. Temple, 14 May (MS. Pierpont Morgan), JB mentions his intention of having DG to dine with him the following week. The existing scraps of journal for May 1768 record the names of many of the famous people who came to pay their respects to the author of *An Account of Corsica*, but DG's is not among them.

[5] Honoré-Camille-Léonor Goyon-Matignon de Grimaldi (1720–95); he arrived in Portsmouth on 6 May (*Lond. Chron.* 7–10 May, xxiii. 446). On 26 May DG played one of his favourite roles, Ranger in *The Suspicious Husband*, "By Particular Desire" (*Lond. Stage* pt. 4, iii. 1334). On 18 Aug. he also played Ranger in honour of the King of Denmark, which, according to a Swiss visitor, was "a part too

all the[6] time I can Spare from the Theatre[7]—I hope You'll excuse Me when I tell You, that a Lawsuit is the Devil, and destroys all Mirth, Pleasure and Goodfellowship. I am, Dear Sir, Most truly Your Obedient Servant,

D. GARRICK

From Garrick,
Tuesday 24 May 1768[1]

MS. Yale (C 1340).
ADDRESS: To ——— Boswell Esqr., in half Moon Street, Piccadilly.

Tuesday, 24th

DEAR SIR: I went out last Sunday with a Small Suspicion of the Gout upon Me,[2] and had intended myself the Pleasure of waiting upon You, but I was in Such pain after dinner, and my foot being much Swell'd, I was desir'd to get home and be quiet—

I found your Card upon the Table,[3] and was very unhappy that I had not the Pleasure of seeing You. My Physician has order'd me into the Air, where I am going directly till Thursday, When, if I am able, I Shall appear in Ranger. I was to have play'd it on Wedy., but I am advis'd Not to Venture till the Night after. I am, Dear Sir, Your most oblig'd, humble Servant,

D. GARRICK

young for him, but which he played as faithfully and agreeably as possible" (D. W. Freshfield, *Life of Horace Bénédict de Saussure*, 1920, p. 106; *Lond. Stage* pt. 4, iii. 1343).

[6] MS. "my" altered to "ye"

[7] Though DG was frequently involved in litigation, either actual or threatened (see *Letters DG* ii. 539–40, 675–76; Sir John Hawkins, *Life of Johnson*, 1st ed. 1787, pp. 428–30; *Biog. Dict.* vi. 51–52), a search of the Chancery records (P.R.O., London) has turned up no trace of this particular lawsuit.

[1] Presumably to be dated in sequence to DG's letter, *ante* 18 May, the Tuesday preceding Thursday, 26 May, when he played Ranger (see below) in *The Suspicious Husband* (*ante* From DG, 18 May, n. 5).

[2] *Ante* From DG, 25 Nov. 1767, n. 2.

[3] JB's journal entry for 22 May records that he "drove about and called at doors"

From Garrick,
Wednesday 12 July 1769

MS. Yale (C 1342). Received 17 July (Reg. Let.).
ADDRESS: To James Boswell Esqr., at Edinburgh, Scotland.
POSTMARKS: ?13 IY, T•W.[1]

Hampton, July 12, 1769

DEAR SIR: You may depend upon giving my utmost attention to Mr. Mickle's Play[2]—It is not in my Power, were it Ever so perfect to perform it this next Winter—We are more than full—I beg leave to congratulate You upon Your Increase of Fame, honest Fame, on account of the Heroes of Corsica: We are told that we shall have the honor of Seeing him in England[3]—I confess Sincerely to You, that I had much rather feast my Eyes with the Sight of Him, than the King of Prussia;[4] Heros with, and without Principles, are to Me very different Creatures, and of very different Estimation To, my Dear Sir, Yours most Sincerly,

D. GARRICK

Pray let Mr. Mickle know the Contents of this for I Don't know where to direct to him.[5]

[1] The initials of the General Post receiver in London; in this case Thomas Wheeler, whose receiving house was in the Strand (J. G. Hendy, *History of the Early Postmarks of the British Isles*, 1905, p. 60).

[2] William Julius Mickle (1735–88), Scottish poet and playwright, best remembered as the translator of Camoëns's *Lusiad* (1776). At this time he was corrector to the Clarendon Press. Having struck up a correspondence with JB the previous year, Mickle sent JB his blank-verse tragedy "Chateaubriant", later called *The Siege of Marseilles*, and JB fell readily into the role of patron; he returned "Chateaubriant" to Mickle on 22 June, enclosing a letter of recommendation to DG, which Mickle duly forwarded with his play (From Mickle, 31 May 1768; To Mickle, 27 June 1768; From Mickle, 8 July 1768; From Mickle, 27 Mar.; To Mickle, 22 June; From Mickle to Miss Mickle, 28–29 June—MS. Osborn Collection; From Mickle 8 July; the following letters were printed in *Univ. Mag.*: To Mickle, 27 June 1768—Jan. 1809, xi. 24; To Mickle, 22 June 1769—Jan. 1809, xi. 24–25).

[3] On 8 May 1769, at the battle of Ponte Nuovo, Paoli and his army of patriots were defeated by the French, and the Corsican struggle for independence came to an end. DG could have read of Paoli's expected arrival in England in *Lond. Chron.* (8–11 July) xxvi. 38, which reports, at the end of a long account of Paoli's flight from Corsica to Leghorn aboard an English merchant ship, that "James Boswell, Esq; received a letter on Friday last from General Paschal Paoli, informing him of his safe arrival at Leghorn, and that he expected soon to be in England." Paoli arrived in London on 20 Sept. (ibid. 21–23 Sept. xxvi. 290), and JB dined with him on the 22nd (Journ.).

[4] Frederick the Great (1712–86).

[5] JB wrote to Mickle on 5 Aug., enclosing DG's letter and recommending that Mickle write to DG for suggestions for improvement. He warned Mickle to remember that "a Theatrical Monarch is a very great Prince", but implied that DG would

To Garrick,
Saturday 30 March 1771

MS. Yale (L 557). A copy in Mrs. Boswell's hand.[1] Sent 31 Mar. (Reg. Let.).

HEADING in JB's hand: To David Garrick Esq.

Edinburgh, 30 March 1771

DEAR SIR: You have good reason to find fault with me for having been so long silent. But you must kindly make allowance for your friend on account of his Changing his Condition as the Phrase is. I married a few weeks after I left you: and I find Myself as happy as I Could wish in a Wife. She brought Me a Son in September last. But that blessing was granted me only for a few hours.[2] I thank god I have a *bene praeparatum pectus*[3] and I am sure it Will give you sincere satisfaction to hear that I am as Well as you Could Wish Me, Comfortably Settled as a Lawyer and a Married Man. *Tempora Mutantur.*[4]

Mr. Donaldson tells Me he has sent you a Copy of his edition of Shakespeare. You Must know the dedication is Written by your Humble servant. I should be glad to know how you like it.[5]

eventually bring on his play. Mickle replied on 21 Aug. that DG had not responded to a letter Mickle had written to him, but that encouraged by JB's expectations he would like to start on alterations immediately so that no other play would be put ahead of his. And he asked JB to write to DG to this effect. On 19 Nov. JB transmitted to Mickle DG's decision that "Chateaubriant" would not do for the stage (To Mickle, 5 Aug.—printed in *Univ. Mag.* Feb. 1809, xi. 102–03; From Mickle, 21 Aug.; To Mickle, 19 Nov.). DG himself wrote to Mickle on 29 Nov. that the play would need "new Modelling" to be made fit for the stage, and suggested that Mickle enlist the aid of Thomas Warton (MS. Osborn Collection; Sim, p. xliv n. where the letter is misdated "Nov. 22th"; *Letters DG* ii. 723, where it is misdated "22 Nov. 1770"). See *post* To DG, 18 Sept. 1771. JB first met Mickle on 5 Sept. 1769, when he was passing through Oxford: "I found myself appearing to great advantage before this Poet, who though of a superiour genius in my opinion as a Bard, was aukward in conversation" (Journ. 5 Sept. 1769).

[1] JB had left London on 10 Nov. 1769 (*Life* ii. 110–11) and married Margaret Montgomerie (?1738–89), daughter of David Montgomerie of Lainshaw, on 25 Nov. 1769 (*Earlier Years*, pp. 441, 568).

[2] On 28 Aug. 1770 (To John Johnston, 29 Aug. 1770).

[3] "A heart well prepared" (Horace, *Odes* II. x. 14–15).

[4] "Tempora mutantur, nos et mutamur in illis", John Owen, *Epigrammatum*, 1620, bk. 8, epigram 58: "Times change and we change with them"—an adaptation of the motto designed by Matthias Borbonius (1566–1629) for the emperor Lothair I (?795–855) (*Delitiae poetarum germanorum*, ed. Janus Gruterus, 1612, i. 685; see also *Corres. HW* xxxviii. 567 n. 66).

[5] Alexander Donaldson (fl. 1750–94), as early as 1761 JB's friend and publisher, later an established bookseller and publish-

We have been kept laughing all this winter by Foote, who has made a Very good Campaign of it here.[6] Woodward has been exceedingly admired and has been a great support to the House;[7] for you know Mr. Foot's drollery Cannot entertain long in a Theatre where there is not a Variety of audiences. I hear he is not to return but has transferred his lease of the Theatre for the two remaining years.[8]

er in London. JB recorded in his London journal of 13 May 1763: "Mr. Garrick was pleased to hear that Donaldson had set up a Shop for cheap Books, and he walked out with me to the Shop, where I introduced Donaldson to him." Donaldson's publication of cheap editions in violation of the gentleman's agreement that copyright existed in perpetuity led to the famous trial, Donaldson *v.* Becket, and decision by the House of Lords against perpetual copyright (*Lit. Car.* pp. 98–100). The edition in question was brought out by Donaldson in Edinburgh in eight volumes in duodecimo, the text from *The Works of Shakespeare*, 1753, prepared by Hugh Blair mainly from the Warburton edition, 1747 (R. M. Schmitz, *Hugh Blair*, 1948, pp. 21–23). In his brief dedication to DG, JB asserted: "An edition of Shakespear is inscribed to you with such peculiar propriety, that it cannot fail of meeting with universal approbation. You, Sir, by animating his characters on the stage, have shewn the British nation the astonishing treasures of the Father of their Drama: And I even question if ever his genius was sufficiently acknowledged by the general voice till you appeared" (*Lit. Car.* pp. 86–88).

[6] Samuel Foote (1720–77), actor, playwright, manager, and mimic, made his first appearance on the Edinburgh stage in 1759. He was "the first legitimate 'star' who ever ventured so far as Edinburgh", and in fact the visit was "quite an innovation on established customs" (Dibdin, p. 153). In 1770 Foote, having taken over the lease of the Theatre Royal from David Ross (*ante* From DG, 8 Mar. 1768, n. 6), returned to Edinburgh with his entire Haymarket company—an excellent one of twenty men and eight women (Jackson, p. 78 and Appendix vii)—with the intention of employing his company during the winter season (the Haymarket was only licensed for plays during the summer months). The 1770/71 season was a financial success—Foote said that he made upwards of £1,000 by it (*post* From DG, 18 Apr. and n. 3).

[7] Before engaging with Foote to appear in Edinburgh in 1770, Henry Woodward (1714–77) had for forty years excelled as a versatile actor in a range of roles, notably as a mimic and comedian, and is said to have been second only to Rich, his teacher, as harlequin. Dibdin credits Woodward with a large share in making Foote's 1770/71 season in Edinburgh a success, and remarks that his benefit—on 2 Mar. 1771, when he played the role of Bobadil in *Every Man in His Humour*—"was perhaps the first benefit in Edinburgh that had been voluntarily supported" (pp. 155–57). *Lloyd's Evening Post* reports that the last play of the season, on 10 Apr., was also a benefit for Woodward, and that he received £260 for the two benefit nights (15–17 Apr. xxviii. 367).

[8] Foote found Scotland disagreeable: the weather was bad, the London jokes had to be explained to the local audience, and the clergy attacked him for continuing to satirize the Rev. George Whitefield, the famous Methodist preacher, after his recent death. Besides, the Scots strongly disapproved of his high style of living, which they considered insolent in an actor: when he drove down the High Street from his house on the Castle Hill in his carriage attended by liveried servants, the mob "would frequently call after the coach in derision 'there goes the *play actor*' ". So that spring he sold his lease, which had two more years to run, to West Digges and John Bland at a loss, and returned to London

His favourite Mrs. Jewel has not taken here. Her poorness of figure and aukward inanimate action disgust us much and we wonder how she has been praised so much in London.[9]

Will you My Dear Sir never favour Scotland with a Visit. Often have you talk'd of it[10] and I realy think our admiration of Shakespeare gives us a Claim to see Mr. Garrick. You have Many friends here whom you esteem and who would be happy to Shew you every Mark of attention. Your Coming among Us would endear you to a people by whom it is worth your while to be remembered. Fame has ever been your darling object. Come and add Caladonia to the dominions which your genius has illuminated. Your health would be the better of a jaunt to our Highlands and you would see Many Scenes of Wild nature Which Would please you. Pray resolve to Come.

Mr. Mickle of oxford writes me that under the auspices of Mr. Thomas Warton and by your direction he is new-Modelling his Tragedy.[11] I would fain hope that he May be able to Make it fit for

(William Cooke, *Memoirs of Samuel Foote, Esq.* 1805, i. 173–75; Murray i. 189–91, and sources cited there; Simon Trefman, *Sam. Foote, Comedian, 1720–1777*, 1971, pp. 194–95; *Memoirs of the Life and Writings of Samuel Foote. Esq; The English Aristophanes* [1777], pp. 24–27).

[9] Ann (Edwards) Jewell or Jewel (d. 1798) had been Foote's servant; he trained her and gave her roles at the Haymarket until, to his displeasure, she married William Jewell (d. 1828), the treasurer of the theatre (*Theatrical Biography*, 1772, ii. 102–06). She first appeared in Edinburgh on 14 Feb. as Polly in *The Beggar's Opera* when, according to the *Courant*, she "made a great impression by her fine vocalisation" (Dibdin, p. 156). Foote wrote to DG c. 1 Apr.: "I had a line last night from the North; Woodward, since my quitting the spot, has not once brought the expenses. Mrs. Jewell has been vastly followed" (Boaden i. 558. This letter is misdated 1 Aug. 1773: the Edinburgh season ended on 10 Apr., but Foote returned to London in March, and the "line" that he received from the North "last night" clearly refers to current performances of Woodward and Mrs. Jewell. Woodward never played in Edinburgh after 1771—Dibdin, pp. 154–55, 157, 496. Also, William Fitzherbert, mentioned in the letter in Boaden, died in 1772.). However, the criticism of Mrs. Jewell's acting style by the author of the *Theatrical Biography* endorses JB's opinion of her: "Many other requisites are necessary beside a *bawling monotony*, and *sawing of the air*, to constitute either sprightly, or sentimental comedy" (ii. 106). She continued in the theatre—at the Haymarket with additional winter seasons in Edinburgh (1773/74, 1774/75) and at DL (1775/76)—until 1781 (*Lond. Stage* pts. 4 and 5; *Biog. Dict.* viii. 161–62).

[10] For example, "he [DG] said he would undoubtedly go to Scotland some one summer, and play a night for each of the charitys at Edinburgh. I told him that he would be adored as something above humanity" (Journ. 13 May 1763). See also *post* To DG, 4 Feb. 1775, 21 Dec. 1775 and n. 10, 22 Mar. 1777.

[11] Rev. Thomas Warton (1728–90), Fellow of Trinity College, Oxford; Professor of Poetry (1757–67); Poet Laureate (1785–90).

the Stage.[12] He Certainly is a Man of genius. His Concubine is a fine Poem[13] and I beleive he will give a good translation of the Luciad of Camoens. He tells me you have been so good as to encourage that publication.[14] Our illustrious friend Mr. Johnson is going on with as Much Vigour as ever. With what dignity and force does he appear in our political disputes. I heartily wish he were in Parliament. I should like to hear him thunder in the Senate.[15]

Pray have you ever Made any use of my little matrimonial

[12] In sending JB an extract of his unfinished poem, "Prospects of Liberty and of Slavery", Mickle had enclosed "Mr. Garrick's Letters": presumably that of 29 Nov. 1769 (*ante* From DG, 12 July 1769, n. 5) and another letter of 30 May 1770 (MS. in a private collection), in which DG had promised to become a subscriber for Mickle's forthcoming translation of Camoëns's *Lusiad.* Mickle's letter to JB must have been written in July 1770 since Reg. Let. records a letter from Mickle received on 3 Aug. 1770; JB answered it on 1 Sept. 1770.

DG had written to Mickle: "Notwithstanding there are many many beautifull passages, it ["Chateaubriant"] wants dramatic Art in my opinion, and I fear it cannot be made fit for the Stage without new Modelling it—If you can Engage Mr. Warton, to whom I beg my best Love and Service to look it over, He will be best able to point out It's defects and shew you how to avoid them for the future. Some attention to the fable, and disposition of the Scenes will be of great Service to you in your future Compositions for the Stage" (29 Nov. 1769—MS. Osborn Collection).

In answer to Mickle, JB had written: "I am glad to hear you have new-Modelled your Tragedy. I hope it shall get forward. But do not trust too much to the most uncertain of all literary pursuits" (1 Sept. 1770, printed in *Univ. Mag.* Feb. 1809, xi. 103). See *post* To DG, 18 Sept. n. 13.

[13] Mickle's *Concubine* (1767), a Spenserian imitation that ran through several editions, was retitled *Sir Martyn* in the edition of 1777.

[14] Mickle published a translation of a passage from the fifth book of the *Lusiad* in *Gent. Mag.* for Mar. and followed it with the entire first book that summer, proposing to print the whole work by subscription (Sim, pp. [x]xxviii–xxxix; *Gent. Mag.* Mar., July, xli. 134, 323–24). The complete translation was published in 1776. For DG's encouragement, see n. 12 above and *post* To DG, 25 Dec. 1772, n. 17.

[15] SJ's "first and favourite pamphlet", *The False Alarm*, was published in 1770 (*Life* ii. 111 and n. 1); his second pamphlet, *Thoughts on the Late Transactions Respecting Falkland's Islands*, was published on 16 Mar. 1771, a long excerpt from it being printed in *Lond. Chron.* (16–19 Mar.) xxix. 265–66. It was withdrawn a few days later, probably by 20 Mar. (*Letters SJ* i. 249–50), and re-released 26 Mar. with a second excerpt printed in *Lond. Chron.* (26–28 Mar. xxix. 297–98; see also *Works SJ* x. 346–49). Copies of the first printing may have reached Edinburgh before the pamphlet was withdrawn, or SJ may have sent JB a copy before publication. By coincidence, SJ's friend William Strahan wrote to one of the Secretaries of State, probably Sir Grey Cooper (J. A. Cochrane, *Dr. Johnson's Printer*, 1964, p. 193), on this same day (30 Mar.) suggesting that SJ be brought into Parliament (*Life* ii. 136–39).

JB's phrasing recalls Pope:

ARGYLE, the State's whole Thunder born to wield,
And shake alike the Senate and the Field.
(*Epilogue to the Satires* ii. 86–87)

thought which Dibdin[16] set to Musick? I have made an alteration in the last line but one. In place of "*o by My Soul* My honest Mat", read "*Alas! Alas!* My honest Mat." This is More of a piece with the Context and goes better with the Musick.[17] Pray let Me have the pleasure of hearing from you soon. I offer my best Compliments to Mrs. Garrick[18] and ever am, Dear Sir, your obliged, Humble Servant, etc.

From Garrick,
Thursday 18 April 1771[1]

MS. Yale (C 1343). Received 30 Apr. (Reg. Let.).
ADDRESS: To James Boswell Esqr., at Edinburgh.
POSTMARK: [London] 20 AP.

London, April 18, 1771

DEAR SIR: I have been confin'd very near two Months with the Gout; Nothing till lately could subdue my Spirits, but I begin to discover that I am growing Old, and tho I have no Apollo at my Elbow, Yet Sickness vellit et admonuit,[2] that it is time for me to get into port, and drop my Anchor. Our Friend Foote has convinc'd Me that he has brought from Scotland a ballance of above one thousand pounds[3]—But his Account of the theatrical

[16] Charles Dibdin (1745–1814), dramatist and song-writer.

[17] *A Matrimonial Thought: To Matthew Henderson, Esq.* had been published in *Lond. Chron.* (20–22 Dec. 1768) xxiv. 599, and DG had "procured" Dibdin to set it to music in autumn 1769. When JB repeated his song to SJ on 10 Nov. 1769, SJ told him he should not swear, so JB altered the line as indicated but not for the reason as given here (*Life* ii. 110–11). Dibdin's setting has not been located.

[18] Eva Maria Veigel (1724–1822) married DG in 1749. JB described her as a "genteel agreable unaffected creature" (Journ. 21 Jan. 1763).

[1] Matters not annotated in this letter are annotated in *ante* To DG, 30 Mar.

[2] "Plucked my ear and warned me" (Virgil, *Eclogues* vi. 4, trans. H. W. Fairclough, Loeb ed.).

[3] Foote had written to DG: "By the last advice from Scotland, the balance in my favour was £1022. 6. 3*d*, which with some little matter the last week will produce, closes the account. Woodward has taken a last night for himself, and offered the public a regale that would disgrace even Bartholomew Fair, cette homme la est bien charlatan." The letter, quoted in part in *Biog. Dict.* (v. 347) from the MS. (Forster Coll. Victoria and Albert Museum, F48 F14 x. 57), is undated, but it must have been written about a week before the Edinburgh season closed on 10 Apr. (see *ante* To DG, 30 Mar. nn. 6, 7).

matters there, differs widely from Yours—He tells me (this is between ourselves) that he was much follow'd and that Woodward was deserted, and likewise that Mrs. Jewell was much approv'd of—The Good People of Edinburgh will not be satisfy'd with the Aristophanical flashes of Merriment,[4] and with the Mere Sallies of Wit, and humour, they require a substantial classical drama—*to cut and come again*, as the vulgar Saying is.[5]—

I must now Sir with the greatest Sincerity and truth beg leave to congratulate You upon Your Marriage. I have been so happy in that State, that I pity all those miserable Mortals who live out of the Pale of my Faith, and lie alone.

Felices ter et amplius
Quos irrupta tenet Copula, etc.[6]

May Your Happiness never diminish, and may Your Lady Soften Every Care, or rather may she prevent their Ever coming near You, may Your natural vigour, and[7] flow of Spirits never fail You, and that You may continue many many Years in that best disposition of Mind You are at Present—is the very sincere Wish of, Dear Sir, Your most obedient, humble Servant,

D. Garrick

I must intreat you not to mention what I have said about the theatre—I shall take care of your Song—

[4] Foote was known as the English Aristophanes.

[5] "To get a full meal." *The Oxford Dictionary of English Proverbs* (3rd ed. 1970) first cites this proverb as of 1699. It appears in DG's own *Irish Widow* (1772) I. i. See OED, Cut, x. 60.

[6] "Thrice happy and more are they whom an unbroken bond unites [and whom no sundering of love by wretched quarrels shall separate before life's final day]" (Horace, *Odes* I. xiii. 17–18, trans. C. E. Bennett, Loeb ed.).

[7] MS. possibly "of spir" with "mind" superimposed on "of" and another "mind" superimposed on "spir", all deleted before "and"

To Garrick,
Wednesday 18 September 1771[1]

MS. Arthur A. Houghton, Jr. On deposit at the Houghton Library, Harvard. A copy at Yale (L 558) in John Johnston's hand,[2] except for the heading, "To David Garrick, Esq.", the last four words of the complimentary close, and the postscript, written by JB. The copy shows no substantive variants. Sent 18 Sept. (Reg. Let.).
ADDRESS: To David Garrick, Esq., London.

Edinburgh, 18 Septr. 1771

DEAR SIR: It gives me concern to find you complaining of sickness, and talking of putting into port. I must be allowed to pay you the compliment that my father did to a valetudinary friend "Long may you complain."[3] You have had more than once the agreable experience of recovering health; and I hope these last summer months have restored you again to your usual state. You are at least happy enough to enjoy at all times the best of Horace's two requisites; for, if the *Corpus sanum* fails, you are never without the *Mens sana*.[4] You are blest with a perennial flow of good spirits and vivacity, which makes the soul live as it were in a southern climate.

Hic ver perpetuum, et alienis mensibus aestas.[5] I will not allow you to think of your Exit when so much of the Play remains, and perhaps some of the best parts of it. I please myself with the prospect of attending you at several more Jubilees at Stratford upon Avon.[6] It is true we must all look forward to the last scene; and you who have so often felt and made others feel its solemnity "must fall"[7] just like others. This puts me in mind of three Essays which I wrote on the Profession of a Player last year, and which

[1] JB's reply to DG's letter of 18 Apr., but, as DG wrote to John Home, this letter was misplaced in the Garrick household (*post* To DG, 27 Feb. 1772). JB summarized this letter in his next one, 27 Feb. 1772.

[2] John Johnston (c. 1729–86), laird of the small estate of Grange in Dumfriesshire and a writer (i.e. a solicitor) in Edinburgh, had been one of JB's closest friends since they met at Edinburgh University in 1755 or 1756.

[3] The friend has not been identified.

[4] "Mens sana in corpore sano", Juvenal, *Satires* x. 356: "A sound mind in a sound body".

[5] "Hic ver adsiduum atque alienis mensibus aestas", Virgil, *Georgics* ii. 149: "Here is eternal spring, and summer in months not her own" (trans. H. R. Fairclough, Loeb ed.).

[6] JB refers to his appearance at the Shakespeare Jubilee at Stratford in Sept. 1769, directed by DG (Journ. 6–9 Sept. 1769; *Earlier Years*, pp. 421–27).

were published in The London Magazine[8] in which I have some concern.[9] Pray have you read them? Since I am upon the serious subject of death, I cannot help expressing to one who feels as you do, that I am affected with much melancholy on the death of Mr. Gray.[10] His Elegy in a Country Church yard has been long like a part of myself; and many passages in his other Poems glance across my soul with a most enlivening force. I never saw Mr. Gray; but my old and most intimate friend the Reverend Mr. Temple Rectour of Mamhead in Devonshire knew him well. He knew his foibles; but admired his genius and esteemed his virtues.[11] I know not if you was acquainted with Mr. Gray. He was so abstracted and singular a Man, that I can suppose you and him never having met.[12]

Permit me now My Dear Sir, again to recommend to your Patronage Mr. Mickle's Tragedy, which I rejoice to hear has now passed through the hands of both the Wartons. By encouraging Mickle you will cherish a very worthy man, and I really think a true poetical Genius. Let me add that your goodness to him will be an additional obligation to your humble servant who will venture to say that you have never had a warmer a more constant or a bolder Admirer and friend at all times and in all places than himself; though you have had multitudes of greater distinction and abilities. All these things considered, I would hope that Mr. Mickle who has waited long in the Antichamber, will soon be

[7] See Pope, *Elegy to the Memory of an Unfortunate Lady*, ll. 75–78. JB quotes these lines in the last of his three essays, "On the Profession of a Player" (see next note).

[8] "On the Profession of a Player", in *Lond. Mag.* (Aug.–Oct. 1770) xxxix. 397–98, 468–71, 513–17. In the first essay, JB describes DG as an actor who "is by study and observation continually adding to his stock of science, and enriching his mind with new ideas". He calls upon DG in the second essay to explain the "mysterious power" or "double feeling" that enables an actor to "live" a character while retaining his own awareness, and so allows him to exercise moral judgement about the part he is playing. The first two essays refer repeatedly and in the most complimentary way to DG.

[9] JB had bought a one-sixth share in *Lond. Mag.* in 1769 (Journ. 14 Oct. 1769; From Charles Dilly, 15 Dec. 1778).

[10] Thomas Gray died on 30 July.

[11] JB had met William Johnson Temple (1739–96) in Robert Hunter's Greek class at the University of Edinburgh in 1755 (*Earlier Years*, p. 28). Temple came to know Gray well during his years at Cambridge, 1763–66. Temple concluded his letter of 3 Sept. to JB with a characterization of Gray, which JB published in *Lond. Mag.* (Mar. 1772) xli. 140, without Temple's name or knowledge. It was later included in William Mason's *Poems of Mr. Gray, with Memoirs Prefixed*, 1775, pp. 402–04.

[12] DG met Gray several times beginning in 1752, and later published some complimentary verses on Gray's *Odes* (*Letters DG* i. 189, 265, 268–69 and nn.; Knapp, no. 179).

introduced, and not be shoved back by others who are more bustling and forward.[13]

I have just been enjoying the very great happiness of a visit from my illustrious friend Pascal Paoli. He was two nights at Auchinleck and you may figure the joy of my worthy father and me at seeing the Corsican Hero in our romantick Groves.[14] Count Burzynski the Polish Ambassadour accompanied him. You know the Count very well; So I need not praise him to you.[15] Why have you not called on General Paoli, since I had the pleasure of presenting you to him in your morning dress "comme un Roi deguisé", and he paid you so handsom a compliment, which I dare say you have added to your cabinet of Jewels. He will be very glad to see you.[16] I had lately a kind letter from our friend Mr. Samuel

[13] In April, Mickle had prodded Thomas Warton into recommending a rewritten "Chateaubriant" to DG (Mickle to Thomas Warton, 18 Apr.—John Wooll, *Biographical Memoirs of the Late Joseph Warton*, 1806, pp. 379–80; Thomas Warton to DG, 26 Apr.—Sim, p. xlv n.); in his reply to Warton, DG virtually rejected it sight unseen. He did, however, add in a postscript, "Has the Dr. at Winchester seen it? A play underwritten by the two Wartons would certainly merit every attention" (DG to Thomas Warton, 30 Apr.—*Letters DG* ii. 734–35). Mickle took the hint and sent off the play to Thomas's brother, Joseph Warton, D.D., Headmaster of Winchester College. Joseph Warton returned it with a general encomium on Mickle's genius, but acknowledging he had been too busy to actually read the play (Joseph Warton to Mickle, 10 June—MS. Osborn Collection: printed in part in Sim, p. xlv n.). JB was literally correct, of course, in saying that the play had passed through both the Wartons' hands.

[14] Paoli, accompanied by Count Burzynski (see next note), arrived in Edinburgh on 3 Sept., fulfilling a promise to visit Scotland and JB. They were at Auchinleck from 6–8 Sept. With JB as guide, Paoli visited the Carron Ironworks, Loch Lomond, and Glasgow, and left Edinburgh for London on 12 Sept. No doubt Lord Auchinleck behaved towards Paoli as he later did towards SJ, with "the dignified courtesy of an old Baron" (*Life* v. 385), but he is supposed to have described Paoli as a "land-louping scoundrel of a Corsican" (*Life* v. 382 n. 2).

[15] Tadeusz Burzynski (d. 1773), former governor of Smolensk, Polish envoy extraordinary to the Netherlands and Great Britain, 1769–73 (S.-A. Poniatowski, *Mémoires*, 1914–24, i. 629, ii. 448; *The Weekly Magazine, or Edinburgh Amusement*, 13 May 1773, xx. 224; *Polski Stownik Biograficzny*). Nothing is known about DG's acquaintance with him.

[16] On some day between 29 Oct. and 1 Nov. 1769, JB and DG called on Paoli at his London lodgings on the spur of the moment, though DG was reluctant because he was in undress. JB's notes of their visit are condensed, partly missing, and employ bad Italian, but they indicate that Paoli told DG Italy would do justice to his merit. When DG apologized for his undress, JB remarked "cest un Roi d<éguisé>". And Paoli added that DG's fame would never die (Notes).

Although we can find no evidence of DG's having called on Paoli after their first meeting, Lady Spencer had reminded DG in Dec. 1770 that he had promised her "a dinner, and a Paoli at Hampton" (Stone and Kahrl, pp. 440–41), which suggests that there had been some contact between DG and Paoli since 1769.

Johnson.[17] He still flatters me with hopes of seeing him among "the rocks of Scotland."[18] I intend being in London next March; and promise myself much happiness with you and my other friends there, now that I am just as you all would wish me to be, as far as I can be while living in Scotland.[19] To be sure Parliament or the English bar are situations "devoutly to be wished".[20] We must look about us. Pray is there any thing in the little note of old Plays belonging to a Scots Gentleman which I left with you? He would most readily give you any that he has.[21] When you have half an hour I beg you may bestow it upon me and be assured that I ever am Your affectionate friend and Servant,

JAMES BOSWELL

I find I must transgress the ordinary bounds of a letter[22] to tell you that Mr. Donaldson[23] who published the last edition of Shakespeare is a prodigious happy man on your having inscribed him among the Freemen of Drury Lane Theatre. He is in the humour of Horace—Quod si me Lyricis vatibus inseres etc.[24] I think I may take a little crop of praise for my Dedication of the Edition, since it has had such an effect.

[17] JB had received a letter from SJ on 27 July (Reg. Let.). On the same day he wrote a letter to SJ introducing James Beattie (*Life* ii. 141–42).

[18] SJ, *London*, l. 10.

[19] That is, a settled married man and practising advocate (*ante* To DG, 30 Mar.).

[20] *Hamlet* III. i. 63.

[21] Although by 1756 DG had all but completed his great collection of early English drama, nearly half having come from the Harleian Library, he continued to fill out the collection with the assistance of such interested friends as JB, who sent him catalogues and attended book sales for him in Edinburgh (*post* From DG, 17 Nov. 1772; To DG, 25 Dec. 1772). The "Scots Gentleman" has not been identified.

[22] The postscript is written on the cover of the letter.

[23] For Donaldson, and JB's Dedication to his edition of Shakespeare, see *ante* To DG, 30 Mar. and n. 5. Presumably DG put Donaldson on the "free-list" of DL, entitling him to free admission, a privilege traditionally granted to playwrights and other authors (*Letters DG* i. 318–19, 320 and n. 3, iii. 1131 and n. 1; Alwin Thaler, "The 'Free-List' and Theatre Tickets in Shakespeare's Time and After", *Modern Language Review*, Apr. 1920, xv. [124]–136).

[24] Horace, *Odes* I. i. 35: "But if you rank me among lyric bards [I shall touch the stars with my exalted head]" (trans. C. E. Bennett, Loeb ed.).

To Garrick, Thursday 27 February 1772[1]

MS. Yale (L 559). A copy in John Lawrie's hand.[2]
HEADING in JB's hand: To David Garrick, Esq.

Edinburgh, 27 February 1772

DEAR SIR: John Home[3] read to me a passage in a letter which he lately received from you where you bid him tell me, that "the reason why I have not had an answer to my last is your having mislaid it; or what is worse, perhaps your maid at Hampton having destroyed it along with some other papers, in which case you would say in imitation of Oedipus

Her hands are guilty, but my heart is free".[4]

For my part, I can only say that if your maid through carelessness malice or otherwise, hath committed the rash and wicked action with which she is charged whereby I have been so long deprived of the pleasure of hearing from you I ought in law and justice to prevail in an action of damages against her, and should be allowed to make oath as to the *pretium affectionis*[5] which I put upon a letter from Mr. Garrick. I need not tell you that I could very honestly swear to a very high value; probably to more than your maid could well spare. If your maid be handsom and I were not a married man I would move that she should give satisfaction by delivery of her person to the Plantiff according to the Maxim of the Civil Law, *Qui non habet in aere luat in pelle.*[6]

[1] See *Ante* To DG, 18 Sept. 1771, n. 1 for matters not annotated in this letter.

[2] Fl. 1770–94. "My Clerk, Mr. Lawrie . . . is a sober diligent attentive lad, very serviceable to me, and I believe very sensible of my kindness to him. He goes to church regularly, which is rare in this loose age, amongst young men of his profession" (Journ. 30 Mar. 1773). In 1784 he had some idea of emigrating to Jamaica with his family (Reg. Let. 1 July 1784), but we do not know what became of the scheme (*Applause*, pp. 250–51 and n. 6).

[3] Rev. John Home (1722–1808), author of *Douglas*. DG rejected *Douglas* for DL, but produced various of Home's later plays. They were good friends (*Letters DG* i. 244–47 and passim).

[4] "My hands are guilty, but my heart is free", John Dryden and Nathaniel Lee, *Oedipus* III. i. 593 (last line). DG cites this quotation elsewhere—for example, in a letter to Home (*Letters DG* ii. 895).

[5] "The imaginary value put upon a subject by the fancy of the owner, or affection he had for it; damage to this extent is not given when there has been no fraud" (Bell ii. 631).

[6] "He who does not have the price in coin shall have it taken out of his hide." This maxim has not been located in the *Corpus Juris Civilis*, but it appears in Sir Edward

The contents of my last letter were a renewal of my solicitation in favour of Mr. Mickle, who has informed me that his Tragedy is altered and improved, and a request to know how you liked three Essays on the profession of a player which appeared in the London Magazine last year—and the Dedication to you of Mr. Donaldson's Edition of Shakespeare, as these performances were by your humble servant.

I hope you will take care this time, and ensure me against suffering by any disaster, whether occasioned by yourself or your maid. I mean that I hope you will favour me with a letter the moment that this comes to your hands. I intend being in London this Spring, and you know it is always one of my most pleasing motives for visiting the Capital, that I can enjoy your society.[7] I offer my best compliments to Mrs. Garrick, and ever am, Dear Sir, Your obliged friend and humble servant,

(signed) JAMES BOSWELL

From Garrick,
Monday 2 March 1772

MS. Yale (C 1344). Received 6 Mar. (Reg. Let.).
ADDRESS: To James Boswell Esqr., at Edinburgh.
POSTMARK: [London] 2 MR.

March 2d 1772, London

DEAR SIR: Had You not again favour'd me with a letter,[1] I shuld have ventur'd a random Epistle to Edinburgh—You must be known Every Where, and Where You are known, my Scribble must have reach'd You—But my Wildness was nipt in the bud by my old cursed disorder,[2] and You were spar'd for a little time more, that has pass'd, and now have at You—

Mr. Mickle Whom You so warmly recommend is a most

Coke, *2 Institutes 173* (*luet* for *luat*, *corpore* for *pelle*) as an "old rule". Coke cites it in connection with *Statute of Westminster* I, 1275, c. 9, which deals with bailiffs in default.

[7] JB arrived in London on 19 Mar. (Journ.).

[1] *Ante* To DG, 27 Feb.; also *ante* To DG, 18 Sept. 1771.

[2] A kidney stone (DG to Lord Chatham, 26 Feb.—*Letters DG* ii. 787). Note DG's later remark, "that has pass'd".

ingenious Man; but I fear from what I have seen, that his talents will not shine in the Drama—His Play before the alteration, was not in the least calculated for representation—There were good passages; but Speeches and mere poetry will no more make a Play, than planks and timbers in the dock-Yard can be call'd a Ship—It is Fable, passion and Action which constitute a Tragedy, and without them, we might as well exhibit one of Tillotsons Sermons[3]—I have heard nothing from him lately, and at present I am full for more than the Next Winter—Mr. Mickle is a rising Genius—A Successful play would mount him Still higher, but the contrary would give him a blow, that would take some time to recover. Perhaps he has chang'd his Mind, or perhaps he has offer'd it to the Other house[4]—Whatever he does, I wish him most heartily success—Genius is of no house or Country, but ought for the Sake of all, to be cherish'd by all.[5]

It gives me great pleasure with the rest of Your friends to hear that you are so happy; it is an old observation, and may be a true one, that Rakes make the best husbands,[6] however between You and Me, I think there is some risque in the Experiment, and I most Sincerely Wish Your Lady joy of her Success in the Tryal.

I must beg a favour of You, to tell me Sincerely (without saying a single word to any body, or your friendship will not be of Service) What You and the wisest folks in Edinburgh think of *Mrs. Heartly the Actress*?—Has <she> the Merit which she is said to have? <Or> is it fashion or Whim, or party to admire her <?> A Word or two of cool, just, and impartial Criticism would greatly oblige me[7]—I repeat it, let it be *cool*, for when Ever You are

[3] John Tillotson (1630–94), Archbishop of Canterbury (1691).

[4] Covent Garden, managed by George Colman.

[5] For Mickle's play, see *post* To DG, 10 Sept. n. 16.

[6] "A reformed rake makes the best husband": a common proverb in the eighteenth century. It appears in Richardson's Preface to *Clarissa*, and EB uses the argument that "the worst rakes were half reformed by becoming Husbands & Fathers" for sending out young women to Botany Bay to provide wives for the convicts ("Extracts from Mr. Burke's Table-Talk at Crewe Hall", no. 4, *Philobiblon Society Miscellanies* [ed. R. M. Milnes] 1862–63, vii).

[7] Elizabeth Hartley (1751–1824) had made her debut in Edinburgh on 4 Dec. 1771. Dibdin reports that her extraordinary beauty "had more to do with her success on the stage than any histrionic ability she possessed" (pp. 157–58; see also Murray i. 190, 194, 197, and sources cited there). JB's opinion of her is unknown. Apparently DG made other inquiries about her because John Moody, in a letter (26 July) to George Garrick, DG's brother, states that she had already been engaged at CG (Boaden i. 476–77). DG saw her there, presumably on 23 May 1774, and remarked

Engag'd, your warmth at least will keep pace with your judgment—Men of Ability are seldom very temperate, so you will excuse my Caution—I beg my best respects to Your Lady and believe me most truly, Your Oblig'd and Sincere, humble Servant,

D. GARRICK

I shall kiss your hands with pleasure in the Spring.

To Garrick,
Thursday 10 September 1772

MS. Yale (L 560). A copy. Sent 10 Sept. (Reg. Let.).

Edinburgh, 10 Septr. 1772

DEAR SIR: Let me in the first place thank you for the obliging care which you took before I left London to have my head externally improved by the addition of a handsom wig made by your own Operatour. Mr. *Gast* acquitted himself to admiration. The wig which you bespoke for me arrived in good time; and, if I may play on words, has made me look the reverse of a*ghast*, giving me indeed an air much superiour to what any other wig did, even those which I had from the celebrated *Courtier.*[1] I have not failed to do justice to Mr. Gast; and at the same time have vaunted my being equipped by Mr. Garrick's Wigmaker. This having given occasion to some pleasantry in divining for what character my wig was fashioned? My friend Captain Erskine observed[2] "to be sure for *Benedict the married man*".[3] My wife however cannot be reconciled to my wearing a wig, let it be ever so well made. I know

"a finer Creature than Mrs. Hartly I never saw" (*Letters DG* iii. 936 and nn. 1, 2).

[1]John Gast, wigmaker, is listed in the London ratebooks at a house on the east side of Rupert St., near Coventry St., from 1765–83 (information kindly supplied by Dr. Francis H. W. Sheppard, General Editor, *Survey of London*; see also *Letters DG* ii. 474). John Courtier, a "hair-merchant", was located at Great Newport St. in Long Acre (*Univ. Brit. Directory* i. 114). DG paid particular attention to appropriate wigs for his actors (James Stewart, *Plocacosmos; or the Whole Art of Hairdressing*, 1782, p. 205); he made fashionable a wig "with five crisp curls on either side" known as the "Garrick cut" (Richard Corson, *Fashions in Hair*, 1965, p. 301).

[2] The Hon. Andrew Erskine (1740–93), third son of the fifth Earl of Kellie, sometime lieutenant in the 24th Regiment of Foot, and co-author of *Letters between The Honourable Andrew Erskine and James Boswell, Esq.* 1763.

[3] *Much Ado about Nothing* I. i. 267–68.

not why it is; but women in general do not like wigs. Did every man's *strength* lie in his hair as Samson's did, the motive would be obvious and natural.

I have delayed writing to you, till I should have it in my power to comply with your desire of having a Copy of the Catalogue of Mr. Samuel Johnson's Writings drawn up by Dr. Percy.[4] As the Catalogue was communicated to me by Percy as a favour, I could not give a copy of it without his permission. This I asked by a letter to him before I left London;[5] but I did not get his answer till the other day. He however freely consents to my letting you have a copy of the Catalogue. He even says that as I contributed to it's formation, I have all the rights of an authour over it. I therefore now send you a copy; and I beg that you may be good enough to give me any additions that you know.[6] I can mention two. The Epigram on Cibber's Birth-day Odes "Great George's praise let tuneful Cibber sing."[7] And the original Epitaph on Claudy Phillips[8] which gave occasion to Mr. Johnson's fine one which I heard you repeat at the Arch-Bishop of York's,[9] and which I find is published in Mrs. Williams's Miscellanies. I wish to have the original one as a foil, and to shew how poor a hint was the occasion of a very bright sally which was in a manner extempore as Mr. Johnson and you sat at breakfast. "Davy I can make a better."[10]—I know you will give me your kind assistance in collecting every thing that may be had with regard to your old Preceptour, of whom you allways entertain a high idea, notwithstanding the *hiatus valde deflendus* in the Preface to his Shakespeare,

[4] Thomas Percy (1729–1811), D.D. For an account of his relationship with JB, see Fifer, pp. lxxix–lxxxvii. The catalogue in question is printed in full in Waingrow, pp. 5–8.

[5] To Thomas Percy, c. 8–11 May. JB left London for Scotland on 12 May (Notes).

[6] For Percy's letter to JB of 24 Aug. see Fifer, p. 16. The original list in the Boswell Papers at Yale (M 148), eight pages in all, includes the following notation: "Thus far [p. 6] I sent to Mr. Garrick with the following Note". JB's note is printed in Waingrow, p. 9 n. 3.

[7] Colley Cibber (1671–1757), actor, dramatist, and theatre manager; Poet Laureate (1730–57).

[8] Charles Claudius Philips (d. 1732), violinist.

[9] On 25 Apr. (Notes). Robert Hay Drummond (1711–76) was translated from Salisbury to York in 1761. He lived in Dartmouth St., Westminster (information kindly supplied by David M. Smith).

[10] The occasion and the verses on both Cibber and Philips were later given in full by JB in *Life* i. 148–49. Anna Williams (1706–83) lived in SJ's household. SJ's epitaph on Philips appeared in her *Miscellanies in Prose and Verse*, 1766, p. 23. See *post* To DG, 29 Aug. 1773; From DG, 14 Sept. 1773 and n. 12.

for which I have often sincerely felt.[11] If I survive Mr. Johnson, I shall publish a Life of him, for which I have a store of materials.[12] I can with pleasure record many of his expressions to your honour; and I think I can explain with truth, and at the same time with delicacy, the coldness with which he has treated your Publick Merit.[13] I had a letter from him, few days ago, informing me that he cannot come to Scotland this Autumn; but he says "I refer my hopes to another year; for I am very sincere in my design to pay the visit and take the ramble."[14]

I send you a Catalogue of Books on sale here just now. Whatever other Catalogues come out shall be sent to you; and I shall be happy to execute any commissions which you may have.[15]

I had a letter the other day from Mr. Mickle. His Tragedy in it's improved state is I understand now with you.[16] I heartily wish that it may be accepted.

[11] "Omission greatly to be regretted" (this formula occurs elsewhere, e.g. Swift's "Battle of the Books", *Prose Works*, ed. Herbert Davis, 1939–68, i. 159). JB refers to a passage in SJ's Preface to his edition of Shakespeare (1765), where SJ wrote: "I collated such copies as I could procure, and wished for more, but have not found the collectors of these rarities very communicative" (*Works SJ* vii. 105). In his journal of 15 Apr. JB remarks: "Mr. Garrick complained of a passage in Mr. Johnson's preface to his Shakespeare, in which he insinuates that Mr. Garrick (for *he chiefly* has the old editions of Shakespeare) was not very ready to communicate them. 'Now', said he, 'not only did his Black get any old Plays that he sent for, but the key of them was left with the maid, with orders to have a fire, and every convenience for Mr. Johnson.' I was sorry to find any coldness between Mr. Johnson and Mr. Garrick. They had misunderstood one another. Mr. Garrick had imagined that shewing his old Plays was a favour. I have since learnt from Mr. Johnson that his idea was that Garrick wanted to be courted for them, and that on the contrary he ought rather to have courted him, and sent him the Plays of his own accord. He denied that his Black ever got any of them." Substantially the same account appears in the *Life* (ii. 192) with a significant additional sentence (see below, n. 13).

[12] So far as we know, this is the first time JB had told anyone that he planned to write a life of SJ.

[13] JB illustrates SJ's varying opinions of DG copiously in the *Life*. On this specific point he adds to what has already been quoted (n. 11 above): "I found Johnson's notion was, that Garrick wanted to be courted for them [plays], and that, on the contrary, Garrick should have courted him, and sent him the plays of his own accord. But, indeed, considering the slovenly and careless manner in which books were treated by Johnson, it could not be expected that scarce and valuable editions should have been lent to him" (ii. 192).

[14] From SJ, 31 Aug. (printed in *Life* ii. 201–02); JB received it on 4 Sept. (Reg. Let.).

[15] MS. "shall shall"

[16] Mickle's letter to JB has not been reported. In his letter to Thomas Warton mentioned earlier (*ante* To DG, 18 Sept. 1771, n. 13), DG wrote that Mickle's play "with some poetical merit, had no dramatic interest; and in my opinion the very names, and that particularly (if I remember right) of the principal character was very un-

I offer my best compliments to Mrs. Garrick, and I ever am with sincere regard, Dear Sir, your obliged friend and humble servant.

From Garrick,
Tuesday 17 November 1772

MS. Yale (C 1346). Received 21 Nov. (Reg. Let.).
ADDRESS: To James Boswell Esqr. at Edinburgh, Scotland.
POSTMARK: [London] 17 NO.

Novr. 17th 1772

MY DEAR SIR: Many thanks to you for Your kind remembrance of Me, and the Catalogues[1]—Your list of Johnson's Works was most agreeable, tho incorrect and incompleat—I will tell you in What when I see You, in the mean time let me hint that You have omitted among his Works the famous *Prologue* which I Spoke, when I first open'd Drury Lane Theatre as a Manager.[2] We go on this Season very briskly—A Farce call'd the *Irish Widow* has had great Success,[3] and will I suppose if taken care of, make you laugh in Scotland—We have a Play call'd the *Duel* now in Rehearsal and

couth, and ill calculated for an English tragedy" (DG to Thomas Warton, 30 Apr. 1771—*Letters DG* ii. 734–35). Presumably this thunderstroke occasioned the metamorphosis of "Chateaubriant" (Osborn Collection) into *The Siege of Marseilles* (published in W. J. Mickle, *Poems and a Tragedy* [ed. John Ireland] 1794). The main character is now called Raymond, and a comparison of the MS. of the first three acts and part of the fourth of "Chateaubriant" with *The Siege of Marseilles* shows many changes. No evidence survives to show how many changes had been made by this time.

Mickle had acquired a new patron in his relation Gov. George Johnstone, a friend of DG. According to Mickle, Johnstone promised him in winter 1772 that his play would be brought on next year (Mickle to William Crowe, 19 Feb.—BL Add. MSS. 28,167 f. 64). JB read the new version of the play "with great pleasure" in April and said that all his endeavours should "be sincerely exerted to second the more powerful interest of Governour Johnstone" (To Mickle, 24 Apr.). But only two weeks after the present letter, JB was trying to prepare Mickle for rejection of his play (To Mickle, 24 Sept.).

As JB learned shortly afterwards, DG refused the play once more, though urged by Johnstone to accept it. Johnstone then took the play to Scotland and John Home "at his desire made some alterations in it. It was returned to Garrick and again absolutely refused by him" (From Mickle, 18 Nov.).

[1] DG is referring to the catalogue of SJ's works (*ante* To DG, 10 Sept. and nn. 4, 6) and to the auction catalogue of the Edinburgh bookseller John Bell (*post* To DG, 25 Dec. and n. 3).

[2] On 15 Sept. 1747. Actually the *Prologue* is included in JB's list (M 148, p. [1]); see *post* To DG, 25 Dec.

[3] DG's comedy, reminiscent of Molière's

written by Mr. O'brien who formerly belong'd to us—It is an interesting Story and very pathetick.[4]

Sir Thos. Mills[5] has this Moment told me that *Serjeant Glynn*[6] is chosen Recorder of the City and that Mr. Bearcroft lost it but by ONE.[7] Our Friend Donaldson, I hear, has had a perpetual Injunction upon him from Chancery not to print some English books; I fear his Situation is not a desireable one, and must End disagreeably with all the English Booksellers against him.[8] I must

Le Mariage forcé, retained its popularity well into the nineteenth century (E. P. Stein, *David Garrick, Dramatist*, 1938, pp. 95–102). DG claimed to have written *The Irish Widow* "in less than a Week" (*Letters DG* ii. 846), designing the part of the Widow Brady—one of his best breeches and dialect parts (Stein, pp. 99–100)—especially for Mrs. Barry, to whom the play is dedicated. It was first performed on 23 Oct. Reviews of the play and the performance were mixed: *Lond. Stage* (pt. 4, iii. 1665), quoting Hopkins's diary, says it was "well perform'd and met with great Applause", but *Lond. Mag.* (Oct. 1772, xli. 458–60) called it "tedious, tame, and disgusting. . . . not worthy of any man of genius".

[4] William O'Brien (d. 1815). Earlier in the year, on 15 Apr., at a breakfast party at DG's, JB met "Mr. obrien formerly the Player who since his marriage with Lady Susan Strångeways, is quite *the fine man about town.* I thought him agreable. His foppishness appeared to be only vivacity and neatness" (Journ.). In 1763 JB had described him as "a lively little fellow; but priggish" (Journ. 13 May). For *The Duel*, see *post* To DG, 25 Dec. n. 6.

[5] Sir Thomas Mills (d. 1793) was born in Perth—a fact that Lord Glenbervie uses to refute the rumour that Mills was a natural son of Lord Mansfield. Mills served with distinction in the French and Indian War, was town adjutant of Quebec in 1762, and was appointed Receiver General on the Council of the Province of Quebec, 30 June 1766 (*Eur. Mag.* Mar. 1793, xxiii. 240; Sylvester Douglas, Lord Glenbervie, *Diaries*, ed. Francis Bickley, 1928, ii. 77; *Documents Relating to the Constitutional History of Canada, 1759–1791*, ed. Adam Shortt and A. G. Doughty, 1907, pp. 37, 195). Returning to England in 1767, he spent the next twenty years living "at a vast expence without any visible means" (*Satirical Poems . . . by William Mason with Notes by Horace Walpole*, ed. Paget Toynbee, 1926, p. 117), frequenting such establishments as the British Coffee-house, where he made the acquaintance of "men of the first eminence for their talents", DG among them (Richard Cumberland, *Memoirs*, 1807, i. 343–44). Towards the end of his life DG was on sufficiently intimate terms with Mills to solicit his influence with Mansfield for friends and neighbours (*Letters DG* iii. 1130, 1182). John Baker attests to Mills's interest in elections (*Diary*, ed. P. C. Yorke, 1931, pp. 405–06). He was knighted in 1772 (W. A. Shaw, *The Knights of England*, 1906, ii. 293). For Mills's later career, see *Letters DG* ii. 828 n. 4 and references cited there.

[6] John Glynn (1722–79), serjeant-at-law and M.P. for Middlesex (1768–79), chiefly remembered as a defender of John Wilkes in various political causes.

[7] Edward Bearcroft (1737–96), M.P. for Hindon (1784–90) and Saltash (1790–96); admitted to the Inner Temple in 1754, K.C. and bencher in 1772, Chief Justice of Chester in 1788 (*Inner Temple* v. 281; *Alum. Cant.*; Namier and Brooke ii. 70). The vote on the Recordership of London, with all the aldermen present, was thirteen for Glynn, twelve for Bearcroft, and one for Hyde, the senior city counsel (DNB, s.v. Glynn).

[8] For the famous case which ensued (still the basis of British copyright law) and JB's part in it, see *Lit. Car.* pp. 98–101. For Donaldson, see *ante* To DG, 30 Mar. 1771 and 18 Sept. 1771.

now look at my Catalogue for 5 minutes, and I have not more time, for the last Bell is expected,[9] and I shall be out of time for the Sale if I don't write to Night—So believe me tho in haste, with great truth most Sincerely yours,

D. GARRICK

In the first Night's Sale among the Quartos—No. 53—*Belezze del Furioso di Ariosto*[10]—Don't let it go for a few Shillings more or less—Night 3d No. 256 Histoire Maccaronique 2 Vol's.[11]—Give any thing in reason—I have not a moment more or I shall lose the Post so adieu!—

To Garrick,
Friday 25 December 1772[1]

MS. Yale (L 561). A copy, including signature, in Lawrie's hand. Sent 26 Dec. (Reg. Let.).
HEADING: To David Garrick Esq.

Edinburgh, 25 Decer. 1772

MY DEAR SIR: Most sincerely do I wish you and Mrs. Garrick the compliments of the season. You are indeed the happiest couple I know. In your family there is *ver perpetuum.*[2]

I send you *Bellezze del Furioso di Ariosto* which cost four shillings. *Histoire Maccaronique* went higher than I thought it was worth.[3] I enclose a new Catalogue where you have the prices marked, and if you have any Commns. I shall readily execute them. I thank you

[9] The bell rung by the postman collecting the mail.

[10] Orazio di Toscanella, *Bellezze del Furioso di M. Lodovico Ariosto*, Venice, 1574. A copy in the Beinecke Library at Yale contains DG's bookplate and a notice in the back which indicates that it was bought at Dr. Malden's sale in 1858, and that Malden had bought the book at the sale after Mrs. Garrick's death. See *post* To DG, 25 Dec. and 29 Mar. 1773. The book in question, however, is not listed in the sale catalogue of DG's library, 1823; the foreword of the catalogue states: "Towards the conclusion of her protracted life, Mrs. Garrick presented the greater part of the Greek and Latin Classics, together with her numerous and highly valuable Italian books, to Christopher Philip Garrick, Esq., the only son of Mr. Carrington Garrick", DG's nephew.

[11] [Teofilo Folengo] *Histoire maccaronique de Merlin Coccaie, prototype de Rabelais*, Paris, 2 vols. 1606.

[1] *Ante* From DG, 17 Nov. clarifies some of the allusions in this letter.

[2] "Perpetuum ver est", Ovid, *Metamorphoses* v. 391: "There is everlasting spring."

[3] JB attended an auction held by John Bell, bookseller, on Tuesday 24 Nov., the auction having begun the previous day (Notes; *Cal. Merc.* 21 Nov. p. [3]).

for your great civilities to my cousen who delivered my last packet.[4] Indeed your kind attention to me from the first hour of our acquaintance has been remarkable. I am much flattered by it and allways retain a warm gratitude.

There must have been a mistake in transcribing the copy of my List of Johnson's works which I sent to you; for the Noble Prologue at your opening Drury Lane Theatre is not omitted in my list. It is a *Chef d'oeuvre*, and does great honour to our illustrious friend. When we meet, I shall without ceremony trouble You to give me all of him that I want. Our friend Langton was a good while [here] this season. I got many *Johnsoniana* from him.[5]

I rejoice that *your House* goes on well. You told me the *Duel* was very *pathetick*. It seems its fate has been so.[6] We are getting quite into the taste of the *Comedie larmoyante*.[7] It is proper that authours should be kept in due tone for it, by having their feelings affected. Was it not rather playing at *Cross Purposes* in Obrien to bring on a peice at each of the rival houses?[8] He can just say with Lottery

[4] Unidentified.

[5] Bennet Langton (1737–1801) with his wife, the Dowager Lady Rothes, had been in Edinburgh off and on from 5 Oct. to 17 Dec. JB lists many engagements with Langton. His notes for 6 Oct. read: "Much Mr. Joh. with L." He also records "good conversation" with Langton on 17 Oct. and 5 Nov. (Notes). For an account of Langton and JB's relationship with him, see Fifer, pp. lii–lxxv.

[6] *The Duel* had only one performance, 8 Dec. (*Lond. Stage*, *Index*). According to Hopkins it was "very much hiss'd from the 2d Act", and the audience "would not Suffer it to be given out again" (*Lond. Stage*, pt. 4, iii. 1677–78). The Advertisement to the printed version (1772) reads: "This play took its rise from the accidental mention in company of a pathetic comedy called *Le Philosophe sans le Sçavoir* [by M.-J. Sedaine], which has been repeatedly acted at Paris, and always with universal applause. It was the wish of a few friends, that this translation of it, executed, perhaps, with too much rapidity, might have a trial on the English stage. It did not escape observation that it was a new species of *drama*, turning altogether upon a single incident, in some passages warm and interesting, but free from the theatrical bustle so much relished in this country, and in the less important scenes, exhibiting a draught of life and manners, easy, natural, but un-adorned. The attempt having been made, the play is now submitted to the candor of the reader." O'Brien's version is an adaptation rather than a translation.

[7] MS. "*Carmoyante*". Strictly speaking, the form of sentimental comedy, introduced from France, which was characterized by tearful scenes and high moral sentiments. This form, of which *The Duel* was an example (see previous n.), had only limited appeal for British audiences, who demanded a greater blending of "sentiment" with comic incident and wit (Arthur Sherbo, *English Sentimental Drama*, 1957, pp. 84, 142). JB may have seen Richard Cumberland's *West Indian*, a play regarded by contemporary and modern critics alike as one of the best examples of the English form of sentimental comedy; it opened the Edinburgh theatre season for this year on 21 Nov. (Dibdin, p. 160).

[8] A pun on the title of O'Brien's farce, *Cross Purposes*, put on at CG 5 Dec.

Advertisers "Not two blanks to a prize." Getting his Farce carried through is a £20 prize.[9]

What do you think of Edinburgh giving five hundred guineas certain to have Mr. and Mrs. Yates, with a benefit to each?[10] The Edinburgh Theatre has the same chance for having Capital Players, as the opposition has for having men of parts. We get them occasionally as they happen to be discontented with administration. While they are here, they are lavish in the praise of Scotland, as the deserters to opposition are in praise of Patriotism. But I observe that the former are as fond of returning to London as the latter are of returning to Court. Digges is steady to us. He is our Sir George Saville and he has as hollow[11] a voice.[12] You draw your sword upon me, when I begin to celebrate him in your presence. But beleive me, he has great merit.[13] Voltaire says that there is but a King and a half in Europe. The King of Prussia

[9] The smallest prize in the contemporary state lotteries (C. L'Est. Ewen, *Lotteries and Sweepstakes*, 1932, pp. 199–204).

[10] Richard Yates (?1706–96) was a leading actor at DL from 1742–67, playing many comic characters, notably Shakespearian clowns—in fact, *Cal. Merc.*, announcing the Yateses' forthcoming visit to Edinburgh, calls him the leading comedian of the British stage (26 Dec. p. [2]). He was also an admirable pantomimist; actually DG first appeared on the London stage as an anonymous substitute for Yates, who was taken ill one night in the spring of 1741 while playing the role of Harlequin in the pantomime *Harlequin Student* at Goodman's Fields (*Letters DG* i. 34 and n. 5).

Mary Ann (Graham) Yates (1728–87), who married Yates, as his second wife, some time before Dec. 1756 (*Lond. Stage* pt. 4, ii. 570), began her career at DL in the first performance of Samuel Crisp's *Virginia* on 25 Feb. 1754 (*Lond. Stage*, *Index*, where Crisp is miscalled "Henry") and later developed into a great tragic actress. In 1767 both Yates and his wife followed Colman to CG when Colman became part-owner of that theatre. They remained there until 1774, when, on Colman's resignation, DG persuaded them to return to DL (Oman, pp. 273, 330; *Letters DG* iii. 929–30). At the time of Mrs. Yates's appearance in Edinburgh in 1773 Henry Mackenzie described her as "an actress of great power, with the finest face and figure in the world" (*Anecdotes and Egotisms of Henry Mackenzie, 1745–1831*, ed. H. W. Thompson, 1927, p. 193). According to *Cal. Merc.* the Yateses were to be paid seven hundred guineas for the winter season of 1773 (26 Dec. p. [2]). See also Murray i. 199–204, iii. 191–92; Dibdin, pp. 160–62. No report of a benefit for either of the Yateses has been traced.

[11] MS. "hallow"

[12] Sir George Savile (1726–84), Bt., a model of conscientious independence. JB admired Savile, who had given an eloquent speech earlier in the year in favour of the Anglican clergyman who wished for relief from subscription to the Thirty-nine Articles. He had a "feeble voice" (DNB).

[13] JB had known West Digges (1720–86) well since 1758 when he first began to associate with actors and actresses (*Earlier Years*, p. 38). At this time Digges was the leading actor and manager of the Canongate theatre in Edinburgh, having arrived there in 1756 via the army and a short but turbulent career as an actor in Dublin (Dibdin, pp. 81–82; Murray iii. 286–88). For a few years in his early twenties JB regarded Digges as an ideal of sophistication and social ease (Journ. 1, 11 Dec. 1762). According to Benjamin Victor, "In

is a King; and the King of Sardinia is half a King.[14] We all acknowledge that there is a Theatrical King at Drury Lane. Why may not Scotland be allowed half a King. Perhaps, your poetical correspondent and I must say Sublime Admirer Lord Chatham would give the same judgement in this case that he did when I had the honour to mention to him Voltaire's *Bon mot*. "If", said he, "I might venture to improve on a saying of Monsieur De Voltaire, I would give all to the King of Prussia, and call him a King and a half."[15]

The *Irish Widow* has not yet made her appearance on our stage. We shall make her wellcome as you say she will make us laugh. You do not mention her being any relation of yours. But there is something in your manner of expressing yourself with regard to her, that I feel myself inclined to take a more than ordinary interest in her.

Mickle has announced to me your refusal of his play. You know the confidence which I have always had in your candour, and how earnestly I have inculcated it on him. I have written a letter of friendly admonition to him. Perhaps he may produce a more perfect Play.[16] In the meantime, I hope you will encourage his translation of the Lusiad, to which I know you subscribed very genteelly.[17]

Mr. Digges almost all the Requisites to form a great Actor seemed to unite; every Advantage of Art and Nature, except an harmonious Voice" (*History of the Theatres of London and Dublin*, 1761, i. 116). He was joint manager of the Edinburgh Theatre Royal from 1771–77 (*Edin. Adv.* 6–10 Sept. 1771, p. [4]; Dibdin, pp. 157–70). See also *post* To DG, 4 Feb. 1775 and n. 10.

[14] Frederick the Great, King of Prussia, and Charles Emmanuel III (1701–73) of Savoy, King of Sardinia. JB described Charles Emmanuel as "a little quiet man" (Journ. 11 Jan. 1765), but despite his insignificant appearance he was a warlike prince and an excellent administrator; during his long reign (forty-three years) he raised his states to a remarkable degree of prosperity (NBG).

[15] JB had heard this *bon mot* of Voltaire's in Genoa (Journ. 7 Dec. 1765). For the comment of William Pitt (1708–78), first Earl of Chatham (Aug. 1766), on Voltaire's saying, see Journ. 23 Feb. 1766. Chatham had addressed a rhymed invitation to DG to visit him, which DG published anonymously in various periodicals (*Letters DG* ii. 787 and n. 1, 790). DG had read the verses to JB the previous spring and shown him a card in which Chatham had written, "Illustrious Shakespeare! but more illustrious Garrick! for the first sometimes goes out of Nature. The other never does" (*Defence*, pp. 119–20).

[16] *Ante* To DG, 10 Sept. and n. 16. Admonition was needed because of Mickle's bitterness towards DG (From Mickle, 18 Nov.). In a long, careful letter JB told Mickle that DG had praised the play's poetry but thought it theatrically deficient, an opinion echoed by John Home (To Mickle, 1 Dec.; JB says in this letter that he did not finish it until 25 Dec. Printed in part in *Univ. Mag.* 1809, xi. 301).

[17] *Ante* To DG, 30 Mar. 1771 and nn. 12, 14. DG's subscriptions had become another source of irritation to Mickle. According to Mickle, he had received a

Let me hear from you when you can, and be assured that nobody is with more sincere admiration your obliged freind than

(signed) James Boswell

To Garrick,
Monday 29 March 1773

MS. Yale (L 562). A copy, in Lawrie's hand. Sent 29 Mar. (Reg. Let.).
HEADING: To David Garrick Esq.

Edinburgh, 29 march 1773

Dear Sir: Though you have not acknowledged the receipt of *Le Bellezze del Ariosto* which I sent you by a Gentleman who carried some books from me to Mr. Johnson, of which Mr. Johnson has acknowledged the receipt,[1] I hope you will wish me joy of my wifes being safely delivered of a daughter.[2] I know that you take a sincere concern in my happiness and I therefore wish for your congratulations.

Your Prologue to: *She stoops to conquer* is admirable. You cannot imagine what satisfaction I have felt at finding my friend Goldsmith come forth with a Prologue written by Mr. Garrick.[3]

letter from DG shortly after the publication of the first book of the *Lusiad* the previous summer authorizing him to draw upon DG for twenty subscriptions to that work. The previous spring in London, Mickle had sent his bookseller around to DG to collect the £12 due him for the subscriptions, and DG asked him to come back another time. Mickle, who had a high-strung sense of delicacy, informed JB: "The Bookseller was ordered never to call again, and I borrowed a trifle of my friend Ballantyne to carry me to Oxford" (From Mickle, 18 Nov.). In response, JB wrote: "Now my dear Sir will you only consider that here was nothing more than what happens upon almost every occasion, when money is asked without any premonition. Few people have twelve pounds at instant command; and, as John Home observed, rich people have it seldomer than others. As then Mr. Garrick shewed no disrespect to you, but only desired your Bookseller to call again, I declare I do not see you have good ground for blaming him. May I request then that this incident may be overlooked, and that you may desire your Bookseller to write a note to Mr. Garrick begging to know when it will be convenient that he should call or send for the money" (To Mickle, 1 Dec.—see preceding note for this letter. This passage was not printed in *Univ. Mag.*).

[1] On 24 Feb., without mentioning the "Gentleman" (*Letters SJ* i. 302). Reg. Let. indicates that JB wrote to SJ on 26 Dec. 1772, and presumably the Pindar that SJ mentions in his reply was conveyed with this letter.

[2] Veronica, born 15 Mar.

[3] The Prologue was spoken by Woodward at CG on 15 Mar., and printed in most of the current periodicals (Knapp, no. 400). Exasperated by George Colman's delay in bringing on *She Stoops to Conquer* at CG in 1772–73, Goldsmith had offered the play to DG, only to be reminded by SJ that

TO GARRICK, 29 AUGUST 1773

I hope to be with you for some time this spring[4] and to profit as usual by your goodness. I must beg and intreat that you will play Macbeth while I am in London. You may remember what an impression you made upon me, by repeating only a few lines of it, while we walked one morning last spring on the banks of the Thames near the Adelphi.[5] I know I am asking a very great favour, But, you have been upon other occasions indulgent to me so far beyond what I could have reasonably expected, that I flatter myself I may obtain a request the granting of which would oblige me indelibly. I offer my best respects to Mrs. Garrick and ever am, Dear Sir, Your much obliged friend and humble Servant,

JAMES BOSWELL

To Garrick,
Sunday 29 August 1773

MS. Yale (L 563). JB's draft. This draft was sent to the printer of the *Tour*, forming Paper Apart "B" at p. 652 of the MS. (*Life* v. 347–48).
HEADING: To Mr. Garrick.[1]

Inverness, Sunday, 29 August 1773

MY DEAR SIR: Here I am and Mr. Samuel Johnson actually with

he had committed himself to Colman, "*who was prevailed on at last by much solicitation, nay, a kind of force*, to bring it on" (John Forster, *Life and Times of Oliver Goldsmith*, 2nd ed., 1854, ii. 365–67; *Life* iii. 320–21). According to Davies, DG, who was "then upon very friendly terms with the author . . . presented him with a very humorous prologue, well accommodated to the author's intention of reviving fancy, wit, gaiety, humour, incident and ch[a]racter, in the place of sentiment and moral preachment" (ii. 157–58).

[4] JB left for London on 30 Mar., but undoubtedly was vague about his plans because he wanted DG to reply to this letter.

[5] Notes, 8 May 1772: "Garrick called on me e'er drest. . . . Took me out to walk in St. J[ames]'s Park. . . . Then on Thames when we talked of lang[uage] repeated 'Hast thou a medecine for a mind diseased' from Macbeth ending 'Throw Physick' etc.—great." DG did not put on *Macbeth* in the spring of 1773. After the death of Mrs. Pritchard (his favourite Lady Macbeth) in Apr. 1768, DG decided never to play the role again (Oman, p. 279); and though he received requests to play Macbeth and even expressed a desire to do so himself from time to time, his last recorded performance in that role was on 22 Sept. 1768, at the particular request of the King of Denmark (Stone and Kahrl, pp. 49, 557–58, 621; Fifer, p. 12 and n. 3; *Lond. Stage* pt. 4, iii. 1352).

[1] In preparing this letter for the printer, EM crossed out JB's heading—supplying in its place, "To David Garrick, Esqr., London"—and signature, provided a footnote (see n. 11 below), and changed the spelling of several words.

me. We were a night at Forres, in coming to which in the dusk of the evening we passed over the bleak and blasted heath where Macbeth met the Witches.[2] Your old Preceptour[3] repeated with much solemnity the Speech

> How far is't call'd to Forres? What are these
> So wither'd and so wild in their attire? etc.[4]

This day we visited the ruins of Macbeth's Castle at Inverness.[5] I have had great romantick satisfaction in seeing Johnson upon the classical scenes of Shakespeare[6] in Scotland, which I really looked upon as allmost as improbable as that "Birnam wood should come to Dunsinane".[7] Indeed as I have allways been accustomed to view him as a permanent London object, it would not be much more wonderful to me to see St. Paul's Church moving along where[8] we now are. As yet we have travelled in Post Chaises; But tomorrow we are to mount on horseback and ascend into the mountains by Fort Augustus, and so on to the Ferry, where we are to cross to Sky. We shall see that Island fully; and then visit some more of the Hebrides; after which we are to land in Argyleshire, proceed by Glasgow to Auchinleck, repose there a competent time, and then return to Edinburgh, from whence the Rambler will depart for old England again, as soon as he finds it convenient.[9] Hitherto, we have had a very prosperous expedition. I flatter myself *servetur ad imum, qualis ab incepto processerit.*[10] He is in

[2] JB was mistaken about the heath (see *Life* v. 504).

[3] MS. "Preceptour" with "u" deleted, presumably by EM.

[4] *Macbeth* I. iii. 39–40. SJ's "recitation was grand and affecting" (*Life* v. 115).

[5] The castle, though associated with Macbeth, had been rebuilt several times since his era. Prince Charles Edward blew it up in 1746.

[6] MS. "Shakespeare" with medial "e" deleted, presumably by EM. Though spelled "Shakespeare" in the First Folio (1623), later editors varied the spelling, most commonly dropping the final "e" (e.g. Rowe, Pope, and Warburton). EM seems to have been the first major editor to drop the medial "e", in the belief that this spelling reflected the pronunciation of Shakespeare's day (see EM's note in his "Life of William Shakspeare", *Plays and Poems of William Shakspeare . . . Comprehending a Life of the Poet*, ed. James Boswell, Jr., 1821, ii. 1–3). In the past JB had used the accepted spelling (e.g. 3 Feb. 1776, 29 July 1780), and no doubt EM deleted the medial "e" in this letter as well as persuading JB to change his usual spelling to "Shakspeare" in his letters (see *intra*) and in the proof-sheets of the *Life* (P 103).

[7] *Macbeth* V. viii. 30.

[8] MS. "with me" deleted before "where"

[9] JB and the Rev. Kenneth Macaulay had laid out most of this route on 27 Aug. (*Life* v. 120–21).

[10] Literally, "Have it [your new character] kept to the end even as it came forth at the first" (Horace, *Art of Poetry*, ll. 126–27, trans. H. R. Fairclough, Loeb ed.). JB

excellent spirits, and I have a rich Journal of his conversation. Look back, *Davy*,[11] to Litchfield,[12]—run up through the[13] time that has elapsed since you first knew Mr. Johnson,—and enjoy with me his present extraordinary Tour. I could not resist the impulse of writing to you from this place. The situation of the old Castle corresponds exactly to Shakespeare's[14] description. While we were there[15] to-day, it happened oddly,[16] that a Raven perched upon one of the Chimney tops, and croaked. Then, I in my turn repeated—"The raven himself is hoarse That croaks the entrance[17] of King [18] Duncan Under my battlements."[19] I wish you had been with us. Think what enthusiastick[20] happiness I shall have to see Mr. Samuel Johnson walking among the romantick rocks and woods of my Ancestors at Auchinleck![21] Write to me at Edinburgh. You owe me his Verses on Great George and tuneful Cibber, and the bad verses which led him to make his fine ones on Philips the musician. Keep your promise, and let me have them. I offer my very best compliments to Mrs. Garrick, and ever am Your warm admirer and friend,

JAMES BOSWELL

adapts this phrase to mean, "It may go on to the end as it started in the beginning." He had used the Latin phrase as the motto to the third of his essays "Remarks on the Profession of a Player", which refer repeatedly to DG (*ante* To DG, 18 Sept. 1771 and n. 8).

[11] In preparing this letter for the printer, EM added a ‡ before the comma, directing the reader to a footnote: "Note. I took the liberty of giving [written over a deleted 'g using'] this familiar appellation to my celebrated friend, to bring in a more lively manner to his remembrance the period when he was Dr. Johnson's pupil" (*Life* v. 348 n. 2).

[12] MS. "Litchfield" with "t" deleted, presumably by EM.

[13] MS. "that" altered to "the"

[14] MS. "Shakespeare" with medial "e" deleted, presumably by EM.

[15] MS. "there" written above a deleted "at it"

[16] MS. "oddly" written above a deleted "strangely". "Note" written below the deletion in EM's hand, but no note was added.

[17] MS. "fatal" added before "entrance" in EM's hand.

[18] MS. "King" deleted, presumably by EM at the time he added "fatal". See preceding note.

[19] *Macbeth* I. v. 38–41. EM marked the run-in quotation to be set off.

[20] MS. "an" deleted before "enthusiastick"

[21] See *post* To EB, 6 Nov. 1778, n. 1.

From Garrick,
Tuesday 14 September 1773

MS. Yale (C 1347). Received Oct. (Reg. Let.).[1] Published in part in *Tour* under the date of 23 Oct. (pp. 436–38; *Life* v. 349–50) following To DG, 29 Aug.
ADDRESS: To James Boswell Esqr., Edinburgh.
POSTMARKS: 16 SE, T•W.[2]

Hampton, Sepr. 14th 1773

DEAR SIR: You Stole away from London, and left us all in the lurch, for we expected You one Night at the Club and knew Nothing of your departure[3]—Had I paid You what I ow'd You for the book you bought for Me, I should only have griev'd for the loss of your Company, and Slept with a quiet Conscience; but wounded as it is, it must remain So till I see you again, tho I am sure our good Friend Mr. Johnson, will discharge the debt[4] for Me, if you will let him[5]—Your Account of Your Journey to *Forres, the Raven old Castles* etc. etc. made me half Mad—Are You not rather too late in the Year for fine Weather?[6] Which is the Life and Soul of Seeing Places—I hope Your Pleasure will continue, qualis ab incoepto etc.[7]—Your friend Mickle threatens me much. I only Wish that he would put his threats in Execution, and if he prints his play, I will forgive him[8]—I remember he complain'd to You

[1] Received at Inveraray, 23 Oct. (*post* To DG, 11 Apr. 1774; *Life* v. 347).

[2] *Ante* From DG, 12 July 1769, n. 1.

[3] JB was elected to The Club on 30 Apr. (*Annals*, p. 12) and left London on 11 May (Notes). DG's election probably took place on Tuesday 9 Mar. In his diary for Friday 12 Mar. Percy recorded, "Tuesday. 2 new members elected to The Club." In Croker's list of Club members, DG is noted as having been elected in Mar. 1773 (JB, *Life of Samuel Johnson*, ed. J. W. Croker, 1831, i. 529).

[4] MS. "the debt" written above a deleted "it"

[5] MS. "fine" written above a deleted "good"

[6] SJ and JB did run into very bad weather, but not until they got among the islands. On 19 Sept. JB recorded, "It was rather worse weather than any that we had yet" (Journ.), and for the next month he reports rain and storms almost daily.

[7] *Ante* To DG, 29 Aug. and n. 10.

[8] Mickle had told JB the previous spring that he intended to print *The Siege of Marseilles* and to criticize DG's choice of plays for DL in its Preface; he persisted in this plan in spite of "two earnest dissuasive letters" from JB (Mickle to John Hoole, 15 Nov.—W. J. Mickle, *Poems and a Tragedy* [ed. John Ireland] 1794, p. xlii[i]). The threat appears in a letter delivered by Richard Fenton to JB in London (JB's reaction is fully recorded in Fenton to Mickle, 10 May—MS. Osborn Collection) and in a short unrecovered note, according to the one "dissuasive" letter from JB known (To Mickle, 12 June; printed in *Univ. Mag.* 1809, xi. 301–02). Mickle also threatened to write a new *Dunciad* with DG as the hero, and told Hoole, "If you think

that his Bookseller call'd for the Money for Some Copies of his Lusiade which I subscrib'd for, and that I desir'd him to call again—The truth is that my Wife was not at home, and that for Weeks togeather I have not ten Shillings in my Pocket[9]—However had it been Otherwise, it was not so great a Crime to draw his Poetical Vengeance upon Me. I despise all that he can do, and am glad that I can so Easily get rid of him, and his ingratitude—I am harden'd both to abuse, and ingratitude.[10]

You, I am sure, will no more recommend Your Poetasters to my

proper you may mention this in any company" (Ireland, p. xlii[i]). We do not know who told DG of these threats, but Mickle may have been spreading them all over London.

In November or earlier, Mickle sent a proof-sheet from the Preface to DG, in a blank cover, which attacked DG as promised (Ireland, p. xlii[i]. A copy of the same proof-sheet, which differs slightly from the text of the Preface as printed later by Ireland, survives in the Osborn Collection. It adds a further denunciation of DG's choice of plays for performance in what may be Mickle's hand). DG sent the proof-sheet to George Steevens (13 Dec.) with the comment, "The Play is to appear after Xmas, & such a Play!" (*Letters DG* ii. 909–10). According to Governor Johnstone (*ante* To DG, 10 Sept. 1772, n. 16), who was much amused, DG had been agitated by Mickle's attack, but Johnstone passed the word on to Mickle "to have no more to say" (William Ballantyne to Mickle, 27 Dec.—MS. Osborn Collection), putting a stop to the printing of *Marseilles*. Johnstone also persuaded Mickle to put aside thoughts of having it produced in Edinburgh until he had finished his translation of the *Lusiad*. *Marseilles* was later revised and rejected by Thomas Harris at CG and R. B. Sheridan at DL (Mickle to Johnstone, 25 May 1774—MS. Osborn Collection; Ireland, p. xliv). For a similar episode involving DG and Tobias Smollett several years earlier, see Oman, pp. 192–93.

[9] Mrs. Garrick seems, at times anyway, to have acted as her husband's paymaster. When JB wanted to borrow five guineas from him at the Stratford Jubilee, DG had to get them from his wife (Journ. 8 Sept. 1769). JB calls DG's lack of cash "a pleasing trait of his domestick life" (*Life* v. 349 n. 1). See also Oman, pp. 199, 209.

[10] *Ante* To DG, 25 Dec. 1772, n. 17. DG was apparently unaware that Mickle had worked up another complaint about the *Lusiad* subscriptions. In spring 1773 Thomas Becket, DG's bookseller, had given Mickle's bookseller £6 as half payment for these subscriptions, "the greatest part" of which, Mickle wrote to JB, "are taken in Becket's shop, and the fruits of my own advertisements, from people unacquainted with Garrick". To pay DG back, Mickle intended to attack him in a footnote to the *Lusiad* (it appears at iii. 1006) which was being set as Mickle translated it; "in the preface I believe I shall spare him" (From Mickle [between 16 Sept. and 5 Nov.]; printed in *Univ. Mag.* 1809, xi. 302–03. This is a portion of Mickle's draft, not the letter as sent).

With the present letter Mickle's name disappears from the correspondence, but when JB published DG's letter in the *Tour* (1785) with blanks for Mickle's name and the *Lusiad*, Mickle was once again enraged. He wanted to rake up the whole business in a review of the *Tour* in *Eur. Mag.*, and Isaac Reed had considerable difficulty in persuading him that the public would care nothing about this long-gone matter (Reed to Mickle, 2 Feb. 1786—MS. Osborn Collection). In his review Mickle restricted himself to one remark about DG's theatrical taste (*Eur. Mag.* 1786, ix. 343). But something or someone (Reed?) impelled JB to add a footnote in the third edition of the *Tour* in which he praises the still anonymous Mickle and his tragedy (*Life* v. 349).

civility and Good Offices—Shall I recommend to You a Play of Eschylus, (the Prometheus), publish'd and translated by poor Old Morrell, who is a good Scholar, and an Acquaintance of Mine[11]—It will be but half a Guinea, and Your Name shall be put in the List, I am making for him—You will be in very good Company. Now for the Epitaphs—Dr. Wilkes's ran thus[12]—

upon Philips the Musician

Exalted Soul! whose harmony could please,
The Love-sick virgin, and the Gouty Ease;
Could Jarring discords like Old *Amphion* move
To beauteous Order, and harmonious Love,
Rest here! till Angels bid thee rise,
And meet thy blessed Saviour in the Skies.

Another.

Philips whose touch harmonious could remove,
The pangs of guilty pow'r, and hapless Love!
Rest here, distress'd by Poverty no more,
Here find that Calm, Thou gav'st so oft before;
Sleep undisturb'd within this peaceful Shrine,
Till Angels wake thee, with a Note Like Thine!

I have no more paper or I should have said more to You—My Love and respects to Mr. Johnson. Yours Ever,

D. GARRICK

I can't write. I have the gout in my hand.

[11] Thomas Morell (1703–84), classical scholar, early friend of DG's, and librettist for several of Handel's oratorios. He wrote "See the Conquering Hero Comes". His edition of *Prometheus Vinctus* of Aeschylus, with a blank-verse translation, was first printed in 1767, and reissued in 1773, with the translation dedicated to DG (*Life* v. 350, 560).

[12] The epitaph on Philips by Richard Wilkes (1691–1760), physician and antiquarian, requested by JB in his letters to DG, *ante* 10 Sept. 1772 and 29 Aug. The epitaph by "Another" below is SJ's. For JB's use of these epitaphs and their correct texts, see *Life* i. 148–49 and 149 nn. 1, 2; *Works SJ* vi. 68–69.

To Garrick,
Monday 11 April 1774

MS. Hyde Collection. A copy at Yale (L 564) in Lawrie's hand omits two words, clearly in error. Sent 19 Apr. (Reg. Let.).[1]
ADDRESS: To David Garrick Esq., Adelphi, London.
POSTMARKS: [Edinburgh] AP 12 [London] 16 AP.

Edinburgh, 11 April 1774

DEAR SIR: When Mr. Johnson and I arrived at Inveraray, after our expedition to the Hebrides, and there for the first time *after many days*[2] renewed our enjoyment of the luxuries of civilized life,[3] one of the most elegant that I could wish to find, was lying for me—a letter from Mr. Garrick.[4] It was a Pine-Apple of the finest flavour, which had a high zest indeed amongst the heath-covered mountains of Scotia.[5] That I have not thanked you for it long e'er now is one of those strange facts for which it is so difficult to account that I shall not attempt it. The *Idler* has strongly expressed many of the wonderful effects of the *Vis inertiae* of the human mind.[6] But it is hardly credible that a man should have the warmest regard for his friend, a constant desire to shew it, and a keen ambition for a frequent epistolary intercourse with him, and yet should let months roll on without having resolution or activity or power or whatever it be, to write a few lines. A man in such a situation is somewhat like Tantalus reversed.[7] He recedes he knows not how from what he loves, which is full as provoking as when what he loves recedes from him. That my Complaint is not a peculiar fancy, but deep in human nature, I appeal to the Authority of St. Paul, who though he had not been exalted to the dignity of an Apostle, would have stood high in Fame as a Philosopher and Oratour, *What I would that do I not*.[8]

[1] The postmarks show that the Reg. Let. entry is incorrect.

[2] A common Old Testament phrase, but no specific reference seems relevant.

[3] On riding in a "comfortable carriage" once again after their journey through the Hebrides, SJ and JB "had a pleasing conviction of the commodiousness of civilization, and heartily laughed at the ravings of some absurd visionaries who have attempted to persuade [them] of the superior advantages of a *state of nature*" (*Life* v. 365).

[4] *Ante* From DG, 14 Sept. 1773.

[5] "I also found a letter [at Inveraray, 23 Oct. 1773] from Mr. Garrick, which was a regale as agreeable as a pine-apple would be in a desert" (*Life* v. 347).

[6] SJ discusses the *vis inertiae* ("the quality of resisting all external impulse") in *Idler* no. 9.

[7] See *Hypochondriack* no. 6 (Bailey i. 142–49 and n. 7).

[8] Romans 7: 15.

You need be under no concern as to your debt to me for the Book which I purchased for you.[9] It was long ago discharged; for believe me, I intended the Book as a Present. Or if you rather chuse that it should be held as an Exchange with the Epitaphs which you sent me,[10] I have no objection.

Dr. Goldsmith's death would affect all the Club much. I have not been so much affected with any event that has happened of a long time.[11] I wish you would give me who are at a distance, and who cannot get to London this spring<,>[12] some particulars with regard to his last appearances.[13] Dr. Young has a fine thought to this purpose that every friend who goes before us to the other side of the river of death makes the passage to us the easier.[14] Were our Club all removed to a future world but one or two, *they*, one should think, would incline to follow.

By all means let me be upon your list of Subscribers to Mr. Morrell's Prometheus.[15]

You have enlivened the Town I see with a musical Piece.[16] The Prologue is admirably fancied *arripere populum tributim*,[17] though to be sure Foote's remark applies to it, that your Prologues have a culinary turn,[18] and that therefore the motto to your collection of

[9] *Ante* To DG, 29 Mar. 1773.

[10] *Ante* From DG, 14 Sept. 1773.

[11] Goldsmith died on 4 Apr. JB's immediate response was to write to DG and others and to publish in *Lond. Mag.* (June 1774, xliii. 295) a song that Goldsmith had written for *She Stoops to Conquer* but which was omitted from the production, with a letter explaining how he came to have it (BP ix. 109–10, 114).

[12] The comma, obliterated from the original by a slight tear, is supplied from the copy.

[13] DG did not provide any details of Goldsmith's last days, but on 20 June JB received a letter from General Oglethorpe (Reg. Let.) written "immediately on My dear Friend Goldsmith's Death", but not posted till 15 June, giving some particulars.

[14] *Night Thoughts* iii. 277–302.

[15] *Ante* From DG, 14 Sept. 1773.

[16] DG's *A Christmas Tale* was first performed at DL on 27 Dec. 1773. Written "in a hurry & on purpose to Shew Some fine Scenes which were design'd by Mons. DeLoutherberg particularly a Burning Palace &c. which was extremely fine & Novel" ("Hopkins Diary", quoted in *Lond. Stage* pt. 4, iii. 1773–74), it created a sensation; but Walpole, though praising the "beautiful scenes", wrote to Lady Ossory on 30 Dec. 1773 that they "have much ado to save the piece from being sent to the devil", and described the play as "a new proof that it is possible to be the best actor and worst author in the world" (*Corres. HW* xxxii. 177). The music, by Charles Dibdin, was said to be "the worst he ever Compos'd" ("Hopkins Diary", quoted in *Lond. Stage* pt. 4, iii. 1774). See also E. P. Stein, *David Garrick, Dramatist*, 1938, pp. 152–53.

[17] "To seize the people tribe by tribe" (see Horace, *Satires* II. i. 69); the Prologue addresses various groups in the audience in turn. JB applies this quotation to DG in the first of his essays, "On the Profession of a Player" (*ante* To DG, 18 Sept. 1771 and n. 8).

[18] "The Prologue was well spoken by Mr. Palmer, in the character of Christmas, represented as a venerable old man, en-

them should be *Animus jamdudum in Patinis*.[19] A Player upon words might answer him—Any *Patinis* rather than your Piety in *Pattens*.[20]—I wonder the Wags have not been quoting upon you

Whose erudition is *A Christmas Tale*.[21]

But Mr. Johnson is ready to bruise any one who calls in question your classical knowledge and your happy application of it.[22]

I hope Mr. Johnson has given you an entertaining account of his northern Tour. He is certainly to favour the World with some of his Remarks. Pray do not fail to quicken him by word as I do by letter.[23] Posterity will be the more obliged to his friends the more that they can prevail with him to write. With best compliments to Mrs. Garrick, and hoping that you will not punish me by being long silent, I remain faithfully yours,

JAMES BOSWELL[24]

To Garrick, Saturday 4 February 1775

MS. Yale (L 565). Sent 6 Feb. (Reg. Let.). A copy in Lawrie's hand. HEADING in JB's hand: To David Garrick Esq.

Edr. 4 feb. 1775

DEAR SIR: Why have you been so long of writing to me? I have not

circled with minced pyes and evergreen; a collar of brawn for his cap, and a carving knife for his sword, preceded by a number of cooks, two of whom carry a-cross the stage a surloin of beef, to the tune of *O! the Roast Beef of Old England*" (*Lond. Chron.* 25–28 Dec. 1773, xxxiv. 624). Foote's remark has not been located; for a discussion of DG's fondness for "culinary prologues", see M. E. Knapp, *Prologues and Epilogues of the Eighteenth Century*, 1961, pp. 125–26.

[19] Adapted from Terence, *Eunuch*, l. 816: "My mind has long been on my dishes" (trans. John Sargeaunt, Loeb ed.).

[20] Foote's puppet-show, *Piety in Pattens*, New Haymarket, 15 Feb. 1773.

[21] Edward Young, *Love of Fame, the Universal Passion* i. 258. JB is alluding to criticism that, like that of Young's Hippolitus, DG's classical learning is no more than a fairy-tale.

[22] SJ would let no one attack DG but himself (*Life* iii. 70, 312 and n. 1), but he criticized DG's knowledge of Latin (*Life* ii. 377).

[23] SJ's *Journey to the Western Islands of Scotland* was published on 18 Jan. 1775 (*Life* ii. 509–10). For JB's assistance with the *Journey*, see *Life* ii. 268–91.

[24] The MS. is mounted and bound in an illustrated, multi-volume set of the *Life*. Due to the tipping-in of an extra illustration the last line of the MS., including the signature, is partly covered by paper, but the reading here can be confirmed from the copy.

had a line from you since your letter[1] which I received at Inverary when Mr. Johnson and I emerged from "the depths of western obscurity".[2] I have wished much to hear from you how he talks of his Journey to the Hebrides, and, I now wish much to hear from you how his Book is received in London.[3] I dare say it will have a rapid and extensive sale and be generally admired though some obstinate Caledonians may perhaps be dissatisfied.[4] What do the Literati now think of Fingal? What has Macpherson to oppose to Mr. Johnsons arguments?[5] How could you let Honest Tom Becket put an Advertisment into the Newspapers gravely asserting that the *originals* of Fingal and other Poems of Ossian lay in his shop for the inspection of the curious,[6] when for any thing that he knows those papers may have been muster rolls of the highland

[1] *Ante* From DG, 14 Sept. 1773.

[2] Quotation not located.

[3] SJ's *Journey*, priced at 5*s*., was published in an edition of 4,000 copies which sold very quickly; a Dublin edition was published in the same year. The work was not reprinted until 1785. SJ told the Rev. Thomas Campbell that he "was better pleased with the commendations bestowed on his account of the Hebrides than on any book he had ever written" (*Johns. Misc.* ii. 6).

[4] SJ "expressed to his friend Mr. Windham of Norfolk, his wonder at the extreme jealousy of the Scotch, and their resentment at having their country described by him as it really was; when, to say that it was a country as good as England, would have been a gross falsehood" (*Life* ii. 306). *St. James's Chron.* printed one such example of resentment, signed "Sandy Aberdeen" (7–9 Feb. p. [1]): "What the Devil do you mean, Sir, by publishing so many scurvy Extracts from your unlucky Travels to the Islands of Scotland? Was it not enough for your Rancour and Malice to publish the infamous Book itself, without retailing it in the Papers, that every English Puppy might have it in his Power to insult over the Venerable Habitations of the generous Highlanders, and turn their more than Roman Simplicity and Oeconomy of Living into Contempt, by miscalling it Penury and Want?" To offset the many Scottish attacks on the *Journey* JB published various recommendations of it in the *Tour* and the *Life* (J. L. Clifford and D. J. Greene, *Samuel Johnson: A Survey and Bibliography of Critical Studies*, 1970, pp. 249–56; W. P. Courtney and D. Nichol Smith, *A Bibliography of Samuel Johnson*, 1925, pp. 119–23; *Life* ii. 303–10, v. 405–09).

[5] James Macpherson (1736–96) had in 1762 published *Fingal*, which purported to be an epic by Ossian, translated from ancient Gaelic manuscripts. SJ repeatedly ridiculed the work, denying both its literary merit and its authenticity (e.g. *Journey*, pp. 117–19; *Life* v. 240–43, 387–89). When Macpherson heard that SJ's forthcoming *Journey* contained a harsh attack on *Fingal*, he tried, through the publisher William Strahan, to persuade SJ to cancel the offending passage. After the *Journey* was published, he attempted to make SJ apologize publicly, and finally resorted to direct threats, prompting SJ's famous reply, "I hope I shall never be deterred from detecting what I think a cheat, by the menaces of a ruffian" (*Life* ii. 298; see also *Life* ii. 295–300, 511–14).

[6] Thomas Becket (?1721–1813), bookseller, and publisher of DG and Ossian. His notice, which appeared in *Lond. Chron.* for 19–21 Jan. (xxxvii. 67), declared that "the Originals of Fingal and other Poems of Ossian, lay in my shop for many months in the year 1762, for the inspection of the curious" (*Life* ii. 294, 510–11).

regiment,[7] or receipts for brewing heathbeer, distilling whisky, or baking oatmeal cakes; for, not a word of erse does he understand.

Your Theatre I see goes on with its usual spirit, and you write Prologues and Epilogues with new varieties of fancy. You have certainly a particular Muse to yourself as an inspirer of that species of writing, for your genius is inexhaustible. I am allways struck with an agreeable surprise, when another of those peices issues from your *forge*, for I cannot imagine how you can give us one of a different form from any of those which we have already had.[8]

Our manager here is doing pretty well.[9] His company is not expensive, which is wisely contrived for this place, where the profits really cannot afford salaries to many capital performers; and we should be satisfied with such entertainment as is suited to our finances.[10] If we have some good common dishes let us be

[7] "The Highland Regiment with the number of the 43rd Foot" was the official title under which the six independent companies known locally as the "Black Watch", in existence since 1730, were formally incorporated, with an additional four companies, into a regiment of line in May 1740 (Archibald Forbes, *The "Black Watch": The History of an Historic Regiment*, 1897, pp. 6–10).

[8] DG had written at least a half-dozen Prologues and Epilogues during the first half of the 1774/75 season, some of which were printed under his name in contemporary periodicals. They tended to be based on varied conceits: the Prologue to Nathaniel Lee's *Rival Queens* (8 Oct. 1774) stressed that this was Willoughby Lacy's first appearance as Alexander; the Epilogue to Gen. John Burgoyne's *Maid of the Oaks* (5 Nov. 1774) compared "counting the house" in the theatre and in Parliament; the Epilogue to Richard Cumberland's *Choleric Man* (19 Dec. 1774) was spoken in the persona of a painter; and so forth. JB's comparison of DG, presumably to a Cyclops at the "forge", seems rather a general reminiscence of various classical passages (e.g. Virgil, *Georgics* iv. 170–75; *Aeneid* viii. 416–53) than a specific allusion; he may be remembering that SJ, in his *Journey*, had called a man they dislodged "black as a Cyclops from the forge" (*Journey*, p. 48). SJ also praised the variety of DG's Prologues (Journ. 27 Mar.).

[9] Although JB presumably is referring to West Digges here (see *ante* To DG, 25 Dec. 1772, n. 13), Digges was never sole manager of the Theatre Royal. Foote had sold his lease in 1771 to Digges and John Bland (1721–1808; see *ante* To DG, 30 Mar. 1771), who had, in fact, been a quarter partner with David Ross since 1767. Graduate of Trinity College, Dublin (Jackson, pp. 79–80), Bland entered the army—after a short period at the Temple in London—and served at Dettingen, Fontenoy, and Clifton Moor under his relation Gen. Humphrey Bland. After becoming acquainted with Digges, he left the army and devoted the rest of his life to the stage. In 1773 he and Digges renewed their lease of the Theatre Royal, and Bland continued as manager for three years after Digges absconded to London in 1777 to escape his creditors (Jackson, pp. 79–81; Murray i. 190–91, 198–99; Dibdin, pp. 159, 170).

[10] "Mr. Digges . . . is now at the head of a company who seem intended as foils to himself; and though they change every year, I am informed they never change for the better. The smallness of the salaries accounts for this; there is only one or two

satisfied. A Turbot or a haunch of venison will of itself cost as much as them all, and the Host have nothing for himself if he serves up an expensive feast at[11] three shillings a head.[12] Mrs. Yates was a very costly dish and really beyond what we can afford.[13]

Publick affairs seem to be cloudy. Whether the clouds will burst out in thunders and storms or be gently dispersed I know not. But I own I have disagreeable apprehensions. I confess that I have not studied the American contraversy as yet, and if I had studied it, should probably be unable to form a decisive opinion. I hope to hear from you soon, and I please myself with the hopes of seeing you in London this[14] spring.[15] Has not Mr. Johnsons Book made you desireous of paying a visit to Scotland? If you neglect it, you will not have used us well; and you will have lost a considerable addition to your fame. But we shall talk of this. With best compliments to Mrs. Garrick I ever am, Dear Sir, your affectionate, humble servant.

From Garrick,
Wednesday 8 March 1775

MS. Yale (C 1348). Received 13 Mar. (Reg. Let.).
ADDRESS: James Boswell Esqr., Edinburgh.
POSTMARKS: 8 MR, 9 MR, T·W.[1]

Adelphi, March 8th 1775

DEAR SIR: Too much business, a severe attack of the Stone, and my Brother's dangerous Situation[2] have prevented me from

whose pay exceeds a guinea a week; which, in a metropolis like Edinburgh, where the necessities of life are almost as dear as in London, is scarce a subsistence; nor can the receipts of the house afford more, while the rent is so high. . . . As the Edinburgh company are very small as well as very bad, Mr. Digges is obliged to perform all the principal parts, and to act every night of representation, which is four times each week" (Edward Topham, *Letters from Edinburgh, 1774 and 1775*, 1776, letter xiv, 7 Jan. 1775, pp. 110–11; see also Dibdin, pp. 163–66).

[11] MS. "at" superimposed upon "of"

[12] "When Mr. Ross obtained the patent, the price of admission was raised to three shillings, pit and boxes; two shillings the gallery; and one shilling the upper gallery" (Hugo Arnot, *History of Edinburgh*, 1788, p. 372).

[13] *Ante* To DG, 25 Dec. 1772 and n. 10.

[14] MS. "this" superimposed upon "next"

[15] JB arrived in London on 21 Mar. He mentions meeting with DG on 23, 24, 25, and 27 Mar. (Journ.).

[1] *Ante* From DG, 12 July 1769 and n. 1.

[2] Little is known about George Garrick (1723–79), DG's younger brother, before 1747 when DG became joint manager of

acknowledging your very obliging and friendly letter[3] Sooner. Our learned Friend's Account of *You*, and *Yours*, has occasion'd much Speculation, and had very near been productive of Mischief—You have heard I am Sure of Letters and Messages (very rough ones indeed) that have pass'd between the Dr. and Mr. Macpherson[4]—but Nine days have done with their business, as they do with all other Wonderful Matters, almost annihilated it—Our friend has this day produc'd another political pamphlet call'd, *Taxation no Tyranny*, a very Strong attack upon the Americans and Patriots—It is said to be well and masterly done—I shall devour it the Moment I have finish'd this letter.[5] How the dispute about Fingal will end, I cannot Yet say; I hope not with bloody Crowns,[6] as seem'd likely at first—An Acquaintance of the Doctor's and formerly an Antagonist of Macpherson, (*Mr. Whitaker* by name) by Some Strange literary Fatality, is bringing forth, in a two Shilling pamphlet, proofs of the Authenticity of Fingal!—! It has likewise been Whisper'd to me, that he will be pert with our Friend[7]—He, you know, is too great a

DL with James Lacy and took George on as general factotum for the theatre. In his later years he was frequently afflicted with illnesses that required long stays in Bath. On this occasion his illness seems to have started as early as the spring of 1774; in May of that year DG wrote several letters telling of his brother's "dangerous situation" (*Letters DG* iii. 929, 932–33), and on 3 July 1774 he wrote to his nieces in Paris that their father "who has been ill, but is now better, is going to Bath" (ibid. iii. 945). Throughout the following winter and spring DG complained of having had to take over much of the routine business at DL which George would normally have looked after. George stayed on at DL after DG retired in 1776, and died on 3 Feb. 1779, two days after DG's funeral (*Biog. Dict.* vi. 112–16; *Letters DG* iii. 977, 994).

[3] *Ante* To DG, 4 Feb.

[4] *Ante* To DG, 4 Feb. and n. 5.

[5] *Taxation No Tyranny* was published on 8 Mar. (*Works SJ* x. 408).

[6] See Shakespeare, *Richard II*, III. iii. 96.

[7] Rev. John Whitaker (1735–1808), antiquarian and historian, had published in 1772 *The Genuine History of the Britons Asserted in a Refutation of Mr. Macpherson's "Introduction to the History of Great Britain and Ireland"*, in which Whitaker claimed that "nearly every important circumstance, every consequential incident, and every essential argument [in Macpherson's *History*], are either frivolous in their nature or useless in their application" (p. 302). He was far less critical of Macpherson's Ossianic poems, however, praising Macpherson in the above work for "calling out the Poems of Ossian from their original obscurity" (p. 5) in a passage he allowed to stand in the "corrected" 2nd ed. of 1773. And in the first volume of his *History of Manchester*, published in 1771, Whitaker had gone as far as to assert that "the Poems of Ossian carry in themselves sufficient proofs of their own authenticity" (i. 16–17), chiding Macpherson merely for what he thought must be an error in Macpherson's *translation* and urging him either to "publish the originals or deposit them in some public library" (ibid. i. 210). It is hardly surprising, then, to find that Whitaker and SJ, whose acquaintance he had made during his brief tenure as morning preacher of Berkeley Chapel, Nov. 1773 to Feb. 1774,

Philosopher, in the best sense of the word, to regard, *The*[8] *Whips and Scorns of* time[9]—He Superiour to the little frail Sensibilities of inferiour beings, like Antaeus, rebounds, and encreases in Vigour from these attacks! and when he has blown up the billows—He

Smiles on the tumult, and Enjoys the Storm![10]

Have *his* Hebrides lost him any friends at Edinburgh?—Fame says—Yes.[11]—

Becket is a fool—and We[12] plague him much about his Erse-knowledge and Learning.[13]

Your theatrical Matters are very ill manag'd—The Stage would have been a very comfortable business in Scotland for any *Sensible, good* Actor, with good Management, but Your Directors[14] are too great Rakes, and too fine Gentlemen, to serve themselves, or please their audiences.

Pray Let us See You Soon, and bring your Spirits, good humour and unaffected Mirth along with You. I am, Dear Sir, Most Sincerely Yours,

D. Garrick

I write in great haste and not in Spirits, but in great pain—the gout has fix'd upon my right thumb, and the post-man can't stay another Moment! Adieu.

were "decidedly hostile" in the Ossian controversy (*Gent. Mag.* 1808, lxxviii. 1035–37). The pamphlet mentioned here has not been traced; however, in the second volume of his *History of Manchester*, published this year, Whitaker criticized SJ for his neglect of British (as opposed to Saxon) etymology in his *Dictionary*, though he apologized for his criticism, hoping that he had executed his own etymological review "with such a respectfulness to the gentleman . . . as is peculiarly due to one . . . [who] ranks equally as the first scholar and the first man in the kingdom" (ii. 235, 240–327 passim, 328).

8 MS. "the *The*"

9 *Hamlet* III. i. 69.

10 We have not been able to trace the source of this quotation. V. J. Liesenfeld has pointed out to us that this is one of two lines which appear at the feet of Britannia/Juno in a satirical engraving, *Aeneas in a Storm*, published in 1737:

She, *While the Outrageous Winds the Deep deform*
Smiles on the Tumult, and enjoys the Storm

(see Plate 35 in Maynard Mack's *The Garden and the City*, 1969, p. 130), but there the trail ends. These lines are probably one of many parodies on the famous line in Addison's *Campaign*: "Rides in the whirlwind, and directs the storm" (l. 292); see, for example, Pope, *Dunciad* iii. 263–64, and *Lines on Curll*, ll. 5–6.

11 *Ante* To DG, 4 Feb. and n. 4; *Life* ii. 305–08.

12 MS. "We" superimposed upon "they"

13 *Ante* To DG, 4 Feb. and n. 6.

14 West Digges and John Bland (*ante* To DG, 4 Feb. and n. 9).

To Garrick, Thursday 21 December 1775

MS. Yale (L 566). A copy in Lawrie's hand, written on sides 2, 3, and 4 of From Lord Kames, 19 Dec. (C 1653), itself a copy. Sent 21 Dec. (Reg. Let.).

HEADING: (To David Garrick Esq.).

Edinr. 21 Decr. 1775

DEAR SIR: You Theatrical Sovereigns are I beleive as much solicited for the places in your gift, as any Monarch in Europe. There is this difference however, that I beleive you never bestow them but according to merit real or imaginary—I am now to apply to your Dramatick Majesty for the vacant place of my Countryman Johnston, not as Prime minister according to the popular cry of scottish influence behind the curtain in Drurylane as at St. James's, but as his successor in the parts which he played.[1] This candidate is Mr. Young who has been upon the stage some time. He was born in this Country and educated in it, but has also spent a part of his life in England.[2] He is recommended to me by Lord Kames who must be allowed to have considerable weight in the *Critick Department.*[3] I enclose his Lordship's letter as it will certainly be more effectual than any thing I can say.[4] Mr. Young desired me to let you know that he

[1] JB refers to Alexander Johnston, who had died 1 Oct. (*Lady's Magazine*, Nov. 1775, vi. 623; Daniel Lysons, *The Environs of London*, 1791–95, iii. 437–38). He had made a name for himself as Gibby, the Scottish servant in Susanna Centlivre's *Wonder*, first performing the role at DL 6 Nov. 1756 (Lysons, p. 437 n. 88; *Lond. Stage* pt. 4, ii. 563), but this seems to have been his only role as an actor (*post* From DG, 26 Dec.). For many years he kept the box-book and was housekeeper at DL, which accounts for JB's reference to him as "Prime Minister" (see *Lond. Stage*, pt. 4, ii and iii passim, which records a benefit for a Mr. A. Johnson, housekeeper and box-book keeper, in May of every year from 1763 to 1775). According to Sir Nicholas Nipclose, Bt., Johnston had once been proprietor of a puppet show in Edinburgh and, during his years as box-book keeper at DL, "accumulated some thousands" as a result of "OECONOMY, obsequiousness and taste in decorations" (*The Theatres: A Poetical Dissection*, 1772, p. 7 n. 2).

[2] Nothing is known of "Charles Young, formerly my Clerk" (From Kames, 19 Dec.), apart from what is found in JB's and Kames's letters. The Young whom the *Edinburgh Rosciad* (1775) describes as "last by far in the theatric rear" (cited in Dibdin, p. 167) is most likely the Thomas Young listed among the Edinburgh performers in 1767 (Dibdin, p. 140).

[3] Henry Home (1696–1782), Lord Kames, judge of the Courts of Session and of Justiciary, who, among his works on many subjects, wrote *Elements of Criticism* (1762).

[4] On 21 Dec. JB recorded in his journal: "Wrote a letter to Mr. Garrick, chiefly to recommend to him one young a Scotsman

would leave the terms of his engagement to be settled by yourself after making tryal of what he can do; he hopes to be at least a decent useful Performer. I have only to add, that it will be obliging to me, and humane to him that[5] you give a speedy answer. If you are pleased to receive him Mr. Digges will allow him to set out for London without delay.

How have you been since I left you in May?[6] I rejoice to see in the publick advertiser[7] that you are playing so often.[8] My season of London is the spring, you must really let us see you more frequently in the months of march april and may. Above all let me intreat as I have formerly done that you would play Macbeth in one of these months.[9]

I shall never cease to renew my claim upon you for a visit to Scotland. Why will you not come and see a country where you have so many friends, and add a northern jewel to your Diadem of Fame? I could write a Rhapsody upon this subject. I indeed wonder much at your neglect of us, and am a little angry, or vexed.[10]

who had gone upon the stage. I enclosed to him a letter to me from Lord Kames, asking me to recommend Young, who had been his Clerk. I suggested to My Lord when he spoke to me, to write such a letter as would be agreable to Mr. Garrick. In writing to Garrick, I felt particles of vivacity rise by a sort of contagion of fancy." (Kames's letter will appear in another volume in this edition. His remarks show a genial admiration for DG.)

[5] MS. "that" superimposed upon "to g"

[6] JB had left London on 22 May (*Life* ii. 377 n. 1).

[7] MS. "publick" superimposed upon illegible word, possibly "papers"; "advertisements" altered to "advertiser".

[8] The first half of the 1775/76 season was a very busy one for DG. This was in fact his last season, though his forthcoming retirement was not announced until mid-Jan. 1776 (*Lond. Stage* pt. 4, iii. 1907). His first role of the season was Lusignan in *Zara* on 25 Oct., and this was followed by Sir John Brute in *The Provoked Wife* on 31 Oct. In Nov. he played Benedick in *Much Ado about Nothing* no less than five times (6, 8, 10, 16, 22 Nov.), the last being a command performance. On 25 Nov. he appeared as Abel Drugger in *The Alchemist*, and on 29 Nov. as Hamlet. In Dec. he played a variety of roles; Leon in *Rule a Wife and Have a Wife* (5, 20 Dec.); Hamlet (8 Dec.); Lusignan (14 Dec.); Kitely in *Every Man in His Humour* (18 Dec.); and Archer in *The Beaux' Stratagem* (23 Dec.—*Lond. Stage* pt. 4, iii. 1922–39). All, of course, were favourite parts.

[9] DG did not play Macbeth in the spring of 1776 (*ante* To DG, 29 Mar. 1773 and n. 5.).

[10] When, in London in the spring of 1772, JB had asked DG why he had favoured Ireland with a visit and not Scotland, DG had remarked: "When I went to Ireland, I went to get money. It was harvest time then with me. But when the Barn's full . . . one grows lazy" (Journ. 15 Apr. 1772). However, the following year DG wrote to William Robertson, 16 [Mar.] 1773, "My heart longs to cross the Tweed . . . Mrs. Garrick and I talk of our Scotch expedition with delight" (Tierney p. 134). The expedition never took place. *Ante* To DG, 30 Mar. 1771 and n. 10; *post* To DG, 22 Mar. 1777.

What says Dr. Johnson of Paris? His remarks are original and nervous upon every subject, and though he had not time to see much his strokes will be masterly. Pray favour me with any of his remarks which you have heard. He has written to me since his return, but reserves himself till we meet.[11]

I have had a son born to me since I saw you so that I have now a wife and three children;[12] and yet I know not how, the cares of the world of which I have read and heard a great deal, do not burthen me much. There is doubtless a knack of carrying our "load of life"[13] with more ease than common, without any remarkable strength of shoulders. It may be a kind of suppleness like the poles of English and Irish chairmen.

I beg you may present my best compliments to Mrs. Garrick, and when you see your brother Mr. Peter Garrick or write to him be so good as let him know I intend to accept of his kind invitation, in my way to London in march next when I propose to view Litchfield[14] the birth place of Samuel Johnson LL.D.[15] I ever am, My Dear Sir, with much regard, Your affectionate, humble servant.

From Garrick,
Tuesday 26 December 1775

MS. Yale (C 1349). Received 30 Dec. (Reg. Let.).
ADDRESS: James Boswell Esqr., Advocate, Edinburgh.
POSTMARK: 26 DE, T•W.[1]

Drury Lane, Decr. 26, 1775

DEAR SIR: Tho I am in the midst of Preparations for Shakespeare's Jubilee, and have my Fool's Coat on to sing his praises,[2] I

[11] SJ and the Thrales had toured France from 17 Sept. to 11 Nov. (*French Journals of Mrs. Thrale and Doctor Johnson*, ed. Moses Tyson and Henry Guppy, 1932). SJ wrote to JB that he had nothing new to say about Paris (16 Nov.—*Life* ii. 387).

[12] Alexander, born 9 Oct. (Journ.). Veronica had been born in 1773 and Euphemia in 1774.

[13] SJ, *Prologue to "The Good-Natured Man"*, first line.

[14] Peter Garrick (1710–95), DG's elder brother and a prosperous wine-merchant, spent most of his life in Lichfield and often entertained SJ. For a record of JB's visit, see the account in his journal of 22–26 Mar. 1776; much of this material was later used in the *Life* (ii. 462–73).

[15] SJ had been awarded the Oxford D.C.L. on 30 Mar. (*Life* ii. 331–33).

---

[1] *Ante* From DG, 12 July 1769 and n. 1.

[2] DG's dramatic entertainment, *The Jubilee* (DL, 14 Oct. 1769), a stage adapt-

will not omit answering your Letter one post,[3] as there is a little business in it—Our Company is So full, and the Parts, or rather part, which Mr. Johnston perform'd,[4] Supplied, that I have not the least room for any new Performer—Indeed my good Friend, we are at present so overburden'd with Histrionic minors, that few Managers could bear their Weight[5]—I am Sorry, that I cannot obey Lord Kaime's Commands, I honour him much and read him often[6]—As for our Friend the Dr., I have seen him but once since his return, he is full of Sarcasm against the french[7]—At present I cannot say more upon this Subject, but You shall have it all in the Spring[8]—I scarce have time to tell You how much I am, Dear Sir, Your most Obedient, humble Servant,

D. GARRICK

From Garrick,
Friday ?3 May 1776

MS. Yale (C 1350).
ADDRESS: ——— Boswell Esqr.

Hampton,[1] Friday

Mr. Garrick presents his Compliments to Mr. Boswell, and begs to have the Pleasure of Seeing his Friend and him at the Adelphi to breakfast on Friday instead of Wednesday[2]—

ation of the pageant originally projected for the Stratford Jubilee in Sept. 1769, ran ninety times the first season—the record run of the century—and often thereafter (*Lond. Stage* pt. 4, iii. 1419). Thomas King took the part of Touchstone and DG that of Benedick (*Lond. Chron.* 14–17 Oct. 1769, xxvi. 370, cited in J. M. Stochholm, *Garrick's Folly*, 1964, pp. 164–65). DG means no more by "have my Fool's Coat on" than that he was to act. He uses a similar phrase in *ante* From DG, 6 May 1768, and *post* From DG, 3 July 1777. See also Boaden i. 648, and Tierney pp. 134–35.

[3] *Ante* To DG, 21 Dec.; Journ. 30 Dec.: "While I sat here [spending the evening at Sir George Preston's] I received a letter from Mr. Garrick in answer to mine of the 21 current mentioned in this Journal [of 21 Dec.]. He could not receive Young; but his letter was very polite. It was a pleasing desert after my comfortable entertainment."

[4] *Ante* To DG, 21 Dec. n. 1.

[5] There were twenty-nine "minor" actors at DL in the 1775/76 season. Sarah Siddons, who was let go after this year, was one of the "minor" actresses (information, including a list of their names, kindly supplied by C. B. Hogan).

[6] *Ante* To DG, 21 Dec. and n. 4.

[7] For some of SJ's critical remarks about the French, see *Life* ii. 402–03.

[8] JB saw DG at least three times in the spring of 1776, and spent part of the evening with him on 18 Mar. (Journ. 19 Mar. 1776), but he does not record their conversation for that day.

---

[1] MS. "Hampton" substituted for "Adelphi" deleted.

[2] JB had called on DG on Friday 3 May,

Mrs. Garrick reminded him after Mr. Boswell had left him, that he had an Engagement of great Consequence on Wednesday,[3] which would Engage him soon in the Morning and keep him late.

To Garrick,
Friday 21 March 1777

MS. Yale (L 567). A copy. Sent 21 Mar. "(Copy). An easy friendly letter" (Reg. Let.).
HEADING: To David Garrick Esq.

Auchinleck, 21 March 1777

DEAR SIR: As you was so obliging as to let me hear from you sometimes, even amidst the cares of your actual Theatrical Reign, may I not as reasonably flatter myself with the hopes of enjoying your correspondence now when you have abdicated as then?[1] Or must I suppose that

Carrying with you all the Stage can boast[2]

into the most compleat state of literary and social ease, you are so happy that you cannot set yourself to write to a friend so far north? I will not think so; but being uncertain if I shall get to London this year,[3] shall eagerly expect an Epistle from you.

Lord Pembroke[4] in a letter which I had the honour to receive

and presumably arranged to have breakfast with him on Wednesday 8 May. On Friday 10 May, JB and Sir William Forbes (1739–1806) of Pitsligo, Bt., had breakfast with DG (Notes, 3–10 May), which suggests that Forbes is the friend DG refers to. Forbes, a highly respectable banker, was a close friend, who served both as JB's general and literary executor; he also wrote a life of James Beattie (1806). It was at breakfast on 10 May that JB and DG competed as mimics of SJ; all except Mrs. Garrick voted for DG (Notes).

[3] This engagement has not been identified.

---

[1] DG retired at the end of the 1775/76 season, with a performance as Don Felix in *The Wonder* on 10 June.

[2] See Pope, *Spring*, ll. 7–10. JB here adapts l. 9 ("Stage" for "World").

[3] JB did not visit London this year, but met SJ at Dr. John Taylor's at Ashbourne, Derbyshire, in September.

[4] Henry Herbert (1734–94), tenth Earl of Pembroke. A cavalry officer, he rose to the rank of general, and in 1761 published *Military Equitation*, which for many years served as a standard work for the cavalry (*Henry, Elizabeth and George*, ed. Lord Herbert, 1939, p. 30). At various times he was Lord of the Bedchamber, Lord Lieutenant of Wiltshire, and Governor of Portsmouth. He was a genial friend of JB's, who visited him at Wilton with Paoli in 1775 (Journ. 19–22 Apr. 1775). Pembroke had

from his Lordship the other day, entertained me with the substance of your Prologue when you read Lethe to the King and Queen.[5] What a fortunate Man am I to have such extraordinary privileges! to be the object of the kind attention of such men as you know are pleased to treat me in a manner far beyond what I can justly claim.

I am exceedingly curious to know how you feel upon your change of life.[6] Hercules with the Distaff must be a strange consciousness to Hercules long used to wield the Club. I know not to what I can with propriety liken your change of situation, as I am unacquainted with your present mode of Existence.

I hope you will not like Congreve disdain or affect to disdain that brilliant favour of the Muse which has conferred such lustre upon you. Mason's defence of him in the Memoirs of Gray will not do.[7] Voltaire told me himself with most critical pleasantry, "Had

also corresponded for many years with DG, whose nephew David for a while held a commission in Pembroke's First (or Royal) Regiment of Dragoons (*Letters DG* ii. 692 n. 1; *Army List*, 1772–75). They were neighbours in Hampton (Oman, p. 344). For Pembroke on DG, see Journ. 21 Apr. 1778.

[5] "We hear that on Saturday evening [15 Feb.] David Garrick, Esq. had the honour to recite a dramatic performance, and to speak a prologue, written by himself for the occasion, before their Majesties, at the Queen's Palace" (*Lond. Chron.* 15–18 Feb. xli. 166). The dramatic piece was an alteration of *Lethe* (*Letters DG* iii. 1153–54, 1167–68; M. E. Knapp, "Garrick's Last Command Performance" in *The Age of Johnson, Essays Presented to Chauncey Brewster Tinker* [ed. F. W. Hilles] 1949, pp. 61–71). It is ironic that what to JB must have seemed a great occasion was one that DG wished to forget. Knapp discusses DG's feelings of humiliation at the chilly reception his performance received.

Pembroke wrote to JB, 9 Mar.: "Garrick says he is running over with liberty, but, for god's sake, ne me citer pas, for it is better, you know, to call names, than name names, I beleive he is dying of ennui. He has read Lethe, in the Texier stile, at the Queen's House. He spoke the Prologue to me, 'an black bird, once a famous singer, grown old, and grey, retires on a branch, meaning to sing no more. The Royal Eagle spys him, and courteously drags him to his Court, makes him tune his voice again, and approves his notes etc.' " Some of the stanzas are quoted in the Knapp article. See also L. L. Martz and E. M. Martz, "Notes on Manuscripts Relating to David Garrick", *Review of English Studies* (1943) xix. 193–96.

[6] *Post* From DG, 3 July.

[7] Temple had contributed a character sketch of Gray to *Lond. Mag.* (Mar. 1772, xli. 140) in which he remarked that Gray "also had in some degree that weakness which disgusted Voltaire so much in Mr. Congreve". This "weakness" was the wish to be thought of as a gentleman rather than as an author (see next note). In his *Poems of Gray to Which Are Prefixed Memoirs*, 1775, William Mason (1725–97) included Temple's character sketch, to which he added this footnote: "I have often thought that Mr. Congreve might very well be vindicated on this head. It seldom happens that the vanity of authorship continues to the end of a man's days, it usually soon leaves him where it found him; and if he has not something better to build his self-approbation upon than that of being a popular writer, he generally finds himself ill at ease, if respected only on that account.

it not been for his Comedies, I might as well have gone to see any Yorkshire Squire."[8]

I should suppose that Mrs. Garrick, to whom pray make my best compliments, will be happy at your quitting the stage; as she will have more of your company. And yet nobody more highly relished your wonderful dramatick exhibitions of genius and art. So I cannot decide. No doubt you will have read the Capital Publication of Memoirs and Letters of Lord Chesterfield.[9] I am impatient to feast on it. I remain, My Dear Sir, allways very much yours.

To Garrick, Saturday 22 March 1777

MS. Yale (L 568). A draft. Sent 22 Mar. "David Garrick Esq. to the above effect" referring to the immediately preceding entry: 22 March 1777, JB to Hugo Arnot: "Hugo Arnot Esq. about procuring him a sight of Mr. Garrick's Robin Hood" (Reg. Let.).
HEADING: To David Garrick Esq.

Auchinleck, 22[1] March 1777

DEAR SIR: Your goodness to me upon every occasion makes it easy

Mr. Congreve was much advanced in years when the young French Poet paid him this visit; and, though a man of the world, he might now feel that indifference to literary fame which Mr. Gray, who always led a more retired and philosophic life, certainly felt much earlier. Both of them therefore might reasonably, at times, express some disgust, if their quiet was intruded upon by persons who thought they flattered them by such intrusion" (p. 403 n.†).

[8] JB had visited Voltaire at Ferney in 1764 (Journ. 24–29 Dec., Notes 25–30 Dec. 1764), but his notes of their conversation do not mention Congreve. In his *Letters Concerning the English Nation*, letter 19, Voltaire writes: Congreve "was infirm, and come to the Verge of Life when I knew him. Mr. *Congreve* had one Defect, which was, his entertaining too mean an Idea of his first Profession, (that of a Writer) tho' 'twas to this he ow'd his Fame and Fortune. He spoke of his Works as of Trifles that were beneath him; and hinted to me in our first Conversation, that I should visit him upon no other Foot than that of a Gentleman, who led a life of Plainness and Simplicity. I answer'd, that had he been so unfortunate as to be a mere Gentleman I should never have come to see him; and I was very much disgusted at so unseasonable a Piece of Vanity" (trans. John Lockman, 1733; rpt. 1926, p. 140).

[9] *Miscellaneous Works of the Late Philip Dormer Stanhope, Earl of Chesterfield . . . To Which Are Prefixed, Memoirs of His Life . . . by M. Maty* [ed. J. O. Justamond] 2 vols. 1777. JB was much taken with some of Chesterfield's correspondence, which he read as this work was going through the press (Journ. 18 Mar. 1776).

[1] MS. "Auchinleck 22" substituted for "Treesbank 9" deleted. JB had been at Treesbank, Ayrshire, on 9 Mar. for the funeral the next day of his wife's sister,

for me at any time to ask a favour from you. It is still easier when the favour is to contribute to the advancement of any species of useful or curious knowledge.

Mr. Hugo Arnot the bearer of this,[2] a brother Advocate of mine at the Scotch bar, is engaged in writing a History of Edinburgh.[3] To trace the Manners of the people is one of his chief objects; and you My Dear Sir know of what consequence Publick[4] Diversions are. The Laureat has elegantly expressed[5] it in Dodsley's Collection of Poems. I need not quote his verses. I trust[6] the fine compliment in them to yourself lives pleasingly in your remembrance.[7]

Our Antiquarians in Scotland are at a loss to know distinctly what was a Game or Play called Robin Hood of which frequent mention is made in our acts of Parliament.[8] Your friend and mine Percy in his Reliques of Ancient Poetry tells[9] us of a little dramatick piece entitled Robin Hood and the Friar, in Mr. Garricks Collection.[10] It is probable that this piece may throw

Mary (Montgomerie) Campbell. Presumably he got no farther than the dateline of a letter to someone on 9 Mar., and converted it to this draft.

[2] Hugo Arnot (1749–86), Edinburgh advocate and antiquarian. Arnot requested JB's aid in a letter dated 17 Mar. JB's reply to Arnot, enclosing this letter to DG, is dated 22 Mar. Arnot also obtained a letter of introduction from Capt. R. B. Walsingham, R.N., which reads: "My Dear Garrick, This is an *introduction* to an *introduction*; Mr. Arnot who will deliver this to you, has a letter of Audience from Mr. Boswell, he is a Scotchman, and wishes to be seconded by an Irishman, therefore put on *your Glove* and take him by *the Hand*, and you'll Oblige Your Friend R. B. Walsingham. Monday Portugal Street" (Forster Coll. Victoria and Albert Museum, F48 E20 xvi. 91).

[3] Arnot's *History of Edinburgh* was published in 1779.

[4] MS. "to Manners" deleted before "Publick"

[5] MS. "expressed" written above a deleted "mentioned"

[6] MS. "trust" written above a deleted "hope"

[7] William Whitehead's "To Mr. Garrick" appears in all the various editions (1748 to 1775) of Robert Dodsley's *Collection of Poems, by Several Hands*. JB presumably refers to ll. 93–104, which begin:

> A nation's taste depends on you
> —Perhaps a nation's virtue too.

[8] Arnot's *History* elaborates on the Robin Hood games which were played in Edinburgh each May, either on a Sunday or a holiday, until the middle or late sixteenth century. His account includes a discussion of the attempts to suppress the games by statute (pp. 77–79). See also Jackson, pp. 411–16.

[9] MS. "mentions" deleted before "tells"

[10] "Robin Hood and Guy of Gisborne", is printed in *Reliques of Ancient English Poetry*, ed. Thomas Percy, 1765. Percy remarks that a different version of this poem, "a little dramatic piece on the subject of Robin Hood and the Friar", appears in DG's collection of old plays (i. 76). "A mery Geste of Robyn Hoode . . . wyth a newe Playe for to be played in Maye Games" is included among the "old and curious Romances" which form the Appendix to William Beloe's listing of the Garrick Collection in his *Anecdotes of Literature and*

light on the Subject and I am to beg, Sir, that you may be pleased to allow Mr. Arnot to peruse it, which will be adding another favour to the many which I have experienced from you. I hope Mr. Arnot's book will entertain you.[11] I have only to wish that you may give him an opportunity to record one very agreable remarkable event in the History of the Caledonian Capital—it's being visited by Mr. Garrick. I am ever, My Dear Sir, your Much obliged, humble servant.

From Garrick, Thursday 3 July 1777

MS. Yale (C 1351). Received 8 July. "David Garrick Esq. that he is in rantipole spirits since he quitted the stage etc." (Reg. Let.).[1]
ADDRESS: ——— Boswell Esqr.

Hampton, July 3d 1777

DEAR SIR: I should have answer'd your letters[2] Sooner, had not I waited to find a curious book for Your friend Mr. Arnott[3]—

You have much oblig'd me by bringing us acquainted—Our Club has flourish'd greatly this last winter, and the addition of Messrs. Dunning,[4] Sheridan[5] etc. etc. etc.[6] give us a great Eclat—However we are incompleat till You add Your Skill to the Concert—

Scarce Books, 6 vols., 1814, 1808–12, i. 406–07. DG gave his Collection to the British Library (Stone and Kahrl, p. 175; G. M. Kahrl, *The Garrick Collection of Old English Plays*, 1982, no. 948.)

[11] In the Preface to his *History*, dated 1 Mar. 1779, Arnot writes, "*Let me not omit to acknowledge the polite and friendly attention with which* DAVID GARRICK, *Esq. communicated to me some curious and valuable manuscripts.—Alas! I little thought that this was to be a tribute to his memory only.*" An extract from "*a Manuscript Play, in the Possession of David Garrick, Esq.*" appears as Appendix I in Arnot's *History*.

---

[1] JB wrote in his journal for 8 July: "Lett[er] from Garrick [but had] Not much relish [for it]."

[2] *Ante* To DG, 21 Mar., and 22 Mar.

[3] Presumably the ms. of the play of which Arnot printed an extract in his *History of Edinburgh* (*ante* To DG, 22 Mar. n. 11).

[4] John Dunning (1731–83), first Baron Ashburton (1782), a prominent London barrister. He had acted for DG in a libel suit against William Kenrick in 1772 (*Letters DG* ii. 811 first n. 3, 821 n. 4). He was first elected to The Club in March (Croker, i. 529).

[5] Richard Brinsley Sheridan (1751–1816), who was elected to The Club in March of this year (Croker, i. 529), had already written four plays and taken over the management of DL from DG.

[6] Three others were elected to The Club this year: Joseph Warton in January, Richard Marlay and John Fitzpatrick, Earl of Upper Ossory, in March (Croker, i. 529).

Tho I am troubled now and then with Short fits of the Stone, and, what I call, long fits of the Gout,[7] No school Boy at a breaking up for the Holidays, had Ever Such rantipole Spirits—I feel such a Weight off my[8] Spirits, that I really feel myself a New Man—However there is no good without some concomitant Evil, I grow fat, and Short-winded[9]—I heard this Morning, that Your Theatre is going to be honour'd with the appearance of Madam Abington[10]—My heart beats to be with You, not to act, or to See your actors, but to converse and be happy with my friends—You may tell Mr. Robertson that he need not be[11] apprehensive of my arrival in Scotland;[12] I shall not *now* insist upon his Seeing Me play the fool, for I have made a vow never to Set my foot upon any theatre again, and I will keep my vow most religiously—You may assure him with my respectful Compliments to him, that I would not Act again one Winter to double my fortune. Dear Sir, most truly Yours,

D. Garrick

I can scarce write for the Nasty Gout in my fingers.

To Garrick,
Tuesday 3 March 1778

MS. Yale (L 569). A copy in Lawrie's hand, except for heading, complimentary close, and brief postscript, written by JB. Sent 4 Mar. "David Garrick, Esq. How he likes Digges—Of Home's *Alfred* etc. etc.—(Copy)" (Reg. Let.).
HEADING: To David Garrick Esq.

[7] *Ante* From DG, 25 Nov. 1767 and n. 2.

[8] MS. "of Care"; "of" changed to "off" and "Care" deleted before "my"

[9] DG may be remembering the Queen's description of Hamlet as "fat, and scant of breath" (V. ii. 287).

[10] Frances Abington (1737–1815) first played at DL in 1756 and, apart from the years between 1759 and 1765, which she spent in Ireland, remained with the company until 1782. She acted in Scotland during race week (19–31 July) and in a benefit on 3 Aug. (Dibdin, pp. 170–71). DG's remark has an ironic edge. He found Mrs. Abington difficult to deal with, and described her to Peter Fountain, 31 July 1776, as "that most Worthless Creature. . . . She is below the thought of an honest Man or Woman—she is as *Silly*, as she is *false* and treacherous" (*Letters DG* iii. 1122; see Stone and Kahrl, p. 594).

[11] MS. "now" deleted before "be"

[12] William Robertson (1721–93), D.D., historian. Robertson and DG had been acquainted since 1758 (Alexander Carlyle, *Autobiography*, ed. J. H. Burton, 1861, pp. 278–80; Boaden i. 95). They met occasionally thereafter, and their correspondence suggests a cordial relationship (*Letters DG* ii. 614; Boaden i. 508–09, ii. 48–49; Tierney pp. 130–35). See also *ante* To DG, 21 Dec. 1775 and n. 10.

TO GARRICK, 3 MARCH 1778

Edinr. 3 March 1778

Dear Sir: Will you have the goodness to forgive me for not thanking you sooner for your obliging letter of last Summer?[1] and the additional goodness to forgive me without my having the aukward labour of making an apology which at present would be as hard as the Egyptian task to make bricks without straw?[2] This will be granting me absolution without pennance; or in the style of His Britannick Majestys Remissions as announced to us in the Newspapers—*a free pardon.*[3]

You have now had an opportunity of seeing Mr. Digges upon a London Stage.[4] Pray tell me how you like him? You may remember how you used to rate[5] me for speaking of him with applause. You must know that he was the first actor that I ever saw; and the impression made upon a warm youthfull imagination is strong and permanent. It was He who threw open to me the portals of Theatrical Enchantment, and therefore He and Pleasure are inseparably associated in my mind.

What do you say to John Home to console him upon the fate of his Alfred? Do you exhort him to acknowledge the justice of his sentence? or do you bid him "die hard, die like a Cock"?[6] I know nothing of this Play.[7]

[1] *Ante* From DG, 3 July 1777.

[2] See Exodus 5: 7.

[3] As, for example, in the case of three soldiers convicted of mutiny at Leith on 20 Apr. 1779 and sentenced to death, the King, "having regard to the . . . distinguished behaviour of the 42d regiment" was "most graciously pleased to grant" to the offenders "a free pardon, in full confidence, that they will endeavour . . . to atone for this . . . atrocious offence" (*Cal. Merc.* 29 May 1779, pp. [2–3]).

[4] For Digges's relationship with JB, and his previous career, see *ante* To DG, 25 Dec. 1772 and n. 13. Digges decamped from debtors' prison in Edinburgh in 1777 (Dibdin, p. 170) and surfaced as Cato at the Haymarket 14 Aug. of the same year. He also played Sir John Brute in *The Provoked Wife*, Macheath in *The Beggar's Opera*, and Cardinal Wolsey in *Henry VIII* among other roles that season (*Lond. Stage* pt. 5, i. 97, 99, 100, 117).

[5] MS. JB himself has inserted "rate" over "write" deleted.

[6] We have been unable to trace this quotation. 3 Mar. 1778 was Shrove Tuesday, the principal day for the practice of cock-throwing (tying a cock to a stake and stoning it to death), one of the more barbarous of Shrovetide sports common until well into the nineteenth century (OED; M. D. George, *London Life in the XVIIIth Century*, 1925, pp. 17, 326, 352).

[7] CG, 21 Jan. for three nights only, with an epilogue by DG, spoken by Mrs. Barry (Knapp, no. 272; *Lond. Stage* pt. 5, i. 142–43). Home withdrew the play himself after the third performance (*Pub. Adv.* 24 Jan. p. [3]). *Alfred* was received "with great Applause" after the second performance, according to *Pub. Adv.* (23 Jan.) p. [4], but *West. Mag.* (Jan. 1778) vi. 47 was not enthusiastic, and pointed out that, among other defects, "the language . . . frequently descends into offensive vulgarity". The

TO GARRICK, 3 MARCH 1778

Lord Pembroke in his last letter to me which I had the honour to receive a few days ago, seems to think a French War inevitable.[8] If there should come one I doubt if you will be able to make a better Song than you did for the last "Hearts of Oak".[9] Perhaps you will not have such a good subject.

Our Club is by your account much enriched since I was last in London. I hope to be with you again this spring.[10] Be kind enough to let me hear from you were it but to tell me you are free from your complaints. I beg you may present my best Compliments to Mrs. Garrick. I am ever, Dear Sir, Yours sincerely.

What is our friend Dr. Johnson doing with the English Poets?[11]

play was brought out by DG's publisher, Thomas Becket, on 14 Feb. (*Pub. Adv.* p. [1]).

[8] Pembroke wrote to JB, 22 Feb.: "By the orders Hood, and De La Motte Piquet have in the Bay, a war seems inevitable. . . . All in France is in motion. The Duc of Lauzan, with me, the other Eveng., received orders to join at Brest immediately. . . . To help the State, My Son too is raising a company."

[9] Verse by DG and music by William Boyce (1759), during the Seven Years' War. (*ante* From DG, 8 Mar. 1768 and n. 3).

[10] As he was to be from 17 Mar. to 19 May (Journ.).

[11] On 29 Mar. 1777 SJ signed the contract for *Prefaces, Biographical and Critical, to the Works of the English Poets* (*Life* iii. 109; *Works SJ* i. 263–64). He was slow to get started, but in early Nov. 1777 he told Mrs. Thrale that he had begun to work "diligently" (*Letters SJ* ii. 231), and on 17 Mar. JB read his "Life of Denham". On 19 Mar. the Dillys showed JB "a good portion of the 'Life of Cowley' " (Journ.), and by 17 Apr. SJ had proof of his "Life of Waller" (*Life* iii. 313). At the end of July SJ sent all of "Cowley" to John Nichols, his printer, telling him that he was already "far advanced" in "Dryden", and that Milton's was to be his next extended Life. In the same letter he asks Nichols "to gather the Lives of *Denham*, *Butler*, and *Waller*, and bind them in half binding in a small volume, and let me have it to shew my friends, as soon as may be" (*Letters SJ* ii. 254). The first four volumes, containing the longer lives of Cowley, Waller, Dryden, and Milton and eighteen shorter lives, came out in 1781 (Courtney and Smith, p. 132).

From Garrick,
Saturday 25 April 1778
MS. Yale (C 1352).
ADDRESS: James Boswell Esqr.

April 25[1]

MY DEAR SIR: The Ladies[2] commanded Me to breakfast at Hampton—I could not but Obey, tho I should have been particularly happy to have breakfasted with you this Morning.[3] Most truly Yours,

D. GARRICK

From Garrick,
Sunday[1]
MS. Yale (C 1352.2).
ADDRESS: To J. Boswell Esqr.

Sunday

MY DEAR SIR: I must desire You not to say a Word where You are going of my design to play at Drury-Lane next Summer. I will give You my reasons when I see You. Yours most truly,

D. GARRICK

[1] MS. "26". The date is inferred from Journ. 25 Apr. (see n. 3 below).

[2] Presumably Mrs. Garrick and her niece Elisabeth Fürst, who had been living with the Garricks since 1777 (*Letters DG* iii. 1194 and n. 3, 1272 and n. 2). The "Ladies" may also have included Tabitha Flasby, a frequent summer visitor at Hampton House (*Letters DG* ii. 615 and n. 4). Hannah More (1745–1833), who had been staying off and on with the Garricks, returned to Bristol some time in April (Roberts i. 139–40; *Life* iii. 256).

[3] On 24 Apr. JB called on DG, who was just going out. JB records in his journal: "I said Id breakfast with him tomorrow. He then said he was going to the Country. But he'd stay a morning on purpose to have my company at a breakfast. . . . I accompanied him to near Northumberland House; and promised to call next morning and take my chance to break[fast] with him if he was not gone. For he had proposed to send me a card in case it should not be convenient for Mrs. Garrick to wait." JB writes in his journal for 25 Apr.: "Met Garrick's coach in Piccadilly and Servt said he was ["Break" deleted] not at home and there was letter for me."

[1] Letter not dated. The only instance of DG's acting in the summer after he became manager of DL is his performance on 18 Aug. 1768 of Ranger in *The Suspicious Husband* "By Particular Desire" of the King of Denmark (*Lond. Stage* pt. 4, iii. 1343). DG did not know that he would be called upon to act on that occasion until the previous month (*Letters DG* ii. 620–21).

INTRODUCTION TO THE BOSWELL-BURKE CORRESPONDENCE

THE portrait of Edmund Burke in Boswell's *Life of Johnson* is its most notorious failure. Other principals, like David Garrick and Oliver Goldsmith, emerge in all their natural liveliness, and even bit players, like Oliver Edwards and the Rev. William Tasker, make brilliant cameo appearances. But Burke is dimly outlined in circumlocutions: "one of the most luminous minds of the present age", "one of the company", "a celebrated orator", "one of our friends". At least once he is hidden in a dash. Most often Burke is "eminent": "an eminent publick character", "an eminent person whom we all greatly admired", "an eminent friend of ours", "a very eminent literary character", "a certain eminent political friend of ours".[1]

Eminent but indistinct. Burke seldom comes forward in his own voice and gestures. Nor do others often describe him; Boswell restricts even himself to a few respectful compliments. Only Johnson is allowed extensive comment and he praises and criticizes Burke without stint. He looked forward at the beginning of Burke's Parliamentary career: "Burke is a great man by nature, and is expected soon to attain civil greatness" (*Life* ii. 16–17). Years later he explained one source of this greatness, Burke's immediacy of impact:

> If a man were to go by chance at the same time with Burke under a shed, to shun a shower, he would say—"this is an extraordinary man." If Burke should go into a stable to see his horse drest, the ostler would say—we have had an extraordinary man here (*Life* iv. 275–76).[2]

This admiration was already plain in the *Journal of a Tour to the Hebrides*. Boswell reports there that Johnson, "said, he did not grudge Burke's being the first man in the House of Commons, for he was the first man every where" (*Life* v. 269). Yet Johnson is also free in censure: he depreciates Burke's jocularity, criticizes

[1] These references are all easily located in the index to the Hill-Powell edition of the *Life*.

[2] For the variants of this famous tribute, see Waingrow, pp. 93–94 and n. 2, and *Herbrides*, pp. 409–10.

his conversation as ostentatious, questions his honesty as a politician, and damns him as "a *bottomless* Whig".[3]

Burke is given few opportunities to respond *viva voce* in the *Life*. He praises Johnson's opinion on a legal case as "workman-like", says modestly that to elicit Johnson's talk is enough for him to do in conversation, excuses Johnson's rough remarks to others, and pays homage on Johnson's deathbed. His most memorable comment is pseudonymous. When Boswell said that Herbert Croft in his "Life of Young" had imitated Johnson's style successfully, "a very eminent literary character" denied it: " 'It has all his pomp without his force; it has all the nodosities of the oak without its strength. . . . It has all the contortions of the Sybil, without the inspiration.' "[4] And that is about all.

Given Boswell's eagerness to exhibit Johnson in all the perspectives contrast could offer—as Dr. Major and Dr. Minor with Goldsmith, as hedgehog and fox with Garrick, to cite a couple of examples[5]—it may seem inexplicable that he did not juxtapose Johnson and Burke. Johnson's superiority to other learned men lay in "the art of thinking", the ability to convert knowledge into wisdom (*Life* iv. 427–28), expressed memorably in speech. Burke was his one formidable rival in those conversational encounters that contemporaries prized as the highest form of entertainment. Johnson praised him as "the only man whose common conversation corresponds with the general fame which he has in the world. Take up whatever topick you please, he is ready to meet you" (*Life* iv. 19–20). And once when Johnson was ill, he remarked, "That fellow calls forth all my powers. Were I to see Burke now, it would kill me" (*Life* ii. 450). But more than emulation was involved. In a calmer moment, Johnson epitomized Burke's social virtues: "I love his knowledge, his genius, his diffusion, and affluence of conversation" (*Life* ii. 181).

Once, with easy virtuosity, Boswell reports both men's parts in a long general conversation at The Club (*Life* iii. 230–38), which, together with many instances in his journal, demonstrates that he was able to record Burke clearly and vividly. He did not lack materials; Burke appears more often in his journal than either

[3] Respectively, *Life* iv. 276, iii. 24/, ii. 348, iv. 223. Boswell does report Johnson as admitting that two of Burke's "conceits" were admirable (iii. 322–23).

[4] Respectively, *Life* iii. 62, iv. 26–27, iv. 280, iv. 407, iv. 59.

[5] *Life* ii. 253–57, ii. 82–83.

Garrick or Goldsmith, and what it failed to preserve, memory and the reports of others would have supplied. Nor did a fear of wounding sensibilities usually deter Boswell; he includes, for instance, embarrassing episodes involving Bishop Percy. The reasons for Boswell's reticence about presenting Burke, to which the present correspondence provides essential clues, extend beyond embarrassment.

Like Johnson and Garrick, Burke had been one of Boswell's early heroes. On seeing Burke installed as Lord Rector of the University of Glasgow in 1784, Boswell recalled "that the first time I had contemplated the character of Mr. Burke, was at Glasgow, four and twenty years ago, when I was a Student of law there, and viewed him like a Planet in the heavens" (Journ. 10 Apr. 1784). Johnson and Garrick, however, had been famous in 1760, while Burke was still an obscure compiler of the *Annual Register*; all Boswell knew about him was that he had written *Of the Sublime and Beautiful* (1757), which presumably Adam Smith discussed in those lectures on rhetoric and *belles-lettres* that Boswell praised so warmly.[6]

By the time Boswell first met Burke at Sir Joshua Reynolds's on 6 May 1772, both had come into notice as authors, Boswell for *An Account of Corsica*, and Burke for several political treatises, most notably *Thoughts on the Cause of the Present Discontents* (1770), which provided the Rockingham Whigs with a *raison d'être*. But Burke's fame derived mainly from his talents as a speaker in the House of Commons, where Boswell thought himself fortunate to hear him:

> It was astonishing how all kinds of figures of speech crowded upon him. He was like a man in an Orchard where boughs loaded with fruit hung arround him, and he pulled apples as fast as he pleased and pelted the ministry. It seemed to me however that his Oratory rather tended to distinguish himself than to assist his cause. There was amusement instead of

[6] Boswell says that he first heard of Burke as the author of *The Sublime and Beautiful* (Journ. 22 Apr. 1788), but he did not read it until many years after it was published (Journ. 18–19 July 1779). That Smith discussed it is the plausible inference of Boswell's editors, I. S. Lustig and F. A. Pottle (*Applause*, p. 204 n. 9). Though Burke is not mentioned in Smith's *Lectures on Rhetoric and Belles Lettres* (ed. J. M. Lothian, 1963, which was printed from a student's notes of 1762–63), neither are the two dicta that Boswell assigns to these lectures (F. A. Pottle, "Boswell's University Education", *Johnson, Boswell, and Their Circle*, 1965, p. 248 n. 1).

persuasion. It was like the exhibition of a favourite Actor (Journ. 5 Apr. 1773).

When he came to write the *Life*, Boswell overlooked their initial encounter, stating it was at his election to The Club (30 Apr. 1773) that he had first met Burke. Boswell had the excuse that he seems not to have found his notes for 1772 until after he had written up this section of the *Life*, but to make this mistake he had also had to forget his discussion with Johnson, published in the *Tour*, of his election, when Johnson told him, "Several of the members wished to keep you out. Burke told me, he doubted if you were fit for it: but, now you are in, none of them are sorry. Burke says, that you have so much good humour naturally, it is scarce a virtue" (*Life* v. 76). This certainly implies some degree of familiarity but their relationship had become so strained after the publication of the *Tour* that Boswell may have unconsciously repressed these early patronizing judgements.

Yet in a deeper sense Boswell was right to date their acquaintance from the meeting at The Club, for the next day, eager as always to cultivate someone he admired, he felt free to call on Burke: "not in" (Journ. 1 May 1773). This situation was rectified over the next few springs. Boswell, both assiduous and relaxed, exerted his usual appeal. On 13 May 1776, to cite a fuller journal account than most, he heard Burke speak in Parliament, then called on him to ask some unspecified question, was given wine and tea and supper, listened to Burke on various topics "run on fine", and was "kindly" invited to call often. Two years later they were "charmingly easy and well at breakfast", and Boswell was so absorbed in their conversation—politics, puns, Johnson, Hume, death—that he missed an engagement. "With thee conversing I forget all time", he quotes in his journal. It had been worth it. Burke called him "ingenious", and he in turn suggested that Burke write the history of the times.[7]

During these years Boswell formed an imaginative model of Burke with which he could identify when he was pleased with himself. Especially after distinguishing himself in company, he felt "a kind of Burke".[8] This model, in its public aspect, formed

[7] Journ. 12 Apr. 1778. Burke also appreciated Boswell's social adeptness; he said of Boswell's arranging his first Johnson-Wilkes dinner meeting that "there was nothing to equal it in the whole history of the *Corps Diplomatique*" (*Life* iii. 79).

[8] Journ. 28 Sept. 1774; see also Journ. 3 Feb. and 30 Nov. 1775.

part of a happy conjunction, "London and Parliament and Burke" (Journ. 22 Feb. 1775) that Boswell envisaged as the most desirable of futures. But Burke also furnished a model of private life. On that "charmingly easy" occasion just referred to, Boswell says, "I told Burke he was the only man I could wish to be. And this not till I had seen how happy he was with his wife and son. For I thought no man happy who had not domestick happiness." How could Burke not enjoy continued happiness, he asked W. J. Temple, when he had "so much knowledge, so much animation, and the consciousness of so much fame"?[9] Boswell's sense of identification with Burke and concern for Burke's welfare were later to make him assume that Burke was equally concerned for his.

A correspondence, initiated in 1778 by Boswell, was intended to cement friendship, but its only immediate result was Burke's response to Boswell's warning from Edinburgh in early 1779 that if a bill for abolishing certain penal statutes against Scottish Catholics was passed in Parliament, Presbyterian bigotry would lead to a desperate rebellion. The amusing ironies of Burke's long reply did not much disguise that excited seriousness with which he always regarded what he took to be vital public questions. While not directly critical of Boswell, it was not a letter one would write to a friend whose views were regarded with much respect.

In fact, Burke did not pay enough attention to Boswell's political opinions to let them spoil the enjoyment he took in his company, though Boswell liked to emphasize that he was both a "Tory and an American" (Journ. 12 Apr. 1778), an unusual combination of attitudes, and to warn Burke against becoming too deep-dyed in Whiggery (Journ. 29 Apr. 1781). In turn, Boswell enlisted him as a confidant (he told Burke he would like a "Seraglio of young girls"—Notes, 5 May 1776) and a counsellor on such everyday problems as how to respond to a malicious newspaper paragraph (Journ. 20 Apr. 1779). (Ignore it, Burke said.) He also elicited Burke's opinions on more significant subjects, like religion and sexual behaviour; when asked how he would react to a son's licentiousness, Burke replied, as he would to his own, "with tenderness and regret" (Journ. 31 Mar. 1779). Like many observers then and now, Boswell thought Burke

[9] To Temple, 12 Aug. 1775—MS. Pierpont Morgan.

demonstrated such intellectual superiority that no ordinary mind could judge his. Entangled in an old nightmare of Liberty vs. Necessity, Boswell wrote indignantly in his journal: "A presbyterian Minister in an obscure parish may speculate on the *Motives* of Burke, and be *clear* that he is a *Machine*. This is a provoking thought" (Journ. 23 Aug. 1782).

Despite their political differences, the situation after the fall of North's Ministry (March 1782) even seemed to improve their relationship. Burke became Paymaster of the Forces, the most lucrative of Government offices, under the uneasy Rockingham-Shelburne Ministry, and Boswell, as discontented in Edinburgh as "a cat in an airpump", immediately applied for assistance: a post of £600 a year would enable him to live in London (To Burke, 18 Mar. 1782). When Burke failed to respond, Boswell was prepared to sulk in the dignity of "an old Scottish Baron and Tory" (Journ. 14 Apr. 1782), but the death of the Judge Advocate (a legal sinecure in the army, worth about £180 a year) changed his mind. The Judge Advocate had to be a member of the Faculty of Advocates, and Boswell eagerly urged on Burke that he had been the only member of the Faculty to express the pro-American sentiments congenial to the new Ministry, while appealing as well to "private freindship" (To Burke, 18 Apr. 1782).

Burke did what he could, or at least went through the motions.[1] He applied on Boswell's behalf to Henry Seymour Conway, the Commander-in-Chief, who was politely non-committal. The post fell, as Burke must have anticipated, to a candidate with more Parliamentary influence, but Boswell was so impressed by Burke's recommendation of him as "a Lawyer of Ability and of general Erudition, and the pleasantest and best tempered Man in the World"[2] that years later, in his "Memoirs", he proudly mentioned Burke's having drawn his character "in glowing colours" and declared that he valued the recommendation more than the office (*Lit. Car.* p. xl). Burke's "real kindness", Boswell told him at the time, his "active benevolence", showed that he was "a very very good man" (To Burke, 30 Apr. 1782). The model had proved its worth: in a spirited moment a few months later,

[1] Henry Dundas, the most powerful of Scottish political figures, later told Boswell "that he *knew* Burke wished to assist" him (Journ. 16 July 1782).

[2] EB to Conway, 23 Apr. 1782, enclosed in From EB of the same date.

Boswell told himself, "I now have as full satisfaction in my own existence as Mr. Burke has—only that I wish for greater objects" (Journ. 18 June 1782). Then, much too quickly, Burke went out of office, but with the shrewd advice that Boswell turn his attention to Dundas: "Pay your Court there, my Dear Boswell. It will answer I tell you" (From Burke, 1 Sept. 1782).

When Burke came back in as Paymaster with the Fox-North Coalition (April 1783), both Boswell and he were under new and severe pressures. His father's death (August 1782) had made it possible for Boswell, if he dared, to move himself to London and the English bar but, besides moral support, he badly needed some office that would cushion his loss of income and additional expenses.

Burke's crisis was more acute: morally, the Coalition was a betrayal of those principles of party purity he had long advocated, and could only be justified by the blackness of its predecessor, the Shelburne Ministry. Practically, he was trying to carry through the reform of the Pay Office, an establishment combining the notable features of the Augean Stables and the Circumlocution Office. And, generously and unwisely, he had reinstated two important officials, Charles Bembridge and John Powell, accused of malfeasance, justifying a fierce criticism that left him constantly on the defensive in the House of Commons. The embarrassing outcome of this scandal was that Bembridge was fined and sentenced to gaol, while Powell committed suicide. Finally, Burke was trying, in approved contemporary fashion, to secure lucrative, permanent government posts for his relations, with particular urgency in the cases of his son and brother (Richard Jr. and Richard Sr.) and his "cousin" Will.

But these strains had no immediate effect on Boswell and Burke's relationship, which was at its closest in the spring of 1783. Apparently after some reminder, Burke invited Boswell to Gregories, his country place in Buckinghamshire, an invitation so valued that Boswell prepared himself with a memorandum, "You're going to enjoy as much as can be had on earth perhaps." His stay in Eden, however, was to be as short as that of our grand parents; he had only time to be shown around, to admire the collection of expensive paintings, and to be lectured on farming, when an express with the news that his nephew David Cuninghame had been critically wounded in a duel recalled him to

London.[3] But that spring he remained several days longer in London than planned in order to accompany Burke to the annual dinner at Chelsea Hospital: "I drank liberally and was in high spirits", says Boswell, "and very happy in my talk, being much encouraged by Mr. Burke" (Journ. 29 May 1783).

On this occasion, too, Boswell finally engaged Burke in that "close conversation" on his prospects which Burke had evaded all spring. (Boswell, a lawyerlike Rasselas, had even intended to present him with a "Memorial on choice of life".)[4] Was it not a proper topic? Hadn't Reynolds written the previous autumn that Burke "says you are the pleasantest man he ever saw and sincerely wishes you would come and live amongst us"? (From Reynolds, 1 Oct. 1782). Didn't Burke have a virtual obligation to provide the means? When pushed to the point, however, Burke was not encouraging: Boswell should fix his mind on some employment in Scotland, and only come to London on visits (Journ. 29 May 1783). Johnson had given him the same advice and Boswell knew it was sensible, but what he wanted to hear was that Burke would take care of him.

Enveloped by the melancholia with which Scotland paralysed him, Boswell could hardly rouse himself to exertion when the Scottish legal establishment faced restructuring after Dundas was forced out as Lord Advocate (principal law officer) in August 1783. Eventually he sent a feeble letter asking for Burke's recommendation to be made Lord Advocate or Solicitor-General (the second office) or joint Solicitor-General or anything. Again he called on "generous friendship" to rescue him from "provincial obscurity". In return he would assist the Coalition's unpopular cause in Scotland (To Burke, 8 Aug. 1783).

Whenever Boswell solicited political help from the powerful (Lord Mountstuart, Dundas, Burke, Lord Lonsdale), he simultaneously insisted on his independence. This attitude was so rigid and unrealistic as to suggest he was compulsively repeating his way of behaving towards his father, when he had vacillated between a deep dependence and assertions of independence that indicated not an emerging self-assurance but a recklessness

[3] Mems. 20 and 21 Apr. 1783; Journ. 31 Mar. and 21 Apr. 1783; *Applause*, pp. 116–17. Cuninghame survived. Boswell wrote a letter to Sir William Forbes about his visit to Gregories which he was afraid was so "hyperborical" that he burned it (Reg. Let. 5 May 1783).

[4] Journ. 31 Mar. 1783; Mems. 20 and 21 Apr. 1783.

defiant of consequences. Mountstuart, the previous spring, had outlined the cold facts of political life: to get ahead, a man needed talents, Parliamentary interest, or money to buy Parliamentary interest (Journ. 18 May 1783). Boswell ran to Johnson for reassurance:

> I mentioned my expectations from the interest of an eminent person [Burke] then in power; adding, "but I have no claim but the claim of friendship; however, some people will go a great way from that motive." JOHNSON. "Sir, they will go all the way from that motive."[5]

Perhaps. Boswell was already putting that possibility to a severe test. On meeting Burke for the first time that spring, Boswell reports, "I most heartily thanked him for his freindly behaviour to me. I enjoyed the consciousness of independence. But I hoped that by his influence I might obtain the pleasurable lot of an employment in London" (Journ. 22 Mar. 1783). Still, for some reason, making his general position plain didn't suffice; Boswell repeatedly insisted to Burke, the most ideological of politicians, that he was a Tory of the Johnsonian school who vehemently opposed Burke's strong Whig views. When Burke talked of Indian affairs, a non-partisan concern in which he had already developed an intense interest, Boswell "told him he was mad Elephants in his brain Nabobs etc." (Journ.? 1 May 1783). These differences in opinion would not have deterred Burke from helping Boswell to a sinecure, but the Lord Advocate's post was politically central. How much reliance could the Coalition put in one who had been a self-proclaimed enemy and who, in any case, was unimportant? Burke could hardly have given this application a serious thought. He replied warmly with, "My dear Boswell", but tactfully (and truthfully) emphasizing his lack of influence, discouraged any hopes.

The year before, Boswell had coyly remarked to Burke that a friend who encouraged and then disappointed expectations was the political equivalent of a jilt (To Burke, 18 Mar. 1782); now his delayed response to what he admitted was Burke's "kind and candid answer" to his application showed that he had worked himself up into a personal, and quite unjustifiable, anger. He was

[5] *Life* iv. 223, some time between 17 and 26 May 1783, but apparently a response to Mountstuart's remarks.

ill-used and the Ministry discredited by the appointment of another (the inoffensive Alexander Wight) as Solicitor-General. While he would welcome Burke on his forthcoming visit to Scotland, Boswell continued:

> I should think meanly of myself did I entertain no resentment of the total neglect which I have had the mortification to experience, at a time when I had reason to think and when it was generally thought that I could not fail to receive some mark of attention from administration (To Burke, 20 Nov. 1783).

(This general expectation seems not to have impressed anyone else.) Burke, caught up in what was to be the Coalition's death-struggle over Fox's East India Bill, failed to reply.

Ignored by all parties, Boswell determined to make his presence felt; he reverted to his convictions and, at the end of December 1783, joined in the attack on Fox's Bill with an effective pamphlet called *A Letter to the People of Scotland on the Present State of the Nation*. His long-time counsellor General Paoli now warned him that he must stick to his new friends and prepare to find his old ones "disgusted and offended."[6] But, characteristically, Boswell wanted to have it both ways. On sending a copy of the *Letter* to Burke, he assured him, "Your prosperity is almost as dear to me as my own."[7] (Burke must have thought he had an odd way of demonstrating this sentiment.) When again no response came to this and to a subsequent letter, Boswell started to worry. A cordial welcome from Burke, at Glasgow for his installation as Rector, momentarily dispelled these fears, and the fragmentary journal of 1784's whirlwind London jaunt records one more of those calls on Burke that had once been frequent: "much pleasantry" (Journ. 30 May 1784). But for Burke, unquestioning loyalty based on shared beliefs was basic to intimacy; their fun and friendship rapidly began to thin out.

Boswell must have hoped that the publication of the *Journal of a Tour to the Hebrides*, with its evocation of the recent past and glorious Johnsoniana, would revive closeness. It had the opposite effect. The *casus belli* was this passage near the beginning:

> We talked of Mr. Burke.—Dr. Johnson said, he had great

[6] From Paoli, 20 Feb. 1784, extracts from which are translated in Joseph Foladare, *Boswell's Paoli*, 1979, pp. 130–131.

[7] To EB, 3 Jan. 1784. He repeated this statement in *LPS 85*, p. 71.

> variety of knowledge, store of imagery, copiousness of language.—[PRINCIPAL] ROBERTSON. "He has wit too."—JOHNSON. "No, Sir; he never succeeds there. 'Tis low; 'tis conceit. I used to say, Burke never once made a good joke*. What I most envy Burke for, is, his being constantly the same. He is never what we call hum-drum; never unwilling to begin to talk, nor in haste to leave off."—BOSWELL. "Yet he can listen."—JOHNSON. "No; I cannot say he is good at that. So desirous is he to talk, that, if one is speaking at this end of the table, he'll speak to somebody at the other end."

Then Johnson adds a version of his remark about how one would immediately recognize Burke as an extraordinary man.

Boswell had too strong an artistic conscience to suppress or euphemize these remarks: Johnson on Burke, one great man's observations on another were essential to his presentation. But he realized that they might give offence and so at the asterisk above (which appeared in the 1st ed.), he added a footnote:

> This was one of the points upon which Dr. Johnson was strangely heterodox. For, surely, Mr. Burke, with his other remarkable qualities, is also distinguished for his wit, and for wit of all kinds too; not merely that power of language which Pope chooses to denominate wit . . . but surprising allusions, brilliant sallies of vivacity, and pleasant conceits (*Life* v. 32–34).

And so on for about four hundred more words, mostly examples. Then Edmond Malone, his quasi-collaborator on the *Tour*, told him after publication that these examples were considered inadequate and (as the correspondence in the present volume shows) piled another four hundred words onto Boswell's original note. Much impressed, Boswell insisted on giving Malone credit for his dazzling contribution when he sent Burke a copy of the second edition.

Burke hated having Johnson's opinion of his wit memorialized, and Boswell and Malone's blundering refutation merely gave it more prominence. Yet he had to recognize they had meant well, and his answer to Boswell combines an acknowledgement of their good intentions with a coldly ironic commentary on their stupidity. "I shall be well content," Burke wrote,

> to pass down to a long posterity in Doctor Johnsons authentick Judgment, and in your permanent record, as a dull fellow and a tiresome companion, when it shall be known through the same long period, that I have had such men as Mr. Boswell and Mr. Malone as my friendly counsel in the Cause which I have lost.

But anger almost betrayed him into what would have been too open an expression of his contempt:

> I am sure there are very few, (let them be qualified as they will) shall be indiscreet enough to interrupt, by the intrusion of their Ideas, the strong flow of your real Wit, and true humour, who will not be great Enemies to their own entertainment, as well as to the satisfactions of the rest of the Company (From Burke, 4 Jan. 1786).

Perhaps the comments on his wit were among the "absurdities" that Burke, according to Michael Lort, fell "hard upon" in the *Tour* (*Later Years*, p. 547).

How could Boswell not have realized that Burke would be so offended? (For that matter, how could the usually tactful Malone have compounded the offence?) One possibility is that Boswell could never be convinced that others were as sensitive to public depiction as they proclaimed. And, in any case, hadn't he made Johnson's "heterodoxy" on this point quite plain? But Boswell's insensitivity may also have resulted from simple blind admiration. About Burke's political opinions and performances as a speaker in Parliament, Boswell often felt some reservations.[8] But Boswell (and Malone too) thought Burke the private person far beyond the petty vanities of ordinary men.

If Boswell failed to grasp the complexity of Burke's character, he had good reason. It combined sharply contrasting qualities while suggesting an underlying consistency at the same time. Contemporaries agreed with Johnson that Burke's intellectual force had an immediate impact. He displayed a wide-ranging, fertile mind with extraordinary powers of expression. Like Johnson, he could reason close or wide as the subject demanded, and he brought to every subject clear thought, extensive learning, and an excellent memory. His phrasing fit his thinking with the smoothness and flexibility of a glove. In particular, he had an

[8] See, for example, Journ. 29 July 1782 and 17 Feb. 1786.

enviable ability to elicit memorable generalizations from the events of everyday life. Burke also had a deeply generous nature: he was always ready to help an individual in need or to defend large classes of the oppressed, like the Roman Catholic Irish or the natives of India. And, as even an unfriendly commentator concedes, he had "enormous persistence, courage, concentration, and energy".[9]

It was the social rather than the political Burke, however, who so impressed, and in part misled, Boswell. Burke could be the pleasantest of companions, his talk characterized by a lively play of ideas and what his disciple, French Laurence, remarked was "not so much wit or humour, as a certain sportive vivacity" (Journ. 15 Nov. 1787) that could animate any gathering. Burke, Malone wrote typically to Boswell of one dinner, "was in great spirits—various, talkative, and delightful. I need not tell you it was a good day" (From Malone, 12 Aug. 1788).

But, in public, Burke was noted for the intensity, sometimes verging on loss of control, with which he discussed issues and personalities. Though his topics often were prudence and moderation, and he paid the conservative's respect to the accumulated wisdom of institutions and tradition, he imagined life in terms of extremes and spoke in superlatives. Every period was the most critical of periods, every crisis the most acute England had ever faced. No respecter of persons, in one speech he compared Lord Shelburne (whom he hated) to Catiline, Cesare Borgia, and the wolf in Little Red Riding Hood.[1] During the Regency crisis he went so far as to declare that George III had been "smitten by the hand of Omnipotence, and that the Almighty had hurled him from his throne".[2] Late in life he implicitly defended his character by arguing that "vehement passion does not always indicate an infirm judgment. It often accompanies, and actuates, and is even auxiliary to a powerful understanding".[3] But while contemporaries admired the richness and fluency of his rhetoric, they distrusted his ever-ready zeal.

[9] John Brooke, in Namier and Brooke ii. 147.

[1] See To Burke, 19 July 1782, n. 9.

[2] *Parl. Hist.* xxvii. 1213, cited in *Corres. EB* vi. 7 n. 2.

[3] *Letters on a Regicide Peace,* III — *Works EB* v. 407.

INTRODUCTION: BURKE

The modern reader tends, says Conor Cruise O'Brien, "to see a Burke more mellow than the Burke of reality".[4]

In fact Burke's understanding was auxiliary to his passion; he trusted his intuitions, though externalizing them as the product of those most eighteenth-century English standards, observation and experience.[5] Something of a seeming paradox is involved: he always emphasized the practical and contingent, circumstances and consequences, but starting as the theoretician of the Rockingham Whigs, he went on to become an international figure during the French Revolution because he was able to articulate the assumptions ("prejudices", he was proud to call them) that plausibly justified the ruling classes' exercise of power. George III paid him an accurate compliment on the *Reflections*: "You have supported the cause of the Gentlemen" (*Corres. EB* vi. 239). The difference between his conclusions and those of the theorists of revolution, Burke claimed, was that his were drawn from a solid empirical knowledge of human nature and theirs deduced through an abstract, and therefore absurd, process of ratiocination. So he felt able to assert, without providing evidence, that the British Constitution was in accord with nature, which he defined as "wisdom without reflection, and above it".[6]

A prominent aspect of Burke's pragmatism was his refusal to investigate the bases, theoretical and historical, of the existing system. "A sacred veil", he said, should "be drawn over the beginnings of all governments."[7] Prescription, the right through long possession to hold property and power unquestioned, must prevail; otherwise the peaceful framework of society would always be in danger of disruption.[8]

Similarly Burke avoided any exploration of his own convictions. He had a deep need for certainty, and his rare moments of doubt, such as those caused by Philip Francis's criticism of the

[4] *Reflections on the Revolution in France*, ed. C. C. O'Brien, 1968, p. 75. Burke could carry this vehemence over into private life. Garrick was a good friend whom Burke late in life called "the most acute observer of Nature I ever knew" (*Works EB* vi. 47), but when he was displeasing on one occasion Burke said he was "almost ready to have spat in his face" (*Portraits*, p. 93).

[5] "What many . . . have called my passions", he wrote, "are my principles" (*Corres. EB* iv. 274). EB tended to confuse intensity of feeling with truth (e.g. *Corres. EB* vi. 91).

[6] *Reflections*, p. 119.

[7] "Speeches in the Impeachment of Warren Hastings", 2nd Day, 16 Feb. 1788, *Works EB* ix. 401.

[8] A limited exception was his discussion of early Whig principles in his *Appeal from the New to the Old Whigs*.

Reflections, were agonizing.[9] Yet both his vehemence and his reluctance to question his convictions suggest an ambivalence about them, which is strikingly apparent in one very early and one very late work. In his *Vindication of Natural Society* (1756), Burke presented such persuasive objections to the contemporary political system that many readers thought it a posthumous work of Bolingbroke's, and Burke was forced to explain in a preface to the second edition that it was all a satire on Bolingbroke's way of thinking. And his *Letter to a Noble Lord* (1796) attacked the aristocracy, through the example of the Duke of Bedford, so ferociously that both the *Critical* and *Monthly* reviewers thought the pamphlet as damaging as any revolutionary's.[1]

Whatever the extent of Burke's suppressed doubts about his political theories, certain unmistakable traits dominated his behaviour in practical politics. No one more plainly exemplifies the dangerous human tendency to divide the world into clearly defined friends and enemies. Temperamentally he belonged in opposition: "I have always been in the Minority" he himself declared (*Life* iii. 235). And it was difficult for him to believe that his enemies might have worthy motives; he thought of them as "cabals" of conspirators, intriguing behind the scenes. This paranoid outlook emerges from time to time in an unattractive strain of self-pity and self-praise. He saw himself as Lear: in the most dramatic hour of his Parliamentary career, as he was about to break with Charles James Fox, he turned on Fox's young followers who had been heckling him, with Lear's

The little dogs and all,
Trey, Blanch, and Sweetheart, see, they bark at me![2]

Mantling himself in the pathos of that grand ruined king was a magnificent gesture, and possibly he found his subsequent position as a minority of one, which inspired his *Appeal from the*

[9] *Corres. EB* vi. 88–92. Shelburne declared "there is no dealing with Mr. Burke, he is so violently attach'd to his own opinion" (cited in *Corres. EB* iv. xiii). Shelburne was a hostile witness, but even friends like Sir Gilbert Elliot found it awkward to disagree (see Cone ii. 393).

[1] *Crit. Rev.* 2nd series (Mar. 1796) xvi. 342; *Monthly Rev.* 2nd series (Mar. 1796) xix. 316–17. Isaac Kramnick explores this ambivalence in *The Rage of Edmund Burke*, 1977.

[2] Sir Philip Magnus, *Edmund Burke*, 1939, p. 215.

New to the Old Whigs, at least temporarily congenial.[3] But his refusal to look within himself and, consequently, his frequent misjudgement of others, might recall to some Regan's deadly conclusion about her father: "He hath ever but slenderly known himself."

In a famous passage in the *Reflections*, Burke remarks,

> To be attached to the subdivision, to love the little platoon we belong to in society, is the first principle (the germ as it were) of public affections. It is the first link in the series by which we proceed towards a love to our country and to mankind.[4]

This is sound eighteenth-century doctrine—Pope makes a similar point in the *Essay on Man*—but for Burke, in a world where so much was at stake and so few could be trusted, personal and political affections took on overwhelming importance. The love and loyalty of his little platoon of Burkes and disciples were remarkable. His wife Jane writes to Cousin Will (it was preaching to the converted) that her husband "*never* is wrong, he may do wrong by provocation but never by mature reflexion" (*Corres. EB* vi. 238). And on that occasion referred to earlier when Philip Francis had the audacity to criticize Burke, his son Richard Jr. rebuked him bitterly: "I tell you, his folly is wiser than the wisdom of the common herd of able men".[5] Such undiscriminating devotion may have provided essential support; likewise it could only encourage Burke's excessive faith in his convictions. In return, Burke felt his relations and friends could do no wrong.

Equally, it seems almost inevitable that Burke should attach himself to the Rockingham Whigs, those great magnates whose high rank, extensive lands, and splendid fortunes made them appear almost invulnerable to the vicissitudes of ordinary existence. In the Greek, "aristocracy" means "the government of a state by its best citizens" (OED, 1), and Burke applied this definition literally. While he was always careful to respect the distance that separated him from them in society, he identified his interests with theirs. Who could better embody that sense of order and stability which he so sought and valued?

Circumstances conspired with temperament in shaping

[3] He must have thought Milton's Abdiel, "unshak'n, unseduc'd, unterrifi'd", an attractive model; he once compared Elliot to him (*Corres. EB* v. 369).

[4] *Reflections*, p. 135.

[5] Cited in *Corres. EB* vi. 92.

Burke's career. First and foremost he was a House-of-Commons man, and he took the usual contemporary view that its members were the guardians or trustees of the people rather than its representatives. He was proud of being chosen for the important city of Bristol in 1774, but at once felt impelled to inform his constituents that he must prefer "his unbiased opinion, his mature judgment, his enlightened conscience" to any views of theirs.[6] Not surprisingly he grew so unpopular that he was forced to decline the poll at the next General Election in 1780. He then spoke pleasantly to Lady Rockingham of coming into Parliament "by any of the little posterns or sallyports of the constitution" (*Corres. EB* iv. 302), but he was left dangling for a disagreeable length of time before he was returned, as Sir George Savile once phrased a similar situation, "in Lord Rockingham's dining-room", for the pocket borough of Malton.[7]

To his enemies and perhaps even to some of his friends, Burke was an impoverished Irish adventurer, trailing his clan close behind him. Speculation in East India stock enabled the Burke ensemble to buy Gregories in 1768, but in their desperate financial sorties they were commonly thought dishonest and were certainly unlucky. Burke had almost no income of his own; he lived, as T. W. Copeland comments, "on loans, gifts, and windfalls" (*Eminent Friend*, p. 59). This situation could have seriously compromised his integrity; he acknowledged himself that "independence of mind will ever be more or less influenced by independence of fortune",[8] and financially, as well as politically, he was dependent first on Rockingham and then on Rockingham's heir, Lord Fitzwilliam. But to Burke money was never more than a means to an end. Though he tried to make the best of his brief periods as Paymaster of the Forces, he was always ready to refuse help that he felt might compromise his honour.

In office and out, the strain of public life told openly on Burke over the years, and in 1783 when Boswell remarked to Johnson that Burke was represented as "actually mad", Johnson replied, "If A Man will appear extravagant as he does and cry, can he

[6] "Speech at the Conclusion of the Poll", *Works EB*, ii. 95.

[7] Savile's phrase is quoted in *Corres. EB* iii. xi. Burke kept his temper during his wait, but Cousin Will complained furiously: Rockingham's "little mind will be gratifyed to see that Great Man thrown into the dark" (quoted in *Corres. EB* iv. 288 n. 1).

[8] "Speech on Shortening the Duration of Parliaments", *Works EB* vii. 78.

wonder that he is represented as Mad" (Journ. 29 May 1783). The repudiation of the Coalition by the King and the electorate in 1784 stunned him, without diminishing the extravagance of his language. He declared in one outburst that "in a struggle against the intrigues of courts and the perfidious levity of the multitude, we fell in the cause of honor, in the cause of our country, in the cause of human nature itself".[9] Burke tended to turn any situation into a cause, if not a crusade, and in the middle of the 1780s he found his most protracted cause in the impeachment of Warren Hastings.

It is against this background that the next crisis in Boswell's relationship with Burke took place. On returning to London in February 1786 to try his chances at the English bar, Boswell paid Burke a call. They had been talking of his journal record of Johnson when, says Boswell,

> I imprudently touched on a calumny against Mr. Burke, in order to be enabled to refute it. We parted on sad terms. I was very uneasy. . . . This affair was happily settled in letters between us. I need not give the detail (Journ. 7 Feb. 1786).

Still sore from the Boswell-Malone anatomy of his wit in the *Tour*, Burke had exploded. He was constantly vilified in the press as everything from a Jesuit to a sodomite (if *Candide* is representative, the two were more or less equated in the public mind),[1] and he had early and wisely decided never to respond to such slanders. Nor did he wish defenders: when Richard Shackleton, the dearest friend of his youth, was cited in print in his support Burke scolded him sharply (*Corres. EB* ii. 130). Nothing could have infuriated Burke more than Boswell's rushing to his aid; he must have thought Boswell the most blundering kind of busybody.

After that, Boswell unhappily reports Burke as shy or cold, though they met "occasionally on sufficiently easy terms" (Journ. 24 Feb. 1788) for dinner at the homes of their friends—John Courtenay or Malone or, most often, Reynolds—or at the Royal Academy or the theatre or The Club. On various occasions Burke

[9] "Speech on the Nabob of Arcot's Debts", *Works EB* iii. 37.

---

[1] Boswell says he long believed Burke to be a Jesuit (Journ. 7 Apr. 1773) and Kramnick has revived the sodomite charge. The nature of the "calumny" Boswell mentioned is unknown.

was "as usual fertile and playful" (Journ. 19 Jan. 1788), and Boswell lamented when he was insufficiently attentive to record his talk fully.[2] There was a bit of a thaw in their relations in 1788. Burke came to dinner, "quite easy and polite". "For the first time had Edmund Burke at my table", says Boswell (Journ. 22 Apr. 1788); it was also to be the last. Boswell persisted in attributing Burke's aloofness to political differences, made chronic by disagreements over Hastings, even though Malone told him that it was his habit of recording conversation that kept Burke at a distance (From Malone, 14 Sept. 1787).

Certainly their attitudes towards conversation differed. Burke's stock in trade was his verbal skill; he owed everything to it, and the constant punning, as he slid among the meanings of words, showed how conscious he remained, even at those times when he was most relaxed, of the importance of language. To be pinned down forever to what he said at such moments was intolerable. If Sir William Scott was not paraphrasing Burke directly he was certainly expressing Burke's views in explaining to Boswell why on one occasion he had not been invited to dinner. Other guests objected to

> the Practice of publishing without Consent what has been thrown out in the freedom of private Conversation. . . . For believe me, it is not the Gaiety of the present Hour nor the most joyus Display of convivial Talents for the Moment, that are an equivalent with many Men for the Pain of being brought out, against their Consent or without their Knowledge, into the Glare of public Light, when they supposed themselves to be merely discussing in a private Society.[3]

Boswell offered a spirited defence:

> If others, as well as myself, sometimes appear as shades to the GREAT INTELLECTUAL LIGHT, I beg to be fairly understood, and that you and my other friends will inculcate upon persons of *timidity and reserve*, that my recording the conversations of so extraordinary a man as Johnson with its concomitant circum-

[2] Journ. 5 and 22 Apr. 1788.

[3] From Scott, 2 Aug. 1791. Though Burke was not at the dinner under discussion (Fifer, p. 347 n. 2), Scott was writing to congratulate him on his *Appeal* at precisely that time (Scott to EB, 6 Aug. 1791, *Correspondence of Edmund Burke, 1744–97*, ed. Charles William, Earl Fitzwilliam, and Sir Richard Bourke, 4 vols. 1844, iii. 230).

stances was a *peculiar* undertaking, attended with much anxiety and labour, and that the conversations of people in general are by no means of that nature as to bear being registered and that the task of doing it would be exceedingly irksome to me.[4]

Burke was accused of many things in his career but never of timidity and reserve. On the other hand, acting in the *Life* as a shade, despite the most flattering mention, to Johnson's light, must have been highly provoking to an easily aroused temper. Even Johnson's famous compliment, "Yes; Burke *is* an extraordinary man. His stream of mind is perpetual", and Boswell's gloss, "It is very pleasing to me to record, that Johnson's high estimation of the talents of this gentleman was uniform from their early acquaintance" (*Life* ii. 450), could hardly have conciliated him. Also, Burke had Boswell's explicit admission shortly after the publication of the *Life* that pressed by Malone he wished "to resume in some degree" recording conversation "because there is much Wisdom and Wit fresh from the Source in casual talk which should not be lost" (To Burke, 16 July 1791).

Malone surely was right in thinking that Burke dreaded Boswell's journal, but political disagreement could well have reinforced his coldness. Burke's biographer, C. B. Cone, points out that "from about 1782 onward, Burke's friendships tended to become more exclusively political". Not only did he break with R. B. Sheridan, Fox, and Courtenay over the French Revolution, he had earlier ceased to correspond with Sir William Jones when he learned that Jones was an admirer of Hastings (Cone ii. 71–72). Two years after Johnson's death he attacked Johnson's pamphlet, *Thoughts on Falkland's Islands*, in such terms that Boswell in his journal called him "intemperately abusive to a departed great Man" (Journ. 16 Nov. 1786). And though Boswell wrote to Temple a few years later that Burke was as "ably philosophical in political disquisition as ever" (To Temple, 31 Mar. 1789—Pierpont Morgan), even their agreement on the iniquities of the French Revolution could not reconcile him to Burke's obsession with the topic.[5]

[4] To Scott, 9 Aug. 1791. Boswell had presented this same line of argument at the end of the *Tour* (*Life* v. 414–16).

[5] For example, To EM, 4 and 7 Dec. 1790.

One conversation Boswell records is particularly revealing. Burke had reverted to their old badinage:

> BURKE. "This [Revolution] in France would almost make me adopt your tory principles." BOSWELL. "Nay you *are* one of us. We will not part with you." BURKE. "You have the art of reconciling contradictions beyond any man [I know]." BOSWELL. "[Yes, I was] a Tory and an American." BURKE. "You were not always an American." (This an unjust suspicion of time serving.)[6] "And then asking Sir James Lowther to come into Scotland to defend Liberty![7] You are the greatest Encyclopediste in Politicks." He indelicately I thought mentioned Mr. Hastings. I could not but say "I am on the other side there I know not how." He was irishly savage a little, but full and flowing.[8]

Burke's taunting Boswell with his political views must have been sincere enough in itself, but it sounds as if it also expresses an otherwise inadmissible resentment.

When Burke told George III that the *Life of Johnson* was the most entertaining book he had ever read, Boswell, having already learned some details in conversation, asked for a written account of this interview with the King. (This was the same letter of 16 July 1791 in which Boswell had threatened to resume his practice of recording conversation.) In his prompt, elaborately polite reply, Burke, who once had looked forward to Boswell's presence in London, now insinuated that he would do well to retire to Auchinleck and abandon "the further publication of anecdotes" for other forms of writing. As to his conversation with the King, "since then other things, not of much moment I admit", says Burke, had dimmed his memory.[9] He did concede remarking, "I

[6] No evidence survives that Boswell's pro-American attitudes were anything but disinterested.

[7] *LPS 85*, p. 28. Lowther had been made Earl of Lonsdale by that time but Boswell had referred to him as "LOWTHER!"

[8] Journ. 23 Jan. 1790. Speakers' names have been added and regularised, and Boswell's abbreviations silently expanded.

[9] Burke was in the middle of an even more serious crisis than usual. He felt he had been read out of the Whig party, had written to Fitzwilliam to decline further financial assistance—and what would he live on?—and was preparing his *Appeal*, published a few weeks later. Public attention was fastened on the French royal family's flight to Varennes (20 June 1791) and their sad recapture.

had not read any thing more entertaining", in response to the King's commendation of the *Life*, but added,

> though I did not say to his Majesty, what nothing but the freedom of freindship could justify in my saying to yourself, that many particulars there related might as well have been omitted; However in the multitude of readers perhaps some would have found a loss in their omission (From Burke, 20 July 1791).

Faced with that chilling response Boswell gave up; in effect it marked the end of their relationship. They met a few times later, at Scott's, at William Windham's, at The Club; their last recorded encounter took place at Philip Metcalfe's on 6 Jan. 1793.

Boswell's uneasy failure to grasp the complexity of Burke's character caused, in part at least, his greatest disappointment in friendship: his failure to retain Burke's regard. It also led to that timidity and reserve with which he treated Burke in the *Life*. Still, the unwanted disciple never wavered in his belief in Burke's greatness. He wrote to Burke in 1784, "I am grateful for your kindness. I love your virtues. I admire your talents": this was a precise statement of a lifelong attitude.[1] And more is preserved of Burke's personality in Boswell's journal than in any source other than his own writings.

In turn, Burke agreed with James Mackintosh in 1796 that the *Life* was "a greater monument to Johnson's fame, than all his writings put together".[2] His testimony is all the more valuable because he never grasped the magnitude of Boswell's artistic achievement. But their greatest works unite them: the *Reflections on the Revolution in France* and the *Life of Johnson*, published within the same year, are the last two significant distillations of eighteenth-century Britain.

F. B.

[1] To Burke, 10 Apr. 1784. He repeated these remarks in almost the same words in To Burke, 15 Feb. 1785.

[2] R. J. Mackintosh, *Memoirs of Sir James Mackintosh*, 1835, i. 92.

To Burke,
Tuesday 3 March 1778

MS. Sheffield City Libraries, Wentworth Woodhouse Muniments, Burke Papers 1/1032. Sent 3 Mar. "Edmund Burke Esq. to begin a Correspondence—thanking him for civilities. (Copy)" (Reg. Let.). A copy at Yale (L 314) in Lawrie's hand, except for one correction in JB's hand.

HEADING in copy: To Edmund Burke Esq.

ENDORSEMENT in an unidentified hand: Mr. Boswel 3d March 1778.[1]

Edinburgh, 3 March 1778

DEAR SIR: Upon my honour I began a letter to you some time ago, and did not finish it, because I imagined you was then near your *Apotheosis*—as poor Goldsmith said upon a former occasion, when he thought your Party was coming into administration[2]—And being one of your old Barons of Scotland,[3] my pride could not brook the appearance of paying my court to a Minister, amongst the crowd of interested expectants on his Accession. At present, I take it for granted that I need be under no such apprehension;[4] and therefore I resume the indulgence of my inclination.

This may be perhaps a singular method of beginning a

[1] The eight letters from JB to EB now at Sheffield all bear endorsements in ink in an unknown hand; four include additional endorsements in ink in another unknown hand. Five of the eight also bear endorsements in pencil by Sir Richard Bourke, co-editor of the 1844 edition of *Burke's Correspondence*. The second set in pen and those in pencil are ignored here.

[2] In 1765 EB had joined the Rockingham Whigs, who were grouped around Charles Watson Wentworth, second Marquess of Rockingham (1730–82), briefly Prime Minister in 1765–66. EB served first as Rockingham's private secretary and was then brought into Parliament as M.P. for Wendover (1765–74); in 1774 he became M.P. for Bristol. JB may have begun his letter in the period after the fall of Saratoga on 17 Oct. 1777 (see n. 4 below). Goldsmith's remark has not been reported, but he wrote to Bennet Langton on 7 Sept. 1771: "They begin to talk in town of the opposition's gaining ground, the cry of Liberty is still as loud as ever" (*Collected Letters of Oliver Goldsmith*, ed. K. C. Balderston, 1928, p. 105).

[3] In technical Scots usage a "baron" was a freeholder whose lands the Crown had erected into a barony, over which he held civil and criminal jurisdiction in petty cases (Bell i. 68–69).

[4] The arrival in London on 2 Dec. 1777 of the news of the defeat of Lt.-Gen. John Burgoyne at Saratoga on 17 Oct. (*Corres. EB* iii. 406) had provided new ammunition for the Rockingham party's opposition to the American war and, as G. H. Guttridge points out, "was causing all manner of new proposals and schemes of ministerial reconstruction" (*Corres. EB* iii. xvii). Nevertheless, the Government retained a clear majority in the Commons. For example, a motion by Charles James Fox, M.P. for Malmesbury, to halt the flow of troops to America was defeated 259 to 165 on 2 Feb. (*Gent. Mag.* Feb. 1778, xlviii. 91).

Correspondence; and in one sense may not be very complimentative.[5] But I can sincerely assure you, Dear Sir, that I feel and mean a genuine compliment to Mr. Burke himself. It is generally thought no meaness to solicit the notice and favour of a Man in Power; And surely it is much less a meaness to endeavour by honest means to have the honour and pleasure of being on an agreable footing with a Man of superiour knowledge, abilities and genius.

I have to thank You for the obligations which you have already conferred upon me by the wellcome which I have upon repeated occasions experienced under your roof.[6] When I was last in London, you Gave me a general invitation which I value more than a Treasury Warrant.[7] An invitation to the "Feast of Reason", and, what I like still more, "the Flow of Soul"[8] which you dispense with liberal and elegant abundance, is in my estimation a privilege of enjoying certain Felicity; And we know that riches and honours are desireable only as means of Felicity; and that they often fail of the end.

Most heartily do I rejoice that our present Ministers have at last yielded to Conciliation.[9] For, amidst all the sanguinary zeal of my Countrymen, I have professed myself a friend to our Fellow-Subjects in America, so far as they claim an exemption from being taxed by the Representatives of the King's British Subjects. I do not perfectly agree with you. For, I deny the Declaratory Act,[10] and I am a warm Tory in its true constitutional sense.[11] I

[5] Copy, "complimentative" altered to "complimentary" in JB's hand.

[6] JB records only three such visits: 9 Apr. 1775 (Journ.), 5 and 13 May 1776 (Notes). At that time EB was living in the Broad Sanctuary, Westminster, an area adjacent to the Abbey and conveniently close to the House of Commons (*Corres. EB* ii. 301 and n. 3). By June 1779 he had moved to Charles Street, St. James's Square (ibid. iv. 88 and n. 2).

[7] On 13 May 1776, EB had invited JB to visit him often (Notes). A Treasury Warrant is a government order, here for a place or sinecure (see *Calendar of Treasury Books and Papers, 1742–1745*, ed. W. A. Shaw, 1903, [xi] 643, for examples).

[8] Pope, *Imit. Hor. Satires.* II. i. 128.

[9] On 19 Feb. Lord North had proposed to the House of Commons two Conciliatory Bills: the first for appointing a commission with powers to treat with the Colonists; the second for declaring Parliament's disavowal of any intention to tax them. The Bills were debated on 23 and 24 Feb. and passed on 2 Mar. (*Parl. Hist.* xix. 762–815; *Ann. Reg.* xxi. 142; see also Journ. 1 Mar. 1778).

[10] In 1766 the Rockingham Ministry had repealed the Stamp Act in response to Colonial demands, but had passed the Declaratory Act, a formal reassertion of Britain's right to tax America. On 3 Feb. 1766, within three weeks of his entering the Commons, EB had spoken in favour of the Declaratory Act (*Corres. EB* i. 242 and n. 1); he reiterated this support at length in his Speech on American Taxation (19 Apr.

wish I were a Commissioner or one of the Secretaries of the Commission for the grand Treaty. I am to be in London this spring;[12] and if his Majesty should ask me what I would chuse, my Answer will be "to assist at the Compact between Britain and America."[13] May I beg to hear from you; and in the mean time to have my compliments made acceptable to Mrs. Burke.[14] I am, Dear Sir, your most obedient, humble servant,

JAMES BOSWELL

To Burke, Friday 6 November 1778

MS. Yale (L 315). A copy with several abbreviations in the first sentence, later expanded interlinearly: "vis, romant, Famly, Scot, oppos". Sent 6 Nov. "Edmund Burke Esq. wishing to hear from him (Copy)" (Reg. Let.).

HEADING: To Edmund Burke Esq.

Auchinleck, 6 Nov. 78

DEAR SIR: While I am here on a visit to my Father at the romantick seat of our Family[1] which lyes upon the western side of Scotland opposite to Ireland I think of Mr. Burke in all his splendour of mind. But it is not pleasing to me to recollect that you have not been so good as to let me hear from you. I do not desire a Diploma[2] from you; nor that you should honour me *longo sermone*.[3]

1774) and was again to defend the Act to JB on 12 Apr. 1778 (Journ.). On both occasions EB qualified his support by arguing that particular circumstances might render taxation inexpedient.

[11] As a supporter of monarchy.

[12] JB was in London from 17 Mar. to 19 May.

[13] As JB knew well, EB, a member of the Opposition, was in no position to influence appointments to the Commission. Rather than a serious bid for appointment, JB's remark reflects no more than his pro-American views (*Pol. Car.* p. 84 n. 7).

[14] Jane Mary Nugent (1734–1812), whom EB married in 1757. She was the daughter of Dr. Christopher Nugent, one of the founding members of The Club.

[1] MS. "Fayr" and "Famly". JB had spent most of the summer in Edinburgh, and arrived at Auchinleck on 23 Oct. He was back in Edinburgh on 11 Nov. (Journ.). In one of his earliest surviving letters, JB describes Auchinleck as "a most sweet, romantic Place" (To John Johnston, 26 Sept. 1759), and his cliché for it was "the romantick seat of my ancestors" (e.g. *Life* i. 462).

[2] Latin *diploma*, an official document conferring some favour or privilege, here an attestation of EB's friendship for JB.

[3] "With a long discourse", a stock phrase (cf. Horace, *Epistles* II. i. 4; *Aeneid* i. 217).

But I wish you may beleive that it would revive my spirits to have a slight proof sometimes that I am not forgotten by you. Pray present my best compliments to Mrs. Burke and your son[4] and be assured that I am, Dear Sir, very much yours.

To Burke, Monday 22 February 1779

MS. Sheffield City Libraries, Wentworth Woodhouse Muniments, Burke Papers 1/1136. Sent 22 Feb. "Edmund Burke Esq. wishing to be assured by him that the Popish Bill is not to be brought in this year—informing him of the dangerous consequences of such an Act at present" (Reg. Let.). A copy at Yale (L 316) in Lawrie's hand.
ENDORSEMENT in an unidentified hand: Mr. Boswell, Edinburgh, 22d. Febr. 1779.

Edinburgh, 22 February 1779

DEAR SIR: Though I have written twice to you, in hopes of having Mr. Burke amongst my *Epistolary Familiares*,[1] and have had no answer, I cannot refrain from giving you a few lines of request to be satisfied upon a subject of no small immediate importance. The very universal opposition in Scotland to a repeal of the penal Statutes against Roman Catholicks must no doubt however wonderful have been authentically communicated to you.[2] I was a warm freind to the Bill; and I trust that in due time it shall pass.

[4] Richard Burke, Jr. (1758–94), EB's only surviving son. He is to be distinguished from Richard Burke, Sr. (1733–94), EB's only surviving brother. JB called the earnest and sober nephew "Richard Burke", and the rough and boisterous uncle "Dick Burke".

---

[1] JB explains his use of the Latin word *familiaris* (belonging to a household, domestic) in his journal of the previous year: "I mentioned the acquisition I had made of Lord Pembroke's *familiarity*. I may call it in the Roman sense of *familiaris*, as I am admitted without ceremony" (Journ. 30 Apr. 1778). In the present letter JB alludes to Cicero's *Epistulae ad Familiares*.

[2] On 25 May 1778, the Commons had passed a bill introduced by Sir George Savile, M.P. for Yorkshire, repealing those portions of "An Act for the Further Preventing the Growth of Popery" (William III, 11 and 12, c. 4) that imposed stiff penalties on priests for saying mass and gave precedence to Protestant over Catholic heirs (*Statutes at Large, 1763–1800*, iv. 41–42, xiii. 290–91; *Parl. Hist.* xix. 1137–45; E. C. Black, *The Association: British Extraparliamentary Political Organization, 1769–1793*, 1963, p. 133.) Since the original statute had been passed before the Union of England and Scotland in 1707, Savile's bill applied only to England. However, Henry Dundas, M.P. for Edinburghshire and Lord Advocate of Scotland, on 14 May 1778 announced his intention to introduce a bill repealing similar statutes in Scotland (*Parl. Hist.* xix. 1142). Under pressure from

But I know the people of Scotland well; and I am *sure* that if it were now to pass, there would be as desperate a Rebellion against Government as in the days of Charles the Second.[3] It has been announced from the authority of *a Secretary of State* that the design of bringing in the Bill is laid aside.[4] But in order to remove every apprehension, may I beg to hear from *you* that there is no intention at present of moving that affair.[5] Your name shall not be mentioned, if you dissapprove of it. It will be enough for me to say that I have good authority. I am, Dear Sir, your most obedient, humble servant,

JAMES BOSWELL

From Burke, Monday 1 March 1779

MS. Yale (C 683). Received 7 Mar.: "Ommitted 7 Mr. Burke a long letter on the Roman-Catholick Bill" (Reg. Let.).
ADDRESS: To James Boswell, Esqr., Edinburgh.
FRANK: Free Edm. Burke.
POSTMARKS: 1 MR, FREE.

Westminster, Monday, March 1, 1779

MY DEAR SIR: Your goodness is indeed inexhaustible; But great as

the fanatical Protestant Association in Scotland, a number of synods and burghs passed resolutions opposing the measure, and anti-Catholic riots took place in Edinburgh on 2 and 3 Feb. and in Glasgow on 9 Feb. (*Scots Mag.* Feb. 1779, xli. 106–10; Black, pp. 135–47, which is inaccurate in certain details). For JB's role in the riots, see Journ. 2 and 3 Feb. and *post* From EB, 1 Mar. n. 8. A full account of the Catholic situation in Scotland, the riots, and subsequent events appears in J. A. Stothert, "George Hay", J. F. S. Gordon, *Ecclesiastical Chronicle of Scotland*, 1867, iv. chs. ix–x.

[3] For an account of the religious disturbances in Scotland under Charles II, see Sir George Clark, *The Later Stuarts, 1660–1714*, 2nd ed. 1955, pp. 267–73.

[4] On 12 Feb. a letter from Lord Weymouth, Secretary of State for the Southern Department, to Thomas Miller, Lord Justice Clerk, giving assurance that no bill for Catholic relief was "intended to be brought into Parliament, by any member of Government, or by any other person known to his Lordship", was published in Edinburgh (*Cal. Merc.* 13 Feb. p. [2]; *Scots Mag.* Feb. 1779, xli. 109).

[5] EB was a warm supporter of Roman Catholic toleration. He had drafted the address by Catholic peers and commoners presented to the King on 1 Apr. 1778 (*Corres. EB* iv. 45 n. 3), and though he did not speak on the bill for English Catholic relief, he was thought by some to be its author (Prior, *Burke* i. 342; see also A. P. Levack, "Edmund Burke, His Friends, and the Dawn of Irish Catholic Emancipation", *Catholic Historical Review*, 1952, xxxvii. 403). In summer 1778 he intervened effectively in the successful effort to obtain relief for Irish Catholics (Cone i. 346–48; Levack, pp. 403–14).

my faults are they do not make such a demand upon it as you imagine. I have had the misfortune of missing the third Letter you speak of; and before your last, only *one* came to my hands.[1] But as I was not so early as I ought to have been in acknowleging the honour of that one, my fault is greater than I fear I am able to attone for; and I tell you of the failure of the other, because I do not wish that my crime should have any aggravation.

I had heard some account of the Subject of your Letter before I receivd it from you.[2] It would have been against the Spirit of the act of Union if Scotland did not, at some time or other partake of the disorders that prevail in the constitution of the British Family. I do confess indeed, that I did not expect, that our dear Sister, who in the rigour of her Prudery, had shewn such outrageous Zeal, and decreed such severe penances against other frail and offending parts of the houshold, should make such a slip herself as to give her a fair Title to the Stool and White Sheet.[3] But these things will happen as long as the very best of us are only made up of mere rebellious flesh and blood.

As to the Riot which has been performed, and the rebellion which is threatned, they have at least the advantage of diversifying the Scene of our modern contentions. A religious war was not exactly the thing I expected in my time. I thought it possible, that even at the other side of the Tweed, a man might be allowd to say his prayers in Latin without any gross violation of the native, inherent, essential priveleges and immunities of the broad Scotch. I admit,[4] that the Ears of heaven may be more delighted with these accents; yet as the other Tongue may be as intelligible there (though not so pleasing) I think a little of it might be borne at Edinburgh without making a very serious quarrel of the matter. The Romans[5] of our day are not quite so dangerous an Enemy to *Galgacus* and his Warriours, as they were 1700 years ago;[6] or as

[1] JB's first letter (*ante* To EB, 3 Mar. 1778) is still among EB's papers at Sheffield. JB's Reg. Let. indicates that the second letter (*ante* To EB, 6 Nov. 1778) was sent, but since the original has not been reported, it may have gone astray.

[2] See below, n. 10.

[3] In some Scottish country churches it was still customary to make sinners stand on a small unrailed platform, called the "repentance stool", where they were publicly admonished from the pulpit. Fornicators and other serious offenders were clothed in a white sheet (Andrew Edgar, *Old Church Life in Scotland*, 1885, pp. 286–93).

[4] MS. "I may" superimposed upon "In that"; "may" is then deleted before "admit"

[5] MS. "The Romans" superimposed upon erased "You cert"

[6] Calgacus (or Galgacus, in eighteenth-

some of their descendants were a century or two since;[7] I cannot conceive, that Bishop Hay[8] is so dreadful a person as Julius Agricola; or that Mr. Macdonald with all his Grocery, or[9] Mr. Bagnal with all his crockery Ware,[10] are altogether so formidable as Sixtus the fifth with his Bulls.[11]

century editions), the famous Caledonian opponent of Julius Agricola, who "fought the last battle for public liberty" against the Romans (Tacitus, *Agricola*, chs. 29–38; Arthur Murphy, "An Essay on the Life and Genius of Samuel Johnson", *Johns. Misc.* i. 430).

[7] For a summary of the civil disturbances that accompanied the Reformation in Scotland from 1560 to 1690, see T. C. Smout, *A History of the Scottish People, 1560–1830*, 1969, pp. 62–71.

[8] George Hay (1729–1811), titular Bishop of Daulis and Vicar Apostolic of the Lowland District of Scotland. Perhaps EB first met him the previous year when he had come to London to seek relief for the Scottish Catholics (*Corres. EB* iv. 45 n. 3). Hay set out for London again on 21 Feb. to seek restitution for damages Catholics had suffered in the riots; there he had printed and circulated among M.P.s a *Memorial to the Public in Behalf of the Roman Catholics of Edinburgh and Glasgow, Containing an Account of the Late Riot against Them*; EB drafted a petition on their behalf, which he presented in the House of Commons on 18 Mar. (Stothert iv. 164–69; Black, p. 135 n. 7).

On 18 Mar. JB called first at EB's, then spent some time in the Commons with Hay, and finally returned at a late hour to dine at EB's (Notes, 18 Mar.). Hay spent the day in the lobby of the Commons consulting with the Attorney-General (Alexander Wedderburn), the Lord Advocate (Henry Dundas), and Lord North (Stothert iv. 169). The next day JB and Paoli called on Hay, who was out; Hay sent JB a note that evening asking him "as a friend" to write to the Edinburgh Town Council suggesting that they arrange restitution (From Hay, 19 Mar.). Nothing seems to have come of this suggestion, quite possibly because Sir Lawrence Dundas, M.P. for Edinburgh, "wrote at once to the Magistrates, urging them to make Compensation" (Stothert iv. 169). For the rest of the story, see *Corres. EB* iv. 99–101; *Scots Mag.* Aug. 1779, xli. 453–54; Stothert iv. 169–75; Black, p. 146 n. 32.

Hay wrote to a friend (28 May 1779) that "the only man who stood the Friend of the Catholics, in the face of all opposition, was Mr. Burke; with singular kindness, taking their cause to heart as if it had been a private matter of his own" (Stothert iv. 172). On 12 July, Hay wrote to EB directly with warm thanks for his "Countenance and protection!" (*Corres. EB.* iv. 100). In 1780 EB spoke of the unfortunate example and encouragement provided to the Gordon rioters in London by the "absolute and entire impunity attending the same offence in Edinburgh" ("Some Additional Reflections on the Executions", *Works EB* vi. 251).

[9] MS. "or" superimposed upon an ampersand.

[10] In his journal JB wrote that a troop of dragoons attempted to "protect the corner shop possessed by Daniel Macdonald Grocer a Papist. The mob had broke his windows. I was quite keen to disperse them, and had it not been for worthy Grange I should probably have been hurt" (Journ. 3 Feb.). Robert Bagnal, a Glasgow potter, was nearly ruined when his works, which he had allowed to be used as a Roman Catholic chapel, were destroyed in the riots of 9 Feb. (*Scots Mag.* Feb. 1779. xli. 108–09; J. A. Fleming, *Scottish Pottery*, 1923, pp. 122–24). EB's information about them presumably came from Hay's *Memorial*, pp. 25–35.

[11] At Christmas 1586, Sixtus V (1521–90) had renewed the bull of his predecessor Gregory XIII for a crusade against heretics (A. O. Meyer, *England and the Catholic Church under Queen Elizabeth*, trans. J. R. McKee, 1916, pp. 318, 322–26). Sixtus V also gave Philip II of Spain a document deposing Elizabeth, to be promulgated as soon as the Armada forces landed in

You certainly have a right to a rebellion in your Town; and of course we must leave the matter and fashion of that gratification to your own Choice. But without presuming to arraign any ones fancy, I confess, that the American rebellion is more to my Taste than that which you are cooking in the North. I think it relishes[12] as well to resist an act of Taxation as an act of Toleration; and it would hurt me rather more to have the Excise in my own house, than the Mass in my Neighbours.[13] I take it for granted, that there are good reasons for every thing you do. But I am apt[14] to be as much puzzled with moral Mysteries as others are with religious. I do not yet clearly comprehend, why it should be right, to burn mens houses and to despoil them of their Goods, because somebody is supposed to intend them an Act of Kindness; and I should not think the difficulty perfectly removed, though it were proved beyond contradiction, that the sufferers were consenting to, or even actually desirous of such a Benefit.[15] Full as little do I understand why the University should share the Fate of the Masshouses; and why the use of the Citadel of Edinburgh should be to afford a place of refuge to your most learned professors and

England, which consequently was never issued. Meyer, following M. A. Tierney, who refers to this document as a "broadside", thinks it was written in English (M. A. Tierney, ed. *Dodd's Church History of England*, 1839–45, iii. 28 n. 2, app. 12; Meyer, p. 323), but the existence of another English version (H. K. Baker, *Elizabeth and Sixtus*, 1938, pp. 205–12—no source given, but referring to the document as a translation, p. 114) suggests, as one would expect, that it was originally written in Latin. A Latin summary appears in Thuanus, *Historiarum sui temporis*, 1733 ed. bk. 89, ch. 9. In the French translation of Thuanus [by A. F. Prévost d'Exiles, P. F. G. Desfontaines, and others] the Latin *diploma* is translated as "Bulle" (*Histoire universelle de Jacques-Auguste de Thou*, ed. P. F. G. Desfontaines, 1734, x. 173).

[12] MS. "relishes" superimposed upon an illegible word.

[13] The excise, which pertained mainly to alcoholic beverages, was notoriously unpopular in Scotland because its system of inspection subjected manufacturers to frequent visits from excise officers, who were permitted to enter the premises in order to examine production accounts. Where fraud was suspected, excise officers might even be stationed on the premises permanently (Binney, pp. 36–38). When EB once facetiously insisted at The Club that JB pay for his share of the wine, he asserted that Scots ought to be taxed: "If we can get any thing out of Scotland, let us have it. . . . By the Customs and excise we some years literally don't get a shilling" (Journ. 28 Mar. 1781).

[14] MS. "as" deleted before "apt"

[15] Presumably EB is referring to a letter from Scottish Catholics to Lord North, published in *Lond. Chron.* 28 Jan., in which they withdrew their request for relief (Hay, pp. 11–12). Dundas stated in the House of Commons on 15 Mar. that "the principal Roman Catholics" of Scotland thought it prudent to abandon any attempt at relief "till time and cool persuasion should remove the unhappy prejudices of the Protestants of that country against them" (*Parl. Hist.* xx. 280–81).

most eminent Writers.[16] But time I suppose will clear up all those deep Mysteries.

You ask me, whether, after his Majesties Ministers have given up the Scotch toleration Bill, any other Members intend to bring it in? Indeed I am so struck with the admiration of this heroic act of Magnanimity[17] in our Ministers, that I do not aspire to the most distant imitation of it. Besides being at 400 good Miles distance from the coercive Arm of the Edinburgh powers, I *will not* tell what I intend to do, or to give my reasons for it, (as Falstaff says) on compulsion, though they were as plenty as Black-berries;[18] and as to what others intend to do, I really do not know. Oh poor Government, how art thou fallen![19] That Government which so many wise Tories and good nursing loyalists have been cramming and[20] nourishing into Strength, has been so overfed, and so diseased by high living, that instead of standing firm on its legs by all the good things that have been put into its belly, it is got so gouty, that it can hardly be supported by crutches! However we continue the old Course without being discouraged by Events; and are dying according to art and by the best rules that are possible.[21] The loan was voted in the Committee on Wednesday last.[22] Lord North was ill on Friday, and the Taxes are put off until today. They talk of a five per Cent on all commodities subject to the Excise, except Malt; A Tax on Post chaises; but in what

[16] William Robertson, Principal of the University of Edinburgh, had taken an active part in supporting Roman Catholic relief. His house, "forming the south-east corner of the College Buildings" ([Robert Chambers] *Minor Antiquities of Edinburgh*, 1833, p. 284), was attacked but saved from damage by friends and a detachment from the Castle (*A Narrative of the Late Riots at Edinburgh*, 1779, pp. 8, 13; Hay, p. 27; *Ann. Reg*. 1780, p. 30; Alexander Bower, *History of the University of Edinburgh*, 1830, iii. 96; Robertson's speech in the General Assembly, 25 May 1779—*Scots Mag*. 1779, xli. 412). He is said to have taken refuge in the Castle, along with several Catholics (Journ. 3 Feb.; Stothert iv. 160; Hay, p. 25). If EB had any other professors or writers in mind, their names do not appear in accessible contemporary accounts, but, according to Hay, the magistrates ordered the publishers of the Edinburgh newspapers not to print any accounts of the riot "without their Inspection and Approbation" (p. 48).

[17] MS. "Magnamity"

[18] *I Henry IV*, II. iv. 236–40. For EB's continuing interest in the Scottish Catholics, see n. 8 above and *Corres. EB* iv. 53–57, 62–64, 83–88, 94–95.

[19] Isaiah 14: 12: "How art thou fallen from heaven, O Lucifer, son of the morning!"

[20] MS. "cramming and" written above a deleted "supporting and"

[21] Pope, *Moral Essays* iv. 38: "And if they starve, they starve by rules of art."

[22] On 24 Feb. the Ways and Means Committee of the Commons approved the raising of £7,000,000 in loans for the navy, despite vigorous opposition from EB and Fox (*Parl. Hist*. xx. 155–63).

manner to be laid on I cannot collect. The Duties of last year have not produced a great deal more than one third of what they were given for. If we cannot contrive to raise 700,000 a year by the present duties, the publick Creditor must fall on the sinking fund; this[23] last year the Want of a proper and sufficient specifick security diminishd that fund by 400,000 £.[24]

I dined with your friend Dr. Johnson on saturday at Sir Joshua's. We had a very good day, as we had not a sentence, word, syllable, Letter, comma, or tittle, of any of the Elements that make politicks.[25] Adieu and believe me with great Esteem and regard, Dear Sir, your most faithful and obedient, humble Servant,

EDM. BURKE

To Burke,
Thursday 2 March 1780

MS. Sheffield City Libraries, Wentworth Woodhouse Muniments, Burke Papers 1/1283. Sent 2 Mar. "Edmund Burke Esq. complimenting him on his Speech for publick oeconomy. Begging he may send me it in franks, and that my freind Dilly's name may be joined with Dodsley's on his title page" (Reg. Let.).

ENDORSEMENT in an unidentified hand: Mr. Boswell, 2d. March 1780.

Edinburgh, 2 March 1780

DEAR SIR: Your allusion to the birth of Pallas, previous to your Speech upon Publick Oeconomy appears now to be more applicable to the then great future Subject than your Modesty seemed to allow, as it has proved truly *Capital*. I know you love a

[23] MS. "this" superimposed on "?tho"

[24] For the new taxes introduced and passed on this day, as well as EB's opposition to them, see *Corres. EB* iv. 47–48 and 47 n. 4. The preceding year's deficit had been about £300,000 (*Corres. EB* iv. 47 n. 1).

[25] In 1772, when discussing whether people who disagreed on important issues could live together in friendship, SJ declared, "I can live very well with Burke: I love his knowledge, his genius, his diffusion, and affluence of conversation; but I would not talk to him of the Rockingham party" (*Life* ii. 181). When they did talk of each other's politics their criticisms were often harsh: SJ frequently accused EB of dishonesty in public life (*Life* ii. 222–23, 348, iii. 45–46, v. 36; Journ. 28 Apr. 1783); EB accused SJ of false charges against the Opposition in his political writings (Journ. 16 Nov. 1786).

pun so please accept of this. As I hope it is not too early for your freinds to congratulate you after your *delivery*, I beg leave to do it with as much sincere warmth as any of them.[1] But I have two favours to ask. One that if it is agreable to join a City Bookseller with Dodsley as Publisher, you may honour with that distinction my freind Dilly whom I can recommend as a worthy and a spirited man, and who having been some time at New York, thinks on American affairs as I do.[2] The other is that to gratify my impatient ardour of curiosity, you may be so very kind as take the trouble to send me your Speech in franks as soon as it is printed.[3]

You promised to read my freind Temple's *Moral and Historical Memoirs* of which a copy was twice sent to you from the Authour, it having been lost or fallen by, the first time.[4]

[1] EB stated in the House of Commons on 28 Jan. 1780 that "he had maturely considered and digested the matter [of political economy], and was now ready to state it; not that he meant to say the form he should give the business was quite perfect, because he was far from pretending to be that Jupiter who could produce a Pallas from his brain, armed completely at all points; he merely designed to inform the House that he was ready" ([John Almon] *Parliamentary Register*, 1780, xvii. 68–69).

We have not traced JB's source for this allusion. Presumably his "pun" evokes simultaneously the birth of Pallas, the éclat of EB's *Speech on Political Oeconomy* delivered on 11 Feb., and its economic subject.

[2] A pirated version of EB's *Speech* appeared on 17 Feb. and the authorized version, published by James Dodsley (1724–97), on 6 Mar. Charles Dilly (1739–1807) was not associated with any of the various editions of the *Speech* (Todd, pp. 100–04). Dilly, at the end of his apprenticeship, had made a short tour of America in 1764: so far, he has been located only in Philadelphia (*Gent. Mag.* 1807, lxxvii. 478; L. H. Butterfield, "The American Interests of the Firm of E. and C. Dilly, with Their Letters to Benjamin Rush, 1770–1795", *Papers of the Bibliographical Society of America*, 1951, xlv. 294 n. 28, 330–31). In 1765 he went into partnership with his brother Edward (Maxted, p. 66), who was more violently pro-American than Charles. But both sympathized with the Colonists and cultivated their American connections (Butterfield, p. 292 and passim; *Diary of John Adams*, ed. L. H. Butterfield, 1961, iii. 189; *Papers of John Adams*, ed. R. J. Taylor, 1977–79, ii. 18–19, 171–72, 211–12, iii. 2, 72–73; *Adams Family Correspondence*, ed. L. H. Butterfield, 1965, i. 200–02; *Papers of Benjamin Franklin*, ed. W. B. Willcox, 1978, xxi. 154–55, 247). In 1780 Dilly published C. H. Wharton's *Poetical Epistle to His Excellency George Washington* to raise funds for American prisoners in England (Butterfield, p. 296; S. H. Bingham, "Publishing in the Eighteenth Century, with Special Reference to the Firm of Edward and Charles Dilly", Diss. Yale 1937, second p. 136).

The Dillys published JB's *Account of Corsica*, 1768. JB describes Charles as "a good tall smartish civil bowing young man, quite of the city form" (Journ. 23 Mar. 1768).

See *Pol. Car.* pp. 89–90 and n. 9 for JB's pro-American views. JB also has in mind EB's position as agent for the General Assembly of the Province of New York in the 1770s (R. J. S. Hoffman, *Edmund Burke, New York Agent*, 1956, pp. 99–101 and passim).

[3] If EB sent this copy no record remains of it. JB read the *Speech* on 26 Mar. and "both wondered and was delighted" (Journ.).

[4] In early 1779, W. J. Temple (*ante* To

From this cold unimportant place you must not expect any thing worth being communicated to Mr. Burke. But I trust that you will be generous enough to treat me with the luxury of hearing from you, though you can have no expectation of a return in *kind*. In *kindness* however "large is my bounty."[5]

I beg to have my best compliments made acceptable to Mrs. Burke and your son; and I ever am, Dear Sir, your much obliged, humble servant,

JAMES BOSWELL

To Burke,
Monday 18 March 1782

MS. Sheffield City Libraries, Wentworth Woodhouse Muniments, Burke Papers 1/1534. Sent 18 Mar. "Edmund Burke Esq. wishing for employment in London and consulting him if I should now be upon the spot. Etc. (Copy)" (Reg. Let.).
ENDORSEMENT in an unidentified hand: Mr. Boswell.

Edinburgh, 18 March 1782

MY DEAR SIR: I promised to trouble you with a letter in favour of the Corporation of Butchers, or *Fleshers* as we emphatically call them, who have been long in possession of Shambles in this City, but are threatened to be set adrift by an Act of Parliament.[1] I was the only Member of my own Society the Faculty of Advocates who as an *Antistes Justitiae*[2] opposed a Resolution for *unconditional* proscription.[3] I enclose a Newspaper in which you will find my

DG, 18 Sept. 1771, n. 11) had published *Moral and Historical Memoirs*, a collection of thirteen essays on such topics as "Foreign Travel" and "Conversation". William Enfield, a regular contributor to the *Monthly Rev.*, praised the book on the whole, though noting that it might have been written in a more pleasing style (*Monthly Rev.* July 1779, lxi. 46–47; B. C. Nangle, *The Monthly Review, First Series*, 1934, p. 161). In a letter of 3 May, JB mentioned to Temple that he had sent a copy of the *Memoirs* to EB.

[5] "*Large was his bounty, and his soul sincere*" (Gray, *Elegy Written in a Country Church Yard*, l. 121).

[1] On 14 Mar. James Hunter Blair, M.P. for Edinburgh, presented to the House of Commons a "Bill for preventing the Slaughtering of Cattle, and for removing Nuisances, within the City and Liberties of *Edinburgh*" (JHC xxxviii. 893).

[2] *Iustitiae antistes* (Aulus Gellius, *Attic Nights* xiv. 4): "a minister of Justice".

[3] Presumably, "*unconditional* proscription" alludes to EB's speech in the House of Commons, 4 Dec. 1781, on his "Motion for a Committee to enquire into the Confiscation of the Effects of his Majesty's new

reasons.[4] I was once going to advise them to present an Address in favour of the American War making an offer of their *knives* and fortunes,[5] which might have secured the Ministerial party. But as they happen to have *justice* on their side it is my opinion they will

Subjects in the Island of St. Eustatius" (*Parl. Hist.* xxii. 769). The previous February the Dutch island of St. Eustatius in the West Indies had surrendered "at discretion" to British forces led by Rear-Adm. Sir George Brydges Rodney and Major-Gen. John Vaughan, who proceeded to sack this wealthy trading post, sending most of its inhabitants into exile and confiscating the greater part of their goods, valued at over £3,000,000, which the Crown later awarded to the attackers (J. F. Jameson, "St. Eustatius in the American Revolution", *American Historical Review*, 1903, viii. 683–708). In EB's vehement denunciation of the sack, he spoke of "the general proscription of all the inhabitants, by which they were ordered to quit the island; all without exception: the Dutch were banished because they were Dutch; the Americans, because they were the King's enemies. . .banished as enemies from St. Eustatius; surrendered without condition at York-town, though friends!" (*Parl. Hist.* xxii. 773). EB's last phrase refers to the notorious tenth article of the British capitulation at Yorktown the previous October by which Cornwallis had been forced to abandon many of the American loyalists to their unpleasant fate.

"Unconditional", however, might well be a more general allusion to the debate over what terms to offer the American colonies: Fox and the Rockingham Whigs were in favour of offering unconditional independence, Shelburne and the Chathamites were reluctant to cede everything, and a small minority of those supporting North's Ministry still believed the war might somehow be won. See further, for example, the debate on Sir James Lowther's motion, 12 Dec. 1781, opposing continuance of the American war (*Parl. Hist.* xxii. 802–31)—esp. Fox's phrasing in answer "to those, who asserted the impolicy of the motion, on the score of its intention of unconditionally withdrawing our forces from attacking the Americans" (p. 825).

[4] The enclosed newspaper has not been recovered. The magistrates wished to remove the slaughterhouses a mile from the Cross. In his journal for 15 Dec. 1781, JB writes of the meeting of the Faculty of Advocates that day, "I alone opposed it [the scheme], from a principle of *justice* to the Fleshers, and I will own at the same time from a wish to appear the Champion even of *that* Corporation. It is wonderful to what keeness I worked myself up." Edgar's map of 1765 shows that at the time the slaughterhouses stood west of Bridge St., just south of the North Loch. In his *History of Edinburgh* (1779; rpt. 1788), Hugo Arnot speaks of their "inconvenience, and exceeding nastiness" (p. 528).

JB seems to have published two letters in *Cal. Merc.* (12 Jan. p. [3], 21 Jan. p. [3]), the first of which, an anonymous answer to a letter signed "Common Sense" (*Cal. Merc.* 7 Jan. p. [3]), argues that it is "*tyrannical*" to proscribe "an useful body of men", and that conditions would be remedied. The second, signed "Simplex Munditiis", replying to a letter signed "Candidus" (*Cal. Merc.* 16 Jan. p. [3]), argues for remedying conditions at the present site, but also approves of moving the slaughterhouses to Paul's Work in Leith Wynd. (Paul's Work was not much farther from the Cross than the existing Fleshmarket.)

[5] JB's play on words refers to the last clause of the American Declaration of Independence: "we mutually pledge to each other our Lives, our Fortunes, and our sacred Honor".

have a much better chance with Mr. Burke and his freinds;[6] and therefore I presume to recommend them to you.[7]

Will you now My Dear Sir give me leave to apply to you on my own account. I allow that I have no other right to do so, but that *Imperfect right* as we Lawyers speak arrising from your having shewn me much kindness upon every occasion, which naturally founds an expectation of more.[8] When a Lady disappoints such an expectation she is called a Jilt. I beleive there is no particular epithet for a Freind who does so. I am also aware that fancy grafted on a good stock of self opinion produces fallacious blossoms in many cases both of Love and Freindship. But I will venture to trust to those which your beams have cherished in my mind.

When I was last in London, you asked me on one of our pleasant evenings over your homebrewed, "how I *could* live in Edinburgh?"[9] I answered "Like a cat in an airpump."[10] In short in so narrow a sphere, and amongst people to whom I am so unlike, my life is dragged on in languor and discontent. What more years may do I cannot tell. But as yet I do not feel myself a bit easier. I explained to you in confidence my hopes of obtaining by Lord Mountstuart's interest, some place of such an income as to enable me to keep house in London.[11] But alas!

[6] After sixteen years in opposition, the Rockingham Whigs were about to return to power. On 20 Mar., before this letter could have reached EB in London, Lord North announced to the Commons that his Ministry was at an end (*Parl. Hist.* xxii. 1217).

[7] Apparently EB never spoke on the question. On 10 May Parliament passed an Act for preventing the slaughtering of cattle within the city of Edinburgh (JHC xxxviii. 997); for an abstract of the bill, see *Scots Mag*. xli. 281.

[8] An imperfect right pertains to matters which are "vague and indeterminate" rather than clearly accessible to legal interpretation (*Bouvier's Law Dictionary*, 1934).

[9] JB spent the evenings of 29 Apr. and 6 and 10 May with EB during his visit to London in the spring of 1781, but does not record this remark in his journal.

[10] Edward Young had used this proverbial expression in lines well-suited to JB's plight: "Like cats in air-pumps, to subsist we strive / On joys too thin to keep the soul alive" (*Love of Fame* v. 177–78).

[11] Almost four years earlier, JB had decided "not to come live in London unless I got place or pension" (Journ. 17 Apr. 1778). He had travelled with John Stuart (1744–1814), styled Lord Mountstuart, eldest son of the third Earl of Bute, in Italy in 1765, and thereafter adopted Mountstuart as his Maecenas, sometimes complaining of his indolence and neglect, and at other times admiring him for speaking "quite in the style of a Prince" (Journ. 17 Mar. 1776). Mountstuart made many promises of help over the years, or so JB interpreted his remarks, but apart from lending JB money had done nothing for him (*Pol. Car.* pp. 23–27, 50–51, 77 n. 2, 81–85). JB kept his hopes of Mountstuart's

Eheu fugaces Posthume Posthume
Labuntur anni![12]

And I see no prospect of my wish being accomplished.—His Lordship has assured me that he is not well with the present Ministry. Pray would he be better with another?[13] Pray is there not now a certainty of a change, upon which a numerous variety of arrangements will take place? May I not now assure myself that you are near your Apotheosis, as poor Goldsmith said of you *poetically* several years ago;[14] for experience proved that his eye was only "in a fine frenzy rolling".[15] If it is now to be real, may I not desire to be remembered by you? I ardently wish for occupation of more consequence than drudging at the bar in Scotland; and I think I should be very happy in exerting what talents I have, under your Auspices.

The late Sir John Pringle said to me last autumn when he was here "I know not if you will be in rest in London. But you will never be at rest out of it." And I recollect Dr. Johnson observing one day at Sir Joshua Reynolds's upon the subject of a London life "that every body is at rest in its proper place. They who are content to live out of London have minds fitted for it."[16] Pray be

help alive by importuning both his brother, Lt.-Col. James Stuart, and even more persistently Stuart's wife, Margaret, an old, intimate friend of JB's wife. (JB conducted a long, open flirtation with her.) Margaret Stuart reassured JB several times that she was pressing his claims to attention with Mountstuart through her husband (e.g. Margaret Stuart to Margaret Boswell, 14 Sept. 1781), but JB had written to her, only two days before the present letter to EB, "complaining of the indifference of Lord Mountstuart and Col. James. Hoping she my amiable freind will not be indifferent too!" (Reg. Let.).

[12] "Alas, O Postumus, Postumus, the years glide swiftly by" (Horace, *Odes*, II. xiv. 1–2, trans. C. E. Bennett, Loeb ed.).

[13] JB seems not to have heard directly from Mountstuart since his departure for Turin in Oct. 1779 (*Life* iii. 411) as Envoy Extraordinary to the Court of Sardinia. In the spring of 1782, Mountstuart got into trouble by behaving insolently to the King of Sardinia, Victor Amadeus III (*Correspondence of King George III*, ed. Sir John Fortescue, 1927–28, vi. 38–40), and returned permanently to England at the end of Nov. 1782 (D. B. Horn, *British Diplomatic Representatives, 1689–1789*, 1932, p. 126).

JB was never to learn that while at Turin, Mountstuart, on his own initiative, had tried to open peace negotiations with France, using his former tutor and JB's old antagonist, Paul-Henri Mallet, as intermediary with Jacques Necker, French Director-General of Finances. George III put an end to these overtures, but Mountstuart was to renew his efforts in the spring of 1782 with the encouragement of Fox, Foreign Secretary as of 27 Mar. in the new Rockingham-Shelburne Ministry (R. B. Morris, *The Peacemakers*, 1965, pp. 98–104, 108–11).

[14] *Ante* To EB, 3 Mar. 1778, n. 2.

[15] *Midsummer Night's Dream*, V. i. 12.

[16] Sir John Pringle (1707–82), Bt., was Physician Extraordinary in the Queen's Household and President of the Royal

good enough to afford me a little consideration, and tell me as a Philosopher and Freind[17] if my restlessness out of the great scene of exertion be not "the divinity that stirs within me"[18] and points out the line I should take? Would there not be something generous in your giving me your aid to attain greater happiness? You told me £600 a year would defray the difference between keeping house in London and in Edinburgh. How shall I contrive to get £600 from government? Would the King, with whom I related to you an excellent conversation, but of himself transplant me into a better climate, how pleasant would it be![19] But I wish not to indulge romantick visions. I am advancing to be called to the english bar, as another string to my bow.[20] In short I am eagerly looking out.

In the mean time, I have an aged Father, whom it is my pious wish as well as my interest to please; and as he dissapproves of my going to London without a sufficient reason, I beg to hear from you, whether my being up on the spot this spring, may not be of some advantage to me?[21] The Noctes coenaeque Deum[22] which I enjoy there, are a sufficient reason in my own mind. But you can understand at once, that something else must weigh with him.

Society. A close friend of Lord Auchinleck and counsellor to JB, he had been in Edinburgh throughout the summer and early autumn of 1781. Returning to London in poor health, he died 18 Jan. According to JB's journal for 9 Aug. 1781, Pringle had made this remark to JB "one day this summer". The journal for 23 May 1778 mentions SJ's observation, but does not date it; nor is it reported in the *Life*. Cf., however, SJ's remark, 30 June 1784, "They who are content to live in the country, are *fit* for the country" (*Life* iv. 338).

[17] Pope, *Essay on Man* iv. 390.

[18] Addison, *Cato* V. i. 7.

[19] Perhaps JB refers to his conversation with the King about General Paoli, 30 May 1781. The journal does not record a meeting with EB between 30 May and 2 June, when JB left London. He had a briefer conversation with the King on 27 May (Journ.), and he was at EB's on the 29th. JB had expressed the same wish for the King's help in a letter to Paoli, 27 June 1781.

[20] JB had been admitted to the Inner Temple on 19 Nov. 1761, but his father insisted that he become a Scottish advocate ("Certificate on my entry as a Student in the Inner Temple", C 1582; *Earlier Years*, p. 74). To fulfil the formal requirements of admission to the English bar, one had to dine in the Temple commons for a prescribed number of days in each of twelve terms (*Inner Temple* v. iii); JB did not begin to keep his terms until Easter Term, 1775. Since he could attend only occasionally, he did not finish his twelve terms until 9 Feb. 1786, at which point he was called to the bar (A 56; Journ. 9 Feb. 1786).

[21] Lord Auchinleck disapproved of JB's annual visits to London: he disliked SJ, he thought such trips too expensive, and he was sceptical of any political advantage to be gained there (Journ. 27 Dec. 1775, 23 Mar. 1777, 26 Sept. 1779). JB is hoping here that EB will write him a letter he can show to his father.

[22] "Nights and feasts of the gods" (Horace, *Satires* II. vi. 65).

You will be pleased to present my best compliments to Mrs. Burke, and to your son when he returns; as I presume he is now upon the circuit.[23]

I trust this letter to your goodness and honour. To have its contents mentioned to any body might hurt me essentially. I ever am, My Dear Sir, with very high esteem, Your obliged and affectionate, humble servant,

James Boswell

I send you a Pamphlet written by me upon the administration of Criminal Justice in Scotland, to which I wish your attention to be directed.[24]

To Burke,
Thursday 18 April 1782

MS. Sheffield City Libraries, Wentworth Woodhouse Muniments, Burke Papers 1/1603. Sent 18 Apr. "Edmund Burke Esq. asking his interest for the office of Judge Advocate in Scotland (Copy)" (Reg. Let.). ENDORSEMENT in an unidentified hand: Mr. Boswell, for Judge Advocate of Scotland's place, April 18 1782, Ansd.

Edinburgh, 18 April 1782

My Dear Sir: Although I am hurt by your neglect of an anxious confidential letter which I wrote to *my Freind Edmund Burke*, on the 18 of last month, I will not let the pride of an old Baron[1] prevent me from soliciting *Mr. Paymaster General*[2] for his interest to obtain

[23] Richard Burke, Jr., who had been admitted to the bar on 24 Nov. 1780 (*Register of Admissions to the . . . Middle Temple*, 1949, i. 381), was at this time on the Northern Circuit. He was the junior member of the Circuit until the spring of 1786, when he left to join the Oxford Circuit (Fifer, p. 229, second n. 1). JB took his place as junior member, and wrote him a facetious letter on the occasion (To R. Burke, 18 Mar. 1786).

[24] *A Letter to Robert Macqueen, Lord Braxfield, on His Promotion To Be One of the Judges of the High Court of Justiciary*, published anonymously on 8 May 1780 (Journ.).

[1] JB had been depressed since his letter to EB of the previous month: "Saw my ambitious views in London all madness—Vexed at being neglected by Burke. Thought I'd indulge a proud distance and just be an old Scottish Baron and Tory" (Journ. 14 Apr.).

[2] EB had been appointed Paymaster-General of the Forces on 27 Mar. It was a sub-Cabinet post, but "the most lucrative office in the State" (Prior, *Burke* i. 403) with a salary of £4,000 a year, an official residence, and other perquisites. Also, previous Paymasters had enriched them-

for me the office of Judge Advocate in Scotland, which is just now become vacant by the death of Sir James Dunbar.[3] I understand it must be filled up by one of our Faculty of Advocates, of which Society I was the single man who at any of our meetings openly avowed a detestation of the measures of the late Ministry against our Bretheren in America.[4] The Lord Advocate who is our Dean or President will candidly attest this.[5]

But I trust much to your private freindship; and I hope you will lose no time in taking the proper steps. As it is in the military department, I suppose General Conway will have the disposal of it.[6] But you will know well what is to be done. The post is just going off. So I have only time to subscribe myself still, affectionately yours,

JAMES BOSWELL

selves by investing the cash in their hands for their own benefit, but EB paid it into the Treasury (Namier and Brooke ii. 151), and Parliament passed his bill providing that the Paymaster's accounts be kept at the Bank of England (J. S. Watson, *The Reign of George III, 1760–1815*, 1960, p. 247; *Parl. Hist.* xxiii. 134–135).

[3] Sir James Dunbar of Mochrum, Bt. (d. 16 Apr.). A Judge Advocate—a legal position in the military whose duties were frequently redefined—apparently was at this time the legal assessor of courts martial. The office of Judge Advocate in Scotland seems to have been a sinecure, requiring only that the holder be in attendance at all courts martial in his jurisdiction (C. M. Clode, *The Military Forces of the Crown*, 1869, ii. 363–65; Clode, *The Administration of Justice under Military Martial Law*, 2nd ed. 1874, pp. 108–09, 125–26; *Green's Encyclopaedia of the Laws of Scotland*, ed. John Chisholm, 2nd ed. 1912, vii. 92). JB also wrote to Lord Pembroke, George Dempster, and Fox about the post (Journ. 18 Apr.; Reg. Let. 19 Apr.). He told Paoli that the Judge Advocate's was "a genteel easy office in the Military department, but the exercise of which is the proper business of a Lawyer . . . [and] the Sallary . . . is equal to Captains pay" (To Paoli, 19 Apr.), about £180 a year (*Pol. Car.* p. 93 n. 9).

[4] Apparently JB does not remark elsewhere on these meetings.

[5] Henry Dundas (1742–1811) had been Lord Advocate of Scotland—the chief legal officer of the Crown—and Dean of the Faculty of Advocates since 1775. He was the most powerful of Scottish politicians, and his support was essential to the North Ministry. "Candidly" alludes to his strong backing of the American war until late 1781. For JB's complex, shifting relationship with him, see *Pol. Car.*

[6] Henry Seymour Conway (1719–95), who had become Commander-in-Chief on 29 Mar.

From Burke,
Tuesday 23 April 1782

MS. Yale (C 685). Received 29 Apr.: "letter from Mr. Burke enclosing one from Genl. Conway. Burke as freindly as I could wish" (Journ.). Besides two enclosures there is a docketing slip preserved with this letter, inscribed: "Mr. Edmund Burke".
ADDRESS: James Boswell Esqr., Edinburgh, N. Britain.
FRANK: Free Edm. Burke.
POSTMARKS: [London] 24 AP, 24 AP, 25 AP, FREE.

Charles Street, April 23, 1782

MY DEAR SIR, Dont censure me too harshly for not answering your very kind and obliging Letter. I protest I had not time for it. Alas! in that Letter you much overrate my power of serving my friends; you cannot overrate my disposition to please or to arrange them.[1] I have served the publick for seventeen years with great fidelity and Labour, and just at the decline of my Life there comes to me a temporary Office of some emollument, considerable expence, and no power.[2] I have the long arrear of all the obligations and kindnesses that I have receivd as a charge upon any little Interest I may be able to obtain. My friends in power have come in with equally long claims upon them, with a divided Patronage, and a reduced Establishment.[3] If I could serve you I tell you in sincerity, that the bringing you to a residence here would be no mean Bribe to me. But what I can do I will upon all occasions where I am free. I lost not a moments time in applying to Genl. Conway.[4] You have a Copy of what I wrote to Genl. Conway and

[1] "To put them in their proper places." The OED (s.v. Arrange, *v.*) points out that "arrange" is a rare word until modern times; the only meaning it gives prior to this date is "to draw up in ranks or in line of battle". EB is credited with two of its earliest meanings, neither of which is precisely the same as its meaning here.

[2] EB had become private secretary to Rockingham in July 1765 and had been chosen for Parliament in December of the same year.

[3] In the Rockingham-Shelburne Ministry, Rockingham, of course, had to share patronage with Shelburne. Further, various reform measures, including EB's Civil List Act, were reducing the number of available offices (Watson, pp. 246–49). Always fiercely loyal to his relations and close associates, EB did manage, however, to benefit them substantially, if only for the time being (e.g. *post* To EB, 19 July, n. 10; From EB, 13 Aug. 1783, n. 5).

[4] In his "Memoirs of James Boswell, Esq.", 1791, issued as publicity for the *Life*, JB wrote, "In 1781 [sic], when Mr. Burke was in power, that celebrated Gentleman shewed his sense of Mr. Boswell's merit in the warmest manner, observing, 'We must do something for you for our own sakes', and recommended him to General Conway for a vacant place, by a letter in which his

my answer that you may see my diligence at least in obeying your Commands. I conversed also with Mr. Fox on the Subject who has very kind wishes for you.[5] I am ever, My dear Sir, Your most faithful and obedient, humble Servant,

EDM. BURKE

[Enclosure]

From Burke to Henry Seymour Conway,
Tuesday 23 April 1782

MS. Yale (C 686). A copy in an unidentified hand, presumably that of Burke's secretary.

ENDORSEMENT in same hand: Copy Lre. To Genl. Conway, 23d April 1782.

HEADING: To Genl. Conway.[1]

Charles St. April 23d

MY DEAR SIR: Business somewhat urgent prevents me from waiting upon you, as I intended to do this Morning, to sollicit you in favour of a friend of mine in Scotland, who wishes to succeed Sir James Dunbar as Judge Advocate. The Gentlemans name is Mr. Boswell, son of the Judge of that Name. He is a Lawyer of Ability and of general Erudition, and the pleasantest and best tempered Man in the World.[2] I believe this Office is in your Gift as

character was drawn in glowing colours" (*Eur. Mag.* June 1791, xix. 406; *Lit. Car.* p. xl). Bennet Langton also recalled EB's remark (From Langton, 2 Oct. 1790), but JB apparently did not record the compliment elsewhere. The exchange between EB and Conway is printed after the present letter.

[5] JB had also written to Fox about the post (*ante* To EB, 18 Apr. n. 3). Fox was Rockingham's Secretary of State for Foreign Affairs and very friendly with EB. JB did not know him well and wrote years earlier that when he tried to flatter him at The Club, Fox "did not like my vinous compliments, and went to another part of the table from that where I sat" (Journ. 31 Mar. 1775). A year after that JB reported him as "indifferently civil" (Journ. 16 Mar. 1776).

[1] MS. "James Boswell Esqr." deleted before present heading.

[2] EB expressed the same opinion to Reynolds, who reported EB's remark to JB in a letter of 1 Oct. 1782: "Mr. Burke dined with me yesterday. He talked much of you and with great affection. He says you are the pleasantest man he ever saw and sincerely wishes you would come and live amongst us."

commander in Chief. I am sensible that I take a great Liberty in asking for it, but I do not hesitate to promise you that when he has an opportunity of coming to thank you for your protection you will have no cause to repent of having attached to you so agreeable a Man as Mr. Boswell. You will pardon this freedom with your usual kindness—I have the honour to be with very real Esteem and regard, My dear Sir, your most faithful and Obedient, humble Servant.

[Enclosure]

From Henry Seymour Conway to Burke, Tuesday 23 April 1782

MS. Yale (C 820).
ADDRESS: To the Right Honble. Edm. Burke, Esq.,[1] Charles Street, St. James's Square.
FRANK: H. S. Conway.
HEADING: R. Hon. Edm. Burke Esq.

Little Warwick Street, 23 April 1782[2]

DEAR SIR: I had this moment the favour of Your letter recommending Mr. Boswell for the place of Judge Advocate in N. Britain now vacant. Some particular circumstances prevent my being able to give any positive answer at present, tho' You may be assur'd that both the quarter from whence the recommendation comes, and the person so favour'd with Your good opinion and so distinguish'd incline me much to wish it were in my power immediately [to] determine as You desire.[3]

[1] EB had taken the oath of office as a member of the Privy Council on 27 Mar. and from that date was formally addressed as "Right Honourable" (*Corres. EB* iv. 430 n. 3).

[2] Conway lived at No. 4 Little Warwick St., a cul-de-sac running out of Cockspur St., in Charing Cross (Wheatley and Cunningham iii. 449, 451–52).

[3] The office was given to Mark Pringle, grandnephew and heir to John Pringle, friend of Henry Dundas and M.P. for Selkirkshire. Mark Pringle himself later (1786–1802) represented Selkirkshire; in Parliament he usually supported Dundas and the Duke of Buccleuch (Namier and Brooke iii. 333–34). On hearing of Pringle's appointment, JB was "a little disappoint-

I am, Dear Sir, with the greatest truth and esteem, Your most Faithful and Obedient servant,

H. S. CONWAY

To Burke,
Tuesday 30 April 1782

MS. Sheffield City Libraries, Wentworth Woodhouse Muniments, Burke Papers 1/1623. Sent 30 Apr. "Edmund Burke Esq. thanking him warmly for his freindship. That a letter from him will reconcile my Father to my paying him a visit at his Venafranos Agros where I long to be. (Copy)" (Reg. Let.).

ENDORSEMENT in an unidentified hand: Mr. Boswell, 30 April 1782.

Edinburgh, 30 April 1782

MY DEAR SIR: The real kindness, the active benevolence of your freindship for me which I have now experienced, is pleasing beyond expression. I used to say that I was never sure of your being a very happy man, till I was admitted familiarly to your house, and saw how agreably you lived with your endearing connections of Wife and son.[1] I am now satisfied that you are a very very good man. Be assured that your goodness is fully felt by me and that if ever an opportunity shall occur you shall find me warmly grateful.

To have such a character from Mr. Burke as you have been pleased to give of me in your letter to General Conway is to have a pearl of great price.[2] I sincerely thank you; and I shall be ambitious to preserve it.

Although your application for me at this time should not prove

ed, but soon recovered" (Journ. 4 May). On 9 July EB attacked Conway in the House of Commons for adhering to Shelburne after Rockingham's death (*Parl. Hist.* xxiii. 182–83), and complained the next year that Conway "never has done a single particle of service to any one friend or recommendation of mine", but he seems to have exaggerated (*Corres. EB* v. 102 and n. 5).

[1] JB wrote in his journal four years earlier: "I told Burke he was the only man I could wish to be. And this not till I had seen how happy he was with his wife and son. For I thought no man happy who had not domestick happiness. He said, 'As to Wife as pres[ent] shall only say she does not make me very unhappy. Of Son as not pres[ent] never Parents had greater reas[on] to be satisfied' " (12 Apr. 1778).

[2] Matthew 13: 46.

successful I am as much obliged to you, as if I had obtained the office; and I shall upon any future opening, freely solicit you.[3]

Let me now, My Dear Sir! most sincerely congratulate you on your promotion, and most chiefly on the power which I trust it will afford you of doing a great deal of good to the British Empire. When more important objects are settled, I shall take leave to suggest some particulars which I am persuaded would tend to make North-Britain both happier in herself, and a better sister to South Britain. For my own part, I much approve of what you once suggested to me that both parts of the Island should be founded into one Mass. But upon this subject I hope to talk with you at leisure.[4] I regret much that I am not in London this spring. But as my Father is as much pleased as he now can be in his decline, with your freindship for me, your writing to me to come up, when the practice of the law here will allow me, will secure me his approbation of my paying you a visit[5] at your *Venafranos agros* in Buckinghamshire, where I have long wished to be with you.[6] I am sure you will approve of my anxious my almost childish care to humour an aged Parent.

I am much flattered by Mr. Fox's kind wishes. I beg you may present my best respects to him. I have the honour to be, My Dear Sir, with the highest admiration, Your much obliged and affectionate, humble servant,

JAMES BOSWELL

[3] Though EB's letter of 23 Apr. offered little hope of assistance, JB was in high spirits: "Burke as freindly as I could wish. Wife pleased. She said [it showed what] interest [I had]. McLaur[in] said I'd get *this* office or an equivalent" (Journ. 29 Apr.). His spirits lasted long after he found he had not been given the position: on 18 June he wrote, "I now have as full satisfaction in my own existence as Mr. Burke has—only that I wish for greater objects" (Journ.). In his "Memoirs of James Boswell, Esq." (see *ante* From EB, 23 Apr. n. 4) JB wrote of EB's letter to Conway, "The place was not obtained; but Mr. Boswell declared, that he valued the letter more" (*Eur. Mag.* June 1791, xix. 406; *Lit. Car.* p. xl).

[4] JB's journals do not record EB's suggestion, and there is no record of their having discussed the matter further.

[5] JB is repeating his request for a letter from EB to show his father (see *ante* To EB, 18 Mar. and n.21), though he undoubtedly showed his father the letter he had just received from EB on the day he is writing the present one: "Dined at Father's and played cards. Communicated letters from London, shewing what interest I had. Father was pleased" (Journ. 30 Apr.).

[6] "Venafran fields" (Horace, *Odes* III. v. 55). Horace describes Venafrum in southern Italy as a country retreat from the lawyer's city cares. EB's country estate, Gregories, lay near Beaconsfield, Bucks., about twenty-four miles west of London. JB did not visit Gregories until 21 Apr. 1783 (Journ.).

To Burke,
Friday 19 July 1782

MS. Sheffield City Libraries, Wentworth Woodhouse Muniments, Burke Papers 1/1707. Sent 19 July. "Right Hon. Edmund Burke Esq. on his Resignation, on my intention to visit him in autumn—and of my Wifes illness (Copy)" (Reg. Let.). The original was enclosed in a letter to Charles Dilly. A copy at Yale (L 317) is in Lawrie's hand, except for all of the last page of the letter as sent, beginning "We have five children", which is in JB's. JB also headed the copy "To Edmund Burke Esq." and "Edinburgh, 19 July 1782".
ENDORSEMENT in an unidentified hand: Mr. Boswell, July 19. 1782.

Edinburgh, 19 July 1782

MY DEAR SIR: Give me leave to embrace you "Unplaced, unpensioned"[1]—just my excellent freind again as I left him, with the additional endearment of having proved to me that I am undoubtedly honoured with his regard and affection.[2] Be you henceforth My Dear Sir in whatever situation, depend upon my grateful attachment.

But I am pained, more than I chuse to discover, by your going out of Administration. Long long did I earnestly wish for your benignant Abilities to have full scope for the reciprocal advantage of the Sovereign and of the People. Your speech upon His Majesty's gracious Message in unison with your celebrated Bill, delighted my Monarchical, I *will* say my Tory Soul.[3] I flattered

[1] "Un-plac'd, un-pension'd, no Man's Heir, or Slave" (Pope, *Imitations of Horace, Satires*, II. i. 116).

[2] In the imbroglio following Rockingham's death, Shelburne became First Minister, and Fox resigned as Secretary of State because of his many points of disagreement with Shelburne. He carried with him a number of the Rockingham group, including EB, who thereby relinquished a chance to enrich himself. EB's resignation took place officially on 10 July.

[3] As one of the stipulations for accepting office, Rockingham had forced the King to agree to EB's reformation of the Civil List, and after further wrangling in the new Cabinet the Royal message urging the reform was read in the House of Commons on 15 Apr. EB then moved the Address of Thanks in which he "congratulated the House and the kingdom on the happy aera when his Majesty, freed from that secret and injurious counsel which stood between him and his people, now spoke to them in the pure and rich benevolence of his own heart" (*Corres. EB* iv. 434; R. J. S. Hoffman, *The Marquis: A Study of Lord Rockingham*, 1973, pp. 372–81; *Parl. Hist.* xxii. 1269). EB's Bill received the Royal Assent on 11 July.

Though in agreement here, EB and JB frequently discussed their differences about Whig and Tory (Journ. 12 Apr. 1778, 29 Apr., 8 May 1781, and *post* To EB, 20 Nov. 1783 and n. 9), and on 4 July, before learning of the dissolution of the Rockingham-Shelburne Ministry, JB had written to Paoli, "My Tory or monarchical enthusi-

myself that by your influence and activity a great deal of good would be done; and I regret from my heart that it should be suspended.[4] The Lord Advocate who I think has Fortunatus's cap,[5] declares he is sorry you have resigned. He spoke of you to me the other day in very pleasing terms.[6] Could you not have waited a while? Would it not have been better to stay, and powerfully counteract any measures of which you might disapprove?[7] But I beg pardon. I am ignorantly intruding upon *political Arcana*; for, from any fragments of your late Speech which I have seen, there is a Mystery in your conduct. You retire in thunder and lightening. There[8] remains a troubled darkness in the Sky. I have full faith in your Virtue and Magnanimity. But I cannot but wish you would explain, by publishing your Speech at length or a Letter to your Constituents.[9]

asm does not perfectly accord with the present majority. I am the Kings friend. I am ambitious of his majestys own protection."

[4] Copy, "suspected"

[5] In the stories that coalesced in the German *Volksbuch* of *Fortunatus*, 1509, and in Thomas Dekker's comedy, *Old Fortunatus*, 1600, Fortunatus has a cap that transports its wearer wherever he wishes. JB is reflecting on Dundas's ability to shift from Ministry to Ministry. Shelburne had just offered to make Dundas Treasurer of the Navy and Keeper of the Scottish Signet for life (Journ. 16 July).

[6] JB records in his journal that during a long, encouraging conversation with Dundas, "He told me that he *knew* Burke wished to assist me. I had mentioned this; and I concluded from what he said that Burke had expressed himself warmly to him" (16 July).

[7] EB had urged his fellow Rockinghamites to consider remaining in office but they thought it proper to resign (*Corres. EB* v. 3–6; Cone ii. 63–66).

[8] MS. "There" altered from "there", preceded by an illegible deletion.

[9] The hidden struggle for power that followed Rockingham's death had aroused intense general interest, and the House of Commons was packed on 9 July, when various leading politicians explained their positions. When EB rose to speak at a late hour there was a certain amount of noise and several Members left. EB then said that "if any of them had any exception to his person, 'they know, (he cried with great warmth, and striking his side) where to find me' " (*Edin. Adv.* 16 July, p. [35]). He then eulogized Rockingham, praised his own sacrifices for the public good, and compared Shelburne to Catiline, Cesare Borgia, and the wolf in "Little Red Riding Hood" (*Pub. Adv.* 10 July, p. [3]). Newspaper accounts, such as *Lond. Chron.* (9–11 July, p. [2]), *Cal. Merc.* (13 July, p. [2], 15 July, p. [2]), and *Edin. Eve. Cour.* (13 July, p. [3]), printed disjointed accounts of EB's speech, playing up details like the Members' rising to leave, EB's challenge, and the allusion to "Little Red Riding Hood". JB found EB's initial outburst comic, and compared it to a condemned man's saying, "What! will you not stay and see my execution?" (Journ. 29 July). A more detailed report of EB's remarks appeared in *A Complete and Accurate Account of the Very Important Debate in the House of Commons . . . in Which the Cause of Mr. Fox's Resignation, and the Great Question of American Independence Came under Consideration*, dated 12 July 1782, pp. 29–33, 38–39. Apparently his speech was never published separately (see Todd).

TO BURKE, 19 JULY 1782

May I have the pleasure to beleive that my young freind your Son has a permanent office secured to him? I am warmly interested in every thing that concerns you.[10]

I am in distress at present in which you who are blest with domestick happiness will sympathise with me. My Wife is ill of breast complaints, which it is to be feared are symptoms of a consumption, her family having been sadly subject to that fatal disease.[11] She has recovered several times when thus threatened which gives hope. But I am in miserable anxiety. We[12] have five children, the eldest of which is only nine years old. I therefore cannot but have dreary imaginings. *Ora pro nobis.*

As she is rather better, I flatter myself that it may be in my power in our Autumn vacation which lasts from 12 August to 12 November, to fulfill my intention of visiting you at your *Venafranos Agros* in Buckinghamshire.[13] Some confidential conversations with you may be of great value to me. I beg to hear from you, if you will be at home and at leisure, during the time I have mentioned; Or if only during a part of it, be pleased to tell me when.

[10] When EB resigned his post as Paymaster, Richard, Jr., Deputy Paymaster of the Forces (at £500 a year) and Richard, Sr., Secretary to the Treasury (at £3,000 a year), followed suit (*Corres. EB* v. 10). *St. James's Chron.* praised the nobility of the family's self-sacrifice (11–13 July, p. [4]). At the same moment, EB was trying to secure an appointment for life for Richard, Jr., and for Dr. Walker King as joint Receivers General of Land Revenues for Essex, Hertfordshire, Middlesex, Norfolk, Huntingdonshire, and London. This appointment, just vacated by the death of the incumbent on 29 June, was held up until granted under the Fox-North Coalition, 5 June 1783 (*Corres. EB* v. 8, 51–53). King, long after, said he made no money from his share, but held it for the benefit of EB and his family (ibid. v. 82 n. 7). Receiverships paid little directly, but Receivers traditionally made money by retaining large balances in their own hands (see *Parl. Hist.* xxii. 204–08; W. R. Ward, *The English Land Tax in the Eighteenth Century*, 1953, esp. pp. 145–58; Binney, pp. 49–60). To extrapolate from later figures, Burke and King might have held as much as £40,000 in balances, but any figure is very uncertain (see House of Commons, *Eighth Report from the Select Committee on Finance*, 1797, pp. 4–6, 18, 39–40).

Also, at the last minute EB tried, through a reluctant Horace Walpole, to secure an assignation to Richard, Jr., of the Clerkship of the Pells, worth, according to Walpole, £7,000 a year, from Walpole's brother Sir Edward Walpole, but this attempt failed (*Corres. EB* v. 10–14; *Corres. HW* xlii. 24–28; see also Martin Kallich, "Horace Walpole against Edmund Burke", *Studies in Burke and His Time*, 1968, ix. 838–46).

[11] Margaret Boswell had suffered from tuberculosis, accompanied by a severe cough and periodic spitting of blood, since 1776. Her latest relapse so preoccupied JB that he kept a separate journal of it (Journ. 22 June–11 Nov.). Mrs. Boswell's two sisters, Elizabeth Beaumont (d. 1776) and Mary Campbell (d. 1777), and her niece Annie Cuninghame (d. 1779) all died of tuberculosis (Journ. 11 Nov. 1775, 8 Jan. 1776, 3, 6 Mar. 1777, 7 Feb., 10 Aug. 1779).

[12] Copy, "We" in Lawrie's hand deleted before "We" in JB's hand.

[13] *Ante* To EB, 30 Apr. and n. 6.

My best compliments to Mrs. Burke and to your son. I ever am, My Dear Sir, your much obliged and faithful, humble servant,

JAMES BOSWELL

To Burke,
Thursday 15 August 1782

MS. Yale (L 318). A copy in Lawrie's hand, to which JB has added the heading, dateline, and salutation. Sent 15 Aug. "Right Hon. Edmund Burke Esq. that it is about a month since I wrote to him of paying him a visit this autumn" (Reg. Let.).

HEADING: To The Right Honourable Edmund Burke Esq.

Edinburgh, 15 August 1782

MY DEAR SIR: Do not think me troublesome or endeavour to get free of the thought I pray you. It is about a month since I wrote to you wishing to know if you would be at your Place in the Country, during all the recess; as I had a warm intention to pay you a visit. Perhaps my letter has not reached you; for I enclosed it to Mr. Dilly my Bookseller not being *quite certain* that it would go directly to you by the publick post.[1] I have the honour to be with the highest esteem and most sincere affection, My Dear Sir, Your much obliged, humble servant.

From Burke,
Sunday 1 September 1782

MS. Yale (C 687).

ADDRESS: James Boswell Esqr., Edinburgh.

FRANK: Free Edm. Burke.

POSTMARKS: BEACONSFIELD, 2 SE, FREE.

Beconsfield, Sept. 1, 1782

MY DEAR SIR, I have been at home but little since I receivd your

[1] EB wrote to his successor as Paymaster, Isaac Barré, on 16 July that he would vacate the Paymaster's house in Whitehall by 22 or 23 July (*Corres. EB* v. 18–19), but he dated a letter from Whitehall as late as 29 July (ibid. v. 26). "Not being *quite certain*", however, may imply that JB was afraid the letter might be opened in the Post Office (cf. *Corres. EB* iv. 437; Ellis, pp. 63–64, 71–72).

very obliging Letter, or I should have thanked you for it much earlier.[1] Your intentions towards me are very kind; and Mrs. Burke and my Brother, the only parts of us now together[2] are much flatterd by your kindness and will[3] be extremely happy to see you here, if it otherwise suits you, and your Business, should call you into this southern Hemisphere, any time in October, for towards the End of this Month I promised to be with Lord Fitzwilliam in Yorkshire.[4]

I wish you may be able to make your way with the present Minister. He, who is, most certainly, neither Whigg nor Tory, can have no objection to you for your principles; upon any other account than that they are principles. He is, I believe taking all proper Steps to fulfil his contract and to bring round the old System, and most of the old actors.[5] "Your Tory Soul", you say

[1] EB seems to be fibbing a bit. He was still at Whitehall on 29 July, then at Beaconsfield on 10 Aug. and later, and had returned to Charles St. by 27 Aug. (*Corres. EB* v. 26, 28, 31, 32). He refers here to JB's letter of 19 July; if he had received that of 15 Aug. he must have decided diplomatically to ignore it.

[2] Presumably Richard Burke, Jr., was at Scarborough for his health (*Corres. EB* v. 35–36).

[3] MS. "will" superimposed upon "shall"

[4] William Fitzwilliam (1748–1833), second Earl Fitzwilliam, Rockingham's nephew and heir, was now EB's patron. EB and Walker King, who had been Rockingham's private secretary, had been putting his papers in order in London. At the moment, they were preparing to visit Wentworth Woodhouse, Rockingham's Yorkshire seat, which had been inherited by Fitzwilliam (*Corres. EB* v. 18 n. 4, 35–36, 45–46).

[5] EB had long shared the common mistrust of Shelburne, calling him by his nickname, Malagrida (a notorious Portuguese Jesuit), as early as 1773 (*Corres. EB* ii. 491; see also ii. 509, iii. 427), but his dislike of Shelburne must have been much intensified by the infighting of the Rockingham-Shelburne Ministry. EB's denunciation of Shelburne in the House of Commons on 9 July has already been cited (*ante* To EB, 19 July, n. 9), and by 3 Mar. 1783 he was characterizing Shelburne as "this wicked man, and no less weak and stupid, than false and hypocritical" (*Corres. EB* v. 72). Also, he wrote in an unpublished sketch that Shelburne "totally wants a uniform rule and scheme of life" (Magnus, *Burke*, p. 317 n. 15).

Personal dislike compounded a basic disagreement about the relationship between the King and the Cabinet. Shelburne adhered to the "old System", which, deprecating party, regarded members of the Cabinet as so many department heads appointed by, and responsible to, the King (*Parl. Hist.* xxiii. 191–93). The Rockingham group was moving towards the idea of the "collective responsibility" of the Cabinet (on this issue see, among many discussions, J. W. Derry, *Charles James Fox*, 1972, pp. 157–59; Frank O'Gorman, *The Rise of Party in England: The Rockingham Whigs, 1760–82*, 1975, pp. 463–68; and O'Gorman, "Party in the Later Eighteenth Century" and the following "Colloquy" in *The Whig Ascendancy*, ed. John Cannon, 1981, pp. 77–99). EB's terminology reflects Fox's, when Fox wrote to Richard Fitzpatrick, his close friend and supporter, on 11 May about "the old system, revived in the person of Lord S." (*Memorials and Correspondence of Charles James Fox*, ed. Lord John Russell, 1853, i. 325), and in his speech on 9 July in

was delighted with my Language on the Bill—You thought it particularly right with the Bill it accompanied. I see you look at things with good optics.[6] I take the true Genius of this constitution to be, Tory[7] Language and Whigg measure; Langua Toscana in Bocca Romana.[8] There have been pretty rapid Revolutions since you left us.[9] I wish you would bring another; though that is not very likely, as the last Shake of the Earthquake did, as second shocks sometimes do, resettle what was disturbed[10] by the first. As to our friend the Advocate, it not only confirmed, but infinitely improved his Situation.[11] Pay your Court there, my Dear Boswell. It will answer I tell you.[12] Adieu and believe me with the best compliments of this house, My Dear Sir, Your most faithful and obedient, humble Servant,

EDM. BURKE

the House of Commons, when Fox said he feared "the old system was to be revived, most probably with the old men, or indeed with any men that could be found" (*Parl. Hist.* xxiii. 163).

The Rockingham group laid claim to the Whig label, as when Fitzpatrick asserted that if the King were allowed to appoint Shelburne as First Minister, it meant "a total end of *Whig principles*" (Russell i. 459). On 10 July Shelburne stated in the House of Lords that "if a Whig was a man who acted upon Revolution principles, and was a friend to the constitution and to the liberties of the people, he would be proud to call himself a Whig" (*Parl. Hist.* xxiii. 196), but his enemies regarded such statements as the political cant of a man totally without principles, subordinate to the King, and intent only on power.

During the Rockingham-Shelburne Ministry, as EB noted with alarm to Rockingham (*Corres. EB* iv. 448-50), Shelburne was consolidating his support at the expense of his co-First Minister (see John Norris, *Shelburne and Reform*, 1963, pp. 151–54); after forming his own Ministry, Shelburne vied with Fox for the support of North and his followers (see John Cannon, *The Fox-North Coalition*, 1969, pp. 26–30).

[6] EB's comment is ironic, since it was notorious that George III had resisted the Civil List Bill as long as he could (*ante* To EB, 19 July, n. 3).

[7] MS. "that" deleted before "Tory"

[8] "A Tuscan tongue in a Roman mouth." EB misspelled *lingua*.

[9] JB had not been in London since June 1781.

[10] MS. "disturbed" superimposed upon an illegible word.

[11] Under Shelburne, Henry Dundas had been made Privy Councillor, Treasurer of the Navy, and Keeper of the Signet in Scotland for life (*ante* To EB, 19 July, n. 5). Shelburne also gave him "the recommendation to all offices that should fall vacant in Scotland" (Russell ii. 29; see also Cyril Matheson, *Life of Henry Dundas*, 1933, pp. 82–85).

[12] JB was already paying court to Dundas, with whom he was on friendly terms at this point; for details, see *Pol. Car.* pp. 95–96.

To Burke,
Thursday 26 December 1782

MS. Yale (L 319). A copy in John Johnston's hand.
ENDORSEMENT: Copy Letter To The Right Honble. Edmund Burke, 23d decemr. 1782.[1]

Edinr. 26 Decemr. 1782[2]

MY DEAR SIR: Soon after having the honour of your last very kind letter, My Father died,[3] That Solemn event opened to me a great deal of private business, But Such was the eagerness of my impatience to be with you, and with Dr. Johnson, that after Conducting my Wife and Children to our Family Seat, I was actually So far on my way to London, when I was brought back by an express that my wife was taken very ill.[4] It pleased God to recover her, and being obliged to remain at home, I Set my mind to Country affairs, and absolutely acquired, Something almost equivalent to a Sixth Sense, a lively fondness of what formerly appeared to me as dull as a Forge or a tan-Work. I read last night for the first time, an account of your experiments in husbandry published by Young in one of his tours.[5] I See your *vivida vis*[6] acts upon Matter as well as upon Spirit.—"Alike the Senate and the field."[7] I have a very romantick place rich in rock, wood, and water; and I have a very extensive tract of Land Capable of improvement. I flatter myself with hopes of Seeing you at Auchinleck. *Silvae Sint Consule dignae*,[8] you may look at Something well said of it in Dr. Johnson's Journey to the Hebrides.[9]

[1] Johnston wrote the first three words of the endorsement and the date at the end; JB supplied the rest.

[2] Johnston made the date-line "Edinr. 23 Decemr. 1782", but someone (presumably JB) altered his "3" to "6". Since we know that JB: "breakfasted and dined with Sir Tho. Dundas" on 23 Dec. (Journ.; see below, n. 15), it is likely that he also wrote this letter on that day but changed the date when he did not post it until 26 Dec.

[3] Lord Auchinleck died on 30 Aug., before EB's letter of 1 Sept. could reach JB.

[4] JB set off from Auchinleck on 24 Sept. but returned the next day on hearing that his wife had suffered a "violent fit of spitting of blood" (Journ. 25 Sept.). "So far" is a Scotticism for "a good distance".

[5] Arthur Young (1741–1820), the well-known writer on agriculture, had visited EB's farm at Beaconsfield in 1770. The following year he published a description of it, with praise for EB's experiments in deep ploughing, draining, and crop selection, in his *Farmer's Tour through the East of England*, 1771, iv. 69–88.

[6] "Vivida vis animi" (Lucretius, *De Rerum Natura* i. 72): "lively power of mind".

[7] Pope, *Epilogue to the Satires* ii. 87.

[8] "Let the woodland be worthy of a consul" (Virgil, *Eclogues* iv. 3, trans. H. R. Fairclough, Loeb ed.).

[9] SJ devoted over a page near the end of his *Journey to the Western Islands of Scotland*,

This winter I continue my former line of practice at the Scots bar. But I am by no means content. I long to be amongst you;[10] and I am Soon to take the liberty of Sending you a Confidential Memorial[11] on that Subject, upon which I trust you will not refuse me your friendly opinion in the Christmas recess.[12]

The Lord Advocate is indeed a lucky man. When the Ship of war to which he formerly belonged was Sinking, he Jumpt into an India Man, where he remained in a very reputable birth, till another Ship of War the Shelburne received him amongst it's Motley Crew.[13]

Your ridicule of the Speech Spoken by the Sovereign at the opening of this Session of Parliament was exquisite, But I could not But feel for the abasement of Monarchy. The Speech was beneath the dignity of the Elector of Hanover.[14] I am Sorry that I live in Such an age as this. My Loyalty is vexed.

1775, to praising Lord Auchinleck's improvement of the estate, while remarking that the ruins of the "old castle", the Boswells' original dwelling place, "afford striking images of ancient life" (*Works SJ* ix. 161).

[10] JB is responding to Reynolds's report that EB had said he wished JB "would come and live amongst us" (*ante* EB to Conway, 23 Apr. n. 2).

[11] In Scots law, "A statement of facts drawn up to be submitted for counsel's opinion. Also, an advocate's brief" (OED s. v. Memorial, *sb.* B.4.d).

[12] Though reminding himself to do so (Journ. 31 Mar. 1783; Mem. 20 Apr. 1783), JB never seems to have sent the promised statement about his plan to be called to the English bar. But near the end of his next stay in London (Mar.-May 1783), he had "a close conversation" about this possibility with EB, who advised him to fix his mind "on an employment" in Scotland, and to come to London only on visits (Journ. 29 May 1783).

[13] For Dundas's positions under North and Shelburne, see *ante* To EB, 18 Apr. n. 5, and 1 Sept. n. 11. By "Ship of War" JB refers to Dundas's strong support of the American war until 1781. North had appointed Dundas as chairman of a Secret Committee of the House of Commons in Apr. 1781 to investigate the war in the Carnatic. Under Rockingham, when Dundas retained only his post as Lord Advocate, he occupied himself with investigating the mismanagement of Indian affairs, which he condemned in several speeches in the House (Matheson, *Life of Henry Dundas*, pp. 81–82). Shelburne's Ministry was a patchwork of former Rockinghamites and independents, which split publicly at the opening of Parliament in December on the issue of granting unconditional independence to America (Cannon, *Fox-North Coalition*, pp. 41–44).

[14] That is, below the dignity of even the Elector of Hanover, much less that of the King of Great Britain and Ireland. In the Speech from the Throne on 5 Dec., reprinted in *St. James's Chron.*, the King was made to say that in conceding independence to America, "I have sacrificed every Consideration of my own to the Wishes and Opinion of my People. I make it my humble and earnest Prayer to Almighty God, that Great Britain may not feel the Evils which might result from so great a Dismemberment of the Empire; and, that America may be free from those Calamities, which have formerly proved in the Mother Country how essential Monarchy is to the Enjoyment of Constitutional Liberty" (5–7 Dec. p. [1]). According to the paraphrase of

May you my Dear Sir be Soon a bright planet near the throne which is your natural orbit. In the mean time, may I beg to be favoured with a few lines from you when you are at leisure, I am Just going to dine with Sir Thomas Dundas, where we shall drink your health,[15] I ever am with most affectionate regard, My Dear Sir, your obliged and faithfull, humble servant,

(Signed) JAMES BOSWELL

From Burke,
Thursday 29 May 1783

Not reported. Noted in Journ. 29 May: "I took a hackney coach and drove to the *Paymaster's*. There was a card from him to me requesting my being with him this day at two to go to Chelsea College, which had not yet been sent and was delivered to me." EB had returned to the Paymaster's office when the Fox-North Coalition assumed power on 4 Apr. As Paymaster, he was also Treasurer of the Royal Hospital, Chelsea, an establishment for old and disabled veterans. The Oak Apple dinner, held annually on 29 May, celebrated the birthday and restoration of Charles II, the founder of the Hospital (C. G. T. Dean, *The Royal Hospital, Chelsea*, 1950, pp. 35, 149, 241).

EB's response, "*Mr. Burke* . . . made the most ludicrous Comments on almost every Paragraph . . . [calling the speech] the greatest Farrago of Nonsense and Hypocrisy he had ever read. . . . The Dignity of the King was but little consulted in the Speech; for he was made to fall upon his Knees, and put up his Prayers to the Almighty — the first Monarch, he believed, who had been made to pray from his Throne. The Dignity of Parliament was still less consulted than that of the King; these Prayers to Heaven being a direct Insult and Libel upon Parliament; for what were they delivered up? To deprecate Evils that might flow from a Measure which his Majesty indeed condemned, but which had been recommended and enforced by Parliament. What greater insult could be offered to that House than to tell them that their Measures were most likely to bring down such heavy Calamities on the Empire, that a pious King was obliged to drop on his Knees and implore Heaven to avert them!" (5–7 Dec. p. [4]).

[15] Sir Thomas Dundas (1741–1820), of Kerse, Bt., M.P. for Stirlingshire and a loyal adherent of the Rockingham Whigs, was the son of Henry Dundas's opponent, Sir Lawrence Dundas, and the brother-in-law of Lord Fitzwilliam (Namier and Brooke ii. 364–65; *ante* From EB, 1 Sept. n. 4).

To Burke,
Friday 8 August 1783

MS. Yale (L 320). A copy in Lawrie's hand. Sent 8 Aug. "Right Hon. Edmund Burke stating my pretensions for preferment, and complaining of being in a narrow situation unsuitable to me" (Reg. Let.).
HEADING in JB's hand: To The Right Hon. Edmund Burke.

Edinr. 8 augt. 1783

MY DEAR SIR: The dismission of mr. Dundas from the office of Lord Advocate of Scotland[1] makes such an opening in our Law department, that I ought not to neglect such an opportunity of stating my pretensions. I am a Gentleman of respectable birth, and have been seventeen years at the bar.[2] My character and talents I trust to your Opinion.[3]

If mr. Campbell our present Solicitor General shall decline the post of Kings advocate I state myself amongst those who are entitled to it.[4] If it shall be given to him, I claim the office of Solicitor General, or if it shall be thought proper to divide that office as has been done upon former occasions I shall be happy to act as joint Solicitor.[5]

Should I obtain promotion in any of these ways I am confident that administration would find me sufficiently zealous, and were I to be brought into Parliament, I hope I might be of some service.

You, my Dear Sir shewed yourself so sincerely my friend when I

[1] When the Fox-North Coalition, under the nominal leadership of William Henry Bentinck (1738–1809), third Duke of Portland, took office, Dundas was replaced as Treasurer of the Navy by Charles Townshend, but remained Lord Advocate. He received Fox's letter dismissing him from that post on 5 Aug. (G. W. T. Omond, *The Lord Advocates of Scotland*, 1883, ii. 114). JB heard of the vacancy on 6 Aug. (Journ. 7 Aug.).

[2] JB had passed advocate at the Scottish bar on 26 July 1766 (*Earlier Years*, pp. 291–92).

[3] JB and EB were at their closest during JB's visit to London earlier in the year, and JB wrote in his journal for 22 Mar., "I enjoyed the consciousness of independence. But I hoped that by his [EB's] influence I might obtain the pleasurable lot of an employment in London."

[4] Ilay Campbell (1734–1823), later Lord Advocate (Dec. 1783), Lord President of the Court of Session (1789), and Bt. (1808). He insisted upon resigning his office when Dundas was dismissed by the Coalition in August, refusing to accept the post of Lord Advocate in Dundas's place (Namier and Brooke ii. 184). The Hon. Henry Erskine was appointed Lord Advocate on 23 Aug. (*Gent. Mag.* Aug. 1783, liii. 718).

[5] Alexander Wight was appointed-Solicitor-General on 21 Oct. (*Fac. Adv.* p. 219). Patrick Haldane and Alexander Home were joint Solicitors from 1746 to 1755, and James Montgomery and Francis Garden from 1760 to 1764 (Sir David Milne, *The Scottish Office*, 1957, p. 219).

applied to you upon a former occasion,[6] that I am willing to flatter myself you may have been kind enough to exert yourself for me at this time of your own accord. I however think it proper to write to you. I wrote to mr. Fox upon a former occasion but was not honoured with an answer, So, I do not trouble him at present, unless you chuse to mention me to him.[7]

I shall think it exceedingly hard, if at a time, when I beleive such men as I know myself to be, are wished for by his Majestys ministers, in this part of the Kingdom especially, I should be entirely overlooked.[8]

I must repeat to you, that I languish in provincial obscurity; and I would fain hope that your generous friendship will releive me from a state of dulness and discontent.[9]

Pray present my best compliments to Mrs. Burke, to your son and to your brother.[10] I reckon myself sure of all their good wishes.

If my present application should faill may I not be recommended to the Duke of Portland for some other employment? My Father Lord Auchinleck studied in Holland with the late Duke,[11] and had once the honour of entertaining this Duke at Perth as a Judge upon the Circuit.[12] Depend upon it, my influence in establishing his Grace's popularity in Scotland, should not be

[6] *Ante* To EB, 18 Apr., From EB, 23 Apr. 1782.

[7] *Ante* To EB, 18 Apr. 1782, n. 3.

[8] By "such men as I know myself to be", JB means men who are independent of factions and, in Scotland particularly, independent of Henry Dundas. Further, JB knew that the Fox-North Coalition was unpopular in Scotland (Journ. 3 Apr.); here he hints that he had told EB earlier that he regretted the King's having been "overwhelmed by a Faction" (Journ. 22 Mar.).

[9] For JB's earlier complaint about the narrowness of Scotland, see *ante* To EB, 18 Mar. 1782 and n. 10.

[10] EB's brother Richard had been reappointed Secretary to the Treasury. JB thought him "vulgar and fierce" (Journ. 13 May 1781); for an account of his character and his closeness to EB, see Dixon Wecter, "Edmund Burke and his Kinsmen", *University of Colorado Studies*, 1939–41, series B, i. 49–75.

[11] Lord Auchinleck and William Bentinck (1709–62), second Duke of Portland, were contemporaries at the University of Leiden: Portland entered as a student of letters on 20 June 1727, and Lord Auchinleck as a student of law on 29 Dec. 1727 (*Album Studiosorum Academiae Lugduno Batavae, MDLXXV–MDCCCLXXV*, 1875, cols. 911, 915). In his continuation of his father's memoirs, Lord Auchinleck listed the names of those who were his closest friends at Leiden, but Portland is not among them (C 338.7, pp. 44–45).

[12] On 2 Sept. 1762, the same day that Lords Auchinleck and Prestongrange opened the Circuit Court at Perth, the third Duke of Portland was lavishly entertained by the magistrates of Perth at the town hall (*Cal. Merc.* 4 Sept. p. 423, 8 Sept. p. 431; *Scots Mag.* Oct. 1762, xxiv. 566). JB must be referring to some dinner at this time.

altogether despised. I ever am with most affectionate regard, My Dear Sir, Your obliged and faithfull, humble servant.

From Burke,
Wednesday 13 August 1783

MS. Yale (C 688). Received 19 Aug. "Right Hon. Edmund Burke that he is to lay my letter before the Duke of Portland with his recommendation. But that he doubts of his interest. A kind and candid letter" (Reg. Let.).

ADDRESS: James Boswell Esqr. [Edinburgh *deleted*; Haddington *deleted*] Kilmarnock.[1]

FRANK: Free Edm. Burke.

POSTMARKS: BEACONSFIELD, 14 AV, FREE.

ENDORSEMENT: Received 19 August 1783. Right Honourable Edmund Burke that he is to lay my letter for promotion before the Duke of Portland. But he doubts of his success. A kind and candid letter.

Beconsfield, Augst. 13, 1783

MY DEAR BOSWELL, I shall certainly lay your Letter with my best recommendation before the Duke of Portland; for surely I wish you success in your pursuits. But for many reasons I hope you have other friends whose original influence is greater, or is less worn out in Service,[2] to put forward your Claim. It is my good fortune to have met in[3] the Course of a long life with many deserving friends; as a balance to this, that long life has Generally been unimportant, and I have had little intercourse with persons in real power. My political connexions are possessd at present of a partition of it, for about four Months. In that short time all the demands of my whole Life have rushed in upon me from all

[1] Lawrie crossed out EB's "Edinburgh" and wrote "Haddington" beneath it; then he crossed out "Haddington" and wrote "Kilmarnock" beneath that. On 2–4 Aug. JB had visited the Hon. Alexander Gordon, later (1784) Lord Rockville, a judge of the Court of Session, at Rockville, his estate near North Berwick, Haddingtonshire (Journ.; George Brunton and David Haig, *An Historical Account of the Senators of the College of Justice*, 1832, p. 537). JB left Edinburgh for Auchinleck on 12 Aug., three days after the Session rose (Journ.).

[2] Cf. *Measure for Measure* I. ii. 109–11: "You that have worn your eyes almost out in the service, you will be considered."

[3] MS. "with" deleted before "in"

quarters; and I have been assaild with such a number of applications, in such a Variety of ways, that being wholly unable to resist them, I have totally lost my little Credit, and am considerd at every post of patronage as an importunate and injudicious suitor. I have been ill for some days, and am still weak and dispirited.[4] Yesterday I spent near four hours in answering Letters; and there is still a considerable arrear.[5] This I say, My dear Boswel, not as an Excuse; for I shall do what you desire; but to give some account of the want of success which I apprehend. I shall be little consulted about the arrangements of Scotland, or any other places. Whether you believe this or not I cannot tell. But it is true. I am ever with very sincere regard and Esteem, My dear Sir, Your most affectionate and obedient, humble Servant,

EDM. BURKE

To Burke,
Thursday 20 November 1783

MS. Yale (L 321). A copy in Lawrie's hand. Sent 20 Nov. "Right Hon. Edmund Burke an indignant manifesto upon my being totally neglected by Administration. Congratulating him on his election as Lord Rector of the University of Glasgow; and trusting he will come down, and that I shall have his company at Auchinleck. (Copy)" (Reg. Let.).
HEADING: To The Right Hon. Edmund Burke.

Edinburgh, 20 Nov. 1783

MY DEAR SIR, Your kind and candid answer to my last letter came to me at my seat at Auchinleck where the *tout ensemble* arround me enables me to bear disappointments better than where I am of less consequence. But indeed my warm friend! as I have the honour and happiness to beleive you, the choice of a

[4] EB was suffering from an unspecified "disorder" and "badness of . . . spirits" (*Corres. EB* v. 111).

[5] EB's correspondence for this period does include several recommendations for patronage (*Corres. EB* v. 91–93, 97–98, 104–105), but his letters of 12 Aug. have not been reported. As well, however, as securing Richard, Sr.'s reappointment as Secretary to the Treasury (*ante* To EB, 8 Aug. n. 10) and Richard, Jr.'s joint-survivorship (*ante* To EB, 19 July 1782, n. 10), EB also managed to retain for another member of his household, his close friend and "cousin" William Burke, the post of Deputy Paymaster in India, which he had originally created for him and which had been approved by the Treasury Board on 16 Aug. 1782 (Cone ii. 24–25).

Solicitor General in Scotland has not only vexed me, as a Gentleman of such connections in every view as give me good reason to think myself ill used, but I can assure you discredits the present ministry more than they are aware. You flattered me with hopes that they were to have no understrapping Manager of affairs on this side of the Tweed. But this appointment[1] is a wretched proof to the contrary. I have an indignant feeling upon the occasion.[2] My comfort has been that the Gentlemen of my own County have shewn me their regard, by electing me twice last autumn to be their Chairman or Praeses as we call him; once at the Quarter Sessions, and once at a[3] General meeting at which we resolved to petition Parliament, for a correction of shameful abuses which have of late prevailled in our Freehold qualifications.[4]

Let me now congratulate you on your election to be Lord Rector of the university of Glasgow.[5] The truth is I still more congratulate myself upon it, because I hope it will certainly induce you to pay a visit to Scotland. Pray let me know if you will be down in the Christmas Recess. I should rather wish that you would come at a better season of the year. But at whatever time you come, I trust you will give me leave to attend you, and will honour me with your Company at Auchinleck, which is but a few hours drive from Glasgow.[6]

This is to me a more agreeable subject than any thing concern-

[1] MS. "disappointment" with "dis" deleted.

[2] Shortly before JB wrote this letter, a "serious conversation" with Henry Erskine, the new Lord Advocate, had left him angry: Erskine "could make but awkward excuses for my not being appointed Solicitor General; and I plainly saw that Scotland was in the hands of understrapping managers, of which I wrote to Mr. Burke in strong terms" (Journ. 21 Nov.). Sir Thomas Dundas is the "understrapping Manager of affairs" alluded to (*Pol. Car.* p. 103 n. 6). Erskine may have owed his appointment primarily to his brother Thomas's friendship with Fox (W. C. Townsend, *Lives of Twelve Eminent Judges of the Last and of the Present Century*, 1846, i. 447; Namier and Brooke ii. 406) or, as JB suggests, to his own long friendship with Sir Thomas Dundas (Alexander Fergusson, *Henry Erskine*, 1882, pp. 238–39; Namier and Brooke ii. 365). In either case, unlike JB, Erskine could be counted on to support the Coalition (see Fergusson, pp. 243–44).

[3] MS. "a" superimposed upon "the"

[4] JB presided at the Quarter Sessions in Ayr on 28 Oct., and again at a meeting of Ayrshire freeholders on 7 Nov. (Journ.). The abuse to which the freeholders objected was the creation by large landowners of "nominal and fictitious" votes (see *post* To EM, 12 July 1788; *Pol. Car.* pp. 97–99).

[5] EB had been chosen in this student election on 15 Nov. (*Corres. EB* v. 117).

[6] EB visited Scotland from 5–16 Apr. and was installed as Rector on 10 Apr. 1784, but did not visit Auchinleck (Journ. 8–10 Apr. 1784; *Corres. EB* v. 136–42). See *post* To EB, 10, 12 Apr. 1784; From EB, 15 Apr. 1784.

ing publick affairs at present. You think it is not easy to sour my temper. But I should think meanly of myself did I entertain no resentment of the total neglect which I have had the mortification to experience, at a time when I had reason[7] to think and when it was generally thought that I could not fail to receive some mark of attention from administration.[8]

I beg to have my best compliments presented to your family and that you may beleive me to be with old Tory steadiness, though you tell me I have a Whig constitution,[9] My Dear Sir, Your much obliged and affectionate, humble servant.

To Burke,
Saturday 3 January 1784

MS. Yale (L 322). A copy in Lawrie's hand. Sent 3 Jan. On 2 and 3 Jan. JB had sent copies of his *Letter to the People of Scotland*, 1783, an attack on Fox's East India Bill, to several persons. On the 3rd he wrote: "Mr. Edmund Burke with ditto (Copy)" (Reg. Let.).
HEADING: (To The Rt. Hon. Edmund[1] Burke).

Edinr. 3 Janry. 1784

MY DEAR SIR: The enclosed Pamphlet of which I beg your acceptance and candid perusal, will shew you how the East India Bill has alarmed my Tory Soul.[2] All subordinate principles of

[7] MS. "reason" superimposed upon "occasion"

[8] JB's "reason to think" that he would obtain some position under the Coalition was that he had been independent of Henry Dundas (*ante* To EB, 8 Aug. and n. 8). There is no evidence to suggest that "it was generally thought" he would get a position.

[9] Perhaps JB is remembering EB's "I take the true Genius of this constitution to be, Tory Language and Whigg measure" (*ante* From EB, 1 Sept. 1782); but in recent years they had often bantered about Whig and Tory (Journ. 21 Apr. 1783; *ante* To EB, 19 July 1782, n. 3), and JB told himself that EB is "a good Tory I do beleive" (Journ. 27 Mar.). A few weeks after the present letter, JB wrote to Henry Dundas, "My friend Burke said I was 'a Tory with a Whig constitution' " (To Dundas, 2 Jan. 1784). See also *Pol. Car.* p. 14 and n. 2.

[1] MS. "Edward", with "mun" in JB's hand superimposed upon Lawrie's "war"

[2] JB learned of the House of Lords' rejection of Fox's East India Bill (technically, two bills) on 20 Dec. 1783, and between 26 and 29 Dec. wrote his first *Letter to the People of Scotland*, endeavouring "to rouse a spirit for *property* and the *Constitution* in opposition" to the Bill (Journ. 26 Dec.). The *Letter* was advertised as published on 31 Dec. (Journ.). In it JB writes, "My principles being of a Tory cast, that is to say, those of a steady Royalist . . ." (p. 6).

Government are to me as nothing compared with "the King as Supreme".[3] You will forgive me for repeating what I have often taken the liberty to say to you, that I am sure you are too good a man not to value Monarchy. I devoutly wish to see you supporting and cheering Majesty. But in whatever State you may be, your prosperity is almost as dear to me as my own;[4] for, I ever am with affection[5] and gratitude, My Dear Sir, Your obliged and faithful, humble servant.

To Burke,
Saturday 31 January 1784

MS. Yale (L 323). A copy in Lawrie's hand. Sent 31 Jan. "Right Hon. Edmund Burke soliciting him to support the Petition of the Schoolmasters of Scotland for an augmentation of Sallary (Copy)" (Reg. Let.). HEADING: To The Rt. Hon. Edmund Burke.

Edinr. 31 Janry. 1784

MY DEAR SIR: A petition is to be presented to the House of Commons on the 5 of Febry. for an augmentation of Sallary to the established Schoolmasters of Scotland.[1] They are at present so poorly provided that the office is held in disesteem, as our friend Dr. Johnson has well observed in his Journey to the Western Islands.[2] I am afraid that some of my Countrymen will be illiberal

[3] I Peter 2: 13–14: "Submit yourselves to every ordinance of man for the Lord's sake: whether it be to the king, as supreme; Or unto governors. . . ." JB adopted this phrase in the *Letter*, where he asserts that the Americans would have been 'willing faithfully to submit themselves to the King as supreme", had they not been driven to rebellion by the King's "evil counsellors" (p. 6).

[4] JB used a nearly identical expression in his second *Letter to the People of Scotland*, 1785, a pamphlet opposing a bill in the House of Commons to reduce the number of judges in the Court of Session from 15 to 10. Citing EB as a dependable opponent of this proposal, JB adds, "his interest is dear to me as my own" (p. 71).

[5] MS. "affection" superimposed upon "affectionate"

[1] The 1696 Act of Settling of Schools provided that the salary of the parish schoolmaster be between 100 and 200 merks (£11. 2*s.* 3*d.*) a year. The petition JB refers to was presented on 3 Feb., and on 16 Feb. Henry Dundas presented a bill for augmenting salaries (JHC xxxix. 883, 920), but it did not get beyond a first reading. No increases were granted until 1803, when a range of 300–400 merks was established (Alexander Morgan, *Rise and Progress of Scottish Education*, 1927, pp. 70–71; William Ferguson, *Scotland: 1689 to the Present*, 1968, pp. 198–202 and references cited there). EB's attitude towards the Bill is unknown.

[2] "The grammar schools are not generally well supplied; for the character of a

enough to oppose the petition, and therefore I beg leave to recommend it to your protection, as I am sure that in all situations you will be the generous friend of Literature.

Perhaps it is not quite delicate to solicit a Legislator to be *for* one where *Property* is in question. But surely it is all fair to solicit him to be *against* one. This is what I am now doing; for, if the Petition shall be granted and the augmentation take place, I as a Landholder shall be more taxed.[3] Which however I shall not grudge. I trust that there will be a very general coalition indeed to support a Body of men to whom all parties must be obliged.

Will you be so kind as to let me hear from you, and be assured that I ever am with most sincere affection, My Dear Sir, Your much obliged and faithfull, humble servant.

To Burke,
Saturday 10 April 1784

MS. Yale (L 325). A copy, on side five of J 92. A much altered draft (L 324) is on J 92, sides one and two (written on the back of a letter from John Lawrie, C 1708).

HEADING: To The Right Honourable Edmund Burke.

Glasgow, Saturday Morning, 10 April 1784

MY DEAR SIR: Your long silence, and particularly your not complying with my request to be informed of the time of your coming to Scotland[1] have made me apprehend it is possible you may have taken offence at my Tory Zeal against a political system which you have supported.[2] Yet I cannot easily beleive that

school-master being there less honourable than in England, is seldom accepted by men who are capable to adorn it" (*Works SJ* ix. 160).

[3] The heritors (property owners, roughly speaking) of each parish were responsible for paying the schoolmaster's salary (Morgan, pp. 70–71). The average schoolmaster in Scotland in the 1790s earned £13 a year, though in Ayrshire the usual stipend was higher (John Strawhorn, *Ayrshire: The Story of a County*, 1975, p. 162).

[1] JB had made this request in *ante* To EB, 20 Nov. 1783. Parliament was dissolved on 25 Mar., which enabled EB to arrive in Edinburgh on 5 Apr.; on 9 Apr. he reached Glasgow, where he was to be installed as Rector of the University on the following day (*Corres. EB* v. 136–38). JB learned of his coming on 8 Apr., and at once resolved to go to Glasgow to meet him. He reached the inn where EB was staying on the 10th, and encountered EB's servant, who at his request took this letter to EB (Journ.).

[2] Though JB knew, of course, that EB

Edmund Burke is deficient in liberality of sentiment. You will please impute partly to my anxiety, partly to your neglect, that I have for a moment entertained a fear of what I should very much regret, for your sake, as well as my own. I am grateful for your kindness. I love your virtues. I admire your talents. And on hearing of your arrival, I have hastened from my Seat in the Country, to wait on you, to Shew[3] you all the respect I can, and to intreat I may have the honour to see you at Auchinleck.

But if in this cursed strife, you "have ought against me"[4] and will not be fully "reconciled" with me even in *this week*,† pray tell me frankly, that our difference may not be exposed to the profane, and that we may either not meet at all, or, in your ever memorable words to the worthy Langton, "live pleasant."[5] I am, My Dear Sir, your faithful, obliged, humble servant.[6]

†Passion Week.

was one of the foremost adherents of Fox's East India Bill, it seems unlikely he was aware that EB very probably was the author of the bills submitted to Parliament (Cone ii. 125–26).

[3] MS. illegible blot. "Shew" supplied from the draft.

[4] Matthew 5: 23–24.

[5] On receiving the letter from his servant EB came at once into the room where JB was waiting, embraced him, and said: "What has made you go so mad of late. As to quarreling with you, that cannot happen. . . . As to telling you when I should come to Scotland, I did not know myself till we were dismissed" (Journ.).

When EB's advice is quoted in the *Life*, Bennet Langton is described merely as "a grave and anxious gentleman" (i. 344).

[6] We attempt here a reconstruction of JB's first draft (L 324) of the present letter. Stages of the draft cannot be precisely isolated, and many of the additions and deletions which bring the draft close to the copy are ignored.

Glasgow, Saturday morning, 10 April 1784

MY DEAR SIR: Your long silence and your not complying with my request to be informed of the time of your coming to Scotland / Glasgow have made me apprehend it is possible you may be deepl[y] offended / have taken offence at my Tory Zeal against a political system which you have supported. Yet I can not seriously allow myself to beleive that Mr. Burke is deficient/has not the largest liberality / allowance for an honest difference of opinion. Should my apprehension / anxiety / I ask your pardon that my anxiety has entertained a moments doubt/ fear of what I should most / very much regret for your sake as well as my own. I retain a very grateful sense of your kindness a respect for your virtues an admiration of your knowledge and genius. And on hearing of your arrival I have hastened from my Seat in the Country to wait on you, to Shew you all the respect I can and intreat / have the honour of seeing you at Auchinleck. But if you "have ought against me" and cannot "be reconciled" even in *this week*, frankly / be pleased to let me / I / pray tell me frankly and I shall not intrude upon you. I again ask your pardon, My Dear Sir, and ever am your faithful, humble servant.

To Burke,
Monday 12 April 1784
MS. Yale (L 326). A copy.
ENDORSEMENT: Left for Mr. Burke when I left Glasgow (He at Lochlomond).[1]

Glasg. Mond. Morn. 12 Ap. 1784

MY DEAR SIR: Your admir[able] behav[iour] towards me at this time has made me exseed[ingly] hap[py].[2] It convinces me that our freinds[hi]p "shall flour[ish] in im[mortal] youth unhurt amidst" etc. etc. etc.[3] I am going to Ed[inburgh] to meet my f[rien]d Col[onel] J. St[uart][4] and shall wait your arriv[al] there. Since you could not now go to Auch[inleck] you will oblige me very much if you will indulge me with the hon[our] of your presence under my roof in town and sup with me any night you are pleas[ed] to appoint by wr[i]ting it on a slip of pap[er] and sending it to me by post that I may engage some peop[le] whom

[1] Sir John Dalrymple had written to EB on 8 Apr.: "You can see Logh Lomond in three hours from Glasgow. . . . I pawn my credit with you that in those three hours ride you will not see more beautiful scenes on this side of heaven." EB went with Lord Maitland and Adam Smith to see Loch Lomond on 11 Apr. (*Corres. EB* v. 139 and n. 2).

[2] For JB's anxiously sought "reconciliation" with EB see *ante* To EB, 10 Apr. and n. 5. On 10 Apr. EB invited JB in to breakfast, and later that evening JB joined EB for a dinner at the University (*Corres. EB* v. 139).

[3] Addison, *Cato* V. i. 29–31:

But thou shalt flourish in immortal youth,
Unhurt amidst the war of elements,
The wreck of matter, and the crush of worlds.

[4] Lt.-Col. the Hon. James Archibald Stuart (1747–1818), second son of the third Earl of Bute (see *ante* To EB, 18 Mar. 1782, n. 11). Though JB had known him for a number of years, they did not become good friends until Stuart's visit to Edinburgh in Sept. 1779 (Journ. 3–4, 8–9, 21–26 Sept. 1779). At his invitation, JB accompanied him that autumn to visit Leeds, London, and Chester, where Stuart's regiment, the 92nd Foot, which he had raised at his own expense, was stationed. M.P. for Buteshire, 1774–80, Stuart became M.P. for Plympton Erle, 1780–84, after being invalided home from the West Indies in summer 1780 (Namier and Brooke iii. 501; *Life* iii. 399, 411–13).

[5] James Maitland (1759–1839), styled Viscount Maitland, later (1789) eighth Earl of Lauderdale, M.P. for Newport, 1780–84. "A most zealous supporter of Fox", he praised EB in his maiden speech, 26 Feb. 1781, and strongly defended Fox's East India Bill (Namier and Brooke iii. 98). EB had been eager to travel with Maitland on this trip (*Corres. EB* v. 123–24), and had stayed at Hatton, Edinburghshire, Maitland's family seat, between his appearances in Edinburgh and Glasgow (Andrew Dalzel, *History of the University of Edinburgh*, ed. C. Innes and D. Laing, 1862, i. 42). At the French Revolution their paths parted, and Maitland, who criticized the pension

you will like. I flat[ter] Myself Lord Mait[land][5] will be of the party.[6] I am more and more, My Dear Sir, Yours affectionately.

From Burke,
Thursday 15 April 1784[1]

MS. Yale (C 689).
ADDRESS: James Boswell Esqr.

[Edinburgh]

MY DEAR SIR, a thousand thanks for your kind invitation. I came very late last Night, and go off very early, (that is, at five) tomorrow morning. I must therefor go to bed early and of Conce[quence] must deny myself The satisfaction of passing the Evening with you. I am sincerely mortified at my disappointment. Yours ever most sincerely,

EDM. BURKE

To Burke,
Tuesday 15 February 1785

MS. Sheffield City Libraries, Wentworth Woodhouse Muniments, Burke Papers 1/1967. Sent 15 Feb. "Right Hon. Edmund Burke that if he comes to Glasgow this Easter I will wait etc. (Copy)" (Reg. Let.).
ENDORSEMENT in an unidentified hand: Mr. Boswell, Febr. 15 1785.

granted to EB in Oct. 1795, was one of two peers denounced by EB in his *Letter to a Noble Lord*, 1796. JB's acquaintance with Maitland seems to have been slight (see Journ. 9, 27 Dec. 1780; 8 Aug. 1781).

[6] JB wrote himself a memorandum on the same sheet, just below this letter: "If he comes, have Dr. Cullen and son. Sir W. F. Dalzell. Dundas. Col. James. Lord Mait. He and you. *Nine* and *no more*. Perhaps *Smith*". The persons meant were: William Cullen, M.D., and his son Robert Cullen, advocate; Sir William Forbes, banker; Professor Andrew Dalzel; Henry Dundas; Col. James Stuart; Lord Maitland; Adam Smith. The names of "Robertson" (Principal William Robertson) and "Blair" (Hugh Blair, D.D.) were at first included after "Dr. Cullen and son", but later struck off the list.

[1] EB stayed in Edinburgh for two nights, 14 and 15 Apr., dining with Adam Smith on the 15th and departing the following morning. Since he here writes of arriving "late last Night", and expects to depart "tomorrow morning", this letter must have been written on the 15th (*Corres. EB* v. 142).

TO BURKE, 15 FEBRUARY 1785

Edinburgh, 15 Febry. 1785

MY DEAR SIR: The state of my private affairs with which I will not trouble you, prevented me from returning to the Temple in November as I fully intended;[1] and after being a good deal hurt by the check which my Ambition received[2] I was sadly afflicted by the death of Dr. Johnson.[3] I am not affraid of owning this to you; because amidst all the conflicts of political contrariety, your high esteem of him remained unshaken, and as you knew my intimacy with him as my "Philosopher and Freind"[4] you can seriously see my loss in its full extent.

I am to be in London this spring.[5] But I now write that I may be determined as to the time of my setting out, which depends upon you. If you are to come down to Glasgow again during the Easter Holidays, I am to claim your promise of a visit to me at Auchinleck which is but thirty two miles from it, and I will wait with pleasure for what I shall value very highly. I should indeed be much better pleased to see you amongst the rocks and woods of my Ancestors, at a more favourable season of the year, and when you are in no hurry.[6] But I shall be proud if Mr. Burke honours me with his company there at any time.—My Dear Sir! be assured that in whatever situation you may be, I shall never be found wanting in admiration of your talents, love of your virtues, and gratitude for your kindness.[7] I remain your much obliged and affectionate, humble servant,

JAMES BOSWELL

[1] JB had not yet finished keeping his terms at the Inner Temple (*ante* To EB, 18 Mar. 1782 and n. 20). It was nearly a year after this that he "dined at the Students table for the last time" on the day that he was called to the English bar (Journ. 9 Feb. 1786).

[2] JB is alluding to his decision, in June 1784, to move to London (e.g. To Temple, 6–8 July 1784). However, his bad financial situation, among other circumstances, quickly forced him to change his mind (To Temple, 20 July 1784), and he lapsed into depression. He wrote to John Johnston (12 Sept. 1784): "The state of my affairs really distresses me, and the disappointment at least for a time of my scheme of active ambition vexes me."

[3] SJ died on 13 Dec. 1784. For JB's initial reaction to his death, see Journ. 17–28 Dec. 1784.

[4] Pope, *Essay on Man* iv. 390.

[5] JB arrived in London on 30 Mar. and stayed there until 24 Sept.

[6] EB never paid this visit. He was re-elected Rector, but his second installation at Glasgow did not take place until 1 Sept., when JB was in London (*Corres. EB* v. 187, 221–22).

[7] JB here repeats in variation his earlier remarks: "I am grateful for your kindness. I love your virtues. I admire your talents" (*ante* To EB, 10 Apr. 1784).

To Burke,
Tuesday 20 December 1785
MS. Yale (L 327). A draft.
HEADING: To The Rt. Hon. Edmund Burke, Beaconsfield.

London, 20 Decr. 1785

MY DEAR SIR: I beg you may be pleased to accept of a copy of the second edition of my Journal of a Tour to the Hebrides[1] which I flatter myself you will find less imperfect than the former.[2]

In my defence of your Wit which while he allowed you all other excellence Dr. Johnson attacked,[3] I after general assertion and reference to many publick and splendid proofs of it[4] took the liberty to specify some instances, as to the value of which I still retain my opinion. But some people having thought that these did not do you justice,[5] Mr. Malone who was so kind as to superintend the second edition as it passed through the press in my absence,[6] wrote an[7] admirable additional note upon the

[1] The 1st ed. of the *Tour* was published on 1 Oct. and the 2nd on 22 Dec. (*Lit. Car.* p. 122). EB's name does not appear on JB's list of thirty-eight people to whom he had sent presentation copies of the 1st ed. (M 131).

[2] For JB's and EM's extensive corrections of the text of the 1st ed., see n. 6 below and the letters cited there. The only substantive change in the presentation of EB from the 1st to the 2nd ed. is discussed below in n. 8.

[3] In the *Tour* JB gives a full report of an evening party on 15 Aug. 1773 when EB was one of the topics of conversation. On this occasion and others, JB reports SJ's criticisms of EB's wit, his inability to listen, and his desire to talk on all occasions (1st ed. pp. 24–26 and n., 256; *Life* v. 32–34 and n. 3). Though SJ was sometimes ready to laugh at EB's puns (*Life* iii. 322–23), he almost always judged EB's wit harshly (*Life* i. 453, iii. 323 and n. 2, iv. 276 and n. 2). But in the *Tour* JB also brings out SJ's respect for EB's learning, eloquence, and qualities of mind. Even in discussing SJ and EB's political differences, JB, though he reports that SJ accused EB of "sticking to a certain set of *men* on all occasions" (p. 28; *Life* v. 36), also states that SJ "did not grudge Burke's being the first man in the House of Commons; for he was the first man every where" (p. 332; *Life* v. 269).

[4] JB first wrote "to pointed proofs" interlinearly after "reference". He then deleted "pointed", substituting "splendid", and added at the beginning of this interlineation "to many publick and". But he forgot to delete "to" after the "and", so that the interlineation after "reference" actually reads "to many publick and to splendid proofs of it"

[5] Shortly after the 1st ed. of the *Tour* was published, EM reported to JB in Edinburgh a general feeling of dissatisfaction with his defence of EB's wit (see n. 8 below and *post* From EM, 19 Oct. 1785).

[6] JB put an X after "Malone" and added "who was so kind . . . in my absence" at the bottom of the draft. For EM and his supervision of the 2nd ed., see *post* the Introduction to the JB-EM correspondence and their letters from 5 Oct. to 11 Nov.

[7] MS. "the" written above "that": both deleted, and replaced by "an"

subject and sent it to me in Scotland for my consideration.[8] Finding[9] that it perfectly expressed my sentiments I[10] readily adopted it and made it my own, though I objected to my being decked with borrowed feathers of such elegance, and wished to have publickly mentioned by whom they were furnished.[11] He thought this improper but I cannot but mention[12] it to you. At the same time allow me to say that I subscribe to every part of it and if I could have found stronger or better words to convey the same meaning I should certainly have used them. I ever am with great regard, My Dear Sir, your much obliged and faithful, humble servant.

From Burke,
Wednesday 4 January 1786

MS. Yale (C 690). Received 5 Feb. "Right Hon. Edmund Burke upon receiving a present of the second edition of my *Tour*" (Reg. Let.).
ADDRESS: James Boswell Esqr., General Paoli's, London.[1]
FRANK: Beconsfield, Jany. fourth 1786, Free Edm. Burke.[2]
POSTMARKS: 27[3] BECONSFIELD, 5 IA, FREE.

[8] In the 1st ed. (pp. 24–26) JB had tried to counteract SJ's harsh judgements with a long footnote—a brief critical essay of about 450 words—calling SJ "strangely heterodox" on the subject of EB's wit, and arguing that in fact it was quite passable. To prove this assertion, JB produces three examples, two of which depend on puns.

In the second ed. EM tried to improve the note by extending it to well over 800 words (pp. 24–26; *Life* v. 32–34). JB suggested a few changes in EM's extension, but by the time they reached EM the sheet in which the note appears had already been printed (*post* To EM, 30 Oct. 1785 and n. 2).

[9] MS. "As it" deleted before "Finding"

[10] MS. "my own sentiments upon the subject" written before "I", with "own" and "upon the subject" deleted.

[11] JB and EM carried on an argument through five letters as to whether EM should be given credit for the extension to this footnote before JB yielded on the main point and agreed not to name EM in print, as long as he was allowed to tell EB the full story (*post* To and From EM, 27 Oct.–5 Nov. 1785 passim). In the 2nd ed. of the *Life,* 1793, he explained it to the public as well (iii. 110 n. 4; *Life* iii. 323 n. 2).

[12] At the beginning of this sentence, JB first wrote, "He would", then deleted "would" and wrote "allowed me to". Above "allowed me to" he wrote "thought this improper but", so that this stage in the draft reads, "He thought this improper but allowed me to mention". Then he deleted "allowed me to" and followed "improper but" in the interlineation with "has", deleted that, and finally wrote "I cannot but"

[1] Paoli was living at No. 1 Upper Seymour St., Portman Square (From John Osborn, 6 June 1784). JB, who had spent the Christmas holidays in Scotland (Journ. 22 Dec. 1785–27 Jan. 1786), arrived in London on 1 Feb., spent four days at Dilly's, and moved to his usual lodgings at Paoli's on 5 Feb. (Journ.).

FROM BURKE, 4 JANUARY 1786

Beconsfield, Jay. 4, 1786

MY DEAR SIR, I give you many thanks for your present of the second Edition of your very entertaining Book. By the Date of your Letter I find that I ought to have profited of your kindness much earlier than I had the good fortune to do: And therefore I may appear more slow in my acknowligements than I ought to be for so valuable a mark of your attention.

I am extremely obliged to you and to Mr. Malone (to whom I beg my best compliments) for your friendly sollicitude with regard to a point relating to me, about which I am myself not very anxious. The Reputation for Wit (the *fama dicacis*)[4] is what I certainly am not entitled to; and, I think, I never aimed at. If I had been even so ambitious, I must shew myself as deficient in Judgment as I am in wit, if I thought that a Title to pleasantry could be made out by argument.[5] The feelings of every one you live with must decide without appeal. I am therefore in no sort disposed to bring a writ of Errour on the Judgment pronounced upon me. I admit the Court to be competent; the proceedings regular; and the reporter learned and exact. This is not only what Justice, but what common policy requires: For if I were to weaken the authority which refuses me what I am not intitled to in a smaller Matter, I might undermine it, when it decides in my favour, in points where my claim is full as doubtful, and the Object of much greater moment. I have other reasons besides, though of a[6] similar Nature, for my perfect acquiescence in this decision. I shall be well content to pass down to a long posterity in Doctor Johnsons authentick Judgment, and in your permanent record, as a dull fellow and a tiresome companion, when it shall be known through the same long period, that I have had such men as Mr. Boswell and Mr. Malone as my friendly counsel in the Cause which I have lost. This circumstance will furnish a strong

[2] Until 1784, to frank a letter an M.P. had only to write "Free" and his signature on the cover or outside. A law passed that year obliged him to write in his own hand the full date and name of the post-town from which the letter was sent (*Parl. Hist.* xxiv. 1330–32; see also Ellis, p. 42).

[3] "27" indicates the distance in miles from London.

[4] EB supplies his own translation for a phrase he adapts from Horace (*Satires* I. iv. 83). The passage in Horace censures the man who pursues a reputation for wit at the expense of an absent friend.

[5] EB is referring to JB's argument in a footnote of the *Tour* (*ante* To EB, 20 Dec. 1785 and n. 8).

[6] In the MS. "a" is a catchword not repeated on the following page.

presumptive proof of my being possessd of some qualities much more estimable than the[7] Talent, which all their Eloquence was not able to protect. It will be thought that the body of the place was of some value, when Engineers of their Skills were so earnest to defend a small, and, I fear untenable, outwork of my reputation. I have turned to Mr. Malones Note.[8] It is sound and judicious in every respect, in its general principles; though, by his partiality and condescension only, applicable to me.

You see, My dear Sir, that Vanity always finds its consolation. But Wisdom might draw a Lesson even from this little Circumstance of which we have been too long in the discussion. I ought not to take this publick reprimand amiss. My companions have a right to expect, that, when my conversation is so little Seasond, as it is, with Wit, it should not, out of respect both to them and to myself, to be so light and careless, as it undoubtedly always has been, and is. It is not only in the other World, that "we are to give an account of every Light word".[9] I ought therefore to thank you for informing the World of this censure of our deceasd friend, that I may regulate myself accordingly. Those I have the honour to live with are too well instructed, not to know and feel, that, though pleasantry is not, prudence and circumspection certainly are in a mans own power; and that if he has not the Talent to please, he ought to have the delicacy not to disgust his Company. I am sure there are very few, (let[10] them be qualified as they will) shall be indiscreet enough to interrupt, by the intrusion of their Ideas, the strong flow of your real Wit, and true humour, who[11] will not be great Enemies to their own entertainment, as well as to the satisfactions of the rest of the Company.[12] I am with sincere respect and regard, My dear Sir, Your most faithful and obedient, humble Servant,

EDM. BURKE

[7] MS. "the" superimposed upon "Wit"

[8] EM's extension of JB's note (*ante* To EB, 20 Dec. 1785, n. 8).

[9] Matthew 12: 36: "That every idle word that men shall speak, they shall give account thereof in the day of judgment."

[10] MS. "who" deleted before "(let"

[11] MS. "who" written above a deleted "but"

[12] Michael Lort, writing to Mrs. Piozzi about JB and the *Tour*, says that EB "fell hard upon him for the absurdities in that performance" (31 Dec. 1785, quoted in Clifford, p. 259 nn. 3, 4).

To Burke,
Tuesday 7 February 1786
MS. Yale (L 328). A draft.[1]
HEADING: To The Right Honourable Edmund Burke.

Upper Seymour Street, Portman Square, Tuesday evening
MY DEAR SIR: I am[2] exceedingly uneasy in consequence of your having very much[3] misconstrued (as I think) a circumstance which passed this morning. I took[4] the liberty of occasionally mentioning a matter that[5] I had heard represented[6] unfavourably through the medium [of] prejudice[7] and[8] my sincere anxiety to be enabled to state it rightly[9] should I ever again hear [it] spoken of in company (in case you had thought it worth your while to take notice of it)[10] was my sole motive for saying a word upon the subject.[11]

I apprehend that my casually[12] introducing Dr. Johnson's

[1] Earlier on this same day JB had called on EB at his London lodgings and in the course of a half-hour's conversation, as he wrote in his journal, "I imprudently touched on a calumny against Mr. Burke, in order to be enabled to refute it. We parted on sad terms. . . . Malone's. Wrote to Burke." Differences in JB's hand suggest that the draft was revised in two stages, and since three words (see nn. 5, 18 below) are in EM's hand, JB must have consulted with him about it. In the notes below, the two stages are designated A and B.

[2] MS. B: "am" written above a deleted "have been"

[3] MS. A: "very much" written above a deleted "entirely"

[4] MS. A: "took" superimposed upon an illegible word.

[5] MS. B: "that" written in EM's hand above a deleted "which"

[6] MS. A: "in company talked of" deleted before "represented"

[7] MS. B: "unfavourably through the medium" written above a deleted "with a degree of" before "prejudice". JB failed to replace the necessary "of" after "medium"

[8] MS. A: "which I was confident you could remove" deleted before "and". Written above "you could remove" is "you might possibly think", also deleted.

[9] MS. A: "in answer" deleted above "rightly"

[10] MS. A: JB first wrote "should it ever again be mentioned", deleted "mentioned" and wrote "talke" above it, deleted "talke" and wrote "st" next to it, presumably as the start of "stated". Then he changed the construction to "should I ever again hear" and followed the undeleted "st" with "spoken of in company" in the same interlineation. The parenthetical phrase that follows interlinearly is a MS. B addition. JB failed to replace the necessary "it" before "spoken"

[11] Around this time EB's political enemies reportedly distributed £20,000 to the press to keep in circulation a great variety of innuendoes and lies: that he was secretly a Roman Catholic, that he had been trained by Jesuits, that he was a sodomite, that his financial dealings were dishonest, and the like (Prior, *Burke* i. 478; *Eminent Friend*, pp. 41–44). JB had earlier believed EB to be a Jesuit (Journ. 7 Apr. 1773), but it is impossible to be sure what scandalous assertion had attracted JB's attention in 1786.

[12] MS. A: "casually" written above the line below a deleted interlinear "accidentally"

name[13] led[14] you into an errour and made you imagine that the matter had been or was to be in writing. But you may be perfectly assured that I never wrote or intended to put in writing one word upon[15] the subject. I therefore[16] could not possibly have any view[17] that way nor[18] did what I took the liberty of saying, proceed from any impertinent curiosity but as[19] I have already observed entirely from my good wishes and my anxiety about every[20] thing that concerns you in any degree as I am and ever shall be gratefully sensible of the obligations which I owe you. I remain with sincere regard, My Dear Sir, your faithful, humble servant.

From Burke,
Wednesday 8 February 1786

MS. Yale (C 691).
ADDRESS: James Boswell Esqr., Genl. Paoli's, Somerset St.,[1] Portman Sq.

Wednesday.

Mr. Burkes compliments to Mr. Boswell. He will call upon him this day at twelve o'Clock; and desires that he may be admitted.[2]

From Burke,
Thursday 9 February 1786

MS. Yale (C 692).
ADDRESS: James Boswell Esqr., Upper Seymour Street,[1] Portman Square.[2]

[13] In this conversation they first discussed JB's journal as a repository of material for the *Life of Johnson* (Journ.).

[14] MS. A: "has" deleted before "led"

[15] MS. A: "concerning" deleted before "upon"

[16] MS. A: "could" deleted before "therefore"

[17] MS. A: "such" deleted before "view"

[18] MS. B: "that way" added in EM's hand interlinearly before "nor"

[19] MS. A: "entirely" deleted before "as"

[20] MS. A: JB first wrote "the slightest matter" before "every", then inserted "even" before "the slightest matter", and finally deleted the whole phrase.

[1] Somerset St. is a short street running parallel to Seymour St. in the vicinity of Portman Square. EB must have written "Somerset St." in error; he addressed his letter of the following day correctly (*post* From EB, 9 Feb.; *ante* From EB, 4 Jan. n. 1).

[2] JB was out when this note was delivered at Paoli's (*post* To EB, 10 Feb.—L 329).

[1] MS. "Street" superimposed on "Pl"

[2] MS. "Portman Square" written below a deleted "Grosvenor Square"

FROM BURKE, 9 FEBRUARY 1786

Pall Mall, No. 45,[3] Feb. 9th 1786

MY DEAR SIR, I did not receive your Note until late in the Evening of yesterday. I must confess, that whatever degree of warmth appeard in my conversation with you the day before, did arise from the Cause you supposed. But as you think, and think in a manner very worthy of you, that any thing of that kind would be improper and unjustifiable, and that it never was in your Intention, I am sorry, that I sufferd myself for a moment to conceive, that you could inadvertently, (and it was only by inadvertence that you could) have fallen into it.

As to the matter of the Calumny I assure you, for your own private satisfaction, and for that only, that it is absolutely false; and this is all I shall ever say to Calumnies.[4] I am pretty well known; and my Character must stand on its own Base, or it cannot stand at all. Apologies, defences, and minute discussions cannot serve it. This is, and has been my own Course; and it will continue to be so as long as I can; and if I might recommend any thing to those who are indulgent enough to take any concern in what relates to me, it would be to take the very same Course;[5] and to leave me undefended. I believe, on recollection, they will observe that one of the most known and most successful ways of circulating slander is by stating charges, and anticipating defences, where nothing can come to proof, where there is no judge, and where every man credits and carries away what he pleases, and according to the measure of his Malice.[6] This I am perfectly convinced was never your intention; but hasty friendship sometimes produces the effect of Enmity. I am with very sincere Respect and Esteem, My dear Sir, Your most faithful and obedient, humble Servant,

EDM. BURKE

I am just going out of Town for a day or two.

[3] JB recorded in his journal for 7 Feb.: "Found Mr. Burke at his lodgings No. 45 Pallmall". Previously EB had been living in Charles St., St. James's Square (*Corres. EB* v. 210).

[4] EB disliked having his friends make any public mention of his character or personal circumstances, much less discuss calumnies about him (e.g. EB to Richard Shackleton, 19 Apr. 1770—*Corres. EB* ii. 129–30).

[5] MS. apparently "Excuse" altered to "Course"

[6] EB had given JB virtually the same advice in 1779, when a newspaper asserted falsely that JB had ridden in a coach with a murderer, the Rev. James Hackman, to his execution. EB said "twould make it worse if I controverted. They would put in Mr. B. not in coach" (Journ. 20 Apr. 1779).

To Burke,
Friday 10 February 1786
MS. Yale (L 329). A draft.

Portman Square, 10 Febry. 1786

My Dear Sir: I was unlucky enough to be gone out five minutes before your note was delivered at General Paolis, by which I missed the honour you intended me on wednesday.[1] I did not come home till twelve at night when I found your note.[2] I next morning called at your lodgings; but was told you were gone to the country. I beg you may let me know when you return and I will wait upon you. Trusting that my note has satisfied you, that my intention was good[3] I remain with great regard, My Dear Sir, your faithful, humble servant.

[1] EB's note of 8 Feb. (*ante*). JB had not yet received his letter of the 9th (*ante*).

[2] The same note of 8 Feb.

[3] JB first wrote "satisfied you, of my good", then deleted "good" and continued "having no bad intention but meaning but". He then deleted these false starts and began again by changing "of my" to "that my" and continuing "intention was good though". He finished the revision by deleting "though"

To Burke,
Friday 10 February 1786
MS. Yale (L 330). A copy.

Portman Square, Friday 4 o'clock

My Dear Sir: I wrote to you this morning with my usual date of *Portman Square.*[1] But I was all yesterday and till this day at noon in the *City*;[2] so that is only *now* that I have the happiness of being relieved by your letter for which I thank you; and depend upon it, I shall profit by your counsel. I ever am with warm regard, Your much obliged and faithful, humble servant.[3]

[1] *Ante* To EB, 10 Feb. (L 329).

[2] JB was called to the bar of the Inner Temple on the afternoon of 9 Feb. and spent the night at Dilly's in the Poultry (Journ.).

[3] The quarrel ended with this note, JB later writing in his journal under the date of 7 Feb.: "This affair was happily settled in letters between us."

To Burke,
Sunday 6 April 1788

MS. Yale (L 331). A copy.
ENDORSEMENT by JB: Sent Monday 7.
HEADING: Copy / To The Right Honourable Edmund Burke.

Great Queen Street,[1] Lincolns Inn Fields,
Sunday, 6 April 1788

MY DEAR SIR: Courtenay observed with a kindly satisfaction that you were cordial with me yesterday; and I trust it was so.[2] I am proud enough in all conscience; but when I recollect[3] how much of your company I once enjoyed, and what friendship you shewed me, I have no difficulty in owning to you that I am very very uneasy that there is now such a coldness between us.[4] Surely there is a time for all things. Surely you and I may have "the feast of reason and the flow of soul"[5] exclusive of politicks. Will you be so good as to engage to dine with me next saturday, or any other saturday, and Sir Joshua, and Courtenay and Malone and Windham shall meet you.[6] Pray do. What more can one gentleman say to another, in our unlucky circumstances. I ever am, My Dear Sir, your much obliged and faithful, humble servant.

[1] JB had moved into No. 56 Great Queen St., the house previously occupied by his friend John Hoole, on 16 May 1786 (Journ.; *Survey of London*, ed. C. R. Ashbee et al., 1900, v. 57–58).

[2] For Courtenay, a close friend of JB's, see *post* To EM, 5 Oct. 1785, n. 1. JB had dined with him the previous day, and "Mr Burke hearing of the party fell in upon us" (Journ. 5 Apr.). Courtenay was a member of the Committee of Managers, headed by EB, for the impeachment of Warren Hastings.

[3] MS. "recollect" written above a deleted "consider"

[4] JB attributed EB's apparent coolness to their political differences. Writing of an encounter with EB in Pall Mall on his way to the Commons, JB "lamented that politicks made a cold separation between us, which never could be got over" (Journ. 13 June 1786; see also Journ. 29 Oct. 1787). EM, however, had a different explanation for EB's aloofness. After spending a day in company that included EB, he wrote to JB: "The true cause I perceive, of B.'s coldness, is that he thinks your habit of recording throws a restraint on convivial ease and negligence" (*post* From EM, 14 Sept. 1787).

[5] *Ante* To EB, 3 Mar. 1778 and n. 8.

[6] For Windham, see *post* From EM, 5 Oct. 1785, n. 4.

FROM BURKE, 8 APRIL 1788

From Burke,
Tuesday 8 April 1788

MS. Yale (C 693).

ADDRESS: James Boswell Esqr., etc. etc. etc., Great Queen Street,[1] Lincolns Inn Fields.

ENDORSEMENT: April 1788.

April 8, 1788

MY DEAR SIR, I am afraid, that you have given a wrong construction to some circumstances in my general manner and late way of Life, and have attributed that to some distance with regard to you which has arisen from the little command I have lately had over my time.[2] However your sollicitude upon the Subject is in the highest degree flattering to me; and I know how to set a just value upon it. I feel much sense of Obligation for your Kindness. As we shall be next Saturday in the midst of the Trial and that I may be obliged to a Business dinner with the Committee[3] I cannot indulge myself in a positive engagement, but if you will condescend to let me fall in upon you on that or any day when you invite other friends, I shall be much obliged to you for letting me fall in among them as I did the other day at Mr. Courtneys.[4] I have the honour to be with the most unfeigned respect and regard, my dear Sir, Your most faithful and obedient, humble Servant,

EDM. BURKE

[1] MS. "Great Queen Street" superimposed upon "Temple". Apparently EB thought JB had chambers at the Temple, which JB did not obtain until 1791 (*post* To EM, 12 Mar. 1791).

[2] EB had been preoccupied all spring with the trial of Hastings, which opened in Westminster Hall on 13 Feb. JB was present opening day and again on 18 Feb., when he heard EB "speak astonishingly well" (Journ.). Though an ardent supporter of Hastings, JB was shaken by revelations of oppression in India, and warned himself "not to be so loud in his Defence . . . especially as it would offend Burke to whom I had formerly been much obliged, but between whom and me there had for some time been an unhappy coldness, though we met occasionally on sufficiently easy terms" (Journ. 24 Feb.). For some account of the trial, see From EM, 17 June 1788 and n. 9.

[3] The Committee of Managers of Hastings's trial.

[4] EB made the experiment on the following Saturday, but on arrival learned from JB's servant that JB was dining alone. Leaving his apologies with the servant, EB hurried away and had not returned home when JB called on him later that day (Journ. 12 Apr.). Two days afterwards Reynolds gave a large dinner-party to which he invited JB. Among the guests were EB, his wife, brother, and son. JB records: "Dick Burke was too rough and wild in his manner today, and I could perceive, either liked me worse than his brother did, or had less art to conceal his dislike—on account of politicks" (Journ. 14 Apr.).

To Burke,
Wednesday 16 April 1788
MS. Yale (L 332). A copy.

Great Queen Street, Wednesday, 16 April

Mr. Boswell presents his best compliments to Mr. Burke and begs leave to remind him that Sir Joshua Reynolds, Mr. Courtenay, Mr.[1] Malone, and some more friends are to dine with Mr. Boswell on tuesday next at 5 o clock when he trusts that he shall be honoured with Mr. Burke's company according to his obliging engagement.[2]

It will be a great mortification to be disappointed.

To Burke,
Tuesday 22 April 1788
MS. Yale (L 333). A copy.

Great Queen Street, Tuesday, 22 April

My Dear Sir: Forgive I pray you my solicitude in sending you this Memento that *today* at five I depend upon having you under my roof,[1] an honour which nobody can value more than your much obliged, humble servant,

James Boswell

To Burke,
Saturday 5 March 1791
MS. Yale (L 334). A draft.

Dear Sir: Observing in the Newspaper called the Oracle, of this

[1] MS. "and" deleted before "Mr."

[2] Presumably JB refers to a specific engagement, perhaps made at Reynolds's dinner on 14 Apr. (Journ.) rather than to EB's general promise to dine when he could.

[1] EB dined according to engagement, and JB recorded the occasion as very pleasant (Journ. 22 Apr.).

morning[1] some impudent lines upon you, with the name of *Mr. Boswell*,[2] though[3] I flatter myself you could not possibly suppose they were mine, such is my respect for you that I take the earliest moment of contradicting this impertinence.[4] I am,[5] Dear Sir, your very faithful, humble servant.

From Burke, Monday 7 March 1791

MS. Yale (C 695).
ADDRESS: James Boswell Esqr., Great Portland Street.[1]
ENDORSEMENT: May 1791.[2]

[1] The *Oracle* for 5 Mar. 1791 fixes the date of this letter.

[2] The lines as they appear in the *Oracle* (5 Mar. 1791, p. [3]) read:

For the ORACLE
Mr. BURKE's *New* WHIG quasi WIG
An *Epigram, by* Mr. Boswell*

Burke chang'd his scratch Whig for a well-powder'd Tye!
Well, the fact is as stated—I cannot deny.
As a Whig he has long ceas'd to copy an *old one*;
But pray, Friend, can you prove that he ever has *sold one*?
And if not, 'tis a good thought, you will not deny,
For an old Party Scratch, to take up a Court Tye.

N.B.* Immeasurably his *best*.

JB's own transcription of the lines, found with this draft, is headed "A Curious Fiction. 5 March 1791", and includes a few minor variants.

EB's *Reflections on the Revolution in France* (Nov. 1790) had publicized the widening split between him and the most prominent faction of the Whig Party, Fox and his adherents, who sympathized with the French Revolutionists, and the poem scurrilously reflects the widespread suspicion that EB had become dependent upon the Court (Cone ii. 348–49). A scratch wig was a small undress wig, relatively inexpensive, sometimes worn with the front hair combed into it; a tie (or tye) wig was more becoming and graceful (Richard Corson, *Fashions in Hair*, 1965, pp. 282, 284–86) and, when powdered, presumably more formal. When JB visited EB at Beaconsfield in 1783, he mentioned the first appearance of his host "at window with scratchwig" (Journ. 21 Apr. 1783).

[3] MS. "put to them" deleted before "though"

[4] JB took the matter seriously enough to consider bringing suit against John Bell, publisher of the *Oracle*. Bell promised to mention that JB was not the author of the lines, but JB found his note, which appeared in the *Oracle* for 8 Mar. (p. [2]), equally impertinent (*post* To EM, 9 Mar. 1791). The note reads:

Mr. Boswell *disclaims to us the having written a charming* Epigram, *said to have flowed from his fine* Pen, *published in our Print lately*. Be it so. Rien n'est beau que le vrai.

[5] JB first wrote, "I have the honour to be your much obliged", which he deleted except for an inadvertently retained "to be" before "I am"

---

[1] JB moved to No. 47 Great Portland St. on 19 Jan. (*post* To EM, 18 Jan. 1791; Wheatley and Cunningham iii. 110).

[2] The endorsement is based on the mistaken date of the letter (see n. 3). In a letter

March 7, 1791[3]

Dear Sir: I have never seen the Newspaper which, from your partiality to me, has given you so much trouble. I take in but one paper; and it has a different Title from yours.[4] Even that I take in I do not always read. I never could suspect you of any thing unworthy of your Character. I have been too much libelled to suffer things of that nature to make any impression upon me. Your very polite attention is however not the less obliging. I have the honour to be, Dear Sir, Your most obedient and humble Servant,

Edm. Burke

To Burke,
Saturday 16 July 1791

MS. Yale (L 335). A copy in an unidentified hand, with one word inserted by JB.[1]

endorsement in JB's hand: To The Right Honble. Edmund Burke, 16 July 1791.

London, Great Portland Street, 16th July 1791

My Dear Sir: The placidum lumen[2] with which you were pleased to look upon one of my pleasantries in redicule of the Meeting at the Crown and Anchor on the 14th[3] encourages me to send you a parcel of them.[4]

That Meeting I understand lost all its vivifying principle of

dated 8 Mar., though actually written on the 9th, JB told EM about the "most obliging answer" he had received from EB (*post* To EM).

[3] MS. "May 7. 1791"

[4] EB subscribed to the *Morning Post* at this time (*Corres. EB* vi. 34 n. 6, 296 n. 1).

[1] The hand seems to be that of a clerk in Dilly's publishing house (cf. To Thomas Wright, 7 July 1791, certainly written at Dilly's).

[2] MS. "lumer". "Placido lumine" (Horace, *Odes* IV. iii. 2): "benign gaze".

[3] This meeting of British radicals celebrated the second anniversary of the fall of the Bastille. It has not yet appeared what pleasantry is referred to or when EB looked upon it, but it seems likely to have been between the King's levee on 15 June (see n. 8 below) and 6 July, when EB arrived at Margate for a month.

[4] These pleasantries are missing, but JB wrote a number of surviving squibs and songs about this meeting, which some feared might spark serious unrest. They include an unpublished song, "Let those who abhor all Kings and Priests" (M 328), and three published items: "State Paper Extraordinary", *Times*, 13 July (P 117: 29); "Celebration of the French Revolution", *Pub. Adv.* 13 July (P 117: 30); and "Songs, Parodies, and Choruses for the Celebration of the Glorious Revolution in France", *Times*, 14 July (P 118: 5).

Mischief, which was chilled by fear. They who ventured to attend were with verry few exceptions men of little Consequence; and under the Cloak of decency, they slunk away at an early hour like pusilanimous conspirators who were very glad to get out of a Scrape.[5]

I also send you a fine saying of General Paolis with respect to your Character. You love good painting and you may depend that is in perfect preservation; so pray allow it a place in your Cabinet.[6]

You were good enough to repeat to me his Majestys Conversation with you concerning that excellent Work Boswells Life of Johnson; and the effect was as it should be; for, I have it from undoubted Authority[7] that on his return to Windsor, The King speaking of my Work said Mr. Burke told me it was the Most entertaining Book he had ever read.[8]

You can do me My Dear Sir a great favour; and I do not recollect your having ever refused me any request[9] that it was proper to grant. I[10] have but an Imperfect recollection of that conversation. It is long since I relieved myself from the Anxious and Laborious task of making minutes of conversations of Value, which however I wish to resume in some degree and am pressed to it by[11] Malone because there is much Wisdom and Wit fresh from the Source in casual talk which should not be lost. You gave me a

[5] Though nine hundred people attended (Cone ii. 371), the dinner went off tamely (*Corres. EB* vi. 295–97, and references cited there).

[6] The saying was not copied out, but JB had recorded it in 1781 on a sheet (J 75) with sayings of Paoli's under the date "Monday Morning 7 May":

> Burke truly a great Man a good husband a good Father and he sometimes goes round the atmosphere and takes such a flight that our eyes cannot follow him. But when we think him lost in the clouds he is conversing with the Gods and throwing light on human knowledge.

A slightly expanded version was printed in *Pub. Adv.* for 17 June 1791 (*Corres. EB* vi. 297 n. 3), with the heading "Mr. Burke" and a preliminary explanation: "When General Paoli was in England, he sometimes drew characters of eminent persons. The following sketch by him of Mr. Burke we have from undoubted authority." The Osborn Collection at Yale preserves a cutting of the printed version, on which JB has inscribed in ink: "The above I attest, James Boswell".

[7] Quite possibly that of John Douglas, Bishop of Salisbury and Dean of Windsor, whom JB visited at Windsor in June (To John Douglas, 17 June). See next note.

[8] The *Life* was published on 16 May. EB's conversation with the King, who had been reading the *Life* in June (*Burney Diary* iv. 477–78, 479), took place at the levee at St. James's on 15 June (*post* From EB, 20 July; *Corres. EB* vi. 297 n. 4). The King took up residence at Windsor for the summer on 10 June, returning to London on 15 June only long enough to hold the levee (*Gen. Eve. Post*, 14–16 June, pp. [1, 3]).

[9] MS. "requist"

[10] MS. "grant, I"

[11] MS. "by" inserted in JB's hand.

delicious repast[12] when you Communicated to me what the Sovereign and Yourself said of my Labours, and particularly when you repeated your very friendly defence of my writing down the Conversations of Johnson.[13] If you will in the leisure[14] of Margate take the trouble to let me have for my Archives at Auchinleck a written State of An interview so preceious to me I shall be exceedingly Oblidged to you.

I hope Mrs. Burke is better[15] and I Offer My best Compliments to her and all those of your household who are with you. I ever am, My Dear Sir, Your faithful, Humble Servant,

(Signed) JAMES BOSWELL

From Burke,
Wednesday 20 July 1791

MS. Yale (C 696).
ADDRESS: James Boswell Esqr., Great Portland Street, London.
FRANK: Margate, July twenty first 1791. Free Edm. Burke.
POSTMARKS: MARGATE, FREE JY 21.
ENDORSEMENT: Right Hon. Edmund Burke.

Margate, July 20, 1791

DEAR SIR, I am perfectly sensible of the favour you have done me by your obliging Letter, and by all the Kind things you are so good to report from others, and much more for those you are pleased to say of me yourself.[1]

I wish you all happiness, whenever you retire to Auchinleck, from the entertainment of your friends and the applauses of the publick. We shall I trust find ourselves hereafter as much obliged

[12] MS. "repose"

[13] EB, in 1796, agreed with James Mackintosh that JB's *Life* was "a greater monument to Johnson's fame, than all his writings put together" (R. J. Mackintosh, *Memoirs of Sir James Mackintosh*, 1835, i. 92).

[14] MS. "loisure"

[15] The chief reason for the Burkes' visit to Margate was to give Mrs. Burke, who suffered from rheumatism, the benefits of sea bathing (*post* From EB, 20 July; *Corres. EB* vi. 314).

[1] Perhaps JB had belatedly, if intermittently, realized EB's sensitivity to depiction in print (*ante* From EB, 8 Feb. 1786, n. 4): in any case he handled EB very gingerly in the *Life*. Often EB is introduced in elaborate circumlocutions, such as "an eminent person, whom we all greatly admired" (ii. 348) or "one of the most luminous minds of the present age" (i. 471).

to your invention as hitherto we have been to your recollection. I am sure that something original from you will be well received. Whether, in the present possession of the favourable opinion of the world as you are, it will be prudent for you to risque the further publication of anecdotes, you are infinitely more competent to judge than I am.

As to the conversation I had the honour of having with the King at his Levee with regard to your Work and to Johnson, I gave you the account of it with as much exactness at the time, as I am able ever to relate any thing; not being much in the habit of precision with regard to particular expressions. Since then other things, not of much moment I admit, have made my recollection of the conversation far worse than then it was.[2] I am quite certain, that I am now far less able to furnish you with any detail of that matter; and that you have reason on occasions of this Nature, and indeed of any nature, rather to trust to your own Memory than mine. Be assured that this is the fact, and that I do not decline an obedience to your Commands, either from Laziness or inattention to you. In the Substance of the conversation you are certainly right. The King by his manner of questioning me, seemd to be affected properly with the merit of your performance;[3] and I said, what I thought, that I had not read any thing more entertaining; though I did not say to his[4] Majesty, what nothing but the freedom of friendship could justify[5] in my saying to yourself, that many

[2] The spring and summer of 1791 was one of the most crucial periods in EB's life. On 6 May, during the debate on the Quebec Bill, came the dramatic break with Fox, and on 12 May EB could read in *Morn. Chron.*, Fox's public voice, that he had, in effect, been read out of the Whig Party. At the moment of writing this letter, EB had just finished correcting the proofs of his response, *An Appeal from the New to the Old Whigs*, Aug. 1791 (*Corres. EB* vi. 298–99). Also, he was heavily engaged in French affairs. Louis XVI's flight to Varennes in late June had aroused deep suspicion of the King in France, while the *émigrés*, led by the King's brothers, the Comte de Provence and the Comte d'Artois, through their representative, Charles-Alexandre de-Calonne, were vainly seeking the support of the British Ministry. Some time around 20 July, EB conducted a secret, highly significant interview with Calonne (*Corres. EB* vi. 300–02).

[3] Fanny Burney also reports (on 5 June) the King's questioning her about the *Life*: "The King, who was now also reading this work, applied to me for explanations without end. Every night at this period he entered the Queen's dressing-room, and delayed Her Majesty's proceedings by a length of discourse with me upon this subject." Again, in July she reports, "He talked over all Mr. Boswell's book" (*Burney Diary* iv. 477, 479). As late as 1811 the *Life* was one of the books the King asked to have read to him (John Brooke, *King George III*, 1972, p. 384).

[4] MS. "to his" superimposed upon "to the"

[5] MS. "justifying"

particulars there related might as well have been omitted; However[6] in the multitude of readers perhaps some would have found a loss in their omission.

Mrs. Burke finds some Benefit from the use of the seabathing and presents her compliments. I have the honour to be with very great respect and regard, Dear Sir, your most faithful and obedient, humble Servant,

EDM. BURKE

[6] "However" written above a deleted "though"

INTRODUCTION TO THE BOSWELL-MALONE CORRESPONDENCE

I

SAMUEL Johnson died on 13 December 1784. While James Boswell, then in Edinburgh, felt "just one large expanse of Stupor" on hearing the news, his publisher Charles Dilly, "in the true spirit of *the trade*", immediately began to shower him with letters agitating for a four-hundred-page biography to be ready in February.[1] Boswell had been collecting materials for that purpose since at least 1772. He knew exactly what he should do: first publish an account of his tour to the Hebrides with Johnson in 1773, then set to work "deliberately" on the "large Work his Life".[2] But he could not apply himself. Alive, Johnson had been generous with advice and encouragement; now his steadying influence was gone, and Boswell became unsettled and depressed. Faced with the awesome task of writing "the Life of him who excelled all mankind in writing the lives of others", Boswell vacillated: as late as February 1785, he still had not decided whether to print the journal he had kept while on the tour or prepare a conflated narrative as he had done for his *Corsica*.[3]

Perhaps a change of scene would do the trick: "I resolved that I would set myself down quietly in London, and get the Work executed easily" (Journ. 21 Feb. 1785). But as Messrs. Pottle and Bennett have written, after his arrival in London on 30 March he "allowed himself to be swept round for a month in an eddy of dinners, executions, and girls" (*Hebrides*, p. xiv). Then on 29 April he dined with Edmond Malone, a fellow member of The Club: "Sat with him till two in morning full of bar scheme and encouraged". Apparently Boswell's plan to move from the Scottish to the English bar was not the only topic of conversation that night; Malone somehow switched on Boswell's literary machine as well, and he spent the whole of the next morning

[1] Journ. 17, 18 Dec. 1784; Reg. Let. 18, 20, 25 Dec. 1784.

[2] Journ. 18 Dec. 1784; Reg. Let. 23 Dec. 1784.

[3] *Life* i. 25; Journ. 21 Feb. 1785.

"writing *Tour*" (Journ. 29–30 Apr. 1785). From now on, Malone would be his literary adviser; he soon would become his confessor, comforter, and closest London friend. And yet before 29 April he and Boswell had been only casually acquainted. Who, then, was this Edmond Malone, and how did he work such magic on Boswell?

He was born on 4 October 1741 in Dublin, the second son of another Edmond Malone, who had practised at the English bar, later would become a Member of the Irish Parliament, and then a judge of the Irish Court of Common Pleas.[4] The Malones were an ancient Irish family: a story that they had descended from a seventh-century king of Connaught probably owes more to family enthusiasm than to genealogical fact, but it is certain that the "Ó Maoileoins" had owned extensive property in Westmeath since at least the twelfth century, when they had distinguished themselves in local ecclesiastical affairs.[5] The Malones of Baronston, founded by Anthony, second son of Edmond Malone of Ballynahown (fl. 1644), had conformed, and in the eighteenth century were as wealthy and powerful as any Anglo- or Scotch-Irish family. Young Edmond's eldest uncle Anthony Malone of Baronston, a barrister and highly influential Irish M.P., in 1757 became Chancellor of the Exchequer in Ireland. Two other uncles, Richard and John, were barristers; Richard, like Anthony, was an M.P. Edmond's older brother Richard also followed the family profession; he inherited Baronston in 1776 and sat in the Irish Parliament until created Lord Sunderlin in 1785. Two younger sisters, Henrietta and Catharine, completed a family that was, to all appearances, comfortable and closely knit.[6]

[4] Except where noted otherwise, the information in the following biographical sketch is taken from DNB and Sir James Prior, *Life of Edmond Malone*, 1860.

[5] John Lodge, *The Peerage of Ireland*, rev. ed. Mervyn Archdall, 1789, vii. 280–93, lists a number of Malones who became abbots of Clonmacnoise and mentions Gilla-Christ O'Malone (d. 1127), whom contemporary records call "a Chieftain of great wealth". Lodge and Archdall say that the Malones were descended from the O'Conors, Kings of Connaught (vii. 280), and Prior connects them more specifically to Murray Mullathan (d. 701), King of Connaught (p. 1), but according to Edward MacLysaght, no such connection exists (*More Irish Families*, 1960, p. 268). For another account of the Malones of Baronston, see Sir Bernard Burke, *A Genealogical History of the Dormant, Abeyant, Forfeited, and Extinct Peerages of the British Empire*, 1883, pp. 350–51; the account in James Woods, *Annals of Westmeath*, 1907, is too inaccurate to be useful.

[6] Two of Edmond's brothers, Anthony and Benjamin, died in infancy.

Malone's education was that of a gentleman destined for life at the bar: Dr. Ford's school in Molesworth Street, Dublin; Trinity College, Dublin, where he was at the top of his class; the Inner Temple (he and Boswell were entered the same year, but Boswell did not attend);[7] a tour on the Continent; a call to the Irish bar on his return in 1767. Literature and drama provided relief from the tedium of legal studies: Malone acted in a school play, wrote and got published an *Ode on the Royal Nuptials*,[8] and in 1765 was introduced to Samuel Johnson. The man who emerged from this education was not personally impressive—no one records sparkling samples of his wit—but enthusiastic and diligent, with endless patience and superb powers of reasoning, which he used confidently. A sensitive, deeply emotional man, he was awkward and painfully self-effacing with women, but among men he made strong and lasting friends to whom he was generous and fiercely loyal.

Malone spent the decade after his call to the bar dutifully following the family profession. According to Sir James Prior, his efforts met with "the usual fortune of a young barrister" (*Malone*, p. 37)—the Irish courts were crowded with men of experience, business was light—but all agreed that he showed great promise. In 1775–76 he campaigned to represent the University of Dublin in the Irish Parliament, billing himself an independent, a man of conscience opposed to the corrupt practices of government. His stand seems admirable to the modern reader but, as Boswell would find, was not calculated to win support from eighteenth-century politicians, with whom personal loyalty counted more than purity of principles. Malone engaged in newspaper controversy and wrote pamphlets, but the successful candidates were Richard Hely-Hutchinson, son of the powerful provost of the University, and Walter Burgh, an orator of considerable eloquence.

On 1 May 1777, Malone quitted Dublin and the bar to settle in London; our records, unfortunately, tell us little about his reasons. Surely he did not make his decision lightly, for he was breaking with family tradition and giving up all hope of political

[7] Malone was entered between 14 Nov. 1760 and 20 Nov. 1761 (*Inner Temple* v. 133). Boswell was entered on 19 Nov. 1761 (*Earlier Years*, p. 74).

[8] *Gratulationes Juventutis Academiae Dubliniensis in Sereniss. Regis et Reginae Nuptias*, 1761, pp. 51–62.

preferment. The slowness of his advancement in law and politics must have been discouraging, particularly after the death of his father in 1774 and of Anthony Malone in 1776 had deprived him of two powerful patrons. There is no reason to suppose that his participation in the election of 1776 was less than whole-hearted, but his defeat probably convinced him of what he may already have suspected, that he was not cut out for public life: he found that he was no great orator and, being shy by nature, he disliked the self-advertisement so necessary to success in politics. Perhaps over a period of years he came to see that if he was to make his mark in the world, he would not do so in the public forum by brash self-assertion, but in the scholar's study by quiet diligence. Such diligence had always been his strong point; for example, during his first years at the bar he had compiled a manuscript index of Irish law, carefully annotated and cross-referenced. Minute labour of this kind, applied to Shakespeare, would later earn him his reputation as "the patron saint of all modern literary scholars".[9] Once he had decided to set up as a man of letters, the decision to move to London, the literary capital, was inevitable.

Political disappointments alone did not drive Malone from Dublin; in a letter of 8 January 1782 to his friend Lord Charlemont, he gave still another reason: "a most unfortunate attachment", a hopeless love affair that had dragged on since 1769, had distracted him from his legal duties and would periodically depress his spirits for the rest of his life.[1] The woman he loved, and who loved him, was Susanna Spencer, about whom little can be learned; and indeed her very obscurity goes far to explain why marriage was out of the question: probably the Malones considered a woman with no claim to family or fortune a poor match for a rising young barrister of ancient lineage. In 1769 Malone tried travel to relieve his love-longing; in 1771 there was talk of sending Susanna to America. By 1776 she was sliding into a deep depression, perhaps tormented by the long continuance of an affair that could not end happily. She wrote to Malone, "I cannot get up my spirits at all I have such violent fits of crying seise me that it almost overpowers me".[2] The letter continues

[9] W. J. Bate, *Samuel Johnson*, [c. 1977], p. 396.

[1] EM to Lord Charlemont, 8 Jan. 1782 (*Charlemont Papers* i. 394).

[2] Susanna Spencer to EM, 27 Jan. 1776 (MS. Bodleian, Malone 39, fols. 372–73).

with obscure references to financial difficulties, a legal action, and some compromising letters from one "Sir Robert". Her letters, only three of which survive,[3] supply few of the circumstantial details for which the biographer hungers, but they poignantly demonstrate her desperate emotional state: "My Comfort is totally out of the Question for I like you never shall be happy and if to know that I am miserable can add to your love I can tell you there is no person more wretched".[4] If her misery did not increase Malone's love for her, it at least did not decrease it, but any hope these lovers might still have had ended when Susanna's melancholy deepened into madness in about 1781, four years after Malone had migrated to London.[5]

In his letter to Lord Charlemont of 8 January 1782, Malone wrote, "There is little chance of getting over an attachment that has continued with unabated force for thirteen years; nor at my time of life is the heart very easily captivated by a new object." But by August of the same year he had found a new matrimonial prospect in Sarah Loveday of Caversham, a lovely and charming girl twenty years his junior.[6] Miss Loveday, however, was put off by his ardent but clumsy wooing (his friend and her cousin John Byng wrote jokingly of the "violent attacks of the Irish volunteer");[7] besides, she had no wish to marry at all. Malone, imagining despite her assurances of friendship that she scorned him as a nuisance, was left to write her self-pitying letters in which he bitterly accused himself of ugliness and bad manners, and her of coldness. Poor Malone! Had he wished to make her despise him, he could not have written more to the purpose:

> . . . what necessity is there for thus distinguishing from *all the rest of the world* one, whose only offence has been the aspiring to a happiness that he did not deserve, who is at least entitled to

[3] See the preceding and next notes; her third letter to Malone, MS. Malone 38, fols. 177–78, is dated 1 Jan. 1806. No letters from Malone to Susanna Spencer have been recovered.

[4] Susanna Spencer to EM, undated (MS. Bodleian, Malone 39, fol. 376).

[5] On Susanna Spencer's madness, see Prior, *Malone*, pp. 286, 289, 290–91. I infer the approximate date of the onset of her insanity from Malone's letter of 8 Jan. 1782 to Lord Charlemont, which mentions that the affair "has ended most unhappily", and from a deed of 14 Feb. 1781, mentioned in Malone's will (see *post*, p. 170 and n. 5). Still, a date of 1780 or even 1779 is possible.

[6] I am grateful to Mrs. Sarah Markham of Wotton-under-Edge, Gloucestershire, for providing information on Sarah Loveday.

[7] *The Torrington Diaries*, ed. C. B. Andrews, 1934–38, i. 91 (29 Aug. 1782).

your pity, and who, be assured, is sufficiently unhappy without the additional weight that you have now laid upon him, by making him believe he is the object not merely of indifference, but of aversion.[8]

Malone swore that he would never recover, but did; Sarah Loveday died unmarried in 1832.[9]

We have no reports of Malone's amorous adventures over the next twelve years, except that Boswell once mentions having found him with a "Dulcinea".[1] But in 1794 Malone courted, without success, Maria Bover, a Cheshire lady of considerable wit and beauty. He wrote to Lord Charlemont that their marriage had been prevented by her having "some years ago entered into an engagement . . . from which she could not disentangle herself, though the person to whom she had plighted her troth had not acted in such a manner as to secure her esteem".[2] Boswell's explanation was a little different: "though Malone is obliging in his manners, He has never been a favorite of the Ladies, He is too soft in his manners."[3] In 1800 William Windham reported that Malone had, "by an unfortunate Irish stare, not at all belonging to his character, lost the favour of a woman who might have made him happy, and probably herself too".[4] This woman has not been identified. Despite his other attempts to marry, Malone's affection for Susanna Spencer continued. Shortly after the onset of her madness he had executed a deed encumbering his estate with an annuity of £100 which provided for her maintenance in a succession of private asylums and homes in England and in Ireland. He visited her, wrote to her, and in his will, made in 1801, left her the sum of £100 to be paid three months after his death and an annuity of £150 to be paid her in semi-annual instalments.[5]

Malone considered his bad fortune with women the greatest source of pain in a life not otherwise unhappy. In 1804 he confided

[8] Winifred Hoper, "Some Unpublished Windham Papers", *The Nineteenth Century and After* (1919) lxxxvi. 674. Mrs. Markham's communications have enabled me to correct the printed text of Malone's undated letter.

[9] *Gent. Mag.* July (1832) cii. 93.

[1] Journ. 13 Dec. 1789. JB used "Dulcinea" elsewhere to mean "prostitute"; see Journ. 9 Nov.–18 Dec. 1779.

[2] *Charlemont Papers* ii. 238–39.

[3] Boswell reported the affair to Joseph Farington (*The Farington Diary*, ed. James Greig, 1922–28, i. 88, 222 n.).

[4] *Windham Papers* ii. 160.

[5] Malone's will, P.R.O. 11/1533 ff. LH 276–RH 277.

to Joseph Farington that he "had lived a life of much anxiety from being disappointed in hopes and wishes which related to domestic union (marriage) that must now no longer be looked for".[6] The illustrious scholarly career that began with his move to London in 1777 must be viewed against this background of personal disappointment and tragedy. He was, as he wrote to Lord Charlemont (8 Jan. 1782), "not at all adapted for solitude"; literature became not only his delight, but also his companion and his escape from painful introspection: "I endeavour to employ my thoughts with books and writing, and when I am weary of them fly into company; and then, disgusted with that, return back to the other; but all will not do." Malone threw himself into his friendships and his scholarly pursuits with the desperate energy of a man in flight. For all his contributions to literary scholarship and to the careers of his friends, he never did outdistance his frustration and anxiety.

Malone seems to have left the Irish bar with little regret; the blandishments of friends and relatives (his brother urged that competition at the bar had slackened and a seat in Parliament could easily be bought)[7] henceforth never induced him to return to Ireland for more than a few months at a time. The death of his father had left him with an income of about £800 a year, enough to live on comfortably, if not magnificently.[8] Now he quickly gained acceptance in London society. He already had some experience as a literary scholar: the year before his move he had prepared an edition of Goldsmith's plays and poems, published in Dublin in 1777 and in London in 1780. He had often visited London and already had many acquaintances there, including George Steevens, the irascible and sometimes malicious scholar who had collaborated with Johnson in an edition of Shakespeare's plays, and who now became Malone's mentor in Shakespearian studies. Steevens printed Malone's "Attempt to Ascertain the Order in Which the Plays Attributed to Shakspeare Were Written" in the 1778 Johnson-Steevens Shakespeare and encouraged him to publish his two-volume *Supplement to the Edition of Shakspeare's Plays Published in 1778* (1780), followed by *A Second Appendix to Mr. Malone's Supplement* (1783). In 1782 Steevens declared himself

[6] *Farington Diary* ii. 186.

[7] Richard Malone to EM, 10 Nov. 1777 (Prior, *Malone*, pp. 55–57).

[8] Prior, *Malone*, p. 42; *Farington Diary* i. 88. Boswell reported Malone's income to Farington.

finished with Shakespeare and the next year gave out that he considered Malone his successor. Malone already was working on his own monumental edition, which would appear in 1790, and at the same time was supplying notes to Isaac Reed, who had charge of the fourth edition of Johnson-Steevens. By 1785 these two projects had lost him the friendship of Steevens, who was infuriated to find that the pupil was not afraid to differ with his master.

During these busy years Malone's life was not all dismal love affairs and Shakespeare: he sat for Sir Joshua Reynolds in 1778, composed an epilogue for Robert Jephson's *Count of Narbonne* in 1781, and wrote a pamphlet on the Rowley forgeries, for which he was vigorously attacked, in 1782. By 1779, when he tried and failed to be elected to The Club (he did not succeed until 1782), he could claim the friendship not only of Steevens, but also of Johnson, Burke, and Reynolds;[9] by 1781 he had made friends with the fastidious Horace Walpole.

Boswell and Malone were acquainted long before they became intimate. They met on 14 April 1781 at a dinner given by Reynolds (Boswell knew whom he was meeting, for he had read Malone's *Supplement*); they met twice more that spring, at the sale of Topham Beauclerk's library and at Johnson's house.[1] They dined together at The Club twice in 1783, twice in 1784, and again in early April 1785; but in all this time neither made much impression on the other.[2] Thus the astonishingly rapid development of their friendship after 29 April 1785 requires some explanation. Malone was unimpressive in company, not at all a Johnson or a Burke; Boswell later described him as "respectable and gentlemanlike rather than shining".[3] He was at his best in small groups and tête-à-tête conversations like the one he had with Boswell on 29 April; there, where he could not be overshadowed by more flamboyant personalities, his own quiet, elegant qualities became apparent. Boswell no doubt was first attracted by Malone's enthusiasm for his literary and legal

[9] EM to Lord Charlemont, 5 Apr. 1779 (*Charlemont Papers* i. 344).

[1] Journ. 29 July 1780; 14, 15, 30 Apr., 7 May 1781. I am not convinced by J. M. Osborn's argument that Boswell and Malone had met before 14 Apr. 1781 ("Edmond Malone and Dr. Johnson", *Johnson, Boswell, and Their Circle*, 1965, p. 10).

[2] Entries in The Club's book of minutes for 8 Apr., 6 May 1783; 25 May, 22 June 1784; 3 Apr. 1785.

[3] *Farington Diary* i. 44.

schemes—but more than one of Boswell's friends were enthusiastic about his Johnsoniana. More impressive to Boswell were Malone's extensive knowledge and cool self-assurance. Malone held firm opinions as to what was correct in language and literature and could back up his opinions with detailed evidence and appeals to authority. This self-assurance, which comes through clearly in his Shakespearian works and in this correspondence, must have been immensely comforting to Boswell, who could waver endlessly over difficult decisions.

Malone, for his part, was quite won over by the legendary Boswellian charm; but there was more. He, like Boswell, had been a friend and admirer of Johnson, whose sayings he had been collecting for years, and he saw in Boswell's journals both a literary masterpiece and a true portrait of his "Great Friend". He was no doubt impressed by Boswell's passion for accuracy—a passion that he shared. And he saw that without steady encouragement Boswell might never print a word of his splendid journals. But Malone did more than encourage Boswell; he stole long hours from his own studies and spent them helping to prepare the *Tour* for press. From June through September 1785 Boswell and Malone met several times a week: "Went to Malone and corrected well" (22 June). "Malone all morning" (28 June). "Long with Malone" (30 June). Malone was always glad to help his literary friends: since his early days in London he had been buying books for Lord Charlemont;[4] in 1786 he helped John Courtenay revise his *Poetical Review of the Literary and Moral Character of the Late Samuel Johnson, L.L.D.*;[5] in 1793 and 1794 he helped Robert Jephson compose his *Roman Portraits* in much the same way that he helped Boswell revise for the second edition of the *Tour*—laboriously, through the post.[6] He also helped Reynolds with four of his *Discourses*.[7] Malone the literary scholar found such work enjoyable, Malone the generous friend found it satisfying, and Malone the grieving lover found that it directed his attention away from himself.

By 23 February 1785, Boswell had decided that his Hebridean

[4] J. M. Osborn, "Edmond Malone: Scholar-Collector", *Transactions of the Bibliographical Society* (1964) xix. 11–37.

[5] See the letters To and From EM, 13 Jan.–7 Apr. 1786.

[6] Prior, *Malone*, pp. 199–201.

[7] F. W. Hilles, *The Literary Career of Sir Joshua Reynolds*, 1936, pp. 142–43.

journal "might be printed with little variation", but he still intended to transcribe it for the printer (Journ. 21 Feb. 1785). Now Malone, Reynolds, Sir Joseph Banks, and others convinced him that the original journal would serve as printer's copy.[8] Extensive additions and substitutions could be written on "Papers Apart"; minor revisions could be made on the pages of the journal itself. Where the journal lapsed, Boswell prepared fresh copy from notes or from memory; he brought all to Malone for correction. A single quotation from near the end of the "Tour" manuscript will show how extensive the revisions could become. I give the passage as Boswell first wrote it, then as revised, with words and letters in Malone's hand in italics:

> My Father called Dr. Johnson Ursa Major. But it is not true as has been said in Newspapers that there was any preparation for it by my saying that he was a Constellation of Genius and Literature. It was a droll abrupt image at Edinburgh after Dr. Johnson was no longer my Father's guest.
>
> My Father*'s opinion of Dr. Johnson may be conjectured from the name he afterwards gave him—which was Ursa Major. But* it is not true as has been *reported, that it was in consequence of my saying* that he was a Constellation of Genius and Literature. It was a *sly* abrupt *expression to one of his bretheren on the bench of the Court of Session, in which Dr. Johnson was then standing; but was not said in his hearing.*[9]

The reader may well wonder whose journal he is reading—Boswell's or Malone's. The present correspondence shows that, despite the many revisions in Malone's hand, it is still Boswell's journal. The first letter that survives (a mere scrap, in fact) is a list of twenty-one proposed emendations which, rather than mark up the manuscript itself, Malone wrote out separately. The final decisions were up to Boswell, who accepted only twelve of these suggestions; the others he passed over or replaced with emendations of his own (From Malone, between 3 and 10 June 1785 and nn.). Clearly, as F. A. Pottle has written, Boswell "was not giving Malone *carte blanche*" (*Hebrides*, p. xvi). This letter is the only one that concerns revisions for the first edition, for soon the two

[8] Proof-sheets of the *Tour* (P 84), pp. 54–55; see *Hebrides*, pp. xv, 411–12.

[9] "Tour" MS. (M 132), p. 708; cf. *Life* v. 384. In the MS., "Constellation" and "Ursa Major" are underscored; to avoid confusion, they are printed here in roman type.

friends were meeting rather than corresponding. We may imagine that during most of these sessions Malone held the pen and read the journal aloud, suggesting revisions for Boswell's approval, while Boswell in turn dictated revisions to Malone.

It has long been supposed that Malone suggested most of the revisions in the second edition of the *Tour*. We know that Malone supervised the printing of much of the book while Boswell was in Scotland, and R. W. Chapman, noting that Malone had entered most of the changes in his own copy of the first edition, concluded that "Boswell made very few changes, merely verbal, except those which were suggested by Malone."[1] Chapman's conclusion proceeds from the assumption that Malone jotted revisions in his copy as he thought of them—a plausible assumption which the present correspondence proves to be false. Malone wrote, "I keep no memorial of the alterations I propose" (5 Nov. 1785 and n. 15); and to confirm it we find in his copy only those revisions that Boswell suggested or approved—Malone's rejected proposals are conspicuously absent. The method followed in revising for the second edition was far more complex than the evidence of Malone's copy of the *Tour* would suggest: Malone sent his proposals to Boswell, who commented on each of them and added his own. On receiving Boswell's letters, Malone went to the printing house and entered the revisions in the copy from which the new edition was being set. He also entered the revisions in his own copy (not used as printer's copy), perhaps so that he could refer to them quickly when reading proof.

F. A. Pottle has recognized that the "elegance" that Malone urged upon Boswell "was dictated by the neo-classical love of generality most memorably expressed in Sir Joshua's dictum that the beauty of art consists in being able to get above all singular forms, local customs, particularities, and details of every kind" (*Hebrides*, p. xi). Boswell accepted many of Malone's "generalizing" suggestions, but mostly he wanted stylistic advice. He was eager to purge his book of Scotticisms and bowed to his Irish friend's determinations as to what was English and what not. Further, he relied on Malone to make his direct, vigorous, but often paratactic style smoother and more periodic. A good example is the description of Coll, which Malone revised in the

[1] *Life* iii. 323 n. 2; *Tour*, ed. Chapman, p. xix.

proof of the first edition. First I present a sample passage as Boswell wrote it, then as revised:

> There is a great number of horses in Col, mostly of a small size. They have too many horses, but they sell some in Tirey and on the main land. Their black cattle are reckoned remarkably good. They are mostly rough-haired. They never put their beasts in any house in winter. Indeed the climate is very mild.

> There is a great number of horses in the island, mostly of a small size. Being over-stocked, they sell some in Tir-yi, and on the main land. Their black cattle, which are chiefly rough-haired, are reckoned remarkably good. The climate being very mild in winter, they never put their beasts in any house.[2]

Malone, it should be said, acted here on his own authority (Boswell was out of town), but he knew that this was exactly the kind of revision Boswell wanted and depended on him to suggest. Boswell resisted those of Malone's suggestions that tended to sacrifice strength of expression to "elegance". When Malone thought the phrase "sore rubs" vulgar and suggested "smart blows", Boswell resisted the change, but was vanquished when told that "*sore* was certainly unjustifiable and must be a scotticism" (Boswell always capitulated when Malone decreed that a word was Scottish). By the third edition the phrase had become "severe strokes"—more Latinate, less Scottish, and less colourful than the original.[3] Malone also objected to the description of Sir Adolphus Oughton as having "a charming sweet temper", and Boswell reluctantly acquiesced in the change of "charming" to "very".[4] But Boswell drew the line at changing "quarrel" to "altercation" in the sentence, "I was afraid of a quarrel between Dr. Johnson and Mr. M'Aulay", saying, "no word that I can think of but *quarrel* is strong enough".[5] Here he goes to the heart of the matter. "Elegance", for the scholarly Malone, was not only grammatical, periodic, and "English" (qualities that Boswell

[2] The original MS. of this passage has not been recovered; the earlier version is from the proof-sheets (P 84), p. 372. The later version is from the 1st ed. p. 372. Cf. *Life* v. 300 and From EM, 23 Aug. 1785 and n. 2.

[3] From EM, 5 Oct.; To EM, 13 Oct.; From EM, 21 Oct.; To EM, 27 Oct. 1785 and n. 36.

[4] From EM, 28 Oct.; To EM, 2 Nov. 1785 and n. 6.

[5] From EM, 28 Oct.; To EM, 2 Nov. 1785 and n. 13.

admired) but also objective, even, and unemotional. Boswell recognized Malone's superior knowledge of English usage, but at the same time was determined to preserve the warmth and vigour of his journalistic style. Near the end of October 1785, when he was beginning to tire of revising the *Tour*, he wrote plaintively to Malone, "Are you not too desireous of perfection? We must make *some* allowance for the Book being a *Journal*" (To Malone, 30 Oct. 1785).

I have emphasized that Malone generally treated Boswell's text with great respect, but now must undercut my argument by admitting that on a very few occasions he introduced changes not only without Boswell's approval, but against his directives. This he did to soften Boswell's expressions of his own emotions or opinions, which might (Malone feared) expose him to public ridicule. Boswell wrote in the first edition, "I loved to behold Dr. Samuel Johnson rolling about in this old magazine of antiquities [the Advocates' Library]". Malone thought "I loved" should be changed to "It gave me pleasure", but Boswell rejected the change, writing, "I think 'I loved' a good warm expression". Malone nevertheless substituted "I was pleased" without Boswell's knowledge.[6] Again, Boswell wrote in the first edition that he "several times burst into tears" on hearing the story of the battle of Culloden. When Malone suggested a change to "I could not refrain from tears", Boswell replied, "Since I have once acknowledged the *fact* let *burst into tears* remain." Malone made the change anyway.[7] Finally, when Boswell wished to insert a paragraph excusing his "wild" note on the Americans and the Devil, Malone declined to do so, saying that the sheet containing the note had already been printed. But in fact, this sheet had *not* been printed when the proposed addition arrived; the real reason Malone did not insert it was that "it would only make the matter worse".[8] Most modern readers of this correspondence will find themselves taking Boswell's side when disputes arise; we enjoy Boswell's warmth of feeling, his attention to detail, and even his extravagance. But from the eighteenth-century point of view, Malone was certainly right in urging Boswell to adopt a more

[6] From EM, 5 Oct.; To EM, 13 Oct. 1785 and n. 17.

[7] From EM, 28 Oct.; To EM, 2 Nov. 1785 and n. 16.

[8] To EM, 27, 30 Oct.; From EM, 5 Nov. 1785 and n. 6.

restrained style, and even in overruling him on occasion, for the prevailing literary fashion was discreet and understated. Malone acted only to save Boswell from himself.

In July 1786, after months of collecting and sorting materials, Boswell began to write the *Life of Johnson* (Journ. 9–11 July). In the writing itself Malone could be of little direct help; instead he became Boswell's cheerleader and his conscience. Boswell read Johnsonian passages from his journals to Malone, whose praise urged him forward; he apologized to Malone when he had done no writing and asked to be "let off" when he had promised to write but wished to dine out.[9] Malone urged him to put the *Life* before all other activities. Though he had encouraged Boswell to try the English bar, he now advised him to "attend laxly" in Westminster Hall (Journ. 16 Nov. 1787). Too, he saw that Boswell could write nowhere but in London. When Boswell was in Scotland or on the circuit, Malone urged him to return to London; when Boswell was in London, Malone urged him to stay.

By the beginning of 1789 Boswell had nearly finished a rough draft of the *Life* (then, it appears, the writing of the first draft stalled until 1791); on 13 October 1789 he and Malone began to revise.[1] The journal shows that they worked together at least once a week, and usually more, in November, December, and January, but the manuscript of the *Life* shows fewer revisions in Malone's hand than that of the *Tour*. The reason is that Boswell and Malone precisely reversed the procedure they had followed in revising the *Tour*: this time Boswell read aloud to Malone and entered most of the revisions in his own hand.[2] From the manuscript, then, we cannot tell who suggested what changes, but in the margins of the proofs and revises Malone wrote occasional queries and comments that show us what kind of revision he was most likely to suggest.[3] In the story of John Eccles, where the proof reads, "He had been at the pains to write the whole book in his own hand,

[9] Journ. 27 June, 7 Nov. 1786; 21 July, 17, 28 Oct. 30 Mar. 1787; 1 May 1788; From EM, 14 Sept. 1787; To EM, 18 Sept. 1788.

[1] To W. J. Temple, 10 Jan., 13–14 Oct. 1789, MS. Pierpont Morgan.

[2] In the Advertisement to the 1st ed. of the *Life*, JB wrote that he had read the MS. to EM, who had "made such remarks as were greatly for the advantage of the Work" (*Life* i. 7).

[3] The surviving proofs and complete revises (second proofs) of the *Life* are now in the Hyde Collection; see also R. W. Chapman, "Boswell's Revises of the Life of Johnson", in *Johnson & Boswell Revised*, 1928, pp. 19–50.

with blottings, interlineations, and corrections", Malone wrote, "or else, 'to transcribe the whole book', with blottings, etc.", and Boswell accepted the change.[4] In the account of the *Adventurer*, where Boswell had repeated the phrase "literary labours" in neighbouring lines, Malone suggested substituting "performances" for the first occurrence of the phrase, but Boswell instead substituted the less Latinate "works".[5] A passage on Johnson's prejudice against actors appears as follows in proof:

> It is remarkable, that in this biographical disquisition there appears a very strong symptom of Johnson's prejudice against players; a prejudice, which may be accounted for by the following considerations: first, his organs were so imperfect, that he was not susceptible of the fine impressions which theatrical excellence produces upon the generality of mankind.

For "may be accounted . . . so imperfect", Malone suggested "may be attributed to the following causes: first the imperfection of his organs, which were so defective"; the substitution, which Boswell accepted, introduced a relative clause.[6] In the *Life*, as in the *Tour*, Malone favoured the Latinate word and the periodic sentence, but again Boswell did not give him *carte blanche*.

Three years after Boswell's death, Malone wrote to Sir William Forbes that he had managed to persuade Boswell to reduce the amount of objectionable matter in the *Life*.[7] This correspondence shows that he deleted a passage he thought would anger his Whiggish friend Lord Charlemont (From Malone, 8 July 1790 and n. 17); another example of his moderating influence can be seen in the margin of a revise, opposite a passage that reads, "Garrick sometimes used to take him off, squeezing a lemon into a punch-bowl, with uncouth gesticulations, and calling out, 'Who's for *poonsh*?' " Boswell had inserted "and hands not over clean" after "gesticulations", but Malone wrote, "Would not this be better omitted?" and Boswell substituted "looking round the company". Malone may have been thinking, as Chapman suggests, of the difficulty of Garrick's mimicking a man with dirty hands, but more likely he objected to the gratuitous reminder that Johnson was not always clean.[8] Malone worried about Boswell's

[4] 1st ed. i. 195; *Life* i. 360.

[5] 1st ed. i. 127; *Life* i. 234.

[6] 1st ed. i. 90; *Life* i. 167.

[7] EM to Forbes, 5 July 1798, MS. Somervell, deposited in the National Library of Scotland (summarized by Waingrow, p. 598).

[8] 1st ed. ii. 35; *Life* ii. 464; Chapman, "Boswell's Revises", pp. 37–38.

depictions not only of others, but also of himself. In the Dedication to the *Life*, Boswell wrote that he had become more cautious, since the publication of the *Tour*, about telling stories in which he was himself the object of Johnson's wit; Malone's concern for Boswell's reputation, so evident in his comments on the *Tour*, suggests that Boswell's greater discretion in the *Life* may have been due, in part at least, to his urging.[9]

Boswell's plan was to send the *Life* to press as soon as he and Malone had revised half of the manuscript.[1] In January 1790 he consulted with Baldwin, Dilly, and Malone about the book's format; printing began in late January or early February and proceeded concurrently with the revision of the manuscript.[2] Time was precious: by the beginning of July, Malone was finishing the last volume of his edition of Shakespeare and planning a visit to Ireland as soon as he had seen the last sheet through the press. And while Malone was wrapping up his project, Boswell was being forced to waste a month in Carlisle on Lord Lonsdale's political business, far from the press. Only a third of the *Life* was in print, and although Malone was able to proof-read five sheets in Boswell's absence, 350 pages of the manuscript still had to be revised.[3] By the time Malone left for Ireland on 19 or 20 November he very likely had helped to revise as much manuscript as Boswell had written, but many documents relating to Johnson's last years had yet to be inserted as Papers Apart; also, as much as the last year of the *Life* remained to be written, and the printing had advanced no farther than about sheet Z.[4] Malone's assistance with the *Life* did not entirely stop

[9] *Life* i. 3. I have discussed Malone's concern over Boswell's depiction of himself above, p. 177. He showed the same concern in his comments on *LPS 85* (From EM, 5 Nov. 1785 and n. 36). I suspect that the same motive was behind Malone's partly successful attempt to make Boswell delete a passage of "Rhodomontade" from the Advertisement to the second edition of the *Life*; see From EM, 13 May, and To EM, 17 May 1793.

[1] To W. J. Temple, 10 Jan. 1789—MS. Pierpont Morgan.

[2] Journ. 6, 9, 11, 13 Jan., 2, 4 Feb. 1790.

[3] To EM, 30 June; To Sir William Forbes, 2 July, MS. Somervell (summarized by Waingrow, pp. 328–29); From EM, 8 July 1790.

[4] 1st ed. ii. 169–76; *Life* iii. 198–209. In the Advertisement to the 1st ed. Boswell wrote that he had read "almost the whole" MS. to Malone, presumably meaning he had read all that he had written (see To EM, 4 Dec. 1790; 18 Jan., 29 Jan., 10 Feb. 1791, for references to the progress of the writing). I estimate the point to which printing had progressed by the time of Malone's leaving London from references in To Lord Hawkesbury, 4 Nov. and To

with his leaving London; he wrote with instructions to "condense as much as possible, always preserving perspicuity and do not imagine the *only* defect of stile, is repetition of word" (From Malone, 23 Dec. 1790). We again see his "neo-classical love of generality" in his advice to omit from the character-sketch a reference to Johnson's "*bow-wow way*" and a comparison of his voice to the Canterbury organ, both of which had appeared in the *Tour* (From Malone, 5 Mar. 1791 and n. 1). But the Boswell-Malone letters from December 1790 to April 1791 have more to do with the *Life*'s value than with its content; Boswell finished his great work with little help from anyone.

As far as Malone was concerned, Boswell was Johnson's only biographer. Soon after Sir John Hawkins's *Life of Samuel Johnson* appeared in 1787, he wrote to Lord Charlemont, "Though he [Hawkins] hung about Johnson at the latter end, he never knew him. His denying that Johnson ever loved his wife, and that he had merely talked himself into thinking so, is one of the most curious assertions that ever biographer produced. There is scarcely a material fact in his book truly stated."[5] Malone was even more violent against "that despicable woman Mrs. Piozzi",[6] who, in the opinion of Johnson's friends, had abandoned him in his final days to elope with a low-bred Italian musician, Gabriel Piozzi. Readers of this correspondence will find that Malone perhaps helped to revise, and certainly approved the publication of, Boswell's scurrilous *Ode by Dr. Samuel Johnson to Mrs. Thrale upon Their Supposed Approaching Nuptials*, and that he, almost alone among eighteenth-century readers, took seriously the wild accusations that Joseph Baretti had made against her in the *European Magazine*.[7] The marginal notes in Malone's copy of Mrs. Piozzi's *Anecdotes of the Late Samuel Johnson, LL.D.* are vitriolic: "This writer", he complains, "can never represent anything correctly and justly;—all is to be overcharged and wrought up so

EM, 4 Dec. 1790, each of which mentions the progress of the press, which also allows us to determine the average speed of the press during the month of November 1790.

[5] EM to Lord Charlemont, 7 Nov. 1787 (*Charlemont Papers* ii. 62).

[6] Prior, *Malone*, p. 412.

[7] Malone could not have assisted with the first version of the *Ode*, written on 12 Apr. 1781, for he and Boswell were not then acquainted (*Laird*, pp. 316–21). He may well have helped with the 1788 revision (reprinted by Mary Hyde, *The Impossible Friendship*, 1973, pp. 131–32), and he certainly had the *Ode* advertised a second time when it did not sell well (From EM, 17 June 1788 and n. 21). On Baretti's "Strictures", see From EM, 17 June 1788.

as to make a high finished picture."[8] He several times writes of her "gross misrepresentation" of Johnson and calls her anecdotes "slip slop"; she is a "mendacious lady" and an "impudent hussy".[9] Though Boswell was jealous of Mrs. Piozzi's closeness to Johnson and annoyed with her as a rival biographer, he probably did not hate her. But Malone clearly did, and here he entirely abandoned his usual scholarly objectivity. He did not know, or would not believe, that Johnson could be a difficult house guest, and it did not occur to him that Mrs. Thrale, with a family to care for, could not afford to sacrifice as much time to Johnson as Malone habitually sacrificed to his friends. Malone's own impulses were affectionate, loyal, and generous; to him, it appeared that Mrs. Thrale had acted in the most ungenerous manner towards an old, sick, and great man who loved and depended on her. To a man of his temperament this was intolerable behaviour.[1]

Malone's severe opinions of Boswell's rivals resulted partly from literary considerations and respect for the memory of Johnson, but partly, too, from his extreme partiality for Boswell the man; for although I have emphasized the literary side of their friendship, there was also a powerful personal attraction between them. By August 1785 they were signing their letters "Yours affectionately"—according to F. A. Pottle "a rare formula in eighteenth-century letters, and particularly striking when occurring in a friendship of only a few weeks".[2] Soon, we find, they were consulting each other on more than literary matters: on 10 September Malone confessed to Boswell the history of his sad loves, and on 19 September Boswell wrote in his journal, "Was *ennuyé*. Away to Malone's, and complained."[3] It would be rash to say that Malone was to Boswell what Johnson had been, that he in any way filled the gap left by Johnson's death. Boswell and

[8] Note to *Anecdotes*, p. 85, from a transcript made by Mona Price in 1919.

[9] Notes to *Anecdotes*, pp. 4, 140, 219 ("gross misrepresentation"); 42, 51, 142, 161, 287 ("slip slop"); 118 ("mendacious lady"); 252 ("impudent hussy").

[1] Interestingly enough, Mrs. Piozzi appears to have thought well of Malone. Amid a good many acid remarks about Boswell written in the margins of her copies of the *Life*, she wrote, opposite one of Malone's footnotes, "Bravo Malone! almost always right" (*The Life of Samuel Johnson . . . with Marginal Comments and Markings . . . by Hester Lynch Thrale Piozzi*, ed. E. G. Fletcher, 1938, ii. 485 n. 1; see also ii. 464 n. 2 and iii. 426 n. 2).

[2] From EM, 9 Aug. 1785; *Hebrides*, p. xviii.

[3] Boswell's journal entry for 10 Sept. is ambiguous, but see *Applause*, p. 340, n. 5.

Malone were more equal in age and intellect than Boswell and Johnson; Malone could not be an object of veneration. But he was, like Johnson, someone to whom Boswell could go for advice and encouragement. Almost alone among Boswell's London friends, Malone had the ability to steady his wavering nerves and lift his sagging spirits. In June 1790, when Boswell, trapped in degrading servitude to Lord Lonsdale, was forced to leave London, his friends, and his work on the *Life* to attend the election in Carlisle, he wrote to beg Malone to give his sunken spirits a lift:

> Every thing that ever vexed me has returned. I feel myself a poor forlorn being; with no permanent vigour of mind, no friend that can enable me to advance myself in life—A fortune sadly encumbered—children whom I can with difficulty support, and of whom I am at a loss how to dispose with advantage and propriety—Such is the general prospect. And for *immediate* feelings, added to *ennui* and selfupbraiding I am again unfortunate enough to have *one* sore of a certain nature contracted I think monday forthnight, which *alone* gives me more pain and alarm than *several* which I had lately. . . . My dear Friend! for God's sake if you possibly can let me have some consolation (To Malone, 30 June 1790).

Malone's reply was soberly optimistic, steady, and practical:

> The first and great consideration is, that the whole is but *temporary*, and that as soon as you return to town and have got completely rid of the *aristocrate* [Lonsdale], you will be just as well as ever. Where misfortunes happen that are likely to give a colour to a man's whole life, there is reason enough for being cast down, if not for complaining: but this is not your case (From Malone, 8 July 1790).

As further consolation Malone sent a quotation from "the wise Bacon" and—what was perhaps stronger medicine—a progress report on the *Life*, which was proceeding through the press in Boswell's absence. Such was Malone's technique for handling Boswell: to calm his wild emotions with clear-eyed realism and to distract him from his anxieties with business. The last, after all, was Malone's prescription for his own malady.

After the publication of the *Life of Johnson* on 16 May 1791, it became more difficult to distract Boswell with literary tasks.

Though he continued to attend in Westminster Hall, his experiment at the English bar was a failure, and he knew it. He had now given up nearly all hope of political preferment.[4] Only Malone could give him relief from his fits of depression. "Like a practical philosopher", Malone could direct his thoughts to the brighter side of things.[5] Boswell at his lowest saw his life as finished and looked back with discontent on his unfulfilled ambitions. But, Malone replied, had he not made valuable additions to his family estate, and had he not achieved great literary fame? Even without satisfying every ambition, had he not done a great deal? However, such relief as Malone could give was temporary, and Boswell wrote, "I was dejected by contrasting my idle, dejected state, with his occupation and prosperity" (Journ. 30 Oct. 1793). Not only was Malone carrying on his Shakespearian studies with characteristic zeal, he was also beginning to work on editions of Dryden and Reynolds, with biographical sketches. Boswell felt himself inferior in his company.[6]

Nevertheless, their friendship continued unabated until the last hour. On 21 May 1795, just two days after Boswell's death, Malone wrote to William Windham,

> I suppose you know poor Boswell died on Tuesday Morning, without any pain. I don't think he at any time of his illness, knew his danger. I shall miss him more and more every day. He was in the constant habit of calling upon me almost daily, and I used to grumble sometimes at his turbulence; but now miss and regret his noise and his hilarity and his perpetual good humour, which had no bounds. Poor fellow, he has somehow stolen away from us, without any notice, and without my being at all prepared for it.[7]

To this eloquent testimony of affection Malone added a more public memorial when he wrote a defence of Boswell's character for the *Gentleman's Magazine* and, contrary to his usual practice, allowed it to be attributed to him. Here he answered the old charges, recently revived in the newspapers, that Boswell had attached himself to great men merely to share in their glory, that

[4] On Boswell's political hopes after 1791, see *Pol. Car.* pp. 171–79.

[5] Journ. 13 Feb. 1794, when Malone discussed Boswell's finances.

[6] Journ. 12 Nov. 1792, 12 Sept. 1793.

[7] *Windham Papers* i. 297–98.

he had little intellectual power of his own, that he was "convivial without being *social* or *friendly*", and that his melancholy was an imitation of Johnson's. Malone concluded, "He will be long regretted by a wide circle of friends, to whom his good qualities and social talents always made his company a valuable accession; and by none more sincerely than by the present vindicator of his fame."[8]

In his will, made 28 May 1785, Boswell had named Sir William Forbes, William Johnson Temple, and Malone his literary executors. In a codicil, added 22 December 1785, he had given Malone charge of the *Life*.[9] Temple outlived Boswell by little more than a year; Malone, with occasional help from Forbes, brought out the third (1799), fourth (1804), fifth (1807), and sixth (1811) editions of the *Life*.[1] Malone did not hesitate, in these later editions, to add new material that came to light, but he continued his policy of treating Boswell's text with respect, and resolutely refused to excise passages that offended those whom Johnson had "tossed and gored", though Forbes pressed him to do so.[2] He would correct only errors of fact. In the preparation of these later editions he was helped by James Boswell the younger, to whom he had become, since the elder Boswell's death, both close friend and mentor. Malone also set young Boswell to work collecting materials for his great "third variorum" edition of Shakespeare, which Boswell brought out in 1821, nine years after Malone's death on 25 May 1812. In 1814 Boswell published *A Biographical Memoir of the Late Edmond Malone*. It is more than a little satisfying that the Boswell-Malone friendship should thus have come full circle, that a James Boswell should have edited the greatest work, as well as written a memorial, of the man to whom his father owed so much.

P. S. B.

II
Editorial Procedures

The letters that Boswell and Malone exchanged in 1785 while

[8] June 1795, lxv. pt. 1. 471–72.

[9] The MSS. of Boswell's will and its codicil are in the Register House, Edinburgh.

[1] *Lit. Car.* pp. 160–61, 171–75.

[2] See Waingrow, pp. 597–607 for Malone's correspondence concerning the third through sixth editions of the *Life*.

revising for the first and second editions of the *Tour* present special problems, for as the letters stand they are unintelligible to the reader who does not have access to the manuscript, the proof-sheets, and the first two editions of the *Tour*. The particular editorial method adopted here is designed to allow the reader to understand the 1785 letters while referring only to the third edition of the *Tour* as reprinted in the fifth volume of the Hill-Powell edition of the *Life*.

Additions to the text. Material enclosed in square brackets is not part of the letter proper, nor is it to be thought of as emendation to the text; it only supplies the context for Boswell's and Malone's proposed emendations to the *Tour*. The editors have at times kept such added material separate from the sense of the text, and at times have made it continuous with Boswell's or Malone's own syntax. For example: "P. 39: 'Mr. *Nairne* Advocate' etc. [was to go with us as far as St. Andrews.] 'It gives me pleasure that by mentioning his name I connect his title' etc. [to the just and handsome compliment paid him by Mr. Johnson]" (From EM, between 3 and 10 June 1785). To read the passage as it stood in the "Tour" MS. before revision, one need only ignore the single quotation marks and the et ceteras. Note that the letter is punctuated and otherwise treated as if the bracketed material were not there. Another example: "P. 29: [The shield of Achilles shews a nation in war, a nation in peace—Harvest sport—nay stealing.] 'A nation in war' etc. Does not this want a little expanding?" (From EM, between 3 and 10 June 1785). In this case it seemed simpler to allow the bracketed material to precede the fragmentary quotation of the "Tour" MS.

Paragraph divisions. Each suggested emendation is presented as a separate paragraph, regardless of manuscript usage, except where two items, appearing in the same paragraph of the manuscript, are so close together that they can be cited in a single quotation.

Style of references. All page and line references in the text are normalized; for example, "P. 8. l. 12. 13" becomes "P. 8, ll. 12–13". All such references are followed with a colon, unless they are continuous with the syntax of the sentences in which they occur. "P." or "pp.", "l." or "ll." are supplied silently where they are lacking.

Quotation marks. These are supplied silently around material from the *Tour* quoted in the texts of the letters, unless the quotation is italicized (underscored in the manuscript). If only part of the quotation is italicized, quotation marks are placed around the entire quotation. Quotation marks are supplied even for one-word quotations. They are also placed around phrases suggested by Boswell or Malone, whether or not these phrases were adopted. Quotation marks already in the manuscript are normalized according to the usage of the Boswell Editions.

Capitalization and Punctuation. After page references followed by a colon, the usage of the manuscript is retained, even if a bracketed passage intervenes. Otherwise, if a complete sentence in the manuscript begins with a lower-case letter, it is capitalized. All capitals already in the manuscript are retained. Punctuation is regularized. For example: the manuscript reads literally, "whose gaiety of manners["] etc., while the edited text reads, 'whose gaiety of manners' etc. (From EM, between 3 and 10 June 1875). Where square brackets would ordinarily appear in the texts of letters, they are replaced by braces.

Annotation. The editors have noted whether each proposed emendation was adopted in the *Tour*. When Malone sends a query, only Boswell's reply is annotated. Boswell's own queries are always annotated. Annotations to suggested emendations of the "Tour" MS. (June–August 1785) include page references to the first edition and to the third as reprinted in *Life* v. Annotations to suggested emendations of the first edition (October–November 1785) include page references to the second edition, where its pagination differs from that of the first, and to *Life* v. Where the text of the letter does not make clear how the revised passage should read, the note supplies this information. In the letters for 1785, and elsewhere in this edition, we have assumed that the reader will have access to the Hill-Powell edition of the *Life*. We have therefore been more generous with quotations from relatively inaccessible sources (e.g., eighteenth-century newspapers and magazines) than with quotations from the *Life*.

Changes. Because of the textual complexity of the 1785 letters, certain substantive but inconsequential changes have been ignored.

Letter pairs. The reader who is interested in following the revision of the first edition of the *Tour* will find it more convenient to read the letters in pairs than to read chronologically. The following table pairs Malone's lists of queries with Boswell's replies. Several of Boswell's letters (15 Oct., 29 Oct., 8 Nov.) do not reply directly to Malone's queries and so are not included in the table.

For		find reply in	
For	From EM, 5 Oct. 1785,	find reply in	To EM, 13 Oct. 1785
	From EM, 19 Oct. 1785		To EM, 27 Oct. 1785
	From EM, 21 Oct. 1785		To EM, 27 Oct. 1785
	From EM, 24 Oct. 1785		To EM, 30 Oct. 1785
	From EM, 28 Oct. 1785		To EM, 2 Nov. 1785
	From EM, 5 Nov. 1785		To EM, 11 Nov. 1785

J 33 designates JB's original journal of his tour with SJ of the Highlands and Hebrides (18 Aug.–26 Oct. 1773). M 132 designates the manuscript of the *Tour* as distinct from J 33: it includes the opening and closing sections of the *Tour.* M 133 designates Papers Apart for the *Tour*, separate sheets sent along with J 33 and M 132 to the printer.

Letters in the Boswell-Malone correspondence after 1785 are printed according to the general Editorial Procedures detailed at the beginning of this volume.

From Malone,
between 3 and 10 June 1785[1]
MS. Yale (C 1888.1).
ADDRESS: Mr. Boswell.

P. 35: [He {Maclaurin} produced two Epitaphs upon his Father the celebrated Mathematician one in English of which Dr. Johnson did not change one word.] "In the other, which was in Latin, he said several alterations." Would it not be[2] better—"he proposed several alterations".[3]

P. 36: [I read to him my notes of the opinions of our Judges upon the Question of Literary property. He did not like them, and said, "They make me think of your Judges not with that respect"] "which I should[4] wish to do". Perhaps better—"which I wish to do".[5]

Ibid.: "when a man's house falls into *disrepair*". I doubt whether Dr. J. used this word—because, I believe, it does not exist. Perhaps—"decay" may do.[6]

P. 37: [He {JB} cannot deny himself the vanity] "of finishing with Dr. J's encomium upon him—'whose gaiety' " etc. Perhaps

[1] This letter lists EM's proposed emendations to a section of the "Tour" MS. running from about the middle of the entry for 17 Aug. through the first few sentences of 24 Aug. 1773 (*Life* v. 49, line 23 to v. 96, line 17). On 1 June 1785 (Journ.) JB was searching for a passage from Butler's *Remains* quoted in this section of the MS. (M 132, p. 42; *Life* v. 57); thus on that date the MS. was still in his possession. EM first helped to revise the "Tour" MS. on 3 June, and JB dined with him on 4 June (Journ.); perhaps on one of these dates JB gave him the section of MS. discussed here. On 10 June JB sent the next section of the "Tour" MS. to EM (*post* To EM, 10 June). The present letter, then, was very likely written between 3 and 10 June.

[2] MS. "be be"

[3] EM's proposed emendations to pp. 35–40 (this and the following seven items) refer to JB's transcript of his original journal (M 132). It seems a reasonable inference that EM (who wrote "I can't endure transcribing"—*post* From EM, 19 Oct. p. 230) convinced JB that the original journal (J 33) could be used for printer's copy (*Hebrides*, p. xv). Accordingly, the "Tour" was printed from the original journal beginning with the fifth sentence under 19 Aug. 1773 ("His daughter, a very pleasing young lady, made breakfast"—1st ed. p. 55; *Life* v. 58. References to *Life* v., which prints the 3rd ed., are given where the readings of the 1st and 3rd eds. are identical or nearly so). In the "Tour" MS., JB rejected EM's "proposed", substituting "made" for "said" (1st ed. p. 45; *Life* v. 50). This and other revisions in the "Tour" MS. listed in the notes below are in JB's hand, unless otherwise noted.

[4] MS. "could" written above "should". So also in the "Tour" MS., which EM quotes.

[5] JB rejected this suggestion and in the "Tour" MS. deleted "could" (1st ed. p. 46; *Life* v. 50).

[6] So changed in the "Tour" MS. (1st ed. p. 46; *Life* v. 51). The first citation of "disrepair" in OED is dated 1798.

better—"of finishing with the encomium of Dr. Johnson, whose[7] friendly partiality to the companion of his tour represents[8] him as one, 'whose gaiety of manners' " etc.[9]

P. 39: "Mr. *Nairne* Advocate" etc. [was to go with us as far as St. Andrews.] "It gives[10] me pleasure that by mentioning his name[10a] I connect his title" etc. [to the just and handsome compliment paid him by Mr. Johnson.] Perhaps better—"It gives me pleasure that the mention of this gentleman gives me an opportunity of subscribing to the just and handsome" etc.[11]

Loose paper:[12] "I insisted *to* scottify his palete"—perhaps better—"*on scottifying* his palete".[13]

P. 40: "but *rather* a profusion of thistles." Might not *rather* be omitted?[14]

—: "there were 16 *cattle*[15] grazing." I believe this is not quite right. It strikes my ear that when any particular *number* is specified, it is better to say "beasts".[16]

P. 25:[17] [There were several points of similarity between them; Learning, clearness of head, precision of speech, and a belief of many things which people in general do not believe.][18] Better Perhaps—"a love[19] of research on many subjects which people in general do not investigate."[20]

Second Loose paper to p. 26: [I was a little acquainted with Mr.

[7] MS. "who has perhaps been too partial" deleted before "whose"

[8] MS. "tour represents" written above deleted "travels has here been represented"

[9] JB adopted EM's alteration and addition and also expanded the quotation from SJ's *Journey*, which "represents him as one 'whose acuteness would help my inquiry, and whose gaiety of conversation . . .' " (1st ed. p. 47; *Life* v. 52).

[10] MS. "does me" deleted before "gives"

[10a] MS. "*name*" with underlining deleted. Italicized in 1st ed. (p. 48; *Life* v. 53).

[11] Unchanged in 1st ed. (p. 48; *Life* v. 53).

[12] A Paper Apart keyed to p. 40 of the "Tour" MS. (see n. 17 below).

[13] So changed in Paper Apart (1st ed. p. 50; *Life* v. 55).

[14] Unchanged in 1st ed. (p. 51; *Life* v. 55).

[15] EM apparently wrote "15 cattel" and changed it to "16 cattle" (the "Tour" MS. reads "sixteen cattel").

[16] Altered in the "Tour" MS.: "There were sixteen head of black cattle grazing" (1st ed. p. 51; *Life* v. 55).

[17] This and the remaining items in EM's letter are keyed to the pages of JB's original journal (J 33). Major changes and expansions in this journal are written separately as Papers Apart. Here EM refers to a Paper Apart keyed to p. 25 of the journal (M 133, p. 30).

[18] Paper Apart, "regard to" written above "belief of" and "consider" written above "believe". JB deleted the whole passage from "and a belief" through "believe", including the alternatives, without indicating which phrases he preferred.

[19] MS. "disposition to" deleted before "love"

[20] So changed in Paper Apart (1st ed. p. 73 n.; *Life* v. 74 n. 3).

Forbes, the minister of the parish. I sent to inform him that a Gentleman desired to see him. He returned an[21] answer, that he would not come to a Stranger. I then gave my name, and he came. I rebuked him for not coming to a Stranger.] *Rebuked* seems too strong a word, yet I have not better to put in its room.[22]

P. 27: "A wild *muir*". This I believe is a Scotch word. We call it[23] *moor*.[24]

P. 28 continued:[25] [This was an Assault upon one of Lord Monboddo's capital dogmas and I was affraid there would have been] "a violent quarrel". Perhaps—"a warm altercation" better.[26]

Ibid: [He produced a very long stalk of corn, as a specimen of his crop, and] "*said you* here the laetas segetes".[27] Is there[28] not some error here?[29]

P. 29: [The shield of Achilles shews a nation in war, a nation in peace—Harvest sport—nay stealing.] "A[30] nation in war" etc. Does not this want a little expanding? Perhaps— "In his book we have an accurate display of a nation in war and a nation in peace;—the[31] peasant is delineated[32] as accurately as the general;—nay even harvest sport and the modes of antient theft are described." ☞ I don't like this much; but the original appears to me much too short.[33]

[21] Paper Apart (M 133, p. 34), "for" written above "an"; "for" adopted in 1st ed. (p. 75; *Life* v. 76).

[22] Paper Apart, "rebuked" changed to "remonstrated to" (1st ed. p. 75; *Life* v. 76).

[23] MS. "it it"

[24] In the "Tour" MS. "muir" changed to "moor" (1st ed. p. 76; *Life* v. 76).

[25] The second of two Papers Apart that replace the crossed-out p. 28 of the "Tour" MS. (M 133, p. 36).

[26] MS. "an altercation", with "an" altered to "a" and "warm" inserted before "altercation". In the Paper Apart EM wrote "warm altercation" above "violent quarrel". JB deleted "violent quarrel" and "warm", substituting "violent" for the latter. 1st ed. "violent altercation" (p. 77; *Life* v. 77).

[27] "Joyous crops" (Virgil, *Georgics* i. 1).

[28] MS. "not this a" deleted before "there"

[29] In the Paper Apart JB inserted "see" before "here" (1st ed. p. 77; *Life* v. 78).

[30] MS. "In" deleted before "A"

[31] MS. "harvest sport, nay stealing, are not om" deleted before "the". "Om" is doubtful.

[32] MS. "por" deleted before "delineated"

[33] JB retained the original wording, and in a Paper Apart for a footnote (M 133, p. 38) argued that he was "resolved that *the very Journal which Dr. Johnson read* shall be presented to the Publick". In the same note he included EM's expansion of the passage, attributing it to "One of the best Criticks of our age" (1st ed. p. 78 and n.; *Life* v. 78 and n. 5).

P. 32: "Dr. J. went downstairs a little"—perhaps better "Dr. J. having retired for a short time".[34]

P. 34: ["I have allways applied to Good breeding what Addison in his Cato says of Honour."] "what Addison says of honour". Perhaps it would be best to add the first line of the passage in Cato here alluded to. I see you have done it.[35]

P. 37: [I hoped then there would be no fear] "of *fulfilling* our wild tour". Perhaps *finishing* or *completing* better.[36]

P. 38: "a little *box* bed". I believe this is what we call a *press*-bed.[37]

P. 42: [He then repeated Dryden's celebrated lines, "Three Poets in three distant ages born" etc. and a part of a latin translation of it done at Oxford—perhaps his own. I must ask.] At the end of the par.—about Dryden's verses on Milton—"I must ask". What is this?[38]

P. 45[39] at bottom: [that he lived in a cave and had a bed in the rock—and she should have a little bed cut opposite to it. Yet he spoke well on the point as to prescription of murder.] "*Yet* he spoke well" etc. What need of this *yet*? I see no opposition between this and what has gone before.[40] After "as to prescription of

[34] So changed in 1st ed. (p. 81; *Life* v. 81). In the "Tour" MS. JB expanded "Dr. J." to "Dr. Johnson", but the rest of the change is in EM's hand, except for a hole in the MS. where the "airs" of "stairs" (in the original) and "for" (in the revision) were.

[35] JB had added four lines from *Cato* in a Paper Apart (M 133, p. 41); apparently EM at first missed the reference "see loose paper" in the "Tour" MS. (see 1st ed. p. 82; *Life* v. 82). In EM's letter the whole passage from "what Addison" through "here alluded to" is deleted. Although the policy of this edition is to report deleted words and phrases in the footnotes, here and in the entry below for p. 42 of the "Tour" MS., deleted material is retained in the text for the sake of clarity.

[36] In the MS. JB wrote "getting through" after "better", and substituted this phrase for "fullfilling" in the "Tour" MS. (1st ed. p. 84; *Life* v. 84).

[37] So changed in the "Tour" MS. (1st ed. p. 85; *Life* v. 84).

[38] MS. "'I must ask.' What is this?" deleted (see n. 35 above). In the "Tour" MS., "perhaps his own" deleted with a horizontal stroke and "I must ask" deleted with vertical strokes. In a Paper Apart for a footnote (M 133, p. 42) JB wrote, "London 2 May 1778. Dr. Johnson dictated to me the following Translation which he made of Dryden's Verses on Milton", followed by six lines of Latin verse. Apparently EM was puzzled by "I must ask" in the "Tour" MS. until he noticed an asterisk following "ask", drawing attention to the Paper Apart that explained the remark. EM then deleted his query, but JB nevertheless deleted "I must ask" and, possibly later, "perhaps his own". EM later decided that it would be best to indicate that SJ had not acknowledged the Latin translation until after 1773, and in the proofs he added "he did not then say by whom" after "Oxford" and revised the footnote. For these revisions and the Latin verses, see 1st ed. p. 87 and n.; *Life* v. 86 and n. 1.

[39] MS. "5" superimposed upon "6"

[40] In the "Tour" MS. JB deleted "Yet" and marked what follows as a new paragraph. In the proofs, "He spoke well on the

murder"—should you not add "in Scotland".[41] We have no such rule in the English Law.

P. 53: "*worthy-like* Clergyman". This is a Scotticism.[42] I don't know what it means and therefore know not how to supply its place.[43]

In p. 58: mark +++. There is a loose paper wanting here.[44]

To Malone,
Friday 10 June 1785
MS. Yale (L 918).
ADDRESS: To Edmond Malone Esq.

[London] Friday, 10 June

DEAR SIR: From Baldwins[1] where I lay last night I send you from p. 59 to p. 82 inclusive.[2] I think the little Original Book will do surprisingly.[3] At the foot of p. 58 is the passage which I *now* keep in instead of the reference which you missed.[4] On p. 79 is a *blank*

point" was changed to "He thus treated the point" (1st ed. p. 88; *Life* v. 87).

[41] Added in the "Tour" MS. (1st ed. p. 88; *Life* v. 87).

[42] Addition of "-like" to adjectives to form new adjectives is especially common in Scottish; see OED, -like, *suffix*, 2. a. and *Scot. Nat. Dict.*, -like, 1.

[43] In the "Tour" MS. "-like" was deleted (1st ed. p. 93; *Life* v. 91).

[44] What EM took as a mark to indicate a Paper Apart actually was JB's start of a line beneath "Johnson" (to italicize his name as speaker), with three perpendicular marks to delete (see 1st ed. p. 98, last line, and *Life* v. 96, line 1). However, JB thought EM was referring to a mark lower on the page (*post* To EM, 10 June and n. 4).

[1] Henry Baldwin (c. 1734–1813), proprietor of the Britannia Printing Office, Fleet Street, was the founder of *St. James's Chron.*, whose contributors included "a phalanx of the first-rate wits, Bonnel Thornton, Garrick, Colman, Steevens, etc. etc." (*Gent. Mag.* 1813, lxxxiii. pt. 1. 190). JB had known Baldwin since at least 1769 (Journ. 14 Oct. 1769), and on 30 Apr. arranged with him for the printing of the "Tour" (Journ.). Baldwin also printed EM's edition of Shakespeare, published in 1790 but already in the press (*post* From EM, ?23 June and n. 2), and the *Life* in 1791.

[2] This section of the "Tour" MS. runs from near the beginning of the entry for 24 Aug. to the end of the entry for 25 Aug. (*Life* v. 96, line 17 to v. 110, line 4).

[3] JB refers to his original journal (J 33), now serving as copy for the printer (*ante* From EM, between 3 and 10 June, n. 3).

[4] *Ante* From EM, between 3 and 10 June and n. 44. JB thought EM's query at the end of the previous letter referred to a passage crossed out at the bottom of p. 58 of the "Tour" MS. rather than to the mark near the top of the page, which EM mistakenly interpreted as a *signe de renvoi* for a missing Paper Apart. Above the crossed-out section (the beginning of the entry for 24 Aug.) JB had written, then deleted, "N.B. go to folio leaf", and had written

after *due* because I forgot whether due *east* or due *what*. Can you supply it from any Book of antiquities?[5] I ever am very much yours,

James Boswell

Pray see if I have ommitted any additional member of our Club. Do you know I had ommitted Steevens—Monstrous![6]

From Malone, Saturday 11 June 1785

MS. Yale (C 1889).
ADDRESS: Mr. Boswell.

[London] June 11

Dear Sir: I send you a few very hasty notes. In your projected University[1] there is some difficulty. When you were on your tour,

"stet" five times in the margin of the crossed-out passage. The cancelled Paper Apart ("folio leaf") is missing.

[5] The passage in the "Tour" MS. is mutilated but can be restored by reference to the 1st ed. (p. 113; *Life* v. 107): "<all that re>mains is the two stone<s s>et up on end with a l<on>g <one> laid between them <as wa>s usual, and one stone due from them." EM apparently being unable to supply the missing word, JB crossed out "due" and substituted "at a little distance", the reading of the 1st ed.

[6] This query refers to a Paper Apart (for a footnote) to p. 82 of the "Tour" MS. (M 133, pp. 47–48; 1st ed. p. 115 n.; *Life* v. 109 n. 5), listing the members of The Club. For EM's answer to JB's query, see *post* From EM, 11 June and n. 7. George Steevens (1736–1800), editor of Shakespeare and at one time EM's mentor in Shakespearian studies, was elected to The Club on 4 Mar. 1774 (*Annals*, p. 142). In January a number of anonymous reviews and essays containing anecdotes of SJ had appeared in *St. James's Chron.*; on 25 Jan. Henry Baldwin had written to JB identifying Steevens as the author of almost all the items. In the issue of 8–11 Jan. Steevens had praised JB's projected "Life of Johnson" in glowing terms: "To Mr. Boswell the Publick will be indebted, on the Subject of our Author's Life, for genuine and ample Information as well as Entertainment. . . . During his long Association with the Doctor in England, as well as throughout his Hebridian Tour, he may be pronounced to have lost no Opportunity of Search respecting the past Occurrences of our Author's Life, or his Sentiments relative to Men and Literature; nor will it be suspected by those who are acquainted with Mr. Boswell's active Mind, that his Curiosity permitted one Circumstance to escape him that might illustrate the Habits, or exalt the Character of the Sage whom he respected almost to Adoration." Later, however, Steevens was critical of JB's Johnsonian projects (*post* To EM, 25 Feb. 1791 and n. 7). For Steevens's relations with EM, see *post* To EM, 4 Dec. 1790 and n. 23, 16 Dec. 1790 and n. 13; 17 May 1793 and n. 1.

---

[1] *Ante* To EM, 10 June and n. 6. SJ and JB thought the members of The Club would make a fine faculty to revive the declining University of St. Andrews (*Tour*, 1st ed. pp. 114–15; *Life* v. 108–09).

Mr. *Vesey* could not be speculated[2] on as Professor of[3] any thing, for I strongly suspect he was not in 1773 a member;[4] but you may ascertain that matter by the book at Baxter's.[5]

You will find an exact list of the Club in the order they were chosen, in the Gentleman's Magazine for Feby. last—p. 98.[6] Yours very truly,

E. MALONE

P. S. You have omitted the two WARTONS GIBBON and Dr. Scott—Quere, was the latter a Member in 1773?[7]

From Malone, Thursday ?23 June 1785[1]

MS. Yale (C 1890).
ADDRESS: Mr. Boswell.

[London] Thursday Evening

MY DEAR SIR, I would wait on you to-morrow with the greatest

[2] MS. "pro" or "per" deleted before "speculated"

[3] MS. "for" deleted before "of"

[4] Agmondesham Vesey (d. 11 Aug. 1785). Accountant-General of Ireland, 1736–81, and a member of the Irish Privy Council, he was elected to The Club 2 Apr. 1773 (*Annals*, pp. 9, 139; *Liber Munerum Publicorum Hiberniae*, ed. Rowley Lascelles, 1852, I. ii. 137, iii. 121; *Roy. Kal.* 1785, p. 252). His wife Elizabeth was well-known as a bluestocking hostess (*Annals*, pp. 9–10; *Life* iii. 424 and n. 3).

[5] In 1785 The Club was meeting at Baxter's in Dover St. The "book at Baxter's", the folio volume recording attendance at Club meetings (Minute Book), is now deposited in the British Library.

[6] *Gent. Mag.* (1785) lv. 98–99. On 2 Mar. EM had written to Thomas Percy, Bishop of Dromore since 1782, "you will see a complete list [of The Club] in the *G. M.* for this month, I suspect sent by Mr Steevens" (*Percy Corres.* p. 22). EM's surmise was confirmed by a note from George Steevens to John Nichols, publisher of *Gent. Mag.*, sent with the copy for the list of Club members (MS. Osborn Collection). The list is not entirely accurate.

[7] Apparently EM refers not to the list in JB's Paper Apart (*ante* To EM, 10 June, n. 6), but to the text itself, which lists those who were members in 1773. All of the names listed by EM are found in the Paper Apart (Steevens's was the only name added later); none of them, however, were members in 1773, and so none are mentioned in the text. As for the two Wartons, Joseph (see *ante* To DG, 18 Sept. 1771, n. 13) was elected in Jan. 1777, Thomas (see *ante* To DG, 30 March 1771, n. 11) in Mar. 1782. Edward Gibbon (1737–94), who in 1785 was in Lausanne completing his *History of the Decline and Fall of the Roman Empire*, 1776–88, was elected in 1774. William Scott (1745–1836), lawyer and one of SJ's executors, was elected in 1778. For dates of members' election to The Club, see Croker, i. 529.

[1] The dating of this letter depends on the dates of JB's attendance at the levee at St. James's, which was held on Wednesdays

pleasure, but I have an accumulation of *Sheets*[2] on my hands, that have been growing into a heep by my negligence these some days past.—If you can give me an hour before or after levee,[3] I am much at your service; or at any time on Saturday morning.—Yours very truly,

E. MALONE

From Malone,
?July 1785[1]
MS. Yale (C 1891).
ADDRESS: Mr. Boswell.

[London] Tuesday Nine o'clock

MY DEAR SIR: What is the hour fixed for our seeing the Queen's Palace[2] to-day, and where are we to meet? Be so good as to let me know, that I may acquaint the ladies.[3]—Yours most faithfully,

E. MALONE

and Fridays during the summer of 1785 (*Roy. Kal.* 1785, p. 95). EM's letter, written Thursday, clearly refers to a Friday levee; JB's journal shows that he attended the levee on Friday 20 May and Friday 24 June. If JB wished to meet with EM to revise the "Tour" MS., as seems likely, then the date 23 June seems most probable for this letter. It should be noted that there is a gap in the journal for 19–26 Aug., so we cannot show that JB did not attend the levees held on Friday 19 Aug. and Friday 26 Aug. (*Lond. Chron.* 18–20 Aug. lviii. 174, 25–27 Aug. p. 198). The formality of the closing formula suggests that the letter belongs among the first few that EM and JB exchanged; see *Hebrides*, p. xviii.

[2] Presumably sheets of EM's edition of Shakespeare, which was in the press as early as March (*Percy Corres.* p. 22).

[3] The levee was generally held in early afternoon; on 24 June it broke up at about 3 p.m. (*Lond. Chron.* 23–25 June, lvii. 606).

[1] The date of this letter is uncertain. July 1785 is suggested by the mention in JB's journal of two similar excursions with EM and his "ladies" (n. 3 below) in July, though this one is not mentioned. On 3 July JB, EM, the "ladies", Courtenay, and Windham visited Richmond. On 7 July the same party (except Windham) saw Strawberry Hill and Pope's grotto at Twickenham, and dined in Bushey Park.

[2] Buckingham House, which had been settled on Queen Charlotte by act of Parliament in 1775.

[3] By "the ladies" EM presumably means his sisters Henrietta (c. 1745–1824) and Catharine (c. 1748–1831) (*Gent. Mag.* 1824, xciv. pt. 2. 189; 1831, ci. pt. 1. 476) and his sister-in-law Philippa Rooper (d. 1831), married to Richard Malone (c. 1738–1816), who on 30 June had been created Baron Sunderlin of Lake Sunderlin [I.]. Lord Sunderlin and "the ladies" had stopped in London on their way to the Continent (Prior, *Malone*, p. 129).

From Malone,
?Summer or December 1785

MS. Yale (C 1892).
ADDRESS: Mr. Boswell, at General Paoli's, Upper Seymour Street.
NOTE by Malone: The packet is gone to Baldwin's.

Wrapper only. Enclosure not reported. The date is uncertain because the "packet" could refer to copy either for the first or the second edition, though copy for the first edition is perhaps more likely. See *post* From EM, 26 Aug., "Your packets are gone to Baldwin's", which suggests that at least some of the copy for the first edition was sent to the printer from EM's.

From Malone,
Tuesday 9 August 1785[1]

MS. Yale (C 1893).
ADDRESS: Mr. Boswell.

[London] Tuesday Evening

MY DEAR SIR: I am so much in arrear that I must devote the whole of to-morrow to preparing some copy for my compositors, who are at a dead stand-still in consequence of my late neglect; but I will give you the *whole of thursday*[2];—I shall expect you at breakfast, and we will have a beefstake above stairs.

Thank you for your information about Sir J. R. I will send to him to-morrow, and also to G. P. etc. for next Monday.[3] Yours Affectionately,

E. MALONE

[1] JB wrote in his journal for Wednesday 10 Aug., "Malone was busy with his Shakespeare. So we did not *sit* upon my Tour." Thus 9 Aug. is the most likely date for this letter; it is confirmed by the journal entries for Thursday 11 Aug. and Monday 15 Aug. (nn. 2 and 3 below).

[2] See Journ. 11 Aug.: "Malone devoted the whole of this day to me, that we might get forward with my Tour. I breakfasted dined drank tea and supt with him, and sat till near two in the morning. Yet we did not get a great deal winnowed, there was so very much chaff in that portion of it."

[3] See Journ. Monday 15 Aug.: "Dined at Malone's with General Paoli Sir Joshua Reynolds. . . . Tour till late." For Pasquale Paoli, see *ante* From DG, 25 Nov. 1767, n. 4; From DG, 12 July 1769, n. 3. JB had known Sir Joshua Reynolds since 1772; probably EM's information about him had to do with whether he was available for dinner on the 15th.

From Malone,
Tuesday 23 August 1785[1]
MS. Yale (C 1894).
ADDRESS: Mr. Boswell.

[London] Tuesday 6 o'clock

MY DEAR SIR, I enclose the Revise of Aa, which is now to be *for press*; but you had best take a last look at it.

You have also the new proof, Bb, which was brought here about four o'clock.—The description of *Col*, you may remember, I had some apprehensions about, on account of the great number of small particulars, and *short* paragraphs.[2] I have endeavoured to remedy the latter, by running sometimes two into one, and hope it will meet your approbation. Yours most faithfully,

E. M.

From Malone,
Friday 26 August 1785[1]
MS. Yale (C 1895).
ADDRESS: Mr. Boswell.

[1]The date of this letter is inferred from information in JB's letters, journal, and expense account. Sheet T (pp. 273–88) of the "Tour" had been printed by Wednesday 3 Aug. (To Thomas Barnard, 3 Aug.), and the last proofs arrived from Baldwin's on 20 Sept. (Journ.). The printing was finished on 22 Sept. Ten sheets remained after Aa (pp. 353–68). Since JB, EM, and Baldwin's compositors were producing about two sheets a week, and this letter was written on a Tuesday, the most likely date is 23 Aug. This inference is supported by evidence that EM was left in charge of the revise of sheet Aa: the proof of this sheet has corrections by both JB and EM, but the revise shows corrections in EM's hand only. There is a gap in the journal from 19 to 26 Aug., but JB's expense account (A 39.1) shows that on 20 Aug. he hired a "Horse to London returning from Mr. Barnard's", on 21 Aug. he spent two shillings on coach-hire, and at some time before 23 Aug. he took a "Jaunt to Streatham". Apparently JB was out of town while EM finished sheet Aa.

[2] EM mistakenly wrote "paragraphs" for "sentences". He combined a number of short sentences in the description of Coll in the proof of sheet Bb (P 84, pp. 372–74; see Introduction, p. 176).

[1] The date of this letter is established by EM's reference to "the parchment you talked of, from your brother's". The "parchment" was a pedigree or "diploma" drawn up for Thomas David Boswell ("T.D.") (1748–1826) in 1775, when he was a merchant in Spain. It had been signed by Robert Boswell, Deputy Lyon King of Arms for Scotland, and his signature had been authenticated by John

FROM MALONE, 26 AUGUST 1785

[London] Friday 12 o'clock

MY DEAR SIR: Mr. Strutt, the engraver,[2] called on me yesterday evening, and I find (as I once suspected) your scheme is not practicable in copper,[3] without a great deal of trouble.—When any thing is cut in copper, the operation is exactly the reverse of the printing types. The former is cut in, the latter stand out:—The consequence is, that the copper cut must be worked off in a *Rolling* press— either before or after the sheet is worked off in the Printing House, so that the sheet is wetted twice; and it is very difficult to make the engraving stand even in the page. To avoid this difficulty, the curious sometimes get the *whole* title page *engraved*, and then there is but one operation. But this certainly is not worth while.[4]

You can however have your crest cut in wood, the wooden block being contrived to fit in along with the printing types, so as to be worked at the same time with the rest of the page.—I wrote last night by the penny post to the most famous hand in London in that way,[5] to call here to-morrow at eleven; but as he is obliged to follow his pattern exactly from not being a draftsman, will it not be best to get the parchment you talked of, from your brother's, to shew him? My servant is going to Norfollk Street, and can carry your dispatch to Thanet Place.[6]

Your packets are gone to Baldwin's. Yours most faithfully,

EDMOND MALONE

Wilkes, Lord Mayor of London (see *post* From EM, 5 Oct. n. 22), and the Principe di Masserano, Ambassador from Spain (To Wilkes, 26 May 1775; From Wilkes, 5 June 1775). JB wrote to Robert Boswell on Friday 26 Aug. asking for a copy of the crest on his brother's diploma; Robert replied on 30 Aug., enclosing a drawing of the crest (a hooded hawk) and adding, "I dare say there is a painting on the Diploma sent to your brother." JB used a slightly altered version of the drawing (To Robert Boswell, 19 Dec.); his expense account shows that on 7 Sept. he paid five shillings to have the woodcut made (A 39.1), which was used on the title-page of the 1st ed.

[2] Joseph Strutt (1749–1802), author, antiquary, painter, and engraver.

[3] MS. "copper" written above deleted "brass"

[4] For the 2nd ed. JB's crest was engraved in copper. See *post* To EM, 30 Oct. and n. 16; From EM, 5 Nov. p. 268; To EM, 11 Nov. and n. 9.

[5] Unidentified.

[6] T.D. lived in Thanet Place (From T. D. Boswell, 2 June 1784) in the Strand, just west of Temple Bar, and close by Norfolk St.

FROM MALONE, 5 OCTOBER 1785

From Malone,
Wednesday 5 October 1785

MS. Yale (C 1896).

ADDRESS in Courtenay's hand: Jams. Boswell Esq., Auchinleck, Cumnock, Dumfries.

FRANK: London Octbr. fifth 1785. Free J. Courtenay.[1]

POSTMARKS: 5 OC, FREE.

London, Octr. 5, 1785

MY DEAR SIR, I heartily congratulate you on the astonishing success of your labours. Dilly[2] called upon me yesterday, and told me that before the end of this week a thousand copies will probably have been issued;[3] so that there will [be] an immediate call for a second edition, which must be put to press before you return to town.

I see so very few people that I can tell you little of the vox populi. Sir J. R. has read the Tour *twice* over, and is very lavish in its praise. Windham is returned to town and I have seen him, but not since he has read it.[4] I understand however from Sir J. R. that one of his remarks is that he thinks you do not seem sufficiently warm and hearty towards Dr. J. I cannot say I think there is any foundation for this. Another person[5] thinks you have paid too much court to your countrymen. Mr. Courteney is just come from Bath and is highly pleased as far as he is gone. He wishes with me that Veronica had been left quietly in her nursery.[6] He agrees

[1] John Courtenay (1738–1816), Irish-born M.P. for Tamworth, 1780–96, and Appleby, 1796–1807, who, though poor and in ill health, gained wide admiration for his political skill and caustic wit. Courtenay first appears in JB's journals in the summer of 1785. Doubtless the two were introduced by EM, and soon Courtenay became one of JB's closest friends. He supplied both JB and EM with franks, helped mediate JB's dispute with Lord Macdonald, and shored up JB's sagging spirits while EM was in Ireland in 1790–91. Philip Metcalfe (*post* From EM, 12 Aug. 1788, n. 10) called Courtenay, JB, EM, and Sir Joshua Reynolds "the Gang" (Journ. 4 Jan. 1790). Courtenay also wrote poetry; among his productions was *A Poetical Review of the Literary and Moral Character of the Late Samuel Johnson, L.L.D.*, 1786 (see *post* To and From EM, 13 Jan.–7 Apr. 1786).

[2] For Dilly, see *ante* To EB, 2 Mar. 1780, n. 2. JB called Dilly's establishment at No. 22 Poultry "my literary headquarters" (To John Wilkes, 23 Mar. 1779), and when in London often received mail there.

[3] Fifteen hundred copies of the 1st ed. had been printed (EM to Charles Burney, 17 Oct.—MS. J. R. G. Comyn, Turnastone, Herefordshire). This information was kindly supplied by John Riely.

[4] William Windham (1750–1810), M.P. for Norwich since 1784, member of The Club since 1778, and close friend of SJ and EM.

[5] Unidentified.

[6] In the *Tour* JB relates that his four-month-old daughter Veronica (1773–95)

entirely also with me in thinking that is no defence to say—"that is my mode or turn"; and that any part or passage of a book that is vulnerable does[7] not barely operate by itself against the writer, but also casts a shade over other parts that are excellent and invulnerable. Thus, for example, had your admirable character of Johnson[8] been published by Hume or Robertson,[9] everyone would instantly allow its merit; but some people will always be weak enough not to credit their own understanding, and will be so staggered by what they have found elsewhere wrong[10] or out of place, that they will *doubt* about what is incontrovertibly excellent.

I see but one newspaper, and enclose you a couple of scraps from it.[11] I gave Dilly an extract or two for the *Publick Advertiser*; for extracts, when the printer owns from whence he took them, are always of use.[12] Your original advertisement mentioned "some

greeted SJ with "a little infantine noise" and other signs that JB interpreted as showing fondness for him. JB resolved that "she should have five hundred pounds of additional fortune" (1st ed. pp. 16–17; *Life* v. 25–26). Veronica died (four months after her father) before she had received her inheritance, but the money was paid into her estate (see F. A. Pottle, "Notes on the Importance of Private Legal Documents for the Writing of Biography and Literary History", *Proceedings of the American Philosophical Society*, 1962, cvi. 327–30).

[7] MS. "is not only" deleted before "does"

[8] 1st ed. pp. 6–11; *Life* v. 16–20.

[9] EM is referring to the histories of David Hume and Principal William Robertson (see *ante* From DG, 3 July 1777, n. 12).

[10] MS. "wrong" written above deleted "weak"

[11] Two clippings from an untraced issue of *Morn. Her.*, between 1 and 5 Oct., are preserved with EM's letter. The first reprints an anecdote from the *Tour* about George Faulkner and SJ (1st ed. pp. 37–38; *Life* v. 44); the other pokes fun at JB: "Pray why are the various *Commentators* on Dr. Johnson, so careful of his reputation,—*Editor Boswell*, among the rest? Is there no way of getting into notice, but by paniering a Corsican General, or a Literary Doctor, and making them carry *rubbish*?"

[12] Soon after the publication of the *Tour*, numerous quotations from and allusions to it appeared in the newspapers. *Pub. Adv.* 1 Oct. p. [2] carried excerpts headed "Boswell's Version of Johnsoniana", including passages on Thomas Cooke, translator of Hesiod (1st ed. p. 30; *Life* v. 37), on Lord Hailes (pp. 31–32; v. 38–39), on Kennicott's Bible and the bulging wall at Edinburgh College (pp. 35–36; v. 42–43), and on George Faulkner (pp. 37–38; v. 44). The same selection had been printed in *Gazetteer*, 30 Sept. (*post* From EM, 19 Oct. and n. 39), and the last item was reprinted in *Morn. Her.* (see preceding note) and in *Lond. Chron.* (1–4 Oct.) lviii. 323. *Pub. Adv.* 5 Oct. p. [3] printed the anecdote of George Graham and Oliver Goldsmith (p. 100; v. 97), the issue for 6 Oct. p. [2] printed some of JB's anecdotes of EB (p. 24 n.; v. 32 n. 3), and the issue for 7 Oct. p. [4] printed SJ's remark that "being in a ship is being in a *jail*, with the chance of being *drowned*" (p. 151; v. 137). To this was added an anecdote not found in the *Tour*: "Dr. Johnson, though a professed enemy to punning, yet, occasionally, could not help indulging himself in this species of wit, particularly if it tended to satire. When the Doctor visited the University of St. Andrews, a place famous for bestowing academical honours without much discrimination, he took occasion to enquire of one of the Professors into the state of their funds, and being told that they were not so

Latin Poems", and that has been copied in all the papers, instead of "Some poetical pieces", the words of the title. It has done some harm; for it has a tendency to cut off one class of purchasers; females, who (as the words are so general) may think half the book is Latin. An instance of this has come within my knowledge. To guard against it, and to puff *obliquely*, I gave D[illy] a paragraph importing that the Latin poems were only three, all very *short*, but so exquisite that every classical reader must[13] wish them much longer.[14]

Now for the second edition. I have read the whole once more over, and with great delight. As I went along, I put down a table of errata, which cover two half sheets. Many of them however are very minute. Your practice of writing a large B instead of a small one, in[15] the middle of a sentence, has hurt some paragraphs, and they will look better hereafter.—[16]

affluently endowed as many of their neighbours,—No matter, said the Doctor dryly, persevere in the plan you have formed, and you will get rich by *degrees*." This anecdote had appeared earlier in *Gen. Eve. Post*, 1–4 Oct. p. [4]. Cf. *Journey*, where SJ wrote, "The indiscriminate collation of degrees has justly taken away that respect which they originally claimed as stamps, by which the literary value of men so distinguished was authoritatively denoted" (p. 17). *Pub. Adv.* printed further extracts from the *Tour* in the issues for 12 Oct. p. [2], 31 Oct. p. [2] (an especially lengthy collection of extracts), and 1 Nov. p. [3]. Since the extracts in *Pub. Adv.* for 1 Oct. are apparently reprinted from *Gazetteer*, and the extract in the 7 Oct. issue is accompanied by an apocryphal anecdote that EM probably would not have inserted, perhaps EM refers here to the extracts printed in the issues for 5 and 6 Oct.

[13] MS. "must" written above deleted "would"

[14] The earliest advertisements for the *Tour* stated that it would contain "some Latin Poems, by Dr. Johnson, relative to the Tour, and never before published" (*St. James's Chron.* 10–13 Sept. p. [3]; *Lond. Chron.* 10–13 Sept. lviii. 255). The title-page of the 1st ed. reads, *Containing Some Poetical Pieces by Dr. Johnson, Relative to the Tour, and Never Before Published*. The paragraph that EM gave to Dilly was printed in *Pub. Adv.* 5 Oct. p. [3]: "The Latin Poems by Dr. Johnson, inserted by Mr. Boswell in his tour, are very short, consisting only of two Odes, and an Elegy of about twenty lines; but they are so highly finished, that every classical reader must wish them longer." The paragraph, slightly altered, was reprinted in a later issue of *Pub. Adv.* (21 Oct. p. [3]), and in *St. James's Chron.* 18–20 Oct. p. [4].

[15] MS. "has hurt half" deleted before "in"

[16] EM refers to JB's habit of beginning sentences with "But", an example of which occurs on p. 48 of the 1st ed. of the *Tour*, where, in a paragraph of seventeen lines, JB began three sentences with "But". In the 2nd ed. EM changed the first and third examples, reducing the "B" of "But" to lower case and substituting colons for periods to link sentences (*Life* v. 53, paragraph beginning "From an erroneous". In this and the following letters dealing with revisions for the 2nd ed. of the *Tour*, page references to the 2nd ed. are not given except where its pagination is different from that of the 1st ed. References to *Life* v. are given where the reading is identical or nearly identical to that of the 2nd ed.).

[He spoke well in favour of entails, to preserve lives of men whom mankind are accustomed to reverence.] Think of "*lives* of men" escaping us both in p. 106, l. 8, instead of *lines*, I suppose.[17]

A friend of Dilly's has suggested an errour, not of the press, but the pen,—in 35 at bottom. [We talked of *Kennicot's* Translation of the Bible, and hoped it would be quite faithful.] Dr. Kennicot did not translate the bible but publish an edition of the Hebrew text, collated with various Mss.—so it must run, "we talked of Kennicot's edition of the Hebrew Bible"—

I will not trouble you with a number of small typographical errours, which you may safely trust to me, if the second edition should go to press before you return;[18] but there are a few paragraphs that might be improved, and I should be glad to have your opinion. I have also some queries for you.

P. 4, note: [Our friend *Edmund Burke*, who by this time had received some pretty sore rubs from Dr. Johnson . . .] "sore rubs". Is not this a vulgar phrase—"smart blows" would be better, though I do'nt like it much.

P. 8, ll. 12–13: [though grave and aweful in his deportment, when he thought it necessary or proper, he frequently indulged himself in pleasantry and sportive sallies.] would not the sense be more nicely marked if the sentence run—"he frequently indulged himself, when he thought it necessary or proper, in pleasantry" etc.

P. 9, l. 4: [*While therefore Doctor Johnson's sayings are read, let his manner be*] "taken *along*". I believe this is not legitimate, and that it should be "along *with them*". A lady to whom I read it, did not *understand* it. This is always a good criterion.

Ibid.: "He was now" etc. [in his sixty-fourth year]: "he was become a little deaf". Would it not be better (to avoid such short sentences) to read—"sixty fourth year; *and* was become" etc.

P. 33, l. 7: [I loved to behold Dr. Samuel Johnson rolling about in this old magazine of antiquities.] "I *loved* to behold" etc. Perhaps better—"It gave me pleasure to behold"—

P. 49: [When we came to Leith, I talked with perhaps too

[17] For JB's replies to the comments and queries in this letter, see *post* To EM, 13 Oct.

[18] In a collation of the first three editions, Chapman (pp. 461–79), records a number of minor changes. JB did not return to London until 17 Nov. (Journ.), by which time a good part of the 2nd ed. had been printed (e.g. sheet D, pp. 33–48, apparently was printed on 4 Nov.; see *post* From EM, 5 Nov. and n. 2). JB and EM revised the last sheets on 20 Dec. (Journ.).

boasting an air, how pretty the Frith of Forth looked; as indeed, after the prospect from Constantinople, of which I have been told, and that from Naples, which I have seen, I believe the view of that Frith and its environs, from the Castle-hill of Edinburgh, is the finest prospect in Europe. "Aye (said Mr. Johnson) that is the state of the world."] "Water is the same every where"—The train of thought here wants a little expansion. To a common reader it is by no means clear.

P. 63: "I was pleased, *curiously pleased*"—[to see Dr. Johnson actually in St. Andrew's, of which we had talked so long.] May not the two words underscored be well spared? *Curiously* you know, I have long objected to.

P. 65: [*Watson* said, "Dr. Hugh Blair took a week to compose a sermon."—*Johnson.* "Then, Sir, that is for want of the habit of composing quickly, which I am insisting one should acquire."—*Watson* said, "Blair was not composing all the week".] "Watson *said*"—twice—Both the *saids* may be omitted; or if not, it then should be "*Dr.* Watson said".

P. 67, l. 13: [Dr. Johnson enforced the strict observance of Sunday. Said he, "It should be different from another day."] "*Said* he, 'It' " etc. This is the only *Said he*, at the *beginning* of a sentence, that has escaped us. It is peculiarly ungraceful; and may be easily changed. "It should be different, he observed", etc.

P. 82, l. *ult.*: [*Gory*, my lord's black servant,] "was sent as our guide *so far*". What is this? I really know not. Is it that Gory was sent to attend you *to a certain distance from Lord M.'s house*? If so, it should be said, and "[Gory"[19] etc. should begin a new paragraph.

P. 160, l. 2: "*Hay's* were the two best"—Here is a difficulty that I cannot solve. In p. 142 you call your two Highland guides John *Gray* and Laughlan Vass. Now, who is *Hay*? In the former page should it be "John *Hay*", or in the latter "*Gray's* were the two best"?

P. 70, l. penult.: [He said our judges had not gone] "deep in literary property". Quere "deep in *the question concerning* literary property".

P. 85, l. 18: [He asked, if weaving the plaids was ever a domestick art in the Highlands, like spinning or knitting. He could not be informed here. But he conjectured probably, that

[19] The square bracket before "Gory" is EM's paragraph marker.

where people lived so remote from each other] "it *would* be a domestick art".—This is a Scotticism.[20] Better "it was likely to be a domestick art".

P. 107, l. 1: ["Sir Joshua Reynolds, Sir, is the most invulnerable man I know; the man with whom, if you should quarrel, you would find the most difficulty how to abuse."] Would it not run neater thus?—"the man, whom, if you should quarrel with him, you would find the most difficulty how to abuse".

P. 171, l. 3: [Dr. Johnson said, the inscription should have been in Latin, as every thing intended to be universal and permanent, should be.] "the inscription *should* have been" etc. "as every intended" etc. *should be*. Quere "as every thing intended" etc. "*ought to* be".

P. 263: [Mr. M'Queen had often talked to me of a curious piece of antiquity near this, which he called a temple of the Goddess *Anaitis*. Having often talked of going to see it . . .] "Mr. McQ. had often *talked*". Better *mentioned* to avoid the repetition; for *talked* occurs just afterwards.

P. 355, l. 16: [He was about seventy-seven years of age, a decent ecclesiastick, dressed in] "a suit of black"—Surely it should be "a suit of black *clothes*"—.

P. 414, l. 13: [Upon the left of its entrance there is a cascade, almost perpendicular] "from top to bottom". Quere "from the top to the bottom".

P. 447, l. 5: "I knew it was not the rule" etc.—[of modern high life to drink to any body.] Should it not rather be—"I knew it was the rule of modern high life *not* to drink" etc.

P. 467, l. 11: [He was a very distinguished scholar, was long abroad, and part of the time lived much with the learned Cuninghame.] "and part of the time". Should it not be, "and *for* part of the time", or "*during* part" etc.

P. 477, l. 19: [My learned friend's doubts appear to have had no foundation; for my respectable neighbour, Mr. Fairlie, who, with all his attention to agriculture, finds time both for the classicks and his friends . . .] "My learned friend's doubts" etc. Would it not be better—"*His* doubts" etc. for just afterwards you have—"for the classicks and his *friends*".

[20]"Would be" meaning "is likely to be" does not appear to be exclusively Scottish (OED, Will, v^1, B. II. 32. b), but "will be" meaning "is likely to be" is predominantly Scottish and Northern (Will, v^1, B. I. 15. d).

P. 279, l. 3: "No, Sir, there *is* none of the French Literati" etc. ["now alive, to visit whom I would cross a sea."] Should it not be—"there *are* none". I am not certain on this point.

P. 243, l. 1: [In conformity with this doctine, I myself, though fully persuaded that the House of *Stuart* had originally no right to the crown of *Scotland*; for that *Baliol*, and not *Bruce*, was the lawful heir; should yet have thought it very culpable to have rebelled, on that account, against Charles I.] Would it not run neater thus? "In conformity with this doctrine, though fully persuaded" etc. "I yet should have thought" etc.

P. 446, l. 10: [Dr. Johnson was much struck by the grandeur and elegance of this princely seat. He said, "What I admire here, is the total defiance of expence." I had a particular pride in shewing him a great number of fine old trees, to compensate for the nakedness which had made such an impression on him on the eastern coast of Scotland.—He thought the castle too low, and wished it had been a story higher.] "He thought the castle" etc. This is rather out of place. It would perhaps be better higher up, after "princely seat". "He thought *however* the castle" etc.

Don't forget Sir Joshua R.'s observation about Johnson's extraordinary motions not being *involuntary*; and therefore not exactly described.[21]

Sir J. says you have given Wilkes what does not belong to him, for that it was to him Burke quoted "Lege solutis" and that he told it to you: and he thinks B. so very fertile and ingenious that he would hardly have repeated the same joke to Wilkes, or in another company.[22]

[21] The reference is to a part of JB's description of SJ: "His head, and sometimes also his body, shook with a kind of motion like the effect of a palsy: he was frequently disturbed by cramps, or convulsive contractions, of the nature of that distemper called *St. Vitus's* dance" (1st ed. p. 9). F. W. Hilles suggests that Reynolds commented on the passage on 22 Sept., when the "jury" of JB's friends met to discuss the *Tour* (*Portraits*, p. 67; Journ. 22 Sept.). See further *post* To EM, 13 Oct. and n. 6; From EM, 19 Oct. and n. 7.

[22] EM refers to JB's note on EB's wit, which contains the following anecdote: "When Mr. *Wilkes*, in his days of tumultuous opposition, was bor'n upon the shoulders of the mob, Mr. Burke (as Mr. Wilkes told me himself, with classical admiration) applied to him what *Horace* says of *Pindar*,

——*Numeris*que fertur
LEGE *solutis*.

Sir Joshua Reynolds, who agrees with me entirely as to Mr. Burke's fertility of wit, said, that this was 'dignifying a pun' " (1st ed. p. 25 n.; *Life* v. 33 n. 3). John Wilkes (1725–97), M.P. for Middlesex (1768–69, 1774–90) and City Chamberlain for London (1779–97) had met JB in London in 1762 (Journ. 27 Nov. 1762), and they had become friends in Italy in 1765 (*Earlier*

Though I have scribled very fast, I shall barely save the post and have only just time to assure you that I am, my dear Sir, your much obliged and affectionate servant,

EDMOND MALONE

I forgot to tell you that Dilly talks of getting an Index made, which he says will help the second edition.[23]

To Malone,
Thursday 13 October 1785[1]
MS. Yale (L 919).

Auchinleck, 13 Octr. 1785

MY DEAR SIR: I found my Wife and five children all well on my arrival here, the 3d. current;[2] and I have since been favoured by you with most agreable accounts of my Literary child so kindly adopted by you. The success of the Tour truly exceeds even *our* expectations. I wonder at Windham's objection; for I am sure affection as well as veneration ever attend our illustrious Traveller, though as one of his *school*, I practise *discrimination.*[3] Neither do I think I have paid more court to such of my countrymen as are praised than they deserve. Sir Joshua's approbation is very flattering. He is in a mistake as to Burke's "LEGE *solutis*". I have not said that Burke said or repeated the joke to Wilkes; but that Wilkes *told* it to me; which is the fact for, I have it down in my *Boswelliana* at the time.[4] Sir Joshua and I at an after

Years, pp. 202–05, 207–09). For further discussion of this pun, see *post* To EM, 13 Oct. and n. 4; From EM, 19 Oct. and n. 19.

[23] See *post* To EM, 13 Oct. and n. 75; From EM, 5 Nov. p. 267; To EM, 11 Nov. and n. 8.

---

[1] An answer to EM's letter of 5 Oct., which it follows paragraph by paragraph.

[2] For JB's wife, Margaret Montgomerie, see *ante* To DG, 30 Mar. 1771, n. 1. His five children were Veronica, Euphemia (1774–1837), Alexander (1775–1822), James (1778–1822), and Elizabeth (1780–1814). JB had left London on 24 Sept. (Journ.) and arrived at Auchinleck on 3 Oct. (Book of Company). He had stopped *en route* to visit John Lee at Staindrop, co. Durham (*Pub. Adv.* 29 Sept. p. [3], 30 Sept. p. [2]).

[3] Sir Joshua Reynolds said of SJ, "He was fond of discrimination, which he could not show without pointing out the bad as well as the good in every character" (*Life* ii. 306; see also iii. 282).

[4] "Boswelliana" contains the following entry: "When Wilkes was borne on the shoulders of the unruly Mob Burke applied to him what Horace says of Pindar, Fertur

period talked of it, which has made him think that *he* told it.—I still remain of opinion that Dr. Johnson's extraordinary motions were *involuntary*. Had not that been the case, he surely would have restrained them in the publick streets. I therefore cannot omit or alter that part of his character. If you think it proper there may be a note to "convulsive contractions" as follows. "*Sir Joshua Reynolds is of opinion that Dr. Johnson's extraordinary gesticulations[5] were not involuntary. But I still think they were; for had not that been the case" etc. *as above*.[6]—Perhaps you and Mr. Courteney are right as to Veronica. I am convinced you are right as to the effect in *general* of weak parts in a Book and that *my way* is no excuse. But to omit Veronica *now* would do no good. It would not be put to *my* credit; Besides I am fond of it. So I insist on retaining it. But in the last line but two of that note for "Nihll" read "nih*i*l".[7] Let me add however that had Veronica not been printed I should *perhaps* have left it out. To omit it *now* would be to invite attacks, by flying.[8]

I am sorry that *Latin Poems* stood in the Advertisements instead of *Poetical Pieces*. Your *oblique* help was very good. Let us take care again.

I shall follow your letter paragraph by paragraph. It is amazing how many typographical errours have been discovered. I can entirely trust to you for the correction of all that you observe. *Lives* for *lines* in p. 106 makes strange nonsense.[9] If a second edition be

numeris legibus solutus, Mr. Wilkes, London, April 1778. N.B. Dr. Johnson thought this an admirable double pun. And he will seldom allow any merit to that species of witticism" (MS. Hyde Collection; see also *Boswelliana*, p. 291). Because JB trusted his contemporary record, Wilkes continued to receive credit for passing on the anecdote (*Tour*, 2nd ed. p. 25 n.; *Life* v. 33 n. 3). Horace's phrase, "numerisque fertur / Lege solutis" (*Odes* IV. ii. 11–12) means "is borne along in measures freed from rule" (trans. C. E. Bennett, Loeb ed.). EB's version may be translated, "[Wilkes], sprung from gaol is carried by his mob" (*Extremes*, p. 315 n. 6). The version in the *Tour* ruins the pun by reading "solutis", which agrees with "numeris", rather than "solutus", which would refer to Wilkes. The version in the *Life* reads "solutus" (iii. 323).

[5] MS. "gestures" written above "gesticulations"

[6] "As above" refers to the earlier clause in this letter, "he surely would have restrained them in the publick streets". For the note in its final form, see *post* From EM, 19 Oct. and n. 7.

[7] The misprint in *Nihil est, nisi hoc sciat alter* ("a thing is of no value unless someone else knows it") was corrected in the 2nd ed. (p. 16 n.; *Life* v. 25 n. 2). JB is adapting a line from Persius, *Satires* i. 27.

[8] The passage from "Let me add" to "flying" is crowded in as an afterthought between the previous sentence, which was to have been the last of the paragraph, and the first line of the following paragraph.

[9] Corrected in 2nd ed. (*Life* v. 101).

printed, I will have a table of all the Errata of any consequence (in which I include *alterations*) thrown off and given to the purchasers of the first edition, who may help their books with a pen.[10] Nice people no doubt will purchase the second edition though they have the first, and let the first go to the kitchen, or at least among the *Ladies maids*.

Capel Lofft suggested to Dilly the errour as to Kennicot which must as you suggest be altered to "edition of the Hebrew Bible".[11] Enclosed is an Extract which Dilly sent me from Loffts Letter which please keep for me.[12]

Now for your Queries.

P. 4, Note: "sore rubs" may not be elegant. But I think it does well connected with "oil of vitriol" which had been *applied*.[13]

P. 8, ll. 12–13: I find I am not understood here{:} "when he thought it necessary or proper" refers to "deportment" at which therefore there should be a semicolon or a hyphen—to prevent ambiguity.[14]

P. 9, l. 4: Most certainly—"along *with them*". The criterion of the Lady not understanding is infallible.[15]

Ibid.: "He was now" etc.—yes insert *and*.[16]

P. 33, l. 7: I think "I loved" a good warm expression.—And I declare I think my long Epithetical *Worthy* and *good* designations do very well. And they *cannot* now be omitted without giving room for reflection against the Gentlemen. So they must stand.[17]

[10] *Post* To EM, 27 Oct. and n. 39.

[11] So changed in 2nd ed. (pp. 35–36; *Life* v. 42).

[12] Capel Lofft (1751–1824), barrister and miscellaneous writer, first met JB at the Dillys' on 19 Mar. 1778 (Journ.). JB and Lofft had recently exchanged compliments, Lofft praising JB's *Letter to the People of Scotland*, 1785, and JB praising Lofft's *Essay on the Law of Libels*, 1785 (From Lofft, 7 June; To Lofft, 3 Aug.; From Lofft, 17 Aug.). JB published Lofft's letters in a broadside dated 27 Aug. 1785 (P 132), in *St. James's Chron.* 27–30 Aug. p. [4] and in *Edin. Adv.* (2–6 Sept.) xliv. 153. The extract from Lofft's letter sent by Dilly has not been reported.

[13] MS. "*severe*", in EM's hand, written above "sore". See *post* From EM, 21 Oct. p. 238; To EM, 27 Oct. and n. 36.

[14] In the 2nd ed. a dash was inserted after "proper" (*Life* v. 17).

[15] So changed in 2nd ed. (*Life* v. 18).

[16] So changed in 2nd ed. (ibid.).

[17] EM nevertheless changed "I loved" to "I was pleased" (*Life* v. 40), apparently without JB's approval, for sheet D, containing the passage, was printed before JB returned to London (*post* From EM, 5 Nov. and n. 2), and the phrase is not mentioned again in the extant correspondence. EM had not mentioned JB's "*Worthy* and *good* designations" on the same page, but JB, perhaps because he knew EM would object to such openly affectionate epithets, or perhaps because EM already had objected to them, takes this opportunity to defend the phrases "*Worthy Mr. James Kerr*" and "*Good Mr. Brown*". "Worthy" and "Good" were retained in the 2nd ed., but set in roman type.

P. 49: I am determined not to alter *now* in *any* degree *any* saying of Dr. Johnson's. So "Water" etc. must remain—though I see the obscurity. But *Authenticity* is my chief boast. So *maneat.*[18]

P. 63: I have no objection to dele "curiously pleased". But before the first "pleased" let there be "much" or "greatly" or "highly", or what *you* please to strengthen it.[19]

P. 65: Both the *saids* may be omitted. But after the first *took* must be changed to "*has taken* a week". For when put in the form of immediate relation, it is different from what it must be when told as of past relation. You will understand me here, and will alter either to "has taken" or in some other way. I think "has taken" better than "will take" (a common phrase) because—afterwards it is said "Blair *was* not composing" etc.[20]

P. 67: "*Said he*" out by all means and change it either to "saying 'it should' " etc. or to " ' It should be different' he observed", as you have suggested.[21]

P. 82: I thought *so far* had been clear enough. But since it is not, please add—and let *Gory* begin a new paragraph. Instead of *so far* it may be said *to the high road.* Or "to shew us *into* (is that english) the high road".[22]

P. 142: *Gray* should be *Hay* and therefore *Hay's* on p. 160 is right. Wonderful escape of all our vigilance.[23]

P. 70, l. penult.: "deep *in the question*" by all means.[24]

[18] "Let it remain." The passage was unchanged in the 2nd ed. In the "Tour" MS. and the 1st ed. a line from Ovid's *Amores*, "Una est injusti coerula forma maris" (II. xi. 12) had followed the quotation from SJ; in the 2nd ed. "coerula" was changed to "caerula" and the Latin line was made a part of SJ's speech. In the sentence preceding "Water is the same", "Mr. Johnson" was changed to "Dr. Johnson" (*Life* v. 54). EM apparently made these minor changes on his own, though JB certainly would have approved the change of "Mr." to "Dr." (*Life* v. 37 n. 2).

[19] 2nd ed.: "I was much pleased" (*Life* v. 65).

[20] 2nd ed. "*Watson.* 'Dr. Hugh Blair has taken a week to compose a sermon.' . . . *Watson.* 'Blair was not composing all the week' . . ." (*Life* v. 67).

[21] 2nd ed.: "It should be different (he observed) from another day" (*Life* v. 69).

[22] Following this paragraph EM wrote in square brackets in the MS. of JB's letter, "to conduct us to the high road"; accordingly, the 2nd ed. begins a new paragraph: "Gory, my lord's black servant, was sent as our guide, to conduct us to the high road" (*Life* v. 82). EM then wrote, "mem. 'This was another point' etc. not suff[icientl]y clear", thus reminding himself to draw attention to the sentence following the one just corrected (*post* From EM, 19 Oct. p. 233, To EM, 27 Oct. and n. 15).

[23] In the 2nd ed. "Gray" on p. 142 changed to "Hay" (*Life* v. 131). "Gray" in the 1st ed. was not a misprint, but an undetected mistake in the "Tour" MS.

[24] 2nd ed.: "He said, our judges had not gone deep in the question concerning literary property" (*Life* v. 72).

P. 85: Thank you for detecting the Scotticism "it *would* be". It may be altered to "it was likely to be" or "it must have been" or, "it was probably".[25]

P. 107, l. 1: Another saying of Dr. Johnson *now* printed and must be sacred. So *maneat*.[26]

P. 171, l. 3: Another *maneat*.[27]

P. 263: "Mr. M'Queen had often *mentioned*" instead of *talked*—Certainly.[28]

P. 355: Is not "a full suit of *black*" a common phrase? We say "clothed in purple" "drest in scarlet". But add *clothes* if you think it better with the addition.[29]

P. 414, l. 13: "from *the* top to *the* bottom". Yes.[30]

P. 447, l. 5: "I knew it was *not* the rule".—A good deal better.[31]

P. 467: "*during* part of the time" better.[32]

P. 477, l. 19: *His* better than "my learned friend's".[33]

P. 279, l. 3: Clearly *are* for *is*.[34]

P. 243: I like the passage as it stands. I like *myself—Moi*: It is more *avowed*. So let it remain.[35]

P. 446: "He thought however the Castle" etc. will come in better after "princely seat".[36]

And Now for my own Corrections.

Pages second and third of my Address to you, let there be a running title DEDICATION.[37] I wonder how I missed this.

P. 74: After "most sincerely yours" put the subscription JAMES BOSWELL. It was in the Original and there is a blank without it.[38]

P. 87, l. 17: [He told us Aberdeen exported stockings to the

[25] 2nd ed.: "it was likely to be" (*Life* v. 85).

[26] In the 2nd ed. the comma after "whom" was omitted; otherwise the passage was not changed (*Life* v. 102).

[27] Unchanged in 2nd ed. (*Life* v. 154).

[28] 2nd ed.: "Mr. M'Queen had often mentioned a curious piece of antiquity near this" (*Life* v. 218).

[29] So changed in 2nd ed. (*Life* v. 287).

[30] So changed in 2nd ed. (*Life* v. 331).

[31] JB approved EM's rephrasing, but miscopied the correction. 2nd ed.: "I knew it was the rule of modern high life not to drink to any body" (*Life* v. 356).

[32] So changed in 2nd ed. (p. 470; *Life* v. 373).

[33] So changed in 2nd ed. (p. 480; *Life* v. 380).

[34] So changed in 2nd ed. (*Life* v. 229).

[35] "Charles I." was expanded to "Charles the First", but otherwise the passage was not changed (*Life* v. 204).

[36] In the 2nd ed. the passage was rearranged as EM had proposed (*Life* v. 355).

[37] Added in 2nd ed. (pp. [v]–vii).

[38] JB refers to his letter to Lord Monboddo, 21 Aug. 1773 (*Life* v. 74). By "the Original" JB means the letter sent to Monboddo, which has not been reported; the copy he made in his journal, used as printer's copy, is not signed. The signature was added in the 2nd ed.

value of a hundred thousand pounds in peace, and to one hundred and seventy in war.] "*to* one hundred" etc. seems not right. Pray see and correct as you please.[39]

Ibid., l. 19: [Dr. Johnson asked, What made the difference? Here we had a proof of the different sagacity of the two professors.] I wish to get rid either of *difference* or *different* if you think it worth while. It must be the latter that is changed, if any; the former being Johnsonian. Would *comparative* do?[40]

Ibid., Note: [Dr. Johnson acknowledged that he was himself the author.] read Auth*ou*r. With the *u*.[41]

P. 93, Note, l. 6: [Gulielmi Rainie, Decani Guildae . . .] after "Rainnie" dele the comma. "Decani Guildae" is his official designation; but now it looks like a *name*.

Ib., l. 4: [honora bilium] "honorabilium".

Ib., l. 6: for "B*u*llivorum" read "B*a*llivorum". See if double l. right.

Ib., l. 7: [Thesaurii] "Thesaur*ar*ii".

Ib., l. 11: for "ex*e*miae" read "ex*i*miae".[42]

P. 95, l. 5: ["Warburton, by his extending his abuse, rendered it ineffectual."] Quere is *his* right before *extending*? I should think *not*.[43]

[39] EM made two trial revisions in blank spaces of the MS. of JB's letter: " 'He told us the [export of *deleted*] stockings exported from Aberdeen amounted in peace to a quantity which produced a hundred thousand pound' etc. or—'He told us that the value of the stockings exported from Aberdeen was one hundred' etc." Another draft is found in EM's copy of the 1st ed. (MS. Hyde Collection): "He told us that the value of stockings exported from Aberdeen was a hundred thousand pounds in peace, and amounted, in time of war, to one hundred and seventy thousand pounds." For further discussion of this passage see *post* From EM, 21 Oct. p. 241; To EM, 27 Oct. and n. 44.

[40] 2nd ed.: "the comparative sagacity of the two professors" (*Life* v. 86).

[41] So changed in the 2nd ed. (*Life* v. 86 n. 1). For a discussion of JB's devotion to spellings such as "authour", see *Earlier Years*, pp. 359, 545. SJ spelled the word "author" in his *Dictionary*, 1755.

[42] This and the preceding four items are corrections to the text of the burgess-ticket presented to SJ by the magistrates of Aberdeen; all of the changes were made in the 2nd ed. (*Life* v. 90 n. 2). "Ballivus" could be spelled with one "l" or two; JB's printer's copy read "Ballivorum", but EM chose to print "Balivorum" in the 2nd ed. In a burgess-ticket presented to JB's brother John at Aberdeen on 7 May 1764 (C 6.4), the word is spelled "Ballivorum". In the 2nd ed. "Abredoniae" in line 1 of the note was incorrectly changed to "Aberdoniae", perhaps by the printer.

[43] This difficulty resulted from confusion in marking the proofs for the 1st ed. The proof first read, "Warburton, by his extensive abuse". EM, who marked the proof, substituted "the" for "his" and changed "extensive" to "extensiveness", apparently intending to make the phrase "by the extensiveness of his abuse". Changing his mind, he deleted his alterations and wrote "stet" under "his"; he then changed

Ibid., l. 14: [He called Warburton's "Essay on Grace" a poor performance.] for "Essay on" read "Doctrine of". I think so. Please see.[44]

Ibid., l. 19: ["people had spoken with tongues, had spoken with languages which they never knew before".] dele *with* before *languages*. Should it not be done?[45]

P. 115, Note, l. ult.: [it will be acknowledged that we might have established a second university of high reputation.] "might have established". Quere? if "might establish" is not better.[46] Should there be a Note upon this note to observe that since the first edition it has been suggested by one of the Club who knew Mr. Vesey better that we had not assigned him a proper place. For that he was quite unskilled both in irish Antiquities and Celtick Learning; but might have been a good professor of Architecture which he really understood.[47]

P. 270, l. 12: ["Most of the great families of England have a secondary residence, which is called a jointure-house: let this be of that kind."] Is not *this* improper here applied to the house at some distance? Would not *it* be better?[48]

P. 281: [At breakfast, Dr. Johnson told us, that there was once a pretty good tavern in Catharine-street in the Strand. . . . When he returned to Lichfield, after having been in London, his mother asked him, whether he was one of those who gave the wall, or those who took it? "Now, said he, it is fixed that every man keeps to the right".] Should there not be inverted commas before "there was once a pretty good tavern" etc. and none in the middle of the last line, as also no "said he"?[49]

"extensive" to "extending his", but forgot to cancel the "stet" under the deleted "his". As a result, the 1st ed. reads "by his extending his abuse". 2nd ed.: "Warburton, by extending his abuse" (*Life* v. 93).

[44] So changed in 2nd ed. (*Life* v. 93).

[45] So changed in 2nd ed. (ibid.).

[46] So changed in 2nd ed. (p. 116 n.; *Life* v. 109 n. 5).

[47] The member of The Club who suggested this change of assignment for Vesey was Thomas Barnard (1726–1806), D. D., Bishop of Killaloe, who in a letter to JB of 14 Aug. stated that Vesey "knew as much of Irish Antiquities as Johnson himself; and as much of Celtick as Japonese. Architecture was really his Fort, which he understood better than any thing else, and had really a very good Taste in it, as well as some Knowledge, and in that Branch there was a Vacancy for him to fill, as the club had then no other adept to rival him." EM incorporated JB's remarks in a note to the 2nd ed. (*Life* v. 108 n. 8).

[48] 2nd ed.: "let the new house be of that kind" (*Life* v. 223).

[49] EM put the whole passage beginning with "there was once a pretty good tavern" in direct discourse, changing pronouns from third to first person as necessary, and dropping "said he" and other markers of indirect discourse (*Life* v. 230).

P. 341, l. 6: [*Johnson.* "Yes, said he; Goldsmith, rather than not speak, will talk of what he knows himself to be ignorant".] dele "said he" and read "Sir". Strange that after *Johnson* "said he" should have been left.[50]

P. 359, l. 19: [*Johnson.* "Aye, sir; but if you were shut up here . . ."] for "Aye" read "Ay".[51]

P. 386, l. 4 from the foot: [We sent to hire horses to carry us across the island of Mull to the shore opposite to Inchkenneth, the residence of Sir Allan M'Lean . . . to whose house we intended to go the next morning.] for *morning* read *day* or say "towards whose house we intended to proceed the next morning". *Day* is best. A long day's journey it is to *go to Sir Allan's.*[52]

P. 387, l. 2 and l. 4: [Dr. Johnson and I sat by ourselves at the inn, and talked a good deal.—I told him, that I had found, in Leandro Alberti's Description of Italy, a good deal of what Addison has given us in his *Remarks.*] *a good deal* occurs in both. Might not the second be *much.* Vary as you please.[53]

P. 480, l. 10: [My father . . . owned to me afterwards, himself, that he was somewhat at a loss how to answer.] I see no use for *himself.*[54]

P. 514, l. 16: [Pray unbend the busy brow, and frolick a little in a letter.] for *brow* read *bow.* It is "bow" in the original. But if *brow* will do as well it may remain.[55]

P. 519, l. 1 of the Advertisement: [*THE authour of* The Journey to the Western Islands . . .] make *The* roman and with a small *t.*[56]

P. 524, ll. 3 and 10: [and with those lighter strokes of Dr.

[50] "*Johnson*" is not in the "Tour" MS.; the printer apparently inserted it without authority, and it passed undetected both in the proof and the revise. 2nd ed.: "*Johnson.* 'Yes, sir; Goldsmith . . . ' " (*Life* v. 277).

[51] So changed in 2nd ed. (*Life* v. 290).

[52] 2nd ed.: "to whose house we intended to go the next day" (*Life* v. 310).

[53] 2nd ed.: "much of what Addison has given us" (p. 386; *Life* v. 310).

[54] Omitted in 2nd ed. (p. 483; *Life* v. 383).

[55] JB refers to the closing words of George Dempster's letter to him, 16 Feb. 1775, printed in part in the *Tour.* The original letter, edited by JB and EM and used as printer's copy, clearly reads "Pray unbend the busy bow". Apparently suspecting the inadvertent omission of a letter, JB changed "bow" to "brow" in the proofs. In the 2nd ed. "brow" was retained (p. 517; *Life* v. 409).

[56] SJ's advertisement in the newspapers extended his apology to MacLeod of Raasay for asserting incorrectly that Raasay acknowledged the chieftainship or superiority of the MacLeods of Skye. Probably JB wanted "The" before "Journey" to be italicized and lowercased so as to remove it from the title; but he wrote "make *The* roman" by mistake. The 2nd ed., however, was changed as JB wished: "*THE authour of the* Journey to the Western Islands" (p. 522; *Life* v. 412).

Johnson's satire. . . . I trust that they who are the object of them have good sense and good temper enough not to be displeased.

I have only to add, that I shall ever reflect with great pleasure on a Tour which has been the means of preserving so much of the enlightened and instructive conversation of one whose virtues will, I hope, ever be an object of imitation.] *Object* occurs in both. May not the first be *subject*?[57]

Additions to my Errata.

P. 76, l. 4 and l. 2 from the foot: [Monboddo is a wretched place, wild and naked, with a poor old house; though, if I recollect right, there are two turrets which mark an old baron's residence. . . . But his lordship is distinguished not only for "ancient metaphysicks," but for ancient *politesse.*] "*old* house" and "*old* Baron's residence". Is it worth while to vary. *Ancient* might do for the second. But "*ancient* Metaphysicks" and "*ancient* politesse" come in soon after. Do as you will.[58]

P. 81: [My lord was as hospitable as I could have wished, and I saw both Dr. Johnson and him liking each other better every hour.

Dr. Johnson having retired for a short time, my lord spoke of his conversation as I could have wished.] *As*[59] *I could have wished* occurs both in the second and third paragraphs. In the second *My Lord* seems a little aukward perhaps. Yet it would degrade him to change it to "He". So I fancy it must remain. Might it run thus: "My Lord behaved"—or "My Lord conducted himself hospitably and agreably".—Make a hog or a dog of it. Only change it.[60]

P. 73, l. 7: [Dr. Johnson gave a shilling extraordinary to the clerk. . . . Dr. Johnson went into an apothecary's.] May not *Dr. Johnson* be *He*?[61]

P. 108: "From perhaps a weakness" etc. [or, as I rather hope, more fancy and warmth of feeling than is quite reasonable, I could, with the most perfect honesty, expatiate on Lord Errol's

[57] So changed in 2nd ed. (p. 527; *Life* v. 416).

[58] Unchanged in 2nd ed. (*Life* v. 77).

[59] MS. "As hospitable" deleted before "*As*"

[60] 2nd ed.: "My lord was extremely hospitable. . . . Dr. Johnson having retired for a short time, his lordship spoke of his conversation as I could have wished" (*Life* v. 81). In his copy of the 1st ed. EM altered the second "my lord" to "lord Monboddo", but apparently changed his mind. "Make a hog or a dog of it", an English proverb, means, "Bring it either to one use, or another" (M. P. Tilley, *A Dictionary of the Proverbs in England in the Sixteenth and Seventeenth Centuries*, 1950).

[61] 2nd ed.: "He afterwards went" (*Life* v. 74). At the end of this query, in the MS. of JB's letter, EM wrote "made already so".

good qualities; but he stands in no need of my praise.] Has not this passage the appearance of its being *weak* or *fanciful* to praise Lord Errol. My meaning is *general* as to people of high birth. May not there be after *quite reasonable* what follows{:} "my mind is ever impressed with admiration of people of high birth *and* I could" etc. Perhaps *admiration* is not the best word that may be found. I beg you may either insert what I have suggested, or express the *general sense* in that place in a better manner.[62]

P. 491, ll. 16 and 19: [Every body had addressed us with some studied compliment on our return. Dr. Johnson said . . . "We are addressed as if we had made a voyage to Nova Zembla.] *addressed* occurs twice. Let the first be changed to *accosted*.[63]

P. 4, Note: [Our friend *Edmund Burke*, who by this time had received some pretty sore rubs from Dr. Johnson, on account of the unhappy difference in their politics . . .] "politic*k*s" wants a *k*. The King never omits it.[64]

P. 9, l. 9: [His person was large, robust, I may say approaching to the gigantic.] the same at "gigantic*k*".[65] Pray wherever the *k* is awanting let it be supplied.

P. 519, l. 17: ["MR. Boswell has this day shewn me a letter, in which you complain of a passage in 'the Journey to the Hebrides.' "] transfer the inverted commas from *the* to *Journey*.[66]

By the way I see your prophecy is fulfilled. A new edition of Dr. Johnson's Journey is coming out. I "carry double".[67] I hope they

[62] 2nd ed.: ". . . quite reasonable, my mind is ever impressed with admiration for persons of high birth, and I could . . ." (*Life* v. 103).

[63] So changed in 2nd ed. (p. 494; *Life* v. 392).

[64] EM added a note on "King": "2 better reasons[:] Dr. J. never omitted it—and it ought not to be omitted." JB's source of information regarding the King's spelling habits is not known. SJ, in his *Dictionary*, 1755, spelled the word "politicks". In this instance the printer was at fault, for the "Tour" MS. reads "politicks"; this spelling was restored in the 2nd ed. (*Life* v. 15 n. 1).

[65] Changed to "gigantick" in 2nd ed. (*Life* v. 18). Here again the printer of the 1st ed. did not follow the spelling of the "Tour" MS.

[66] Unchanged in 2nd ed. (p. 522; *Life* v. 412). JB's copy of SJ's letter, used as printer's copy, does not contain the inverted commas, which were added in the proofs.

[67] JB's *Tour* contains an anecdote about a man who pretended to be SJ's brother. By this imposture he "was well received for two years, among the gentlemen of Northamptonshire", and even "grew so impudent as by his influence to get tenants turned out of their farms". SJ commented, "It pleased me to hear that so much was got by using my name. It is not every name that can carry double; do both for a man's self and his brother" (*Life* v. 295). A similar anecdote was printed in *Pub. Adv.* 25 Oct. p. [3], but in this account the impostor was located in Ipswich.

will take care to correct his errour as to Rasay's chieftainship. Please suggest it to them.[68]

I have had a letter from Wilkes, who affects to find fault, as if there were "a horrid deal of trash".—He points out two inaccuracies without mentioning the pages where—"Please send" is not English. Read "Please *to* send".—"You *was*" should be "you *were*".[69]

Langton[70] promised to write down some corrections. Be so good as put him in mind of it. I hope you have attended to ευχαιτε on p. 60.[71]

Would it not be of advantage to subjoin translations into english of the greek and latin quotations, at the foot of the pages where they occur.[72]

A running title "Journal of a Tour To the Hebrides" will have a very agreable effect.[73]

I think the Book may be well compressed into less space, so as to

[68] Strahan and Cadell published the new edition of SJ's *Journey* late in 1785, but the amendment was not made in the text. The publishers, however, prefixed a note, dated "Strand, Oct. 26, 1785", in which they reprinted SJ's advertisement of retraction, which had been published, "by Dr. Johnson's desire", in Edinburgh newspapers in 1775 and was later reprinted in the *Tour (Works SJ* ix. 167).

[69] Wilkes had written to JB on 1 Oct. with general praise for the *Tour*, but had found, he wrote, "many passages, which I thoroughly disapprove, and some at which I am indignant—. . . *Please send* is not English. *Please to send. You was* should be *you* were. Can you write *you is*? cum 1,000,000, 000,000,000,000,000,000,000,000,000,000, 000 aliis. Your book wants an index. His [SJ's] account of Burke for instance is dispersed thro' the volume. . . . What a horrid deal of trash you have made the press groan under? If it were possible, you would kill his reputation. The pocket pistol of your *8vo* has sorely wounded him. Your blunderbus *4to* will be his coup de grace, but should he linger, the stilletto of Piozzi will give the finishing stroke." See *post* From EM, 19 Oct. p. 235, 5 Nov. and n. 38.

[70] For Bennet Langton, see *ante* To DG, 25 Dec. 1772, n. 5.

[71] In a quotation from Hesiod, JB wanted the κ of 'ευκαιτε (prayers) changed to χ. EM made the change in the 2nd ed., but left uncorrected other anomalies in this word (a modern editor would print εὐχαὶ δὲ) and elsewhere in the line (*Life* v. 63 and n. 1). Gentlemen scholars of Greek in the eighteenth century allowed themselves great latitude in the handling of accents, spelling, and word division.

[72] EM wrote at the end of this paragraph, "mem. the *greek* of Epictetus should be in a note", referring to 1st ed. p. 344 (*Life* v. 279) where SJ quotes Epictetus in translation. The Greek quotation was not added. To the 2nd ed. EM added eleven translations, six his own, four by Dryden, and one by Francis (2nd ed. pp. 49, 52, 60, 216, 256 [two], 350, 388, 454, 494 [two]; *Life* v. 54. n. 1, 56 n. 1, 63 n. 1, 187 n. 1, 213 nn. 2, 3, 283 n. 2, 311 n. 4, 361 n. 2, 392 nn. 3, 4). He left various lines by Horace untranslated and, in particular, gave no translations of Latin poems by John Locke (2nd ed. p. 96 n.; *Life* v. 94 n. 1), SJ (pp. 173–74, 177, 407–08; v. 155, 158, 325–26), and John Macpherson (pp. 328–29; v. 265–66). See JB's acknowledgement of EM's translations, p. 454 n.; v. 361 n. 2).

[73] Added in 2nd ed.

save two or three sheets, and look better than when so very widely done.[74]

I am not sure if an Index will be of great advantage. But I am against a *copious* one as Dilly proposes.[75] A Blockhead may put in nonsence if allowed to say much. If it is made at all I would have it very slight. For instance instead of "Burke Edmund his extraordinary powers—24—contest concerning his wit. Ibid. resembles a character drawn by Sir George Mackenzie 256—neither like Cicero nor Demosthenes 257" etc. etc. etc. I would have merely "Burke Edmund 24–256" and so on mentioning no more than the pages where he appears, and in the same manner as to other people.

I wish to have four or perhaps six copies thrown off on writing paper for you and me. *Rex meus* (if he *tastes* the Book) should have one. One I will give to the Advocates Library. Your Dedication Copy must be as elegant as possible.[76]

I had almost omitted a remark as to p. 500, l. 4 from the bottom: [Upon which Dr. Johnson wrote one of his *sesquipedalia verba*, which was] "pronounced *by the deaf and dumb*". Is not that very like a Bull. The *meaning* as in all Bulls is clear enough. But the expression is not accurate I fancy. Should it not be "by the *Scholars*"? or some other word.[77]

If an Index is to be made, will you take the trouble to direct how it should be made. The trouble I have given and still give you is really too much, and I cannot enough thank you.

Should a second edition be wanted, how many should be printed. Might I venture another 1500.[78] It will be printed a very great deal cheaper than the first.

I am uneasy to think that the irish edition and the translations (if any are made) will have the wretched blunders in them. If I could find out who is to translate I would send my Alterations.[79]

[74] *Post* To EM, 30 Oct. n. 14.

[75] Dilly wrote to JB on 5 Oct.: "A Correct and Copious Index in the New Edition will be very acceptable to the readers of your Journal." See *post* From EM, 5 Nov. p. 267; To EM, 11 Nov. and n. 8.

[76] Though EM ordered six fine-paper copies of the 2nd ed. (*post* From EM, 19 Oct. p. 236), none has been located.

[77] 2nd ed.: "pronounced by the scholars" (p. 503; *Life* v. 399).

[78] See *post* To EM, 15 Oct. p. 225; From EM, 19 Oct. p. 225; To EM, 27 Oct. p. 249 for the press run of the 2nd ed. Fifteen hundred copies of the 1st ed. had been printed (*ante* From EM, 5 Oct. n. 3).

[79] The first Irish edition, dated 1785, is a relatively faithful reprinting of the 1st ed., corrected by JB's table of errata (*Lit. Car.*

Having now I think said all that I can say about my Book, I have only to add that my Wife thinks it will be better for me to remain all the winter in London, attending the Courts and studying that I may be properly prepared before I start at the bar. I depend much on your good counsel in the bold attempt which I have resolved to make; and if I succeed, we shall I hope talk of it with triumph *here*.[80] Whether I succeed or not, *here* we shall

Nobly pensive sit and think.[81]

I ever am with the highest esteem, My Dear Sir, your much obliged and affectionate friend,

JAMES BOSWELL

Please read seal and send Dilly's Letter.[82]

Pray continue to let me have accounts of my Tour. I wish Langton would let me know what the Sovereign says.[83]

There is still one circumstance to be considered. In my note on p. 134[84] I mention[85] that the conversation of a great Personage will appear in my Life of Dr. Johnson. Queritur[86] if this be quite proper. Jack Lee objects to publishing the conversations of living Princes especially when those who are the subject of them are alive.[87] Should I add "if it be not signified to me that it ought not

p. 116). The only early translation of the *Tour* is a German version by Albrecht Wittenberg, dated 1787 but actually published in 1786. Made from the 2nd ed., it is accurate but somewhat abridged (*Lit. Car.* pp. 129–31).

[80] That is, at Auchinleck. JB arrived in London from Edinburgh on 17 Nov. (Journ.). With EM's encouragement he now determined to realize his old dream of practising at the English bar. He returned to Edinburgh for the Christmas holidays and arrived again in London on 1 Feb. 1786. He was called to the bar on 9 Feb. 1786 (Journ.).

[81] An allusion to Pope's "Verses on a Grotto", l. 10:

> Approach: But aweful! Lo, th' *Aegerian* Grott,
> Where, nobly-pensive, ST. JOHN sate and thought.

[82] JB's letter to Dilly has not been reported.

[83] Langton was well known at Court; his son Peregrine reported that the King particularly enjoyed discussing literature with him (Fifer, p. lxvii n. 52).

[84] *Life* v. 125 n. 1.

[85] MS. "mention" written above deleted "promise"

[86] "It is asked".

[87] John Lee (c. 1733–93), barrister and M.P. for Clitheroe since 1782, was a close friend of JB. Upon leaving London on 24 Sept., JB had announced in *Pub. Adv.* his intention to visit Lee at Staindrop, Co. Durham (see n. 2 above); Lee, in fact, had invited JB to call in his "Passage Northwards" (From John Lee, 28 Aug.). On his journey home, JB departed from Harrogate in the Carlisle coach on 28 Sept. (Journ.); the journal breaks off at this point. The road from Harrogate to Carlisle passed seven miles from Staindrop (*Cary's New Itinerary*, 1806, col. 318); presumably JB arrived there on 29 Sept. On 3 Oct. Lee wrote from Staindrop to JB at Auchinleck, mentioning JB's "late short Visit . . . at this

yet to appear" or some such phrase. I believe it is better to let the Note remain as it is. And *if* it is not agreable to the Great Personage that the Conversation should appear, it can be quietly left out in my Life of Dr. Johnson.—Yet Let the Note stand as it is.[88]

To Malone,
Saturday 15 October 1785[1]
MS. Yale (L 920).

(2)[2] P. 68, l. 16: [I could have shewn him more than two {trees} at *Balmuto*, from whence my ancestor came.] after *came* add "and which is now the property of"—or "which now belongs to"— "a branch of my family".[3] This may seem of no con-

Place". Lee proceeded to discuss JB's *Tour*: "I think there are many Passages that had better have been omitted, respecting living Characters, and I particularly point, to a supposed Conference with his Majesty (which it seems is reserved for the Life of Dr. Johnson,) respecting the Controversy between the Bishops Warburton and Lowth. There are many Reasons, why the Conversations of Princes, respecting the Conduct or Character or Attainments of their Subjects, should be held secret, and especially during the Lives of those Princes and most of all during the joint Lives of those who hold the Conversations and the Persons concerning whom they are held." Warburton had died in 1779, but Lowth lived until 1787. JB got permission from the King to publish this conversation, which was printed separately in 1790 and then in the *Life (Lit. Car.* pp. 137–41).

[88] Only the last sentence of the note was altered. Where the 1st ed. reads, "It will appear in Dr. Johnson's LIFE", the 2nd ed. reads, "It may perhaps at some future time be given to the publick" (*Life* v. 125 n. 1).

[1] We infer the date from EM's reference to "your second letter of the 15th" (*post* From EM, 19 Oct. p. 227; the "first letter" would be To EM, 13 Oct.); however, most of these corrections were probably written down before that date, and the whole list posted on 15 Oct. with a covering letter that has not been reported. The emendations cover two conjugate leaves, written on all four sides. The first three sides contain notes to pp. 63–478 of the *Tour*; these notes were probably made on JB's first close reading of the published book, perhaps at "Squire" Dilly's, where he spent two nights after leaving London (Journ. 24–26 Sept.). In any case, a blank on p. 3 of the MS. suggests that JB was away from his library when he wrote this part of the list (n. 31 below). The fourth page, written in a different ink, contains "Additions", written perhaps after JB returned to Auchinleck, but probably before he received EM's letter of 5 Oct. (n. 38 below). Certainly a note on Veronica crowded into the top margin of the first page was written at Auchinleck, and very likely after JB received EM's letter of 5 Oct. (n. 42 below).

[2] The "(2)" indicates that this item should follow the next one, which is marked "(1)".

[3] 2nd ed.: "from whence my ancestors came, and which now belongs to a branch of my family" (*Life* v. 70).

sequence; but it marks my *superiority* in blood over the Laird who has the *ancient* inheritance; and *in Scotland* that is something.[4]

(1) P. 63, l. 25: [We saw in one of its streets a remarkable proof of liberal toleration; a nonjuring clergyman, with a jolly countenance and a round belly, like a well-fed monk, strutting about in his canonicals.] there is an ambiguity as to the *canonicals* which it may be supposed are meant only as the drapery of the *monk*—Therefore trans. and read "strutting about in his canonicals, with a jolly countenance" etc.[5]

P. 105, l. 10: [Lord Errol, who has so large a family, resolved to have a surgeon of his own.] for *so* read *a* or *a very* and dele *a* after "large".[6]

Ibid., l. 3 from the foot: [as God knows best what should be . . .] "God" Capitals. Johnson always did it.[7]

P. 134, l. 8: [at the governor's house . . .] read "govern*o*ur".

P. 135, l. 1: ["I can see no superior virtue in this."] read "superi*o*ur".

P. 148, l. 4: [Governor Trapaud was much struck with Dr. Johnson.] read "Govern*o*ur".[8]

P. 151, Note, l. penult. and ult.: [One day, when we were dining at General Oglethorpe's, where we had many a valuable day . . .] *one day* and "valuable *day*" come too close. Might not the first be *Once*. I believe this may be *too* nice, and I do not insist on it.[9]

P. 157, l. 7: [Governor Trapaud had made us buy . . .] read "Govern*o*ur".[10]

Ibid., l. 3 from the foot: [The poor M'Craas, whatever may be their present state, were much thought of in the year 1715.] is not "much thought of" a scotticism? Should it not be "of considerable estimation," or some such phrase. Pray take care of it.[11]

[4] Balmuto belonged to Claud Irvine Boswell, later (1799) Lord Balmuto of the Court of Session, whose sister Elizabeth was Lord Auchinleck's second wife. Claud's father, John, who bought Balmuto from the Boswells of Balmuto, was the younger brother of JB's grandfather James Boswell (*Life* v. 70 n. 1). Boswell of Auchinleck was a cadet branch of Boswell of Balmuto.

[5] 2nd ed.: "a nonjuring clergyman, strutting about in his canonicals, with a jolly countenance and a round belly, like a well-fed monk" (*Life* v. 66).

[6] 2nd ed.: "Lord Errol, who has a very large family" (*Life* v. 101).

[7] 2nd ed.: "God" (ibid.).

[8] This and the two preceding spelling changes were made in the 2nd ed. (*Life* v. 125, 135).

[9] Unchanged in 2nd ed. (*Life* v. 138 n. 2).

[10] So changed in 2nd ed. (*Life* v. 142).

[11] 2nd ed.: "were of considerable estimation in the year 1715" (ibid.). In his copy of the 1st ed., EM had written "in high estimation". "Much" used to qualify a past participle does not appear to be exclusively Scottish (*Scot. Nat. Dict.*, Muckle, *adv.* II. 2:

P. 159, ll. 22 and 23: [It is a terrible steep to climb, notwithstanding the road is made slanting along it; however, we made it out.] "*made* slanting" and "*made* it out" too close. The first may be "formed" or the second may be changed to "got over it" or some such phrase. The *first* change will be easiest.[12]

P. 160, l. 20: [Here now was a common ignorant Highland horse-hirer.] is *horsehirer* english for *locator equorum*? If it is not, I know not how to express myself unless by saying *clown.*[13]

Ibid., l. 3 from foot: [It grew dusky; and we had a very tedious ride for what was called five miles; but I am sure would measure ten. We spoke none.] "we *spoke none*" Langton told me is a scotticism. It must be—"We did not speak"—Or "We did not exchange a word" or "we had no conversation".[14]

P. 161, l. 3: [I was riding forward to the inn at Glenelg, on the shore opposite to Sky, that I might take proper measures, before Dr. Johnson, who was now advancing in dreary silence, Hay leading his horse, should arrive. He called me back with a tremendous shout, and was really in a passion with me for leaving him.] To justify myself from a suspicion which may be formed that I meant to leave Dr. Johnson with only one strange highland attendant in the desert—the full fact[15] must be added, "Vass also walked by the side of his horse, and[16] Joseph followed behind; so as he was thus attended and seemed to be in deep meditation, I thought there could be no harm in leaving him for a little while."[17]

P. 167, l. 9: [one of those regiments which the late Lord Chatham prided himself in having brought "from the mountains of the North" . . .] the commas must be transferred to "the mountains". Pitt's phrase was "found them *in* the" etc.[18]

"a muckle thocht o' man"; OED, Much, *adv.* C. 5).

[12] 2nd ed.: "notwithstanding the road is formed slanting along it; however, we made it out" (*Life* v. 144).

[13] "Horse-hirer" is a Scottish expression meaning "one who lets saddle-horses" (John Jamieson, *An Etymological Dictionary of the Scottish Language*, 1879–87). 2nd ed.: "Here now was a common ignorant Highland clown" (*Life* v. 144).

[14] "None" as an emphatic negative adverb (often following the verb) had been obsolete in English since the seventeenth century, but was still used in Scottish (*Scot. Nat. Dict.*, Nane, III). 2nd ed.: "We had no conversation" (*Life* v. 144).

[15] MS. "the full fact" written above deleted "it"

[16] MS. "and and"

[17] Added before "He called me back" in 2nd ed., with suggested "so as he was" altered to "as therefore he was" and a comma added after "attended" (*Life* v. 144–45).

[18] By "commas" JB means inverted commas or quotation marks. They were transferred so that the phrase read "having brought from 'the mountains of the North' " (*Life* v. 150). JB quotes William

P. 191, l. ult.: [I the last night obtained my fellow traveller's permission . . .] dele *the.*[19]

P. 214, l. 19: [she {Flora Macdonald} heard upon the main land, as she was returning to Sky about a fortnight before . . .] for *to Sky* read *home.*[20]

P. 223, l. 1: [Dr. M'Leod being informed of this difficulty, said he would risk his life once more for Prince Charles; and it having occurred, that there was a little boat upon a fresh-water lake in the neighbourhood, the two brothers, with the help of some women, brought it to the sea.] *the two brothers* does not make it clear *who*—read "young Rasay and Dr. McLeod".[21]

P. 227, l. 21: "John Mackenzie *is* alive." [I saw him at Rasay's house.] The chronology of my Tour is not quite distinct for the *present* sometimes refers to the time when written *first,* sometimes to *this* year. For instance of the latter p. 42 Sir Alexr. Dick. [he was then on the verge of seventy, and is now eighty-one.][22] Might not a note be put to *Alive** thus "*1773".[23]

P. 237, ll. 9 and 10: [Kings and subjects may both take a lesson of moderation from the melancholy fate of the House of Stuart; that the former may not suffer degradation and exile, and the latter may not be harrassed by the evils of a disputed succession.]

Pitt's speech in Parliament in favour of the repeal of the Stamp Act, 14 Jan. 1766: "I have no local attachments: it is indifferent to me, whether a man was rock'd in his cradle on this side or that side of the Tweed.—I sought for merit wherever it was to be found.—It is my boast, that I was the first minister who looked for it, and I found it in the mountains of the north" (*The Celebrated Speech of a Celebrated Commoner*, 1766, pp. 3–4). Pitt refers to his having raised two regiments of Highlanders to serve in America in 1757 (*Gent. Mag.* 1757, xxvii. 42, 333). These regiments, Montgomery's (77th) and Fraser's (78th) Highlanders, were the first Highland regiments that had been raised since 1745 (Frank Adam, *The Clans, Septs and Regiments of the Scottish Highlands*, 2nd ed., 1924, pp. 279–80). For Pitt, first Earl of Chatham, see *ante* To DG, 25 Dec. 1772, n. 15.

[19] So changed in 2nd ed. (*Life* v. 168).

[20] So changed in 2nd ed. (*Life* v. 184).

[21] So changed in 2nd ed. (*Life* v. 190).

[22] On p. 42 of the 2nd ed. EM added a footnote, "In 1773", to "he was then". Because Sir Alexander Dick (b. 1703) died on 10 Nov. 1785, the footnote was dropped and the passage revised for the 3rd ed.: "he was then on the verge of seventy, and is now (1785) eighty-one" (*Life* v. 48). For a second note on Sir Alexander, see *post* To EM, 30 Oct. and n. 13.

[23] "*1773" is written slightly below the line, presumably so as to look like a footnote. In the 2nd ed. the two short sentences were revised and combined: "John M'Kenzie was at Rasay's house, when we were there." A footnote was added to this sentence: "This old Scottish *member of parliament*, I am informed, is still living (1785)" (*Life* v. 193 and n. 1). In his copy of the 1st ed. EM wrote, "Since the first edition of this book"; then deleting this phrase, he continued, "I am informed that this old Scottish *member of parliament* is still living (1785)." See *post* To EM, 27 Oct. and n. 31.

take care to read *Kings* for *the former* and *Subjects* for *the latter*. It is corrected in some copies; but not in that which is now before me.[24]

P. 240, l. 22: [The abstract point of *right* would involve us in a discussion of remote and perplexed questions.] should not "abstract" be in Italicks to mark that the *plain* right is not dubious.[25]

P. 281, l. 11: [At breakfast, Dr. Johnson told us, that there was once a pretty good tavern in Catharine-street in the Strand, where very good company met in an evening. . . . He was introduced to this company . . .] Is it not better to make Dr. Johnson talk by deleting *that* and putting commas before "there was" etc. and making it "*I* was introduced" etc. etc.[26]

P. 340, ll. 1, 2, and 3: ["You are admitted with great facility to the prince's company, and yet must treat him with great respect. At a great court, you are at such a distance that you get no good."] does not *great* occur too often? might the first be *much*.[27]

P. 448, l. 16: [on the blank page of my Journal opposite to that which contained what I have now mentioned . . .] would it not be better to say *contains*.[28]

P. 466, l. 15: [though his {John Campbell, Earl of Loudoun's} interest in our county was great, and had been generally successful . . .] Why *had been* might not that be omitted? Pray decide.[29]

(2) P. 478, l. 22: [the road to the church, made by my father at a great expence, for above three miles . . .] after "three miles" "upon his estate" or "upon his own estate" to mark the extensive domain. *Now mine*. I *must* have this.[30]

(1) P. 468:[31]

[24] Leaf Q7 (pp. 237–38) of the 1st ed. exists in two states, the first of which reads "the former" and "the latter", and the second, "Kings" and "subjects" (*Lit. Car.* p. 113). EM's copy of the 1st ed. read with the first state, but EM altered it to read with the second. The 2nd ed. reads with the second state of the 1st ed. (*Life* v. 199).

[25] So changed in 2nd ed. (*Life* v. 202).

[26] See *ante* To EM, 13 Oct. and n. 49, where the same point is discussed. The present entry was probably written before JB's letter of 13 Oct.

[27] In the 2nd ed. "great respect" was changed to "much respect" (*Life* v. 276). The change is also found in EM's copy of the 1st ed., where "great" in "great facility" was also deleted; however, the word was not deleted in the 2nd ed.

[28] So changed in 2nd ed. (p. 449; *Life* v. 357).

[29] Omitted in 2nd ed. (p. 469; *Life* v. 372).

[30] 2nd ed.: "made by my father at a great expence, for above three miles, on his own estate" (p. 481; *Life* v. 381).

[31] JB here left a blank space of about three lines near the bottom of the third page of the MS., apparently intending to add a note on Robert III of Scotland when he

Pp. 237–38: I think it would be better to print Voltaire's reflections in *Italicks*. There is a kind of *surprise* on finding the *french* suddenly in the same form with the english. It is a *ha ha*![32]

Additions.

P. 293, l. 17: ["the heart is as tender when a man is in health as when sick".] for "as when Sick" read "as when *he is* sick".[33]

P. 294, l. ult.: [He said, he could never get the meaning of an *Erse* song explained to him. . . . "I take it, said he, they are like a song which I remember".] for "erse song" read "erse song*s*" to correspond with *they* on p. 295, l. 3.[34]

P. 319, ll. 19 and 20: [While the examination was going on, this Talisker . . . could not resist the pleasantry of asking . . .] for "*this* Talisker" read "*the present* Talisker". I suppose *this* is a scotticism in the sense there used.[35]

Col should have only one *l passim*; not *Coll*.[36]

In the first sheets there are too many proper names in Italicks.[37]

It still appears to me, with submission, that you are wrong in not putting the *name* as well {as} the *Work* in Italicks. "Gataker *on lots*" seems *half* done. I would have *Gataker on lots—Burnet's History* etc. etc. Humour me in this in the second edition, if there shall be one.[38]

could get access to a reference work. The note was added later (presumably after his return to Auchinleck) on the last page of the MS. (see n. 39 below).

[32] See *post* From EM, 5 Nov. and n. 20.

[33] So changed in 2nd ed. (*Life* v. 240).

[34] See *post* From EM, 21 Oct. p. 240; To EM, 27 Oct. and n. 43 for further discussion of this passage.

[35] So changed in 2nd ed. (*Life* v. 260). "This Mr. M'Sweyn" on p. 358 of the 1st ed. was changed to "The present Mr. M'Sweyn" in the 2nd ed. (*Life* v. 289), and "this Mr. Waller" on p. 86 was changed to "the present Mr. Waller" (*Life* v. 86). Both of these changes were presumably suggested by JB's proposed emendation of "this Talisker". The usage does not seem to be a Scotticism (see OED, This, *dem. pron. and adj*. II. 1).

[36] Beginning with this entry, JB's handwriting becomes more expansive, and he apparently also changed pens. Since this and the next entry discuss material near the front of the book, it is likely that some time has elapsed since JB wrote the preceding entry, and that he is again working through the book from the beginning. In the 1st ed., *Coll* (as it is now generally spelled) is usually printed with one "l", and only rarely with two (twice on p. 98). These instances are corrected in the 2nd ed. (*Life* v. 95).

[37] See, e.g. 1st ed. p. 3: "To *attract* him, we had invitations from the chiefs *Macdonald* and *Macleod*; and, for additional aid, I wrote to Lord *Elibank*, Dr. *William Robertson*, and Dr. *Beattie*." In the 2nd ed. the names in this passage were all set in roman type (*Life* v. 14).

[38] These changes were made as JB requested (e.g. 1st and 2nd ed. pp. 353, 375; *Life* v. 285, 302). The phrase "if there shall be one" suggests that JB wrote this section before he received EM's letter of 5 Oct., which confirms that there was to be a 2nd ed.

P. 468: [As we passed very near the castle of Dundonald, which was one of the many residencies of the kings of Scotland, and in which, Robert the Third was born . . .] for "Robert the third was born" of which I cannot find evidence read "Robert the second lived and died".[39]

Ibid., l. 21: [from whence there is an extensive prospect of the rich district of Cuninghame, the western sea, and the Isle of Arran.] dele *and* before *the* and after *Arran* read "and a part of the north of Ireland" or "northern coast of Ireland".[40]

P. 72, l. 26: [When we came down from it, I met Mr. Gleg, the merchant here.] *the* should be delete. It looks as if there were only *one* merchant—or *two* Mr. Glegs, and the *merchant* were a distinctive appelation.[41]

Veronica is herself so fond of her appearance that she would be much mortified if I should delete her.[42]

From Malone,
Wednesday 19 October 1785

MS. Yale (C 1897).

ADDRESS in Courtenay's hand: Jams. Boswell Esqr., Auchinleck, Cumnock, Dumfries.

FRANK: London Octbr. nineteenth 1785. Free J. Courtenay.

POSTMARKS: 19 OC, FREE.

Queen Anne St. East, Octr. 19, 1785[1]

O brave we![2] I have this moment received an answer to a note that I

[39] JB originally intended to write this note in a blank space on the third page of the MS. Neither the precise date (c. 1340) nor the birthplace of Robert III of Scotland is known with certainty. The 2nd ed. was changed as JB requested (p. 471; *Life* v. 373).

[40] 2nd ed.: "Cuninghame, the western sea, the Isle of Arran, and a part of the northern coast of Ireland" (ibid.).

[41] 2nd ed.: "Mr. Gleg, a merchant here" (*Life* v. 73). Crowded into the top margin of the last page of the MS., this note, which was apparently an afterthought, seems to have been written with the same pen as was used for the note on Veronica.

[42] This note is crowded into the top margin of the first page of the MS. Presumably JB is responding to EM's criticism of the passage on Veronica (*ante* From EM, 5 Oct. and n. 6). In any case, JB must have written the note after he returned to Auchinleck on 3 Oct., the earliest date on which Veronica could have known that she appeared in the printed *Tour*.

[1] From 1779 until his death in 1812,, EM lived at No. 55 Queen Anne St. East (Prior, *Malone*, pp. 45–46). For descriptions of this house in later years, see ibid., pp. 300, 321.

[2] This exclamation, according to JB's *Tour*, was Dr. Johnson's: "a peculiar expression of his when he rejoices" (*Life* v. 360).

sent to Dilly's, informing me that there are now in his warehouse but 230 copies—I begin with this, because I choose to set off well.—I thought, my dear Sir, your letter of the 13th *long of coming*;[3] for behold! the first two sheets were actually set up before it arrived, and I was environed with difficulties. However all is safe, for not a page of the second edition is yet worked off. Just as I was sitting down to write, your second letter of the 15th was brought to me. I will go through them both regularly; but first let me tell you the state of things here. Dilly went out of town last thursday for ten days; finding the sale so rapid he thought it prudent to put the second edition immediately to press, lest all his copies of the former should be exhausted, and it is not safe to let the publick ardour cool. On this principle I find from[4] Baldwin that he urged him to get through *five* sheets a week, but that will be utterly impossible on my part, nor indeed is it necessary. Dilly is not quite accurate in his calculation; for besides the 230 copies in his shop, it must be considered, that there are probably not less than 200 now scattered in the various shops in London; so that this quantity will certainly suffice till the other edition can be ready. I suppose 4 sheets a week is the most we can do.—And now for some of my difficulties. My first was about the "contractions". I drew up what I conceived to be Sir J. R.'s idea about them by way of note and sent it to him. He approved, but sent me a much larger and very valuable discussion of the subject, which I shall[5] enclose with this letter. It could not have been got in without a good deal of trouble; besides I thought it too valuable to be thrown away and better to be reserved for the LIFE. His solution of the startings and gestures being connected with ideas from which he shrunk, is surely very ingenious. It meets with your observations about his not restraining these motions in the streets, for such ideas were as likely to intrude into such a mind there as any where else;—in reverie. However I have added what you sent as you will see by the[6] enclosed. It will do very well for the present, Johnson's character you know must be worked up again for the life; part of

[3] EM underlines "long of coming" as a Scotticism, like "long of being" (see *Life* v. 15 and n. 4). "Of" was often used in Scottish where English used other prepositions, and "long of" was an especially common idiom (e.g. Journ. 7 Oct. 1774, 24 Mar. 1780; *Scot. Nat. Dict.* Of, *prep.* 4.3).

[4] MS. "he urge" deleted before "from"

[5] MS. "enclose" deleted before "shall"

[6] MS. "the" written above deleted "what"

the present omitted, and some new added.[7] As for *Veronica* (for I am still now in the first sheet) it stands just as you desired. It would be foolish *now* to omit it. I wish however I could persuade you to omit the *tail* of the note in p. 29. [To find a thought, which just shewed itself to us from the mind of *Johnson*, thus appearing again at such a distance of time, and without any communication between them, enlarged to full growth in the mind of *Markham*, is a curious object of philosophical contemplation.—That two such great and luminous minds should have been so dark in one corner,—that *they* should have held it to be "wicked Rebellion" in the British subjects established in America, to resist the abject condition of holding all their property at the mercy of British subjects remaining at home, while their allegiance to our common Lord the King was to be preserved inviolate,—is a striking proof to me, either that "He who sitteth in Heaven," scorns the loftiness of human pride,—or that the evil spirit, whose personal existence I strongly believe, and even in this age am confirmed in that belief by a *Fell*, nay, by a *Hurd*, has more power than some choose to allow.] You will see by a scrap I enclose from Sir Joshua it is not

[7] Before EM received JB's letter of 13 Oct. containing instructions for a footnote on SJ's "contractions", he had already written a note, which had been set in type along with the rest of sheet B but not yet printed: "Such they appeared to me; but since the former edition, Sir Joshua Reynolds has observed to me 'that they were only habits, in which he indulged himself at certain times. When in company, where he was not free, or when engaged earnestly in conversation, he never gave way to such habits, which proves that they were not involuntary.' " In the proof (P 85), EM altered "that they were only" to "that Dr. Johnson's extraordinary gestures were only" and added at the end of the footnote, "I am still however of opinion that they were involuntary, for if that had not been the case, he would surely have restrained them in the publick streets." The proof of the conjugate leaves B4 and B5 (pp. 7–10), containing the emended footnote, was enclosed with this letter. For the final form of the note, see 2nd ed. p. 9 n.; in the 3rd ed. "former edition" was changed to read "first edition", but the note was otherwise not changed (*Life* v. 18 n. 4). Sir Joshua Reynolds's "very valuable discussion" of SJ's "contractions" was written on a folio sheet consisting of four pages of text, in the form of a footnote by JB. For the *Life*, JB cut the two leaves apart and used the first (M 145) as printer's copy (*Life* i. 144–45). The second leaf (C 2368) he drew on in writing the *Life* (i. 128–29, 142–43) but did not print verbatim. (For Reynolds's note, see Waingrow, pp. 119–22.) At the end of his note EM wrote, "Mem. what Mr. Langton says about Dr. Johnson's *owning* that his gestures or habits or whatever they may be called were very similar to those of the *kissing* Dr. Barton of Christchurch, Oxford." Dr. Philip Barton (d. 1765), canon of Christ Church College, Oxford, was nicknamed "Kissing Barton" (*Gent. Mag.* 1765, xxxv. 347; *Thraliana*, ed. K. C. Balderston, 1942, i. 20, 156). JB did not use this information in the *Life*. See *post* To EM, 27 Oct. for JB's answers to this and the following comments and queries.

my opinion alone.[8] It is indeed that of every creature I have spoken to. As far as the word *contemplation* is very right and *apposite*; but to start away to a totally different subject is alway very *unscholarlike*; and you should never forget you are writing a *book*, not a *pamphlet*,[9]—and that merely saying, I wish at all hazards to hitch in my opinion on another subject, is no excuse at all. So much for the general complexion of that excrescence;—the *prince of the darkness*[10] at the end renders it a thousand times worse. If it be your opinion, what absolute necessity for stating it *there*? Non est his locus.[11] Pray do consent to omit. We were hampered before, because the cancel could not be filled up;[12] but now we are free: and it is not here as in the case of Veronica, where you say, to omit would be "like flying". Every author on revising his book not only may, but ought, to omit what does not appear pertinent or in its proper place;—to consider it in that light alone.

Sir Joshua, you will see, has made a good hit about the *fore*-legs of the hare, and I shall adopt it; for the[13] sheet must be printed before I can have your answer.[14]

So also as to a note on *doggedly* in p. 33. [Somebody talked of happy moments for composition; and how a man can write at one time, and not at another.—"Nay (said Dr. Johnson) a man may write at any time, if he will set himself doggedly to it."] something of this import: *Note* "I suppose Dr. Johnson meant with obstinate[15] resolution. It commonly means *sullenly*, and in that sense only is it found in his Dictionary."—[16]

[8] In his "scrap" or list of corrections (C 2366), Reynolds wrote, "The note p. 29 is the wildest part of the book. The unprepared transition after the words *philosophical contemplation* and his declaration at the end of his believing in the Devil is too bad."

[9] EM alludes to the personal digressions included in JB's *LPS 85* (see *post* From EM, 5 Nov. and n. 36).

[10] Cf. *All's Well that Ends Well* IV. v. 42; *King Lear* III. iv. 143; *Paradise Lost* x. 383; *Paradise Regained* iv. 441.

[11] An adaption of "Sed nunc non erat his locus", Horace, *Ars Poetica*, l. 19: "For such things there is a place, but not just now" (trans. H. R. Fairclough, Loeb ed.).

[12] Apparently EM did not object to (perhaps he had not seen) the footnote until sheet C (pp. 17–32) of the 1st ed. had been printed. Getting rid of the footnote would have necessitated cancelling C6 (pp. 29–30). Since JB and EM did not have material to fill the space that would have been left blank by the deletion of the note, they let it stand.

[13] MS. "for it the"

[14] In his list of corrections (C 2366), Reynolds had written, "pag. 27 'from her legs being short' 'from her *fore*legs being short' ". The passage he referred to in the 1st ed. was, "A hare will run up a hill best, from her legs being short; a dog down." In both the 1st and 2nd editions, the passage occurs in sheet C.

[15] MS. "obstinatete"

[16] Reynolds had written, "page 33 *doggedly*—requires a note[:] its common

Pray when you write answer his Quere on p. 76 "Sir you got into our club"—etc. and send me a little note for that place—[17]

Sir Joshua is wrong in p. 268, l. 23. "He has *not* said" etc. ["what he was to tell; so you cannot find fault with him, for what he has not told."] He has misapprehended the passage.[18]

At last I have brought you to your second sheet C. and here I had a great difficulty about Burke. This sheet I found yesterday was also set up; however we got it so arranged as to admit what I wanted.[19] Windham, Courtney, Mr. Hamilton,[20] every one in short, talk loudly that the specimens you have given of Burke's wit are not good ones, that they have more of pun and conceit than of wit in them. I was, you may remember, apprehensive of this, and thought it dangerous to stake his character in this point of view on particular instances. Mr. Hamilton, who lived long in great intimacy with him, says, he could have given twenty better. To satisfy therefore all parties, and at the same time to strengthen your argument, I have tacked a rider to your note, which I sent last night to Baldwin's, and hope to have a proof of it before I seal this, that I may enclose it, (for I can't endure transcribing); I think you will approve of it, as it is entirely congenial with your sentiments on the subject, and at the same time pays B. a handsome compliment. Send me your opinion upon it and any alterations you think proper, as I will endeavour not to have it worked off till I hear from you: if that should not be practicable, and you should disapprove, then it must be a cancel; and I hope you will excuse me as acting for the best.

* * *

Thus far I had written when Langton (whom I had called on yesterday came in) and he has obligingly suggested many

meaning is *sullenly*." See *post* To EM, 27 Oct. and n. 4.

[17] Reynolds had written, "page 76 'Sir you got into our Club by doing what a man can do.' Quere what is the meaning."

[18] Reynolds had written, "268. line 23 [*Life* v. 221]. 'He has not said what he was to tell'. The word 'not' is superfluous."

[19] JB had added to the *Tour* a footnote disputing SJ's charge that "Burke never once made a good joke" (1st ed. pp. 24–26 n.; *Life* v. 32–34 n. 3). Pp. 24–26 of the 2nd ed. were in sheet C (C4v–C5v). See *ante* From EM, 5 Oct. and n. 22; To EM, 13 Oct. and n. 4 for a discussion of a part of JB's footnote. See JB's account of the footnote to EB and EB's response (*ante* To EB, 20 Dec. 1785 and n. 3; From EB, 4 Jan. 1786).

[20] William Gerard Hamilton (1729–96), M.P. for Wilton, known as "Single Speech Hamilton", had employed Burke from 1759 or 1760 until they quarrelled and parted in 1765 (Namier and Brooke ii. 146). See also *post* To EM, 25 Feb. 1791 and n. 12.

things—but the discussion of them has taken so long (an hour at least) that I am afraid I shall not have time to say half what I intended for[21] it is now near four, and[22] the bellman goes by at half after five (to say nothing of dinner). The point that took us most time was the settling the passage in p. 92 in which he is alluded to, though not mentioned. [We talked of one of our friends taking ill, for a length of time, a hasty expression of Dr. Johnson's to him, on his introducing, in a mixed company, a religious subject so unseasonably as to provoke a rebuke.] He did not at all press the altering it, but very truly said it was but right to state it correctly, which is not the case at present. The fact was there was a vague and loose disquisition carrying on, how far toleration in a state should go; and L. in order to bring it to a point put the case, whether if a preacher[23] were publickly to argue against the Trinity, that should be endured by the *State*. Johnson, who did not hear well, did not know exactly how it was introduced, and burst out into a violent explosion. I made him therefore write down his own idea—which is—"on his attempting to prosecute a subject that had a reference to religion, beyond the bounds within which the Doctor thought such topicks should be confined, in a mixed company". This surely is more correct. The question concerning the Trinity was not *unseasonable* for it had immediate relation[24] to the conversation then pursued.—He gave me a[25] very good addition to the story about Graham and Goldsmith, which Johnson always mentioned when he told the story,—and therefore you may safely add it, and[26] rely upon it that your memory failed you. [P. 100: He told me a good story of Dr. Goldsmith. Graham, who wrote "Telemachus, a Masque," was sitting one night with him and Dr. Johnson, and was half drunk. He rattled away to Dr. Johnson: "You are a clever fellow, to be sure; but you cannot write an essay like Addison, or verses like the *Rape of the Lock*." At last he said, "*Doctor*, I should be happy to see you at Eaton."—"I shall be glad to wait on you," answered Goldsmith.—"No (said Graham) 'tis not you I meant, Dr. *Minor*; 'tis Dr. *Major*, there."—Goldsmith was excessively hurt by this. He

[21] MS. "The point that took us most" deleted before "for"

[22] MS. "& and" ("and" written at the top of a new page).

[23] MS. "preacher" written above deleted "min"

[24] MS. "relig" deleted before "relation"

[25] MS. "a g" deleted before "a"

[26] MS. "on the" deleted before "and"

afterwards spoke of it himself. "Graham (said he) is a fellow to make one commit suicide."] After "half drunk" add, "and was now got to about the pitch of looking at one man and talking to another". This accounts for Goldsmith's mistake and makes the whole much neater. Give me your opinion. There can, I think, be no impropriety in adding it. But at all events, if you differ with me, it may go in a note "Mr. L. says" etc.—but this is awkward—Johnson used also always to say in telling the story—"and this to Goldsmith, Sir, who was as irascible as a hornet"!—But that is of less consequence than the other.

With respect to George Rex, L.[27] says he seldom gives his opinion on books, but dives into that of others;—that he entered into the subject *warmly*, and continued a considerable while upon it—He wished to hear L.'s opinion, and L.[28] to give it as shortly as he could told[29] the great man the story of the gentleman "who having got[30] Robinson Crusoe just as he had put one stocking on, read the two volumes through before he drew on the other".[31] There's for you!—G. did not talk of particular parts but shewed that he read the book. He asked L. whether you did not run some danger of offending the Kirk in Scotland. He said he thought not, and that you had so happy a way of treating your antagonists in conversation, that you could not suffer much. He then told him the story of Foot's attack on Johnson, and your method of putting F. down by the repetition of Johnson's bon mot about the *dog*.[32] G. laughed heartily and was much pleased—But I am losing time about such *little* matters, when more material call on me.

I will attend to all your corrections. It is impossible for me now to enter into a discussion of them. I had discovered many more than I sent you—and I find you have hit on many of the[32a] same.

[27] MS. "L." written above deleted "he"

[28] MS. "to hear L.'s opinion, and [he *deleted*] L." written above deleted "to L.'s opinion"

[29] MS. "L." written above deleted "he" before "told"; then "L." deleted.

[30] MS. "having got" written above deleted "read"

[31] This story has not been traced.

[32] Samuel Foote, while at Edinburgh, "thought fit to entertain a numerous Scotch company, with a great deal of coarse jocularity, at the expence of Dr. Johnson". JB's response was to repeat SJ's remark on Foote: "I do not know, Sir, that the fellow is an infidel; but if he be an infidel, he is an infidel as a dog is an infidel; that is to say, he has never thought upon the subject" (*Life* ii. 95–96 and 95 n. 2). For Foote, see *ante* To DG, 30 Mar. 1771, n. 6. From JB's invitation to this gathering, we learn that the occasion was a contest in mimicry between the advocate Robert Cullen (d. 1810) and Foote (Lord Kellie to JB, between Nov. 1770 and Apr. 1771).

[32a] MS. "them" deleted before "the"

Each however has some peculiar to himself. L. has just now pointed out some that escaped us both:—[P. 68: In the grotto, we saw a wonderful large lobster claw.] "Lobster-claw" he says is Scotch.[33] Read "lobster's claw".

P. 81: [Dr. Johnson examined young *Arthur*, Lord Monboddo's son, in Latin. He answered very well; upon which he said, with complacency, "Get you gone!"] "When *James* comes back, you shall be in the Muses Welcome." L. asks *what* James was meant. Did he mean "when the king shall have his own again" as they say in your country—or "When James I. comes back"—i.e. ad Graecas Calendas.[34]

[P. 160: Here now was a common ignorant Highland horse-hirer.] *Horse-hirer* he says is Scotch.

[P. 82: When he took up his large oak stick, he said, "My lord, that's *homerick*".] "*That's* Homerick" he says should be "*This* is Homerick"—J. being in the act of speaking. It may perhaps be justified by his pointing to the stick;—so spoken δεικτικῶς.[35] I must add from my self before I leave that passage, that "Here was another instance of similitude between him and Lord Monboddo"—wants *opening*. [*Gory*, my lord's black servant, was sent as our guide so far. This was another point of similarity between Johnson and Monboddo.] What is the similitude? It is in fact their both having *black* servants. You and[36] I know that Francis Barber was a black, and it is told in a former page; but the reader may remember nothing of that, and it should be told here.

L. also pointed out several errors in Locke's Latin Verses.[37]

He doubts about *injusti* in "Una est injusti caerula forma maris". I don't see the force of the epithet. Are you sure it is in Ovid's *Epistles*?[38]

I send you some scraps from the newspapers. They have been living on you, as it might be supposed they would do, for this fortnight. The *Gazeteer* went to unreasonable lengths, as you will

[33] Cf. *Scot. Nat. Dict.* Lapster, *n.*: "labster tae".

[34] The Greek calendar had nothing to correspond to the Roman Calends, hence the Latin proverb "ad Graecas Calendas" means "never". Cf. "ad Kalendas Graecas soluturos", Suetonius, "Augustus", *Lives of the Twelve Caesars*, sect. 87: "They will never pay".

[35] "Demonstratively".

[36] MS. "happen" deleted before "and"

[37] 1st ed. pp. 96–97 n.; *Life* v. 94–95 n. 1.

[38] The 1st ed. incorrectly identifies the line as being from Ovid's *Epistles*; see *post* From EM, 24 Oct. for the correct citation and a translation.

see by his extracts; "he uttered them by great *swarths*".[39] I made Dilly threaten him, and he has been more moderate since.[40] The St. James's Chron. did very well; gave the character of J. and the concluding 3 pages of the book.[41] These were good inflamers. I sent a Letter, which will appear tomorrow—with "Raderotoo"—I thought it a good morceau.[42]—I have not seen any abuse; but I am told a constant fire has been kept *against* you in the *Morn. Post*. I do not take in the paper, and could not meet with it in two or three coffeehouses where I enquired.[43]

I am writing away *ventre a terre* this hour past (now almost five) and can observe no method—Did you strike out or put in Mrs. Thrale ("neither Beauclerk nor I nor Mrs. T.") at the press? [P. 299: I spoke of Mrs. Montague's very high praises of Garrick.—*Johnson*. "Sir, it is fit she should say so much, and I should say nothing. Reynolds is fond of her book, and I wonder at it; for neither I, nor Beauclerk, nor Mrs. Thrale, could get through it."] Sir J. R. and I had a dispute about it. He says, she is not in his copy. I know she is in mine. Both of us may be right.—[44]

[P. 22, note: A worthy friend of mine in London was lately consulted by a lady of quality, of most distinguished merit, what

[39] "And utters it by great swarths" (*Twelfth Night* II. iii. 150). Two clippings from *Gazetteer*, 30 Sept. and 1 Oct., are preserved at Yale. For the first, see *ante* From EM, 5 Oct. n. 12; the second reprints anecdotes from the *Tour* on atheism (1st ed. p. 42; *Life* v. 47–48), on Lord Hailes (p. 44; v. 49), and on the view of the Firth of Forth (pp. 48–49; v. 53–54).

[40] The editor of the *Gazetteer* was James Perry.

[41] *St. James's Chron.* 29 Sept.–1 Oct. p. [4], carried a letter entitled "Edinburgh Effluvia" and signed "Hud Your Haunde", which included JB's account of his walk up the High Street in Edinburgh with SJ (1st ed. pp. 13–14; *Life* v. 22–23). In the issue for 1–4 Oct. p. [2], a full column was devoted to JB's character-sketch of SJ (pp. 6–10; v. 16–19). The next issue, 4–6 Oct. p. [2], devoted another full column to the *Tour*. The article began with a laudatory paragraph in which the *Tour* was commended as "a Book fraught with more curious Information, and interesting Anecdotes of Persons and Things, than any Publication that has made its Appearance for some Time past"; and noting that some persons might be offended by their appearance in Boswell's pages, replied: "To Cavillers of this Class, the ingenious Journalist replies in a Manner, in our Opinion, highly convincing, and which we shall therefore take the Liberty of laying before our Readers in the Writer's own Words." The last three pages of the *Tour*, in which JB defended his procedure of recording conversations, are then quoted (pp. 522–24; *Life* v. 414–16).

[42] *Post* From EM, 21 Oct. and n. 18.

[43] *Post* From EM, 21 Oct. and n. 19.

[44] No copy of the 1st ed. with Mrs. Thrale's name omitted is known to exist; it may be that Reynolds was mistaken. See *post* To EM, 27 Oct. p. 249 and n. 19; and J. C. Riely and Alvaro Ribeiro, "'Mrs. Thrale' in the *Tour*: A Boswellian Puzzle", *Papers of the Bibliographical Society of America* (1975) lxix. 151–63. On the controversy concerning this passage, see *post* From EM, 25 Mar. 1786; To EM, 31 Mar., 3 Apr. 1786; From EM, 7 Apr. 1786 and n. 5.

was the best History of England for her son to read. My friend recommended Hume's. But, upon recollecting that its usher was a superlative panegyrick on one, who endeavoured to sap the credit of our holy religion, he repented.[45]] I forgot to say that L. wished instead of his *repented* (about Hume) we should say—"revoked his recommendation". His name is not mentioned.

Courtney has found out *Quantum cedat virtutibus aurum*. [P. 217: Upon the table in our room I found in the morning a slip of paper, on which Dr. Johnson had written with his pencil these words: "Quantum cedat virtutibus aurum." What he meant by writing them I could not tell.] He was certainly thinking of the attachment of the Highlanders to Prince Charles (as we must now call him)[46] being superior to the love of money. They did not discover him, and rejected the reward offered by Government. This had been talked over before you went to bed.—So it will make a note, if you please. "An ingenious friend observes" etc.

Wilkes, I am told, says, "you have now fired a pocket pistol at Johnson's reputation; presently you mean to discharge a blunderbuss at it; and afterwards Madam Piozzi is to stab at him with a stiletto." Is this in his letter to you, or only oral?—Poor man! how little he knows! But I am sure he has no taste for *good sense*, and would rather have the name of saying a good thing, than benefit mankind by instructing them, if he were capable of doing so; which I believe he is not.

[P. 17: She {Veronica} would be held close to him; which was a proof, from simple nature, that his figure was not horrid.] Is not—"which shews his figure was not quite *horrid*"—too strong? Would not "very[47] displea{si}ng", or "very disagreable" be better. But it is too late to talk of this;—as the first sheet must be worked off before I can have your answer.

Would you have Goldsmith's lines on the English Nation, inserted in the proper place? I think you said so. [P. 431: We talked of Goldsmith's *Traveller*, of which Dr. Johnson spoke highly; and, while I was helping him on with his great coat, he

[45] The "usher" to Hume's *History* is an account by Adam Smith of Hume's last days and character.

[46] EM refers to JB's insistence on calling the Young Pretender "Prince Charles Edward". See JB's letter to, and conversation with, George III about this designation (To George III, 6 June; Journ. 15 June); also *Applause*, pp. 307–08, 310–12, and his footnote in the *Tour* justifying the use of this title (1st ed. p. 215 n.; *Life* v. 185 n. 4).

[47] MS. "very" written above deleted "quite"

repeated from it the character of the English nation, which he did with such energy, that the tear started into his eye.]

Send me translations of as many passages as you can—[48]

Where is "*ευκαιτε γεροντων*" etc. You say Hesiod. Langton says *Theognis*.

I am much vexed that they have not sent me the addition to Burke's note. I have been expecting it every moment—I must send it to you on friday.

I forgot to say that I voted for only 1000 copies. It is safest. If a third edition be necessary, so much the better. It will be creditable.—(I have ordered the six fine paper copies.) I can easily get your cypher cut in copper.

I find it impossible to add more, for I am now writing almost in the dark; however on the prospect of future acquaintance I must beg you to present my best compliments to Mrs. Boswell, (who I am persuaded is the very reverse of what the satirical Wilkes chooses to describe as "a true Montgomery")[49] and to believe me always your faithful and affectionate,

E. M.

From Malone,
Friday 21 October 1785
MS. Yale (C 1898).

London, Octr. 21, 1785

MY DEAR SIR: I now proceed in continuation. I was so hurried in finishing my last letter, that I had not time to read the latter part of it over, and if it had not been for the irresistible douceur of sixpence, which tempted the bellman to stay while I sealed the packets, you would not have received them by Wednesday's post.—And now for criticism.—

[48] *Ante* To EM, 13 Oct. and n. 72; *post* To EM, 29 Oct.

[49] Mrs. Boswell's maiden name was mentioned in *LPS 85*, p. 55: "having the honour and happiness to be married to his lordship's [the eleventh Earl of Eglinton's] relation, a true *Montgomerie*, whom I esteem, whom I love, after fifteen years, as on the day when she gave me her hand". JB's presentation copy of the *Letter* to Wilkes is preserved in the British Library; in it Wilkes underlined this passage (*Lit. Car.* p. 110). Wilkes's comment has not been traced.

P. 58, l. 2: ["Many more conveniences and elegancies are enjoyed where money is plenty, than where it is scarce."] "where money is *plenty*".—Langton observes very justly that it is impossible Johnson could have used this phrase, because it {is} quite ungrammatical. It is either a Scotticism or a Provincialism—Read "plentiful".[1]

P. 84: [We had tedious driving this afternoon and] "we[2] were a *good deal* drowsy".—A scotticism he says.[3] Have you any objecn. to "*somewhat* drowsy". If you meant a stronger expression, it must be "*very* drowsy".—

P. 92, l. 4 from bottom: [Principal Campbell, Sir Alexander Gordon, Professor Gordon, and Professor Ross, visited us in the morning, as did Dr. Gerard,] "who had come *in* six miles from the country" etc. You mean, "who had come *into Aberdeen* from the country"—This he justly observes is a Scotticism.[4] It is avoided by deleting *in*.

Now for myself.

In p. 10 [His prejudice against *Scotland* was announced almost as soon as he began to appear in the world of letters. In his *London*, a poem, are the following nervous lines:

> For who would leave, unbrib'd, *Hibernia*'s land?
> Or change the rocks of *Scotland* for the Strand?
> There none are swept by sudden fate away;
> But all, whom hunger spares, with age decay.

The truth is, like the ancient *Greeks* and *Romans*, he allowed himself to look upon all nations but his own as barbarians: not only *Hibernia*, but *Spain*, *Italy*, and *France*, are attacked in the same poem.] you mention "His prejudice against *Scotland* was early announced"—In the next page you go on to say—"not only *Hibernia*, but Spain" etc. It certainly should be "not only Hibernia *and Scotland*, but" etc. for the lines quoted from Johnson relate to both, and *Scotland* is the principal object of consideration, and

[1] "Plenty" used as an adjective was a colloquialism found in several contemporary dialects (OED, Plenty, II. 1; Joseph Wright, *English Dialect Dictionary*, 1898–1905, Plenty, 2). And cf. From EB, 1 Mar. 1779 and n. 18. For JB's answers to this and the following comments and queries, see *post* To EM, 27 Oct.

[2] MS. "we we"

[3] "A good deal" used to modify an adjective was not exclusively Scottish (OED, Deal, *sb.*[1], II. 6. b; *Scot. Nat. Dict.*, Dale, *n.*[1] and *v.* I. 6).

[4] Not exclusively Scottish (OED, In, *adv.* A. 1; Come, *v.* VIII. 59. a; *Scot. Nat. Dict.*, In, *prep.*, *adv.*, *v.*, *n.* I. A. 1).

therefore should not be omitted. I have ventured on this insertion, it being necessary to print off the first sheet yesterday.

P. 16, l. 1: [Sir *William Forbes* . . . who, with distinguished abilities, and application in his profession of a Banker, is at once a good companion, and a good christian . . .] "*profession* of a Banker" is not right. A Banker's is no *profession*. It certainly should be "his *business* of a banker"—but as I feared you might think that word *degrading*, I would make no change.[5]

P. 42, l. 9 from bottom: ["But stay! (said he, with one of his satyrick laughs). Ha! ha! ha!"] I wish the *Ha ha ha* were omitted. It is only fit for the drama. What can a reader do with it? It adds nothing.

P. 53, l. 4: "Is not a great *proportion* of it chosen by peers?" This was a cancelled leaf. Strange that we should pass over the inaccuracy. *Proportion* has 5 senses in Johnson's Dictionary, not one of them justifying this use of the word; "relation of one quantity to another" etc. etc.—but never the *quantity itself* so related. It undoubtedly should be "Is not a great *part* of it, or a great portion of it"—. The first appears to me the best.

P. 37, penult. of note:

["A cowardly Scot came John behind,
And ran him through the fair body!"]

"A cowardly *Scott*"—I find Rizzio was first stabbed by one Thos. *Scott*, so that perhaps this is not merely a national designation. Is this worth observing? See the histories.

P. 4: "sore rubs"—I had changed to *smart blows*, but on receiving your letter changed it back again to "sore rubs". But on talking it over with Langton he said *sore* was certainly unjustifiable and must be a scotticism.[6] A rub cannot be *sore*, though it may make the person rubbed *sore*. So to avoid impropriety, and to keep to your *idea*, it is printed "severe rubs" considering *rubs* metaphorically.

[5] JB ignored or overlooked this paragraph, and the passage remained unchanged in the 2nd ed. (*Life* v. 24–25). EM apparently thinks of "profession" as applying only to the learned professions—to divinity, law, and medicine (OED, Profession, III. 6. a). But SJ's *Dictionary* and OED show that the word had long been used in a wider sense, of any occupation.

[6] "Sore" could be used as an intensifying adjective both in Scottish (sair) and in English, but was more common in Scottish (*Scot. Nat. Dict.*, Sair, *adj.*, *n.*, *adv.*, I. 7; OED, Sore, *a.* I. 4. d).

P. 6, l. 9: "I beg *to be* understood, *that I* insert" etc. This is perhaps not ungrammatical, but yet it is certainly not neat. I have therefore ventured to make it—"I beg *it may be* understood, that I" etc.—The difference is minute, but yet I think you will on considering it see that I am right. It should be either "I beg to be understood *as* inserting" etc. or "I beg it may be understood that I insert" etc. I have preferred the latter.

I called on *Reed* yesterday.[7] He pointed out one mistake, and promises more. [P. 202: I was here amused to find Mr. Cumberland's comedy of the *West-Indian*, in which he has very well drawn a Highland character, Colin M'Cleod, of the same name with the family under whose roof we now were.] It is not in the *Westindian* that a Scotchman is introduced, but in the *Fashionable Lover* by the same author. This is easily corrected.—"A comedy of Mr. Cumberland's" would have been safer.

[P. 178: a mezzotinto of Mrs. Brookes the actress (by some strange chance in Sky) . . .] R. says Mrs. Brookes was sister to Houston the Engraver by whom her print was done, and that she was *not* an actress. He is generally correct in such matters; but I think you said, you saw her play. How is this?[8]

When he was at Cambridge,[9] he took the trouble to transcribe

[7] Isaac Reed (1742–1807), an authority on the drama, was a friend of SJ, JB, and EM. He helped SJ with the *Lives of the Poets* and, later, JB with the *Life*. JB praised his knowledge of English literary history (*Life* iv. 37).

[8] Hester Brooke, or Brooks (d. 1782), the actress with whom JB had an affair in 1761–62, is the subject of the only engraving of a "Mrs. Brooks" made by Richard Houston (c. 1721–75), the Irish-born engraver (*Earlier Years*, p. 78; J. C. Smith, *British Mezzotint Portraits*, 1884, ii. 649). However, according to John Taylor, who knew Mrs. Brooke in London and wrote the fullest account of her life, she was "the daughter of a respectable tradesman in the city" (*Records of My Life*, 1832, i. 32), which contradicts Reed's assertion. She was married to James Brooke, an apprentice engraver who later became a writer and succeeded John Wilkes in producing the *North Briton* (Anthony Wilson [Henry Bromley, pseud.], *Catalogue of Engraved* British Portraits, 1793, p. 309; *Gent. Mag.* Nov. 1807, lxxvii. 1080). JB met her in Edinburgh, after she had abandoned her husband and their three children, presumably driven by Brooke's violent temper, to pursue a career on the stage (*Earlier Years*, p. 78; Taylor, *Records*, i. 33–34). On 28 Dec. 1761, "Mrs. Brooks" appeared on the Edinburgh stage as Miranda in Susanna Centlivre's comedy *The Busybody* (Dibdin, p. 112). See further, *Earlier Years*, pp. 77–78, 82, 478.

[9] Reed visited Richard Farmer (1735–97), Master of Emmanuel College, each year at the time of the Stourbridge Fair. The fair, "formerly by much the most considerable in England", and still of great local interest, was held annually for a fortnight beginning on 18 Sept. (*Univ. Brit. Directory* ii. 497). In 1785 Reed was in Cambridge from 12 Sept. to 15 Oct. ("*Isaac Reed Diaries, 1762–1804*", ed. C. E. Jones, *University of California Publications in English*, 1946, x. 4, 139).

the title page of Archibald Campbell's Book. [P. 447: I know not how a *middle state* came to be mentioned. Her grace wished to hear him on that point. "Madam, (said he,) your own relation, Mr. Archibald Campbell, can tell you better about it than I can. He was a bishop of the nonjuring communion, and wrote a book upon the subject."] It is a very long and remarkable one. It was printed in folio in 1721. Being on so curious a subject, and so much being said of the author, he thinks the title should be given in a note, and has promised to send it to me. Do you approve?—

[P. 337: He said, he was angry at a boy of Oxford, who wrote in his defence against Kenrick; because it was doing him hurt to answer Kenrick.]—He says the name of the Oxford boy who defended Johnson against Kenrick was Berkeley;[10] and thinks it ought to be told in a note.

P. 162: "As we passed the barracks" etc. [at *Bernéra,*] "I looked wishfully at them as soldiers" etc. [have always every thing in the best order. But there was only a serjeant and a few men there.] I wish this paragraph was omitted. It appears a very slight and an[11] insignificant one. You had in your mind the recollection of having early wished to[12] enter into a military life,—but this not being stated *here* the paragraph seems very idle.

P. 295, l. 1: [He said, he could never get the meaning of an *Erse* song explained to him. They told him, the chorus was generally unmeaning. "I take it, said he, they are like a song which I remember: it was composed in Queen Elizabeth's time, on the Earl of Essex; and the burthen was "Radaratoo, radarate, radara tadara tandore."] "They told him the chorus was always unmeaning." Do you mean that the persons *then present* when you were in the Isle of Sky, told him,—or that Johnson on former occasions had always been told etc. If the latter it would be more explicit thus: "He added, 'I could never get the meaning of an

[10] William Kenrick (c. 1725–79) had attacked SJ in *A Review of Dr. Johnson's New Edition of Shakespeare: in Which the Ignorance, or Inattention, of That Editor Is Exposed, and the Poet Defended from the Persecution of His Commentators*, 1765. James Barclay (c. 1747–c. 1770) of Balliol College, Oxford, then published *An Examination of Mr. Kenrick's Review . . . By a Friend*, 1766. EM's copy of Kenrick's *Review* is now in the Bodleian Library, Oxford (*Alum. Oxon.*; *Life* i. 498, 556, v. 273, 549–50). In his copy of the 1st ed., EM wrote "His name was Berkley" at the bottom of p. 337, but no note to that effect was added in either the 2nd or 3rd ed. (*Life* v. 273). James Barclay's name was later used in the *Life* (i. 498).

[11] MS. "imprude" deleted before "an"

[12] MS. "for a" deleted before "to"

Erse song explained to me. I have been told[13] the chorus was generally unmeaning. I take it they are like' " etc.—or something of that sort.

Pray, as the passage stands at present and supposing no need of the above change,—is "*they* are like a song" right? Perhaps it may be justified by referring it to "Erse song" and "the chorus".

P. 87, l. 17: One of your own remarks. Will this do? "He told us that the value of the stockings exported from Aberdeen in time of peace was one hundred thousand pounds, and in time of war amounted to one hundred and seventy thousands pounds."

In same page every second line of the Latin should be indented.[14]

P. 523, l. 23: [They whose inferiour exertions are recorded, as serving to explain or illustrate the sayings of such men,] "may be proud of being thus associated, and *having their names carried* down" etc. This appears to me not quite accurate or at least not elegant. Perhaps better thus—"may be proud of being thus associated and *of* their names *being transmitted* to posterity" etc.

Next line but two: [Before I quit this subject, I think it proper to say, that I have suppressed every thing that I thought could really hurt any one now living. With respect to what *is* related, I thought it my duty to "extenuate nothing, nor set down aught in malice".] "that I have suppressed every thing *that* I thought" etc. Better—"*which* I thought". Ibid. last line but four: "I *thought* it my duty"—Better: "I *considered* it as my duty"—to avoid repetition of *thought*.

P. 47, l. ult.: [He {Joseph Ritter} was the best servant] "I ever saw *in my life*". Why the words underscored? It is too colloquial, not book-language, and nothing got by it.

I wrote ευκαιτε, I believe, in my hurry, in[15] my last letter, but don't be afraid; it shall be printed right: and you shall have your *Gataker on Lots* etc. to your own mind; though you are wrong, I think.

Pray in reading over Sir Joshua Reynolds's paper about Dr. J.'s contractions, don't forget it is written in *your name*. Hence he says, "Mr. Pope had the same opinion with *me* (i.e. with me, *Boswell*) on

[13] MS. "alway" deleted before "told"

[14] JB did not respond to this comment. EM made the alteration to SJ's Latin translation of Dryden's "Lines on Milton" in his own copy of the 1st ed. and in the 2nd ed. (*Life* v. 86 n. 1).

[15] MS. "to you" deleted before "in"

this subject." I puzzled myself there, and thought he had made some mistake, but he is very right.

I enclose my *rider* to Burke's note. I hope you will like it, and think you cannot *disapprove*, as it is entirely agreable to your own sentiments, justifies the former note, and at the same time pays him a handsome compliment.[16]

* * *

Here has my foolish Joseph[17] let in a prating tiresome egotist upon me, who has staid above an hour. Servants can never distinguish whom one wishes to see, and whom to exclude.—I must conclude therefore hastily, for it is now three o'clock, and I am engaged to dinner at four.

You have, enclosed, the Letter I mentioned in my last—[18] I tumbled over some *Morning Posts* yesterday, but could find none of the attacks that I had heard of, except a very paltry epigram, which however you shall have.[19]

[16] The proof-sheet containing EM's addition to the note on EB has not been reported; however, its original state can to some extent be reconstructed from the corrections EM later sent to JB together with the note that was finally printed (*post* From EM, 24 Oct. and n. 2).

[17] EM's servant Joseph Parkes, who with EM had witnessed the codicil to JB's will on 30 May (MS. Register House, Edinburgh).

[18] See *ante* From EM, 19 Oct.: "I sent a Letter [to *St. James's Chron.*], which will appear tomorrow—with 'Raderotoo'—I thought it a good morceau." EM's long letter, signed "*One* not *of 'other Times'* ", appeared in the issue for 18–20 Oct. p. [2]. Writing of "that *bra' Child*, and incomparable Poet, Ossian, the Son of Fingal", EM said, "The late Dr. Johnson always avowed his entire Disbelief in the Authenticity of these *moderno-antique* Poems; but it was in the Isle of Sky that he gave that silly Fiction its *coup de Grace*; for among the many curious and entertaining Anecdotes which Mr. Boswell has lately given to the World, in his *Tour to the Hebrides*, is the following." EM then quoted SJ's opinions on Ossian as reported by JB in the anecdote he calls "Raderotoo" above (1st ed. pp. 294–98; *Life* v. 240–43). EM enclosed a clipping (P 82:7) of his "good morceau" in this letter; the clipping is initialled "E.M." and contains a marginal note drawing attention to two corrections he had made in quoting from the 1st ed., which read: "Mr. M'Leod said, that was much liker than Mr. M'Pherson's translation of the former passage. . . . He [SJ] did not require Mr. M'Pherson's Ossian to be liker the original than Pope's Homer." EM altered both instances of "liker" to "more like", with a marginal comment, "better than *liker*". JB adopted these emendations in the 2nd ed. (p. 296; *Life* v. 242; see *post* To EM, 27 Oct. and n. 49).

[19] A clipping preserved among the Boswell Papers at Yale (P 82:5) may be this "paltry epigram":

A COMMENTARY *on* JOHNSON'S COMMENTATOR.

BOSWELL, first to raise a name,
And puff a literary fame,
Laid violent hands on PASCAL's glory;
Then ITCHING with a Patriot fire,
For SCOTIA's cause in bombast ire,
Hails William Pitt a Tory.
And now to raise a little cash,

FROM MALONE, 21 OCTOBER 1785

Pray can you solve the problem about the *hairs*, in the letter in the St. J. Chron. abusing Johnson, that I sent you?[20] It puzzled me. Courteney made it out at once. Farewell. Ever yours most sincerely,

E. MALONE

This Quack of Caledonia,
Crams JOHNNY BULL [with] sickly trash,
And calls it the JOHNSONIA.

J.M.

Grosvenor-street, Oct. 10, 1785.

See *post* To EM, 29 Oct. EM seems to have missed several attacks that appeared in *Morn. Post* between 30 Sept. and 14 Oct.: 30 Sept. p. [2]: "It is truly of *vast* consequence to the public, that Mr. *Boswell* has 'at *last*, quitted the Metropolis and gone into the country'. What great pains some weak people take to *puff* themselves into *notice*."

8 Oct. p. [2]: "By what appellation are we to style *Jemmy Boswell's* new mode of puffing himself? It might be with some propriety be styled the Puff *Posthumus*; we cannot help comparing Poor Dr. Johnson, as treated by Boswell, to a dead whale thrown on the sands of Leith, of whom every penny is made by his Caledonian Proprietor; the huge monster is first exhibited as a shew, and then all the blubber and bone sold to the highest bidder."

10 Oct. p. [3]: "*Boswell*, says Johnson, condemned the Scotch for their nationality, while in the same paragraph he tells us that Johnson thought no country so good as his own; how is this, good Master Boswell?" This paragraph was reprinted in *Pub. Adv.* 11 Oct. p. [4] .

14 Oct. p. [2] : "A Scotch correspondent informs us that *Master Boswell* is busily employed from morning to night in sounding his own praises; and that the Printer of a certain Morning Paper may shortly expect another packet of *puffs*, which he will be expected to distribute in proportional quantities in his different publications; but the Commissioners of the Stamp-office will no doubt make a scrutiny.

"Poor *Boswell* is destitute of original ideas. He possesses no stamina of true genius; and therefore to obtain a temporary but perishable reputation, he has, on two occasions, clung to the trains of great men. *Paoli* brought him from his literary obscurity; and that story being now forgot, *Jemmy's* fame was on the rapid decline, when suddenly the great Doctor's *death* proved the Caledonian's *resurrection*. What would the literary Hercules say if he saw his name bandied about in such trash?—*Rest perturb'd spirit*!"

[20] The letter appeared in *St. James's Chron.* 27–30 Aug. p. [2]; a clipping is preserved at Yale (P 82:1). Commenting on SJ's *Prayers and Meditations*, the writer observed that "the poor Doctor had, in religious Matters, and, perhaps, in religious Matters *only*, a distempered Brain." To prove that "a Man may be a good Scholar, a fine Poet, an excellent Critick, and yet be at Bottom but a weak Man", the writer told of "a Gentleman now living, whose Writings and Style are justly admired, and who is considered as an able Scholar, and a sensible Man; yet he is incapable of perceiving the following unquestionable Truth, *i.e.* Supposing there are more Men upon the Face of the Earth than there are Hairs on any one Man's Head, there must then be two Men with the same Number of Hairs on their Heads." See further *post* To EM, 30 Oct.; From EM, 5 Nov. pp. 271–72.

From Malone,
Monday 24 October 1785
MS. Yale (C 1899).

London, Oct. 24, 1785

MY DEAR SIR: I write you three words just as I am sitting down to dinner.—I forgot, I believe, in my last letter to tell you that I will not suffer them to work off Sheet C, but go on with D, E, etc. so that you will have it in your power to make what alterations you please in Burke's note, and with respect to the *Prince of darkness.* I have made Burke's note something better. For "on the look and action of the speaker" read, "on the peculiar manner of the speaker". For "a thousand concomitant circumstances" read "a thousand minute particulars". For "to set it before the eye of the spectator *naked and divested of* those ornaments which" etc. read "to set it before the eye of the spectator *divested of*[1] those concomitant circumstances which" etc. For "that my opinion is well founded" read, "that what I have asserted is well founded"—*Opinion* occurs just afterwards. In the beginning—"which they think with me, he undoubtedly merits". Which do you prefer, that, or this—"which they agree with me in thinking he" etc.[2]

I had struck out the inverted commas in p. 15, before I received your letter.[3]

I have been this moment at Payne's shop[4] to find out *Una est injusti* etc. p. 49. You are wrong. It is in Ovid's *Amor.* L. II. El. 11:[5] I think it will be best to quote two lines in the *note*, as they will somewhat explain Johnson's idea:

Non illic urbes, non tu mirabere sylvas;
Una est injusti caerula forma maris.

[1] MS. "(without)" written above "*divested of*"

[2] These changes were adopted in the note added to the 2nd ed. (pp. 24–26 n.; *Life* v. 32–34 n. 3). For JB's choices between the alternatives EM offers, and for his replies to the other comments in this letter, see *post* To EM, 30 Oct.

[3] On p. 15 of the 1st ed. quotation marks had been printed at the beginning of each of ten lines of a quotation by SJ; this was inconsistent with the usage of the rest of the book. This matter is not mentioned in any extant letter from JB; perhaps it was discussed in the covering letter of 15 Oct. now missing (see *ante* To EM, 15 Oct. n. 1).

[4] Thomas Payne (1719–99) and his son of the same name (1752–1831) were booksellers in Castle St. near Mewsgate; their shop was a gathering-place for the literati of the day, including EM, Steevens, and Windham (Maxted).

[5] *Amores* II. xi. 11–12. EM supplied the reference in his copy of the 1st ed. where he wrote "xi" over "11".

I have this moment hammered out a bad translation (for I could not get Garth's Ovid.)[6]

Nor groves nor towns the faithless ocean shows;
Unvaried still its azure surface flows.

I don't like it, but I believe it must do.

In the same sheet p. 60 [*Εργα νεων, βουλαιτε μέσων, 'έυκαιτε γερόντων.*] will this do for old Hesiod?

Let active enterprize the young engage,
The more adult be famed for counsel sage;
Prayer is the proper duty of old age.

It expresses the sense and that is all that can be said of it.

P. 51, l. 4 from bottom: [Dr. Johnson afterwards bid me try to write a description of our discovering Inch Keith, in the usual style of travellers, describing fully every particular; how we concluded that it must have once been inhabited, and introducing many sage reflections.] "how we concluded" is awkward, stuck in between *describing* in the former member, and *introducing* in the subsequent one. I have ventured to make it—"describing fully every particular; *stating the grounds on which we concluded* that it must have been" etc.[7]

P. 52, l. 14: [I happened luckily, in allusion to the beautiful Queen Mary, whose name is upon the fort, to think of what Virgil makes Aeneas say, on leaving the country of his charming *Dido*. Invitus regina tuo de littore cessi.] *on leaving*. It should be "on *having left*". Aeneas did not speak the words on his going away from Carthage,—but when he met Dido in the shades below, as an apology for *having* left her. Drydens translation is not very good, but will do better than Pitt's.[8]

Ibid., l. 2: [All that was said might be true, and yet in reality

[6] EM refers to *Ovid's Metamorphoses in Fifteen Books. Translated by the Most Eminent Hands*, 1717, which included translations by Dryden, Pope, Congreve, Addison, and others. The dedication was signed by Sir Samuel Garth (1661–1719), M.D., who also translated part of the work, so the whole came to be known as "Garth's Ovid". It does not include a translation of the *Amores*.

[7] A draft of this revision in EM's copy of the 1st ed. shows that EM first wrote "stating the reasons", and then substituted "grounds" for "reasons".

[8] Dryden's translation (1697) of the line, "invitus, regina, tuo de litore cessi" (*Aeneid* vi. 460), reads "Unwilling I forsook your friendly State". Christopher Pitt's translation (1740) reads, "I left your Realm reluctant".

there might be nothing to see. He said, "I'd have this island."] "All that was *said*". Better "All that was *told*"—*said* occurs just afterwards.

P. 53, l. 4: I have changed *proportion* to *part*. I have made all the other corrections in that sheet, that you desired.

Verte nocturna manu et diurna[9] your first ten sheets, as we shall want them first.

I hope to hear soon from you, and am ever faithfully and affectionately Yours,

EDMOND MALONE

Can you read this vile scrawl? I write in the greatest hurry, having some company to dine with me; Courteney among others, from {whom} I shall get a frank.

To Malone,
Thursday 27 October 1785
MS. Yale (L 921).

Auchinleck, 27 Octr. 1785

MY DEAR SIR: On my return home today after an absence of three days,[1] I found your most valuable packets of the 19 and 21 current. I am affraid I shall be too late to catch this day's post; so shall proceed directly to business.

P. 9: The *contractions* are well stated for the present.[2] Sir Joshua's note at *large* will be admirable in the *Life*; But it must be in Sir Joshua's own name.[3] "*Fore*legs" and the note on *doggedly* are an improvement.[4]

[9] "Turn with nightly and daily hand". See Horace, *Ars Poetica*, ll. 268–69: "vos exemplaria Graeca / nocturna versate manu, versate diurna": "For yourselves, handle Greek models by night, handle them by day" (trans. H. R. Fairclough, Loeb ed.).

[1] JB's Book of Company shows that he had gone to Ayr for the Quarter Sessions on 25 Oct., and that he and his wife had spent that night at Lady Crawford's at Rozelle and gone the following day, for dinner and the night, to John McAdam of Craigengillan's at Berboth.

[2] EM's note (*ante* From EM, 19 Oct. n. 7), with only minor verbal alterations, was added to the 2nd ed. (*Life* v. 18 n. 4). JB's comments in the main body of this letter were written in response to EM's letter of 19 Oct. The comments in the long postscript respond to EM's letter of 21 Oct.

[3] "But . . . name" is an interlineation in the MS., and "*Fore*legs" (which originally followed the semicolon) is written with a lower-case "f". For Sir Joshua's "note at *large*", see *ante* From EM, 19 Oct. and n. 7.

[4] See *ante* From EM, 19 Oct. and nn. 14, 16. In the 2nd ed. "legs" was changed to "fore-legs" (p. 28; *Life* v. 35); the note on

As to the note on p. 29 I wish the objectionable part had not been printed. But I cannot consent to omit it for my reason as to another passage that it looks like *flying*—And I am the more averse to it, that my omission might very plausibly be ascribed to a *mean* shrinking from an opinion which is not pleasing at St. James's. And as to the *Devil* I will not *fly* from *him*. "Resist the devil and he will *flee* from you" says the text.[5] If you please you may add, "Some of my most respected friends wished I would omit the latter part of this note, as unconnected with the former part and somewhat wild. I am satisfied that it would have been better it had not been printed at first. But I retain it lest I should be supposed to have abandoned opinions as to which I am firm";—If this requires correction, do as you will but preserve the meaning. I am sorry I cannot *yield*.[6]

P. 25, Note: Your *Rider* is excellent. But I *positively* will not impose it on the publick as *my own*. I beg it may be retained, and changed so as to suit[7] a third person and then put under it A FRIEND. Or if you would grant me MALONE it would honour it greatly. Then add, "I am greatly obliged to my friend for this Note to which I freely subscribe" (Express it as you please.)

P. 76: at "Man can do" put a Note "*I suppose he meant that I assiduously and earnestly recommended myself to some of the Members as in[7a] a canvas for an election into Parliament."—This is what I thought his meaning. You may express it better.[8]

P. 92: I cannot alter after Dr. Johnson's death what I constantly maintained when he was alive that the *Trinity* was *unseasonably* introduced in a company consisting of people who probably would have *attacked* the doctrine or LAUGHED at it. Dr. Johnson *heard* very well how it was introduced, and again and again afterwards persisted in being offended at it. He thought it was done on purpose to have a *contest*. As our worthy friend's name is not mentioned he need not be uneasy. But if he is very desireous of

"doggedly" was added not to p. 33 of the 2nd ed., but to a second occurrence of the word (p. 116), and in the 3rd ed. was moved to the earlier occurrence (*Life* v. 40 n. 3).

[5] James 4: 7.

[6] The note was reprinted without additions or omissions (*Life* v. 36–37 n. 3; see *post* From EM, 5 Nov. p. 267).

[7] MS. "the" deleted before "suit"

[7a] MS. "in" written above a deleted "upon"

[8] EM rephrased the note to read: "This, I find, is considered as obscure. I suppose Dr. Johnson meant, that I assiduously and earnestly recommended myself to some of the members, as in a canvass for an election into parliament" (*Life* v. 76 n. 2).

the alteration, let him have it—as it does not *contradict* what I hold.[9]

I am *sure* Dr. Johnson said no more to me of Telemachus Graham but *half drunk*. Please then put in a note Mr. Langton's additions—*looking* and *talking* and the *hornet*.—[10]

"Lobster'*s* claw"—to be sure.[11]

I take it "King James comes back" was "when a King is to be entertained"—or perhaps he *might* have a sly allusion to *Redeat* in Dr. King's sense. Let every Reader have his own conjecture.[12]

Let *horsehirer* be *altered* as you see best.[13]

"*That's* Homerick" will do.[14]

P. 82: for "*this* was another point" read "having a black servant was" etc.[15]

Lock's verses were printed from Dr. Brocklesby's copy of Sydenham. Please compare.[16]

[9] "As our worthy . . . I hold" is an interlineation in the MS. The passage was altered to read as Langton had suggested (*Life* v. 89).

[10] The note was added in the 2nd ed.: "I am sure I have related this story exactly as Dr. Johnson told it to me; but a friend who has often heard him tell it, informs me that he usually introduced a circumstance which ought not to be omitted. 'At last, sir, Graham, having now got to about the pitch of looking at one man, and talking to another, said, *Doctor*, &c.' 'What effect (Dr. Johnson used to add) this had on Goldsmith, who was as irascible as a hornet, may be easily conceived' " (p. 100 n.; *Life* v. 97 n. 3).

[11] 2nd ed.: "In the grotto, we saw a lobster's claw uncommonly large" (p. 68). This sentence was omitted from the 3rd ed., which substituted, "The grotto was ingeniously constructed" (*Life* v. 70).

[12] Nevertheless, a note was added to the 2nd ed.: "I find, some doubt has been entertained concerning Dr. Johnson's meaning here. It is to be supposed that he meant, 'when a king shall again be entertained in Scotland' " (p. 81 n.; *Life* v. 81 n. 3). Presumably the purpose of the note was to obviate any suspicions that SJ had Jacobite leanings. William King (1685–1763), D.C.L., Principal of St. Mary Hall, Oxford, delivered a famous speech at the opening of the Radcliffe Library (1749), in which he introduced the word "redeat"—"may he [the Old Pretender] return"—six times (*Oratio in Theatro Sheldoniano Habita Idibus Aprilibus, MDCCXLIX. Die Dedicationis Bibliothecae Radclivianae*, 1749; see also *A Translation of a Late Celebrated Oration. Occasioned by a Lible, Entitled, Remarks on Doctor K—g's Speech*, 1750).

[13] 2nd ed.: "a common ignorant Highland clown" (p. 160; *Life* v. 144).

[14] Unchanged in 2nd ed. (p. 82; *Life* v. 82).

[15] See *ante* To EM, 13 Oct. n. 22. 2nd ed.: "The circumstance of each of them having a black servant was another point of similarity between Johnson and Monboddo" (pp. 82–83; *Life* v. 82).

[16] This entry was crowded into the margin of the MS. without any sign to show where it should be inserted. It is placed here so as to follow the order of EM's letter of 19 Oct. Dr. Richard Brocklesby (1722–97), physician, attended SJ in his last illness and supplied JB with an account of his final days (From Brocklesby, 27 Dec. 1784). L. F. Powell notes that "Locke's complimentary verses were first appended to the second edition of Sydenham's *Methodus curandi Febres*, 1668: there are a few variants, chiefly of spelling and punctu-

Let *revoked* be inserted as to Langton on Hume's History. If he would give us his *name* it would add authority.[17]

Mr. *Courteney* is right as to *Quantum cedat*. By all means a Note. Solicit him for his *name*.[18] I wish to have as many stars in my firmament as I can get.

Mrs. Thrale was *re*inserted at the press upon Mr. Courteney's recommendation and she must remain—[19]

Horrid as to our great friend's *figure* must stand. It is *Churchill's* epithet which I shew not to be just.[20]

G. R. has done greatly. But I am much obliged to worthy Langton.

1000 Copies will be enough for this edition. But surely it should be printed *closer*. Pray *order* this.[21]

I am pretty sure that *Una est injusti* etc. is in Ovid's Epistles. But pray consult a *Delphini* Copy.[22]

I am *sure* Dr. Johnson said "Εργα Νεων" etc. was a saying "as old as *Hesiod*", for he read it so stated. If Langton can shew it in another Poet please put in a note "*The line is in . . ."[23]

ation, from Boswell's text" (*Life* v. 496). Apart from changes in capitalization, more than a half-dozen typographical corrections were made in the 2nd ed. (pp. 96–97 n.; *Life* v. 94 n. 1).

[17] 2nd ed.: "he revoked his recommendation" (p. 22 n.; *Life* v. 30 n. 3). Langton's name was not added; it has not hitherto been certain that he was JB's "worthy friend . . . in London".

[18] In the 2nd ed. a translation was given of "Quantum cedat virtutibus aurum": "With virtue weigh'd, what worthless trash is gold!" (p. 216 n.; *Life* v. 187 n. 1). A note was also added: "Since the first edition of this book, an ingenious friend has observed to me, that Dr. Johnson had probably been thinking on the reward which was offered by government for the apprehension of the grandson of King James II., and that he meant by these words to express his admiration of the Highlanders, whose fidelity and attachment had resisted the golden temptation that had been held out to them" (p. 217 n.; *Life* v. 187 n. 2). Courtenay's name does not appear; he is here first identified as JB's "ingenious friend".

[19] JB struck out Mrs. Thrale's name in the "Tour" MS. (J 33) and reinserted it in the first proof (P 84). See *ante* From EM, 19 Oct. n. 44. Her name was retained in the 2nd ed. (p. 299; *Life* v. 245).

[20] Unchanged in 2nd ed. (p. 17; *Life* v. 26). Charles Churchill (1731–64) satirized SJ in *The Ghost*, 1762, as "Pomposo", who has "Features so horrid, were it light, / Would put the Devil himself to flight" (ii. 687–88).

[21] *Ante* To EM, 13 Oct. and n. 78; From EM, 19 Oct. p. 236; *post* To EM, 30 Oct. and n. 14.

[22] *Ante* From EM, 24 Oct. and n. 5 for the correct citation; for JB's response, see *post* To EM, 30 Oct. The "Delphin Classics" were published in sixty-four volumes, Paris, 1674–1730; the title-pages read, "ad usum serenissimi Delphini": "for the use of His Royal Highness, the Dauphin". Ovid's works, which appeared in the series in 1689, were edited by Daniel Crespin.

[23] The Greek line on p. 60 is from Hesiod (*Life* v. 63 and n. 1).

I find I must now stop or lose the post. So adieu till the 29th when I shall write again. I am ever most faithfully and gratefully yours,

JAMES BOSWELL

P. 58: *plentiful*—certainly.[24]

P. 84: "*somewhat* drowsy".[25]

P. 92: dele *in* after "come".[26]

P. 10: Certainly insert *Scotland.*[27]

P. 37: "A cowardly SCOT" does not apply to Rizzio but to Johny Armstrong.[28]

P. 42: I resign the "Ha ha ha" to your deleting pen.[29]

P. 53: read "a great *part* of it".[30]

N.B. P. 227: Please put a note to l. 21 "alive". "*Since the first edition of this Book I am informed that John M'Kenzie still lives (in 1785) and that he was the first who introduced in the Hebrides a good method of curing fish which is at present considered as an object of parliamentary attention. Some consideration from Government to this useful old scottish *Member of Parliament* would be a liberal bounty."—Perhaps this note is *pamphletical.* If you think so omit it. Only let his being *still* alive remain.[31]

P. 183, l. 15: [I never saw a figure that was more perfectly a representative of a Highland gentleman.] "more perfectly *a representative*" seems a bad phrase. Would it not {be} better "that gave a more perfect representation"—or "a more perfect idea".[32]

Yes, I would have Goldsmiths lines on the English Nation inserted.[33]

If before this reaches you, your Rider to Burke and the Note on Johnson and Markham be printed off, I think instead of

[24] So changed in 2nd ed. (*Life* v. 61). Edward Gibbon also made this change in his copy of the 1st ed. (Osborn Collection). This and most of the following items were written in response to EM's letter of 21 Oct.

[25] So changed in 2nd ed. (*Life* v. 83). In his copy, Gibbon wrote "very" above "a good deal".

[26] So changed in 2nd ed. (*Life* v. 90).

[27] So changed in 2nd ed. (p. 11; *Life* v. 20).

[28] Unchanged in 2nd ed. (*Life* v. 43).

[29] Nevertheless, the passage remained unchanged in the 2nd ed. (*Life* v. 48).

[30] So changed in 2nd ed. (*Life* v. 56).

[31] This longer note was not added, but the phrase "old scottish *Member of Parliament*" was adopted in a shorter note (*ante* To EM, 15 Oct. n. 23).

[32] 2nd ed.: "that gave a more perfect representation of a Highland gentleman" (*Life* v. 162).

[33] Here JB responds to a query in EM's letter of 19 Oct. In his copy of the 1st ed. EM wrote, "Mem. to insert the lines". In the 2nd ed., "the character of the English nation" was changed to "the character of the British nation", and Goldsmith's lines were added (p. 431; *Life* v. 344–45).

cancelling them I shall *add* at the end of the Book—That the Rider though put in my name when I was at a distance from the press is written by one of the best Criticks of the age—or by Mr. Malone, to whom I am greatly obliged for it; but cannot allow myself to neglect the maxim of my own profession *Suum cuique tribuito*[34]—And as to the *Omission* of the Americans and the devil say it was done to please some of my most respected friends who thought it unconnected with the subject and rather too wild. But I still adhere to the opinions in it.[35]

Your corrections on pp. 4 and 6 "*severe* rubs"[36] and "it *may* be understood"[37] are for the better.

P. 202: *Fashionable Lover*. One is vexed at such mistakes.[38]

I hope you will approve of my printing a sheet of all the Corrections etc. in this edition and let it be sold for 6d. or 3d. to the purchasers of the first.[39]

Perhaps it is a different Mrs. Brookes that Mr. Reed means. *Mine* was an *Actress* and lived (perhaps lives yet) with Mr. Griffiths once a Player brother of *Frances* wife of *Henry*.[40]

I am obliged to him both for Archibald Campbell's title page,

[34] "To each man his due", a legal maxim adapted from Cicero, *De Officiis* I. v. 15; see also *Life* ii. 201, iii. 323 n. 2.

[35] See n. 6 above.

[36] So changed in 2nd ed. (p. 4 n.); the 3rd ed. was changed to read "severe strokes" (*Life* v. 15 n. 1).

[37] So changed in 2nd ed. (p. 6; *Life* v. 16).

[38] 2nd ed.: "I was here amused to find Mr. Cumberland's comedy of the *Fashionable Lover*" (*Life* v. 176).

[39] JB had already proposed the publication of a separate list of errata (*ante* To EM, 13 Oct. p. 209), but the idea seems to have been dropped.

[40] See *ante* From EM, 21 Oct. and n. 8. The only change made in the passage concerning "Mrs. Brookes" for the 2nd ed. was that her name was spelled "Brooks" (2nd ed. p. 178; *Life* v. 158). In the proofs of the 1st ed. of the *Tour* JB had called her "my fair friend" but later struck out the phrase. Hester Brooke and actor- manager Richard Griffith both joined the Theatre Royal, Norwich, in 1763, and during her long tenure with the company Mrs. Brooke's name was closely associated with Griffith's (D. H. Eshleman, *The Committee Books of the Theatre Royal, Norwich, 1768–1825*, 1970, p. 161). JB had seen Griffith perform in 1761 in Edinburgh, where he had played as early as 1754, specializing in the portrayal of "fops and fine gentlemen" (Journ. 21 Dec. 1761; Jackson, p. 42). Griffith was acting-manager of the Theatre Royal from 1766 until 1780, when he resigned from the job because of poor health (he continued as an actor in Norwich and, later, in London); Mrs. Brooke resigned the following year, having contracted cancer, and died in 1782 (Eshleman, p. 159, 161–62; Taylor, *Records* i. 35–36). JB was apparently unaware of her death when he was revising for the 2nd ed. of the *Tour*.

JB's phrase, "brother of *Frances* wife of *Henry*", alludes to *A Series of Genuine Letters between Henry and Frances*, 1757–70, a collection of letters between Griffith's sister Elizabeth (c. 1727–93) and her husband, another Richard Griffith (c. 1716–88; Eshleman, p. 159).

and the Boy at Oxford's name, and approve of both being put in *notes*.[41]

P. 162: the Barracks of Bernéra are mentioned to have been looked at *wishfully* on account of the *good order* in which soldiers have every thing. It was the just apprehension of bad quarters, made me look wishfully. So the sentence is proper enough.[42]

P. 295, l. 1: I think I sent an alteration of this in my last. My meaning is that the Company present told him. The alteration should be "I take it erse songs are like a song which I remember. It was composed" etc.[43]

P. 87, l. 17: Your alteration of the Aberdeen stockings exported is good. Or it may be "and to the value of one hundred and seventy thousand pounds in time of war".[44]

P. 523, l. 23: I think the present reading as good as the alteration to "and of their names being transmitted" etc. But if you like the alteration I submit.—The other corrections on that page "*which* I thought"—and "I *considered* it as my duty" are good.[45]

P. 47, l. ult.: *in my life* may to be sure be delete. Would it be right to mention that my Bohemian was of the Roman Catholick persuasion?[46]

[41] Archibald Campbell (1668–1744), nonjuring Bishop of Aberdeen, the immeasurably long title of whose *Doctrines of a Middle State between Death and the Resurrection*, 1721, is printed in full as a note in the 2nd ed. (pp. 447–48; *Life* v. 356 n. 2), but no note on Barclay was added (*ante* From EM, 21 Oct. n. 10).

[42] Unchanged in 2nd ed. (*Life* v. 145).

[43] In his preceding letter (*ante* To EM, 15 Oct. p. 245) JB had proposed altering the passage to make "an *Erse* song" agree with "they": "He said, he could never get the meaning of *Erse* songs explained to him. They told him, the chorus was generally unmeaning. 'I take it, said he, they are like a song which I remember' ". EM then queried whether "they told him" referred to the company present or to those with whom SJ had discussed Erse poetry "on former occasions" (*ante* From EM, 21 Oct. p. 240). Here JB affirms that "they told him" refers to the company present and returns to his earlier point. This time, however, he proposes to resolve the disagreement of "an *Erse* song" and "they" by changing "they" to "Erse songs". 2nd ed.: "He said, he could never get the meaning of an *Erse* song explained to him. They told him, the chorus was generally unmeaning. 'I take it, (said he,) Erse songs are like a song which I remember' " (*Life* v. 241).

[44] *Ante* To EM, 13 Oct. and n. 39; From EM, 21 Oct. p. 241. None of the alterations so far proposed was adopted in the 2nd ed., which reads: "He told us that the value of the stockings exported from Aberdeen was, in peace, a hundred thousand pounds; and amounted, in time of war, to one hundred and seventy thousand pounds" (*Life* v. 86).

[45] All of these changes were made in the 2nd ed. (p. 527; *Life* v. 415–16), except that the 2nd ed. reads "considered it my duty", not "considered it as my duty".

[46] The phrase was omitted in the 2nd ed., but no reference to Joseph Ritter's Catholicism was inserted (*Life* v. 53). JB did mention it in the *Life*: "I asked Dr.

P. 487, l. 21: [That *Fingal* is not from beginning to end a translation from the Galick . . .] "Galick" I beleive should be spelt "Ga*e*lick".[47]

P. 496, l. 17: [one evening, a great many years ago, when Dr. Blair and I were sitting together in the pit of Drury-Lane playhouse . . .] read "Dr. Hugh Blair" to distinguish clearly Dr. Hugh the Rhetorician from Dr. John the Chronologist.[48]

P. 296: *more like* is better than *liker.*[49]

The Post town being four miles from me, this was not in time, so will come two days later. But I do not regret it, as some things will be better.[50]

From Malone, Friday 28 October 1785

MS. Yale (C 1900).

ADDRESS in Courtenay's hand: Jams. Boswell Esqr., Auchinleck, Cumnock, Dumfries.

FRANK: London Octbr. Twenty Eighth 1785. Free J. Courtenay.

POSTMARKS: 28 OC, FREE.

London, Octr. 28, 1785
Four o'clock

MY DEAR SIR: Hang the Scotch Post! I was in hope to have received a line from you to-day relative to Burke's note; and yet on consideration I believe you could not have received the printed note, so as to answer it, though you might have received a former

Johnson whether his [Ritter's] being a Roman Catholick should prevent my taking him with me to Scotland. JOHNSON. 'Why no, Sir. If *he* has no objection, you can have none' " (*Life* ii. 103).

[47] Changed to "Gallick" in 2nd ed. (p. 490; *Life* v. 389). Both "Gaelic(k)" and "Galic(k)" were standard spellings (OED, Gaelic).

[48] So changed in 2nd ed. (p. 499; *Life* v. 396). Hugh Blair (1718–1800), D.D., minister of the High Church, Edinburgh, and Regius Professor of Rhetoric and Belles Lettres in the University of Edinburgh, had long been JB's friend. John Blair (d. 1782), LL.D., was the author of *The Chronology and History of the World, from the Creation to the Year of Christ, 1753*, 1754.

[49] For EM's changes of "liker" to "more like" in a newspaper extract, see *ante* From EM, 21 Oct. n. 18; here JB approves them for the 2nd ed. (*Life* v. 242).

[50] This paragraph was added at the top of the first page of the MS., above the date-line and salutation. The post-town was Cumnock.

letter about it.[1]—The Tour goes on swimmingly. There are as you will see but 112 copies left, and Dilly is pressing for expedition.[2] I long to see the Remarks on you, which are advertised, but not published. I suspect they will come from some friend of Lord Macdonald's[3]—I enclose you a fair copy of your first sheet, which is the only one printed off. The paper is better than the former.[4] You see it to disadvantage, not being pressed.—The Letter in the St. James's is a very sensible one, and must be of service. I don't know the author. Selfe says *a very considerable man indeed*[5]—But I must proceed to business.

[1] EM had enclosed a proof of his "rider" to the note on EB in his letter of 21 Oct., and had mentioned the rider in his letter of 19 Oct. The letter of 21 Oct. probably did not arrive at Auchinleck until about 26 Oct., and JB did not see it until his return from the Quarter Sessions on 27 Oct. (*ante* To EM, 27 Oct. and n. 1).

[2] EM enclosed a note from Dilly dated "Friday 28th Octr.", which reads: "Mr. Dilly respectful Compliments to Mr. Malone with the letter to Mr. Boswell which Mr. M—— will please to forward—Mr. Dilly has now about 112 Copies of the Tour—and the reprint should go on with all possible expedition." JB returned Dilly's letter to him to EM (*post* To EM, 2 Nov.) and it has not been reported.

[3] The pamphlet, signed "Verax" and entitled *Remarks on the Journal of a Tour to the Hebrides, in a Letter to James Boswell, Esq.*, was printed for John Debrett and dated "London, October 27, 1785". Nevertheless, the pamphlet seems not to have been available until at least 7 Nov. (*post* From EM, 5 Nov. p. 271). *Pub. Adv.* first advertised the pamphlet as published "this day" in the issue for 8 Nov.; *St. James's Chron.* first advertised it in the issue for 8–10 Nov. Verax attacked JB's vanity, and faulted his writing for its "inelegancy of style"; he also criticized SJ's poetry and appended an ode by "a friend of mine"—but probably Verax himself—on the loss of SJ's oak stick (see *Life* v. 318–19). The criticisms in the pamphlet were considered rather mild; in *Crit. Rev.* (Dec. 1785) lx. 474, an anonymous reviewer wrote, "we are almost ready to suspect this to be a friendly attack." The pamphlet is discussed by Charles Ryskamp, in "Boswell and Walter James; Goethe and Daniel Malthus", *Eighteenth-Century Studies in Honor of Donald F. Hyde*, ed. W. H. Bond, 1970, pp. 207–24. Ryskamp suggests that Verax was probably the novelist and poet Richard Graves (1715–1804). Sir Alexander Macdonald (c. 1745–95), Bt., later (1776) first Baron Macdonald [I.], had entertained JB and SJ meanly at Armadale in Skye and had come under attack in the *Tour* (1st ed. pp. 165–66; *Life* v. 148 n. 1). Macdonald apparently had nothing to do with Verax's attack, but was soon to prepare an attack of his own; see *post* To EM, 11 Nov. and n. 15, 10 Mar. 1786 and n. 3, 12 Mar. 1786 and n. 3.

[4] By "fair copy" EM means not a proof, but the sheet (B, pp. [1]–16) in final form for the 2nd ed. This sheet, which survives at Yale (P 86), contains the text from *Life* v. 13 to v. 26. The paper of the 2nd ed. is thinner than that of the 1st.

[5] EM refers to a letter signed "M. M.", which appeared in *St. James's Chron.* 22–25 Oct. p. [1]. "M. M." praised JB's *Tour*, which he said had made him "impatient to see the Life of his [JB's] Fellow-Traveller". A regular correspondent in *St. James's Chron.*, "M. M." apparently was not a member of SJ's circle, for in his letter he says, "Mr. Boswell has made me personally acquainted with a Man to whom I was before a Stranger; he has drawn his Picture better than Sir Joshua could have drawn it." He also criticizes Sir Joshua Reynolds for placing "himself and Mr. Jarvois in that inimitable painted Window at New College as Parties in the Adoration, and yet *looking*

P. 35, l. 11: [We then conducted him down the] "Post-house stairs, Parliament close". Should it not be—"*and* parliament" etc.[6]

P. 39, l. 7: [But Sir Adolphus, who had a charming sweet temper . . .] "a *charming* sweet" etc. I have ventured to substitute *very* for *charming*. The latter quite a Lady's word.

P. 38: [I once took the liberty to ask him, if Swift had personally offended him, and he told me, he had not.] Swift was never in London after 1737 so could not have personally affronted Johnson. But the passage requires[6a] no change.

P. 43, l. 10 {from bottom} [*vicious intromission*, that is to say, intermeddling with the effects of a deceased person, without a regular title, which formerly was understood to subject the intermeddler in payment of all the defunct's debts.] "*in* payment". Surely this should be—"*to* payment".

P. 92, l. 8:[7] ["What is to come of society, if a friendship of twenty years is to be broken off for such a cause?"] "What is to *come* of society" etc. This is certainly not English, and should be, "what is to *become*" etc. and so I am sure Johnson said. I suspect it merely a misprint.[8]

P. 110, l. 5 from bottom: [Dr. Johnson, who did not admire it, got off very well, by taking it out, and reading the two second stanzas with much melody.] "the two second stanzas"—What does this mean? We say the *first two*, the *first four* stanza{s} etc. (and some improperly say, the *two first*)—but what is "the two second"?—If I should not get your answer to this quere I will venture[9] to substitute—"and reading two stanzas"—as that will be perfectly safe.

P. 115, *Club note*: [Our club, formerly at the Turk's Head, Gerrard street . . .] I know you don't like parentheses; but will it[10]

at those who come to admire two such excellent Artists". Reynolds had designed the west window in the chapel of New College, Oxford. A clipping of "M. M.'s" letter, dated in EM's hand, is preserved at Yale (P 82:9). Selfe was the corrector at Baldwin's press (Journ. 6 Jan., 24 July 1790; see also *post* From EM, 5 Nov. p. 268).

[6] JB replies to this and the following comments and queries in *post* To EM, 2 Nov.

[6a] MS. "?wants" deleted before "requires"

[7] MS. "l. 2"

[8] "Come of" was not a misprint, but the reading of the "Tour" MS. SJ used "come" to mean "become" in *Rasselas*, chap. 44.

[9] MS. "will venture" written above deleted "venture"

[10] MS. "it it"

not be for the honour of the club to ascertain its *birth*, and add after "Gerrard Street" "(where it was[11] first instituted in the year)".

P. 159, l. 10 from bottom: [We rode on well, till we came to the high mountain called the *Rattakin*, by which time both Dr. Johnson and the horses were a good deal fatigued.] "It is a *terrible* steep to climb." I imagine you had the idea of *labour* not *danger* in your mind. If so, *painful* will be better than *terrible*, which is a vulgar word, (as applied here) like *mortal* strong, etc.

P. 154, l. penult: [As he narrated the particulars of that ill-advised, but brave attempt, I] "*several times burst* into tears". Is not this too strong? Would it not be better—"I could not refrain from tears".

P. 125, note: [In Scotland, there is a great deal of preparation before administrating the sacrament.] *administrating*—is obsolete. Even Hooker uses *administering*.[12]

P. 127, l. 9: [I was afraid of a quarrel between Dr. Johnson and Mr. M'Aulay.] "of a quarrel"—Would not *altercation* be better.

P. 129: [It had only two of the Latin fathers, and one of the Greek ones in Latin.] "Greek *ones*". I have a horrour of this plural.[13] "Greek *fathers*" will avoid it, and the *repetition* is not so bad as the other.

P. 162,[14] l. 6 from bottom: [he did not hear of us till we had passed his house, otherwise he should have insisted on our passing the night there.]—"*passed* his house"—"*passed* the night". I don't know how to mend it. I believe we tried before in vain.

P. 145, l. 7: [Dr. Johnson would not hurt her delicacy, by insisting on "seeing her bed chamber," like *Archer* in the *Beaux Stratagem*.] I think it would be more elegant—"by insisting like

[11] MS. "first met, or" deleted before "was"

[12] "Administrate" is less common than "administer", but does not seem to have been obsolete in the eighteenth century (OED, Administrate and Administer). SJ, in his *Dictionary*, 1755, for "Administrate" gives only the definitions, "To exhibit; to give as physick". Under "Administer" he quotes Richard Hooker (c. 1554–1600), *Of the Laws of Ecclesiastical Polity*, 1593, IV. x: "Have not they the old popish custom of *administering* the blessed sacrament of the holy eucharist with wafer-cakes?"

[13] See SJ's *Dictionary*, 1755, One, *n. s.*, 12: "*One* has sometimes a plural, either when it stands for persons indefinitely; as, *the* great ones *of the world*: or when it relates to some thing going before, and is only the representative of the antecedent noun. This relative mode of speech, whether singular or plural, is in my ear not very elegant, yet is used by good authors."

[14] MS. "161"

Archer in the comedy, on 'seeing her bedchamber' ". There is no need of naming such a well known play.

[P. 261: He was too proud to submit, even for a moment, to be the object of ridicule, and instantly retaliated with such keen sarcastick wit, and such a variety of degrading images, of every one of which I was the object, that, though I can bear such attacks as well as most men, I yet found myself so much the sport of all the company, that I would gladly expunge from my mind every trace of this severe retort.] I find great objection has[15] been made to your suppression of D. J.'s retort in the *Seraglio* conversation. I wish it had been given; but yet I think you have a very good defence, and therefore beg leave to suggest the addition of a note to this purpose.

After stating the objection—"The objectors forget that I have said in the conclusion of my work that I have suppressed whatever I thought could really[16] hurt any one now living. I have in various places in this work shewn that I did not wish to spare myself; but in the present instance I had surely a right to the same indulgence that I gave to others; I mean the suppression of what at the time particularly wounded my private feelings." Or something of that sort—

"Please send" is certainly as Wilkes observes not good English; and it was to vex him that you used the expression several times in your long letter to me.[17] Whenever I meet with him, I shall inform him of your malice. You are not to be reviewed in the Gent. Magazine this month. If in the others, I will send them.[18]—Ever Yours Affectionately,

E. MALONE

[15] MS. "about" deleted before "has"

[16] MS. EM first wrote "omitted whatever could give" and then wrote "suppressed" above a deleted "omitted", inserted "I thought" above the line with a caret between "whatever" and "could", and deleted "give" before "really"

[17] "Please send" does not occur in JB's letters of 13 and 15 Oct., but cf. "Please read seal and send" in *ante* To EM, 13 Oct. p. 219. Perhaps EM is referring to the covering letter of 15 Oct., now missing (*ante* To EM, 15 Oct. n. 1).

[18] JB's *Tour* was favourably reviewed in *Gent. Mag.* (Nov. 1785) lv. 889–94. Preserved with this letter is a transcription in EM's hand of a passage from *Pub. Adv.* 28 Oct. p. [2]. The transcription, contained in its own wrapper and addressed "Mr. Boswell", reads, "*Boswell.*—You may ever know a man of merit from the noise and nonsense vented against him by the dullness or dishonour of the times. Thus may Boswell repel each puny attack, while he further sooths himself with the eulogy on himself from Sam. Johnson, and in the dining parlour of Jack Lee."

To Malone,
Saturday 29 October 1785
MS. Yale (L 922).
ADDRESS: To Edmond Malone Esq., Queen Anne Street East.

Auchinleck, 29 Octr. 1785

MY DEAR SIR: The success of our Book is very flattering indeed. Wilkes has[1] written to me what you mention. But it does not in the least affect me. The Epigram you sent is not so very bad. I suspect *a certain penurious gentleman.*[2] I am much obliged to you for your *defence* in the St. James's Chronicle.

I wish the note on *Quantum cedat* etc. to be "Mr. Courteney not less distinguished by private[3] virtues and accomplishments than by parliamentary talents has obligingly helped me" etc.[4]

I am anxious that the Americans and the Evil Spirit may remain since they have been once in; and I believe must cancel if they are delete. I will also cancel rather than falsely assume such an excellent note as yours on Burke's Wit. If *one of the best criticks*[5] etc. is to remain in two other places, it should be there too, to mark *identity*. But I would be obliged to you for *Mr. Malone* in all. Please add to that note the fullest and clearest avowal of its being my own sentiments and altogether just. *There* I give you leave to *speak for me*.

I find myself not disposed to translate the quotations. My spirits are quite different from what they were in London. Such as cannot be found already translated or are not easily done may be omitted.[6]

My Wife returns you her best compliments. I have made her perfectly well acquainted with you.

I hope to be with you on the 16 Novr. On thursday 3 friday 4 or

[1] MS. "indeed" deleted before "has"

[2] For the epigram, see *ante* From EM, 21 Oct. and n. 19. In the *Tour* JB twice speaks of a "penurious gentleman of our acquaintance" (*Life* v. 277, 315), meaning Lord Macdonald (in 1773 Sir Alexander Macdonald). The "penurious gentleman" is named in the "Tour" MS. (*Hebrides*, p. 242).

[3] MS. Originally "Courteney whose private"

[4] *Ante* From EM, 19 Oct. p. 235; To EM, 27 Oct. and n. 18. The note for the 2nd ed. referred to Courtenay only as "an ingenious friend" (p. 217 n.; *Life* v. 187 n. 2).

[5] Other references to EM as "one of the best criticks of our age" occur in *Life* v. 78 n. 5 and v. 399 n. 4.

[6] *Ante* To EM, 13 Oct. and n. 72.

saturday 5 a letter directed to me *Edinburgh* will come before I set out.[7]

I owe to worthy Langton all that can be properly done. So let him have his own way of the *censurable* dispute as it does not *contradict* my opinion.[8] I ever am, My Dear Sir, most faithfully yours,

James Boswell

I shall bring all my materials for the Life with me.

To Malone,
Sunday 30–31 October 1785
MS. Yale (L 923).

Auchinleck, 30 Octr. 1785

My Dear Sir: I did not (by a neglect of one of my *people*) receive your favour of the 24th till today, when I should have received it yesterday. But I could not have answered it sooner. How happy am I that Sheet C is not thrown off. I am quite *inflexible* as to my note, on the Americans and the Evil Spirit. (Which my *addition* will soften or more properly it will soften criticism.)[1] And I am quite *positive* that I will not borrow such feathers as the rich plumage of your note on Burke. I greatly approve of your variations upon it, and where you write *double* I prefer "*without* those concomitant circumstances"—to *divested of*—The former agrees better with *concomitant*. I like also "they agree in thinking"—better than "they think".[2] You surely can have no difficulty in altering your note so as to apply to—"one[3] of the best Criticks of the age"—or—"Mr. Malone"—Let a —— be put between my Note and it. Perhaps it may be introduced thus

[7] JB's Book of Company shows that he departed for Edinburgh on 4 Nov. He left Edinburgh on 12 Nov. and arrived in London on 17 Nov. (Journ.).

[8] *Ante* To EM, 27 Oct. and n. 9.

[1] *Ante* To EM, 27 Oct. and n. 6; *post* From EM, 5 Nov. and n. 6. JB wrote this and the following remarks in response to EM's letter of 24 Oct.

[2] EM did not receive the present letter until after sheet C had been printed (*post* From EM, 5 Nov. p. 267 and n. 6); thus he could not follow JB's preferences here. The note in the 2nd ed. reads "which they think with me, he undoubtedly merits" and "divested of those concomitant circumstances" (p. 26 n.; *Life* v. 32 n. 3).

[3] MS. "A friend" deleted before "one"

"Since the first edition some persons have objected" etc. "upon which One of the best Criticks of the age has remarked"—And then take it in and instead of "*my* opinion" say "the Authour's"—"the Journalist's" or "Mr. Boswell's". If you hesitate might not C stand till we meet?[4]

I thank you for your accurate attention to "Una est injusti"—Your translation is good. Only I doubt if *unvaried* conveys fully what is meant by *una* or rather what Dr. Johnson meant viz. that the sea is the same *every where*.[5]

As to *Hesiod* is it not a reflection on *english* that it requires three lines of *it* for one line of *greek*. I approve however of your translation except the second line. *The more adult* is I think too formal and does not sound well. Suppose we make it

Be vigorous manhood famed for counsel sage.

Might not the first line be as well thus

In youth let active enterprise engage.

or

Let active enterprise our youth engage.

But do as you will. If no *name* is put to the translations, I must *thank* a *friend* for them in a *Note* or *Advertisement to the second edition*.[6]

P. 51 I think might have stood as before, though you have made it better.[7] Are you not too desireous of perfection? We must make *some* allowance for the Book being a *Journal*.

P. 52: *on leaving* is very advantageously changed to "on having

[4] Since we lack any earlier versions of EM's addition to this note, it is not easy to tell exactly where JB's suggested revisions were supposed to fit. One plausible guess is that "upon which One of the best Criticks of the age has remarked" was intended to replace "I was well aware" (*Life* v. 32 n. 3—p. 2 of note). The first-person pronouns in the note were to be replaced with "the author", "Mr. Boswell", or third-person pronouns. JB intended "the Authour's" to replace the "my" of "my opinion", a phrase that appeared in the proof of the note, but that EM changed to "what I have asserted" (*ante* From EM, 24 Oct. and n. 2; *Life* v. 32 n. 3—p. 3 of note). Thus the reading that JB proposes is, "the being in company with him, for a single day, is sufficient to shew that the Authour's opinion is well founded".

[5] *Ante* From EM, 24 Oct. and n. 5; *post* From EM, 5 Nov. and n. 29.

[6] For further discussion of the translation, see *post* From EM, 5 Nov. and n. 25. JB acknowledged EM's translations as the work of "the friend whose observations are mentioned in the notes, p. 78 and 503" (2nd ed. p. 454 n.; *Life* v. 361 n. 2). These are the notes in which EM is described as "one of the best criticks of our age" (*ante* To EM, 29 Oct. n. 5).

[7] So changed in 2nd ed. (*Life* v. 55).

left".[8] Wherever there is essential errour I am clear for correction.

(A strange parenthesis.—I cannot for my life recollect the *name* of your Housekeeper and Cook Mrs. —— I mean Betty's surname and I am disturbed by hunting for it.)[9]

Please add *Dryden* to the translation of "Invitus" etc.[10] I know not whether it be better to print the translations in text or notes.[11] I would not have the Epitaphs or Dr. Johnsons Poems translated in this edition.[12] And as the translations and additional notes[13] will take up room—the compositor should surely *set closer*.[14]

I should think my Crest and Cypher might be done on a plate of Copper[15] as thick as the wooden one so as to be struck off at once

[8] So changed in 2nd ed. (*Life* v. 56).

[9] *Post* From EM, 5 Nov. p. 272.

[10] The translation added from Dryden was "Unhappy queen! / Unwilling I forsook your friendly state" (*Life* v. 56 n. 1). EM also set off "regina" with commas in the Latin quotation: "Invitus, regina, tuo de littore cessi."

[11] The translations were printed as notes.

[12] MS. "in this edition" is an interlineation, which includes several words, now deleted and illegible, before "in". For further discussion of the epitaphs on Maclaurin and Smollett, which were not translated in the 2nd ed., see *post* From EM, 5 Nov. p. 266; To EM, 11 Nov. and nn. 3, 4. For other Latin poems not translated, see *ante* To EM, 13 Oct. n. 72. Latin verses by Sir Alexander Macdonald were added to the 2nd ed. as an appendix; these were not translated (pp. 533–34; *Life* v. 419–20).

[13] Additional notes were added to the 2nd ed. at pp. 9 (*Life* v. 18 n. 4: SJ's "contractions"), 76 (v. 76 n. 2: JB's election to The Club), 81 (v. 81 n. 3: the *Muses' Welcome*), 100 (v. 97 n. 3: Graham and Goldsmith), 115 (v. 108 n. 8: Vesey), 116 (v. 110 n. 1: "doggedly"; see *ante* To EM, 27 Oct. n. 4), 217 (v. 187 n. 2: "Quantum cedat"), 227 (v. 193 n. 1: John M'Kenzie), 402 (v. 320 n. 2: *Mercheta Mulierum*), 428 (v. 342 n. 1: "to *stultify* himself"), 447 (v. 356 n. 2: Campbell's *Middle State*), 462 (v. 367 n. 3: epitaphs; see *post* To EM, 11 Nov. nn. 3, 4), 524 (v. 413 n. 3: Sir William Forbes), and 527 (v. 415 n. 4: on passages omitted from 2nd ed.; note expanded in 3rd ed.). Two notes on Sir Alexander Dick were added to the 2nd ed. but omitted from the 3rd; for the first (p. 42; v. 48), see *ante* To EM, 15 Oct. n. 22. The second (p. 525; v. 414), added to "*Requiescant in pace*", reads: "While these sheets were passing through the press, my valuable friend Sir Alexander Dick, mentioned in p. 42, has been added to the number." Also the note on EB (pp. 24–26; *Life* v. 32 n. 3) was greatly expanded in the 2nd ed.

[14] The compositor did, in fact, "set closer" to compensate for the additional notes, so that the two editions correspond closely in pagination up to p. 447, where the note on Campbell's *Middle State* was added. Other notes, especially the long one containing the epitaphs on Smollett and Maclaurin (pp. 462–63) caused further divergence in the pagination, so that the main text of the 2nd ed. runs to 528 pages as contrasted with the 524 of the 1st. Two appendices were added to the 2nd ed. (pp. [529]–34) and, on the unnumbered page at the end of the book, the advertisement for the *Life of Johnson* was expanded to fill the space left by the omission of the errata on the corresponding page of the 1st ed. In both editions, the verso of this last leaf is blank. The 2nd ed. also added an advertisement (p. [viii]) and a table of contents (pp. [ix]–xx). The 3rd ed., which was set much closer than the 1st and 2nd, comes to only 442 pages, plus sixteen pages of front matter and the unnumbered leaf at the end.

[15] MS. "*stout*" deleted before "Copper"

with the printed Title.[16] There is no hurry as to this. I may perhaps get a better drawing or even engraving at Edinburgh and bring with me, or have it sent up.

Ibid.: "All that was *told*" is an improvement.[17]

I should suppose we have now made all the corrections we can well do.

My Wife says she wishes I would set out so as to be with you as soon as possible that we may confer as the edition proceeds. It is humiliating to experience how much I depend upon *situation* for happiness. My Wife says my spirits are like brandy set on fire. If not constantly stirred the flame will go out. The weather here at present is exceedingly cold—snow, frost, sleet. I suffer from it.

Tomorrow I have a sale by auction of my crop etc. and am to let the fields about my house for three years, in the view of my London settlement.[18] My Wife goes with me to Edinburgh in a day or two. It will take me[19] some days there to collect my papers and pack up books etc.—as I shall not return to my house there.[20] I am ever, My Dear Sir, your much obliged and affectionate friend,

JAMES BOSWELL

I puzzled myself long with the Aenigma as to the *hairs* but could make nothing of it. My sons tutor at length discovered it.[21] *Two* men with each *one* hair. Is he right? I see this to be a solution.[22]

N.B. The *red* you see on this paper is currant jelly not claret or port. I have been remarkably *moderate*.

31 Octr. I see in the Publick Advertiser *Remarks* on my Tour

[16] JB misunderstood the problem of printing with an engraved plate and lead type on the same page. The problem is not the thickness of the copperplate, but that, as EM said, "The former [copperplate] is cut in, the latter [type] stand out" (*ante* From EM, 26 Aug.); thus they are inked by different methods and must be printed on different presses. The design on a wooden block, such as that used for the 1st ed., "stands out" like type, and so can be set with the type. See further *post* From EM, 5 Nov. p. 268; To EM, 11 Nov. and n. 9.

[17] 2nd ed.: "All that was told might be true" (p. 52; *Life* v. 56).

[18] JB's Book of Company shows that the auction went on for two days. JB planned to settle in London after being called to the English bar (*ante* To EM, 13 Oct. n. 80).

[19] MS. "me me"

[20] JB means that he will not return again to his house in James's Court once he has taken care of his papers and books.

[21] The Rev. Alexander Millar (d. 1804), later (1787) minister of Kilmaurs.

[22] *Ante* From EM, 21 Oct. and n. 20; *post* From EM, 5 Nov. pp. 271–72.

advertised.[23] Well done Battledore![24] *Euge*! as Dr. Fordyce called out to young Courtaney.[25]

To Malone,
Wednesday 2 November 1785
MS. Yale (L 924).

Auchinleck, 2 Novr. 1785

MY DEAR SIR: This morning I had the favour of yours of the 28 Octr. and I thank you by the return of the post. The Letter in the St. James's Chronicle *must* do service.[1] I should be glad to know the Authour of it. *The Ambassador says well.*[2] The paragraph in the Publick Advertiser is cheering.[3] It will be thought my own. But it is not, upon my honour.

The first sheet you have sent me looks a good deal better I think than the first edition. Your *and* in p. 9 after "sixty fourth year" I adopt.[4]

P. 35, l. 11: The posthouse stairs are *from* the Parliament Close or adjoining to it. *Stet* therefore. Tis like Duke Street Grosvenor Square.[5]

[23] For "Verax's" *Remarks*, see *ante* From EM, 28 Oct. and n. 3. The pamphlet was first advertised in *Pub. Adv.* 26 Oct. p. 1.

[24] "Dr. Johnson said . . . 'It is advantageous to an author, that his book should be attacked as well as praised. Fame is a shuttlecock. If it be struck only at one end of the room, it will soon fall to the ground. To keep it up, it must be struck at both ends.'—Often have I [JB] reflected on this since; and, instead of being angry at many of those who have written against me, have smiled to think that they were unintentionally subservient to my fame, by using a battledoor to make me *virum volitare per ora*" (*Life* v. 400–01; Virgil, *Georgics* iii. 9, "fly on the lips of men", trans. H. R. Fairclough, Loeb ed.).

[25] Latin "euge", from Greek "εὖγε", means "well done". George Fordyce (1736–1802), Scottish physician at St. Thomas's Hospital, had been a member of The Club since 1774. Kenneth (c. 1769–1838), son of John Courtenay, in 1789 was enrolled in Trinity College, Cambridge, and later took orders (*Gent. Mag.* June 1838, n. s. ix. pt. 1. 665; *Alum. Cant.* II). The anecdote to which JB alludes has not been reported.

[1] *Ante* From EM, 28 Oct. and n. 5.

[2] " '*The Ambassadour says well*,' became a laughable term of applause, when no mighty matter had been expressed" (*Life* iii. 411).

[3] *Ante* From EM, 28 Oct. n. 18.

[4] JB seems to have forgotten that he had already approved this emendation; see *ante* From EM, 5 Oct. p. 203 and To EM, 13 Oct. and n. 16.

[5] Unchanged in 2nd ed. (*Life* v. 42). For the Post House stairs, see *Hebrides*, p. 454.

P. 39: "charming" might have remained. Sir Adolphus was *gentle* and *fine*. But your *very* must do now.[6]

P. 43: I beleive it should be "*to* payment". In our scotch law language we say *in*—as liable *in* damages.[7]

P. 92, l. 2: Certainly "*be*come" not "come".[8]

P. 110, l. 5 from bottom: "the *two second* stanzas" is bad indeed. I mean the second and third stanzas.—Your *two stanzas* (if this does not come in time) will do well.[9]

P. 115: By all means add the *epoch* of the institution of our Club.[10]

P. 159, l. 10 from bottom: the steep is really *terrible*; for there is danger. I am not fond of the change to *painful*. *Desperate* or *monstrous* or some such strong word is required. But I think *terrible* should remain.[11]

P. 125, Note: read "administering".[12]

P. 127, l. 9: no word that I can think of but *quarrel* is strong enough.[13]

P. 129, l. 5: for *ones* read "Fathers".[14]

P. 145: I am for retaining *Beaux Stratagem*. The Comedy is not so well known by *Archer* as to you and me.[15]

P. 154, l. ult.: Since I have once acknowledged the *fact* let *burst into tears* remain.[16]

Of Duke Street, Edward Walford wrote, "Grosvenor Square is connected with Oxford Street, at its north-east corner, by a thoroughfare of inferior appearance, built about 1770, and called Duke Street, probably after the Duke of Cumberland" (*Old and New London*, [1873–78] iv. 343). This and the following items, as far as the one on "passed" and "passing" (1st ed. p. 162), respond to EM's comments in his letter of 28 Oct.

[6] So changed in 2nd ed. (*Life* v. 45).

[7] So changed in 2nd ed. (*Life* v. 48).

[8] So changed in 2nd ed. (*Life* v. 89).

[9] 2nd ed.: "the second and third stanzas" (*Life* v. 105).

[10] 2nd ed.: "Our club, originally at the Turk's Head, Gerrard-street, then at Prince's, Sackville-street, now at Baxter's, Dover-street, which at Mr. Garrick's funeral acquired a *name* for the first time, and was called The Literary Club, was instituted in 1764, and consists of thirty-five members, beyond which number, by a late rule, it cannot be extended. It has, since 1773, been greatly augmented." New information in the note includes the date of The Club's founding and the limitation of the number of its members (see *post* From EM, 5 Nov. and n. 19). The remainder of the note was reprinted with only one minor change (*ante* To EM, 13 Oct. and n. 46).

[11] Unchanged in 2nd ed. (*Life* v. 144). In his copy of the 1st ed., EM changed "terrible" to "painful", but later cancelled the correction.

[12] So changed in 2nd ed. (*Life* v. 119 n. 1).

[13] Unchanged in 2nd ed. (*Life* v. 120).

[14] 2nd ed.: "fathers" (*Life* v. 121).

[15] Unchanged in 2nd ed. (*Life* v. 133).

[16] Nevertheless, the passage was changed in the 2nd ed. to read, "I could not refrain from tears" (*Life* v. 140).

P. 162: *passed* and *passing* must not remain. Suppose we should say "he did not hear of us till *it was too late* otherwise he should have insisted on our passing the night at his house"—Or "he did not hear of us till we had passed his house otherwise he should have insisted on our *being there* all night"—or "*being his guests* that night" or "our *spending* that night" or "*being* that night under his roof".[17]

P. 58, ll. 8 and 12: [After what Dr. Johnson has said of St. Andrew's, which he had long wished to see, as our ancient university, and the seat of our Primate in the days of episcopacy, I can say little. Since the publication of Dr. Johnson's book, I find that he has been censured for not seeing here the ancient chapel of *St. Rule*.] *ancient* and *ancient*. It will be too late I suppose and indeed hope to correct this. The first should be *oldest*.[18]

It is curious that I should have written *please send* several times to you *after* Wilkes's correction. I enclose you *Jack's* letter to amuse you.[19] Pray keep it and all *papers* concerning the *Tour*.

As to the *Seraglio* conversation—Unless some publick animadversion should appear on my omitting the *Retort* I do not think I am obliged to offer any Apology. At any rate it will come much better from *One of the best Criticks of the age*. Or MALONE if he will honour me with his *name* which for his own credit as well as mine I hope he will do in several instances. Lest you should not have kept a copy of the apology I write it out from your letter—only changing it for another than myself.

"The objectors forget that the Authour has said in the conclusion of his Tour that 'he has suppressed whatever he thought could really hurt any one now living.' He has in various places in this Work shewn that he did not wish to spare himself; but in the present instance he had surely a right to the same indulgence that he gave (or that he *gives* or has *given* or with which he has *treated* others) I mean the suppression of what at the time particularly wounded his private feelings"—(I think the expression too strong. I would rather have it "the suppression of what

[17] 2nd ed.: "otherwise he should have insisted on our sleeping there that night" (*Life* v. 146).

[18] So changed in 3rd ed. (*Life* v. 61), but the alteration apparently was not in time for the 2nd ed. Sheet D (pp. 33–48) had been printed by 5 Nov. (*post* From EM, 5 Nov. p. 266), and EM received the present letter probably about 7 Nov. By that time sheet E (pp. 49–64), which contained the passage JB proposed to emend, had almost certainly been printed.

[19] *Ante* To EM, 13 Oct. and n. 69; From EM, 28 Oct. and n. 17.

from the recollection of what he felt at the time, he apprehends might lessen him too much in the eyes of partial observers".)—I do not like my own way of it either. Might not the note stop at *others*? as the text has expressed my earnestness to have the *retort* obliterated.[20]

Your kind attention to my Book is wonderful. I send you Dilly's letter to me to shew his earnestness for dispatch and his *reason*.[21] Let us therefore *now* resolve not to look any more on the Book with a nice critical eye, but let the press work away. Yet the improvements are such we cannot regret the *curious* attention that has been bestowed. I ever am your much obliged and affectionate friend,

JAMES BOSWELL

From Malone,
Saturday 5 November 1785
MS. Yale (C 1901).

London, Novr. 5, 1785

MY DEAR SIR: Your letter, containing the full Epitaph on M'claurin,[1] did not come in time, the sheet having been worked off that morning.[2] But I wish you would get, if you can, before you leave Edinburgh, the entire epitaph on Dr. *Smollet*, or lay such a train as that it shall be transmitted to you here; and it can be printed as a note to Johnson's part of that epitaph; and in the tail

[20] *Post* To EM, 11 Nov. and n. 5.
[21] *Ante* From EM, 28 Oct. n. 2.

[1] Colin Maclaurin (1698–1746), mathematician and natural philosopher, was the father of JB's friend John Maclaurin (1734–96), later (1788) Lord Dreghorn of the Court of Session. In the 1st ed. of the *Tour*, JB told how SJ had suggested several alterations in John's epitaph on his father, and listed the alterations, but did not print the entire epitaph (p. 45).

[2] EM refers to JB's letter of 30 Oct., whose postscript shows that it could not have been posted before 31 Oct. In that letter JB mentions "the Epitaphs" (on Maclaurin and Smollett) and discusses the note on the Americans and the Devil, which EM comments on next. References in these letters show that mail between Auchinleck and London normally took five days, though varying (presumably because the new mail-coach system was not operating with perfect consistency) between four and six. JB's letter of 30 Oct. probably reached EM about 4 Nov.; the sheet "worked off that morning" was sheet D, which was to have contained Maclaurin's epitaph. Presumably JB enclosed the epitaph in his letter of 30 Oct.

of that note you can draw in M'claurins Epitaph,—saying you were at a distance from the press, when the former sheet was worked off.[3]—You have given yourself unnecessary uneasiness about the American note and the fiend; you have them both; they are actually printed off without the smallest variation or addition.[4] As for the *addition* I think it would only make[5] the matter worse; however this was not a thing of choice, for neither did the addition come in time.[6] Now as you have carried these points, you must positively yield to me about the *rider* to Burke's note. I kept the sheet back as long as I could, but as Dilly is crying out for five sheets a week, it was absolutely necessary to work it off; accordingly I went to Baldwin's the moment I received your letters of the 27 and 29th of Octr. and signed the death warrant. Courteney agrees with me entirely in thinking it will not have at all the effect intended, if it were to be ascribed to another person than the author; to say nothing of the awkwardness of the business. With respect to your *nolo assumere*,[7] this is very easily settled by your telling Burke himself that the note was written by me in your absence, and sent to you, and that you approved of every part of it and made it your own. To this I have no objection—but I will prove to you decisively when[8] we meet that nothing more should be done.[9]

I have struck out a better plan than an Index. It is to have *short* contents of each day. This will excite curiosity and not discover too much:—something like the heads of a chapter in Hume's History.[10]

"Dr. Johnson's character—arrives in Scotland—views the

[3] *Post* To EM, 11 Nov. and n. 4.

[4] *Ante* To EM, 27 Oct. and n. 6.

[5] MS. "hurt the w" deleted before "make"

[6] For JB's proposed addition to the note, see *ante* To EM, 27 Oct. p. 247. EM had originally intended to hold back sheet C, containing the note on the Americans, until after D and E had been printed (see *ante* From EM, 24 Oct.); however, it is apparent from what follows that he allowed it to be printed about 2 Nov., when he probably received JB's letters of 27 and 29 Oct. See n. 2 above on the timing of the post. If so, then EM's statement that JB's addition to the note on the Americans did not arrive in time cannot be true, for he received the letter of 27 Oct., as he says immediately below, just before sheet C was printed. It appears that EM rejected JB's addition on his own authority, not because it arrived too late to be inserted but because "it would only make the matter worse".

[7] "I do not wish to receive (credit)", perhaps an echo of "nolo episcopari": "I do not wish to be made a bishop."

[8] MS. "that we" deleted before "when"

[9] *Post* To EM, 11 Nov. and n. 7.

[10] *Ante* From EM, 5 Oct. p. 207; To EM, 13 Oct. and n. 75; *post* To EM, 11 Nov. and n. 8. The reference is to David Hume's *History of England*, 1754–62.

Castle etc. of Edinburgh" etc. etc. Selfe[11] can do it as well as any one. It will be putting a little money too in his pocket, which will be right; for I forgot to tell you, before you went, that he should have been considered. I believe it is always customary in the case of *Gentlemen Authors*; and indeed he had a great deal of the trouble and the merit in decyphering the MS.; for in all difficulties Loder applied to him.[12]

With respect to the engraving, it will be much the best way to engrave the *whole* title page; it will add very little to the expence; and works off much cleaner and evener, than when the paper is to be twice wetted and to go through two hands. I have spoken to Strutt,[13] the engraver about it. It can be done in two or three days; so I will give no order till you come.[14]

You did not answer some of my queries—"painful *steep*" 159—"*two second* stanzas" "refraining from tears" 154 "Greek fathers" 129 etc. but there will be time enough for them.[15]

Do not forget to bring up the original MS. of the Journal, as some things, you know, were struck out that are to be in the Life; and also my Letters, for I keep no memorial of the alterations I propose, and you sometimes refer me back to my own remark, when I have forgot what my remark was[16]—Pray send me the

[11] *Ante* From EM, 28 Oct. n. 5.

[12] Loder was Baldwin's compositor; JB found him "an accurate obliging man" (Journ. 10 May) and on 22 Sept. gave him a bonus of two guineas (A 39.1). There is no record of JB's having given Selfe a bonus.

[13] *Ante* From EM, 26 Aug. n. 2.

[14] *Ante* To EM, 30 Oct. and n. 16; *post* To EM, 11 Nov. and n. 9.

[15] JB answered these queries in *ante* To EM, 2 Nov., which had not yet reached EM.

[16] EM kept no record of the suggestions he sent to JB. His own copy of the 1st ed. was used largely to record emendations that JB had proposed or approved. To cite only a few examples, EM's emendation on p. 70 of "deep in literary property" to "deep in the question concerning literary property" (*ante* From EM, 5 Oct. p. 204) was approved by JB (*ante* To EM, 13 Oct. and n. 24), and the emendation was entered in EM's copy. But EM's emendation, proposed in the same letter, of "should be" on p. 171 to "ought to be", was rejected by JB, and the emendation was not made in EM's copy. JB's proposal to omit the word "himself" on p. 480 (*ante* To EM, 13 Oct. and n. 54) was adopted in the 2nd ed., and the change was made in EM's copy. For apparent exceptions to the rule that EM recorded in his own copy only those emendations that JB himself approved or proposed, see *ante* To EM, 15 Oct. n. 11; From EM, 28 Oct. p. 256; To EM, 2 Nov. and n. 11. Because EM kept no separate list of his proposed emendations, he relied on JB to refer, in his replies, to the pages where emendations had been proposed. However, JB did not always do so, particularly in his letters of 27 and 30 Oct.

note[17] ready cut and dry to be added to the Seraglio story—as I shall want to send it (as copy) to the press, before you can be here; though it cannot be *worked off* before then.[18] In the note on the Club should not the number to which it is limited (35) be mentioned as its smallness is an honourable circumstance; and also its first institution? This last I asked before.[19]—I should think inverted commas all down the paragraph from Voltaire will do better than Italicks, and sufficiently prepare the reader for a quotation.[20]

It is a rule in the H. of Commons, when any one objects to a tax, to call on him to propose a *better*. But it seems a very absurd[21] one. When[22] therefore you object to the three English lines for one Greek one, I am authorized by precedent to ask, why you did not send a *shorter* translation. But I will not rest on authority. The truth is, I was aware of the impropriety, and laboured hard to compress them, but I could not succeed. It is a very singular line; containing more perhaps than the famous incompressible latin line, *Victrix causa* etc.[23] for there are three distinct propositions in it. The most one could do, would be to get them into two lines; and then one proposition must be in one line, and the *two* remaining in the other. Courteney proposed to me to contract them thus.

In active enterprize let youth engage;
In council, man; let pray'r employ old age.

But "let man *engage* in council", is not elegant,[24] nor perhaps accurate; and "*employ* old age" is not so good as "*proper duty* of old age". So I thought it better to give the sense fully, which the three

[17] MS. "add" deleted before "note"

[18] *Post* To EM, 11 Nov. and n. 5. The "Seraglio" anecdote occurs in sheet S (pp. 257–72) of the 2nd ed.

[19] *Ante* To EM, 2 Nov. and n. 10. If EM was able to produce four or five sheets a week, sheet I (pp. 113–28), containing the note on The Club, must have been printed before JB's arrival in London on 17 Nov. If so, EM probably inserted the information on the number of members on his own authority, for the matter is not mentioned again in the extant correspondence.

[20] *Ante* To EM, 15 Oct. p. 225. In the 1st ed. the long French quotation had been set in the same style as an English quotation. EM's change was made in the 2nd ed. (pp. 237–38) and in the 3rd ed. (pp. 196–97); in the Hill-Powell ed. of the *Tour* (v. 199–200) the marginal quotation marks are not reproduced.

[21] MS. "bad" deleted before "absurd"

[22] EM first wrote "one, I"; the "W" of "When" is superimposed upon "I", but no attempt was made to change the comma to a period.

[23] "Victrix causa deis placuit, sed victa Catoni", Lucan, *Pharsalia* i. 128: "The victorious cause pleased the gods, but the vanquished one pleased Cato."

[24] MS. "accurate or" deleted before "elegant"; "or" is doubtful.

lines do. For "the more adult" I printed "The *riper man* be famed" etc. which is better.[25]

With respect to "*Una* est injusti"—it would not[26] have been allowable[27] to have given a translation that imported *water is the same every where* (though J. applied it so,) for that is not Ovid's meaning, as appears clearly from the context. His mistress is going to sea, on which account he chooses to abuse the poor ocean. "There blow all the winds of heaven, east, west, north, and south;—there you have no variety—no groves, no cities;—the face of the unjust ocean, (that spares neither the innocent child, nor the pious father,) is *one* dull blue surface, not[28] *diversified* and enlivened as the land is, by variety of objects."[29] Before we have done with translation, pray set yourself a task at some inn on the road, after you are duly refreshed—I mean to translate the lines from Juvenal "Esto bonus miles"—I had hoped to have found a good translation in Dryden,—but unluckily the 8th Satire was *done*[30] into English by Stepney, and very miserably.—I will work at it too; and we will compare.[31]

[25] *Ante* From EM, 24 Oct.; To EM, 30 Oct. In EM's copy of the 1st ed. there are three drafts of this translation. The first is found at the bottom of p. 60:

Let active enterprize the young engage,
The [more adult *deleted*] riper man be famed for counsel sage;
Prayer is the proper duty of old age.

This is the version used in the 2nd ed. (p. 60 n.). Near the bottom of p. 61 of EM's copy is another version:

Let youth in deeds, in counsel man engage;
Prayer is the proper duty of old age.

This version was used in the 3rd ed. (*Life* v. 63 n. 1). Under it is written Courtenay's version; however, where the version in the present letter reads "man", the one in EM's copy of the *Tour* reads "men".

[26] MS. "however" deleted before "not"

[27] MS. "allowable" written above deleted "allowed"

[28] MS. "unvaried by" deleted before "not"

[29] *Ante* From EM, 24 Oct.; To EM, 30 Oct. The translation added in the 2nd ed. (p. 49 n.; *Life* v. 54 n. 1) reads:

Nor groves nor towns the ruthless ocean shows;
Unvaried still its azure surface flows.

[30] MS. "transl" deleted before "*done*"

[31] George Stepney (1663–1707) contributed to Dryden's translation of Juvenal's *Satires* (1693). His translation of the present passage (viii. 79–84) is as follows:

Be a good Souldier, or upright Trustee,
An Arbitrator from Corruption free,
And if a Witness in a doubtful Cause,
Where a brib'd Judge means to elude the Laws;
Tho *Phalaris his Brazen Bull* were there,
And *He* wou'd dictate what he'd have yuo [*sic*] swear,
Be not so Profligate, but rather chuse
To guard your Honour, and your Life to lose,
Rather than let your Virtue be Betray'd;
Virtue, the Noble Cause for which you're made.

In a paragraph added to a note, the translation used in the 2nd ed. (p. 454 n.; *Life* v. 361 n. 2) is attributed to EM (*ante* To EM, 30 Oct. n. 6).

I called at Debretts yesterday. The pamphlet addressed to you is not to be out till Monday.[32] Mr. Dempster has just called on me.[33] I find from him and others, that the generality of your countrymen are displeased about Lord M—d.[34] The fact, I believe is, that they all know every particular passage that *looks* towards him; and they all talk as if he was mentioned by name in each. This I know was the case with your friend Mr. Bosville, whom I happened one day to meet.[35]—You cannot imagine how much mischief your own pamphlet has done you and how slow people are to allow the praise of good thinking and good writing to one whom they think guilty of such indiscretion in that pamphlet as a man of sound sense (they allege) would not be guilty of.[36] I venture to tell you this, because perhaps you will not hear it from others; and it proves decisively my doctrine, that a man should in his writings have as few *weak* places as possible. Pray turn this to account hereafter.—If we had happened to have laid our heads together on that business, I think we could have made out of your materials,—a short, argumentative, witty and biting piece, which would not have been open to any just animadversion:—but it is now in vain to think more of it.

You have not hit off the hairs, I will therefore add the solution, to gratify your son. It is no enigma, no riddle, but a plain

[32] John Debrett (d. 1822), publisher of "Verax's" *Remarks*, had his shop opposite Burlington House in Piccadilly (*ante* From EM, 28 Oct. and n. 3).

[33] George Dempster (1732–1818), M.P. for Perth Burghs, had long been a close friend of JB, who printed his letter praising SJ's *Journey* in the *Tour* (*Life* v. 407–09). Dempster was also on the "jury" of friends who approved the *Tour* on 22 Sept. (Journ. 21, 22 Sept.).

[34] Macdonald.

[35] William Bosville (1745–1813), Lord Macdonald's brother-in-law and son of JB's friend Godfrey Bosville, later served as an intermediary in the quarrel between Macdonald and JB.

[36] MS. "of." written above deleted "?often". *LPS 85*, published on 26 May (Journ.), attacked a bill introduced into the House of Commons on 27 Apr. which proposed to reduce the number of Lords of Session from fifteen to ten and to augment the salaries of the remainder. JB pointed out that the bill infringed the Articles of Union, and argued, among other points, that it would serve to concentrate political power in the hands of the Pitt Administration. The pamphlet received favourable reviews and was instrumental in preventing the number of judges being diminished, but it was considered indiscreet in the number and extravagance of its personal remarks about JB and several prominent Scots. JB claimed that his "sallies of vivacity" were included to hold the reader's attention; besides, personal remarks were permissible in political pamphlets. In the *Letter* itself, JB justifies the inclusion of material about himself by saying, "you who censure it, have read it, and *must* therefore know it". The *English Review*, with its comment on JB's "eternal vanity and egotism", illustrated a common reaction (*Pol. Car.* pp. 119–29).

demonstrative proposition, as clear and incontrovertible as any in Euclid. The proposition is, that if the number of persons in the world be greater than the number of hairs on any person's head, some *two* persons must have the same number of hairs.

The total number of persons in the world must be either even or odd. First, suppose it even,—and the total number of persons, *six*; for that will do as well as millions:—A. B. C. D. E. F. The greatest number of hairs on any one of them (ex concessu)[37] can only be *five*. A. has one, B. two, C. three, D. four, E. five; or change them round as you may. What becomes of F.? Must he not have either one hair, or two, or three, or four, or five? Certainly yes; and of consequence, *two* persons *must* have the same number of hairs. Q. e. d.

If the number of persons in the world be odd, five for example, A. B. C. D. and E.,—the number of hairs is four, and E. will be just in the same situation with Mr. F. and must be covered in the same manner as some one of his friends A. B. C. D.

I have found out three "you *was's*" and corrected them; but cannot find your *friend* Wilkes's "Please—send" any where—but in your letters.[38]

I have put DRYDEN to the lines from Virgil—but no signature to the new translations—Surely they are not worth noticing. The translations I have put in notes.[39]

I had almost forgot to tell you, my cook's name is *Hacket*, which must be a considerable consolation to you.[40]

I intended to have written only a few words, and have scribbled almost two sheets:—but I must now go to dress for dinner; for I am to dine with a most punctual man—Mr. Agar.[41] Courteney is

[37] "From what is given", i.e. following from the premise that "there are more Men upon the Face of the Earth than there are Hairs on any one Man's Head" (*ante* From EM, 21 Oct. n. 20).

[38] Chapman, in his edition of the *Tour*, noted six instances where "you was" in the 1st ed. was changed to "you were" in the 2nd (Chapman, pp. 466, 475, 476, 478). Neither Chapman nor the present editors have had better success than EM in locating "please send" in the 1st ed.

[39] *Ante* To EM, 30 Oct. and nn. 6, 10, 11.

[40] *Ante* To EM, 30 Oct.; *post* To EM, 17 Nov. 1788; 9 Mar. 1791.

[41] Welbore Ellis Agar (1735–1805), Commissioner of Customs and prominent art collector (*Life* iii. 118 n. 3). On 13 Sept. JB had dined with Agar at Reynolds's (Journ.). On 31 July 1790, JB reports, "Agar entertained us with the most extravagant fictions of vanity" and, on 23 Aug. 1790, the "pomposity and splendour of Agar diverted me" (Journ.). In 1791 Agar helped JB to procure for his old classmate Alexander Dawson a position as tide-waiter in Customs (*Pol. Car.* p. 172 and n. 3).

to call on me. He talks of going to Italy with Genl. Dalrymple (who has lost his wife) in a few days; to stay three or four months: but he is not quite decided.[42] Farewell—and believe me ever, my dear Sir, Your sincerely Affectionate Friend,

E. MALONE[43]

To Malone, Tuesday 8 November 1785

MS. Yale (L 925).

ADDRESS: To Edmond Malone Esq., Queen Anne Street East.

Edinburgh, 8 Novr. 1785

MY DEAR SIR: I have had a very disagreable business with young

[42] William Dalrymple (1736–1807), brother of John, fifth Earl of Stair, was at this time a major-general in the army and M.P. for Wigtown Burghs (Namier and Brooke ii. 295–96). In 1783 he married Marianne Dorothy, daughter of Sir Robert Harland of Sproughton Hall, Bt. Born in 1759, she died at Streatham, which was being rented by Dalrymple during the Piozzis' stay in Italy, on 28 Oct. 1785 (*Scots Peer.* viii. 151; *Gent. Mag.* 1785, lv. 919; Clifford, p. 352 n. 1). Dalrymple was reputedly "a man of the most amiable manners and temper" (*Gent. Mag.* 1807, lxxvii. 280), and was a close friend of Courtenay (Namier and Brooke ii. 296). Courtenay did not go to Italy with Dalrymple, who returned to London in June 1786 (Journ. 15 June 1786).

[43] Preserved at Yale is a slip containing two extracts from *Pub. Adv.* copied in EM's hand; it was probably enclosed with this letter. The first, from the issue of 3 Nov. p. [2], reads: "Boswell has been nick-named. By the bye contumilious denominations ought not to affect, what they cannot alter, the nature of truth. *Bozzy* has with some turn [for 'truth'?], however, been likened to the *Save-all* of Sam. Johnson. To go on allusively from adjoining objects, Adams of Pembroke may be called Johnson's *Extinguisher*." This item answers an attack in *Pub. Adv.* 25 Oct. (printed *post* To EM, 8 Nov. n. 11). "To nickname", according to SJ's *Dictionary*, means "to call by an opprobrious appellation". For William Adams, Master of Pembroke College, Oxford, see Waingrow, p. 10 n. 1. In the Preface of SJ's *Prayers and Meditations*, ed. George Strahan, 1785, Adams is said to have urged SJ to write a devotional work. But in a letter to *Gent. Mag.*, dated 22 Oct. 1785, Adams wrote that he had not been consulted about the publication of the book, and if he had been, would certainly have advised against it (Oct. 1785, lv. 755–56).

EM's transcript of the item from the issue of 5 Nov. p. [4] reads, "the only *deep* observation of Boswell in his *Johnsoniana* is his remark that a man may *dance* gracefully and *walk* awkwardly. As an illustration, the Scottish authors *speak* as if they were never out of the Isle of Sky, and write as anglicisedly pure as a Chesterfield." This paragraph was reprinted from *Morn. Post*, 4 Nov. In the *Tour* JB wrote, "It has been often remarked, that in his [SJ's] poetical pieces, which it is to be regretted are so few, because so excellent, his style is easier than in his prose. There is deception in this: it is not easier, but better suited to the dignity of verse; as one may dance with grace, whose motions, in ordinary walking,—in the common step, are awkward" (*Life* v. 17). Also with the present letter was found a receipt for the plate used to engrave the crest on the title-page of the 2nd ed. of the *Tour*. Dated 15 Dec., it clearly does not belong with this letter. For the text, see *post* To EM, 11 Nov. n. 9.

Mr. Tytler[1] who has totally forgotten his having told me he had no objection to the passage concerning him being inserted in my Tour, though upon my honour I am as certain of the fact as of any circumstance in the whole course of my existence. You shall have all the particulars when we meet. [Pp. 485–86: Young Mr. Tytler stepped briskly forward, and said, "*Fingal* is certainly genuine; for I have heard a great part of it repeated in the original."—Dr. Johnson indignantly asked him, "Sir, do you understand the original?"—TYTLER. "No, sir."—JOHNSON. "Why, then, we see to what this testimony comes:—Thus it is."—He afterwards said to me, "Did you observe the wonderful confidence with which young Tytler advanced, with his front ready *brased*?"] It is now settled by my consenting that his name and the *brasing* shall be suppressed in the second edition, to which I most willingly agree, as I never should have mentioned his name, had he not as I thought been quite satisfied.[2]

I enclose the correction, though I hope I shall be with you long before it is wanted.[3]

[1] Alexander Fraser Tytler (1747–1813), Scottish advocate, since 1780 had been joint Professor of Universal Civil History at Edinburgh. (His colleague, John Pringle, had held the chair since 1765, but had never lectured.) In 1790 Tytler became Judge Advocate of Scotland, and in 1802 he took a seat in the Court of Session as Lord Woodhouselee (*Fac. Adv.* pp. 174, 210; A. Grant, *The Story of the University of Edinburgh*, 1884, ii. 367–68).

[2] On 31 Oct. Tytler wrote to JB strongly objecting to the anecdote about him in the *Tour* and demanding that his name be omitted from the 2nd ed. (A transcript of the letter, from Tytler's commonplace book, is printed in Claire Lamont, "James Boswell and Alexander Fraser Tytler", *The Bibliotheck*, 1971, vi. 4). JB, replying on 6 Nov., insisted that Tytler had agreed to the use of his name, but declared himself willing to suppress it. Tytler supplied a revised version of the passage and conceded that JB had not injured him intentionally (From Tytler, 7 Nov.; Lamont, p. 7). But when JB asked, through their intermediary Dugald Stewart, for an apology "for the expressions in his hasty letter" (To Stewart, 8 Nov.), Tytler, citing the injury already done, declined to supply it (Tytler to Stewart, 9 Nov., enclosed in From Stewart, 9 Nov.). There the matter rested until JB consulted EM and Courtenay, who "both agreed it was absolutely necessary to have an Apology" (Journ. 18 Nov.). So JB wrote to Tytler that some reparation was necessary "for the *terms* in which you expressed yourself in your first letter" (To Tytler, 18 Nov.). In reply, Tytler once again insisted that he had never approved the insertion of the anecdote. But, he continued, "As you have now done every thing possible to repair this Injury, I, for my part, do sincerely regret the harsh terms of that letter, and requesting you to excuse them, I have just now committed it [i.e. his copy] to the flames, as a monument of the intemperance of passion which ought not to exist" (From Tytler, 24 Nov.). JB declared that Tytler's letter gave him "perfect satisfaction" (To Tytler, 1 Dec.), and the matter was at an end.

[3] The following changes were made in the 2nd ed.: shortly before the passage quoted in square brackets, "Mr. Tytler . . . and his son, the advocate" was changed to

I also enclose you the Edinburgh Review of my Tour which is wonderfully well. I have no guess who did it.[4] Shall we take the hint and make my Parish minister disappear as the Hottentot, and mention the saying as applied to *one* of the Presbyterian Clergy. We shall talk of this. [Pp. 478–79: Mr. Dun, though a man of sincere good principles, as a presbyterian divine, discovered a narrowness of information concerning the dignitaries of the church of England. . . . Dr. Johnson was so highly offended, that he said to him, "Sir, you know no more of our church than a Hottentot."] It might be easily done, by observing the day of our dining at Mr. Dun's, that "Dr. Johnson though he held notions far distant from those of the presbyterian Clergy,[5] yet could associate on good terms with them.[6] He indeed occasionally attacked them.[7] One of them discovered[7a] a narrowness" etc.[8]

It is strange that Scotland affects my spirits so woefully. It acts

"Mr. Tytler . . . and some other friends" (1st ed. p. 485; 2nd ed. p. 487; *Life* v. 387). The passage quoted in square brackets was revised as follows: "One gentleman in company expressing his opinion 'that *Fingal* was certainly genuine; for that he had heard a great part of it repeated in the original.' Dr. Johnson indignantly asked him, whether he understood the original; to which an answer being given in the negative, 'Why then, (said Dr. Johnson,) we see to what *this* testimony comes:—thus it is' " (2nd ed. p. 488; *Life* v. 388). The sentence beginning "He afterwards said to me" was omitted from the 2nd ed. In the following paragraph, the clause "This gentleman's talents and integrity are unquestionable" (referring to Tytler) was changed to "The talents and integrity of the gentleman who made the remark, are unquestionable" (2nd ed. p. 489; *Life* v. 388).

[4] The review of JB's *Tour* in the *Edinburgh Magazine; or, Literary Miscellany* (Oct. 1785) ii. 187–92, had previously appeared in *Cal. Merc.* (2 Nov.) p. [1]. Most of this long review consists of excerpts from the *Tour*; however, the unidentified reviewer's own remarks are generally favourable. The writer cites JB's "uncommon success" in developing a style for anecdote which is "lively, characteristic, and epigrammatic", and remarks, "Though Dr Johnson be the principal figure in this journal, the author himself often appears sometimes in amiable and respectable points of view. He has considerable merit in bearing with the peculiarities, promoting the contentment, and drawing forth the wisdom of his fellow-traveller." The enclosed copy of the review has not been reported.

[5] MS. "persuasion" deleted before "Clergy"

[6] MS. "(many of)" deleted before "them"

[7] MS. "occasionally attacked them" written above deleted "gave them occasional hits"

[7a] MS. "?having" and illegible word above it both deleted before "discovered"

[8] The reviewer in the *Edinburgh Magazine* (n. 4 above) had written, "He has occasion to speak of living characters, and of those whose relations are yet alive. It is delicate ground, and he treads with caution. . . . The table-talk of his parish-minister at Auchinleck will give that gentleman no pleasure in the perusal; he may even think it hard that words spoken at a venture, possibly to fill up conversation, and which perhaps he regretted, should nevertheless be taken down, and told to all the world." The offending passage was changed as JB suggested (2nd ed. p. 481; *Life* v. 381).

upon me like the *grotto del cane* when I am brought close to it.[9] What *right* have I to be thus disgusted by *my own* country and *my own* countrymen. I wish I were in Queen Anne Street East. And there's an end on't.[10]

I can trace your friendly correcting hand in the Publick Advertiser.[11] Adieu, My Dear Sir, I am ever most faithfully and affectionately yours,

James Boswell

To Malone,
Friday 11 November 1785
MS. Yale (L 926).

Edinburgh, 11 Novr. 1785

My Dear Sir: I am much obliged to you for your long friendly letter of the 5th and I shall henceforth *to a certain degree* be more cautious to leave as few *weak* places (in the opinion of my friends) in what I publish.[1] The original M.S. of the Journal lyes in my Bureau in Portman Square,[2] and I have all your letters since we parted, with me. I shall try to get the entire epitaph on Smollet (if

[9] JB visited the Grotta del Cane near Naples on 18 Mar. 1765 (Notes).

[10] A favourite expression of SJ's (e.g. *Life* v. 83).

[11] After the publication of the *Tour*, *Pub. Adv.* printed several derogatory items aimed at JB and SJ (e.g. 18 Oct. p. [2], 24 Oct. p. [2], 25 Oct. p. [2], 1 Nov. p. [3], and 5 Nov. p. [4]). One of the attacks reads: "A correspondent considers Mr. Boswell as Dr. Johnson's *Save-all*. And as he has taken so much pains to pick up whatever dropped from the learned author, perhaps so very curious a gentleman, and so great an oeconomist of learned productions may be able to tell us (and truly it will be a curious anecdote) how many of the Doctor's f—ts went to an ounce. As he appears to be well skilled in the puffing art, it is imagined this experiment could not escape him" (25 Oct. p. [2]). Probably JB refers to an answer to this item, printed in *Pub. Adv.* for 3 Nov. (*ante* From EM, 5 Nov. n. 43), which he thinks is by EM. JB could not have received EM's transcription of the item before he wrote the present letter, but he probably had seen it in his own copy of the newspaper. Cf. *ante* To EM, 30 Oct. and n. 23, where JB mentions having seen the advertisement of "Verax" 's *Remarks* in *Pub. Adv.* before EM's report of having seen the same advertisement could have reached him (*ante* From EM, 28 Oct.).

[1] This and the following comments respond to those in EM's letter of 5 Nov.

[2] JB had made Paoli's house his London headquarters since 1775. Paoli now lived in Seymour St., Portman Square.

it be *in esse*) sent after me.[3] M'Laurin's may be left to another edition.[4] I enclose the Seraglio Note; though I am not sure if it be necessary to obviate an objection not publickly made, unless where there is so good a reason as in the case of Burke's wit.[5] I acquiesce in your *jackdawing* me with so fine a feather,[6] and I shall satisfy myself with telling privately to whom I owe it.[7] Your *Heads* instead of an *Index* will be much better.[8] You have certainly the art of Bookmaking and Bookdressing in the utmost perfection. I am sorry I did not know of Selfe's claim from a Gentleman Authour. But it shall be made up to him by the Heads.

I am not fond of an engraved title page. But we shall settle this, when I come.[9]

I thank you for Mrs. *Hacket*. It absolutely relieved me from a disagreable straining after what I could not reach more than Sam could *fugaces* in the Ode "Posthume Posthume".[10]

[3] Tobias Smollett's epitaph, composed in part by SJ, was inscribed on the monument erected by the novelist's cousin James Smollett (d. 1775), Commissary of Edinburgh. In the 1st ed. (pp. 460–61) JB included only those portions of the epitaph proposed by SJ as improvements to the Latin text. In the 2nd ed. he added a footnote giving the full inscription (pp. 462–63 n.; *Life* v. 367 n. 3).

[4] Nevertheless, JB followed EM's suggestion (*ante* From EM, 5 Nov. p. 266) that Maclaurin's epitaph be appended to the Smollett note together with an explanatory paragraph, which reads: "That the reader might be enabled to judge of the propriety of the additions made by Dr. Johnson to the epitaph on Mr. Maclaurin, mentioned in p. 45, I wished to have inserted it at large, but being at a distance from the press when the former part of this work was printed, the note intended for that page did not arrive in time. I shall therefore introduce it here" (2nd ed. p. 463 n.). In the 3rd ed., Maclaurin's epitaph was shifted to its proper position and the explanatory paragraph deleted (*Life* v. 50 n. 2).

[5] JB's note on the "Seraglio" conversation (*ante* From EM, 28 Oct.; To EM, 2 Nov.) has not been reported; it was not added to the 2nd ed.

[6] The jackdaw is proverbially a thief of precious and glittering objects.

[7] Although EM did not permit JB to acknowledge his authorship of the Burke note in the *Tour*, JB did so in the *Life*, presumably without his permission (iii. 323 n. 2). Also, see *ante* To EB, 20 Dec. 1785.

[8] An analytical table of contents was added to the 2nd ed. (pp. [ix]–xx; *Life* v. 5–11).

[9] The title-page of the 2nd ed., like that of the 1st, was set in type, but rather than the woodcut used for JB's crest in the 1st ed. (*ante* From EM, 26 Aug. and n. 1), a copperplate engraving was used for the 2nd. A receipt for the making of the plate was found with EM's letter of 5 Nov.; it reads as follows:

1785 Mr. Malone	To F. Vincent		
	£.	s.	d.
Decr. 15 Engraving Plate with Falcon etc.		10	6
Recd. the contents for Mr. Vincent By Andw. Pollock.			

The receipt is in an unknown hand, except for "Recd. . . . Pollock", which is in EM's hand. Francis Vincent, engraver, lived at No. 10 Bateman's Buildings, Soho (*Univ. Brit. Directory* i. 319).

[10] "We talked of memory, and its various modes.—JOHNSON. 'Memory will play

I shall do my best at an Inn to translate "Esto bonus miles".[11] I am very lucky. Instead of the abominable Fly or even some coarse male companion I have engaged a young Lady of quality and an *english* governess three in a chaise.[12] We are to set out tomorrow and travel at our leisure—No bad hours in this cold weather. I hope to be in *Town* on Wednesday night, or thursday to dinner.[13]

When you and I look back upon the accumulation of just censure concerning L—d M——d and think how little appears with his *name* (and nobody has a right to apply any thing said without it) we must wonder that the little we suffered to escape displeases. Yet I declare I am sorry that *any* part of it appears (with his *name* I mean). My Wife says that attacking his *cheer*, is adopting Dr. Johnson's *lowbred* notion of the importance of a *Good table*;[14] and she thinks I had no right to *report* Dr. Johnson's saying that Sir A. was "utterly unfit for his situation" which she thinks a severe reflection which will stick both to himself and his family. She has been in sad anxiety lest he should call me out and was going to write to you intreating you would prevent it. I have no great fear of *that*. But why be in any degree a publick executioner? I therefore enclose for your consideration what I would propose to introduce instead of "Instead of finding the Chief of the Macdonalds" etc. and if you approve that leaf shall be cancelled a second time.[15] I have the milk of human kindness in abundance.[16]

strange tricks. One sometimes loses a single word. I once lost *fugaces* in the Ode *Posthume, Posthume*' " (*Life* v. 68). SJ refers to Horace, *Odes* II. xiv. 1.

[11] *Ante* From EM, 5 Nov. n. 31.

[12] JB's companions were Lady Elizabeth Hope (1768–1801) and her governess Mrs. Dawkins (Journ. 12 Nov.). JB could travel to and from London by public stage-coach (fly, diligence) or hire a post-chaise with one or more companions.

[13] JB arrived in London on Thursday, 17 Nov. and dined with EM the same day (Journ.).

[14] "When invited to dine, even with an intimate friend, he [SJ] was not pleased if something better than a plain dinner was not prepared for him. I have heard him say on such an occasion, 'This was a good dinner enough, to be sure; but it was not a dinner to *ask* a man to' " (*Life* i. 470).

[15] F. A. Pottle gives a connected account of the quarrel between JB and Lord Macdonald (BP xvi. 221–59). After seeing Macdonald at the theatre and feeling "remorse for having printed so much severity against him" (Journ. 8 Aug.), JB had cancelled a leaf of the 1st ed. (pp. 167–68). EM and he now made several minor changes and replaced one sentence in which SJ compared Macdonald to "an attorney who has twenty houses in a street"; this, however, reappeared later in the book as part of "the character of a rapacious Highland Chief" (1st ed. p. 474; *Life* v. 378; see BP xvi. 230–31).

[16] *Macbeth* I. v. 17.

I have been much disconcerted by my Wife's affectionate fears. If the *Remarks* come from him, he has retaliated, and we have no more to do. Yet I still doubt if it would not be better on my own account, to make the proposed change. Indeed much changing may have the appearance of wavering. So it must be well weighed, when our heads are laid together.—If you could have an opportunity to know for *certain* that Lord M——d does not take it *hot*, a few lines to Mrs. Boswell James's Court Edinburgh would relieve an excellent woman. To say that a man does not *entertain* liberally—and that a Gentleman educated in England is totally unfit for the Hebridian situation are surely no *severe* reflections. And what is *anonymously* said ought not to be taken as *levell'd at me.*[17]

It is sad that there should be such mixtures of alloy in human happiness. The fame of my Tour is darkened somewhat by censures as if I were ill natured. But I am now amidst narrow-minded prejudiced mortals. Adieu, my Dear Sir. I cannot express how warmly I am yours,

JAMES BOSWELL

To Malone,
c. Sunday 25 December 1785

Not reported. *Post* From EM, 3 Jan. 1786: "Many thanks for your letter from York." JB reached York on the night of 24 Dec. and left early on 26 Dec. (Journ.).

[17] Gay, *Beggar's Opera* II. x: "If you mention Vice or Bribe, / 'Tis so pat to all the Tribe; / Each crys—That was levell'd at me." The passage deleted from the 1st ed. (pp. 165–66) is printed in *Life* v. 148 n. 1. The three paragraphs substituted for this passage (2nd ed. pp. 165–66; *Life* v. 148–49) begin, "The most ancient seat" and end with "they will be tamed into insignificance". For anonymous references to Macdonald in the *Tour*, see n. 15 above and *ante* To EM, 29 Oct. n. 2.

To Malone, Tuesday 3 January 1786

MS. Yale (L 927). Sent 3 Jan. "Edmond Malone Esq. of my safe arrival etc. etc. enclosing Mr. W. James's letter" (Reg. Let.).
ADDRESS: To Edmond Malone Esq.

Edinburgh, 3[1] Janry. 1786

MY DEAR SIR: I got well home, and found my Wife much better and my children all in good health. The Cloud was quite dispelled; nor did I meet here with any of the disagreable things which I apprehended.[2] Nay I had the satisfaction to perceive that my trial of a more enlarged sphere was by no means condemned as irrational. So let me be content.

Dilly informs me that the second edition "is welcome amongst the trade fully to his expectation and that he conceives he shall by the 10th be able to give a very good account of its progress." Should it come to a third I would venture 1500, as I suppose there will be no more.[3]

[1] MS. "2" written in error. According to Reg. Lèt. the present letter was sent on 3 Jan. The surviving draft of the letter to Walter James, mentioned in the third paragraph of this letter, is dated 3 Jan., and JB's journal records that Lunardi, mentioned in the last paragraph, supped with the Boswells on 3 Jan.

[2] JB was in London from 17 Nov. to 22 Dec. and arrived in Edinburgh on 28 Dec. 1785 (Journ.). While in London, he had been in low spirits, no doubt the combined effects of the controversy with Lord Macdonald (see BP xvi. 221–59), concern over the practicality of practising at the English bar, and apprehension about the reactions of his Scottish friends to the *Tour*. On his arrival in Edinburgh, however, JB wrote, "Had the highest consolation in seeing my dear Wife and children, and the cloud of melancholy was quite dissipated by *experiencing* that I could so soon be at home from London" (Journ. 26 Dec. 1785).

[3] Reg. Let. records that the letter from Dilly arrived on 2 Jan. Dilly reported, JB notes, "that the second edition of my Tour to the Hebrides is doing well." On 3 Jan. JB replied, "glad that my Tour to the Hebrides does so well. If the second edition goes off speedily I think to print a third of 1500" (Reg. Let.). Neither letter has been reported. 1,500 copies were printed of the 1st ed. of the *Tour*, and 1,000 of the 2nd (*ante* From EM, 5 Oct. 1785 n. 3; To EM, 27 Oct. 1785, p. 249). JB's use of the word "venture" here and in *ante* To EM, 13 Oct. 1785, p. 218 suggests, perhaps, that he was bearing at least a part of the expense of printing the *Tour*. He records having written to Dilly on 23 Dec. 1784, "I intend to publish in the Spring my tour with Dr. Johnson, a good Prelude to my large Work his Life. Will he go halves in an edition?" (Reg. Let.). Before 13 Jan. 1785 JB received word from Dilly that he was "desireous to have my 'Tour to the Hebrides' speedily published"; Dilly wrote again on 29 Jan. that he wished JB to have "all the profits" from the "Tour" (Reg. Let.). Unfortunately, these letters have not been reported, and we have no way of ascertaining precisely the financial arrangements between JB and Dilly. It is unlikely that JB sold the rights to the *Tour*, for we know that

Enclosed is a very handsom letter from the Authour of the "Defence" of my Journal, which pray preserve. Perhaps it may be necessary to produce it publickly. I have written to him.[4]

The weather is excessively cold.[5] Lunardi is to sup with me tonight.[6] We all join in best compliments to you. Pray assure Mr. Courtenay of my most grateful regard.[7] I ever am, My Dear Sir, your much obliged and affectionate, humble servant,

JAMES BOSWELL

From Malone, Tuesday 3 January 1786

MS. Yale (C 1902). Received 7 Jan.[1] "Edmond Malone Esq. about my Tour" (Reg. Let.).

ADDRESS in Courtenay's hand: Jams. Boswell Esqr. Edinburgh.

FRANK: London Janry. third 1786. Free J. Courtenay.

POSTMARKS: [London] 3 JA, 3 JA, FREE [Edinburgh] JA 8.

he paid certain incidental costs, such as the expense of cutting the crests for the 1st and 2nd eds. (JB's expense account, A 39.1; *ante* To EM, 11 Nov. 1785, n. 9).

[4] Soon after the attack on the *Tour* by "Verax" (*ante* From EM, 28 Oct. 1785, n. 3) appeared *A Defence of Mr. Boswell's Journal of a Tour to the Hebrides; in a Letter to the Author of the Remarks Signed Verax*. The author of the anonymous *Defence* was probably Walter James James (1759–1829), a literary dabbler and Bennet Langton's cousin by marriage (Fifer, pp. 308–09 n. 4; Charles Ryskamp, "Boswell and Walter James; Goethe and Daniel Malthus", *Eighteenth-Century Studies in Honor of Donald F. Hyde*, ed. W. H. Bond, 1970, pp. 209–19). James's letter to JB of 26 Dec. 1785, written in a pompous style but an elegant hand, notes, "I find, by the public prints, that this trifle of mine, has had the honour of being ascribed to your pen. . . . It may possibly afford you some satisfaction to silence those who may, either seriously or jocularly, ascribe the 'Defence' to your pen, by producing this Letter, which I shall be happy to hear of your receiving". James enclosed a copy of his pamphlet. JB replied on 3 Jan. "to beg that you may be so good as to let me know something more of so kind a friend than his name; and be assured that I shall be very happy to have an opportunity of cultivating your acquaintance." There is no record that they ever met.

[5] In his journal for 3 Jan. JB wrote, "Having drank wine the day before, both at dinner and supper, and the frost being intense, I had a headack, and breakfasted calmly in bed." *Edin. Adv.* (30 Dec. 1785–3 Jan. 1786) xlv. 5, reported that for several days past the weather in Scotland had been the coldest "ever remembered since the year 1740".

[6] On 15 Sept. 1784, Vincenzo Lunardi (1759–1806) had made the first balloon flight over England. Since Sept. 1785 he had been in Scotland, where he put on five exhibitions between 5 Oct. and 20 Dec. (John Kay, *A Series of Original Portraits*, 2nd ed., 1877, i. 79–85). JB invited him to sup, he says, "at the earnest desire of my children" (Journ. 3 Jan.).

[7] JB was grateful to Courtenay for serving as adviser and intermediary in the controversy with Macdonald (Journ. 6–12 Dec.; BP xvi. 221–59).

[1] As the Edinburgh postmark reads "JA 8", presumably Reg. Let. is in error.

FROM MALONE, 3 JANUARY 1786

London, Jany. 3, 1786, 5 o'clock

My dear Sir: Many thanks for your letter from York—Est aliquid prodire tenus, in such piercing weather.[2]

Here has Courteney been with me this hour and a half, which we have employed in making two additional Stanzas to his Ode—At last we shall launch it in a day or two.[3] However the time has run away so, that I can only say three words. All goes on well. Of the new edition I understand near 300 are gone off already, including the presents and 50 sent to Edinburgh—Devaynes has had a book,[4] and I desired one also to be sent to Langton and T. Warton.[5] The last was peculiarly proper on

[2] "It is something to go so far", an inexact quotation of Horace, *Epistles* I. i. 32, "est quadam [*in some editions* quodam] prodire tenus". In London the temperature did not rise above freezing between 23 Dec. 1785 and 4 Jan. 1786 (*Gent. Mag.* 1786, lvi. 914). JB reached York on 24 Dec. (when there was sleet, a harsh wind, and a temperature of 29°F. in London), attended Christmas services the next day in York Cathedral, and dined that night with the prebendary in residence, William Mason, who "was very angry that he was not attacked by Johnson" in the *Tour* (Journ.). That night in Scotland "there was a violent storm of wind from the N. E. accompanied by snow and hail. Accounts from different parts of the country mention, that there was a great deal of thunder and lightning" (*Edin. Eve. Cour.* 26 Dec. 1785, p. 2). From 23 to 27 Dec. there was intense cold and a violent storm in Newcastle, about halfway between Edinburgh and York (*Edin. Adv.* 30 Dec. 1785–3 Jan. 1786, xlv. 5). JB left York early on the morning of 26 Dec. (Journ.).

[3] Courtenay's *Ode* was first printed in *Pub. Adv.* for 9 Jan. p. [2], with the following paragraph, signed "B. J." (JB?) prefixed: "The following elegant Ode having accidentally fallen into my hands, if you think it worth a place in your Poet's Corner, it is at your service. It is the production, if I am rightly informed, of a gentleman well known in the political world, who has long been deservedly admired for the happiest vein of wit and humour, and is not less distinguished by his various and extensive knowledge in almost every branch of literature and science." The *Ode*, addressed "*To* ——— ———, *Esq.*" and dated "*Bath, Sept.* 22, 1784", begins as follows:

Whilst you illumine Shakspeare's page,
And dare the future critick's rage,
Or on the past refine,
Here many an eve I pensive sit,
No B—e pours out a stream of wit.
No B——ll joys o'er wine.

The speaker compares the state of man to that of an "air balloon" blown about by metaphysical winds, but finds comfort in "music, love, and wine" tempered by "Reason and science". The *Ode* was reprinted in *Gent. Mag.* (Jan. 1786) lvi. 66–67, where the blanks were filled with the names Malone, Burke, and Boswell.

[4] John Devaynes (c. 1726–1801), Apothecary to George III, moved in the circle that included JB, EM, and Courtenay, and was a member of the Essex Head Club. He attended JB in his last illness (*Gent. Mag.* 1801, lxxi. 93; Journ. 22 Feb.; James Boswell the younger to W. J. Temple, 8 [May] 1795—MS. Pierpont Morgan).

[5] No list survives of presentation copies of the 2nd ed., as does of the 1st (M 131). Copies were sent not only to Devaynes, Langton, and Warton, but also to Francis Barber (From Barber, 7 Jan.—MS. Hyde Collection), EB (*ante* To EB, 20 Dec. 1785), Lord Eglinton (Reg. Let. entry for 3 Jan.), Richard Sharp (reported to F. W. Hilles, c. 1930), and the fourth Viscount Townshend

account of his budget of letters.[6]—I enclose you the G. M. There is a pretty severe attack and sufficiently unjust. I mean to answer it in the Mag. for next month, and to sweep in two or three other Reviews.[7]—You are not reviewed this Month in the Monthly R. So much the better as Griffith has got your 2d Edn.[8]—It is very provoking that[9] such a quantity of nonsense should be talked and written about Johnson. I have not time to answer half of it but I positively will do something. Facit indignatio.[10]—There is a very sensible review of you in the European Mag. which I have just this moment cast my eye on.[11] I cannot send it, lest I should make my packets too heavy.—Dilly thinks your attacker in the G. M. is St——s.[12] I don't think it his style, but he works in so many different shapes, that there is no certainty.—

"Amid all this *criticism*, I must sit down to dinner"[13]—So farewell—Ever Yours most faithfully,

E. M.

(K. D. Duval catalogue, Dec. 1973, pp. 5–6). Also, JB intended to present copies on fine paper to the King, the Advocates' Library, and EM, though no record exists to testify that he actually did so (*ante* To EM, 13 Oct. 1785, p. 218; From EM, 19 Oct. 1785, p. 236).

[6] Warton had written to JB on 5 Nov. 1785, offering to send copies of "about twenty of Dr. Johnson's Letters written to me in the years 1755, 1756". JB gratefully accepted this unsolicited offer (To Warton, 18 Nov. 1785). See *post* To EM, 10 Mar. and n. 2.

[7] The enclosure from *Gent. Mag.* is missing, but this attack, signed "D. H." (Dec. 1785, lv. 959), criticizes JB for his vanity, forwardness, impertinence, nationality, and absurdity. "D. H." also asserts that SJ had said "as plainly as an *Englishman* can speak, that the Journal *was not fit to be printed*". "D.H." was Richard Gough (*Lit. Anec.* vi. 271). The issue for the previous month (pp. 889–94) contains a favourable review of the *Tour*. Aside from a number of squibs that had appeared in the newspapers since the publication of the *Tour* (*ante* From EM, 21 Oct. 1785, n. 19, 5 Nov. 1785, n. 43; To EM, 8 Nov. 1785, n. 11), several longer essays and reviews had attacked the *Tour*. For example, an essayist in *Pub. Adv.* 21 Dec. 1785, p. [1], had asserted that the *Tour* should not have been published. *Crit. Rev.* (Nov. 1785) lx. 337–45 had found much both to criticize and to praise, and the *English Review* (Nov. 1785) vi. 369–78 had been decidedly unfavourable.

[8] Ralph Griffiths (1720–1803) was founder and publisher of the *Monthly Rev.*

[9] MS. "the great" deleted before "that"

[10] "Si natura negat, facit indignatio versum", Juvenal, *Satires* i. 79: "If nature refuses, indignation writes the verse." This phrase was to be used as the title of EM's essay (*post* From EM, 1 Feb. n. 5).

[11] *Eur. Mag.* (Dec. 1785) viii. 448–52. The review was continued in the issues for Mar. (ix. 168–73), May (340–44), and June 1786 (413–16). The author was William Julius Mickle (Isaac Reed to Mickle, 12 and 30 Nov. 1785, 2 Feb.—MSS. Osborn Collection).

[12] George Steevens (*ante* To EM, 10 June 1785, n. 6) was already notorious in literary circles for his fondness for perpetrating hoaxes and inserting in newspapers and magazines malicious pseudonymous attacks on his friends (*Life* iii. 281 and n. 3).

[13] On 19 Aug. 1773 SJ and JB surveyed the ruins at St. Andrews. "Dinner was mentioned.—JOHNSON. 'Ay, ay; amidst all these sorrowful scenes, I have no objection to dinner' " (*Life* v. 63).

TO MALONE, 13 JANUARY 1786

To Malone,
Friday 13 January 1786

MS. Yale (L 928). Sent 13 Jan. "Edmond Malone Esq. that I have found things in Scotland by no means so disagreable as I apprehended" (Reg. Let.).

Edinburgh, 13 Janry. 1786

MY DEAR SIR: I am much obliged to you for the Gentleman's Magazine, in which the Shuttlecock is excellently kept up.[1] I do not feel the Attack as severe because the *references* are never supported when the pages are looked at. The only thing in it that appears to me worth obviating, is the *misunderstanding* of Dr. Johnson's meaning as to the *subject* of the Journal being *fit for publishing*. It will however be very kind in you to knock this foe and two or three more against one another.[2] I have seen the European Magazine which really reviews me very sensibly, as you have observed; and I think also very favourably. I am glad to see the Review is to be continued. I shall meet the continuation[3] and I hope also the Monthly Review[4] in London on the 2d of february.

I am wonderfully recovered, and I am agreably surprised to find the people here by no means hostile as I apprehended. Dr. Blair has declared himself to me very well pleased nay something more, and he even takes the *Cow* pleasantly.[5] I had a long walk t'other day with Dr. Robertson to whom I said I hoped he was not offended at my having honoured my Book with him. He said by no means, and we talked a great deal of Dr. Johnson of whom he has a high opinion, but not to *idolatry*[6] as some of us are thought to

[1] *Ante* From EM, 3 Jan. n. 7. In his attack, "D. H." had written, "the hardest rap on the knuckles is but a 'battledoor to make Mr. B. *virûm volitare per ora*' ". For an explanation of the reference, see *ante* To EM, 30 Oct. 1785, n. 24.

[2] *Post* From EM, 1 Feb. nn. 5, 6.

[3] The continuation did not appear until the Mar. issue (*ante* From EM, 3 Jan. n. 11).

[4] The *Tour* was not reviewed in *Monthly Rev.* until April (lxxiv. 277–82). Written by Samuel Badcock (1747–88), a dissenting clergyman (B. C. Nangle, *The Monthly Review, First Series*, 1934, pp. 2, 65), the review was rather unfavourable.

[5] JB wrote in his journal for 1 Jan., "Visited him [Dr. Blair] between sermons, and found him wonderfully pleased with my Tour and Court of Session letter." On Hugh Blair, see *ante* To EM, 27 Oct. 1785, n. 48. For the incident with the cow, see *Life* v. 396.

[6] Ben Jonson wrote of Shakespeare, "I lov'd the man, and doe honour his memory (on this side Idolatry) as much as any" (*Timber: or Discoveries*, in Ben Jonson, *Collected Works*, ed. C. H. Herford *et al.*, 1925–52, viii. 583–84).

have.[7] He said the Dr. wrote letters admirably and that those to Lord Elibank and the Duke of Argyle in my Journal are as courtly letters as he ever read;[8] that Johnson was a man of great wit in conversation, great taste in his own writings and still more in judging of the writings[9] of others. I shall have these two "good and wise Doctors"[10] to dine with me, before I leave this town. The weather is so unfavourable that I am not going to Auchinleck. I met *Monbod* yesterday in the Advocates Library; but he did not speak to me. This being the case, and as he persists to abuse Dr. Johnson, he will be fair game in the LIFE.[11]

Lady Colvill who I thought was offended as a *Scotchwoman* has no *personal* quarrel with the Journalist, which I am very glad at as she is one of my most respectable friends.[12] I am to dine with her today on a boiled Turkey and oyster sauce. I shall think with social cordiality of worthy hospitable Courtenay, whom her Ladyship admires exceedingly, but has imaged him to be a neat smart brisk little man.[13] I shall be happy to see his Ode now that it

[7] On 14 Jan. JB wrote, "I had one of these days walked with Principal Robertson who was much pleased with the print [from JB's portrait of Mary Queen of Scots], and in good humour with my Tour" (Journ.). But on 29 Apr. 1778, when JB had said that he "worshipped" SJ, Robertson had said, "You should not worship him; you should worship no man" (*Life* iii. 331).

[8] For these letters, see *Life* v. 182, 363.

[9] MS. "writings" written above deleted "taste"

[10] After a visit with Robertson and Blair in Edinburgh, SJ told JB, "Sir, these two doctors are good men, and wise men" (*Life* v. 397).

[11] James Burnett (1714–99), Lord Monboddo (1767) in the Court of Session, had entertained SJ and JB for dinner at Monboddo House, Kincardineshire, on their Hebridean tour (21 Aug. 1773). But despite a courteous comment about the "magnetism of [Monboddo's] conversation" in the *Journey* (*Works SJ* ix. 12), SJ and he never liked each other, and Monboddo, who had helped mediate between JB and his father during his marriage crisis of 1769 (*Earlier Years*, pp. 413–14, 417–18), must have felt his friendship for JB betrayed when he read a series of jeering remarks about himself in the *Tour* (*Life* v. 45, 46, 111, 248, 330).

In his journal for 12 Jan. JB wrote: "Was at a meeting of the Curators of the Advocates Library. Felt myself very easy. Lord Monboddo came into the Library. I bowed to him, but he did not speak to me. I understood afterwards that he was violent against me. I did not care. I considered that it would make him *fair game* in Dr. Johnson's 'Life'." JB did in fact record several of SJ's criticisms of Monboddo in the *Life* (e.g. ii. 147, 219, 259–60).

[12] Elizabeth, Lady Colville (c. 1735–94), sister of JB's friend and literary collaborator in early life, the Hon. Andrew Erskine, first married (1760) Walter Macfarlane of Macfarlane, the antiquary (d. 1767); she then married (1768) Alexander, seventh Lord Colville of Culross. She and JB were close friends from early in life, and JB "had once serious thoughts of proposing marriage to her" (Journ. 23 Nov. 1776). In his *Tour* JB mentioned her as one "to whom I am proud to introduce any stranger of eminence, that he may see what dignity and grace is to be found in Scotland" (*Life* v. 395).

[13] We know little of Courtenay's appearance. Contemporary cartoons suggest he

is completed. I also long to see his Johnsonian verses in print,[14] not however without the excuseable selfishness of hoping that the *Recorder* of his wonderful conversations will not be forgotten.

You did well to send Devaynes a Book and not ill to give Langton a second. I hope Mr. Courtenay has had a second.

Did I beg of you to secure me six proofs of my own Mezzotinto by Jones.[15] Pray do it.

I trust I am now *resolved* to make *a fair trial* in Westr. Hall, without *anxiety*. My Wife thinks it will be better that she and the children come first to furnished lodgings, that she may take the house herself.[16] We shall talk of all these things. My kindest compliments to Courtenay. Ever most affectionately yours,

JAMES BOSWELL

My second edition (50 copies) not yet arrived here.[17]

P. 284[:] Monday 20 Septr. It is suggested that the Lion is not in Valerius Maximus but in Aulus Gellius.[18]

From Malone, Friday 13 January 1786

MS. Yale (C 1903). The verso of the wrapper is addressed and franked in Courtenay's hand: "Jas. Boswell Esq., Edinburgh. London Janry. Eleventh 1786. Free J. Courtenay." As the letter for which the frank was intended was not written until 13 Jan., the wrapper was addressed and franked again. Received 17 Jan. "Edmond Malone Esq. encouraging me to remove to London" (Reg. Let.).

was fairly tall, lank, with a long nose and jutting chin; Wraxall never remembered "a more complete cynic in his dress, manners, and general deportment", and spoke of his "neglected exterior" (quoted in Namier and Brooke ii. 262–63).

[14] *Post* From EM, 13 Jan. and nn. 5, 6, 8, 10.

[15] John Jones (c. 1745–97), engraver, had his residence and shop at No. 63 Great Portland St. He made the engraving, dated 17 Jan. 1786, from Reynolds's portrait of JB, painted in 1785 (Journ. 5 July, 10 Sept. 1785).

[16] *Post* To EM, 24 Jan. n. 7; From EM, 1 Feb. and n. 4.

[17] The 2nd ed. of the *Tour* was not advertised in Edinburgh until 20 Jan. (*Edin. Adv.* 17–20 Jan. xlv. 45); it was to be sold by William Creech, bookseller at the Cross (*Williamson's Directory for the City of Edinburgh*, 1784–85).

[18] The passage in the 2nd ed. reads as follows: "Nature seems to have implanted gratitude in all living creatures. The lion, mentioned by Valerius Maximus, had it." In the 3rd ed. JB altered the passage to read, "The lion, mentioned by Aulus Gellius, had it", and added a note with the reference "Aul. Gellius, Lib. v. c. xiv" (*Life* v. 232 and n. 3). The story referred to is of Androcles and the lion.

FROM MALONE, 13 JANUARY 1786

ADDRESS in Courtenay's hand: James Boswell Esqr., James's Court, Edinburgh.
FRANK: London Janry. thirteenth 1786. Free J. Courtenay.
POSTMARKS: [London] 13 JA, FREE [Edinburgh] JA 17.

London, Jany. 13, 1786

MY DEAR SIR: You will see by the inside of the cover that I intended to have written to you two days ago; but I have been much out of spirits this week past,[1] and have not been able to rouse myself to do any thing for the G. M. as I intended, though I still hope to do something in time for this month.[2]—I am very glad to find that you do not think your movement here so formidable a business. Be assured, you consider it much too deeply;[3] and so perhaps you would say to me concerning what constantly preys upon me, though at some times, from accidental circumstances, more than at others. There is no arguing about feelings. "Sensation is sensation"[4] still.

Courteney is going on with his Verses on Johnson.[5] They are swelled from about 30 Lines to 170. He dined with me yesterday, and we revised them, and I think it is probable, from our talking over matters, they have by this time extended to 200. His opening now runs thus:

Scotia, rejoice! your terrour now is fled;
Unrivall'd Johnson's number'd with the dead:
MacOssian's sons may now securely rest,
Safe from the taunting sneer, the frolick jest.
Lost is the man etc.[6]

[1] EM's phrase, "what constantly preys upon me", in the second sentence following, suggests that his low spirits were caused by his grief for Susanna Spencer, with whom he had fallen in love in 1769, and who had been insane since about 1781 (see Introduction, pp. 168–70).

[2] *Ante* From EM, 3 Jan. and n. 7. Because periodicals were not published until at least the end of each month, EM still had time to submit a piece. See further *post* From EM, 1 Feb. and n. 5.

[3] Cf. *Macbeth* II. ii. 27: "Consider it not so deeply."

[4] "But he [SJ] owned to me that he was fatigued and teased by Sir Alexander's doing too much to entertain him. I said, it was all kindness.—JOHNSON. 'True, sir; but sensation is sensation' " (*Life* v. 95).

[5] Courtenay's *Poetical Review of the Literary and Moral Character of the Late Samuel Johnson, L.L.D.* was published by Charles Dilly on 6 Apr. (*Morn. Her.* 6 Apr. p. 1). The poem contains 294 lines.

[6] The 1st ed. of Courtenay's *Poetical Review* begins:

A Generous tear will Caledonia shed?
Her ancient foe, illustrious Johnson's dead:
Mac-Ossian's sons may now securely rest,
Safe from the bitter sneer, the cynick jest.

At the end of the lines in which he describes Johnson's[7] talents for conversation, he has introduced these:

With Reynolds' pencil, vivid, bold, and true,
Thus fervent Boswell gives him to our view:
With fond delight we praise his happy vein
Grac'd with the naïvete of the sage Montagne.

I am not quite satisfied with the last couplet. He means to introduce two more lines, after the second, to tie what follows better to the preceding couplet.[8]

It is really now a very good performance; I wish I could persuade him to leave[9] out "Bell and the Dragon", which is not of a piece with the rest, and his "never reading the bible",—which is not true.[10]

I dined at Sir J. R. the day before yesterday; we had too large a party to be pleasant (12) though many of them were good men and true:[11]—Langton, Scott, Dr. Warren, Dr. Brocklesby, Sir C. Bunbury, Mr. Seward, Mr. Cambridge, Dr.[12] Burney etc.[13]—

Lost is the man, who scarce deigns Gray
to praise. . . .

[7] MS. "Johnson's" written above deleted "his"

[8] In the 1st ed. (p. 21) the lines were altered and expanded:

With Reynolds' pencil, vivid, bold, and true,
So fervent Boswell gives him to our view.
In every trait we see his mind expand;
The master rises by the pupil's hand;
We love the writer, praise his happy vein,
Grac'd with the naiveté of the sage Montaigne.

[9] MS. "live"

[10] The offending lines were retained in the 1st ed. (p. 6):

He sleeps and fasts, pens on himself a libel,
And still believes, but never reads the Bible.
Fame says, at school, of scripture science vain,
Bel and the Dragon smote him on the brain. . . .

In notes to these lines, Courtenay quoted SJ's *Prayers and Meditations*: "I resolved last Easter to read, within the year, the whole Bible; a great part of which I had never looked upon." And, "I have never yet read the Apocrypha. When I was a boy I have read or heard Bel and the Dragon" (*Works SJ* i. 147, 151).

[11] *Much Ado about Nothing* III. iii. 1.

[12] MS. "Dr." superimposed upon "Mr."

[13] Richard Warren (1731–97), M.D., the King's physician, whom William Gerard Hamilton called "a coxcomb, but a *satisfactory coxcomb*" (*Life* iii. 245 n. 1, vi. 452–53), attended both SJ and JB in their last illnesses. Sir Thomas Charles Bunbury (1740–1821), Bt., M.P. for Suffolk (1761–84, 1790–1812), though more a "racing man" than a politician, was a follower of Charles James Fox. He was one of the pallbearers at SJ's funeral (Namier and Brooke ii. 136–40). William Seward (1747–99), literary dilettante and hypochondriac, became a good friend of JB (*Life* iii. 123 n. 1). Richard Owen Cambridge (1717–1802), minor poet, is chiefly remembered for his beautiful villa at Twickenham. JB praised him at length in the *Life* (iv. 196). Charles Burney (1726–1814), Mus. Doc., appears frequently in the *Life*. Langton, Scott, Warren, Bunbury, and Burney were members of The Club.

The alterations in your 2d Edition were talked of. An idea, I find, has gone about, that they are very numerous. Sir C. B. mentioned as a proof that they must be so, that the new volume was much *thinner* than the former. I told him, the book was so far from being diminished in bulk that there were 30 pages more in the second edition than the first. The fact is, that the second is printed on a thinner paper, and therefore looks lanker. I am sorry that you did not mention in your final note, that the omitted passages[14] amounted to about 20 lines. It can be done hereafter.[15]—I find from Dilly that all goes on very well. I think, if you print a 3d Edition you may safely venture 1500.[16]

I shall preserve Mr. James's Letter very safely.—I hope that you will come to us before the end of the month, and that you will always believe me most faithfully and affectionately Yours,

E. MALONE

To Malone,
Saturday 14 January 1786

MS. Yale (L 929). Sent 14 Jan. "Edmond Malone Esq. suggesting an addition to the Advertisement of my Tour" (Reg. Let.).
ADDRESS: To Edmond Malone Esq.

Edinburgh, 14 Janry. 1786

MY DEAR SIR: By a letter which I received from Dilly today dated 10 Janry. I find that the sale of the Tour "had not been so quick for ten days and that he should therefore assist the circulation by fresh advertising near the close of the month."[1]

As he does not appear to me to be *expert* in advertising (as I

[14] MS. "passages" written above deleted "pages"

[15] For the pages added to the 2nd ed., see *ante* To EM, 30 Oct. 1785, n. 14. The "final note" mentioned by EM was added to p. 527 of the 2nd ed.; it explained that some indiscreet passages in the 1st ed. had been dropped in the 2nd. In the 3rd ed. the corresponding note explained that the deleted passages "did not amount in the whole to a page", and was expanded to rebut an attack on the *Tour* by Peter Pindar (*post* To EM, 10 Mar. n. 3; From EM, 17 Mar. n. 9).

[16] *Ante* To EM, 3 Jan. and n. 3. Dilly apparently had trouble selling the 3rd ed., which he advertised as late as 1799 (*Lit. Car.* pp. 122–23).

[1] The letter from Dilly is not reported; Reg. Let. records that JB received it on 13, not 14, Jan.

perceive the old *latin Poems* etc. still retained)[2] I beg you may be so kind as to take a little trouble to set him right. And I really think it would be proper to add ***This Edition is improved by several corrections,—many additional notes—a Table of Contents—and an Appendix.[3]

You will consider if it should proceed "containing a letter to the Authour from Dr. *Blacklock*, with the Authours remarks—and Verses written and presented to Dr. Johnson in the Isle of Sky by Sir *Alexander* (now *Lord*) *Macdonald*." *This* or a *part* of it, I imagine may be of use.[4]

As Mr. James allows me to *produce* his letter to vindicate me from the *newspaper reflection* of having written the *Defence* myself, might it not be produced in the *same channel*?[5]

If Mr. Jones has not yet published my Portrait, I wish to have OF AUCHINLECK added to my *name*. May I also trouble you with this? My title of *Baron d'Auchinleck* is known on the Continent. You may smile at my vanity, but humour it.[6]

[2] *Ante* From EM, 5 Oct. 1785 and n. 14. The phrase "some Latin Poems" appeared in the advertisements as late as Jan. 1786 (e.g. *Gen. Eve. Post*, 13–15 Dec. 1785, p. [2], 20–22 Dec. 1785, p. [4], 3–5 Jan. 1786, p. [2]; *Lond. Chron.* 22–24 Dec. 1785, lviii. 603, 27–29 Dec. 1785, lviii. 620; *Pub. Adv.* 27 Dec. 1785, p. [1], 30 Dec. 1785, p. [1]; *Whitehall Evening Post*, 15–17 Dec. 1785, p. [1], 22–24 Dec. 1785, p. [1]).

[3] The revised advertisement reads as follows: "This Day was Published, With the Addition of a Table of Contents, and an Appendix, In One Volume Octavo, price 6s. in boards, the Second Edition, revised and corrected, THE JOURNAL of a TOUR to the HEBRIDES, with SAMUEL JOHNSON, LL.D. By JAMES BOSWELL, Esq. Containing some Poetical Pieces, by Dr. Johnson, relative to the Tour, and never before published; a Series of his Conversation, Literary Anecdotes, and Opinions of Men and Books. Together with an authentic account of the distresses and escape of the GRANDSON of KING JAMES II in the year 1746. London: Printed for Charles Dilly, in the Poultry" (*Morn. Her.* 20 Jan. p. [1]).

[4] Neither Thomas Blacklock (1721–91), the blind poet, nor Lord Macdonald is mentioned in the advertisements in the London papers; however, the advertisement in *Edin. Adv.* (17–20 Jan.) xlv. 45, adds the following paragraph: "This edition, besides being more elegantly printed, is improved by several corrections—and many additional notes—by a Table of Contents—and by an Appendix, containing a Letter to the Author from Dr. *Blacklock*, with the Author's remarks upon it; and verses written and presented to Dr. Johnson in the Isle of Sky, by SIR ALEXANDER (now LORD) MACDONALD." Clearly, the Edinburgh advertisement was the work of JB, while the London advertisement was by EM.

[5] James's letter was never printed, and James was not mentioned in the newspaper advertisements; however, in the "Advertisement" to the 3rd ed. JB mentioned him as "a gentleman who published a Defence of my Journal, and has added to the favour by communicating his name to me in a very obliging letter" (*Life* v. 3).

[6] JB's letter doubtless arrived too late, for the mezzotint, entitled "James Boswell of Auchinleck, Esqr.", was published on 17 Jan. (*ante* To EM, 13 Jan. n. 15). "Baron d'Auchinleck", a title allowed to a gentleman of JB's standing by German heraldry,

TO MALONE, 14 JANUARY 1786

If you have not yet looked at *Pinkertons's* two volumes of Ancient Scottish Poems just published by Dilly, pray do. His notes rather exceed the Drawcansirship[7] of Robert Heron Esq. He abuses superlatively not only Johnson, but Swift—Arbuthnot etc. etc.[8]

I have not yet read much of Blackstone at this time.[9] I fear that I shall not be able to study even sufficiently to have a superficies of english law. But you shall command me, as Guide Philosopher and Friend.[10]

The *last day* on which you are to write to me during this recess is Monday 23 Janry.[11] I am ever, with most sincere esteem and gratitude, affectionately yours,

JAMES BOSWELL

was used by JB during his Continental tour, 1764–66 (*Earlier Years*, pp. 158, 213, 227, 500).

[7] Drawcansir, a swashbuckling character in *The Rehearsal*, 1672, by George Villiers, second Duke of Buckingham (1628–87), et al. parodied Almanzor in Dryden's *Conquest of Granada*. Drawcansir's name was often applied to those who were enemies to friends and foes alike (see OED, Drawcansir).

[8] John Pinkerton (1758–1826), whose *Ancient Scotish Poems*, 2 vols., 1786, was published by Charles Dilly in London and William Creech in Edinburgh, had written, "Any schoolmaster might have done what Johnson did. His dictionary is merely a glossary to his own barbarous works. Indeed, that a man of very small learning (see his works), but confessedly quite ignorant of the Northern tongues, should pretend to write an English dictionary at all: that a man, confessedly without taste, should attempt to define the nicer powers of words, a chief province of taste: that a man, confessedly the very worst writer in the language save Sir Thomas Brown, and whose whole works are true *pages of inanity* wrapt in barbarism, should set up for a judge of our language: are all ideas to excite laughter" (ii. 404). Pinkerton also attacked Swift (ii. 384, 412) and Arbuthnot (ii. 412). JB's interest in this publication may have been due partly to a reference to "a MS. belonging to James Boswell Esq. of Auchinleck" (i. lxxxix). This sixteenth-century MS., known as "The Asloan Manuscript", is now in the National Library of Scotland. *Ancient Scotish Poems*, though dated 1786, was advertised as "this day . . . published" as early as 17 Dec. 1785 (*Whitehall Eve. Post*, 15–17 Dec. 1785, p. [3]). Earlier in 1785, Pinkerton had published *Letters of Literature* under the pseudonym "Robert Heron, Esq."; this book, like *Ancient Scotish Poems*, was noted for its attacks on established literary figures, including Virgil. In three of the letters Pinkerton also attacked the 1778 edition of Shakespeare by SJ and Steevens (*Letters*, pp. 105–16, 162–78, 301–15).

[9] *The Commentaries on the Laws of England*, 1765–69, of Sir William Blackstone (1723–80), was widely recognized as the classic textbook on English law. Since Scots law is founded on Roman civil and not English common law, JB was reading Blackstone in preparation for his move to the English bar (Journ. 2 Jan.).

[10] Pope, *Essay on Man* iv. 390.

[11] JB was to leave for London on 27 Jan. (Journ.).

To Malone,
Tuesday 24 January 1786

MS. Yale (L 930). Sent 24 Jan. "Edmond Malone Esq. enclosing letter to Mrs. Strange open, and begging he may look at Mr. Hoole's house. Account of my good appearance in the court of Session etc." (Reg. Let.).
ADDRESS: To Edmond Malone Esq.

Edinburgh, 24 Janry. 1786

MY DEAR SIR: Your kind letter of the 13 current did me much good. I most sincerely sympathise with you in being out of spirits. Yet you raised mine. For, without flattery of any species I tell you, that I am (as our great Friend wrote to the Chancellor) *mihi carior* when I find myself so much regarded by you.[1] Courtenay's elogium too elevated me much. It is beyond my warmest expectation. How much am I obliged to him. I wonder why you are "not quite satisfied with the last couplet"

With fond delight we praise his happy vein
Grac'd with the naiveté of the sage Montaigne.

I cannot give it up. It is perhaps too much in the opinion of many. But I grasp it. The similarity to Montaigne is quite characteristical.[2] I long to see the whole Poem.

I have boldly resumed my practice in the Court of Session. The Court had given judgement unanimously against "my respectable neighbour Mr. Fairlie".[3] I drew a Petition which fortunately had such an effect as to turn the tide.[4] The Lord President said

[1] When SJ wrote to Lord Thurlow on 9 Sept. 1784 thanking him for his offer of a loan—in effect a gift—of five or six hundred pounds, he concluded, "from your Lordship's kindness I have received a benefit which only Men like You can bestow, I shall live *mihi charior* with a higher opinion of my own merit." In *Letters SJ* iii. 221, R. W. Chapman thus annotates *mihi charior*: "The phrase occurs in Ovid, *Metam.* viii. 405, *Tristia* IV. vi. 46, but with a different application, e.g. in the former passage 'o me mihi carior' is 'dearer to me than myself'. Here it means 'more valuable to myself' (than formerly)."

[2] *Ante* From EM, 13 Jan. and n. 8. JB liked to compare himself to Montaigne, quoting Pope: "I love to pour out all myself, as plain/As downright *Shippen*, or as old *Montagne*" (*Imit. Hor. Satires* II. i. 51–52). He had done so in his journal (10 Apr. 1776), in *Hypochondriack* no. 70, Aug. 1783 (Bailey, p. 301), and in *LPS 85*, p. 101 n.

[3] Quoted from the *Tour* (*Life* v. 380). Alexander Fairlie of Fairlie (c. 1722–1803), a noted agricultural improver, was for a time factor to Archibald, eleventh Earl of Eglinton (*Ayrshire*, pp. 291, 293; *Gent. Mag.* 1803, lxxiii. 1259).

[4] Fairlie was involved in a dispute with a plasterer named Thomas Clayton in Leith Wynd, Edinburgh (*Williamson's Directory for the City of Edinburgh*, 1782–83), over a bill, the sum involved being £27. 9*s*. 5*d*. Despite

from the chair: "My Lords, I must say to my friend Mr. Boswell (whom I am happy[5] to see here) that this paper is very well drawn, both as to matter and manner."—This publick praise made a good deal of noise, and it is now said that whenever I chuse it, I may return to the bar here with a good prospect of success. This is well. His Lordship had me to dine with him, and we took our wine jovially. Excellent all this after my Letter on the Judges Bill.[6]

You speak philosophically when you say that I consider my movement to London much too deeply. It *must* be now, after going so far.

Enclosed is a letter about securing a House in Great Queen Street which I beg you may read, seal and send; and if you could look at it and give your opinion it would be very kind.[7] I am too late for the post I fear. Ever most faithfully yours,

J. B.

To Malone,
Saturday 28 January 1786

Not reported. Sent from Newcastle 28 Jan. "Edmond Malone Esq. that I am to be in *town* on Wednesday. Begging (if not engaged) he may give me some dinner on thursday and have Courtenay" (Reg. Let.).

JB's petition (dated 18 Jan.—MS. Signet Library, Arniston Collection), Fairlie lost his cause, but only by one vote (From Fairlie, 24 Apr.).

[5] MS. "very" deleted before "happy"

[6] In *LPS 85* (*ante* From EM, 5 Nov. 1785, n. 36), JB had attacked the judges of the Court of Session in general as political appointees. Its Lord President, Robert Dundas (1713–87), a vigorous, domineering judge and astute politician, was the elder half-brother of Henry Dundas, whom JB had also attacked in the pamphlet. For JB's earlier relations with Robert Dundas, see *Earlier Years*, pp. 398–99 and *Pol. Car.* index.

[7] JB was thinking of renting No. 56 Great Queen St. in preparation for his family's move to London.

From Malone,
Wednesday 1 February 1786
MS. Yale (C 1904).
ADDRESS: James Boswell Esqre., at Mr. Dilly's, Poultry.

Wednesday Five o'clock

MY DEAR BOSWELL: I have this moment received your Letter from Newcastle, and hope this will find you safe in the Poultry.[1] I wish you had come and dined with me today, for our friend Courteney, is now with me, and we are just going to sit down to a piece of roast beef—But he has promised to meet you here tomorrow, if possible.[2]

I have seen Hoole's house, and tho'[3] it is old, it has some advantages, and I think will suit you for one year at least. There is an excellent drawing room, and a study formed exactly for writing the life of Dr. Johnson.[4]

I suppose you have got the Gent. Magazine today. I have, you see, worked hard for you. I was so pressed in point of time that I was forced to send my *first* copy to the press, with a very hasty revisal; so you must make allowances[5]—There is but one material error—*juntos* for *junto*.[6] You are not reviewed today in the Monthly R. How is this?[7]

I ordered a copy of the Tour to be sent to Windham, who expressed himself very warmly about you, with respect to the town talk about Lord M.—C. has given all the papers to W. for his

[1] In 1769 Edward Dilly had invited JB to stay at his house, No. 22 in the Poultry (Journ. 1 Sept. 1769; *Life* iii. 65 n. 2), and JB often took advantage of this invitation, especially upon his arrival in London, and now was staying with Edward's younger brother Charles Dilly.

[2] On 2 Feb. Courtenay and JB dined with EM (Journ.).

[3] MS. "thouh" altered to "tho' "

[4] John Hoole (1727–1803), principal auditor of the India House, is best remembered as the translator of Ariosto, Tasso, and Metastasio. He was a friend of SJ's, and wrote a detailed account of SJ's last days. JB, who had dined with SJ at this house as Hoole's guest, inspected it on 2 Feb., and though he found it "old fashioned and part of it dark" (Journ.) determined to take it. See *ante* To EB, 6 Apr. 1788, n. 1.

[5] EM's defence of JB, entitled "Facit Indignatio" and signed "Anti-Stiletto", appeared in *Gent. Mag.* (Jan.) lvi. 17–23 (*ante* From EM, 3 Jan. and nn. 7, 10; From EM, 13 Jan.).

[6] EM defended JB's recording of minute details of SJ's behaviour and conversation by citing Sir Philip Warwick's use of similar details to depict Cromwell's character in his *Memoires of the Reigne of King Charles I*, 1701: "What a trait of character have we in the well-known story of that artful, hypocritical, canting tyrant's having thrown the cushion of his chair at the head of one of his juntos . . ." (*Gent. Mag.* lvi. 20).

[7] *Ante* To EM, 13 Jan. n. 4.

perusal.[8] He is a good man to lay them before, as his opinion has great weight and very deservedly—Yours Affectionately,

E. M.

To Malone,
Friday, 10 March 1786[1]

MS. Yale (L 931). Sent 10 Mar. "Edmond Malone Esq. from Grantham about my fortification Ballad and as to contradicting a Report as to alterations in the Second edition of my Hebrides" (Reg. Let.).
ADDRESS: To Edmond Malone Esq.

Stamford, Friday at dinner

MY DEAR SIR: The weather has proved much milder, and the roads are excellent. I shall write to Mr. Warton from York. I envy you the reading of the Letters with his Notes.[2] I am very desireous that the second edition affair should be well settled: And to the World who know me not as you do, I should think that in case the *fact* as to a Letter being actually written to me should be mentioned in the Papers it would be of great consequence that you and Mr. Courtenay as my friends while I am absent on the Circuit should state the matter in my letter to the Papers to consist with your knowledge, that a letter from the noble Lord was *afterwards* received—and it also consists with your knowledge that an explanation honourable (or proper, or some such expression) to both parties took place. This would knock it on the head.[3]

[8] Before he returned to Scotland on 22 Dec. 1785, JB enclosed in a wrapper all the correspondence and other papers concerning his quarrel with Lord Macdonald, and turned them over to EM, who made sure that all were numbered and enclosed them in a second wrapper (BP xvi. 257). Courtenay showed this packet to Windham.

[1] JB had been in London from 1 Feb. to 9 Mar., when he left to attend the Northern Circuit (he had been called to the English bar on 9 Feb. and, since then, had been regularly attending the sittings in Westminster Hall and Guildhall). In his journal for 12 Mar. he records that he "wrote well to Malone" from Grantham two days earlier.

[2] *Ante* From EM, 3 Jan. n. 6. Thomas Warton's packet was a notebook containing transcripts of eighteen of SJ's letters (seventeen to Warton, one to Robert Chambers) "illustrated with notes" (*Life* i. 270). Warton's notebook, used as printer's copy for the *Life*, is now at Yale (M 145); the original letters are at Trinity College, Oxford (Waingrow, p. 144 n. 1). JB did not receive the notebook until his return to London in April (Journ.); he wrote to thank Warton for the notebook on 13 Apr. (Reg. Let.).

[3] Before his quarrel with Lord Mac-

Enclosed are six of my Ballad which I neglected to give you.—After COURTENAY's verse I would insert the following

Nor can we to SHERIDAN's fame be unjust
Who cleared the whole question from sophistry's dust
Nor to DEMPSTER's who ill even at peril of death
Risk'd that night in the Senate[4] to yield his last breath.[5]

The last evening we were at Courtenay's[6] I imagine I perceived some alteration in the verses on me. I hope *the keen research* is not omitted. I think "By him was taught the sacred love of truth" etc. etc. were well.[7] This Letter for Mr. Courtenay as well as yourself.

donald, JB had ordered the deletion of an offensive passage from the *Tour* (*ante* To EM, 11 Nov. 1785 and nn. 15, 17); however, the satirist John Wolcot, writing under the name Peter Pindar, asserted in his *Poetical and Congratulatory Epistle to James Boswell, Esq.*, 1786, p. 16, that JB had deleted the passage at Macdonald's insistence. When JB read Wolcot's *Epistle* on 24 Feb. (Journ.), he immediately wrote a circumspectly worded denial for *St. James's Chron.* (2–4 Mar. p. [1]): "It having been asserted, in a scurrilous Pamphlet, that some Alterations were made in the second Edition of a late Work, in Consequence of a Letter from a noble Lord to the Authour, we have Authority to say that the Assertion is false." Apparently finding this reply inadequate, JB on 9 Mar. sent a signed letter to the newspapers, asserting that "soon after the Publication of the first Edition of my Work . . . without any Application from any Person whatever, I ordered twenty-six Lines, relative to the Noble Lord, to be omitted in the second Edition (for the Loss of which, I trust, twenty-two additional Pages are a sufficient Compensation); and this was the sole Alteration that was made in my Book relative to that Nobleman" (*Morn. Her.* 11 Mar. p. [4]; *St. James's Chron.* 11–14 Mar. p. [2]; *Morn. Chron.* 13 Mar. p. [2]; *Pub. Adv.* 14 Mar. p. [2]. This letter was reprinted in *Gent. Mag.* April, lvi. 285, and *Eur. Mag.* June, ix. 397). JB is now worried that the abusive letter he received from Lord Macdonald after he had ordered the alteration in the 2nd ed. of the *Tour* may be adduced in the newspapers to support Wolcot's charges; he suggests that if the letter is mentioned, EM and Courtenay should reply in the newspapers.

[4] MS. "in the Senate" written above illegible deletion.

[5] As the Reg. Let. summary cited at the head of this letter shows, JB is referring to his "fortification Ballad". Though it was then at the printer's (*post* To EM, 12 Mar.), neither printed copy nor contemporary printed references to it have been found. The enclosure of "six" (lines?) mentioned has not been reported, and only six lines of the "Ballad" survive in manuscript elsewhere (M 9:5). It is apparent, however, that JB's poem attacked a plan proposed by Charles Lennox, third Duke of Richmond, for a highly expensive fortification of the dockyards at Portsmouth and Plymouth. The plan was opposed on 18 Feb. by Richard Brinsley Sheridan, whose speech "on this occasion was the subject of much admiration" (*Ann. Reg.* 1786, first p. 104), and also by Dempster (Namier and Brooke ii. 317). For the debate, see *Parl. Hist.* xxv. 1096–1157. The controversy is summarized in A. G. Olson, *The Radical Duke*, 1961, pp. 81–85.

[6] 8 Mar., when JB had dined with EM at Courtenay's. He left London for the Northern Circuit the next day (Journ.).

[7] JB refers to the lines on himself in Courtenay's *Poetical Review*, pp. 23–24:

Amid these names can BOSWELL be forgot,
Scarce by North Britons now esteem'd a Scot?

I hope to hear Barrister[8] at law York. Yours most affectionately,

J. B.

Grantham at night

I am now quietly passing my evening at the house of the Rev. Dr. Palmer an old Clergyman a very reading man, who knew Warburton at an early period.[9]

I *intreat* that *Neck or nothing* as Mr. Courtenay worded that *tendresse* of mine, may be *entre nous*. There is no harm in talking of it with levity as I do at large. But no *particulars*.[10]

I tax your friendship exorbitantly. But believe me I am very sensible of your kindness.

To Malone,
Sunday 12 March 1786

MS. Yale (L 931.1). Sent 12 Mar. "Edmond Malone Esq. from Tadcaster—more as to the above.[1] Also as to Courtenay's Verses on Dr. Johnson. That whatever good may come of the english bar trial, I shall owe it to him, he having *held* me to it—in great spirits.—" (Reg. Let.).

[Tadcaster] Sunday Morning

Upon better consideration it appears to me that Mr. Courtenay and you cannot attest that the *Letter* from a noble Lord to me was

Who to the sage devoted from his youth,
Imbib'd from him the sacred love of truth;
The keen research, the exercise of mind,
And that best art, the art to know mankind.—

[8] MS. "at York" deleted before "Barrister"

[9] When in Grantham, JB often visited Richard Palmer (c. 1714–1805), prebendary of Canterbury and rector of St. Swithin's in London (*Gent. Mag.* 1805, lxxv. 493; *Alum. Cant.* I). On 19 Mar. 1775 Palmer told JB that William Warburton had once belonged to the Literary Society at Grantham, "and then used to abuse Pope both as a Philosopher and a Satyrist. He afterwards was wiser, and defended Pope, and became his intimate freind" (Journ.).

[10] Almost certainly this *tendresse* was *Lurgan* (or *Larghan*) *Clanbrassil*, a lyric celebrating JB's mistress, Margaret Caroline Rudd (see *Later Years*, pp. 294–95, 319–20, 322, 325). His son Alexander printed it, in all innocence, in his *Songs, Chiefly in the Scottish Dialect*, 1804, p. 17, with the title "Song to an Irish Air by the Late James Boswell, Esq." but our MS. fragment (M 343.3) gives the title as "Lurgan Clanbrassil".

For the probable origin of the phrase "neck or nothing", see *Extremes*, p. 304 n. 3. As applied here by Courtenay, the phrase most likely refers to Mrs. Rudd's acquittal on a charge of forgery (a capital crime) at her celebrated trial in 1775 (see *Ominous Years*, pp. 352–55).

[1] *Ante* To EM, 10 Mar., headnote.

settled on *honourable* terms for *both* parties. I still have *some* uneasy doubt that I was wrong in not firing at once at the unsigned absurd abuse, and calling on him to *name* the *atonement* or to ask pardon for the letter. But I had the friendly counsel of you both to act as I did, and you may recollect the sad depression of spirits in which that letter found me. And after all as Courtenay said to me tother day[2] I was *right* as a man of *good principles*, for as I was to a certain degree the Agressor, had I acted with hasty violence and the consequence been fatal I should have been reckoned a *Ruffian*. The truth is that a man who fears fear is anxiously jealous of himself. But on the other hand I cannot think it *quite* honourable to annihilate what a man has written to another, *after* a very *intelligible* message has been received.[3] Mr. Courtenay and you may concert how to express that by the interposition of friends the affair was settled. I own I should wish exceedingly that an attestation by such men as you and him should be brought out, so that the Matter might be forever quashed, without all the circumstances being disclosed, as to which there might be room enough for ill disposed cavilling.[4]

I am so exceedingly well at present, that nothing whatever appears too difficult for me. I am going to church here and then to proceed to York, to take my place at the *Counsel* Board as Junior.[5]

If I do succeed as an english Barrister, and add something to my Family, I shall owe it to you; for, you *held* me to it. If I do not succeed I shall owe to you the tranquillity produced by having made the trial, and the better existence in a better country.

I have written the additions to my Ballad on a separate leaf, to save you trouble in transcribing; for, after settling how it should be, you may send the leaf to Marshall's in Aldermary Churchyard with J. B.'s compliments.[6] I think in *equity* they have a right to the

[2] Presumably on 8 Mar., when he and EM had dined at Courtenay's (Journ.).

[3] *Ante* To EM, 10 Mar. n. 3. To end his quarrel with JB, Lord Macdonald had agreed to produce a "second edition" of the unsigned abusive letter to JB that had begun the quarrel, by deleting the most offensive passages.

[4] Apparently Macdonald's letter was never made public, so EM and Courtenay did not have to publish the reply JB is here discussing.

[5] For JB's duties as the junior member of the bar on the Circuit, see *post* To EM, 22 Mar. and n. 17.

[6] John Marshall was a printer and book and print seller at No. 4 Aldermary Churchyard (Maxted; *Bailey's Western and Midland Directory*, 1783). JB's use of his initials here perhaps suggests that he had signed his "Ballad" with his initials.

best edition. If you have the curiosity to call yourself, and view the great *Officina Cantilenarum*,[7] you may deliver the leaf. And as they may have thrown off a number of the *first*, you will please *to* send[8] or give them a crown to reprint it, if you think it worth while. But let a parcel of them be sent to you, of which send me half a dozen. I really wish the PEOPLE to be warm and vigilant upon this *antinaval* business.[9]

Dr. Palmer asked me—"When are we to have your friend Mr. Malone's Shakespeare?" My answer was "I am affraid not till next winter." Pray what answer am I to give when that question is put to me at any time?[10] He shewed me the translation of Crousaz which has been ascribed to Dr. Johnson; But which is certainly not his. I agree with you that the translation itself is not a test. But the Preface is.[11]

Be so good as *to* tell Mr. Courtenay that I am now[12] for *fortemque Gyan fortemque Cloanthum.*[13]

I enclose a leaf of Knox's Essays wrapped round my shoe-buckles at Dilly's, in which are paragraphs wonderfully Johnsonian. I think perfectly so, except the first three lines of the second as to which I doubt.[14]

[7] "Manufactory of songs".

[8] Both John Wilkes and EM had criticized JB's use of "please send" as "not English", and recommended "please to send" (*ante* To EM, 13 Oct. 1785 and n. 69; From EM, 28 Oct. 1785 and n. 17).

[9] Opponents of the Duke of Richmond's fortification plan (*ante* To EM, 10 Mar. n. 5) feared that the fortification of the dock-yards at Plymouth and Portsmouth would decrease the prestige and power of the navy. For example, Sir William Lemon, M.P. for Cornwall, argued, "That period . . . may be marked as the aera of maritime decline, when it [the fortification bill] is adopted" (*Gent. Mag.* May, lvi. 401).

[10] *2 Henry IV*, in vol. 5 of EM's Shakespeare, was printed by April, and in September vols. 6 and 7 of the ten-volume set were in the press (*Percy Corres.* pp. 34–35), but the edition was not published until 1790.

[11] JB repeats in the *Life* that the Preface in itself "long ago convinced" him that this translation was not SJ's work. In fact it was by Elizabeth Carter. For the confusion between the two translations of works by Jean-Pierre de Crousaz (1663-1750) concerning Pope's *Essay on Man*—the other one was by SJ—see *Life* i. 137–38, iv. 494–96.

[12] MS. "?still" deleted before "now"

[13] Virgil, *Aeneid* i. 222, 612, "brave Gyas and brave Cloanthus". Gyas and Cloanthus are participants in a boat race held to commemorate the death of Aeneas's father (*Aeneid* v. 104–248). Presumably JB alludes to a line or passage which was being considered for inclusion in the *Poetical Review*, but that did not appear in the printed version.

[14] Vicesimus Knox (1752–1821), miscellaneous writer, whose *Essays, Moral and Literary* were published anonymously in 1778 by Charles Dilly on SJ's recommendation. They were reprinted frequently thereafter, with Knox's name on the title-page; the 8th ed. appeared in 1786. When JB first read extracts from the *Essays* in *Lond. Chron.*, he thought them better than his *Hypochondriack* (Journ. 7 Jan. 1778). On

I would have

> Croft[15] Knox and Nares to this great[16] school belong
> And many more than can be nam'd in song.

Croft—because his Young (notwithstanding Burke) is for the most part undistinguishable—Knox because he is very like, and is a Writer of prodigious popularity—Nares because he is also very like, and has I think uncommon merit which deserves to be pointed out to the World.[17]

After that Couplet will come the *Names* amidst whom He who now sits over Coffee and toast and Muffin cannot be forgot.[18] My most cordial compliments to Courtenay.

I intend to return from *Lichfield* by *Oxford* to forage at Pembroke and University Colleges for my GREAT WORK.[19]

Knox's imitation of SJ's style, see *Life* iv. 390–91, where JB cites a passage from Knox's third essay as being in a Johnsonian style; perhaps it was a leaf from this essay that JB found wrapped around his shoe-buckles.

[15] MS. "Crofts" altered to "Croft"

[16] MS. "Johnson's" written as alternative above "this great"

[17] This couplet was not, as JB hoped, inserted in Courtenay's *Poetical Review*. Herbert Croft (1751–1816), later (1797) Sir Herbert, Bt., was vicar of Prittleworth, Essex, from 1786 until his death. His life of the poet Edward Young was abridged and adopted by SJ for his *Lives of the Poets*. Though JB thought his style "undistinguishable" from SJ's, EB called Croft "a bad imitation of Johnson [:] all the warts and contortions without the ——— All the panting and convulsions of the Sybil without the inspiration" (Journ. 8 May 1781). An expanded and revised version of EB's remark, attributed to "a very eminent literary character", appears in the *Life* (iv. 59). Robert Nares (1753–1829), philologist, was also quoted in the *Life* (iv. 389–90) as an imitator of SJ. Of his *Elements of Orthoepy*, 1784, JB wrote, "I know no book which contains, in the same compass, more learning, polite literature, sound sense, accuracy of arrangement, and perspicuity of expression" (*Life* iv. 389 n. 6).

[18] The *Poetical Review* (pp. 22–24) named those whom SJ had influenced: Goldsmith, Reynolds, Burney, EM, Steevens, Hawkesworth, Sir William Jones, and of course JB, who alludes to the line about himself: "Amid these names can BOSWELL be forgot" (*ante* To EM, 10 Mar. n. 7).

[19] JB left the Northern Circuit early in order to return to London in time for an Appeal before the House of Lords (*post* To EM, 25 Mar. and n. 5). There is no record that he stopped at Oxford on this return trip, but he and EM visited it from 27 Apr. to 1 May when he called on William Adams, Master of Pembroke College, and Nathan Wetherell, Master of University College.

From Malone,
Friday 17 March 1786

MS. Yale (C 1905). Received 19 Mar. "Edmond Malone Esq. a most agreable letter of various particulars—enclosing more verses by Courtenay on Dr. Johnson" (Reg. Let.).

London, March 17, 1786

MY DEAR SIR: Many thanks for your remembrances from Stamford etc. I was[1] very glad to find you were in so good spirits, and intended to have told you so yesterday, as you may perceive by the inside of this cover,[2] but Mr. Courteney dined with me, and we work'd upon the inclosed lines, so that it was not in my power to write and send them to you, for they were not finished then:—and now it is past five oclock and I can say but three words; but my *inclosures*[3] must compensate. I did not like the poem concluding unfavourably to our great friend, and therefore proposed the thoughts that are now versified, for the conclusion; and in the Evening we hammered out the lines together.[4] I think the account of his Latin Poetry is a good addition, and a good answer to those who talk so lightly of it and abuse it for not being Virgilian and Ovidian and I know not what:[5]—C. struck out *the deep research* for a very good reason; because in every piece there ought to be a subordination, or *keeping*, as the painters call it; and *deep research* had before been applied to the *hero*.[6] But you may be well satisfied—You have a knowledge of mankind, a love of truth, and Exercise of mind.—The lines on Jones are much improved:

Replete with science etc.
———————— filial awe;

[1] MS. "intend" deleted before "was"

[2] The wrapper for this letter is not preserved; apparently EM had Courtenay frank it on one side on 16 Mar. and on the other side on 17 Mar. (cf. *ante* From EM, 13 Jan.).

[3] Presumably EM enclosed transcripts of Courtenay's conclusion, his lines on SJ's poetry, and his lines on JB (nn. 4, 5, 6 below). The enclosures have not been reported.

[4] A long passage (pp. 25–26) beginning,

Yet Learning's sons, who o'er his foibles mourn,
To latest time shall fondly view his urn,

may represent the lines EM and Courtenay "hammered out . . . together".

[5] In acknowledging that SJ's Latin verse is not strictly classical, Courtenay argues that it displays his own genius rather than that of Ovid or Virgil.

[6] EM refers to the verses on JB (*ante* To EM, 10 Mar. n. 7), which in the final version read "The keen research". Apparently the phrase "deep research" had been used in praise of SJ's labours on his *Dictionary*; however, the final version reads "His wide research" (p. 11).

Harmonious Jones! who in his splendid strains
Sings Camdeo's sports on Agra's flow'ry plains,
In Hindu fictions while we fondly trace
Love and the Muses deckd with Attick grace.[7]

Your Letter appeared in Mor. Herald—M. Chron. Pub. Ad. and St. J. Chron.—I was obliged to pay a guinea to the *Herald*. The rest were honourable men, and inserted it gratis.[8]—Not a word of reply as yet from *P. P.*—You may re[p]ly, if necessary. C. will take care of you—[9]

I have been so hurried that I have done nothing about the new edition of the Ballad; but will tomorrow.[10] Downpatrick and the source of the Nile shall be equally secret.[11] You are more likely to blab than we.

I forgot to tell you another improvement made in the *School*. After "He like a Titian formed his brilliant school":

new { * While from his lips impressive wisdom fell,
* He taught congenial spirits to excell.[12]

I shall but just save the post and have not time to read over.

I hope the fees come in very fast—Adieu—Ever Yours most faithfully,

E. M.

[7] "Replete . . . filial awe" does not appear in the published version of the *Poetical Review*. Sir William Jones (1746–94), jurist and orientalist, had been a member of The Club since 1773; the allusions in Courtenay's lines are to his "Hymn to Camdeo" (*Poetical Works of Sir William Jones*, 1810, ii. 55–59).

[8] For JB's answer to Peter Pindar, see *ante* To EM, 10 Mar. n. 3. The phrase "honourable men" may recall its reiterated use in *Julius Caesar* (III. ii).

[9] Wolcot again lampooned JB (as well as Courtenay, Sir John Hawkins, and Hester Lynch Piozzi) in *Bozzy and Piozzi*, 1786. Because he had "persevered in 'the lie o'erthrown' ", JB replied in a footnote to the 3rd ed. of the *Tour* (*Life* v. 415, n. 4). Courtenay also was interested in rebutting Wolcot, and had suggested bringing an action against his publisher, George Kearsley (*post* To EM, 22 Mar.).

[10] *Ante* To EM, 10 Mar. n. 5.

[11] Proverbially, the source of the (White) Nile was a mystery. "Downpatrick" was JB's code-name for Mrs. Rudd; see *post* To EM, 3 Apr.: "I have had a charming letter from Downpatrick." She had once attended school in Downpatrick, Northern Ireland (*Authentic Anecdotes of the Life and Transactions of Mrs. Margaret Rudd*, 1776, p. 14).

[12] The two new lines were transposed in the *Poetical Review* (p. 22):

He, like a Titian, form'd his brilliant school,
And taught congenial spirits to excel,
While from his lips impressive wisdom fell.

To Malone,
Wednesday 22 March 1786

MS. Yale (L 932). Misdated 20 Mar. in Reg. Let.: "Edmond Malone Esq. that I am *learning* wonderfully, and am assured that my assiduous attendance will procure me business—his letters make me *carior mihi.* A few remarks on Courtenay's verses—Proposing to prosecute the publisher of Peter Pindar, for the *false* dialogue to injure my life of Dr. Johnson the *eclat* of which might be raised by the Action—by Erskine expatiating etc. (a confidential note within)."[1]

York, 22 March 1786

MY DEAR SIR: The additional lines you have been so good as to send me are exquisitely fine, particularly those upon our Great Friend's latin poetry, in which I cannot perceive one fault or one line or word that should be altered, unless *soothing* Lyre be too *gentle* for a giant. Those too on Jones and the additional couplet to the *School* are admirable. The *Conclusion* is also a valuable improvement. But I have some difficulty as to the first line of the couplet as to which I observe Mr. Courtenay and you are undecided. "Whose mind *discursive*" is very well suited to "every Science *traced*", but not so well to *embraced*, as "Whose *ample* mind"; But then an *ample* mind is not so well suited to "each path of science traced". I prefer the first reading; and upon better consideration a *discursive* mind may be *enlarged* enough to embrace morals arts and languages.[2] We shall have a most respectable Poem of it at last. I certainly agree with you that I may be well satisfied with the honour done me. It was not "*deep* research", but "*keen* research", which I missed. *Deep* I should have objected to as not just. I am quite pleased with my share of praise, as the lines now stand.

I have read my Letter in the Morning Chronicle and St. James's Evening.[3] I am much obliged to their Editors and to that of the P. A. for their genteel behaviour. It was however worth a guinea to have it in the Herald.

[1] For the possible contents of this enclosure, which has not been recovered, see *post* From EM, 25 Mar. n. 2.

[2] The lines in Courtenay's *Poetical Review* concerning SJ and the "lyre" read:

He felt the tuneful Nine his breast inspire,
And, like a master, wak'd the soothing lyre (p. 19).

The couplet rhyming "traced-embraced" does not appear in the poem as printed. (Quotation marks are supplied in this paragraph.)

[3] *St. James's Chron.* carried the subtitle *British Evening-Post.*

Courtenay once proposed that an Action should be brought against the Publisher of Peter Pindar's Attack[4] which we have now repelled. But what would you think of prosecuting him for the Post[s]cript in which he *falsely* asserts that a conversation passed between *him* and Dr. Johnson in which the Doctor spoke of me in the most contemptous manner, and *particularly* enlarged on my being incapable to write his Life.[5] Absurdly[6] malignant as this really is, it *may* be believed by many people, and therefore *may* injure the success of my GREAT WORK. I own I am not much affraid of this. But if I thought that a verdict would be obtained merely to proclaim the falsehood[7] of the fellow and punish him in the most *tender* part his *purse*, I certainly should prosecute. And you will consider if this would not give an opportunity to announce the Work in the most splendid manner. Erskine[8] would expatiate upon it as not only to be the Life and Conversation of the first Genius etc. etc. etc. but the History of Literature and Literary Men during a[9] considerable period.[10] A letter or two of Dr. Johnson's to me might be *proved*[11] and read;[12] as might Dr. Blair's to me,[13] and if necessary a good deal of parole evidence might be

[4] Wolcot's publisher was George Kearsley (d. 1790), bookseller at No. 46 Fleet St. Being held responsible for the work of his authors was nothing new to Kearsley, who had been arrested for publishing no. 45 of Wilkes's *North Briton* (Maxted).

[5] In the Postscript to his *Poetical and Congratulatory Epistle* (*ante* To EM, 10 Mar. and n. 3), Wolcot wrote, "As Mr. Boswell's Journal hath afforded such universal pleasure by the relation of minute incidents, and the great Moralist's opinion of men and things, during his northern tour; it will be adding greatly to the anecdotal treasury, as well as making Mr. B. happy, to communicate part of a Dialogue that took place between Dr. Johnson, and the Author of this Congratulatory Epistle, a few months before the Doctor paid the great debt of nature." Wolcot has SJ abuse JB's literary powers and his *Corsica*, and end by discussing JB's plan to write his life: "Were I sure that James Boswell would write *my* life, I do not know whether I would not anticipate the measure, by taking *his*". And later: "BOSWELL write my life! why the fellow possesses not abilities for writing the life of an *ephemeron*" (*Works of Peter Pindar*, 1794, i. 324–26).

[6] MS. "ly" of "Absurdly" written above deleted "and"

[7] MS. "faleshood"

[8] JB's distant cousin, the Hon. Thomas Erskine (1750–1823), later Lord Chancellor as Baron Erskine of Restormel Castle (1806) and K.T. (1815).

[9] MS. "a" superimposed upon "the"

[10] JB used similar phrasing on the title-page of the *Life: The Whole Exhibiting a View of Literature and Literary Men In Great-Britain, for Near Half a Century*.

[11] Used here in its legal sense, "established as genuine".

[12] None of SJ's extant letters to JB mention JB's qualifications as a biographer, but he had praised JB's Hebridean journal highly (*Life* v. 226–27, 279) and read there of JB's intention to write his biography (v. 312 and n. 2).

[13] In a letter to JB of 3 Mar. 1785, Hugh Blair had reported SJ's praise of JB; the letter was printed in the *Tour* (*Life* v. 398).

produced to shew how gross the calumny is. Perhaps even Lord Carmarthen's letter containing the polite approbation of a Great Personage might be introduced.[14] Do consult with Mr. Courtenay as to this; for, it appears to me a very good use might be made of such an Action.[15]

I am *learning* wonderfully as I shall prove to you by my Note-Book.[16] I am assured that my assiduous attention will procure me Brieffs against the Summer Assizes. But I do not expect one here at this time. There is a number of provincial Counsel who previously secure the small business, and a great many Yorkshire Counsel come from London, so that a new man must have some *particular* recommendation to get himself fairly introduced: I have not the least doubt but that when I am once started, I shall be in request. You see I am just in the patient and hopeful frame that I should be.

It is amazing how I do my duty as *Junior* of our law society; how I regulate our Mess, and how I dance with the Ladies.[17] I at first lived too hard, which is very wrong in every view. But I have taken up, and am shewing that I can be an *Aristippus*.[18]

Do let me hear from you as often as you can. I cannot express what good you do me. You make me live *mihi carior* as poor Sam wrote to Lord Thurlow.[19]

After *friday* direct *Lancaster* and insert *on the Northern Circuit.* My cordial compliments to Courtenay. Ever most warmly yours,

J. B.

[14] Francis Osborne (1751–99), styled Marquess of Carmarthen, later (1789) fifth Duke of Leeds, was from 1783 to 1791 Pitt's Secretary of State for Foreign Affairs, which gave him frequent access to the King. In the *Life* JB did print this letter from Carmarthen, which he had received on 1 Mar. (Journ.), giving the King's approval to publish an account of his famous conversation with SJ in 1767 (*Life* ii. 34 n. 1).

[15] Courtenay's idea was quietly dropped, and no action was brought against Wolcot's publisher.

[16] JB's "Legal Notebook" for 1786–87 (Lg 40) shows that he had so far taken twenty-five pages of notes at the Lent Assizes at York.

[17] JB's duties as junior member of the bar on the Northern Circuit also included writing letters and keeping the records (To Richard Burke the younger, 18 Mar. and Fifer, p. 229 n. 1).

[18] Aristippus (c. 435–c. 356 B.C.) was traditionally considered the founder of the Cyrenaic school of philosophy, which taught that present enjoyment was the highest good, but that one should develop the capacity to enjoy without becoming a slave to pleasure. JB's expression "taken up" here means "reformed" (OED, Take, B. XII. 90 n.).

[19] *Ante* To EM, 24 Jan. and n. 1.

To Malone,
Thursday 23 March 1786

Not reported. Sent to London from York 23 Mar. "Edmond Malone Esq. All confidential, for advice concerning an unfortunate matter" (Reg. Let.). See *post* From EM, 27 Mar.; To EM, 31 Mar.).

To Malone,
Saturday 25 March 1786

MS. Yale (L 933). Sent 26 Mar. "Edmond Malone Esq. to send me Sigra. Piozzi's Book in franks etc." (Reg. Let.).
ADDRESS: To Edmond Malone Esq., London.

York, 25 March 1786

MY DEAR SIR: I am *as well as can be expected*;[1] but am in great uneasiness that I have not a letter from *home* for a forthnight. *There* believe me my *heart* is. My consolation is that Norton (under whose cover my letters come) is gone to Lancaster to the Election.[2]

There was in the General Evening of tuesday last, a pretty keen attack upon me under the title of "Dr. Johnsons Ghost" a Parody on William and Margaret. I *felt* it to be well done, though conscious of its injustice, but I viewed it as I supposed many will do. Pray secure the paper for me while one may be had.[3]

[1] An expression commonly used of women in childbed or the late stages of pregnancy (Eric Partridge, *A Dictionary of Clichés*, 4th ed. 1950, p. 19). According to Partridge, it dates from the late nineteenth century, but it appears at least as early as *Tristram Shandy* IV. xii. JB is referring to his attack of gonorrhoea.

[2] The Hon. Edward Norton (1750–86), M.P. for Carlisle on Lord Lonsdale's interest, was at the Lancashire by-election as Lonsdale's chief agent. But when he arrived on the 29th, JB discovered that Norton was dead, according to rumour as the result of fatigue following the election (Namier and Brooke iii. 214). JB did have "the comfort to find at Norton's a good letter from *home*" (Journ. 29 Mar.).

[3] *Gen. Eve. Post*, 18–21 Mar. p.[4]: *Dr. Johnson's Ghost. By a Lady*. Reprinted in *Gent. Mag*. (Apr. 1786) lvi. 427–28, it was written by Elizabeth Moody and appears in her *Poetical Trifles*, 1798. This parody of David Mallet's ballad, *William and Margaret*, in sixteen quatrains portrays SJ's ghost rebuking JB for depicting his character unfavourably and for cultivating his friendship for profit. Moody's title suggests that she knew the version of Mallet's poem published in Percy's *Reliques*, 1765, where it

I see "My Dear Lady" Signora Piozzi is come forth this day Lady Day.[4] I envy you at this moment. Pray send her to me in franks *on the Northern Circuit.*

The Appeal in the House of Lords in which I am Counsel is to come on the 12 April. I must therefore be with you on the 10, unless I can get it put off till after Easter,[4a] which I doubt will not be, as one delay has already been granted on my Account. Yet I am to make our Solicitors try, as the Assizes at Lancaster will not be over by the 10, and I wish to attend all through.[5] We have this morning lost Sir Thomas Davenport who has languished in a fever for ten days.[6]

I have had the happiness to prevent a duel between two of my bretheren here, the particulars of which I will tell you at meeting.[7]

When you pass through Great Queen Street will you be kind enough to call on Mrs. Strange and talk with her about *my* house in *town.*[8] I intend to take possession of it in a few days after my return and to set myself down *fervently* to Johnson and English Law which I have the pleasure to find grows more familiar to me every day. *She* is to find me a Maid of all work and my brother and Dilly are to look me out a man servant whom I am to approve or disapprove when I see him.

[4] "My Dear Lady" was one of SJ's terms of endearment for Hester Lynch Thrale (now Piozzi). Mrs. Piozzi's *Anecdotes of the Late Samuel Johnson, LL.D.* was advertised to appear on Lady Day, the feast of the Annunciation (25 Mar.). JB probably saw the advertisement on p. [3] of the same issue of *Gen. Eve. Post* that contained *Dr. Johnson's Ghost.*

[4a] 16 Apr.

[5] JB was to appear before the House of Lords as counsel for Henry Drumlanrig Cuninghame and others against William Cuninghame, who had appealed an earlier decision in favour of JB's clients. For an account of the cause, see Appendix 2 below. On 26 Mar. JB wrote to John Spottiswoode, a London solicitor acting as agent for JB's clients, to try to have the appeal put off again. Spottiswoode replied that it could not be done (Reg. Let.), and so JB returned to London on 10 Apr. (Journ.). But the Lords did not in fact hear the cause until 24 Apr.

[6] Sir Thomas Davenport (1734–86), M.P. for Newton, Lancashire, and a serjeant-at-law, died of "an inflammation in his bowels" (*Gent. Mag.* Mar. 1786, lvi. 270; Namier and Brooke ii. 302–03).

[7] JB published a long report of this quarrel between Serjeant James Bolton and Edward Law (later first Baron Ellenborough) with his own part in it in *Gen. Eve. Post,* 20–22 Apr. p. [1], and shorter accounts appeared in *Lond. Chron.* (18–20 Apr.) lix. 376, and *Morn. Her.* 21 Apr. p. [3].

[8] Isabella Strange (1719–1806), wife of Robert Strange, the engraver, lived at No. 52 Great Queen St. She was one of JB's advisers about Hoole's house (see To EM, 24 Jan.). JB had met her through her brother, his old friend Andrew Lumisden.

My best compliments to "the brilliant Courtenay".[9] You see I am *up* again. I ever am most affectionately yours,

J. B.

From Malone, *Saturday 25 March 1786*

MS. Yale (C 1906). Received 29 Mar. "Edmond Malone Esq. friendly as to my confidential affair—concerning Signora Piozzi's Anecdotes of Dr. Johnson" (Reg. Let.).

ADDRESS in Courtenay's hand: Jams. Boswell Esqr., Barrister at Law, Lancaster.

FRANK: London March Twenty fifth 1786. Free J. Courtenay.

POSTMARKS: [London] 25 MR, FREE.

March 25, 1786, Four o clock

MY DEAR SIR: I have been so employed all the morning that I have only time to write[1] three words. I received your letter from York yesterday—and am glad to find you have a *due sense of* what has past. Sam would tell you you were a *sad dog*.[2]—Mrs. Piozzis book came out this morning. I have only been able to *devour* half of it. It is very entertaining—but the stories are *strung* too thick on each other—and she does not *dramatise* sufficiently. She has got many of your unpublished stories and some of them not so well as you have them.[3]—The last leaf of the book relates to you. It[4] is dated

[9] This quotation has not been traced. JB may be quoting someone's comment on Courtenay's *Poetical Review* or his own comments on Courtenay in his unrecovered "fortification Ballad" (*ante* To EM, 10 Mar. and n. 5).

[1] MS. "say" deleted before "write"

[2] Since EM treats JB's attack of gonorrhoea as news in his next letter (*post* From EM, 27 Mar.), his remarks here most likely refer to JB's "confidential note" enclosed in To EM, 22 Mar., which JB alludes to in the head-note to the present letter as "my confidential affair". Presumably the note contained some confession of bad behaviour; it may have given details of JB's actions on the circuit, where he admitted he had "at first lived too hard" (*ante* To EM, 22 Mar.).

In his 1887 edition of the *Life* (vi. 298) G. B. Hill documents SJ's fondness for "dog" as a term of reproach, and in *Johns. Misc.* he notes further that "the reproach is often mixed with good humour" (i. 245 n. 1). SJ called Thomas Pennant "a *Whig* . . . a *sad dog*" (*Life* iii. 274).

[3] For examples of stories that Mrs. Piozzi and JB tell differently, see *Life* i. 416 and n. 2, ii. 188 and n. 3, 194 and n. 2, iii. 336 and n. 2, iv. 94 and n. 4. JB cites several examples of the inaccuracy of her story-telling in his "animadversions" (Journ. 22 Feb. 1791) on her *Anecdotes* (*Life* iv. 340–47).

[4] MS. "She says some" deleted before "It"

Naples feb. 10, 1786 and runs[5] thus—"Since the foregoing went[6] to press, having seen a passage from Mr. B.'s T. to the H. in which it is said that *I could not get through Mrs. M.'s Es. on Sh.*, I do not delay a moment to declare, that on the contrary I have always commended it myself, and heard it commended by every one else; and few things would give me more concern than to be thought incapable of tasting or unwilling to testify my opinion of its excellence."[7]—You see she does not state fairly. She should have said—"in which Dr. J. is reported to have said that neither he nor I" etc.—Dilly will send you the book by the Stage on Monday directed to Lancaster—It will be a high Treat.—Only 160 of the Tour left. D. thinks there should be immeadiately another edition put to press—Yours most faithfully and affectionately,

E. M.

Calamo rapidissimo.[8] The Poem will be ready for publication by thursday or friday.[9] The 1st Sh[eet] goes to press today, and a proof of a second is to be ready this evening.—It will make 4 Sheets. Our *absent* friend, I see, has forgot *Esqr.*[10] No matter.

From Malone, Monday 27 March 1786

MS. Yale (C 1907). Received 29 Mar. "Edmond Malone Esq. (supposing me much more indisposed than I proved to be) advising me to leave the Circuit directly, and return to London, to take care of my health. More concerning Signora Piozzi's Anecdotes—A good trimming of that Lady" (Reg. Let.).

London, March 27, 1786

MY DEAR SIR: I did not receive your Letter of the 23d till after my last was dispatched on Saturday—This is not a time for preach-

[5] MS. "the purport is" deleted before "runs"

[6] MS. "was printed off" deleted before "went"

[7] For the passage referred to, see *Life* v. 245. Mrs. Piozzi's Postscript is printed in *Anecdotes*, p. 307, and *Johns. Misc.* i. 351.

[8] "With most rapid pen".

[9] 30 or 31 Mar. Actually, Courtenay's *Poetical Review* was not published until 6 Apr. (*ante* From EM, 13 Jan. n. 5).

[10] "Absent" refers to Courtenay's absent-mindedness as well as his physical absence. In addressing and franking this letter, he apparently forgot to add "Esqr." to JB's name in the address. However, EM got him to do so before he posted the letter, for "Esqr." does appear in the address in Courtenay's hand.

ing, or I could hold forth very handsomely.—C. agrees with me in thinking you ought to lose no time in leaving the Circuit.—As you have not probably briefs to detain you, it will be the less observable; and you can put it on your family being daily expected in London, (sooner than you thought for) and that you go to meet them. People seldom are interested enough about one to discuss these matters minutely.—I have not sent you what you desired, because a poor friend of mine, G. Canning, shortened his life by them.[1]—Make use of common milk and water, *warm*, to wash the part with, 2 or 3 times a day. You are mistaken in having so very low an opinion of country surgeons. In such a town as Lancaster, it is[2] impossible but there must be some one of credit and skill, and I would by all means apply to him; because by his giving you a few pills of a slight preparation of mercury, to take every night, tho' on the road, he[3] will prevent the disorder from making a rapid progress and it will be the more manageable when you come to town. Pray attend to this.

I have read Mrs. Piozzi's book twice through; there is a great deal of good stuff in it; but many of your stories, not half so well told. The story of Graham, whom she ignorantly calls *Eaton* Graham, is murdered;[4]—as are some others, but many are told well.—I suppose you have got it by this time and found yourself in p. 261.[5] I think the conclusion is *pointed*, on purpose to gratify

[1] Presumably the Irishman George Canning (d. 1771), failed lawyer and minor poet, who died of an "inflammation in his bowels" when his son George, the future Prime Minister, was only a year old (Wendy Hinde, *George Canning*, 1973, p. 12). It is not known what medicine shortened Canning's life.

[2] MS. "it"

[3] MS. "he" written above deleted "you"

[4] The Rev. George Graham (1728–67), dramatist and assistant master at Eton. Her anecdote runs: "They [SJ and Goldsmith] had spent an evening with Eaton Graham too, I remember hearing it was at some tavern; his heart was open, and he began inviting away; told what he could do to make his college agreeable, and begged the visit might not be delayed. Goldsmith thanked him, and proposed setting out with Mr. Johnson for Buckinghamshire in a fortnight; 'Nay hold, Dr. *Minor* (says the other), I did not invite you' " (*Anecdotes*, p. 180; *Johns. Misc.* i. 270). For EM's gloss on this story in his copy of the *Anecdotes*, see Waingrow, p. 140 n. 2.

[5] "I fancy Mr. B—— has not forgotten, that though his friend one evening in a gay humour talked in praise of wine as one of the blessings permitted by heaven, when used with moderation, to lighten the load of life, and give men strength to endure it; yet, when in consequence of such talk *he* thought fit to make a Bacchanalian discourse in its favour, Mr. Johnson contradicted him somewhat roughly as I remember; and when to assure himself of conquest he added these words, You must allow me, Sir, at least that it produces truth; *in vino veritas*, you know, Sir—'That (replied Mr. Johnson) would be useless to a man who knew he was not a liar when he

Mrs. Mountague. I long to see your *report* of the same story.[6] She seems clearly to mean that it should be understood that Dr. J. called you a *liar*; whereas it is manifest that his argument is *general*, and not ad hominem—otherwise than thus: "if you wish to avail yourself of that position[7] (*in vino veritas*), to make it of any use to you you must confess yourself not a man of truth, when you are sober. I do not say this is the case, but such is the dilemma you are driven to, to give your argument any weight."—Such I think was his meaning—She does not, I think, write[8] about Johnson *cordato animo*;[9]—and there is an evident weakness, and flimzy statement, when she comes at the end to account for her going to Bath.—She contradicts all the former part of her book, and would have the reader think that the eighteen years intercourse with J. was a *bondage*, which she endured *to please Mr. Thrale*, but when he was dead it became insupportable;—and so she was forced to fly to Bath:—when in truth she was flying not *from* Dr. J. but *to* a new husband; who does not appear upon the canvass.[10]

She hints at a quarrel between Dr. J. and Master *Pepys*, but does not tell the particulars. I think you have them.[11] I can't guess

was sober.' " (See also *Johns. Misc.* i. 320–21, and Waingrow, p. 140 n. 3.)

[6] For JB's version, see *Life* ii. 187–88 and n. 3. See *post* To EM, 31 Mar. and nn. 18, 19 and Waingrow, p. 141 n. 6.

[7] MS. "argum" deleted before "position"

[8] MS. "wrigh" deleted before "write"

[9] "With a judicious mind." If this is a quotation, the editors have been unable to locate it.

[10] "I was forced to take advantage of my lost lawsuit, and plead inability of purse to remain longer in London or its vicinage. I had been crossed in my intentions of going abroad, and found it convenient, for every reason of health, peace, and pecuniary circumstances, to retire to Bath, where I knew Mr. Johnson would not follow me. . . . Veneration for his virtue, reverence for his talents, delight in his conversation, and habitual endurance of a yoke my husband first put upon me, and of which he contentedly bore his share for sixteen or seventeen years, made me go on so long with Mr. Johnson; but the perpetual confinement I will own to have been terrifying in the first years of our friendship, and irksome in the last; nor could I pretend to support it without help, when my coadjutor was no more" (*Anecdotes*, pp. 291–93; *Johns. Misc.* i. 339–41). Ostensibly when Mrs. Thrale left London for Bath on 6 Apr. 1783 she had agreed not to marry Gabriel Piozzi (1740–1809), the Italian musician she loved. But they renewed their "vows" to each other before parting that day (*Thraliana*, ed. K. C. Balderston, 1942, i. 561) and were married on 23 July 1784.

[11] SJ disliked William Weller Pepys (1740–1825), later Bt., Master in Chancery, perhaps, as Mrs. Piozzi suggests, because his manner was so artificial (*Thraliana* i. 56). They quarrelled repeatedly. Though Mrs. Piozzi does not specify the present occasion in her *Anecdotes* (pp. 141–42; *Johns. Misc.* i. 244–45) Fanny Burney does in the account she gave: it took place at Streatham in June 1781 and concerned SJ's "Life" of Lyttelton (*Burney Diary* i. 497–502). For Pepys's version of it, see A. C. C. Gaussen, *A Later Pepys*, 1904, i. 129. JB does not mention this quarrel in the *Life* but says that SJ at another time blamed

which of the members of the Club it was that was so completely *down'd* in p. 202.[12] She[13] has written a most flaming letter of panegyrick to Mrs. Montague, which Mrs. M. says she considers as the greatest honour that ever was done her.[14] So the ladies, you see, will be bien d'accord, when Mrs. P. arrives; a point that I make no doubt she labours at as of great consequence, to secure a good reception in the same set she formerly frequented.—

I hope to see you before the end of the week, in somewhat a better state of body and mind than when you wrote your last, and am, Very truly and Affectionately Yours,

E. M.

To Malone,
Friday 31 March 1786

MS. Yale (L 934). Sent 31 Mar. "Edmond Malone Esq. that I am much better, and shall stay out the Circuit—obviating Signora Piozzi's insinuation that it is *not true* she ever disapproved of Mrs. Montagu's Book" (Reg. Let.).

Lancaster, 31 March 1786

MY DEAR FRIEND: I feel with all possible warmth of gratitude your kindness to me, and I am determined more and more to

Mrs. Thrale for arousing his dislike of Pepys: " 'You praised that man with such disproportion, that I was incited to lessen him, perhaps more than he deserves. His blood is upon your head' " (*Life* iv. 82).

[12] Mrs. Piozzi's diary shows that the man referred to was not a member of The Club. He was Richard Pottinger (d. 1794), Clerk to the Privy Seal (*Gent. Mag.* Feb. 1794, lxiv. 181; *Roy. Kal.* 1778), who contradicted SJ "petulantly enough" at dinner one day. The host, the Hon. Thomas Fitzmaurice, said, "Our friend here has no meaning now in all this, except just to relate at club to-morrow how he teized Johnson at dinner to-day—this is all to do himself *honour*." When Pottinger replied, "I see no *honour* in it, whatever you may do", SJ said, "Well, Sir! . . . if you do not *see* the *honour*, I am sure I *feel* the *disgrace*" (*Johns. Misc.* i. 285; cf. *Thraliana* i. 166). JB disputed Mrs. Piozzi's version of the story (*Life* iv. 342–43, 542).

[13] MS. "She" superimposed upon erased "Mrs."

[14] This letter has not been reported, but Mrs. Piozzi acknowledged in a letter of 1 Mar. to Samuel Lysons that she had written to Mrs. Montagu contradicting SJ's statement about the *Essay on Shakespear* (*Bentley's Miscellany*, 1850, xxviii. 442). Charlotte Lewis wrote to Mrs. Piozzi on 8 May that Mrs. Montagu was "monstrously proud of your letter, & shews it every-where" (*Thraliana* ii. 745 n. 1); Horace Walpole reported having seen it in a letter of 16 Mar. to Sir Horace Mann (*Corres. HW* xxv. 634).

deserve it. I found here both your letters of the 25 and 27. By my last you would see that my illness was by no means such as I had just reason to apprehend, and *now* it is very gentle. I therefore do not take your advice borrowed from King Duncan "Go get him Surgeons."[1] The truth is I cannot lie; and I fear that one on whom it is not proper perfectly to rely might order me some *course* which I should not like to venture upon, and should not know how to evade. I thank you for not sending what killed Canning though I cannot conceive why what has been so beneficial to thousands should be so fatal to *him*. I am to take slight mercurial pills which I have directed a Chymist to make up.[2] It is much better that I attend the Assizes here. I am gaining practical knowledge, habituating myself to english modes, and making myself observed for assiduity. My *misfortune* I have with my *facility of manners* (which Dr. Adam Smith early allowed me)[3] rendered scarcely the subject even of raillery. So all is wonderfully well in this *last* ex[c]ursion into the *wilds* of Venus.

I rejoice to hear that Courtenay's admirable Verses are to appear so soon. I suppose they *have* appeared by this time. It is too late now for the first edition of them to mention, that in the passage on Dr. Johnson's latin verses, I am not sure if *soothing* be a good epithet for his Lyre.[4] Yet I know not what other to suggest. I wish for one more *sounding* more *grand*. Also I doubt if his *classick* strains be right,—after shewing that they are *not* taken from the <classic>ks.[5] Yet as they are shewn to be the true <Horatian>[6] fruit raised in British soil, I may be wrong. Pray give my most cordial compliments to our worthy Friend. What an accession to my happiness have I had in you two! If we could but make him a Christian "altogether such as I am", except these *sins*.[7] In case

[1] *Macbeth* I. ii. 44.

[2] According to the expense account JB kept while on the Northern Circuit, he spent 3*s*. 4*d*. for medicine on 21 Mar., 6*d*. on 22 Mar., 5*s*. 2*d*. on 27 Mar., and 1*s*. on 1 Apr. (A 40). Probably all of these medicines were for treatment of JB's gonorrhoea, but the 1*s*. spent on 1 Apr. was specifically for the "slight mercurial pills".

[3] JB was fond of quoting this phrase from a letter from Smith that has not been reported (*Earlier Years*, pp. 43, 466).

[4] *Ante* To EM, 22 Mar. and n. 2.

[5] *Ante* From EM, 17 Mar. n. 5. The phrase "classick strains" does not occur in Courtenay's account of SJ's Latin verse (*Poetical Review*, pp. 18–19).

[6] This reconstruction of the damaged text is far from certain, but see *Poetical Review*, p. 19:

Horatian strains a grateful heart proclaim,
While Sky's wild rocks resound his Thralia's name.—

[7] Acts 26:29, "And Paul said, I would to God, that not only thou, but also all that

you should not recollect the passage of scripture to which I allude, I am sure he will. As Voltaire's old grayheaded domestick Jesuit *Père Adam* said to me in benevolent hope of the conversion of *that* brilliant Genius "J'espere que quelque beau moment le bon Dieu lui accordera la grace."[8] I am no *Hypochrite*, though sadly *inconsistent*.

And now for La Signora Piozzi. I received her by the coach only last night *Thursday*, and her journey down cost me within 6d. of her original price.[9] I however did not grudge the cost, and *devoured* her as you say. I had before the Book arrived, two *whets* in the *Herald*.[10] She is a little artful impudent malignant Devil. She relates that Johnson in reference to her *littleness* said Insects have gay colours.[11] I will add Insects are often *venomous* have often *stings*. It is *clear* that she *means* to bite me as much as she can, that she may curry favour with Mrs. Montague. P. 44 is *undoubtedly* levelled at me;[12] for, it *describes* what the Jade has often seen me do—but with Dr. Johnson's *approbation*; for he at all times was flattered by my preserving what fell from his mind when shaken by conversation, so there was nothing *like* treachery.[13] I must have the patience of *Job* to bear the Book of *Esther*. But I shall trim her *recitativo* and all her *airs*.[14]

The *retort* upon *in vino veritas* which she affects to *remember* as if she had been *present* was told to her by myself, and she has either forgotten or misrepresented[15] the true state of it. The argument in favour of drinking was maintained by me one evening at the Crown and Anchor[16] where Dr. Johnson supt with Lord Binning

hear me this day, were both almost, and altogether such as I am, except these bonds."

[8] Père Antoine Adam (b. 1705). For this remark, see Journ. 29 Dec. 1764.

[9] Mrs. Piozzi's *Anecdotes* was advertised in *Gen. Eve. Post* at 4*s*. "in boards" (*ante* To EM, 25 Mar. n. 4).

[10] *Morn. Her.* printed extracts from the *Anecdotes* on four consecutive days (27–30 Mar.). JB had received the first two instalments.

[11] Reported in the *Anecdotes*, p. 279 (*Johns. Misc.* i. 331); JB quoted SJ's remark in the *Life* (i. 495).

[12] Gay, *Beggar's Opera* II. i. (see *ante* To EM, 11 Nov. 1785 and n. 17).

[13] Mrs. Piozzi wrote that she had once asked permission to record some of SJ's conversation, but added, "a trick, which I have however seen played on common occasions, of sitting steadily down at the other end of the room to write at the moment what should be said in company, either *by* Dr. Johnson or *to* him, I never practised myself, nor approved of in another" (*Johns. Misc.* i. 175).

[14] An allusion not only biblical, but also to Handel's oratorio *Esther* and to Gabriel Piozzi's profession.

[15] MS. "misrapresented"

[16] A tavern in Arundel St., Strand (Edward Walford, *Old and New London* [1873–78] iii. 75).

and his tutor, Langton, myself, and <one or two> more.[17] But I have it all in writing. It was I think in <1772; my> Journal will ascertain it all exactly. I am pretty certain his answer to *in vino veritas* was "Sir a fellow is not much to be regarded who cannot speak truth till you fill him drunk."[18] I am *sure* he did not *point* his fire personally to *me*, till after I had teased him long, to bring out all I could. When I at last said, "But Sir would not you drink to forget care, to forget every thing disagreable?" JOHNS. "Yes,—if I sat next *you*."[19] *Madam* as *Sam* said "has no care about truth."[20] We shall concert a genteel Reply to her, to this effect.[21] She should have stated *fairly*—not said by *me* as might be supposed from her manner of expressing it, but *reported* by me to have been said by Dr. Johnson. Two particulars are to be considered. 1st. If Dr. Johnson said it his sacred love of truth as acknowledged by herself and his remarkable accuracy, must counterballance what she is *now* pleased to set forth. I should rather suppose *her* forgetful, than *him* mistaken.—Then 2d. Whether my *Report* is to be credited? It is in my Journal written at the time, and that Journal was revised by Dr. Johnson. I had no motive whatever to *invent* it. Nay so far was I from wishing it should appear that upon correcting the proof sheet in which it occurs, I said (As Mr. Malone and Mr. Courtenay will remember) "Why should I set two women to pull one anothers caps? Besides had Mrs. Thrale been still in the state she formerly was, I might have been less scrupulous; but now that she is under a cloud, and may probably desire to have the protection of Mrs.

[17] Charles Hamilton (1753–1828), styled Lord Binning, later (1795) eighth Earl of Haddington, was the stepson of Langton's mother-in-law; his tutor's name was Oliphant (Journ. 15 Apr. 1772). Also present at this supper was "a young Gentleman of Eton" and Peter Johnston of Carnsalloch, Dumfriesshire, in 1772 a student in Lincoln's Inn, and now (1786) M.P. for Kirkcudbright Stewartry (ibid.; Namier and Brooke ii. 683).

[18] SJ said, "I would not keep company with a fellow who lyes as long as he is sober, and whom you must fill drunk before you can get a word of truth out of him" (Journ. 15 Apr. 1772). Cf. *Life* ii. 188.

[19] In the *Life*, JB reported this part of the conversation separately, and in the third person, calling himself only "a gentleman" so as to prevent any impression that SJ's earlier remark was indeed *ad hominem* (ii. 193 and n. 1). However, Mrs. Piozzi identified the "gentleman" as JB in the margin of her copy of the *Life* (ibid.).

[20] SJ once said to JB, "I told Mrs. Thrale, 'You have so little anxiety about truth, that you never tax your memory with the exact thing' " (*Life* iii. 404). On another occasion, SJ mentioned her "laxity of narration, and inattention to truth" (*Life* iii. 243). For references to other examples of her inaccuracy, see *Life* vi. 380.

[21] JB now reverts to the issue of Mrs. Piozzi's Postscript on Mrs. Montagu's *Essay on Shakespear* (see *ante* From EM, 25 Mar. and n. 7).

Montagu should she venture to return to England, it might hurt her; and I dare say she would deny it." Upon these considerations I struck it out, and some hundreds of the first edition were actually thrown off without it: Sir Joshua Reynolds's copy has it not.[22] Mr. Courtenay however insisted that as Dr. Johnson had done Mrs. Thrale the honour to quote her as an authority on taste and to class her with himself and Beauclerk, I had no right to deprive her of such a distinction to which she had an authentick title under my own hand. I was convinced, and ordered her[23] name to be reinstated. Thus it is—between my unbiassed record, and Mrs. Thrale's accuracy of remembrance as to which I must be forgiven for entertaining some doubt, especially where she will not deny that she has a little interest to forget. It is strange that she has heard *every one* commend Mrs. Montagus Book, for she surely cannot reckon Dr. Johnson *nobody* and it is very well known how *He* talked of it. I shall then tell his criticism on it at length to Sir Joshua's face when they were dining at my lodgings, as also what he said at Sir Joshua's table in the hearing of Sir Joshua and his nephew the Rev. Mr. Jo. Palmer that "When Shakespeare has ——— for a rival and Mrs. M. for a defender he is in a pitiful state indeed."[24]

We shall have all this (on which I have dwelt too long; but I wish to speak a little to the *Blue* World) well drest.

Eaton Graham is I fancy only an errour of the press; for, he was an under Master or Usher at Eton School.[25]

She seems to have had no *affection* for our great friend, but merely the attachment of vanity.

She describes him as barbarous and dirty. The story of spitting her relations is I suppose exagerated; or she must have provoked him confoundedly by *affectation* of grief.[26] The Book however has a

[22] *Ante* From EM, 19 Oct. 1785 and n. 44; To EM, 27 Oct. 1785 and n. 19.

[23] MS. "the" altered to "her"

[24] JB refers to two discussions about Mrs. Montagu, the first on 16 Oct. 1769 (*Life* ii. 88), and the second reported immediately afterwards in the *Life* (ii. 89), but in fact to be dated 1775 or later. It is virtually certain that Shakespeare's "rival" was Robert Jephson (1736–1803), the Irish poet and playwright, whose first play was not produced until 1775 (*Life* ii. 486–87). Reynolds's nephew is presumably the Rev. Joseph Palmer (1749–1829), whose tragedy "Zaphira" Reynolds unsuccessfully urged DG to produce (*Letters Reynolds*, p. 40 n. 2). Reynolds, however, had another clerical nephew, the Rev. John Palmer (c. 1729–90), a Unitarian minister in Islington.

[25] *Ante* From EM, 27 Mar. n. 4.

[26] "When I one day lamented the loss of a first cousin killed in America—'Prithee, my dear (said he), have done with canting: how would the world be worse for it, I may

great deal of valuable Memorabilia, which prove themselves genuine. But there is seldom the true *zest*. She puts cherries in the brandy.[27]

I am glad that a third edition of my Tour is thought not unadviseable. But let it not be begun till I return, that I may make it quite correct. I *positively* will give you your note on Burke, it has been so much admired.[28] I hope to be with you on the 10 or 11. I had this day one *motion* in Court; so I am in practice.[29] Do not let the third edition be put to press till I come. I ever am with most perfect regard, Yours very gratefully,

J. B.

There is no post from this till tomorrow morning.[30]

To Malone,
Monday 3 April 1786

MS. Hyde Collection. Sent 3 Apr. "Edmond Malone Esq. enclosing a refutation of Signora Piozzi upon *recollecting* that she had read my Tour in manuscript and had not denied what is reported of her slighting Mrs. Montagu's Book—leaving to him to publish or not in the newspapers with my name and more or less as he might think best" (Reg. Let.).

Lancaster, 3 April 1786

MY DEAR SIR: O brave We![1] I am now completely armed against

ask, if all your relations were at once spitted like larks, and roasted for Presto's supper?' Presto was the dog that lay under the table while we talked" (*Anecdotes*, p. 63; *Johns. Misc.* i. 189–90). In the *Life*, JB quoted this story as an example of Mrs. Piozzi's "exaggeration and distortion", confirmed by Baretti's account of the same incident (*Life* iv. 347). Baretti's account came to JB through EM, who recorded it in "Maloniana", his commonplace book (Prior, *Malone*, p. 398; see J. C. Riely, "The Biographer as Advocate: Boswell and the 'Supper of Larks' Case", *Greene Centennial Studies: Essays Presented to Donald Greene* , ed. P. J. Korshin and R. R. Allen, 1984, pp. 307–19).

[27] Cherry brandy, milder and less alcoholic than unflavoured brandy, was made by soaking cherries in brandy for about a month (Peter Jonas, *The Distiller's Guide*, 1816, pp. 65–67). SJ called brandy a drink for heroes (*Life* iii. 381); flavoured liqueurs were generally thought to be ladies' drinks.

[28] For the discussion of the note on EB, see *ante* To and From EM, 5 Oct.–11 Nov. 1785, passim. JB did not acknowledge EM's authorship of the note in the 3rd ed. of the *Tour* but did so in the *Life* (iii. 323 n. 2).

[29] JB's list of "English Fees" (Lg 41) reveals that this was the first business he received while on the Northern Circuit; his fee was 10*s*. 6*d*. See also Journ. 31 Mar.

[30] This sentence is written upside-down in the top margin of the last page of the letter. Also in the top margin, but right side up, is "York 19 March 1786" deleted.

[1] *Ante* From EM, 19 Oct. 1785, n. 2.

Signora Piozzi—She read the three volumes of my original Journal, and did not deny as to Mrs. Montagu.[2] Only think of my not recollecting this, when I last wrote to you.

As you are upon the spot and can better judge than I can of the *effect* of her *denial* which from *le bon Dillys* account is *strong*,[3] you will please to decide whether the enclosed should not be immediately put into the newspapers. Consult with Courtenay. I will not send it to the venal *Chanticleer*.[4] But I am sure the *Publick*—the *St. James s* and probably the Morning Post will insert it liberally. I should think too the Gentlemans Magazine would give it a place. I myself think it ought to appear, and that I should pay for it rather than that it should not. Its appearing speedily too I think of some consequence; otherwise it might do in my "THIRD EDITION—With a Postscript concerning Signora Piozzi". I shall at any rate have such a Postscript. But it appears to me that an *immediate* trimming may be of service.

I leave it to you entirely to correct vary abridge enlarge my Reply, as you think best.[5]

May I not appeal to Sir Joshua who often heard our friend upon Mrs. Montagu's Essay—particularly when[6] Shakespeare has —— for a[7] rival and Mrs. M. for a Defender, he is in a pitiful state indeed.[8] Might not we add Mr. Langton and others. Pray see as to this.

I have put the passage as to the great Brewer's Wife within hooks,[9] for consideration. It would I dare say vex her; but is it not too coarse? Yet it shews *how* she might talk *differently* then from what she now does of Mrs. M.

Shall the addition with *** appear at all? and if it does would it be better to be inserted *before* my subscription?

Would it be proper to introduce into this Reply the Account of

[2] Mrs. Thrale wrote to JB on 18 May 1775, after reading a part of his journal: "I return you a thousand Thanks for your entertaining Manuscript. . . . Your Journal has almost blinded me, and I can but just see to tell you how earnestly I wish you a happy meeting with your family."

[3] The letter that Dilly enclosed with Mrs. Piozzi's *Anecdotes* has not been reported; JB received it on 30 Mar. (Reg. Let.). "Le bon Dilly" is perhaps an echo of David Hume's epithet "le bon David", which he earned by his amiability (see e.g. E. C. Mossner, *Life of David Hume*, 1954, p. 439).

[4] That is, the *Morning Herald*, which had charged for the insertion of JB's letter refuting Peter Pindar (*ante* From EM, 17 Mar. and n. 8).

[5] *Post* From EM, 7 Apr. and n. 5.

[6] MS. "when" written above deleted "if"

[7] MS. "a" superimposed upon "his"

[8] *Ante* To EM, 31 Mar. and n. 24.

[9] Brackets, printed below as parentheses.

the passage being first left out etc.—and the pulling of caps, and the *prophesy* that she would *deny*? You can indent it charmingly if you think fit.[10]

I am quite ashamed, or rather am sensible I *ought* to be ashamed of giving you so much trouble. But I am conscious I would do as much for you, if I could have an opportunity.

I long much to see Courtenay's Poem in print, and I hope it will come to me here in franks. After this you will direct to me no more at Lancaster; for we leave it, I beleive on thursday or friday. If my Cause in the House of Lords is to come on the 12, I shall proceed directly to London. If it is put off, I shall go round by Lichfield and Oxford.[11] I have not yet written to Mr. Thomas Warton, which is wrong. I may delay it now, till I have read his communications, in case I do not pay him a visit.[12] I expect every day a letter from the Solicitor in the appeal to inform me as to the time fixed.

I long much to be with you again. Yet I am vastly well upon the Circuit. My accessions of knowledge please me much, and I value myself on my assiduity. I was Counsel for a prisoner on Saturday, and cross examined boldly.[13] Yours with great regard,

J. B.

I have had a charming letter from Downpatrick.[14] I believe I shall be quite comme il faut very soon.

[Enclosure]

Having read a Postscript (dated *Naples*) to *Signora Piozzi's* Anecdotes of Dr. Johnson in which after mentioning that "it is *said*

[10] MS. "proper" deleted before "fit"

[11] *Ante* To EM, 12 Mar. and n. 19, 25 Mar. and n. 5.

[12] *Ante* From EM, 3 Jan. n. 6; To EM, 10 Mar. and n. 2.

[13] JB's "Legal Notebook" (Lg 40, pp. 44–51) contains an account of the trial of Margaret Hamilton *alias* Margaret Montgomery for house-breaking and theft. The case was heard on Saturday 1 Apr. and JB served as counsel for the accused. Despite his "bold" cross-examination of witnesses, Margaret Hamilton was convicted of the felony. JB's account is printed in BP xvi. 291–94. Another account, almost certainly by JB, was published in *Edin. Adv.* (12–16 May) xlv. 305: "A curious incident happened at the last assizes at Lancaster. A woman was indicted for house breaking by the name of Margaret Hamilton, alias *Margaret Montgomery*;—upon which Mr. Boswell was instantly called on by his brethren at the bar to be counsel for the prisoner. He readily undertook the office; but his client, instead of a *true Montgomery*, turned out to be a *false thief*, and was convicted of felony." The phrase *true Montgomery*, from JB's *LPS 85*, had been ridiculed by Wilkes (*ante* From EM, 19 Oct. 1785 and n. 49); by this time it seemingly had become a public joke. JB's juxtaposing *true Montgomery* and *false thief* echoes *1 Henry IV*, which juxtaposes "true prince" and "false thief" (e.g. I. ii. 154–55) and "true man" and "false thief" (e.g. II. i. 92–94).

[14] Mrs. Rudd, here discreetly called "Downpatrick" (*ante* From EM, 17 Mar. n. 11).

in my Tour to the Hebrides that *She could not get through Mrs. Montagu's Essay on Shakespeare*", she declares as follows[15] "*On the contrary* I[16] have *always* commended it myself, and heard it commended by *every one* else." —I beg leave to observe that it would have been fairer[17] to have mentioned *who* said it, which was not *I* but *Dr. Johnson* for whom she once professed both respect and affection whatever she at last felt from his frowns, and however she may venture to treat his character.[18]

And[19] as there seems to be an oblique *stiletto*[20] in the paragraph, the *Signora* will pardon *me* for *now*[21] saying that I trust more to the accuracy of the *Report* in my Journal, than to her memory at this distance of time, especially when it is a little biased.

My reasons for this confidence are, *first*[22] that the Report so far as Dr. Johnson himself is concerned is perfectly agreable to the opinion which he at all times expressed of Mrs. Montagu's Essay, for which I shall appeal to Sir Joshua Reynolds; and I *wonder* that he *never* expressed it to *Mrs. Thrale. Second* He would not have told the circumstance of Mrs. Thrale's not relishing the Book had he not been *sure* of the fact and as he read over my Journal he would have corrected the passage had I mistaken him. But *Third Mrs.*[23] *Thrale herself* many years ago perused[24] my Journal in the original Manuscript as far as to the Isle of Col;[25] as to which I *have a letter under her own hand* in very flattering terms;[26] and therefore as the passage in question was[27] read[28] by her,[29] she certainly would have objected to it, had she *then* thought it erroneous. (But she was *then* the great Brewer's Wife in all the pomp of wealth.)

[15] MS. "as follows" written above deleted "that"

[16] MS. "she" deleted before "I"

[17] MS. "but" inserted as interlineation before "fair", then deleted; "fair" altered to "fairer"

[18] MS. "affection however she may now treat his memory" (with "venture to" written above deleted "now". "Now" is uncertain.) JB then deleted "however . . . memory" and substituted "whatever . . . character"

[19] MS. "And" preceded by "N.L." and bracket to indicate new paragraph.

[20] Wilkes used "stiletto" of Mrs. Piozzi's then forthcoming book (see *ante* To EM, 13 Oct. 1785, n. 69).

[21] MS. "*now*" inserted as interlineation.

[22] MS. "*first*" inserted as interlineation.

[23] MS. "it must be considered that" deleted before "*Mrs.*"

[24] MS. "many years ago perused" written above deleted "read over"

[25] MS. "in the original . . . Isle of Col" written above deleted "as far as to *Dunvegan* when She was recovering from her last childbirth,"

[26] See n. 2 above.

[27] MS. "occurs before Dr. Johnson and I left the mainland of Scotland and therefore" before "was" deleted except for "the mainland" (an oversight).

[28] MS. "read" written above deleted "perused"

[29] MS. "her" written above deleted "the *Signora*"

FROM MALONE, 7 APRIL 1786

If *Signora Piozzi* wishes to make the experiment of returning to England, and taking a place in the *Bluestocking* Circles, it is very proper that she should pay her court to Mrs. Montagu. But I do not chuse that she should do it *in this way*.

JAMES BOSWELL

*** I shall by and by[30] have occasion to speak more fully concerning the above, and several other passages of Signora Piozzi's Book.

From Malone,
Friday 7 April 1786
MS. Yale (C 1908).

London, April 7, 1786

MY DEAR SIR: My hand is so wearied with filling five sides of very large paper that I have just dispatched to Marseilles,[1] that I am[2] only able to send you three words with the Poem[3] which I enclose on the chance of its finding you at Lichfield—Salve magna parens![4] C. agrees with me in thinking that it will be very right to make some reply to the *Signora*, in the course of this month, and not to defer it to a note in your third edition, which may not come out till the matter is forgotten, and which when it does appear but few will read:—but great *address* will be necessary in constructing the answer,—which we will sit down to, when you return to

[30] MS. "soon" written as alternative above "by and by"

[1] EM's brother, Lord Sunderlin, was travelling in the south of France with his wife and sisters (*ante* From EM, ?July 1785, n. 3).

[2] MS. "know" deleted before "am"

[3] Courtenay's *Poetical Review*, which had appeared the day before (*ante* From EM, 13 Jan. n. 5).

[4] "Hail, great mother" (Virgil, *Georgics* ii. 173). In his *Dictionary* SJ used the salutation to pay tribute to Lichfield, his birthplace (*Life* iv. 372 and n. 1). JB's expense account (A 40) indicates that he had dinner in Lancaster on 6 Apr.; probably he left either that evening or early on 7 Apr. He arrived in London before breakfast on 10 Apr. (Journ.). Resting only one night, one could travel the 234 miles between Lancaster and London (*Univ. Brit. Directory* i. 569) in only two and a half days (JB did so on 17–19 June 1790—Journ.) but any more relaxed journey would have left little time for a stop in Lichfield. If, against probability, JB did stop briefly in Lichfield (see *ante* To EM, 25 Mar. and n. 5), he probably would have arrived on 8 Apr. EM's letter could well have met him there, but the absence of a wrapper or an entry for this letter in Reg. Let. makes it impossible to determine whether JB received the letter in Lichfield or whether it was returned to London.

town[5]—I have thoughts of sending some strictures on her book to the G. M. for this month, and also on C.'s too *highly coloured* statement of our great friend's foibles. I told him I meant something of this kind and he has no objection. I shall throw in a good deal of praise, you may be sure;—so it will be the very best way of *advertising* the poem.[6] A very sensible man (Mr. Flood)[7] who sate some time with me this morning, said of it (for C. sent him one yesterday) that he has proved *himself* truly of the school, by following Johnson's own steps, in[8] his biography, and mixing with great panegyrick a rather exaggerated and *sometimes* not sufficiently grounded *invective* against him.[9]

We had a very pleasant dinner a few day's ago at Sir J. Reynolds's, where I saw for the first time your old friend Lord Monboddo.[10] I am quite vexed that you struck out *pocket*.[11] It was a great deal too good for him. He is the most surly disagreable fellow I ever saw, and with all his parade of learning, I suspect is shallow at bottom. Never did a man fall into a more unlucky set—for we had a strong band of Johnsonites:—Dr. Parr, a very clever fellow, a great admirer of *Sam's*, who had been under

[5] Little of JB's first version of his reply to Mrs. Piozzi's Postscript (*ante* To EM, 3 Apr.) survived the revision that JB, EM, and Courtenay made on 15 Apr. (Journ.). Instead the final version was a coolly argued statement of fact: the remark on Mrs. Thrale's opinion of Mrs. Montagu's book was SJ's, not JB's; SJ's opinion of the book was well known to be that expressed in the *Tour*; both SJ and Mrs. Thrale had read the journal from which the *Tour* was printed; and JB had struck out Mrs. Thrale's name, then restored it in the printed *Tour*. JB's reply appeared in *Gazetteer*, 17 Apr., and in many other newspapers and periodicals. It was reprinted in *Gent. Mag.* (Apr. 1786) lvi. 285–86, and in *Eur. Mag.* (June 1786) ix. 397–98. In the 3rd ed. of the *Tour* (*Life* v. 245 n. 2) this reply appeared as a footnote with the exception of the last paragraph (inappropriate here). That paragraph is reprinted, following the footnote, in *Life* v.

[6] If EM wrote such strictures, they have not been reported.

[7] Henry Flood (1732–91), celebrated Irish politician and briefly M.P. for Winchester (1783–84), was now contesting the seat for Seaford. He was returned on petition on 26 Apr. (Namier and Brooke ii. 441–42).

[8] MS. "and" deleted before "in"

[9] *Ante* To EM, 13 Oct. 1785, n. 3.

[10] The dinner took place either on Saturday 1 Apr. or Sunday 2 Apr. Reynolds's Engagement Books show that Monboddo dined at five o'clock on both days.

[11] EM refers to the footnote in the *Tour* that reports Samuel Foote's description of Monboddo as "an Elzevir edition of Johnson". (That the addition was entered in EM's copy does not prove that it was EM's suggestion; see *ante* From EM, 5 Nov. 1785, n. 16). However, after the sheet of the 2nd ed. containing the note had been printed, JB cancelled the leaf (F5, pp. 73–74) and restored the original reading. Perhaps at EM's insistence, JB added in the 3rd ed., "It has been shrewdly observed that Foote must have meant a diminutive, or *pocket* edition" (*Life* v. 74 n. 3; Chapman, pp. 466, 481; *Lit. Car.* p. 117).

Sumner at Harrow and is reckoned one of the best Greek scholars in England:[12]—Dr. Burney, Steevens, Langton, and Seward.—Parr and Monboddo began to spar a little before dinner and after dinner there was a pitched battle. Monboddo maintained as usual that Johnson was no scholar, did not understand Greek etc. and Parr made an eloquent elogium on our friend, and beat Monboddo out of the field on the subject of Greek Literature. Aristotle was talked of[13] and M. maintained, that is *asserted*, for he does not condescend to *argue*, that he was superior to all the moderns put together. Parr allowed him great merit but not quite so much as this. M. maintained he could know nothing about the matter unless he had read *all* the *commentators* on Aristotle, and intimated that he had but a slight opinion of his knowledge of Greek. P. said "he had read *some* of the Commentators pretty carefully—what his knowledge of Greek was or was not could only be proved by bringing down the books and producing particular passages";—however he would not let old Monbod. off with respect to Aristotle, but challenged him to shew how he excelled all of the moderns. The other growled, but did not say a word—and soon after surlily got up. Sir[14] J. R. asked him where he was going—"I'll go to the Ladies",—was his reply.—He fell from Scylla into Charybdis; for he found Mrs. Gwatkin, Sir Joshua's niece,[15] reading Mrs. Piozzi's book—She[16] asked him, if[17] he had read it. "No (he said) nor shall I. I hated and despised the fellow when he was living. Indeed when after his death they published his Prayers and Meditations, I *pitied* him." O indelible disgrace! to be pitied by Monbod.!! If you have any mercy on such a fellow, may your right hand forget its cunning![18]

We had a most pleasant day till one o clock in the morning—all

[12] Samuel Parr (1747–1825), LL.D., schoolmaster and curate at Hatton, Warwickshire. SJ disputed with Parr more than once, admired the way he argued, and wrote him a letter of recommendation for the mastership of Colchester Grammar School (*Life* iv. 423 n. 3; see *post* To EM, 13 Apr. 1795). Robert Carey Sumner (1729–71), D.D., was Headmaster of Harrow and an acquaintance of SJ. Parr was Sumner's first assistant master from 1767 to 1771.

[13] MS. "off" with final "f" erased.

[14] MS. "and went of" (for "and went off") deleted after "up"; EM attempted to make the "f" of "of" into the "S" of "Sr", but deleted his attempt and began again.

[15] Theophila Palmer Gwatkin (1757–1843), who lived with Reynolds for most of the time from 1770 until her marriage to Robert Lovell Gwatkin in 1781 (*Letters Reynolds*, pp. 54 n. 1, 78 n. 2). She was the subject of several of Reynolds's paintings.

[16] MS. "She" superimposed upon erased "The"

[17] MS. "he" deleted before "if"

[18] Psalms 137: 5: "If I forget thee, O Jerusalem, let my right hand forget her cunning."

on Johnson.—Many elucidations and corrections of Mrs. P. came out in the course of conversation from Seward and Sir Joshua. I wished much for you to have enjoyed and preserved them.—I endeavoured to recollect a few particulars next day.—Adieu. Both C. and I miss you much—I hope you mean soon to return to us—Meanwhile believe me most faithfuly and affectionately yours,

E. MALONE

To Malone,
Saturday 19 August 1786
MS. Yale (L 935).
ADDRESS: To Edmond Malone Esq., London.

Carlisle, 19 August 1786

Safely[1] arrived here My dear Friend, I write, to mention a few things—My address is Auchinleck Cumnock Dumfries, the postdays from London, Monday Wednesday friday. I get the Publick Advertiser. So you have only to mention any squibs in the Herald. Be so good as to get my crest engraved again from the title page of the second edition.[2] I would have little advertising till winter—I would say "This day is published carefully corrected and enlarged[3] with additional notes particularly suitable animadversions on Hester Lynch Piozzi etc. The THIRD EDITION of etc." Do as you will. I think *She* should be mentioned.[4] If the Advertisement be not thrown off—instead of wit etc. *exhibited* I would say *recorded* because it is the word of most *import* and has been *laughed* at by the Buffoons; so I would *brave* them. Let the Advertisement be dated London 15 August 1786.[5] I do not mean

[1] MS. "Saefely". Presumably JB left London on 16 or 17 Aug.; he arrived at Auchinleck on 21 Aug. (Book of Company).

[2] *Ante* To EM, 11 Nov. 1785, n. 9. EM found the copperplate for the title-page of the 2nd ed. and used it again for the 3rd (*post* From EM, 4 Sept.).

[3] MS. "enriched" written as alternative above "enlarged"

[4] The advertisement of the 3rd ed. in *Lond. Chron.* (7–10 Oct.) lx. 350 did not mention Mrs. Piozzi.

[5] JB replaced the one-paragraph Advertisement of the 2nd ed. of the *Tour* with a three-paragraph Advertisement in the 3rd ed. There he defended it against "animadversions in the periodical Journals of criticism" and elsewhere, especially on the part of "shallow or envious cavillers, who

to make *presents* of the third edition. It shall have a fair chance. The Dedication copy must be elegantly bound by Searlè Mr. Kirkley's son in law;[6] and Dr. Barnard Bishop of Kilaloe must have one for St. Woolstans.[7]

Adieu. I am quite comfortable, and very happy in the prospect of being so soon with my true Montgomerie[8] and our children, and not being long from you and my other London friends. I am ever most warmly yours,

J. B.

How much do I owe you! I have now the Home Circuit *intus*.[9] I am <*in*> *cursu*[10] of I know not what success.

From Malone, Monday 4 September 1786

MS. Yale (C 1909).

ADDRESS in Courtenay's hand: James Boswell Esqr., Auchinleck, Cumnock,[1] Dumfries.

FRANK: London Septembr. fourth 1786. Free J. Courtenay.

POSTMARK: [London] 4 SE.

ENDORSEMENT: Mr. Malone about Dr. Johnson's Life.

London, Sep. 4, 1786

MY DEAR SIR: Though it is so long since you left this, I did not get a fair copy of the *Advertisement* till Saturday,[2] and your post did not then go out.[3]—I think you will allow it to be *firm* and manly,

have endeavoured to persuade the world that Dr. Johnson's character has been *lessened* by recording such various instances of his lively wit and acute judgment, on every topick that was presented to his mind" (*Life* v. 3–4). The Advertisement is dated "*London*, 15th Aug. 1786".

[6] Perhaps John Searle, in 1791 a stationer and bookbinder at No. 35 Brewer St., Golden Square, and later (1794) in South Molton St. His wife's name was Mary Anne, but her maiden name is not known. She operated the bindery as late as 1828 (Charles Ramsden, *London Bookbinders*, 1780–1840, 1956, p. 127; *Univ. Brit. Directory* i. 281). Kirkley may be "Old Mr. Ralph Kirkley", Reynolds's servant for twenty-five years (Journ. 12 Feb.).

[7] *Ante* To EM, 13 Oct. 1785, n. 47. St. Wolstans in Co. Kildare was Thomas Barnard's seat.

[8] *Ante* From EM, 19 Oct. 1785 and n. 49; To EM, 3 Apr. and n. 13.

[9] "From within". JB shifted back and forth from the Northern to the Home Circuit.

[10] "[Headed] in the direction".

[1] MS. "Cumnock" written above deleted "Crumlin"

[2] Probably proofs of the Advertisement to the 3rd ed. of the *Tour* were enclosed with the present letter.

[3] *Ante* To EM, 19 Aug.: "the postdays from London, Monday Wednesday friday".

without *capering* too much.—I found the cypher-plate, so there was no need of new engraving. I remember giving it to you, and I suppose you replaced it again in its old corner where it lay in perfect safety.—I hope the *Life* goes on well. Did you attend to a laboured attack in the Pub. A. against[4] S. J. signed *Erica*.[5] It has all a *foundation*, but is monstrously exaggerated; the surest, and most wounding kind of abuse. I have no doubt it is Macpherson's—Where he speaks toward the end of Ossian, he lets the Cat out.[6]—Yet you were tender about this fellow—surely without any reason.[7] Pray keep that paper. I think towards the end of the Life, where the smaller traits of character are to be investigated, it would be very right to answer this and Mrs. Piozzi, and all other artful *misrepresentations* that are well done; and to mark distinctly how far true and where the falsehood commences.[8]—Learning has suffered an irreparable loss in the death of poor Mr. Tyrwhitt. He was assuredly, if not the best, one of the best scholars in England, and a man of most amiable manners. He was carried off in a fortnight by a dyssentery. I believe you saw him here one day.[9]—I have been walking all the morning (a great effort for me) and am come home at half past five; and the bellman dinning in my ears.—Courteney and I and Sir J. Reynolds have been a good

[4] MS. "sign" deleted before "against"

[5] "Erica's" letter appeared in *Pub. Adv.* 26 Aug. p. [2] and in *Eur. Mag.* (Aug.) x. 128–30. It is a long attack on SJ's character as presented by his biographers. *Pub. Adv.* 2 Sept. p. [2] carried a letter signed "M. M." warmly commending "Erica's" opinions. It seems unlikely that the same "M. M." who wrote, "he [SJ] stands much higher in my Estimation now than ever" (*St. James's Chron.* 22–25 Oct. 1785; *ante* From EM, 28 Oct. 1785, n. 5), now commends "Erica's" attack.

[6] "Erica" wrote, "It is certain that he [SJ] returned from the Hebrides persuaded of the truth of the second sight, and convinced of the spuriousness of Ossian's Poems. The improbability of the former recommended itself, but the extreme probability of the latter obstructed its reception. He was ignorant of the nature of internal evidence, nor thought of comparing the poems with the avowed productions of the Translator. He might possibly have suspected them less, had they been announced as imparted by Ossian to Macpherson through the visionary medium of the second sight."

[7] JB had subscribed to the fund which enabled Macpherson as a young man to search for a long Erse poem, and Macpherson and he had known each other in London in 1762–63 (see *London Journal*, index). In the *Tour* he hedged about the authenticity of *Fingal*; his doubts were more pronounced in the *Life* (*Life* v. 389–90, ii. 302).

[8] Although JB criticized Mrs. Piozzi's *Anecdotes* at length in the *Life* (iv. 340–47), he did not mention "Erica's" letter.

[9] Thomas Tyrwhitt (1730–86), a classicist but best remembered for his exposure of Chatterton's forgeries and his edition of the *Canterbury Tales*. He died on 15 Aug. No record of JB's having met him at EM's has been reported.

deal together. We had a very good day in Leicest.-Field[10] with Burke on Sunday Sennight,[11] and not a bad one on friday at Brocklesby's with Sir J. R., C., Govr. Ellis (the Voyager),[12] old Macklin,[13] Mr. Cooke,[14] *Murphy*,[15] cum multis aliis.—A select party adjourned to Sir Joshua s and supped. There's for you—We visited old *Adee* in time, for he is dead, I see.[16]—Pray present the best Compliments of an unknown gentleman to Mrs. B. and believe me ever Most faithfully yours,

EDM. MALONE

From Malone,
Friday 24 August 1787
MS. Yale (C 1910).

London, Aug. 24, 1787

MY DEAR SIR: As I know the value of even a very few lines when one is four hundred miles from London,[1] I write three words to inform you that I had yesterday a letter from Dr. Farmer,[2] saying that he had actually received from Miss Lawrence the letter to her

[10] MS. "Field."

[11] Sir Joshua Reynolds lived in Leicester Fields.

[12] Henry Ellis (1721–1806), formerly Governor of Georgia and Nova Scotia. In the expedition of 1746 to seek a north-west passage through Hudson's Bay, Ellis acted as hydrographer, surveyor, and mineralogist. He published a popular account of the voyage in 1748.

[13] Charles Macklin (c. 1697–1797), actor and stage manager, a friend of JB.

[14] Almost certainly William Cooke or Cook (d. 1824), barrister, known as "Conversation Cooke" after the publication of his poem *Conversation* in 1796, subsequent editions of which included "poetical portraits" of SJ, EB, Reynolds, Goldsmith, DG, JB, and others. Cooke wrote memoirs of Macklin and Samuel Foote, and in 1785 published an anonymous *Life of Samuel Johnson, LL.D.*, which EM described as "a very incorrect and hasty life, a mere catchpenny" (*Percy Corres.* p. 19). Cooke, like Arthur Murphy (see next note), was a member of the Essex Head Club, where he often dined with JB (e.g. Journ. 8 Nov.; 28 Mar., 25 Apr. 1787).

[15] Arthur Murphy (1727–1805), playwright and actor, in 1792 published an *Essay on the Life and Genius of Samuel Johnson, LL.D.* On 27 June, Murphy, Cooke, EM, and JB had dined together at Brocklesby's (Journ.).

[16] JB and EM had visited Swithin Adee, M.D. and Fellow of the Society of Antiquaries of London, at Oxford on 30 Apr. (Journ.). He died on 12 Aug. (*Gent. Mag.* Aug. lvi. 716).

[1] JB was at Auchinleck from 20 Aug. to 24 Sept. He arrived in London again on 29 Sept. (Journ.).

[2] *Ante* From EM, 21 Oct. 1785, n. 9. A friend of SJ, Farmer is mentioned frequently in the *Life*.

Father, and also some notices of Johnson; both which I hope to have tomorrow.[3]—You see Fortune favours you on every side. Courteney is at length come to us. I invited him to leave Bath[4] and meet the *Gang*[5] at Mr. Windham's last Tuesday, and he very gallantly did so, and just arrived as we were sitting down to dinner. We had a prodigy there, Dr. Mounsy, who told us he was 93 years old. He talked a good deal and told many stories, but not accurately nor faithfully, but it seem'd not the inaccuracy of old age, but rather as if he had *never* been a strong minded man.[6]—C. dined with me yesterday, and we both agreed that you were a great loss to us.—Come back therefore soon.—We meet again tomorrow at Sir J. R. Farewell. Yours most Affectionately,

E. M.

My best Compliments to Mrs. Boswell.[7] I called at your house, but no news from Bowle.[8]

[3] Elizabeth Lawrence (d. 1790) was the daughter of Dr. Thomas Lawrence (1711–83). JB printed four letters from SJ to Lawrence (*Life* ii. 296, iii. 419, iv. 137, 143–44), extracts of letters from SJ to Miss Lawrence (*Life* iv. 144 n. 3), and an account of SJ by "a lady", transmitted to JB by Miss Lawrence (*Life* i. 82–84). An unsigned, undated MS., apparently in Miss Lawrence's hand, is preserved at Yale among the Papers Apart for the *Life* (M 145, pp. 16–23). It contains three of the four letters printed in the *Life* (the letter of 17 Jan. 1782—*Life* iv. 137—is missing), the extracts of letters to Miss Lawrence, the anonymous lady's account of SJ, and a Latin poem addressed to Dr. Lawrence, not printed by JB (see *Works SJ* vi. 310–11). In this letter and the next, EM mentions only some of the contents of the MS.

[4] Courtenay had been at Bath since 1 June (Journ.).

[5] *Ante* From EM, 5 Oct. 1785, n. 1.

[6] Windham's diary for 21 Aug. reads, "Had company to dinner; that is to say, Sir Joshua, Malone, Courtenay, who came from Bath, and with him, not unwelcomely, old Mounsey, at the age of ninety-three. I don't know that he improved the conversation much, but it was not for want of spirits to talk, nor from any cause that might not equally have existed forty years ago. To me his presence was a satisfaction, independent from what he might add or take from the society" (*The Diary of the Right Hon. William Windham, 1784 to 1810*, ed. C. A. Baring, 1866, pp. 123–24). Messenger Monsey, or Mounsey (1693–1788), physician to Chelsea Hospital, was a favourite among Whig politicians and in Mrs. Montagu's literary circle. SJ disliked his rough manners (*Life* ii. 64).

[7] Mrs. Boswell had been in London from 25 Sept. 1786 to 13 Aug. (Journ.); there she had met EM and several times dined with him.

[8] Since June 1785, William Bowles (1755–1826) and JB had been corresponding about Bowles's Johnsonian materials, but they did not reach him until 9 Nov. and then did not include SJ's letters to Bowles, which JB had been pressing for (see Waingrow, index).

To Malone,
between 10 and 24 September 1787

Not reported. In Reg. Let. for September JB wrote, "During this month which I passed till the 24th at Auchinleck, I sent and received only a few letters . . . two from Mr. Malone. I wrote once to him." From the postscript to *post* From EM, 14 Sept. it appears that EM had not as yet received this letter from JB.

From Malone,
Friday 14 September 1787
MS. Yale (C 1911).

London, Sep. 14, 1787

MY DEAR SIR: As I have some thoughts of going to Cambridge next week for a few days, and may possibly not be in London when you return, I write you three words to tell you that I have received from Dr. Farmer Johnson's letter to Dr. Lawrence, and a few extracts from other letters of his, made by his daughter, chiefly relative to his health. Mr. Windham has also sent me three letters to himself, which are all that he ever received. They are of no great value, but do him honour.[1]—Mrs. Thrale[2] Piozzi, I should say, has, I find, been applying to Mrs. Boothby at Litchfield for letters, but will not I am told succeed.[3]—Courteney has been in town and is gone again to Bath, to bring up his family. He has taken a little house in Bryanston Street, which I am sorry for; as it is quite out of my walk.[4]—We had yesterday, a very good quiet day at Sir J. Reynolds's.—Edmd. Burke, Mr. Lawrence,[5] Sir J. and myself. The true cause I perceive, of B.'s coldness, is that he thinks your

[1] These three letters (*Life* iv. 227, 362–63) are now in the Hyde Collection.

[2] MS. "Thrale" deleted.

[3] For the story of JB's and Mrs. Piozzi's attempts to acquire SJ's letters to Hill Boothby, see Waingrow, p. 237 n. 4.

[4] Bryanston St. runs between Cumberland and Portman Streets, parallel to and one block north of Oxford St. EM's house in Queen Anne St. East was about a mile to the north-east.

[5] EB's protégé French Laurence (1757–1809), later (19 Oct.) D.C.L., in 1796 was appointed Regius Professor of Civil Law at Oxford and elected to Parliament for Peterborough. JB first met him at Reynolds's on 15 Nov. and thought him "a fine fellow" (Journ.).

habit of recording throws a restraint on convivial ease and negligence.[6] I think after once your great work is done, which you seem to refer ad Graecas Calendas,[7] it will be of consequence to declare, that you have no thoughts of that kind more.

I have call'd twice or thrice in Queen St. but Miss B. has happened to be abroad.[8] There seems to be a great deal of business going on.—No packet,[9] or box from Bowles.—What an insufferable procrastinator! almost as great a one as another person of my acquaintance.

I have but just time for this post. So farewell. My best Compliments to Mrs. B. and believe me, Dear Boswell, Your sincerely Affectionate,

EDM. MALONE

I hope you received a Letter from me about a fortnight ago.

From Malone,
Friday 28 September 1787
MS. Yale (C 1912).
ADDRESS: James Boswell Esqre.
ENDORSEMENT: Mr. Malone.

Friday Night, Sep. 28, 1787

MY DEAR SIR: I have been so long such a sedentary creature that the movement to Cambridge for a week or ten days appears to me a great event;[1] and, I have been as busy this whole day (in providing a sufficient quantity of *copy* for my compositors, and arranging matters for the country) as if I was at the head of the Prussian troops before Amsterdam.[2]—However, I have stole a

[6] See pp. 98–100.

[7] "Never" (*ante* From EM, 19 Oct. 1785, n. 34).

[8] Veronica Boswell and JB's other children had accompanied him to London on 25 Sept. 1786 (Journ.). JB had taken only Mrs. Boswell and his son Alexander on this visit to Auchinleck (Journ. 13 Aug.).

[9] MS. "news" deleted before "packet"

[1] EM stayed with Dr. Farmer at Emmanuel College, Cambridge from 29 Sept. to 13 Oct., when he returned to London in a coach with Isaac Reed (Journ. 29 Sept., 13 Oct.; *Isaac Reed Diaries*, ed. C. E. Jones, 1946, pp. 154–57).

[2] A Prussian army invaded Holland when Wilhelmina, Princess of Orange, sister of Frederick William II of Prussia, was arrested on suspicion of intending to incite a rebellion. By 23 Sept. the Prussians had advanced to within four miles of Amsterdam, which capitulated on 10 Oct. (*Ann. Reg.* 1787, pp. 29–64; *Gent. Mag.* Oct. lvii. 919–23).

moment at Eleven at night, to tell you, your Johnsonian letters are all safe in my drawer, and that you are in high luck, for here is Mr. Humphry the painter just come from India, who has three more letters for you.—He is so good as to go with me for two days to draw my friend Dr. Farmer, for my book.[3]—I hope to be in town by Monday se'nnight, or Tuesday Sennight at farthest.—Farewell—Yours most truly,

E. M.

To Malone,
Monday 1 October 1787

Not reported. Sent to Cambridge from London 1 Oct. "Edmond Malone Esq. at Cambridge regretting his absence and hoping for his return" (Reg. Let.).

To Malone,
Saturday 8 March 1788
MS. Yale (L 936).
ADDRESS: To Edmond Malone Esq.

MY DEAR SIR: He who has but one servant must often be sensible of scanty accomodation (We shall *all* get into *rounding* I believe even in our shortest notes).[1] Mine has to go to Langton's where

[3] Ozias Humphry (1742–1810), portraitist and miniaturist, had gone to India in 1785 to find work and had returned because of poor health. At Yale are two undated letters from EM to Humphry, soliciting SJ's letters to him (*Life* iv. 268–69). The first (?16 Nov. 1787) is in the Osborn Collection; the second (?17 Nov. 1787) is bound into a presentation copy of James Boswell the younger's *Biographical Memoir of the Late Edmond Malone, Esq.*, 1814. Humphry accompanied EM to Cambridge on 29 Sept. and left on 3 Oct. (*Isaac Reed Diaries*, pp. 154–55). In the first volume of EM's edition of Shakespeare, facing p. 1, is an engraved collage of portraits of four Shakespearian scholars: SJ, Thomas Tyrwhitt, Richard Farmer, and Thomas Edwards. The engraving, by Thomas Holloway, has no attribution to the original artists, but the engraving of SJ is from the 1778 portrait by Reynolds, and the engraving of Farmer presumably is from Humphry's drawing.

[1] By "get into *rounding*" JB means to write rounded Johnsonian periods.

three of my children are at a Ball.[2] I hope then the *first* Vol. will come in time to go by your servant to Courtenay's with the *second.*[3] If not *Fata aspera*![4]—Upon reading again I am not *so much* disappointed.[5] But still I fear the *wet blanket* as Courtenay said.[6] My Wife is still very uneasy. I shall not fail tomorrow at five I hope and trust.[7] I am in truth most affectionately yours,

J. B.

I am going on with the *Life*—anything to the contrary notwithstanding. It *will* be a valuable Collection.

From Malone,
Saturday 8 March 1788

MS. Yale (C 1913).
ADDRESS: Mr. Boswell.
ENDORSEMENTS: [on recto] Mr. Malone on reading Dr. Johnson's Letters to Mrs. Thrale. [on verso] Mr. Malone on reading Mrs. Thrale's Collection of Johnson's Letters.

March 8

I sat up till four o'clock reading away as hard as I could, and then my candle went out and I could read no more; yet I was not able to finish the first Volume. The letters are, I think, in general very pleasing and exactly what I expected. I think you rate them too low.[1] I would not have one of them omitted.

[2] The ball was given on the birthday of Langton's son George (Journ.; Fifer, p. 21 n. 10).

[3] Mrs. Piozzi's *Letters to and from the Late Samuel Johnson, LL.D.*, 2 vols., was published by Strahan and Cadell on 8 Mar. (*Gazetteer*, 8 Mar. p. 1; *World*, 8 Mar. p. [1]). Dilly sent JB a copy a day earlier (Journ. 7 Mar.).

[4] "Harsh fate!" (*Aeneid* vi. 882).

[5] In his journal JB wrote that he was disappointed by the quality of SJ's writing, as well as by SJ's "fawning" upon Mrs. Thrale because of "luxurious living in her husband's house", which caused him to treat his friends, JB felt, "much more lightly than we had reason to expect". JB continues, "This publication *cooled* my warmth of enthusiasm for 'my illustrious friend' a good deal. I felt myself degraded from the consequence of an ancient Baron to the state of an humble attendant on an Authour. . . . I carried the volumes to Malone" (7 Mar.).

[6] The OED's first citation of "wet blanket" in its usual modern sense is dated 1810. Presumably JB feared that Mrs. Piozzi's volumes would diminish interest in further publications about SJ.

[7] Mrs. Boswell was again very ill with consumption; all the same, JB "went very lowspirited" to dine at EM's with Courtenay the next day (Journ. 9 Mar.).

[1] The first volume of Mrs. Piozzi's *Letters* runs to 397 pages. JB later thought better of them (Journ. 9 Mar.).

I see she has got one of your letters; about the Son who married against his father's consent; where he talks *of small-shot debts*.[2] How comes this?

I love him still more than ever. He had a most tender heart; and as much virtue, I believe, as falls to the lot of humanity. I hope heartily *Madam* will be trimm'd well for her suppression, and evident imposition with respect to his answer to her matrimonial notification.[3] All his documents concerning the value of truth, have been thrown away upon her.

I send you the first Volume, and you shall have the second in the Evening. I hope Mrs. Boswell is better. Yours Affectionately,

EDM. MALONE[4]

To Malone, Thursday 15 May 1788

Not reported. See *post* From EM, 17 June: "The short note which you sent me on the morning of your going away". This note contained directions for addressing letters to Auchinleck. JB left London for Auchinleck on 15 May to seek support for his Ayrshire candidacy in the upcoming Parliamentary election, to travel the Northern Circuit, and to fulfil his duties as Recorder of Carlisle (Journ. 15 May; *post* To EM, 12 July, 7 Oct.).

[2] For SJ's letter to Joseph Simpson, see *Life* i. 346–47 and *Letters SJ* i. 125–27. Copies of the letter were given to JB by both Mary Adey and Daniel Astle (Waingrow, pp. 67–71, 181). Miss Adey also gave a copy to Mrs. Piozzi (Waingrow, p. 67 n. 17). The sentence that EM refers to is, "Small debts are like small shot; they are rattling on every side, and can scarcely be escaped without a wound: great debts are like cannon; of loud noise, but little danger" (*Life* i. 347).

[3] In printing SJ's letters, Mrs. Piozzi had omitted that of 2 July 1784, which contained SJ's condemnation of her marriage to Piozzi ("you are ignominiously married"), and her firm reply of 4 July 1784 (*Letters SJ* iii. 174–75). She did print SJ's letter of 8 July 1784, in which he reluctantly gave his blessing to her marriage (iii. 177–78), immediately after her letter announcing her marriage (iii. 172–73), thus making it appear that SJ had given his blessing without hesitation, if not without misgivings.

[4] JB used the address side of this letter to jot down several notes for the *Life* (M 155:10), which include the comment: "Mrs. T.'s Letters. To see him waiting for letters from her and Queeney shews his mind had green sicknes; eat chalk tobacco pipes etc. etc."

To Malone,
Monday 2 June–Thursday 5 June 1788

MS. Yale (L 937). Sent 5 June. "Edmond Malone Esq. Account of my busy active life in the Country desiring to hear from him. Regretting my absence when Lord Sunderlin and the Ladies are at London" (Reg. Let.).

ADDRESS: To Edmond Malone Esq., London.

Auchinleck, 2 June 1788

MY DEAR SIR: This morning (being the first weekday of the month) I thought with pleasure on our *mensiversary* meeting at breakfast to read the Johnsoniana of the preceeding month in the E.M. G.M. etc. etc. etc.[1] and Monboddo's whim as to the soul being present in the place on which thought is fixed for the moment, was almost realised.[2]

My Wife though she made out the journey in six days and a half, being impatient to get home to her own appartment, has I think been rather worse since she came here.[3] Perhaps the agitation of travelling may have increased the fever; for her pulse is a good deal quicker than it was in London. The Physician whom I called to her from our County town,[4] a sensible honest man, fairly told me that he knew no medecine that could be of any service to her; that her constitutional disorder had been growing[5] worse from year to year, that she could not entirely recover, and that she must depend on light diet, good air, quiet, and moderate exercise for alleviating her complaints and prolonging her life. She is in the mean time sadly distressed and dismally apprehensive.

[1] JB and EM usually breakfasted together on the first of each month to read over the monthly magazines that had appeared that day (see Journ. 1 Dec. 1785; 1 Mar. 1786; 1 May, 1 June 1787; 1 Mar., 1 May 1788).

[2] In his *Antient Metaphysics*, 1779–99, ii. 303–09, Lord Monboddo states that the mind, when it thinks of a distant object, is in the same place as that object: "It is impossible to conceive any thing acting or energizing, where or when it is not. The substance, therefore, of the Mind, must of necessity be where or when it acts. . . . [It is] certain, that our Mind can transport itself to distant Places and Times, and there operate as it does upon objects present."

[3] JB, his wife, and four of his children (Veronica stayed in London) set out for Auchinleck on 15 May (Journ.) and arrived on 21 May (Book of Company).

[4] JB's Book of Company shows that Dr. John Campbell, physician of Ayr, stayed the night of 29 May. Dr. Campbell tended Mrs. Boswell in her last illness and died on 13 June 1789, having outlived her by only nine days (*Scots Mag.* June 1789, li. 310).

[5] MS. "increasin" deleted before "growing"

God may be pleased to recover her as upon former occasions. But I cannot help being much affraid.

As for myself, I have since I left you been blest with health and sound spirits, so that I have been enabled to enjoy and to bear, the good and evil of my existence, wonderfully well. Could such a state but last, I should be apt to contravert Johnson's gloomy notions of Life. But alas! I have had too much experience of a different state; and I may be persuaded that I shall have more. Much comfort and felicity have I had in your society, and much I still hope I shall have.

I have now been here a forthnight and must acknowledge that I have done very little to advance the Life. A few visits from intimate neighbours who notwithstanding my Wife's situation have been with me, and a great variety of business upon my Estate have occupied me, and supplied an excuse for indolence.[6] I shall however task myself as in London, and get on.

I see no paper but The P. A. in which there has been no mention what<ever> of *The Ode*. Pray what be<came> of it? Did it run at all <or was> it crushed in the bud?[7]

I am now writing on the 5th having been interrupted after having proceeded so far on the second. I hope you have had many *good days* in my absence, and that all the *Gang* are well. It will be very kind (if you *can* find a little leisure) to give me an Epitome of what has passed. Have your foreigners as we may now call them returned yet?[8] I regret being prevented from many agreable parties with them. I offer my best compliments to them, to Sir Joshua and Courtenay and young Jephson[9] who was good enough to call before I set out and missed me. I ever am, My Dear Sir, most affectionately yours,

James Boswell

[6] The Book of Company lists over a dozen visitors between 21 May and 2 June. In addition, JB must have been collecting his rents about this time (see From James Bruce, 9 June 1783; To James Bruce, 1 June 1786; To Andrew Gibb, 4 June 1791).

[7] JB's *Ode by Dr. Samuel Johnson to Mrs. Thrale upon Their Supposed Approaching Nuptials*, is dated 1784 but was actually published on 13 May 1788 (*post* From EM, 17 June, n. 21; *Lit. Car.* pp. 131–34). The first version was written on 12 Apr. 1781, the day after Henry Thrale's funeral; it is printed from the MS. in *Laird*, pp. 319–21. JB determined to publish the *Ode* on 9 May 1788 (Journ.), presumably as a riposte to Mrs. Piozzi's *Letters*; this much revised version, which includes a Preface, is reprinted in Mary Hyde, *The Impossible Friendship*, 1972, pp. 131–32.

[8] Lord and Lady Sunderlin and EM's sisters Henrietta and Catharine.

[9] Richard Mounteney Jephson (1765–1825), later (1815) Bt., barrister, son of

From Malone,
Tuesday 17 June 1788
MS. Yale (C 1914).

Queen Anne Street East, June 17, 1788

MY DEAR BOSWELL, The short note which you sent me on the morning of your going away has, with other causes, prevented my writing till now, for I knew not what to make of *Machline*, whether spelt with an *h* or a k, and could not conceive how such a direction could convey a letter to Auchinleck. To make matters quite sure, I wrote a line to your daughter last night, and have followed the address she sent me, though it varies from what I think you formerly used—Auchinleck, Cumnock, Dumfries.—[1]

I have had your letter of the 2d of June some time, and should have sent you a line before now, but that I have been in constant employment by the arrival of my brother and his family, who all *landed* safe in Queen Anne St. on the 3d of this month, the day after Sheridans first exhibition;[2] and for a week afterwards the running about in quest of tickets, and the actual attendance in Westminster Hall was, I assure you, very sufficient employment. It was settled that each of the managers should be entitled to have a Clerk, and Courteney was so good as to name me: so that I had an excellent place in the Managers' box, and went at my own hour. Never was anything like the anxiety for tickets; fortunately two of our ladies would not go through the fatigue of sitting so many hours: I say, fortunately; for my little interest could never have compassed three tickets, but I got one each day for my youngest sister[3] who was down each morning at the door by seven o'clock and supported with my assistance and that of a friend, the most

William Jephson, D.D., and nephew of Robert Jephson the poet and playwright (*Inner Temple* v. 484). Young Jephson's career is summarized in M. D. Jephson, *An Anglo-Irish Miscellany*, 1964, pp. 321–28. JB first met young Jephson at EM's on 12 Nov. 1787 (Journ.).

[1] A post office had recently been established at Mauchline (*post* To EM, 12 July), about two miles north of Auchinleck House. Veronica supplied a different post route (*post* To EM, 12 July). JB's *h* and *k* are ordinarily indistinguishable.

[2] On the first day (of four—3, 6, 10, 13 June) of his famous speech, R. B. Sheridan charged Hastings with having mistreated the Begums of Oudh. EM in some way has misdated his family's arrival.

[3] Catharine Malone (*post* To EM, 12 July).

shocking press I ever remember to have been in, from that hour till nine, when the doors opened. You may easily judge of it, when I tell you that Dr. Lawrence in assisting a lady lost half his coat, and many women and men their shoes, hats etc.[4] My brother also had a ticket each day, and young Jephson who was sitting with me quite in despair the night before the first performance, had the good fortune to be named unsolicited Windham's Clerk.—You have heard probably so much of this speech, as to be now tired of the subject: I will therefore only say in general, that it was one of the finest pieces of regular composition, of conclusive argument, of wit, of humour, of pathos, that I ever heard: and that it was as finely spoken as it was happily conceived. His minute recollection of facts and dates was astonishing; and all that part of the speech was certainly extempore: the very splendid parts undoubtedly were composed, for no human mind could on the sudden produce such an assemblage of beautiful images, always in the happiest words: but even these were spoken with such uncommon energy and rapidity, that for a[5] moment one could not but believe them the effusions of the instant. I am not sure that it will have such an extraordinary effect, when printed, though *in haec verba*;[6] for the action, voice and manner had undoubtedly a considerable share in the impression: but still it may, without any danger of suffering by the comparison, be placed beside any oration either of ancient or modern times; and has put[7] the speaker of it on such a pinnacle, that no one would be surprised if he was made Secretary of State to-morrow.[8]—It is utterly *impossible* Hastings should not be found guilty on this charge.[9]—I send you the Gazeteer, as you probably

[4] The London newspapers were filled with tales of the rudeness of the crowd. The following account, for example, appeared in *Pub. Adv.* 4 June, p. [3]: "A lady went into the Hall, almost in the *pure* stile of Eve. Instead of fig leaves, she had only her *shift* and *under petticoat*, the others were torn off. Her shift being longer than the petticoat, made a very whimsical appearance. Delicacy, however, felt for her situation, and every act that *decency* could suggest, in the midst of a *genteel gentle press*, was done to hide her situation."

[5] MS. "a" superimposed upon erased "the"

[6] In the same words.

[7] MS. "put" written above deleted "placed"

[8] For accounts of this speech and its treatment as a public show, see Walter Sichel, *Sheridan*, 1909, ii. 127, 147–69; Jerome Landfield, "The Triumph and Failure of Sheridan's Speeches against Hastings", *Speech Monographs* (1961) xxviii. 143–56; and F. Chatel de Brancion, *R. B. Sheridan*, 1974, pp. 168–76.

[9] Warren Hastings (1732–1818), Governor-General of India from 1774 to 1784, was being tried on charges of corruption and cruelty. The trial, which was taking place before the House of Lords, lasted from Feb. 1788 to Apr. 1795, when

have not seen it; and though it is very imperfectly taken, it is better than the other papers, and will give you some notion of this extraordinary performance.[10] He was just 14 hours in speaking it. When he had done, he sunk down quite exhausted, and Burke was so delighted, that he threw his arms round him, and embraced him. Just afterwards he shook hands with Jephson and me, who stood just behind,—"I wish you joy, I wish you joy; he is an honour to our country."[11] He[12] is a most amiable man, and has not one grain of envy in his composition. Gibbon was there every day, and was much delighted.[13] Being ask'd how he liked the compliment to himself, he said he must be either very vain or very foolish not to be highly gratified by it.[14] Never was anything better spoken or[15] more happily introduced than the compliment to "the *immortal leader of the prosecution.*"[16] I hope to meet them both at the Club to-day: it will probably be our last meeting.[17] Why are you

Hastings was acquitted. The most recent account of the trial is by P. J. Marshall, *The Impeachment of Warren Hastings*, 1965.

[10] Most of the London newspapers carried lengthy accounts of Sheridan's speech. Versions appeared in *Gazetteer*, 4, 7, 9, 11, 14 June; *Pub. Adv.* 4, 7, 11, 14 June; *Lond. Chron.* (3–5, 5–7, 10–12, 12–14 June) lxiii. 537–39, 549–50, 561, 573–75; *Morn. Her.* 4, 7, 11, 14 June; and *Gen. Eve. Post*, 3–5, 5–7, 7–10, 10–12, 12–14 June. Within a few days after the speech, at least five versions were advertised in book form (*Gazetteer*, 17–19 June, p. [1]; *Morn. Her.* 16 June, p. [3]; *Gen. Eve. Post*, 14–17 June, pp. [2, 4]). One of these, *The Celebrated Speech of Richard Brinsley Sheridan, Esq. in Westminster-Hall, on the 3d, 6th, 10th, and 13th of June, 1788, on his Summing up the Evidence on the Begum Charge against Warren Hastings, Esquire*, was reprinted with some changes from *Gazetteer*. A more complete version than any of these, made from shorthand notes taken at the trial, is printed in *Speeches of the Managers and Counsel in the Trial of Warren Hastings*, ed. E. A. Bond, 4 vols., 1859–61, i. 481–729.

[11] Presumably EM refers to Ireland, the birthplace of all four men.

[12] EB.

[13] MS. "with it" deleted after "delighted"

[14] Sheridan stated, "If you read all past histories—peruse the annals of Tacitus—read the luminous page of Gibbon, and all the ancient or modern writers that have searched into the depravity of former ages to draw a lesson for the present, you will not find an act of treacherous, deliberate, cool, cruelty that could exceed this" (*Speeches*, ed. Bond, i. 676). Gibbon later reflected on Sheridan's speech: "I shall not absolve or condemn the Governor of India, but Mr. Sheridan's eloquence demanded my applause; nor could I hear without emotion the personal compliment which he paid me in the presence of the British nation" (*The Autobiographies of Edward Gibbon*, ed. J. Murray, 1896, p. 336). According to Thomas Moore, when asked how he came to apply the word "luminous" to Gibbon, Sheridan whispered, "I said '*vo*luminous' " (*Memoirs of the Life of the Right Honourable Richard Brinsley Sheridan*, 5th ed., 1827, i. 511).

[15] MS. "than his" deleted before "or"

[16] Sheridan complimented EB, "the *immortal leader of the prosecution*", at length (*Speeches*, ed. Bond i. 621–22), but this particular phrase is not reported.

[17] Gibbon was president for the evening at The Club. Eight others were present, including EM, but EB and Sheridan were absent (Minute Book).

not here to participate in all this?—Courteney and I are often in want of you. We had a very good party on Sunday last at Sir Joshua's at Richmond; our ladies and my brother, Lord and Lady Townshend and his daughter,[18] Courteney, Devaynes, and I. We all regretted you were not with us, as we came home.—Lord Sunderlin means to go to Ireland in about ten days; and I am looking out for some ready furnished house in the country for Lady S. and my sisters and myself for two or three months. I wish to be near town on account of the press, and have some thoughts of trying for one in the neighbourhood of Camberwell or Dulwich; where if you should be able to return to *your wòrk*, I hope we shall be able to give you a bed,—without *ants* to disturb you.[19] In this day's paper there is a house somewhat farther off advertised,—in Kent; about 12 miles from London—This possibly may suit.[20]

The poem has gone off but badly, for want of your assistance. Finding it did not move, I made Faulder advertise it a second time.[21] Charlotte Wishfort was sent to the World, and was acknowledged to be not without humour; but was never inserted:[22] T. is a friend of the pretty Signora, and I suppose was

[18] George Townshend (1724–1807), first Marquess Townshend, and his second wife, Anne Montgomery (d. 1819), whom he had married in 1773, had both sat for Reynolds. Elizabeth (c. 1767–1811), was Townshend's daughter by his first wife Charlotte (d. 1770); she married in 1790 (*Gent. Mag.* May 1790, lx. 274). Reynolds's Engagement Book does not mention this gathering, but shows that he began a portrait of Lady Sunderlin the next day.

[19] On 16 July 1786, JB, EM, Courtenay, and his son John "dined under a tree" near Dulwich. JB wrote, "I wished for a room and table and chairs. We were troubled by ants" (Journ.).

[20] EM later settled on Cobham Park, Surrey (*post* From EM, 12 Aug.). The editors have not located the advertisement that he saw.

[21] *Ante* To EM, 2–5 June, n. 7. JB had written at least one paragraph on the *Ode* for *Pub. Adv.* (12 May, p. [3]); he kept a cutting for his archives (P 116:29): "Dr. Johnson's courtship of Mrs. Thrale, and his rage in being rejected for Signor Piozzi, which is said now to be *promulgated* by Baretti, is one of the most extraordinary things that we have yet had concerning our great Lexicographer. Query, Did Hawkins know this? Does Boswell know it? What are we to believe? Why have we not a detail? Why not some documents? Let us have all out." But JB's absence from London prevented further puffing. The *Ode* had earlier been advertised in *World*, 13 May, p. [1] and *St. James's Chron.* 13–15 May, p. [3]; it was advertised again in *Morn. Her.* 5 June, p. [1]. Robert Faulder (fl. 1779–84), bookseller in New Bond St., published the *Ode* (*Lit. Car.* pp. 131, 134; Maxted).

[22] The *World*, 22 May, p. [2], acknowledged receipt of "Charlotte Wishfort", remarking that it "has some humour, and shall be considered", but it was never published, and no copy is known to exist. The title is probably an allusion to Lady Wishfort, Congreve's ageing siren in *The Way of the World*, 1700. Besides "Charlotte Wishfort" and the *Ode*, JB had written at least two satirical poems on Mrs. Piozzi. One, his "Piozzian Rhimes", was published in *Lond. Chron.* (18–20 Apr. 1786) lix. 373 and *Pub. Adv.* 20 Apr. 1786, p. [2] (re-

afraid.[23] Besides, he[24] likes no body's nonsence but his own.[25] Baretti's *Strictures* in the European on the 1st of this month were very good; more temperate than usual; and prove decisively that Esther Lynch is a sad jade.[26]

I hope by this time Mrs. Boswell's native air has done her some good, and that her complaints are at least alleviated. Miss B. is very well, and Devaynes told me on Sunday that Mrs. Stevenson was much pleased with her frank and good disposition, and had no doubt that she would improve extremely in a short time by being with her.[27]

I have two other letters to write before I dress for the Club—so farewell at once—I beg you[28] will present my best compliments to Mrs. B. and believe me ever, Your sincerely Affectionate and faithful,

EDM. MALONE

P.S. The two vols. of Gray were not sent home with the other books.[29]

printed by Mary Hyde, *The Impossible Friendship*, 1972, p. 112 n. 149). The other, probably written in 1786, survives in manuscript (M 310), but probably was never published. It is an obscene attack on Mrs. Piozzi's second marriage, and contains references to the *Anecdotes* and Mrs. Montagu.

[23] Giuseppe Baretti (below, n. 26) called Mrs. Piozzi "the pretty Signora" in a letter of 20 Mar. to the editor of *Eur. Mag.* (Mar. 1788, xiii. 147; reprinted in Baretti, *Epistolario*, ed. L. Piccioni, 1936, ii. 315–16) and his "Stricture the Second" (*Eur. Mag.* June 1788, xiii. 393).

[24] MS. "the" deleted before "he"

[25] Edward Topham (1751–1820) was the proprietor of *World*, a newspaper known for absurd gossip, much of it written by Topham himself. In addition to serious works like *Letters from Edinburgh*, 1776, Topham wrote four popular farces, produced at DL and CG between 1780 and 1787. *World* was one of the few periodicals that was consistently friendly to Mrs. Piozzi during the publication of her Johnsoniana, but EM is mistaken in thinking this friendliness due to Topham, whom she knew little, if at all. Mrs. Piozzi's friend at the *World* was Topham's co-editor the Rev. Charles Este, a member of her social set who is often mentioned in *Thraliana* (Clifford, pp. 314–15).

[26] Giuseppe Marc' Antonio Baretti (1719–89) had instructed the Thrales' eldest daughter Hester Maria ("Queeney") in Italian from 1773 to 1776. For his notorious three "Strictures", on Mrs. Piozzi, see Clifford, pp. 322–26; and *post* From EM, 12 Aug. nn. 14, 17.

[27] Since May, Veronica Boswell had been enrolled in Mrs. Stevenson's boarding school in Queen's Square (Journ. 12–14 May). See further, *post* To EM, 12 July; From EM, 12 Aug.; To EM, 18 Sept. Veronica had spit some blood, and Devaynes (*ante* From EM, 3 Jan. 1786, n. 4), who visited the school, "had promised to attend to her health" (Journ. 13 May).

[28] MS. "you you"

[29] Presumably the Dublin edition in 2 vols. of *The Poems of Mr. Gray*, 1775. We know nothing further about these volumes.

2 Postscript. John,[30] just as I was sealing this, has told me, that Miss B. only *believes* the direction which she sent, is the true one; so after all perhaps it should be Cumnock. What a careless fellow you were not to write your Address at the end of your last letter!

To Malone,
Saturday 12 July 1788

MS. Hyde Collection (first two leaves); MS. Yale (L 938, last four leaves). See below, n. 8. "In the months of July and August and former part of September, I sent and received many letters which I have neglected to register. I wrote once to Mr. Malone and heard twice from him" (Reg. Let.). The two letters from EM are perhaps *ante* 17 June (JB recorded no letters received in June) and *post* 12 Aug.

York, 12 July 1788

MY DEAR MALONE: Your long letter came safely to me before I left Auchinleck on the 1st of this month, upon my own horse, to join the Northern Circuit here, which I have done. I was not careless as to giving you my address. It was formerly by Cumnock and Dumfries. But a post being now established at Machline the next village to me, I left a note of direction for you, *Auchinleck Machline by Edinburgh*. However my daughter's direction by *Kilmarnock* which is eight miles farther off, did very well.

It was very obliging in you to give me so full an account of Sheridan's celebrated summing up, which has undoubtedly been a very brilliant exhibition of talents; and I see the strong impression which it made upon you from the way in which you express yourself. But now that the fervour is somewhat abated, I hope you can bear to be told that I am still hopeful that for the honour of Britain and that of undoubtedly a great and meritorious Conductor of affairs which, however I may as a humane moralist disapprove, are sanctioned by this country, Warren Hastings shall upon the whole be found not guilty.[1] It is fair to tell you that I dined yesterday with the ArchBishop of York, and that the Wines

[30] EM's servant John Bullock (*post* To EM, 4 Dec. 1790, n. 24).

[1] JB had met Hastings at Reynolds's on 19 Mar. 1787 and called on him a day later. Throughout Hastings's trial JB remained a loyal supporter.

(in particular the Burgundy) were excellent, and given with Archiepiscopal hospitality.[2]

You fully excused yourself for your long silence in the "vacancy" of which my "keen eye"[3] was beginning to see unpleasing possibilities. You must have indeed been a very busy man, and I rejoice that you was so successful, and that our estimable young friend Jephson enjoyed what he deserved. Miss Catharine Malone shewed a spirit truly milesian in repeatedly encountering the perilous struggles at the door of the Hall. As nobody could be admitted without tickets it was surely very illjudged in those who had them to assemble so early. But a good place upon such an occasion is something though I think it was bought too dear.

I am glad that you have had, and are to have so much agreable time with your Ladies. You know what a Circuit is, by supposing something rather better than what you have seen;[4] and you may guess how I contrast my situation with yours. I am however animated with the consciousness of acting with a very manly spirit, and though a dreary remonstrance from my spanish brother, that I am lessening myself when there is not the least probability of my getting business,[5] be seconded by my having no brief here, I am not cast down. I attend diligently, I take good notes, I feel a gradual accession of knowledge, and I look forward with hope. Indeed I was assured of three briefs at Newcastle

[2] JB had met William Markham (1719–1807) at Court on 27 May 1781 (Journ.), but prepared the way for this visit to Bishopthorpe, the Archbishop's residence, with a letter of recommendation from John Thomas Batt (below, n. 17). A long account of this visit appears in JB's journal for 11 July. "It is fair to tell you" may allude to Markham's support of Hastings; years earlier Markham had been a close friend of EB's (Cone i. 217–19, ii. 251; Sir Clements Markham, *Markham Memorials*, 1913, ii. 8–10, 19–25, 36–38, 55).

[3] Cf. *Hamlet* III. iv. 117.

[4] EM had practised law in Ireland (see Introduction, p. 167); perhaps JB is contrasting the English with the Irish courts.

[5] JB calls Thomas David Boswell his "spanish brother" because he had been a merchant for twelve years in Valencia (*ante* From EM, 26 Aug. 1785, n. 1). T. D. had consistently opposed JB's English bar scheme; on 11 June 1787, for example, JB wrote, "He pressed upon me the discreditable appearance which I made here [in London], not being either in parliament, or in practice at the bar, or having fortune sufficient to enable me to make a figure suitable to the rank of my family" (Journ.; see also Journ. 12 Feb., 8 June, 23 July 1786). Reg. Let. mentions "several letters" from T. D. in July, August, and early September (none of which has been reported); presumably he wrote his latest "dreary remonstrance" in early July.

before I left London.[6] This is all *biographical* as we have pleasantly talked.

Before I set out from Auchinleck, my Wife had a very favourable remission of her severe and alarming complaints. The country air, Asses milk, the little amusements of ordering about her family, gentle exercise, and the comfort of being at home and amongst old and valuable friends[7] had a very benignant effect upon her; and I would fain flatter myself that she may recover though not full health, yet such a degree of it as that she may enjoy life moderately well. Her preservation is of great importance to me and my children, so that there is no wonder that I suffer frequently from anxious apprehensions, which make me shrink. I sometimes upbraid myself for leaving her; but tenderness should yield to the active engagements of ambitious enterprise. I am not sure whether I shall go all round this Circuit, though I rather think I shall, unless I hear that she is worse. But you will be very angry when I confess to you, that I have not yet advanced a single page in Johnson's Life, since I left London. The truth[8] is that during the six weeks that I was at Auchinleck I was in some degree indolent or rather averse to sedentary exertion; I had a great deal of business to settle in the management of my estate, and having been a declared candidate for the County ever since the last election I found such an appearance of stirring, that it was proper for me to begin my canvas directly, in which I tell *you*, not ostentatiously, that I have met with more success than I expected.[9] You know that in the scotch counties there are comparatively speaking few freeholders, I suppose not above 300 in any County; and if the votes which I and many others call *nominal and fictitious votes* be struck off according to the Lord Chancellor's opinion, I suppose there will not be above fourscore in Ayrshire. But the uncertainty as to the *sincerity* of each of those votes (as Lord Thurlow well expressed himself) that is to say

[6] Charles Douglas Currie, the London attorney who had assured JB of the briefs, wrote on 20 July to report that he had "found the Parties Plaintiffs and Defendants most inflexibly bent on settling their differences by Arbitration", but that they would pay JB's fee even though they did not require his services.

[7] The Book of Company records a number of visitors to Auchinleck in June.

[8] The fragment from the Hyde Collection ends with the catchword "truth" at the bottom of the page, and the Yale fragment (L 938) begins with the word "truth".

[9] The last election was the General Election of 1784. For JB's Parliamentary ambitions during this period, see *Pol. Car.* pp. 149–53.

being really and true the freehold of the voter, and not a vote *by* the *Grantor through* the voter, will make our county elections curiously dubious if no law be made to ascertain with more precision the legality of our votes.[10] I stand between two parties—the State Coalition interest which is to support one candidate, and a strange coalition between Lord Eglintoune and Sir Adam Fergusson who are both with the present administration, but which has given great offence to many of their friends, who will therefore prefer me who am of the same political way of thinking, without having the exceptionable circumstance of being in a confederacy to enthral the County. Thus I am; and I assure you the business of what we call *riding the County*, and being as civil and agreable to every body as possible is fine training. I return to Auchinleck from the Circuit, that I may complete my round of the Freeholders, and arrange a variety of matters concerning my Estate.[11] Now do not scold me; for, I promise to set apart so much time for the Life, that the rough draught shall be all done, and brought with me to town early in[12] October;[13] and you know that till the rough draught be finished we cannot proceed in the Metropolis. I might come a little sooner; but as I must hold the Michaelmas sessions as Recorder of Carlisle,[14] it would be

[10] For an account of the complicated Scottish electoral system, and the decision of the Lord Chancellor, Edward Thurlow (1731–1806). first Baron Thurlow, on nominal and fictitious votes, see *Pol. Car.* pp. 5–6. The number of Ayrshire votes stood at 224 in 1787, at 221 in 1790, and at 110 in 1791 (*Ayrshire*, p. 102).

[11] The "State Coalition", headed by the Earls of Cassillis, Dumfries, and Glencairn, had supported the late Fox-North Coalition. Archibald Montgomerie (1726–96), eleventh Earl of Eglinton, and Sir Adam Fergusson of Kilkerran (1733–1813), Bt., since 1774 had divided the county in a conflict essentially between aristocratic and gentry interests. But both being supporters of Pitt, Henry Dundas persuaded them in 1784 to share the representation in turn, Hugh Montgomerie of Skelmorlie, Eglinton's heir, being chosen in the General Election of that year for Parliament. This "strange coalition", as JB calls it, easily dominated the political scene in Ayrshire. Now there were rumours that Montgomerie would resign from Parliament to accept a government post, and JB wished to rally those disaffected by the Eglinton-Fergusson alliance behind him (for further details see *Pol. Car.* pp. 108–23, 150–53). Under 11 Sept. JB wrote in the Book of Company, "I was much from home canvassing the County".

[12] MS. "early in" written above deleted "in the beginning of"

[13] Of course, JB did not have the rough draft finished by October; see *post* To EM, 17 Nov.

[14] Since 1786 JB had been connected with James Lowther (1736–1802), first Earl of Lonsdale, a powerful and unscrupulous politician, serving as Mayor's Counsel in the 1786 election in Carlisle and, beginning in Jan. 1788, as Recorder, or principal legal officer, of Carlisle. For a detailed account of JB's involvement with Lord Lonsdale, see *Pol. Car.* pp. 131–49, 161–64.

travelling 300 miles and back again, for being a week or two more in London.

Your kind mention of a bed for me in the rural retreat where I suppose you now are (I hope at dear Dulwich) is very flattering.[15] Pray present my very best compliments to the Ladies, who I hope are to pass the winter in London. Much much do I regret the sad reason which will prevent my having a family to receive them in Great Queen Street, where we have had some days aye and nights never to be forgotten.

Sir Joshua I doubt not is as well as he can be, in the constant enjoyment of his art and the best Society. Do not fail I pray to put him and Courtenay in cordial[16] remembrance of me. Whom did I meet unexpectedly in my way to York but Batt, on a ride out from Harrogate, where I agreed to go three miles out of my road to dine with him at his mess, which I did jovially, in the Reynoldsian style,[17] and we had an ample conversation concerning the fair Palmeria,[18] which I reserve till I have the pleasure of *joying* with you over some old Oporto.[19]

The accounts which you give me through the medium of Devaynes of Veronica please me much. To have a daughter in the capital boarding school of Queen Square is an agreable circumstance. Had I taken your advice sooner it might have been better. But pecuniary deficiency is an embarrassing thing. I trouble you with a letter to my daughter.[20] I intend to bring my two sons with me, and venture them at Westminster school, as I can controul them from time to time.[21] A separation however for a long time of

[15] *Ante* From EM, 17 June, n. 19; *post* From EM, 12 Aug.

[16] MS. "cordial" written above deleted "kind"

[17] For JB's meeting with John Thomas Batt (c. 1746–1831), barrister, see Journ. 5 July. They had met several times at Reynolds's house (Journ. 31 May, 12 Aug., 24 Nov. 1787), and Batt was among the mourners at Reynolds's funeral (C. R. Leslie and T. Taylor, *Life and Times of Sir Joshua Reynolds*, 1865, ii. 633).

[18] Mary Palmer (1750–1820), Reynolds's niece, cared for him during his last years and inherited most of his estate at his death in 1792. In the same year she married Murrough O'Brien, fifth Earl of Inchiquin, later (1800) created Marquess of Thomond.

[19] An allusion to Courtenay's ode "To Edmond Malone, Esq.", one line of which reads, "No B[oswe]ll joys o'er wine" (*ante* From EM, 3 Jan. 1786, n. 3).

[20] Not reported.

[21] EM's "advice" apparently had been to send the children to boarding-school, but JB had been held back by the expense (Journ. 3 Dec. 1787). He wrote in his journal for 12 May, "Waited on Mrs. Stevenson. . . . Stated my difficulties, and how she [Veronica] should have come sooner". James, Jr. went to Westminster School in 1790, but JB sent Alexander to Eton in 1789. Both had entered Soho

my family is dreary. You my dear friend can well believe me in this.

I am somewhat alarmed that the *Ode* though so truly good has not moved. It is I fear a slight symptom of a cooling as to Johnson. I have inquired for it at several shops here, in vain though most of the new publications are to be had. I have not seen a word about it except in the Monthly Review which allows it to be *witty*, but thinks the story improbable. Pray be so good as to inquire for me how many are sold. When I return to town, I will shew you how I shall *puff* the embers into a flame.[22] So let Faulder carefully preserve them. "Look to't I'll do't."[23]

And what becomes of Shakespeare amidst all this hurry of harangues, and parties with Ladies, and rural felicities?[24] "Pray Sir may I be allowed to ask Are not you the Commentator upon Shakspeare?"[25] I need never be ashamed while you stand between me and publication—while Mr. Malone's coach stops the way.

I have written you a still longer letter than that with which you favoured me. Be kind enough to let me hear from you again, if in the course of this month *On the Northern Circuit*, if afterwards *Auchinleck Machline Dumfries*. I ever am yours most affectionately and faithfully,

James Boswell

Academy in 1786, but Alexander was now being tutored at home by an assistant master from Soho. See *post* To EM, 8 July 1789, nn. 3, 5.

[22] *Monthly Rev.* (June) lxxviii. 528, printed only a brief notice, which reads in part, "It is a pity this piece of wit (for witty it is) had not a better foundation. Nature and probability are too much violated in the supposition of matrimonial views on the part of Johnson after the death of his friend Thrale." *Crit. Rev.* (Sept.) lxvi. 252–53, was to be less kind: "We have not seen a more bare-faced catchpenny; for a drauling reader might peruse, with ease, these lines in three minutes. . . . One stanza, however, is not bad, but one alone we can rescue from oblivion." The review then quotes the third stanza. The *Ode* not having been reviewed favourably, JB took it upon himself to praise it in the *Life* (iv. 387 n. 1). *Crit. Rev.* was closer to the truth in its prediction of the poem's oblivion, for a number of loose sheets turned up later at Auchinleck, suggesting that JB was not able to "*puff* the embers into a flame" (*Lit. Car.* p. 134).

[23] JB echoes Mr. Bayes's Prologue in Buckingham's *The Rehearsal*, I. ii: "Look to't, look to't; we'll do't, we'll do't: look to't, we'll do't."

[24] MS. "felicties"

[25] Presumably a reference to an occasion on which someone accosted EM with this question.

From Malone,
Tuesday 12 August 1788
MS. Yale (C 1915).

London, Aug. 12, 1788

MY DEAR BOSWELL: Here is at least the *fifth* frank I have got from Courteney for you without being able to fulfill my intention of writing to you. For near three weeks I was a strenuous election-partizan, from my regard to our friend, who was a principal manager;—"Townshend for ever!" was the word. I was lucky enough to get a few votes[1]—The opposition party are much pleased with their victory and Fox is gone in *triumph* to Switzerland,[2] in spite of all the impudent abuse thrown out against him and his friends by Parson Horne and Mr. Topham.[3] It is manifest that the latter has twice had a cane over his head since the close of the election, by some friend of the Dutchess of Devonshire,[4] and by a country man of mine Mr. D. O'Brien, to whom T. has made a most abject submission.[5] Since the election I have been in a

[1] Lord John Townshend (1757–1833), an intimate friend of Fox's and member of the Devonshire House circle, had defeated Vice-Adm. Samuel Hood, first B. Hood [I.] in a violently contested by-election for Westminster by a vote of 6,392 to 5,569, the poll having closed on 4 Aug. "Our friend" undoubtedly is Courtenay, who had remained loyal to Fox and the Opposition though his patron George Townshend, fourth V. Townshend (John Townshend's father), had gone over to Pitt and been created first M. Townshend in Oct. 1787 (Namier and Brooke i. 336, ii. 262, iii. 553).

[2] Fox remained on the Continent until the Regency crisis in November recalled him post-haste.

[3] John Horne Tooke (1736–1812), clergyman turned politician, had joined with Pitt in a "constitutional club" that supported Hood's candidacy (above, n. 1). He published a pamphlet called *Two Pair of Portraits* (the Elder and Younger Pitts in contrast to Fox and his father), 1788, severely criticizing Fox. Topham's attacks on Fox, in *World*, appeared almost daily in early August. See, for example, 4 Aug. p. [3, cols. b and c], 6 Aug. p. [3, col. 1].

[4] During the Westminster election, *World* published witty but often personal attacks on Fox and his supporters and, in particular, intimated that the morals of the ladies who canvassed for Townshend were less than strict. But in the issue of 8 Aug. [p. 2] *World* regretted the items it had printed in "a spirit of *Calumny against Women*" and apologized especially to Georgiana Spencer Cavendish (1757–1806), Duchess of Devonshire, and Anne Trevor, Lady Dungannon.

[5] Dennis O'Bryen (1755–1832), surgeon turned playwright, journalist, and pamphleteer, was a friend and zealous supporter of Fox. *World*, 4 Aug. [p. 3] printed a ludicrous story about O'Bryen which mentioned, among other things, his having been "actually tried at the Old Bailey for the murder of a Constable" during the Westminster election of 1784. The issue of 6 Aug. [p. 3] printed an apology to O'Bryen, explained that the charge of murder had been lodged anonymously and

constant hurry with family matters. After a six weeks' search we have at length got a country house—Cobham Park, near Cobham, in Surrey, 18 miles from town; and are to go there the day after to-morrow. I have stolen a quarter of an hour to write to you from a morning that is to be entirely devoted to business: for besides packages for the country, enquiries about waggons etc. I have a great deal of arrangement to make in my house, and am presently to[6] engage in an arduous business—the taking down all my books and putting them into my 'drawing room, preparatory to my house being painted, inside and out: a most disagreable business, that I have deferred from year to year till it can be deferred no longer.

Did I tell you in my last that Hayes had published 13 of Johnson's Sermons under the name of Taylor. The title page is cautious. They are "Sermons *left for publication* by Dr. Taylor".[7] They are excellent in my opinion.—You were very right in charging me with having *Frank's* letter.[8] I found it the other day in my drawer of papers, which is in such a *regular confusion* that I am sure of finding whatever I have miss'd, *at some time or other*.—We have had one or two very good days here, and wanted you much to have been with us. During the tumult of the election, Sir J. R. Courteney, young Jephson[9] and Metcalf[10] dined with me and *my*

without any evidence whatever, and asserted, "The prosecution alluded to in that article . . . we considered, together with every person who ever heard the circumstance mentioned, to have been the most wicked and abandoned conspiracy against a Gentleman's life, that villainy ever designed or infamy ever attempted to perpetrate". As late as 23 Mar. 1789, an allusion to Topham's retraction appeared in *Star*, in a poetical dialogue between "The Captain [Topham] and the Curate [Rev. Charles Este]", another editor of *World*:

CURATE.—Oft am I sorry for the words you eat.
CAP.—What! from O'——N? I'd have else been beat.

(Lucyle Werkmeister, *The London Daily Press, 1772–1792*, 1963, pp. 173–74).

[6] MS. "just" deleted before "to"

[7] The Rev. Samuel Hayes (c. 1749–c. 1795), usher at Westminster School, published *Sermons, on Different Subjects, Left for Publication by John Taylor, LL.D.* in two volumes, the second of which appeared in 1789. JB listed them among SJ's works (*Life* i. 24, iii. 181), and modern scholarship has supported his attribution. According to the most recent editors of the sermons, SJ wrote all but one (the eighth in vol. 2), though Taylor probably revised some others (*Works SJ* xiv. pp. xxi–xxxv).

[8] Francis Barber (c. 1742–1801), SJ's black servant and residuary legatee. "*Frank's* letter" is perhaps that of 2 Apr. authorizing JB to demand from Sir John Hawkins all books and papers that had belonged to SJ (From Barber, 2 Apr.; To Barber, 11 Apr.).

[9] MS. "young Jephson" written above deleted "D.J." (see below n. 20.).

[10] Philip Metcalfe (1733–1818), M.P. for Horsham and wealthy brewer, was a friend of Reynolds and SJ, who made him

ladies; and on the morning of the day I was lucky enough to light on Burke, who had come from Beconsfield the night before.[11] He came to us, and was in great spirits—various, talkative, and delightful. I need not tell you it was a good day. He was a great treat to my sisters, who had never seen him before, and who were much flattered by his notice. Having sat[12] between them, and got after into some metaphysical or rather moral disquisition with them, they sustained the argument so well that when they went from table, he exclaimed to me, "Who are those two very extraordinary women?" You may be sure I did not fail to gratify them by the report. I cannot help telling you of a beneficent action of these two most excellent women, which only came to my knowledge last night—When they were at Nice they found a poor man of the name of *Michelle*, who knew a little English and taught french. They soon found his mind to be much above his situation, and finding him very poor, and sickly, and old in constitution, though not sixty, they became interested about him. The poor man to gain a scanty livelihood, was forced to teach 12 and sometimes 14 hours a day, and when he ceased to be able to teach, had nothing but poverty and misery and disease before him. They gave him about 20 Guineas to pay such little debts as he owed and settled a pension upon him of 18 Guineas, a year, for life which they commissioned the Nice Banker to pay him;—a Guinea and a half on the 1st day of every month. The poor man's heart overflowed with gratitude; for the last year he was enabled to attend to his ill health, and to leave off his laborious employment. They had many letters full of gratitude from him at different times after their leaving Nice: but last night received one which brought tears to my eyes. It begins "Quand vouz lizez ceci, je n'existerai plus." It was partly written in April last and he requested the Nice Banker to transmit it after his death. He died on the 27th of July last, and just was able to add a few lines to what he had written before, requesting his kind benefactors would in case he died before the first day of the ensuing month, make one payment more, to enable his widow to bury him. They mean to do more

trustee for Francis Barber's annuity (Namier and Brooke iii. 133; *Life* iv. 505).

[11] On 1 Aug. EB wrote to Charles Burney from Beaconsfield, intending to send the letter when he arrived in London (*Corres. EB* v. 408–09). If EB reached London on the evening of 1 Aug. EM's dinner must have been on 2 Aug.

[12] MS. "got" deleted before "sat"

than that for a daughter of his, about 15, and have more heartfelt satisfaction in having smoothed the latter hours of this poor man than in all the enjoyment that pomp and gold can give.[13]

Reed who called upon me about a fortnight ago told me that Baretti had sent one more *Stricture* on *the pretty Signora*, containing the promised history of the *Bastard*:[14] but it was so stinging that the proprietor had some doubts as to *safety*:[15] and accordingly I find it did not appear the first of this month. The fact it contained was this: La Signora used to say, you know, in her husband's lifetime that her partiality for P. arose from his being as she supposed a natural son of her father's when he was at Rome. Her marriage was somewhat at variance with this. However, says B. very soon after Thrales death she resolved to marry the Signor; but thinking it not decent to do so "ere the funeral baked meats were cold"[16] she proposed to him that he should take a tour to Italy to see his relations. Being pretty *sure* that he was of an amorous constitution, she was afraid he might in his travels defraud her of her rights by anticipation, and so engaged a frenchman, whose name I have forgot, to attend him, and to see that no wrong was done her. This man she promised to pay £100 to for his trouble, but when the service was done, refused to pay him. He has turned informer and on his information B. tells this story.—What a Jade she is![17]

[13] Three letters from Michel to the Misses Malone, dated 25 Jan., 7 and 19 Feb., are in the Bodleian Library (MS. Eng. Letters c. 15, ff. 34–38).

[14] Towards the end of his "Stricture the Second" on Mrs. Piozzi's edition of SJ's letters, Baretti had written, "I will endeavour in my following Strictures to entertain him [the reader] with more sportive details; and, among other diverting subjects, give him some account of a bastard brother; a story not to be matched by any novel in Boccacio's Decameron" (*Eur. Mag.* June, xiii. 398).

[15] *Eur. Mag.* was run by a group of proprietors, of whom Reed was the most active, though he did not wish to be known as the editor (*Lit. Illus.* vii. 48). The present letter suggests that EM may not have realized how prominent a role Reed played among the proprietors.

[16] Cf. *Hamlet* I. ii. 180–81.

[17] According to Baretti's "Stricture the Third", finally published in *Eur. Mag.* (Aug.) xiv. 89–99, Mrs. Piozzi had convinced her first husband, Henry Thrale, that Piozzi was a natural son of her father's born in Brescia. (She did remark in her journal that Piozzi was "amazingly like" her father—*Thraliana* i. 448 n. 7.) Baretti also asserted that before her second marriage Mrs. Thrale promised an Italian named Mecci an annuity of £50 (among other rewards) to accompany and spy on Piozzi during a trip to Italy. After marrying Piozzi she refused to pay Mecci, who had offended Piozzi by a foolish toast at their wedding banquet, and he was forced (following Baretti's advice) to get her solicitor to intervene to secure his annuity. Contemporary readers as well as modern authorities tended to discredit Baretti's

I saw Veronica about a month ago, and she was then well, and seem'd reconciled to her situation. I make no doubt she will be greatly improved by it: but you will never cease to delude yourself with *sounds*.—What has THE GREAT BOARDING SCHOOL IN QUEEN'S SQUARE to do with the matter? Any other place where good English manners could be attained, would do just as well.[18]

Poor Courteney has been much out of order this some time past. I wish he could get to Bath. He promises us a few days at Cobham.[19] I hope you will do the same when you come. D. Jephson[20] is to be with us, and we are in the neighbourhood of a most deligh[t]ful country; so we shall do very well. If you do not bring up *the Life* complete, expect no mercy.

I was rejoiced to hear that Mrs. B. had found such benefit from her native air; and hope she continues to mend. Pray present my best Compliments to her and Euphemia; to whom you will do great injustice, if you do not give her a snatch of Queen's Square.[21]—Here is much more than a quarter of an hour for you—However I must now break off—So farewell at once, and believe me in every place Your most truly Affectionate

EDM. MALONE

The poem, I fear, has done nothing. Here is a strange book come out, called *A History of living authours*. I have escaped very well. The[22] author mentions your Corsica with praise, and barely

strictures *in toto* (Clifford, pp. 323–24; *Thraliana* ii. 616 n. 3), but Baretti at least believed his own stories since it is unlikely, as Norbert Jonard has pointed out, that he would lie to himself in his own marginalia to Mrs. Piozzi's *Letters to and from the Late Samuel Johnson, LL.D.* (*Giuseppe Baretti*, 1963, p. 438; the marginalia are edited by D. C. Gallup, "Giuseppe Baretti's Work in England", Diss. Yale 1939, pp. 216–66). EM's phrase, "Being pretty *sure* that he was of an amorous constitution", may reflect an earlier version of this "Stricture". In a letter to Mrs. Piozzi after her second marriage in 1784, Baretti accused her of having had sexual relations with Piozzi before marriage, which she vehemently denied (*Thraliana* ii. 615–16).

[18] Veronica was homesick in Mrs. Stevenson's boarding-school (To Margaret Boswell, 9 Nov.; Veronica Boswell to Margaret Boswell, 7 Dec.). In To EM, 12 July, JB had written, "To have a daughter in the capital boarding school of Queen Square is an agreable circumstance." It was known as "the ladies' Eton" (Wheatley and Cunningham iii. 132).

[19] For some time, both Courtenay's finances and his health had been precarious; however, the exact nature of his complaint is unknown (Journ. 20 Mar. 1787; 23 Feb. 1788; *post* From EM, 29 Sept.).

[20] Richard ("Dick") Jephson.

[21] Mrs. Stevenson declined to accept Euphemia as her pupil, though JB considered attempting to persuade her to do so (To Margaret Boswell, 28 Jan. 1789—MS. Rosenbach Museum and Library).

[22] MS. "They" deleted before "The"

enumerates your two pamphlets and the Journal.[23] In the Account of Burke, he mentions that his first attempt in Britain was standing as a candidate for a professorship of logick in Glascow; that he had but very few votes, and that the successful candidate Mr. *James Clow* is still living. Can this be true? It is entirely new to me.[24]

To Malone,
Thursday 18 September 1788

MS. Yale (L 939). "Edmond Malone Esq. that my canvas of the County must excuse my not having written a line more of Johnson's Life. I shall sit down *doggedly* in London and perhaps drink no wine till it is finished. My Wife is uneasy at her sons leaving her; but it is for their good. Begging a consolatory letter by return of post" (Reg. Let., misdated 25 Sept.).

ADDRESS: To Edmond Malone Esq., Queen Anne Street East, London.
POSTMARKS: MAUCHLINE [London] SE 22 88.

Auchinleck, Mauchline N. B. 18 Septr. 1788

MY DEAR MALONE: Your very kind and animated letter "upbraids my too tedious delay"[1] every time that I look upon it. But, if you were busy with the Westminster Election I have been more so with that of Ayrshire. My chief object is the General Election. But it is believed that we are to have a vacancy declared as soon as Parliament meets, by our present Member's getting a Place of £500 a year.[2] Lord Eglintoune and Sir Adam Fergusson our County Coalition as heterogeneous as the Great One are

[23] *Catalogue of Five Hundred Celebrated Authors of Great Britain, Now Living*, 1788. Of JB's *Tour* the compiler writes, "In 1786 [*sic*] he published a Journal of a Journey to the Western Islands of Scotland undertaken with doctor Samuel Johnson in one volume octavo."

[24] T. W. Copeland has dismissed this story as "a particularly hardy legend" (*Corres. EB* i. 129). In 1751–52 David Hume competed for the chair of Logic formerly occupied by Adam Smith, who was transferred to the chair of Moral Philosophy; but James Clow (d. 9 July 1788) won the seat (James Coutts, *History of the University of Glasgow*, 1909, pp. 221, 312; J. H. Burton, *Life and Correspondence of David Hume*, 1846, i. 350–51).

[1] Not located.

[2] Hugh Montgomerie (1739–1819), M.P. for Ayrshire, 1784 to 27 June 1789, when he was appointed Baggage-Master and Inspector of the Roads in North Britain (*Pol. Car.* p. 160; Namier and Brooke iii. 158–59). (JB repeats the £500 figure in To W. J. Temple, 2 Aug. 1789—MS. Pierpont Morgan.) Montgomerie's appointment would necessitate a by-election.

attempting to impose upon us a gentleman from another county nominated by Dundas.[3] This a number of us feel as an insult, and are therefore resisting it. I am as yet the only declared candidate in opposition to it. I know not what chance I have of success, as a meeting is called to consider of a proper person;[4] but my exertion at present will be of service to me against the General Election. Pray then accept of this apology for my silence for too long a time, nay for my having done nothing to Dr. Johnson's Life—Literally nothing—not a single line of the remaining part of the first draught which I hoped and trusted should be completely finished here. It will require an exercise both of your philosophy and indulgent friendship to make allowance for me. But just consider half my time on the Circuit—half on politicks, county politicks, and the arrangement of my lands. I see that *the Whole* will be of London Manufacture. I am to be at Carlisle to hold the Michaelmas Sessions as Recorder on the 7th October, and shall proceed *to town* reckoning to be there about the 15th. I shall then set myself *doggedly*[5] to my task, and be *totus in hoc*.[6] I even think of *resolving* not to taste wine till it be done; and *that* I think will make me work hard indeed. I am however seriously uneasy at this delay, and I beg of you to comfort me, instead of scolding me. I have always found you a mild Confessor.

You have had I find some excellent days; that when you drew Burke the 20000£ prize[7] must have been exquisite. But how it was not at first told him who the Ladies were, puzzles me. It was however the occasion of a proud moment to them and to you, with good reason. I am much obliged to you and to Miss Catharine for your visit to *Queens Square*, of which Veronica informed me.[8] I

[3] The Eglinton-Fergusson-Dundas coalition (*ante* To EM, 12 July and n. 11) had selected William MacDowall (c. 1749–1810) of Garthland, Renfrewshire, to stand as a stop-gap for Fergusson, who would be returned at the next General Election (*Pol. Car.* p. 153; Namier and Brooke iii. 83). The "Great One" refers to the short-lived Fox-North Coalition.

[4] This meeting of freeholders, which took place on 25 Sept., unanimously proclaimed JB the candidate of their choice, but seems to have been poorly attended (*Edin. Adv.* 26–30 Sept. 1. 213–14; *Pol. Car.* p. 153).

[5] *Life* v. 40 and n. 3, v. 110; see *ante* From EM, 19 Oct. 1785 and n. 16; To EM, 27 Oct. 1785 and n. 4.

[6] "Wholly (engaged) in that", a legal phrase.

[7] The grand prizes in the State Lotteries were generally £20,000; three such prizes were awarded on 11 Feb. 1788, when £500,000 in all was given away (C. L'Est. Ewen, *Lotteries and Sweepstakes*, 1932, pp. 207–08).

[8] Veronica's letter has not been reported.

confess the influence of *sounds*. The *Great Boarding School* does certainly impress me. *Sound* also incites me to send my boys to one of the *Great Schools*. But I am distressed what to determine concerning them. Their mother who though much recovered is still afflicted with her former complaints in a considerable degree is miserably anxious about them, and allows herself to fancy that their health will suffer when under the care of strangers, and that she will never see them again. Her tender concern would make me leave them here this winter, if I had a good english tutor for them. Yet I consider that her uneasiness will probably abate when they have been a little while from her, and she has heard that they are well; and that it will be of essential advantage to them to have an english education. My present intention is to send them both, but certainly the second to Westminster; so I am to bring them with me. My fear is that when I have them again in London my irresolution may again keep them unsettled with only such advantage as Soho Square affords.[9] I intreat to hear from you by return of post with some *mental bark*.[10] As I imagine Courtenay may be still out of town, I address this directly to your house. If you write as late as the 26 or 27 your letter will come to me before I set out, and I do request it.

The taking down your library etc. etc. must appear mighty operations. But it will be agreable to see the clean freshness. You will *live pleasanter*.[11] Your rural retreat has I hope answered your expectations. Happy shall I be to share it with you, if it does not *dissipate* my *Johnsonian* concentration. Your account of the charity of your sisters has all the *story* of romance and all the *truth* of Christian Benevolence. Pray present my very best compliments to them.

What is Courtenay doing and to do?

I shall shew you how I can make the Ode fly yet *Virum per ora*.[12]

[9] *Ante* To EM, 12 July and n. 21.

[10] "Jesuit's Bark" or quinine was regarded practically as a panacea, useful in treating "mortifications and putrid ulcers, also in petechial and purple fevers . . . [and] small-pox" (*Gent. Mag.* May 1749, xix. 209). It was also used to treat sore throats, measles, suppression of urine, scrofula, and gout. The OED credits JB with the first metaphorical use of "bark" in his comments on the *Rambler*: "in no writings whatever can be found *more bark and steel for the mind*" (*Life* i. 215).

[11] "As Mr. Burke once admirably counselled a grave and anxious gentleman [Langton], 'live pleasant' " (*Life* i. 344; see also *ante* To EB, 10 Apr. 1784).

[12] JB refers to EM's report in his letter of 12 Aug.: "The poem, I fear, has done nothing." For the Latin, see *ante* To EM, 30 Oct. 1785, n. 24.

At present I am under one of those clouds with which Johnson was prest, but which I hope you shall never know. I ever am, My Dear Malone, more and more your affectionate Friend,

JAMES BOSWELL

Be so good as to buy for me the History of the Island of Veritas 2/6 Sewel[13] and put it up in packets addressed Countess of Craufurd[14] and these under cover of Hugh Montgomerie Esq. M.P. Mauchline N.B. and see they are not 2 oz. weight.[15]

Pray remember Mauchline with an H in the middle.

My overseer who stands by me says my letter looks like a Dublin Journal, full all round.[16]

From Courtenay, Jephson, and Malone, Monday 29 September 1788

MS. Yale (C 838, C 1590, C 1916).

ADDRESS in Courtenay's hand: Jas. Boswell Esqr., Recorder of Carlisle.
FRANK: Cobham Septembr. Twenty ninth 1788. Free J. Courtenay.
POSTMARKS: 21 COBHAM [London] SE 30 88, FREE S.
ENDORSEMENT in EM's hand: Mr. Boswell will be at Carlisle on the 7th of Octr.—

Cobham Park, Sepr. 29, 1788

[in Courtenay's hand] DEAR BOSWELL: You would be delighted with the *Aristocratic*[1] dignity and Convenience of this Mansion;—

[13] *A True and Faithful Account of the Island of Veritas* by Jasper Richardson (pseud.) was published in late August by Charles Stalker, bookseller at No. 4 Stationers' Court, Ludgate St. The book was sold by John Sewell (1734–1802), bookseller at No. 32 Cornhill, as well as by Stalker (Maxted; *Gen. Eve. Post*, 23–26 Aug. p. [3]). An account of a Unitarian Utopia imitative of *Gulliver's Travels*, it was reviewed unfavourably in *Crit. Rev.* (Nov. 1788) lxvi. 422–23 and *Monthly Rev.* (Dec. 1788) lxxix. 525–28.

[14] Jean Hamilton Lindsay (c. 1735–1809), Countess of Crawford, was a close friend of the Boswells and is mentioned frequently in JB's journal.

[15] Members of Parliament could send and receive free of charge letters weighing two ounces or less (R. C. Alcock and F. C. Holland, *The Postmarks of Great Britain and Ireland* [1940] p. 185).

[16] JB's overseer James Bruce (1719–90) forwarded parcels of newspapers during JB's absence from Auchinleck. He refers to Thomas Todd Faulkner's *Dublin Journal*, 1725–1825, a newspaper with exceedingly narrow margins. The present letter is on a single sheet folded so as to make two leaves (four pages). The body of the letter is written with virtually no margins; the first postscript is written upside-down between the salutation and the beginning of the text, and the last two postscripts take up the corners of the fourth page.

[1] Courtenay underlines *Aristocratic* be-

especially with the Addition of Malone's Hospitality.—Dont think of quitting the Joys of wine—as you threaten in your last; if you do—Your life of Johnston will resemble—Sir J. Hawkins[2].—Mr. Jephson—is much pleased—with your Connubial *Ode* to the Signora.—He wishes to see—and hear you—Let him speak for himself.[3]—Best Compliments and wishes to Mrs. Boswell—and Believe me—Yours faithfully and Affectionately,

J. COURTENAY

[in Jephson's hand] Mr. Jephson takes the liberty to add in his own hand that he is ambitious of having the honor of being personally known to a Gentleman whom he has so often admired in his writings, and hopes to meet Mr. Boswell here about the 11th or 12th of[4] Octr.[5]

[in EM's hand] You see by the other side that you, as well as we, have had a loss by your sojourning so long in Caledonia. Courtenay and Mr. Jephson (the author) came to us on Thursday, and are this moment (Monday Morn) set out for London. Jephson has not been here for 21 years, so that much is new to him, and he new to many. He is as pleasant as ever, in spite of the creeping on of *non intellecta senectus*.[6] We had a good day at Sir Joshua's last week, and he promised to come to us here, but never came. Jephson's stay in England is to be but short. His wife is gone forward with her brother to Bath,[7] and her husband means to follow her about the middle of next month, and so to proceed to

cause it was a recently imported French neologism (*Oxford Dictionary of English Etymology*, ed. C. T. Onions, p. 49).

[2] Sir John Hawkins's (1719–89) *Life of Samuel Johnson, LL.D.* appeared as the first volume of the collected works of SJ (11 vols.) on 20 Mar. 1787 (Waingrow, p. 197 n. 1), and was issued separately the same year. For EM's remarks on it, see B. H. Davis, *Johnson before Boswell*, 1960, pp. 188–94.

[3] Robert Jephson had been a close friend of EM's since their schooldays. EM wrote an Epilogue for his *Count of Narbonne*, 1781, and a Prologue and part of an Epilogue for *Julia*, 1787.

[4] MS. "instant" deleted before "of"

[5] JB's endorsement on a letter from Lonsdale shows that he did not arrive in London until 26 Oct. (From Lonsdale, 22 Oct.).

[6] "Obrepit non intellecta senectus", Juvenal, *Satires* ix. 129: "old age is creeping on us unperceived" (trans. G. G. Ramsay, Loeb ed.). Jephson was now fifty-two years old.

[7] Jephson's wife (d. 1797) was Jane Barry Jephson, daughter of Sir Edward Barry, Bt., physician and Professor of Physic in the University of Dublin (M. D. Jephson, *An Anglo-Irish Miscellany*, 1964, p. 310; M. S. Peterson, *Robert Jephson*, 1930, p. 14; *Comp. Bar.* v. 384). She had two surviving brothers, John (c. 1727–94), Dean of Elphin, and Robert (c. 1731–c. 1791–94), a barrister (*Comp. Bar.* v. 385 and n. b).

Ireland. However, he has promised us a few days before he goes,[8] and Courteney with him; so that I hope you will decide your causes at Carlisle as expeditiously as you can, and make what haste you can here; that you may not lose some pleasant hours, which as life passes away, become more and more valuable. We have an excellent house here, and four or five spare bed chambers. Pray write me a line from Carlisle, to say whether you think you can get away from thence so as to be here by the 12th of Octr. which is Sunday sen'night.

Your neglect of Johnson's Life is only what I expected. Scotland is not the place for it. If you don't get to press by December, you will not be able to have it out in May. My Shakspeare goes on but very slowly; hardly a sheet a week, and a dreadful outcry for copy. I have three plays yet to revise and prepare, to say nothing of the printing of them: beside the Preface to write, and the History of the old Play houses to amplify and print: So that if I can publish on[9] the first of February, it will be the soonest.[10]

Courteney has been as pleasant and amiable as usual, and is in tolerable good health. His affairs much as they were; except that he has been able to raise a sum of Three hundred Pounds and to pay off an old demand against him at Tamworth. But this does nothing for the future. He hopes to get to Bath for a month, which is always of great service to him: but we will not let him go till after the[11] middle of next month.—I have been two or three times in London to see how they were going on at my house; and must spend two days there the beginning of next week to put my library in order, and to leave the front room (which is now entirely covered with books and lumber) free for the painters. The

[8] MS. "goes," written above deleted "leaves town"

[9] MS. "on" superimposed on erased "by" (first word on page). At the bottom of the preceding MS. page, "by" is not deleted; so MS. reads "by on"

[10] The ninth volume of EM's edition of Shakespeare was to contain *Romeo and Juliet*, *Hamlet*, and *Othello*. Presumably EM had yet to prepare the texts of the sonnets and other poems, which were to be in volume ten along with *Titus Andronicus*, the poem *Romeus and Juliet*, an Appendix of textual notes, and a Glossary. To the Preface and "Historical Account of the English Stage", which were to be prefixed to the first volume, were added Prefaces by SJ, Steevens, and Pope, a biography of Shakespeare, a revision of EM's "Attempt to Ascertain the Order in Which the Plays Attributed to Shakspeare Were Written", first published with Steevens's edition of Shakespeare in 1778, and other material. EM's prolegomena grew so large that the first volume was finally issued in two parts. Like JB, EM was too optimistic about the date of publication of his Shakespeare. It did not appear until Nov. 1790.

[11] MS. "his" deleted before "the"

younger Jephson is still here, and accompanies me generally. We have a hired Phaeton that[12] holds three, and turns to excellent account. It is just gone off to Kingston with our friends: there they will get a postchaise that will carry them to London in little more than an hour. When I go next there, I will get the book that you desire. This Letter will get to Carlisle three or four days before you: but I suppose the Postmaster will have the sense to keep it.—These are but trifling matters for a *grave judge*, but such as they are they are meant to convey the best wishes of your sincerely Affectionate,

EDM. MALONE

To Malone,
Tuesday 7 October 1788
MS. Hyde Collection.

Carlisle, 7 October 1788

MY DEAR MALONE: Was ever any man more unlucky than I am at this time. Such tantalising do I experience. The rich letter—the constellation from yourself, Mr. Jephson and Mr. Courtenay was lying for me here. But alas! I found before I left Auchinleck that I could not raise £500 (which *must* be paid in London about the first of November) in the way that I was flattered to beleive I could do it, so I am under the necessity of going back in order to get it.[1] I hope a few days will suffice, and then I shall hasten to *town*.[2] I

[12] MS. several illegible words deleted before "that"

[1] On 26 Oct. 1787 JB borrowed £300 from Charles Dilly (to whom he already owed £200) and £200 from Henry Baldwin, to repay a debt of £575 to Robert Preston, M.P. for Dover (Journ. 26 Oct. 1787; "View of My Affairs", 1787—A 52; Namier and Brooke iii. 326). JB used the wood on his property of Templand as security for the £500 he owed to Dilly, and set 1 Nov. 1788 as his due date for repayment (A 26). To repay this debt, JB sold his Templand wood for £650, paid in four bills (promissory notes) of £162. 10*s* each. One of these he "discounted", or sold to the bank of Hunter and Co., Ayr, for less than face value, and the other three he used as collateral for a loan of £300 from the same bank. He borrowed £200 from the Bank of Scotland, to be repaid from his December rents, and used the sum of £500 to repay Dilly on 28 Oct. 1788. He borrowed £200 from W. J. Temple to repay Baldwin ("View of My Affairs", 1788—A 52; A 26).

[2] JB left Auchinleck for Carlisle on 3 Oct. and returned on 9 Oct. He set out for London on 20 Oct., arriving there on 26 Oct. (Book of Company; *ante* From EM, 29 Sept. n. 5).

beseech you to prevail on Mr. Jephson not to go till I get to you. I am exceedingly vain of his notice, and should be sadly mortified were I to miss him.[3] O this auri sacra *fames* which I translate this cursed *want* of gold.[4]

Pray give my best compliments to Mr. Jephson and to our excellent friend Courtenay. The description of your present situation enchants me. I trust I shall have one or two noctes coenaeque Deum—ay and Dearum.[5]

The Life shall be finished with assiduous dispatch, and we shall do nobly yet. I ever am, My Dear Sir, most affectionately yours,

JAMES BOSWELL

To Malone,
Monday 17 November 1788

MS. Yale (L 940).
ADDRESS: To Edmond Malone Esq., Cobham Park, Surrey.
POSTMARK: [London] NO 17 88.

London, 17 Novr. 1788

MY DEAR MALONE: I was very sorry that I could not stay longer in the very agreable society at Cobham Park. But in truth I was so very ill (GOD only knows the cause) that I was quite[1] unfit for you.[2] I continued so after leaving you till friday evening, when the cloud began to break, and ever since I have been better.[3] I am now so well as to be a match for Miss Catharine for I do not think the day too long. I dined at home every day last week with my

[3] If JB came to Cobham in time to see Robert Jephson, their meeting has not been reported. JB saw Jephson frequently in London in Jan.–Aug. 1790 (Journ.).

[4] "Accursed hunger for gold" (*Aeneid* iii. 57, trans. H. R. Fairclough, Loeb ed.). JB forces the sense of the Latin.

[5] "O noctes cenaeque deum", Horace, *Satires* II. vi. 65: "O nights and feasts of the gods". JB adds "Dearum", "of the goddesses".

[1] MS. "quite" written above deleted "very"

[2] JB wrote to his wife on Sunday 9 Nov.: "I wearied of the *country* at Mr. Malone's and staid only a day and a half, and two nights."

[3] In the absence of a journal for this period, the chronology is hard to fix. JB reached London on 26 Oct. (*ante* From EM, 29 Sept. n. 5); he stayed at least until 28 Oct. and probably until 2 Nov., when he had Veronica, his brother T. D., and Mrs. and Miss Buchanan to dinner (*ante* To EM, 7 Oct. n. 1; To Margaret Boswell, 9 Nov.). Presumably he paid his visit to Cobham some time before 8 Nov., when he and Veronica dined with Reynolds (ibid.).

children only, and for the five last days of it did not taste fermented liquor. Yesterday I dined at Metcalfe's with Sir Joshua and Miss Palmer, Mr. Townly,[4] Dr. Lort,[5] Sir William Scott,[6] a nephew of Metty's and his Lady.[7] It was a very good day.

Yesterday forenoon I went to make love to Mrs. Hacket,[8] but young Jephson was there before me. I was happy to hear good accounts of you all from him.

During all this time I have laboured at the Life, and what I wonder at, have done very well. I am now half done with 1783, so that there remains no more but a year and a half of the first draught to do. But then the Conversation with the King is to be formed into a complete scene out of the various minutes[9]—my Correspondence with him is to be excerpted—and the whole series of the Composition is to be revised and polished. I intend to make a Skeleton of the Whole, or a Table of Contents in the chronological order, and have it examined by some of the most Johnsonian freinds and by steady Reed—that any omissions may be supplied.[10] Cadel whom I met in the street the other day,

[4] Charles Townley (1737–1805), the engraver and antiquary, whose well-known collection of classical sculpture JB had visited several times (Journ. 12 Apr., 25 May 1781; *Diaries of William Johnston Temple*, ed. Lewis Bettany, 1929, p. 27; BP xv. 229; *Life* iii. 118 n. 3).

[5] Michael Lort (1725–90), D.D., antiquary, was a prebendary of St. Paul's Cathedral and librarian at Lambeth. In the *Life* (iv. 290 n. 4) JB calls him "my late worthy friend . . . of whom it may truly be said, *Multis ille bonis flebilis occidit*" (Horace, *Odes* I. xxiv. 9: "Many are the good who mourn his death", trans. C. E. Bennett, Loeb ed.).

[6] William Scott (*ante* From EM, 11 June 1785, n. 7) had been knighted on 3 Sept. (W. A. Shaw, *The Knights of England*, 1906, ii. 300).

[7] When Philip Metcalfe (*ante* From EM, 12 Aug. n. 10) called JB "Bozzy", a familiarity tolerated only from SJ, JB retaliated by calling him "Mettie" (Waingrow, p. 589 n. 1). The nephew mentioned may have been Christopher-Barton Metcalfe (1759–1801), son of Metcalfe's older brother Christopher; his "Lady", whom he married in 1787, was Sophia, daughter of Robert Andrews of Auberies, Essex (*Burke's Landed Gentry*, 1851, i. 859; *Gent. Mag.* 1787, lvii. 452 and 1794, lxiv. 582).

[8] EM's cook; see *ante* To EM, 30 Oct. 1785; From EM, 5 Nov. 1785.

[9] JB wrote, "The particulars of this conversation I have been at great pains to collect with the utmost authenticity, from Dr. Johnson's own detail to myself; from Mr. Langton, who was present when he gave an account of it to Dr. Joseph Warton, and several other friends, at Sir Joshua Reynolds's; from Mr. Barnard; from the copy of a letter written by the late Mr. Strahan the printer, to Bishop Warburton; and from a minute, the original of which is among the papers of the late Sir James Caldwell, and a copy of which was most obligingly obtained for me from his son Sir John Caldwell, by Sir Francis Lumm" (*Life* ii. 34 n. 1). See Frank Taylor, "Johnsoniana . . . Boswell's Use of the 'Caldwell Minute' ", *Bulletin of the John Rylands Library* (1952–53) xxxv. 235–47.

[10] In an octavo notebook now at Yale (M 147) JB made a chronological list of the events of SJ's life, his letters, and his

raised my hopes by saying he was convinced mine would be the only Life that would be prefixed to Johnson's Works.[11] I forgot to mention another operation that remains to be performed which is selecting and arranging in proper places the Memorabilia furnished by Langton, Maxwell, Steevens, Seward.[12] You see my freind Richard is himself again.[13] I long to be with you again and shew you that I am independent both of more wine, and a hot supper which are indeed the *resources* of uneasy craving. I shall work assiduously to get my Magnum Opus concluded. It will be something for me to rest upon. I may perhaps surprise you with a visit soon by throwing myself into the Guildford Coach. But pray let me hear from you, that I may be sure not to miss you.

I say nothing of the strange state of Government. Only that I could lay a considerable bet that all will be well again. There will be curious doings on thursday when Parliament meets.[14] I hope Courtenay will come.

Pray present my very best respects to the Ladies; and beleive me to be ever most affectionately yours,

JAMES BOSWELL

publications. He also made a chronological list of SJ's writings from 1760 to 1777, which he sent to Isaac Reed, who entered additions and returned it (To and From Isaac Reed, 21 Apr. 1790).

[11] Thomas Cadell (1742–1802), bookseller in the Strand, had been a friend of SJ's; his son Thomas, in partnership with William Davies, published the fourth to eighth editions of the *Life* (*Lit. Car.* pp. 171–75). The life most frequently prefixed to SJ's works was Arthur Murphy's *Essay on the Life and Genius of Samuel Johnson, LL.D.*, 1792, though JB's *Life* was included in one early nineteenth-century edition (Waingrow, p. 282 n. 3).

[12] JB used a large block of Langton's anecdotes to fill in 1780 (*Life* iv. 1–33), a year in which he had not seen SJ, and for the same reason used the anecdotes of William Maxwell (1732–1818), D.D., to fill in 1770 (*Life* ii. 116–33). Steevens's few anecdotes are grouped under 1784 (*Life* iv. 324–25). JB had little faith in the accuracy of the anecdotes supplied by Anna Seward (1742–1809); after condensing them, he inserted them in various places in the *Life* (Waingrow, p. 54 second n. 2; see also index, *Life* vi. 348). Waingrow prints the surviving Johnsoniana from these four sources.

[13] Colley Cibber, *Tragical History of King Richard III*, 1700, V: "Conscience avant; *Richard's* himself again."

[14] George III had fallen ill in the middle of October and was now clearly insane, which if he did not recover would necessitate the establishment of a regency. On Thursday 20 Nov. the House of Commons met only briefly, agreed that it had no power to act in the King's absence, and adjourned for a fortnight, hoping in the mean time for an improvement in the King's health.

FROM MALONE, 19 NOVEMBER 1788

From Malone,
Wednesday 19 November 1788
MS. Yale (C 1917).
ADDRESS: James Boswell Esqre., No. 56, Great Queen Street, Lincoln's Inn Fields, London.
POSTMARKS: 21 COBHAM [London] NO 20 88.

Wednesday, Nov. 19

MY DEAR BOSWELL: I was very glad to find by your letter that you were working so hard. We hoped to have had a glimpse of you when we were in town last, but I suppose the blue devils engaged you at home. If you wish to be a man of *great consequence*, you will come down to us on Saturday next, and bring with you a full and true account[1] of what was done on the preceding day and thursday.[2] Perhaps if Courtenay be come, as I make no doubt he is, and[3] the house adjourns on friday for ten days or a fortnight, he will come with you:—in that case you two could come in a chaise to Kingston and I would send the Phaeton there to meet you. Let me know your plan by a line written on Friday Evening, which I shall get at 8 on Saturday Morning.

I suppose C. is in high spirits:[4]—My best wishes to him. No trimming composition of J——s[5] will do—Horse and foot shall they *all* go.[6] They had better not have held up their heads so high.

I am endeavouring to pull up lost time—but am frightened at what I have yet to do.—Farewell—Ever most faithfully and affectionately yours,

E. M.

[1] "A full and true account" was a stock phrase in the titles of broadsides and pamphlets describing murders, battles, revolts, and various kinds of disaster.

[2] *Ante* To EM, 17 Nov. n. 14.

[3] MS. "he will" deleted before "and"

[4] Courtenay, being a member of Fox's party, would have been delighted with the prospect of a Regency headed by the Prince of Wales.

[5] Presumably EM refers to Charles Jenkinson (1729–1808), created first Baron Hawkesbury in 1786 but popularly called Jenky (e.g. Journ. 24 May 1789). As the King's confidant he was widely credited with great secret influence. The King and he, it seems, had discussed an "all-party Administration" after North's fall in 1782 (Namier and Brooke ii. 677), but EM may have been aware that he had supported the move of the St. Albans Tavern group to bring Pitt and Fox together in early 1784 (*Later Correspondence of George III*, ed. Arthur Aspinall, 1962–70, i. 71 n. 5). If Jenkinson himself proposed some compromise between them it has not been reported.

[6] Proverbial: "They will all be overthrown."

To Malone,
Saturday 2 May 1789

Not reported. Sent from Auchinleck. "Edmond Malone Esq. of my wife's severe illness and that I know not how to leave her, but must if possible be in London 25 May to appear for the Corporation of Carlisle in a Cause in the K[ing's] B[ench] etc." (Reg. Let.). The cause in which JB was to appear had been brought by five men to whom the Corporation had refused licenses to keep inns in Carlisle (Lg 54, 55). JB set out for London via Lowther on 19 May (Journ.).

From Malone,
c. late June 1789

Not reported. See *post* To EM, 8 July: "I thank you for your letter which I cannot doubt is that of a sincere friend." Doubtless a letter of condolence on the death of Mrs. Boswell on 4 June. Reports of her death did not appear in the London newspapers until after mid-June (*Pub. Adv.* 17 June, p. [3]; *Lond. Chron.* 16–18 June, lxv. 578); presumably EM wrote after reading her obituary or, like Paoli, after hearing the news from T. D. Boswell (From Paoli, 19 June).

To Malone,
Wednesday 8 July 1789

MS. Yale (L 941). Sent 8 July. "Edmd. Malone Esq. of my distress. To know when he leaves London as that will regulate my coming" (Reg. Let.).

Auchinleck, 8 July 1789

My Dear Malone: I thank you for your letter which I cannot doubt is that of a sincere friend.[1] The expressions that you *shrunk*

[1] On 4 June JB, having been in London only a week, received word from Euphemia and Dr. John Campbell that Mrs. Boswell was dying of the consumption that had afflicted her since 1776. He and his sons Alexander and James set out that evening

from the subject and that I must have had a *dreadful time* satisfy me that you have conceived my distress. It is indeed a very afflicting complication, upon which it is unnecessary to enlarge. I can freely say to *you* who know me intimately with all my seeming inconsistencies, that Religion affords me much comfort. Of this I am *sure*, so that there can be no question as to the *effect* upon *my own mind.*

Your counsel I take very kindly; but when we meet I will explain to you how I cannot comply with it.[2] Mean time I beg your advice and assistance as to my eldest son. He is a boy of good sense good talents and good dispositions; but from his having a rupture he has been kept at home too long, and been too much indulged. He is now almost fourteen, and I wish much to send him for a year or two to one of the great schools in England, to open his mind as to social life, and get him some genteel companions. He is a very determined Scotch Laird. But I will try to give him a tolerable share of learning and polished manners. Be so good as to ask of Jephson with my best compliments to get me a very particular state of Eton—the education to be had—the expence etc.—And whether there would be any danger there to one with my son's complaint. I *must* send him from me somewhere.[3] Could I get him into the same house with Mr. Tighe's son I should like it.[4] My second son is to be continued for some time at Soho Academy. He is to be a Barrister at Law. I can manage him as I chuse.[5]

And now My Dear Friend let me beg to know when your

and "posted from London to Auchinleck night and day" in just over sixty-four hours, only to find that Mrs. Boswell had died the day they had left London (To W. J. Temple, 4 June and 3 July—MS. Pierpont Morgan).

[2] EM's advice to JB has not been reported.

[3] Sandy enrolled at Eton on 15 Oct. and remained there until 1792. For R. M. Jephson's possible connection with Eton through Edward Tighe, see next note.

[4] Edward Tighe (fl. 1753–97), who had attended Eton in 1753–58, was a Member of the Irish Parliament, 1763–97. A friend and warm promoter of Robert Jephson, in 1775 he had persuaded Horace Walpole to write an Epilogue for Jephson's *Braganza* (R. A. Austen-Leigh, *The Eton College Register, 1753–1790*, 1921, p. 518; *Corres. HW* xli. 287, 458). The Jephson mentioned here, however, must be R. M. Jephson (see *post* From EM, 19 Aug. and n. 2), who no doubt also knew the Tighe family. Tighe's son George William (1776–1837), who had attended Eton since 1785, lived in "Weston's", a house run by Mrs. Catherine Harris; Sandy, too, lived there after his arrival at Eton (Austen-Leigh, pp. xxix, 59, 518; To Alexander Boswell, 28 Oct.).

[5] James Boswell the younger ("Jamie") remained at Soho Academy until he entered Westminster School, 7 June 1790.

elegant Work will really be out, and when you are to go to Ireland; for upon that will depend my time of returning to London.[6] I have been very busy in getting my affairs here put in a proper train. I am to set out for the Northern Circuit on the 20 or 21, for however unpleasant it is, I cannot help thinking that it is necessary for me to go at least once a year to keep up my professional appearance. If I can have the benefit of your revision of my Life of Johnson for any reasonable time were it but three weeks, after the Circuit is over, I would settle matters so before setting out from hence, that I could hasten to town the moment the Circuit is over which will be I reckon about the 25 of August.[7] You will receive this I hope on Monday the 13 or tuesday the 14 instant. If you write to me on either of these days or Wednesday the 15, I shall receive your letter in time *by Mauchline N.B.* You may believe that to be among my *intellectual friends* again will be highly agreable so far as I now can relish any thing; and when I am once more in London, I shall not slacken till my Magnum Opus is launched. What a satisfaction is it to me, My Dear Malone that I have such a friend as you. It will please your truly kind heart to be told that since I parted from you I have not drunk a bottle of wine any one day. My *double* parental charge I trust will make me steady in avoiding what is surely very wrong. My best compliments to Courtenay and Jephson. I ever am your faithful and affectionate,

JAMES BOSWELL

From Malone,
Wednesday 19 August 1789
MS. Yale (C 1918).
ADDRESS: James Boswell Esqre.

London, August 19, 1789

MY DEAR BOSWELL: I received your former letter very safe, but not

[6] EM left London for Ireland as soon as he had read the last proof of his edition of Shakespeare, 19 or 20 Nov. 1790. The edition was published on 29 Nov. 1790 (*post* To EM, 4 Dec. 1790).

[7] In his Book of Company JB wrote, "On Monday the 10th [Aug.] I set out with intention to take a part of the Northern Circuit but felt my mind so sore that I avoided it. . . . I returned on friday the 28th." Most of this interval JB spent at Lowther (To W. J. Temple, 23 Aug.—MS. Pierpont Morgan). He then returned to Auchinleck, staying there except when performing his duties as Recorder of Carlisle (21–24 Sept.) until he left for London on 1 Oct. (Book of Company).

till the day was pass'd, beyond which you said it would be in vain to write to you; and I imagined that you were in the mid carreer of the northern circuit.

Jephson is gone to France with Windham to pay a visit[1] to the new Gallick Patriots. They sailed on Thursday the 13th from Brighton to Dieppe.[2] I however had mentioned to him your inquiry about your son, and he had no doubt that a place might be had in the same house with Mr. Tighe's son.

The town is a desart. Courtenay and I had thoughts of going down to Brighthelmstone for a few days, on last Sunday, but some family affairs prevented him: and one of our inducements was taken away, for Sir J. Reynolds who had been there for a week, came from thence last Saturday. Poor Sir J. has had a great misfortune, he has entirely lost the use of one of his eyes, he fears by a cataract but that is not ascertained; and he is, not without reason, very low spirited, lest the other should fail also. We are all uneasy about him from his plethorick habit, lest he should have some stroke; and counselled him, as strongly as we could last Sunday, without alarming him, to have the best advice, and to lose blood etc. as that might have a great effect on his remaining eye. The failure may possibly be of the paralytick kind, tho' he has no other symptom of complaint.[3] I mean to see him tomorrow, and hope he has consulted both Hunter and Warren or Baker, as he promised us.[4]—If anything should happen to him, the chain of our[5] society at least, would be sadly broken:—but let us hope the best.

[1] MS. "visit" superimposed upon erased "new"

[2] Windham, Richard Mounteney Jephson, and Sylvester Douglas (later Lord Glenbervie) stayed in France until 9 Sept. (*The Diary of the Right Hon. William Windham*, ed. C. A. Baring, 1866, pp. 184–85; *Windham Papers* i. 89; *Charlemont Papers* ii. 123–24).

[3] On 13 July, in the midst of a sitting, Reynolds's career as a painter ended suddenly when the vision of his left eye became impaired. Within ten weeks he entirely lost his sight in that eye and was apprehensive lest he should lose vision in his right eye as well. His ailment was diagnosed as gutta serena, a disease of the optic nerve, but was more likely "a retinal detachment such as often occurs in medium degrees of short sight. What probably lay behind it, however, was a malignant tumour caused by disease of the liver" (Derek Hudson, *Sir Joshua Reynolds: A Personal Study*, 1958, p. 210).

[4] John Hunter, surgeon (1728–93), Richard Warren, physician (*ante* From EM, 13 Jan. 1786, n. 13), and Sir George Baker (1722–1809), President of the College of Physicians, were all friends of Reynolds and his circle. All attended, at one time or another, members of JB's family.

[5] MS. "our" superimposed upon erased "soc"

I proceed as usual diligently, but yet make no great progress. I am resolved not to go to Ireland till I have finished my Shakspeare. I have yet a play and a half to print, beside the History of the Stage which is now at the press, and my preface to write[6] as well as print. I suppose I cannot possibly get away before the 1st of November.

The sooner you come to us the better it will be for us all, and particularly for Your sincerely Affectionate,

EDMOND MALONE

To Malone,
Wednesday 30 June 1790

MS. Yale (L 942). "Wrote to Malone a long complaining letter, anxious lest he should be gone or his Shakspeare ready before my return" (Journ. 30 June).
ADDRESS: To Edmond Malone Esq., Queen Anne Street East, London.
POSTMARKS: CARLISLE [London] JY 3 90.

Carlisle, 30 June 1790

MY DEAR MALONE: I do not think it is in the power of words to convey to you how miserable I have been since I left you. I had just time to mention to you the sudden annunciation of the dissappointment of my vain hopes in one respect, owing indeed more to what I was told by others than to my own opinion—But the disappointment was afterwards aggravated by the harshest and most degrading discovery of the opinion formed of me. You know the wretched state of spirits in which I had been for some time, and you may imagine how I was depressed and fretted, and although there was better behaviour in the course of the journey, how my spirit was tormented, to think what a dupe I had been, and that I was now compelled to a most disagreable service without reward or hope of any advantage.[1] This is the tenth day

[6] MS. "print" deleted before "write"

[1] On 14 June Lonsdale demanded that a reluctant JB accompany him to Carlisle as Recorder to settle some business concerning the poor-rate and to attend the election. On the same day JB heard from Col. James Lowther, M.P. for Westmorland, that Lonsdale had dismissed the idea of giving JB a seat in Parliament, saying, "He would get drunk, and make a foolish speech" (Journ.). On 17 June, the day they were to leave London, JB spoke of his reluctance to go to Carlisle, and Lonsdale said, "You

that I have been at this place. On the first I executed all that was necessary to be done to stop any clamour concerning the poors rates. I might then have returned directly to London—But I had been *peremptorily* told that it was the duty of the office which I had *solicited* to attend both the election, and the Midsummer Sessions, before which there was not time to chuse my successor. I therefore found myself *devoted* I could not tell how long.[2] I remained a few days at an Inn,[3] and then went to lodge and board at the Mayor's, an old grocer, now the Postmaster, with one daughter such as might make a man forget the difference of sex; but they are both very civil, and I have an excellent room.[4] Except one evening that I drank tea with a clergyman, and one morning that Sir James Johnston and I breakfasted together, I have had no other company at any meal, till today when I made one with a few of the corporation at my Inn.[5] I who was lately in London with all its variety and animation. You have had distress of mind. But your active spirit never failed within you. I have heard you say that you

asked the Recordership of me. I did not wish you should be Recorder. But you were so earnest I granted it. And now when duty is required, you would give it up. What have you done for your sallary? . . . I suppose you think we are fond of your company. You are mistaken. We don't care for it. . . . I suppose you thought I was to bring you into Parliament. I never had any such intention. It would do you harm to be in Parliament." JB wrote, "This was a full discovery. I had leave of absence for an hour; went to Malone, and told him". As JB and Lonsdale walked to the coach, "the bringing into Parlmt. was resumed, and he shewed his poor opinion of me, saying I would get drunk and make a foolish speech". They quarrelled again in the coach, and when they stopped at an inn in Barnet, a duel was prevented only by JB's being unable to find pistols. They made peace and drank a glass of wine together, but JB wrote, "I was inwardly mortified to think that I had deceived myself so woefully as to my hopes from the GREAT LOWTHER, and that I was now obliged to submit to what was very disagreable to me, without any reward or hope of any good" (Journ. 17 June).

[2] JB had arrived in Carlisle on 20 June, and the next day signed the orders for the poor-rate (Journ. 20–21 June). Presumably JB underlined *devoted* to emphasize its less usual meaning of "doomed".

[3] JB stayed until 24 June at the Bush in English St., run by James Fairbairn (Journ. 23–24 June; *Univ. Brit. Directory* ii. 631, 633).

[4] Jeremiah Wherlings (c. 1720–1811) was sometime Mayor of Carlisle (*Gent. Mag.* 1811, lxxxi, pt. 2. 487; Samuel Jefferson, *History and Antiquities of Carlisle*, 1838, p. 448). JB went to lodge with him on 24 June (Journ.).

[5] Sir James Johnstone (1726–94), Bt., M.P. for Dumfries Burghs, drank coffee with JB on 22 June. That evening JB had tea with the Rev. Joseph Dacre Carlyle (1759–1804), an Arabic scholar, who somewhat relieved JB's gloom with "his Books and literary conversation" (Journ.). On 30 June JB wrote, "I dined with the Mayor and some more members of the Corporation at the Bush": this gave him a short interval of relief, but he found the company vulgar (Journ.).

never sat listless by the fire. I have during these wretched days sat so, hours and hours. Every thing that ever vexed me has returned. I feel myself a poor forlorn being; with no permanent vigour of mind, no friend that can enable me to advance myself in life—A fortune sadly encumbered—children whom I can with difficulty support, and of whom I am at a loss how to dispose with advantage and propriety—Such is the general prospect. And for *immediate* feelings, added to *ennui* and selfupbraiding I am again unfortunate enough to have *one* sore of a certain nature contracted I think monday forthnight, which *alone* gives me more pain and alarm than *several* which I had lately. Whether it be that it is enhanced by apprehension in my feeble state of mind and body from living very low,[6] or that it is of a worse nature than common I cannot say. I have for twelve days followed Mr. Earle's method, without any seeming effect. I have written to him, and expect his answer tomorrow.[7] Short as the time is since I left you, I can hardly bring myself fully to a persuasion that I have enjoyed such society. How shocking is it to think that I was dragged away from my friend Temple who came from Cornwall almost on purpose to see me, and saw me so little[8]—and was forced to interrupt my Life of Dr. Johnson the most important, perhaps *now* the only concern of any consequence that I ever shall have in this world—and what galls me, and irritates me with impatience is the thought that I lose those hours which you could now have given me for revising my M.S. and that perhaps you may be gone before I get back to town. Even the fear of not being in London when at last your Shakspeare comes out is shocking. My dear Friend! for God's

[6] "I had drunk very little wine since I left London, so that I was low" (Journ. 22 June).

[7] James Earle (1755–1817), surgeon at St. Bartholomew's Hospital, had in January treated JB for a urethral stricture (Journ. 31 Jan., 2 Feb.). On 14 June, JB "rashly went three times in the course of this day to a stranger" (Journ.). It is not certain that JB's present disease was gonorrhoea: on 15 June he already felt hot and feverish, and by 22 June was having difficulty walking (Journ.); Dr. William B. Ober writes that these symptoms are "consistent with ascending infection of the urinary tract with prostatic or renal involvement" ("Boswell's Clap", in *Boswell's Clap and Other Essays*, 1979, p. 24). JB's letter to Earle of 26 June has not been reported, and only a small fragment of Earle's reply, which included a prescription, survives as the verso of a Paper Apart for the *Life* MS. (M 145, p. 229; Journ. 26 June, 1 July). Presumably on Earle's advice, JB went to his barber on 4 and 5 July and himself performed a minor operation on his sore (Journ.). This was JB's nineteenth and last attack of urethral disease before his final illness (Ober, pp. 24–25).

[8] Temple and his daughter had been in London since 14 May (Journ.).

sake if you possibly can let me have some consolation. The melancholy to which I am subject I know cannot be helped. But I beseech you try to alleviate such of my sufferings as can admit of soothing. Sir John Scott wrote me a very sensible and kind letter in favour of my *right* of resignation—but recommending a *quiet* disentanglement.[9] The election begins next saturday 3 July; and to be sure it *may* be protracted till monday the 19 as fifteen polling days may be insisted on. The *very worst* then that can be is my not being in London till *thursday 18 July*.[10] I tremble to ask if you will be *gone* or Shakspearre *ready* by that day—But I have given in my resignation to take place on the conclusion of the Midsummer Sessions which are on the *12 July*.[11] I would fain hope I may obtain leave to depart then or *sooner*. In short I am at the mercy of another person for this once. Lord Lonsdale is to be here in a day or two, and Penn with him, and I hope that Penn may be of some service to me.[12] Never was a mind in a more *dislocated*[13] state than mine now is. Ought I, my dear Malone, to submit to my miserable constitution, and *retire* to my estate by which I may probably extricate my affairs?[14] Or shall I go *ad extremos indos*[15] or what shall I do? But I beg pardon. *Hoc age*.[16] Pray keep this that I may see the sad picture and burn it. This goes off tomorrow morning. You will receive it on saturday. If you write that day I can have your letter

[9] Not reported; the letter arrived on 27 June (Journ.). Sir John Scott (1751–1838), brother of Sir William Scott (*ante* From EM, 11 June 1785, n. 7; To EM, 17 Nov. 1788, n. 6), barrister, M.P. for Weobley, later first Earl of Eldon and Lord Chancellor, in 1788 had advised JB on his English bar scheme (Journ. 27 Apr. 1788), and earlier this year had promised to help JB obtain some preferment (Journ. 10 June).

[10] JB probably meant to write "thursday 22 July". The election ended on 14 July; JB left the next day and arrived in London on 16 July (Journ.).

[11] JB's letter of resignation is dated 23 June and addressed "To the Mayor, Aldermen, Bailiffs, and Capital Citizens of Carlisle" (MS. Hyde Collection).

[12] On 26 June JB had written to Richard Penn (c. 1734–1811), grandson of the founder of Pennsylvania and M.P. for Appleby under Lonsdale's patronage, complaining of poor health and depression and asking Penn to intercede with Lonsdale for permission to return to London immediately. Penn showed his letter to Lonsdale, but to no avail (Journ. 2–3 July).

[13] JB uses the word "dislocated" of his state of mind in Journ. 15 June. Presumably he means "unsettled" or "disordered".

[14] On the same day JB wrote in his journal, "I doubted if I could live cheaper at Auchinleck, and . . . I could not support a country life."

[15] "To the furthest Indies"; cf. Horace, *Epistles* I. i. 45: 'impiger extremos curris mercator ad Indos", "ardent trader that you are, you rush to the furthest Indies". Like JB, Horace's "ardent trader" is fleeing "a slender fortune and the shame of failure at the polls" (trans. H. R. Fairclough, Loeb ed.).

[16] "Get to work"—a piece of self-advice. Cf. Horace, *Epistles* I. vi. 31.

on monday. Kind compliments to Jephson and all friends. How I envy you all. But what could the best of you do in my place?

I am you may believe exceedingly anxious to see Mr. Earle, as I dare not trust any practitioner here.[17] The only sign of life in me at this time is my having read all Waller and two of Terence's Plays.[18]

From Malone, Thursday 8 July 1790

MS. Yale (C 1919).
ADDRESS in Philip Metcalfe's hand: James Boswell Esqr., Carlisle.
FRANK: London, eighth July 1790. P. Metcalfe.
POSTMARKS: [London] JY 8 90, FREE.

London, July 8, 1790

MY DEAR BOSWELL, I have been reproaching myself these three days for not writing to you, but in truth am not much to blame, having been employed from[1] morning till night, and partly with your business. Before I enter on that however, let me say a word on the subject of low spirits. I will not say that your present situation is not an unpleasant one; but surely you have greatly magnified all the evils which you have described. The first and great consideration is, that the whole is but *temporary*, and that as soon as you return to town and have got completely rid of the *aristocrate*,[2] you will be just as well as ever. Where misfortunes happen that are likely to give a colour to a man's whole life, there is reason enough for being cast down, if not for complaining: but this is not your case. The being well or not being well with ——[3] has nothing to do with your changing Scotland for London, with the embarrassments of your fortune, with the difficulty of educating your children, and twenty other circumstances, that you have enumerated by way of aggravating the account.

[17] JB was much recovered by the time he reached London; his journal does not record a further consultation with Earle.

[18] JB had read all the poems of Edmund Waller on 26–28 June, but did not think highly of them. He had finished reading the *Andria* and the *Eunuchus* and begun the *Heautontimorumenos* (Journ. 25, 26, 28 June). JB squeezed this last paragraph onto the first page between the salutation and the opening line of text.

[1] MS. "for"

[2] See *ante* From EM, 29 Sept. 1788, n. 1.

[3] Lonsdale.

Let me now give you a sentence from the wise Bacon, of which I ought to have long since profited myself, but which, though it may not be always applicable to objects that *cling about the heart*,[4] certainly *ought* to serve, in most other cases: "That which is past, is gone and irrevocable; and wise men have enough to do with things present and to come: therefore they do but trifle with themselves that labour in past matters."[5] I happened to be reading his Essays last night when the printers boy called; and though I had ordered a sheet of yours for press in the morning, in which you give an account of Johnson's being offended by your urging the subject of death too far, I could not help writing to Mr. Plympsel,[6] if possible to add the following note—to[7] the words—"it will do him no good to whine":[8] because they appear to me admirably to express and *justify* Johnson's notions on the subject; and both from your representation and that of others (Courteney[9] etc.) the reader might him think a *pusillanimous* fellow.[10] Don't however be alarmed, for I am sure you will approve of the insertion. The note was this:

Bacon in his admirable Essays has delivered a congenial sentiment, which may serve to place Dr. Johnson's notion[11] on this subject in its true light: "Certainly the contemplation of death, as *the wages of sin*, and passage to another world, is holy and religious; but the fear of it, as a tribute due unto nature, is

[4] The editors have not traced this quotation, if it is a quotation. EM presumably refers to his unhappy love affairs (see Introduction, pp. 168–71).

[5] Francis Bacon, "Of Revenge" (*Works*, ed. James Spedding *et al.*, 1857–74, vi. 385).

[6] The "intelligent and accurate" compositor at Baldwin's (Journ. 14 June). On a Paper Apart for p. 37 of the *Life* MS. (M 145) he signed his name "J. Plymsell". Perhaps he was John Plymsell, who opened his own print-shop in 1799 at No. 33 New Street Square (Maxted).

[7] MS. "to" written above deleted "after"

[8] "To my question, whether we might not fortify our minds for the approach of death, he answered, in a passion, 'No, Sir, let it alone. It matters not how a man dies, but how he lives. The act of dying is not of importance, it lasts so short a time.' He added, (with an earnest look,) 'A man knows it must be so, and submits. It will do him no good to whine' " (*Life* ii. 106–07).

[9] Cf. Courtenay's *Poetical Review*, pp. 8–9:
A coward wish, long stigmatiz'd by fame,
Devotes Maecenas to eternal shame;
Religious Johnson, future life to gain,
Would ev'n submit to everlasting pain:
How clear, how strong, such kindred colours paint
The Roman epicure and Christian saint!

[10] Presumably EM is alluding to SJ's reputation for preferring Latinate vocabulary, "pusillanimous" being defined in SJ's *Dictionary* as "meanspirited; narrow-minded; cowardly"; also he seems to be recalling JB's surprise that SJ would apply the low word "fellow" to himself (*Life* ii. 362).

[11] MS. "notions", with "s" deleted.

weak."[12]—I happened to light on the words while the boy was waiting. In a former edition of the Essays printed in 1613, the passage runs somewhat differently, and I had some mind to have taken it from thence as still more apposite.—"Certainly the fear of death, as contemplation of the cause of it and the issue of it, is religious; but the fear of it for itself, is weak."[13]

Your compositor has gone on very smartly; and has not been delayed by me, though I am so busy. I have never seen more than two proofs. The sheet in which was *νυξ ερχεται*[14] you had ordered for press, and no revise of it came to me: so the errour has gone. It is but a trifle and may be corrected in the Errata.[15] That sheet was Qq. I have had 5 sheets Rr. Ss. Tt. Uu. Xx. The last nearly exhausts Maxwell.[16] It will, I believe, be worked off tomorrow.—I took but one liberty more than I have mentioned, which, I think, upon reflection you will approve. It was to strike out two lines in which you mention an expression which you have heard Johnson used originally in The False Alarm, and struck out.[17] Why raise up against him a host of enemies, by telling a

[12] "Of Death" (*Works* vi. 379). Bacon revised and expanded his *Essays* several times; the last revision published in his lifetime, and the one on which later editions are based, is the "newly enlarged" edition of 1625, a copy of which EM owned and annotated (*Bibliotheca Boswelliana . . . Sold by Auction, by Mr. Sotheby*, 1825, p. 10). It is possible that EM here quotes the 1625 edition; if so, he modernizes the spelling. (See next note.)

[13] *The Essaies of Sr Francis Bacon Knight, the Kings Atturny Generall*, 1613, a reprint of the 1612 revision and enlargement of the *Essays*, the first version of which was printed in 1597. EM modernizes the spelling.

[14] MS. "*ερχεται*"; the reading of the 1st ed. of the *Life* (i. 303; cf. *Life* ii. 57) is "Νυξ ερχεται", also the reading of the *Life* MS.

[15] The "Corrections and Additions" to the 1st ed. were printed on the last page of front matter in the first volume. The quotation was corrected to "Νυξ γαρ ερχεται", the first words of a passage from John 9: 4, "the night cometh, when no man can work", which was inscribed on the dial-plate of SJ's watch. The watch was now owned by George Steevens, whom JB probably consulted as to the exact wording of the inscription (M 158).

[16] Since the 1st ed. was printed in quarto, each signature contained only four leaves. Sigs. Qq–Xx contained pp. 297–344 of vol. i (*Life* ii. 43–129). Maxwell had supplied JB with the Johnsoniana printed in the 1st ed. i. 336–45. His anecdotes were much expanded in later editions (*Life* ii. 116–33; *ante* To EM, 17 Nov. 1788, n. 12).

[17] EM apparently deleted these lines in proof, for they are not deleted in the *Life* MS. (M 144, p. 354). Following the phrase, "is but too evident" at the end of a paragraph (*Life* ii. 112), they read: "Indeed I am well informed that there was struck out from it an expression still more degrading than any that now remain 'Had government been overturned by this faction England had died of a *Thyrasis*.' " "Thyrasis", or more properly "phthiriasis", means an infestation of lice. Waingrow (p. 330 n. 10) thinks that the suppressed sentence appeared in the sixth paragraph from the end of *The False Alarm*, 1770 (*Works SJ* x. 343), where it would refer to the uprisings led by Wat Tyler (1381)

thing that need not be told, and in[18] which perhaps your information may have been inaccurate? I do sincerely believe that my friend Lord Charlemont, if he had read that passage in your book, would have thrown it into the fire.[19]

I hope that by Earle's instructions you have before this time got the better of what gave you so much alarm. Your business is now to consider how much you will gain by getting rid of the bad company you have been obliged to keep. With respect to every thing else, your prospects in life are not in the smallest degree better or worse than they were before.

I have had a most curious treasure from Dulwich College on which I have been working this week past, and which will throw me back a fortnight: All the accounts of a playhouse in Shakspeare's time; the contents of the Wardrobe; and various notices relative to the authors of those days. I received it luckily on the very day when I had ordered my last sheet of the *Hist. of the Stage* for press. I immediately stopp'd it, and shall be able to include several curious matters in a couple of sheets.[20] I think it will be impossible for me to get away before the first week in August.

Jephson has been these five days at Cambridge, taking his master's degree, and has been solicited already by lord Euston for his vote.[21] I expect him at dinner.—I had a letter two days ago from Courteney at Bath, where he has received much benefit. He talks of being here next week. He called on Miss Seward at Lichfield. She is very ill of a dropsy, and her physician, Dr. Darwent, has but little hopes of her. She is I suppose at the critical period of 45. C. says, she keeps up her spirits, and is resolved to[22] die en philosophe.[23]—There is not a mortal in town so you have

and Robert Kett (1549). SJ, then, would be comparing Wilkes's supporters to their rebellious mobs or an infestation of lice.

[18] MS. "in" written above deleted "of"

[19] James Caulfeild (1728–99), first Earl of Charlemont, prominent Irish Whig and a member of The Club since 1773.

[20] The new material was the diary of Philip Henslowe (d. 1616), manager of several London theatres. EM printed an account of the diary and papers together with extracts in the "Emendations and Additions" to the front matter in his edition of Shakespeare (i. pt. 2. 288–329).

[21] Richard Jephson took his M.A. at Emmanuel College (*Alum. Cant.* II). George Henry Fitzroy (1760–1844), styled Earl of Euston, later (1811) fourth Duke of Grafton, was M.P. for Thetford, 1782–84, and for Cambridge University, 1784–1811. At the universities of Oxford and Cambridge, the degree of master of arts or doctor qualified the holder to vote for M.P. (Namier and Brooke i. 35, ii. 436).

[22] MS. "to to" with a large gap between the two words (see n. 25 below).

[23] Anna Seward did not die until 1809. Her physician was Erasmus Darwin

no loss. Sir J. R. however contrived to muster up ten or twelve last week. Mr. and Mrs. Cholmondelay—Mrs. Moore, Dr. and Mrs. Lort, Dr. Lawrence etc. etc.[24] I have left the above blank lest I should not get a frank from Metcalf, in which case you must pay a shilling[25]—which place to account of your very Affectionate,

E. M.

I did not know what to do with this. "He repeated Drydens lines on love (gentle tempestuous, *see further*)" for your compositor gave me, you see, *asides* and all. I could not find the passage; so made it—"some lines by Dryden on love, which I have now forgotten."[26]

To Malone,
Saturday 4 December 1790

MS. Hyde Collection.
ADDRESS: To Edmond Malone Esq. [Sackville Street, Dublin *deleted*; *added in unidentified hand*] Mullingar.
POSTMARKS: [London] DE <4> 90.

London, 4 Decr. 1790

MY DEAR MALONE: Let me begin with myself—On the day after your departure[1] that most friendly fellow Courtenay (begging the pardon of an M.P. for so free an epithet) called on me, and took my word and honour that till the first of March, my allowance of wine per diem should not exceed four good glasses at dinner, and a

(1731–1802); she published *Memoirs of the Life of Dr. Darwin*, 1804.

[24] The Hon. and Rev. Robert Cholmondeley (1727–1804) married that "very airy lady" (*Life* v. 248) Mary Woffington (c. 1729–1811), sister of the famous Peg Woffington. "Mrs. Moore" was Hannah More. Michael Lort's wife was Susannah Norfolk (c. 1742–92).

[25] EM left half of the page blank between the two "to's" (n. 22 above) so that he could fold the letter to form its own wrapper. But Philip Metcalfe addressed and franked a separate wrapper.

[26] EM wrote this postscript upside-down above the dateline on the first page of the letter. See *Life* ii. 85 and n. 3. The lines were probably from Dryden's *Tyrannick Love* II. i. 292–95:

Love various minds does variously inspire:
He stirs in gentle Natures gentle fires;
Like that of Incense on the Altars laid:
But raging flames tempestuous Souls invade.

[1] Probably 19 or 20 Nov. (EM to John Jordan, 19 Nov., in *Original Letters from Edmond Malone to John Jordan,* ed. J. O. Halliwell-Phillipps, 1864, p. 48, where it is misdated 1793).

pint after it—And this I have kept, though I have dined with Jack Wilkes[2]—at the London Tavern after the launch of an Indiaman[3]—With dear Edwards[4]—Dilly—at home with Courtenay Dr. Barrow[5]—at the Mess of the Coldstream[6]—at the Club[7]—at WARREN HASTINGS's—at Hawkins the Cornish Member's[8]—and at home with a Colonel of the Guards etc.[9]—This *Regulation* I assure you is of essential advantage in many respects. The Magnum Opus advances. I have revised p. 216.[10] The additions which I have received are a Spanish Quotation from Mr. Cambridge[11]—an account of Johnson at Warley Camp from Mr. Langton[12]—and Johnson's letters to Mr. Hastings—three in all—one of them long and admirable; but what sets the diamonds in pure gold of Ophir is a letter from Mr. Hastings to me illustrating them and their Writer.[13] I had this day the honour of a

[2] Wilkes's dinner was on Sunday 21 Nov. (From Wilkes, 17 Nov.; To Wilkes, 18 Nov.).

[3] The London Tavern, in Bishopsgate St. near Cornhill, had a large upstairs room in which the East India Company often gave dinners (Bryant Lillywhite, *London Coffee Houses*, 1963, pp. 710–11).

[4] Possibly Oliver Edwards (1711–91), a college friend of SJ who had chanced to meet him in London in 1778. JB would soon put to press the famous account of this meeting (*Life* iii. 302–07), so perhaps visited Edwards to obtain his approval. The epithet "dear" seems to mix affection with condescension: Edwards was an amiable man, but ignorant.

[5] The Rev. William Barrow, D.C.L., master of Soho Academy (Journ. 9 June 1786).

[6] JB's host must have been Thomas Bosville (1758–93), a Lt.-Colonel in the Coldstream Guards. JB, who thought the Boswells were a cadet branch of the Bosvilles of Yorkshire, called Thomas's father Godfrey his "Yorkshire Chief" (*Life* iii. 439). But see also below, n. 9. At that date, the first battalion, where the mess apparently was held, was stationed in the Tower of London (Daniel MacKinnon, *Origin and Services of the Coldstream Guards*, 1833, ii. 440).

[7] The first dinner of the Parliamentary session, 30 Nov. (Minute Book).

[8] Christopher Hawkins (1758–1829), later (1791) Baronet, M.P. for Mitchell, 1784–99.

[9] Unidentified. If JB had entertained Thomas Bosville (n. 6 above), presumably he would have given his name since EM must have known of him (e.g. Journ. 6 Dec. 1785). Another possibility, John Sutton (Captain in the Guards, Lt.-Colonel in the army), whom JB had met in 1786 (Journ. 19 May 1786), had retired on 23 Mar. (MacKinnon, *Coldstream Guards* ii. 490–91). JB later mentions knowing Lt.-Col. Edward Morrison, a friend of Bosville's (Journ. 22 Aug. 1793).

[10] Of the second volume (*Life* iii. 273–74).

[11] JB had written to Richard Owen Cambridge (*ante* From EM, 13 Jan. 1786, n. 13) asking about a Spanish passage Cambridge had quoted in a conversation with SJ in 1778 (the letter is not reported). Cambridge recalled the conversation and replied in time for the press (From R. O. Cambridge, Nov. 1790; *Life* iii. 251). The Spanish poet was Quevedo (*Life* iii. 518).

[12] Langton transmitted these anecdotes in a letter of 30 Nov. They are printed in *Life* iii. 361–62.

[13] The three letters from SJ to Hastings and the illustrative letter from Hastings to JB are printed in *Life* iv. 66–70.

long visit from The late Governour General of India. There is to be no more Impeachment. But you will see his character nobly vindicated. Depend upon this.[14]

And now for my Friend.—The appearance of Malone's Shakspeare on the 29th November was not attended with any external noise; but I suppose no publication seised more speedily and surely on the attention of those for whose critical taste it was chiefly intended. I send by this post under cover of Mr. Lees,[15] fifteen newspaper paragraphs collected by Mr. Selfe who offers you his most attached respects.[16] If I find any that escape him, I shall secure them for you. At the Club on tuesday where I met Sir Joshua, Dr. Warren, Lord Ossory,[17] Lord Palmerston,[18] Windham, and Burke in the Chair, Burke was so full of his anti french Revolution rage, and poured it out so copiously that we had almost nothing else.[19] He however found time to praise the clearness and accuracy of your dramatick History; and Windham found fault with you for not taking the profits of so laborious a

[14] *Ante* From EM, 17 June 1788, n. 9. Parliament had been dissolved in June, and there was debate over whether the new Parliament could constitutionally pick up the impeachment proceedings where the old Parliament had left off. However, the trial eventually resumed and dragged on until 1795. "Late" in "The late Governour General" is an insertion above the line.

[15] John Lees (d. 1811), born in Ayrshire, was Secretary of the General Post Office, Dublin. He was created Baronet in 1804, and on his death was reportedly worth £250,000 (*Roy. Kal.* 1790, p. 269; *Gent Mag.* 1811, lxxxi. pt. 2. 666). As an official of the Post Office, Lees could send and receive letters free of charge; in 1785 JB had used him to forward sheets of the *Tour* to Thomas Barnard (Fifer, p. 190 n. 8; From Barnard, 14 Apr., c. 17 July, 14 Aug. 1785). JB once invited him to Auchinleck (From Lees, 10 Aug. 1785).

[16] Selfe was the corrector at Baldwin's printing house (*ante* From EM, 28 Oct. 1785, n. 5). The clippings he sent have not been recovered; however, the newspapers of late Nov. and early Dec. printed many items on EM's edition of Shakespeare. See *Pub. Adv.* 30 Nov. p. [2], 2 Dec. pp. [2, 3], 4 Dec. p. [3], 6 Dec. p. [4], 7 Dec. p. [2], 11 Dec. p. [3], 14 Dec. p. [1]; *Morn. Chron.* 9 Dec. p. [3], 10 Dec. p. [3], 13 Dec. p. [3]; *St. James's Chron.* 27–30 Nov. p. [4], 2–4 Dec. pp. [1, 2, 4], 4–7 Dec. p. [4], 7–9 Dec. p. [4], 9–11 Dec. p. [4], 11–14 Dec. p. [4]; *Gazetteer*, 30 Nov. p. [2], 2 Dec. p. [3], 3 Dec. p. [2], 7 Dec. p. [4], 9 Dec. p. [2]; *Times*, 3 Dec. p. [2], 11 Dec. p. [3]; *Lond. Chron.* (30 Nov.–2 Dec.) lxviii. 534; *Gen. Eve. Post*, 27–30 Nov. p. [4]; *World*, 6 Dec. p. [3]. For extracts from these and later items, see n. 20 below; From EM, 23 Dec. nn. 6, 7, 11; From EM, 23 Jan. 1791, n. 2; Appendix 3, pp. 437–38.

[17] John Fitzpatrick (1745–1818), second Earl of Upper Ossory, M.P. for Bedfordshire and a member of The Club since 1777 (Namier and Brooke ii. 431–33; Fifer, p. xcv).

[18] Henry Temple (1739–1802), second Viscount Palmerston, M.P. for Newport, Isle of Wight, a member of The Club since 1784, and father of the future Prime Minister (Namier and Brooke iii. 519–20).

[19] EB's *Reflections on the Revolution in France*, published on 1 Nov. (W. B. Todd, *A Bibliography of Edmund Burke*, 1982, p. 143), had provoked a storm of pamphlets and newspaper squibs.

Work.[20] Sir Joshua is pleased, though he would gladly have seen more *disquisition* (you understand me).[21] Mr. Daines Barrington is exceedingly gratified.[22] He regrets that there should be a dryness between you and Steevens, as you have treated him with great respect.[23] I understand that in a short time there will not be one of your Books to be had for love or money.

I have called several times on John, who hopes to set out next week; but I am not for his being in a hurry.[24] Pray let me hear from you, and command me most freely. I offer my best respects to the Family—I should say the House[25] and compliments to Jephson. I ever am most affectionately yours,

J. B.

To Malone,
Tuesday 7 December 1790

MS. Hyde Collection.
ADDRESS: To Edmond Malone Esq. [Sackville Street, Dublin *deleted; added in unidentified hand*] Mullingar.
POSTMARKS: [London] DE 7 90 [Dublin] <DE> 11.

London, 7 Decr. 1790

My Dear Malone: It is my intention to send you a weekly packet every Saturday, while there is *stuff* which I suppose there will be

[20] Cf. *Pub. Adv.* 11 Dec. p. [3]: "Mr. Malone's new edition of Shakespeare is already nearly expended. That gentleman accepted of fifty copies of it, as presents to his friends; this was the only remuneration he could ever be prevailed upon to receive for his labour of eight years in commenting that difficult writer. He insisted too with the booksellers, that the new edition should be sold as cheap as possible."

[21] MS. "(you understand me)". EM, in his 1790 edition of Shakespeare, had printed a long note by Reynolds in defence of tragicomedy (i. pt. 1. 143–44). As F. W. Hilles suggested (*Portraits*, p. 121), this may be a part of a longer essay on tragicomedy (parts of which are printed in *Portraits*, pp. 125–38) that Reynolds had hoped EM would make more extensive use of.

[22] Daines Barrington (1727–1800), barrister, antiquary, and naturalist, was a friend of both SJ and JB and a member of the Essex Head Club.

[23] After the publication of the 1778 edition of Shakespeare's plays, George Steevens declared himself a "dowager editor" and let it be known that he considered EM his heir (Prior, *Malone*, pp. 100–01; *Charlemont Papers* ii. 51); in 1780 EM published, with Steevens's blessing, a *Supplement* to the Johnson-Steevens edition. However, Steevens's naturally quick temper was aroused by some of EM's annotations in the 1785 edition of Johnson-Steevens, the production of which Isaac Reed supervised; henceforth their relations became more formal, though neither acknowledged publicly that their friendship was at an end.

[24] EM's servant John Bullock (Bullock to John Jordan, 20 May 1797–– Shakespeare's Birthplace MS. 87. fol. 142), who was to join his master in Ireland; see *post* To EM, 7 Dec.

[25] Presumably because the ennobling of EM's elder brother had turned the "family" of Malone into a "house".

for some time. But this is a Gazette Extraordinary, of which you will not grudge the postage.

I dined last saturday at Sir Joshua's with Mr. Burke, his Lady, son, and niece,[1] Lord Palmerston, Windham, Dr. Lawrence, Dr. Blagden,[2] Dr. Burney, Sir Abraham Hume,[3] Sir William Scott. I sat next to young Burke at dinner, who said to me that you had paid his Father a very fine compliment.[4] I mentioned Johnson to *sound* if there was any objection.[5] He made none. In the evening Burke told me he had read your Henry VI with all its accompanyment, and it was "exceedingly well done". He left us for some time, I suppose on some of his cursed politicks; but he returned. I *at* him again, and heard from his lips, what believe me I delighted to hear, and took care to write down soon after. *I have read his History of the Stage, which is a very capital piece of Criticism and Antiquarianism. I shall now read all Shakspeare through in a very different manner from what I have yet done—when I have such a Commentator.*— Will not *this* do for you my friend? Burke was admirable company all that day. He never once I think mentioned the French Revolution, and was easy with me, as in *days of old*. I *do* upon my honour *admire* and *love* him. Would that he had never seen Lord Rockingham, but had ever "walked in a perfect way."[6] I am assured by a noble courtier that George Rex has said, "Whatever he may have said of me, I now entirely forgive him."[7]

The best answer to him is by George Rous the Counsel.[8] It is

[1] Mary Cecilia French (1766–1816) (*Corres. EB* vi. 66 and n. 4).

[2] Charles Blagden (1748–1820), M.D. and Secretary of the Royal Society.

[3] Sir Abraham Hume, Bt. (1749–1838), formerly (1774–80) M.P. for Petersfield, was a patron of the arts and a collector of minerals and precious stones (Namier and Brooke ii. 652).

[4] In the Preface to his edition of Shakespeare EM mentioned EB as the only competitor to SJ's "extraordinary powers of mind": "a great orator, philosopher, and statesman . . . whose talents and virtues are an honour to human nature" (i. pt. 1. lxviii).

[5] After his quarrel with EB, who disliked seeing printed references to his private life (see p. 98), JB was uneasy about his numerous references to EB in the *Life*.

[6] Psalms 101: 6: "He that walketh in a perfect way, he shall serve me."

[7] During the Regency crisis EB had asserted in the House of Commons that George III was "a Monarch smitten by the hand of Omnipotence, and that the Almighty had hurled him from his throne" (*Corres. EB* vi. 7 n. 2). But the publication of the *Reflections* led George III in early 1791 to say to EB at Court, "There is no Man who calls himself a Gentleman that must not think himself obliged to you, for you have supported the cause of the Gentlemen" (*Corres. EB* vi. 239). The "noble courtier" is unidentified.

[8] George Rous (c. 1744–1802), barrister, counsel for the East India Company, and formerly (1776–80) M.P. for Shaftesbury, published *Thoughts on Government: Occasioned by Mr. Burke's Reflections, &c.* about 4 Dec. His name appeared in the newspaper advertisements (e.g. *Gen. Eve. Post*, 2–4 Dec. p. [4]), but not on the title-page of the first edition.

honest open manly able Whiggism. Courtenay is enraptured with it. But *Jack* is absolutely an *enthusiast* in this french business.

I shall be indebted to you for half the postage of this, as I enclose a letter to the Bishop of Killaloe to send me the *Round Robin*, and wish to be sure of a *certain* and *speedy* conveyance, and therefore trouble you.[9]

As I was going to inquire for your servant John today, I met him in the street, and scolded him for being abroad in a cold rainy day. He intended to have set out this week; but having contracted a fresh cold, and Dr. Warren having said to me that he should be in no haste, I have presumed to advise that he should delay his journey. You will send him your own orders. My daughters join me in best compliments. I have proposed Genl. Burgoyne for the Club having had a very excellent letter from him. I am very anxious for him.[10] Yours ever,

J. B.

To Malone,
Thursday 16 December 1790
MS. Hyde Collection.

London, 16 Decr. 1790

My Dear Malone: You will I hope have received my letter, with one parcel of paragraphs, one only of which was mine, as you would see by our stipulated mark*.[1] I now send you by John a second parcel not one of which is mine.[2] Your *Character* is written by a person whom I guessed, from his having said to me almost

[9] JB's letter to Thomas Barnard has not been reported; Barnard sent him the original Round Robin on 20 Dec; eventually it was returned (Waingrow, p. 375 n. 3). JB had an engraving made and inserted in the *Life* (iii. facing p. 83).

[10] JB had interviewed Lt.-Gen. John Burgoyne (1722–92) after his surrender at Saratoga in 1777, and retained an admiration for him. On 29 Nov. JB wrote to him proposing to submit his name for membership in The Club. Burgoyne replied on the same day with thanks and JB proposed him on 30 Nov. (To Burgoyne, 1 Dec.). See *post* To EM, 16 Dec. and n. 11.

[1] See *ante* To EM, 4 Dec. n. 16. The editors have not determined which (if any) of these paragraphs is by JB.

[2] These clippings have not been recovered.

the very words of the concluding part, in the street—in short a schoolfellow.[3]

Courtenay read to me your letter which is truly affecting.

> —— whence comfort seem'd to flow
> Discomfort swell'd.

I would fain hope that your friend has recovered.[4] I dined on saturday in company with your Apothecary Mr. Atkinson[5] whom I found to be most conversable from his having known Lord Tyrawley[6] and I know not how many great men. He said the best thing for Mr. Jephson would be a saline draught put into a state of effervescence; but that before his advice could reach you, it would be unecessary—one way, or other.

I was sadly mortified at the Club on tuesday where I was in the chair, and on opening the box, found three balls against General Burgoyne. Present besides *moi*—Lord Ossory, Sir Joshua Reynolds, Sir Joseph Banks,[7] Dr. Fordyce,[8] Dr. Burney, Young Burke, Courtenay, Steevens. One of the balls I do believe was put into the *no* side by Fordyce by mistake. You may guess who put in the other two.[9]

The Bishop of Carlisle[10] and Dr. Blagden are put up. I doubt if the latter will be admitted till Burgoyne gets in first.[11]

Steevens owned that your labour on Shakspeare exceeded that

[3] EM's "Character" appeared in *Pub. Adv.* 14 Dec. p. [1]; it is printed in Appendix 3 below, pp. 437–38. EM surmised that the writer was Hervey Redmond Morres (c. 1743–97), second Viscount Mountmorres, who could have been a schoolfellow at Dr. Ford's school in Dublin (*post* From EM, 23 Jan. 1791). JB had met Mountmorres at EM's on 9 Nov. 1789 (Journ.).

[4] EM's letter to Courtenay has not been recovered; Courtenay's reply of 15 Dec. is at Yale. EM's "friend" is William Jephson (see *post* From EM, 19 Dec.). For the quotation, see *Macbeth* I. ii. 27–28.

[5] Joseph Atkinson, whose shop was at No. 196 Bishopsgate St. (*Univ. Brit. Directory* i. 58).

[6] James O'Hara (1690–1773), second Baron Tyrawley, Field Marshal and diplomat, was noted for blunt wit and licentiousness.

[7] Banks (1743–1820), Bt., botanist and President of the Royal Society, had been a member of The Club since 1778.

[8] *Ante* To EM, 30 Oct. 1785, n. 25.

[9] JB marked the names of Banks and Steevens with crosses to indicate that they had voted against Burgoyne.

[10] John Douglas (1721–1807), D.D., Bishop of Carlisle and later (1791) of Salisbury, was a literary scholar and pamphleteer as well as a clergyman. JB, seconded by Sir Joseph Banks, proposed Douglas for membership; however, he was not elected until 1792 (Fifer, p. 361 n. 1).

[11] Blagden was proposed by Reynolds, but not elected until 1794 (Minute Book; Fifer, p. xlii). Burgoyne died (1792) before he could again be put up.

of the whole Phalanx.[12] But he made no secret of his intending in his next edition of *Johnson and Steevens's Shakspeare* (for of that title he boasts) to assume all your Prolegomena, and all your notes which he likes, and that he will put yours *last* where *others* have preceeded you. Also that he will exalt Monck Mason, and give due praise to Ritson.[13]

My work has met with a delay for a little while—not a whole day however—by an unaccountable neglect in having paper enough in readiness. I have now before me p. 256.[14] My utmost wish is to come forth on Shrove tuesday (8 March) "Wits are game cocks etc."[15]

[12] In the Advertisement to his 1793 edition of Shakespeare, Steevens writes that EM's "attention, diligence, and spirit of enquiry, have very far exceeded those of the whole united phalanx of his predecessors" (i. xxi). Earlier editors of Shakespeare included Nicholas Rowe (1709), Alexander Pope (1725), Lewis Theobald (1734), Sir Thomas Hanmer (1743–44), William Warburton (1747), Hugh Blair (1753), SJ (1765), Edward Capell (1767–68), SJ with Steevens (1773, 1778), and Isaac Reed as reviser of SJ and Steevens (1785).

[13] Courtenay reported in his letter to EM, 15 Dec., "Boswell and I had a good deal of conversation with Stephens on the subject [of EM's edition of Shakespeare].—He *seem'd* at least to speak candidly on the merits of it" (MS. Yale). In his 1793 edition of Shakespeare, however, Steevens clearly showed his annoyance with EM while praising him highly (see preceding note). John Monck Mason (1726–1809), a member of the Irish House of Commons, had published *Comments on the Last Edition of Shakespeare's Plays* (i.e. the 1778 edition) in 1785. Steevens wrote of him to Bishop Percy, "He is often ingenious and sometimes right; but occasionally outdoes even Dr. Warburton in absurdity of conjecture. . . . Still, with all his extravagances, I must allow that he is a man of thinking and erudition" (*Lit. Illust.* vii. 3). In the Advertisement to the 1793 edition of Shakespeare, Steevens wrote of Mason's *Comments*, "Any formal recommendation of them is needless, as their own merit is sure to rank their author among the most diligent and sagacious of our celebrated Poet's annotators", but added that he had omitted some of Mason's notes "through honest commiseration" (i. ix–x). Joseph Ritson (1752–1803) had published *Remarks, Critical and Illustrative, on the Text and Notes of the Last Edition of Shakspeare* (i.e. the 1778 edition) in 1783, followed in 1788 by *The Quip Modest*, an attack on Isaac Reed's 1785 edition. Ritson abused nearly all previous editors of Shakespeare, including Steevens, but no one more than EM (B. H. Bronson, *Joseph Ritson: Scholar-at-Arms*, 1938, ii. 394–403, 488–92, 500–14). By 1790 Ritson and Steevens were on friendly terms, partly because of their mutual dislike of EM, and Steevens did admit many of Ritson's notes in his 1793 edition of Shakespeare (Bronson i. 178, ii. 527–28). In 1792 Ritson published *Cursory Criticisms on the Edition of Shakspeare Published by Edmond Malone*, in order "to rescue the language and sense of an admirable author from the barbarism and corruption they have acquired in passing through the hands of this incompetent and unworthy editor" (p. vii). EM answered this pamphlet in *A Letter to the Rev. Richard Farmer . . . Relative to the Edition of Shakspeare, published in MDCCXC, and Some Late Criticisms on That Work*, 1792.

[14] Corresponding to *Life* iii. 337–39.

[15] JB quotes "The Elephant and the Bookseller" (ll. 75–76) from John Gay's *Fables:*

No author ever spar'd a brother,
Wits are game-cocks to one another.

Cockfights are traditional on Shrove

I shall probably trouble you with a packet towards the conclusion. I am affraid of having too much Copy.

Langton is in town, and dines with me tomorrow quietly, and revises his *Collectanea*.[16]

I beg to have my best compliments presented to Lord and Lady Sunderlin and your valuable sisters, and ever am, My Dear Sir, your much obliged and affectionate friend,

JAMES BOSWELL

From Malone, Sunday 19 December 1790

MS. Yale (C 1920).

ADDRESS: James Boswell, Esqre., Great Portland Street, near Portland Chapel, London.

POSTMARKS: MULLINGAR [Dublin] DE 21[1] [London] DE 25 90.

Baronston,[2] near Mullingar, Ireland
Decr. 19, 1790

MY DEAR BOSWELL, I was much obliged to you for your two letters and for the Shakspeare extracts, and should have thank'd you for them before this time but for a sad calamity which has engrossed all my thoughts and has made Shakspeare and fame and all worldly matters appear of very little value. In a very few hours after I arrived in Dublin an express arrived from my brother's house in the country to tell us that a most dear and old friend, Dr. Jephson, father to our young lawyer, lay in extreme danger at this place.[3] As soon as we had got the best physical advice, we hastened down here. He and I from our earliest youth, had lived in the strictest friendship, and had the strongest partiality and affection for each other. He had come here from his living in the

Tuesday (see *ante* To DG, 3 Mar. 1778 and n. 6).

[16] Langton's *Collectanea* is undoubtedly the long MS. printed by Waingrow, pp. 354–74, and used in *Life* iv. 2–27.

[1] The Dublin postmark is under the London postmark and difficult to read; it may be "DE 20".

[2] Lord Sunderlin's estate in Co. Westmeath.

[3] William Jephson (1734–90), D.D., father of Richard Mounteney Jephson. A brief account of him appears in M. D. Jephson, *An Anglo-Irish Miscellany*, 1964, pp. 297–98.

north on purpose to meet me, but alas, before we met, he had lost his senses. When I came into the room, having the whole of that day expressed great impatience to see me, he fell into an hysterick laugh, which made the most dismal impression on me. We could not for a long time ascertain his disorder, because his pulse constantly continued soft and good; but it proved a bilious and miliary fever, and he died last monday (the 21st day) in the extremest agonies. He had from the first such a fatal nausea to every thing that he could take no medecine, and unfortunately had not, as in most fevers, any thirst, so that even whey he only drank by spoonfuls. From some acridness of the bile, I suppose his inside suffered so much at last, that his cries during the last thirty hours were the most heart-rending thing you can imagine. He every moment was imploring the father of heaven for mercy and that he would be pleased to reduce him to powder and to put an end to his sufferings. The day before he died, he became somewhat like rational, and when I press'd him to take a little whey, said to me very slowly and affectingly—"I have something within that tells me Almighty God is going to dispose of me—Leave me to him."—His agonies were at length so great that his last fatal groan, the impression of which I yet feel, was some relief to us: but what a sad situation it is when this can[4] be the case!—I do not know any one man of my acquaintance so much beloved as he was. To the greatest purity of heart and the most generous sentiments was added a cheerfulness and simplicity of character, that was highly engaging. In addition to this he had the warmest feelings and I think the soundest understanding I ever met united together. You will not therefore wonder that the loss of such a man after an intimacy of above thirty years, has made a deep impression on me. I hope the sad scene to which I have been a witness, will never be entirely effaced from my mind, and that the recollection of it will have an effect on all my future life.—Pray throw the following into the Pub. Ad.—(Deaths.)

Decr. 13. At Baronston in Ireland, the[5] seat of the Right Hon. Lord Sunderlin, of a bilious fever the Revd. Dr. William Jephson, Rector of Ray in the diocese of Raphoe, and of Kilbritton in the diocese of Corke; Chanter of the Cathedral of Ross, and Perpetual

[4] EM first wrote "the best", then altered "the" to "this", erased "best", and wrote "can" over the erasure.

[5] MS. "of a bilious fever" inserted above the line before "the", then deleted.

Curate of Monkstown in the diocese of Kildare: a gentleman endeared by many virtues to a numerous circle of the most respectable friends, by whom he is sincerely regretted.[6]

I will on thursday[7] the 23d[8] or perhaps sooner send you something more at large for[9] the Gent. Mag. which you will be so good as to transmit to Nichols.[10]—And in the same letter, I will send you a bill for 50£ for a purpose I shall then explain to you—

I do not know whether you are now in Queen Anne St. or Great Portland St. but imagine you will move to the latter on the 25th and therefore direct there.—[11]

I have two other letters to write, so can add no more—Remember me most kindly to Courtenay and to all that think of me and believe me ever very Affectionately yours,

E. MALONE

From Malone,
Thursday 23 December 1790

MS. Yale (C 1921).

Baronston, Decr. 23, 1790

MY DEAR BOSWELL: I beg you will be so good as to convey to Mr. Nichols for the G. M. what I shall write below and on the last page, which I will manage so that you may cut it off, to save the trouble of transcription. This will, I imagine, reach you on the 27th or at furthest the 28th: pray send it as soon as you can, as I wish it to be in this month.[1] I attended my poor dear friend to the

[6] See *post* To EM, 18 Jan. 1791: "The papers had inserted Dr. Jephson's death before your letter came." The *Pub. Adv.* 28 Dec. p. [4] and certain other newspapers printed an obituary of Jephson which seems to have originated from some other source than this letter.

[7] MS. "thursday" written above deleted "tuesday"

[8] MS. "21st" altered to "23d"

[9] MS. "whi" deleted before "for"

[10] Publisher of *Gent. Mag.*

[11] MS. "The" deleted after "there.—" JB did not move to Great Portland St. until 19 Jan. 1791 (*post* To EM, 18 Jan. 1791).

[1] JB cut off the bottom of the page, as EM instructed; the printer's copy has not been recovered. The obituary appeared in *Gent. Mag.* (Dec. 1790) lx. 1152: "At Baronston, co. Westmeath, in Ireland, the seat of the Rt. Hon. Lord Sunderlin, in his 57th year, the Rev. Wm. Jephson, D.D. rector of Ray, in the diocese of Raphoe, and of Kilbriton, in the diocese of Corke; curate of Monkstown, near Dublin (a perpetual cure), and chanter of the cathedral of Ross—The virtues and talents of this excellent man had so strongly attached to him a numerous circle of most respectable friends, that few

grave last monday se'nnight, and the present is the last office I can do him.

I enclose you a bill for £50, which I beg you to take to Mr. Pujet's,[2] (College of Physicians, Warwick Lane) and to get the amount from him immediately, paying the discount (which is a mere trifle) if he requires it: but he sometimes pays such short bills at sight.—You will, after you receive it, be so good as to pay it to Mr. Dalby, a silversmith, No. 105, New Bond Street,[3] for the use of Mrs. Susanna Spencer; and get a receipt from him, specifying that he receives it for her use.[4]—We received six mails last night, ending with that of the 17th. I find parliament has kill'd Shakspeare, but suppose he will revive on the recess.—[5] I perceive no notice has been taken of the Essay proving old Macklin's account of an ancient pamphlet to be spurious. It is at the end of Vol. 1. Part I. I took a good deal of pains with it and I think have been successful. If you have not read it, pray look at it and draw it into notice, *quietly*—and on no account "overstep the modesty of nature".[6]—I see some one (perhaps the edr.) has said that

have died more sincerely regretted. He had come in November from his benefice in the North, to meet an old and dear friend (after a separation of many years), who was expected to arrive from England; but he was deprived of his intellects before they met, by a bilious and miliary fever, of which he died on the 21st day, in violent convulsions. He was buried on the 15th [actually 13 Dec., according to the present letter], in the family-vault of Lord Sunderlin, his pall being supported by that Nobleman, Sir Pigot Pierse, bart., Alexander Murray, esq. and Edmond Malone, esq.—As a preacher, he was one of the most eminent in Ireland, and was not less distinguished for the energy and propriety with which he read the sacred service. As a companion and a friend, his loss is deeply felt. He married Thomasine, one of the sisters of the Hon. Richard Mounteney, deceased, formerly fellow of King's College, Cambridge, and late one of the barons of the Exchequer in Ireland; by which lady he has left four sons: John, who is in holy orders, Richard Mounteney, a barrister at law, William, and Robert." EM later complained that the obituary was badly edited (*post* From EM, 5 Mar. 1791).

[2] John Puget (d. 1805) of the firm of Puget and Bainbridge, merchants at the College of Physicians (*Univ. Brit. Directory* i. 261; *Gent. Mag.* June 1805, lxxv. 588–89).

[3] John Dalby, jeweller and goldsmith (*Univ. Brit. Directory* i. 119).

[4] EM had been supporting Susanna Spencer, now insane, since 1781 (Introduction, pp. 168–70).

[5] Very little concerning EM's edition of Shakespeare had appeared in the newspapers since mid-December. Since most of the London newspapers were printed in single sheets of four pages, long Parliamentary reports tended to drive out other news.

[6] *Hamlet* III. ii. 20. The essay "Shakspeare, Ford, and Jonson" in EM's edition of Shakespeare (i. pt. 1. 387–414) accused Charles Macklin of fabricating an account of, and prose and verse extracts from, a pamphlet supposedly entitled *Old Ben's "Light Heart" Made Heavy by Young John's "Melancholy Lover"*, which, according to Macklin, contained some anecdotes of Jonson's enmity towards Shakespeare and John Ford. EM printed Macklin's account

Steevens will overtake me in *6* months.[7]—Pray throw in to the P. A. that he is making great exertions for that purpose, and will probably be able to publish in *twenty months*: for that is the utmost he can do, supposing he works off 6 Sheets a week[8]—If the Critical Review should take any notice of me on[9] the 1st of Jan. pray desire Arnold my newsman, in Mortimer St.[10] to send it to me (in the same manner he sends the Monthly, and the G. Mag.)—but otherwise not. I don't suppose I shall be reviewed so soon.[11]—I have had such a letter from Burke as you would reposite among your most precious muniments: and indeed I value it very much. It would be idle to pretend not to be proud of the praise of such a man.[12]—I am very glad to hear the Opus Magnum goes on so well. Pray take care of colloquialisms and vulgarisms of all sorts. Condense as much as possible, always preserving perspicuity and do not imagine the *only* defect of stile, is repetition of words.—Remember me to Courteney, Sir J. etc. and believe me ever, my dear B., faithfully and affectionately Yours,

E. M.

in his edition of Shakespeare (i. pt. 1. 202–05). EM's essay had in fact been noticed in *Pub. Adv.* 6 Dec. p. [4]: "In an Essay, which concludes the first part of his first volume, and which he has entitled—'*Shakspeare, Jonson, and Ford*,' Mr. Malone has made some pretty acute strictures on the production of a *Veteran of the Stage*; as to FORD's *Lover's Melancholy*, which was represented for Mrs. Macklin's benefit in the year 1748, a sly hint is conveyed in one part of the essay, that Mr. Macklin had the assistance of some *learned friend*."

[7] The newspaper paragraph referred to appeared in *Gazetteer*, 9 Dec. p. [2]: "Mr. Steevens's new edition of Shakspeare is at the press; and the booksellers who are the proprietors of it say, they expect to overtake Mr. Malone in six months." EM apparently supposed that the paragraph was inserted by the editor of *Gazetteer*. Since James Perry's resignation on 27 Nov. the paper had been, in effect, without an editor; it was being managed temporarily by J. Beauchamp, whose "position was equivalent to those of the modern production manager and make-up editor" (R. L. Haig, *The Gazetteer, 1735–1797*, 1960, pp. 217, 220). EM, however, probably did not know of Perry's resignation.

[8] No such notice appeared in *Pub. Adv.* for Jan. or Feb. 1791.

[9] MS. "the" deleted before "on"

[10] George Arnold, bookseller at No. 51 or 56 Mortimer St., Cavendish Square (Maxted).

[11] In fact, *Crit. Rev.* did not review EM's edition of Shakespeare for another year (Dec. 1791, n.s. iii. 361–69). The reviewer criticized EM for overannotating his text, but concluded, "Mr. Malone has corrected the text of Shakspeare with uncommon care . . . and his Edition is not only more convenient in size, but in every other respect, superior to any that has hitherto appeared."

[12] EB's undated letter is now at Yale. It was printed in James Boswell the younger's *Biographical Memoir of the Late Edmond Malone*, 1814, pp. 17–19, and in *Corres. EB* vi. 181–82. EB praised EM's "infinite pains", "great sagacity", and "publick Spirited Labours", and sent him a copy of his *Reflections on the Revolution in France*.

TO MALONE, 18 JANUARY 1791

To Malone,
Tuesday 18 January 1791

MS. Hyde Collection.

ADDRESS: To Edmond Malone Esq. at the Right Honourable Lord Sunderlin's [Baronston, near Mulingar *deleted*] Ireland [*added in unidentified hand*] Gone to Sackville Street, Dublin.

POSTMARKS: [London] JA 18 91 [Dublin] JA 24, JA 28, JA 28.

London, 18 Janry. 1791

MY DEAR MALONE: You will have seen from The Gentleman's Magazine that I got your commission as to Dr. Jephson's *obituary* executed, though your letter did not reach me till the 29 Decr. Pray who is the Sir Alexander Murray who attended his funeral?[1] The Bankers on whom your bill was drawn were not at home when I called, so I could not get it discounted by them; but my spanish brother did it very readily, and with his compliments begged you might be informed that he was glad he could accomodate you, and that he would be happy to receive your farther commands.[2] On the 1st current, I paid the neat £50 which my brother gave me, according to your direction, and have the receipt ready to be sent, or kept till your return as you chuse. The papers had inserted Dr. Jephson's death before your letter came.

I have read your *Shakspeare Ford and Jonson* with as much attention and as much admiration of your research, accuracy and clearness of arrangement and expression as you could wish. But I hesitate to introduce it into view in the newspapers, till I hear from you; for to tell you the truth I cannot help dissenting from you as to my old friend Macklin's having been the inventor of the statement which you have refuted with complete nay almost superflous success, I mean with a superfluity of proof and argument. I waited till I should hear others upon it, and started it at the Club. Dr. Warren who I found to my surprise was master of it, said just what I had thought, that you had been too hard on Macklin, and that your dissertation would have been equally

[1] JB apparently was mistaken. The obituary in *Gent. Mag.* listed "Alexander Murray, esq." as having attended the funeral; there was no baronet or knight of that name alive at that time. He is unidentified.

[2] T. D. Boswell after his return from Spain in 1780 had settled in London as a merchant and banker; his business was now at No. 26 Titchfield St., near Oxford St. (*Univ. Brit. Directory* i. 80).

perfect without arraigning his veracity, but only shewing that the pamphlet which he quoted was grossly erroneous; for, you will observe that all its errour though fatal to it's credit does by no means shew that it was a recent invention, for, all of it might have been the effect of ignorance or falsification at the time when the pamphlet is said to have been written. Mr. Steevens agreed with Dr. Warren, and told us that the pamphlet's not having been yet recovered by you did not prove that it did not exist, or had not existed; for more than one which had been supposed fictions had been recovered; and he added that he had never seen your advertisement. Thinking as I do I was affraid to write upon the subject in any way, lest I should either oppose you, or seem to agree in the charge of falshood against poor Charles, who unquestionably could not *himself* be the Authour of the statement, for which more reading than he has, nor of the verses for which more genius than he has, is requisite. I will wait your answer, and one way or other shall have your dissertation drawn into particular view, as it shews what a lawyer and judge you might be if you would.

I have been so disturbed by sad money-matters that my mind has been quite fretful. £500 which I borrowed and lent to a first cousin an unlucky Captain of an Indiaman were due on the 15th to a merchant in the City. I could not possibly raise that sum, and was apprehensive of being hardly used. He however indulged me with an allowance to make partial payments £150 in two months £150 in eight months, and the remainder with the interests in eighteen months. How I am to manage I am at a loss, and I know you cannot help me.[3] So this upon my honour is no hint. I am really tempted to accept of the £1000 for my Life of Johnson.[4] Yet it

[3] On 31 May 1781 JB had borrowed £500 from Alexander Anderson, merchant in Prince's St., Lothbury, to lend to his impecunious cousin Bruce Boswell (1747–1807), who was to go out as Captain of the East India Company's ship, *Earl of Chesterfield*. The voyage (1781–86) was a financial disaster, and Bruce Boswell was dismissed from his command (Journ. 31 May 1781; *Univ. Brit. Directory* i. 53; "A Narrative of the Voyage of the Ship Earl of Chesterfield"—C 306; "View of my Affairs", 1787–93—A 52). The loan was not repaid until after JB's death (Robert Boswell to Sir William Forbes, 3 July [?1795]—MS. Somervell Papers, NLS; *Boswelliana*, p. 188).

[4] George Robinson (1737–1801), bookseller at No. 25 Paternoster Row, was an active purchaser of copyrights, noted for his generosity to authors (Maxted). He had mentioned to EM in early 1790 that he would be willing to pay £1,000 for the rights to the *Life* (To Bennet Langton, 9 Apr. 1790—BL Add. MSS. 3,6747E, ff. 50–51, printed in part in Waingrow, p. 313; *post* From EM, 5 Mar.).

would go to my heart to sell it at a price which I think much too low.—Let me struggle, and hope. I cannot be out on *Shrove tuesday* as I flattered myself. P. 376 of Vol. II[5] is ordered for press and I expect another proof tonight. But I have yet near 200 pages of Copy besides letters and *the death* which is not yet written. My second volume will I see be 40 or 50 pages more than my first.[6]

Your absence is a woeful want in all respects. You will I dare say perceive a difference in the part which is revised only by myself, and in which many *insertions* will appear.

My spirits are at present bad. But I will mention all I can recollect. Did I inform you that Dr. Blagden was blackballed, and that the Bishop of Carlisle shared the same fate the same day, I suppose to keep the other in countenance. Before the ballot there was a question whether your proposal for two blackballs which had *eight* for it and *two* against, was now a law. Sir Joshua alone was *for* it against *eight* of us. He then moved to have it considered by the Club at large and inserted in the cards which was seconded by Dr. Fordyce and settled accordingly; but on tuesday last neither mover nor seconder being present no notice was taken of it.[7] We had last Club Banks, Steevens, Warren, Windham, Burney, Dr. Warton, and Langton, who has been here several weeks at the Queen's Head in Holborn.[8] Warton and he and Seward are to dine with me next saturday at my new house to which I remove tomorrow, having taken this for another quarter, that the other might be seasoned.

I had almost omitted to acquaint you that Humfrey and Man of Harp lane[9] have applied to me twice on *your* account for £17. 19. 2 of charges on the Madeira which is a *joint* concern.[10] I said I should write to you. How shall it be managed? Poor C. has been at

[5] *Life* iv. 78–79.

[6] The first volume contains 516 pages and 28 preliminary pages; the second volume contains 586 pages and a title-page.

[7] A unanimous vote was required for election to The Club. On 3 Mar. 1789 EM had proposed that at least two black balls be required to exclude a new member; but no action was taken until 28 Dec. 1790, when Reynolds moved that the call for the next meeting should announce that a vote would be taken to determine the issue. However, at the meeting of 11 Jan. the proposal was allowed to expire (Minute Book).

[8] JB had supped at the Queen's Head in High Holborn on 8 July 1763 and 26 May 1786 (Journ.). Gentlemen coming from the country often put up at inns in Holborn (Wheatley and Cunningham ii. 222; Bryant Lillywhite, *London Coffee Houses*, 1963, pp. 465–66).

[9] Sugar-coopers (*Univ. Brit. Directory* i. 188); also, one supposes, wine-coopers.

[10] Apparently JB, EM, and Courtenay together had bought some madeira.

Bath for some time. I had a few lines from him a day or two ago. His situation is deplorable. I would fain have the seat in Parliament turned to account, and I found him not averse; but that must be negotiated if at all, by others.[11] Sir Joshua has been out of town a long time, I *really* think more than three weeks, at Burke's and Lord Ossory's.[12] He returned on sunday; but I have not yet seen him. I have his card for dinner on thursday. I am to dine with Erskine on friday.[13] For a wonder he called on me, and then sent his invitation. Jo. Warton is to be there; but he declares that he did not suggest me.

Have I mentioned to you that Steevens told us at the Club he should take you *all* in—"History of the Stage" etc. (which my eldest son pleased me by saying "this is *very* entertaining") and that he is to exalt Ritson and advance Monck Mason.[14] He has not yet begun. I have scarcely left room to offer my best compliments to Lord and Lady Sunderlin and your sisters. Ever gratefully and affectionately yours,

JAMES BOSWELL

From Malone,
Sunday 23 January 1791

MS. Yale (C 1922).
ADDRESS: James Boswell, Esqre., Great Portland Street, Cavendish Square, London, Single Sheet.
POSTMARKS: MULLINGAR, IRELAND [Dublin] JA 24 [London] JA 31 91.

Baronston, Jan. 23, 1791

MY DEAR BOSWELL, I have for some time been in daily expectation of receiving a line from you, which I think you would not have omitted to send me, merely to inform me of the safe arrival of my draft, and can only account for my not hearing from you by supposing you have written by some private hand, a mode of

[11] That is, JB thought the seat might be sold. However, Courtenay sat for Tamworth until 1796.

[12] Reynolds left for Beaconsfield on 1 Jan.; he planned to call at Woburn Abbey, seat of the Duke of Bedford, on 10 Jan., and from there proceed to visit Lord and Lady Ossory at Ampthill, Bedfordshire (*Letters Reynolds*, pp. 208–10).

[13] Thomas Erskine.

[14] Quotation marks supplied in this sentence.

conveyance always uncertain.[1]—I have had also another disappointment; for Arnold the Stationer in Mortimer Street neglected to send me on the 1st of this month the Gent. Mag. and Monthly Review, as I directed him to do regularly. Pray be so good as to call on him about them.—I see I am reviewed in the *Analytical* Review.[2] I shall be much obliged if you will enclose that in *one* packet[3] directed for me at the inside, and the outer cover directed for John Lees, Esq. General Post Office, Dublin. Has the European M. taken any notice of me? If S[teevens] does any thing, it will be there.[4]

Has no body had the charity to rectify that silly account which appeared in the P. Adv. and which by what you say, I suppose was written by Lord Mountmorres?[5] Without any intention to deceive, the representation is as fallacious, as it well could be. Anyone would imagine from it that from my early youth I had been a dangler upon theatres, and were as well acquainted with the birth parentage and education of all the dramatick tribe as Mr. Tighe.[6] My having performed a trifling part in a school-play, when quite a child, has no more relation to my publishing the works of Shakspeare, than any other fact in the world: yet according to this writer, it gave a colour to all my future life.—The truth is, I never thought of commenting on Shakspeare till about fifteen years ago, and am so far from a frequenter of theatres, that I do not go there a dozen times in a winter. If a man pretends to be a biographer, he should mention the father of his hero; he should tell where he was bred; in what college he was educated, with what degree of reputation he passed through it, etc. etc.—In short

[1] JB's letter of 18 Jan. arrived in Dublin on 24 Jan. and was directed to Baronston, about fifty miles away, where it probably arrived on 26 Jan., two days after EM left for Dublin. It was redirected and did not reach Dublin again until 28 Jan. (*ante* To EM, 18 Jan., headnote).

[2] The review appeared in two parts, Dec. 1790, viii. 451–54 and Sept. 1791, xi. 1–13. Though the reviewer objected to some of EM's notes, he was generally complimentary, and concluded, "We do not hesitate to pronounce him [EM] equal or superior to most, or all of his predecessors, in deep, various, and appropriate reading; in unwearied diligence, fidelity, scrupulous exactness, and unremitting perseverance; whether these be always assisted, or set off by an equal degree of discrimination and sagacity, we decline to determine."

[3] MS. "packet" written above deleted "wrapper"

[4] Steevens was a friend of Isaac Reed, who managed *Eur. Mag.*, but EM's edition of Shakespeare was not reviewed there.

[5] *Ante* To EM, 16 Dec. 1790 and n. 3; *post* From EM, 14 Apr. n. 5; Appendix 3, pp. 437–38.

[6] Edward Tighe (*ante* To EM, 8 July 1789, n. 4) had long been a theatrical enthusiast (*Letters DG*, index; Stone and Kahrl, p. 179).

Lord M. had much better confine himself to french translation or Irish Politicks, and leave his school fellows to the care of wiser heads.[7]

I mean to leave this place tomorrow and shall be in Dublin on Wednesday:—So Sackville Street, Dublin, is my address for the future.

Pray write to me soon, if you have not already done it. Where is Courteney? I have had a letter from him a long time by me and have waited to know from you whether he was in London or Bath, before I wrote to him.[8] I will send him the best account I can get when I go to town of our *paltry* Irish Politicks. Remember me most kindly to him and Sir Joshua, and believe me ever, my dear B., your sincerely Affectionate,

EDM. MALONE

To Malone,
Saturday 29 January 1791

MS. Hyde Collection.
ADDRESS: To Edmond Malone Esq. at the Right Hon. Lord Sunderlin's, Sackville Street, Dublin.
POSTMARKS: [London] JA 29 91 [Dublin] FE 4.

London, 29 Janry. 1791

MY DEAR MALONE: You will find this a most desponding and disagreable letter for which I ask your pardon. But your vigour of mind, and warmth of heart make your friendship of such consequence that it is drawn upon like a Bank. I have for some weeks had the most woeful return of melancholy, in so much that I have not only had no relish of any thing, but a continual uneasiness, and all the prospect before me for the rest of Life has seemed gloomy and hopeless.[1] The state of my affairs is exceed-

[7] Lord Mountmorres had written several tracts on Irish politics, and in 1790 had translated *The Danger of the Political Balance of Europe . . . from the French of the King of Sweden.*

[8] MS. "to him" written above deleted "to me". Courtenay had written on 15 Dec. 1790 (*ante* To EM, 16 Dec. 1790, n. 13). He returned to London a few days before 5 Feb. (Journ.).

[1] On 1 Mar., when JB's spirits returned, he wrote that he had been depressed for "ten or eleven weeks", that is, since early or mid-December (Journ.).

ingly embarrassed. I mentioned to you that the £500 which I borrowed several years ago and lent to a first cousin an unfortunate India Captain must now be paid £150 on the 18 of march £150 on the 18 of Octr. and £257. 15. 6 on the 18 July 1792. This debt presses upon my mind, and it is uncertain if I shall ever get a shilling of it again. The clear money on which I can reckon out of my estate is scarcely £900 a year. What *can* I do? My grave brother urges me to quit London and live at my seat in the Country, where he thinks that I might be able to save so as gradually to relieve myself. But alas I should be *absolutely* miserable. In the mean time such are my projects and sanguine expectations, that you know I purchased an estate which was given long ago to a younger son of our family, and came to be sold last autumn, and paid for it £2500 £1500 of which I borrow upon itself by a mortgage.[2] But the remaining £1000 I cannot conceive a possibility of raising, but by the mode of Annuity, which is I believe a very heavy disadvantage. I own it was imprudent in me to make a dear purchase at a time when I was sadly straitened; but if I have had missed the opportunity, it never again would have occurred, and I should have been vexed to see an ancient appanage, a piece of—as it were the flesh and blood of the family, in the hands of a stranger. And now that I have made the purchase, I should feel myself quite despicable should I give it up. In this situation then my Dear Sir, would it not be wise in me to accept of 1000 guineas for my Life of Johnson, supposing the person who made the offer[3] should now stand to it, which I fear may not be the case, for two volumes may be considered as a disadvantageous circumstance. Could I indeed raise £1000 upon the credit of the Work, I should incline to *game* as Sir Joshua says;[4] because it *may* produce double the money, though Steevens *kindly* tells me that I have overprinted, and that the curiosity about

[2] Knockroon belonged to the Boswells of Auchinleck in the sixteenth century, but about the year 1600 John Boswell of Auchinleck gave it to his fourth son William, the only son by his second marriage. William's great-great grandson, John Boswell of Knockroon, tax collector in Ayr, was left impoverished by the collapse of Douglas, Heron, and Co. in 1772; his estate was sold in Oct. 1790 (James Paterson, *History of the Counties of Ayr and Wigton*, 1863, i. pt. 1. 192, 198–99; *Ayrshire*, pp. 133, 302–03; From John Boswell, 13 Sept. 1790). JB had borrowed the £1,500 from Alexander Fairlie (Journ. 20 Feb.).

[3] George Robinson (*ante* To EM, 18 Jan. and n. 4).

[4] Reynolds had said that "human nature loves *gaming*—agitation, uncertainty" (Journ. 6 July 1785).

Johnson is *now* only in our own circle. Pray decide for me; and if as I suppose you are for my taking the offer inform me with whom I am to treat. In my present state of spirits, I am all timidity. Your absence has been a severe stroke to me. I am at present quite at a loss what to do. Last week they gave me six sheets. I have now before me in *proof* p. 456.[5] Yet I have above 100 pages of my copy remaining, besides his *Death* which is yet to be written, and many insertions were there room. As also seven[6] and thirty letters exclusive of twenty to Dr. Brocklesby most of which will furnish only extracts.[7] I am advised to extract several of those to others and leave out some; for my first volume makes only 516 pages and to have 600 in the second will seem aukward, besides increasing the expence considerably. The *Counsellor*[8] indeed has devised an ingenious way to thicken the first volume, by *prefixing* the Index.[9] I have now desired to have but one compositor.[10] Indeed I go sluggishly and comfortlessly about my work. As I pass your door I cast many a longing look.

I am to cancel a leaf of the first volume, having found that though Sir Joshua certainly assured me he had no objection to my mentioning that Johnson wrote a Dedication for him, he now thinks otherwise.[11] In that leaf occurs the mention of Johnson having written to Dr. Leland thanking the University of Dublin for their Diploma. What shall I say as to it?[12] I have also room to

[5] *Life* iv. 223–25.

[6] MS. "seven" superimposed upon "four"

[7] *Life* iv. 353–69.

[8] Thomas Edlyne Tomlins (1762–1841), a corrector at Baldwin's, "who having contracted debt was obliged to quit the bar, and was now honestly getting his livelihood by *certain* diligence" (Journ. 14 Feb.). "Counsellor Tomlins" (Journ. 3 Oct. 1793) edited *St. James's Chron.* and had already written two books on legal matters.

[9] The "Alphabetical Table of Contents" prepared by Tomlins added only fifteen pages to the first volume.

[10] J. Plymsell (*ante* From EM, 8 July 1790, n. 6), who had been sharing the task with at least "Mr. Manning" (*Life* iv. 321).

[11] A specimen of the cancelled leaf, pp. 271–72 of the first volume, is now at Yale. For the cancelled passage on p. 272, see *Life* ii. 2 n. 1, iv. 555–56.

[12] The passage mentioning Thomas Leland (1722–85), D.D., Fellow of Trinity College, reads: "Johnson acknowledged the favour in a letter to Dr. Leland, one of their number; but I have not been able to obtain a copy of it." JB first struck out the latter part of the sentence from "I have" and substituted "though his son has been so good as to make a search it has not been found." However, he decided to retain the first version (*Life* i. 489; see *Letters SJ* i. 179). In 1786 JB had unsuccessfully solicited a copy of the letter from Leland's son John, who had replied that the letter was "at present" on loan to a friend of his father's (From John Leland, 29 July 1786). In 1787 EM appealed to his friend Lord Charlemont for help in obtaining the letter, because, he wrote, "a story has gone abroad that Johnson set no value on this Irish degree, which this letter would confute". Charlemont, however, was unable to

state shortly the anecdote of the College Cook, which I beg you may get for me.[13] I shall be very anxious till I hear from you.

Having harassed you with so much about myself, I have left no room for any thing else. We had a numerous Club on tuesday. Fox in the chair, quoting Homer and Fielding etc. to the astonishment of Jo. Warton, who with Langton and Seward eat a plain bit with me, in my new house last saturday. Sir Joshua has put up Dr. Lawrence, who will be blackballed as sure as he exists.[14] Pray give me some particulars of your irish life. Present my best respects to Lord Sunderlin and the Ladies and believe me to be ever affectionately yours,

J. B.

We dined on Wednesday at Sir Joshua's. 13 *without* Miss P[almer]. Himself—Blagden—Batt—Erskine—Langton—Dr. Warton—Metcalfe—Dr. Lawrence—His brother a Clergyman[15]—Sir Charles Bunbury—myself.

Your cook has left at my house for you, four penny post letters, and two sealed notes. I know none of the hands. What shall I do with them.

We all think that Palmeria will be Mrs. Blagden.[16]

help (*Charlemont Papers* ii. 62–63). Leland eventually supplied a copy of the letter for the fifth edition of the *Life*, 1807 (i. 467 n. 9).

[13] When he wrote to Lord Charlemont about the Leland letter (see preceding note), EM also mentioned a letter "to some man who was employed in the college kitchen, who had a mind to breed his son a scholar, and wrote to Johnson for advice." This letter, Charlemont replied, "is also well remembered, and John Kearney has promised, if possible, to find it, though he seems almost to despair" (*Charlemont Papers* ii. 62–63). John Kearney had been EM's classmate at Trinity College, Dublin, where he was now Professor of Oratory. In 1799 he became Provost of Trinity College, and in 1806 was made Bishop of Ossory.

[14] *Post* To EM, 10 Feb. and n. 4.

[15] The Rev. Richard Laurence (1760–1838), D.C.L., vicar of Coleshill, Berkshire, in 1814 was appointed Regius Professor of Hebrew and canon of Christ Church, Oxford, and in 1822 became Archbishop of Cashel, Ireland.

[16] Mary Palmer married the Earl of Inchiquin in July 1792 (*ante* To EM, 12 July 1788, n. 18), so Blagden eventually was disappointed. In June 1792 JB, William Seward, and William Parsons, barrister, composed a short poem (M 66) on the subject while dining at the house of John Cator, a timber merchant, friend of SJ, and one of Henry Thrale's executors. The first five lines are in JB's hand, the remainder in Seward's:

For fair Palmeria Blagden breath'd his sighs
Blagden the grave the narrative the wise
But she the loftiest of all lofty dames
Thus in aspiring haughtiness exclaims
"Shall I this philosophi[c] Fellow take
On *me* his vile experiments to make
One who will analize me joint by joint
And after all may freeze below the point

From Malone,
Saturday 5 February 1791

MS. Yale (C 1923).
ADDRESS: James Boswell, Esqre., Great Portland Street, Cavendish Square, London, Single Sheet.
POSTMARKS: IRELAND [Dublin] FE <5> [London] FE 9 91.

Sackville Street, Feb. 5, 1791

MY DEAR BOSWELL: I have received both your letters, (18th and 29th of Jany.) the latter yesterday, and the other not so soon as I might have done, in consequence of its having gone to Baronston and being returned from thence.[1] I have at present time only to write three words on the spur of the occasion, but will answer them both very soon—Pray be so good as to buy, or to get the Don[2] to buy, for me, a half of a Lottery ticket. I will send you a bill for eight guineas, which I suppose will be the purchase, on Monday or tuesday next and at the same time enough to pay my own share of the duty on our Madeira and also Courteney's.—This Letter may possibly get to you the day before the first day's drawing;[3] but in case it should not reach you till thursday or friday, buy the half ticket warranted undrawn from your old friend Hazard.[4]—My last letter from Baronston I imagine reached you the day after you wrote last.[5] Pray be so good as to remember what I said in it about *Reviews*, and give Arnold the Stationer a slight reproof for his want of punctuality—I will write to Courteney in a day or two[6]—Yours ever, my dear Boswell, most sincerely,

E. MALONE

I mean the half ticket to be one of those stamped by

I cannot stoop to be a thing so mean
A Dutchess I—no—every Inch a Queen."

The pun in the last line is of course on the name "Inchiquin". This *jeu d'esprit* caused JB some concern when a copy was given to Cator, and JB wrote to ask that it be circulated no farther (To John Cator, 8 June 1792).

[1] *Ante* From EM, 23 Jan. n. 1.

[2] T. D. Boswell, who had lived in Spain.

[3] The letter arrived on 9 Feb.; the drawing was to begin "on or before 9 Feb. 1791, at the Guildhall" (C. L'Est. Ewen, *Lotteries and Sweepstakes*, 1932, p. 210).

[4] Probably Robert Hazard of Hazard, Burne, and Warner, stockbrokers, No. 93 Cornhill (*Univ. Brit. Directory* i. 175). His firm was among the most prominent licensed dealers in lottery tickets from 1789 until the State Lottery was abolished in 1826 (Ewen, pp. 232, 271).

[5] Actually two days after, on 31 Jan.

[6] Not reported.

Government;[7]—and be so good as to write the names Edmond, Henrietta, and Catharine Malone on the back of it and to let me know the number; for expectation, you know is half the sport.

From Malone,
Monday 7 or Tuesday 8 February 1791

Not reported. See *ante* From EM, 5 Feb.: "I will send you a bill for eight guineas, which I suppose will be the purchase, on Monday or tuesday next and at the same time enough to pay my own share of the duty on our Madeira and also Courteney's." EM also answered JB's objections to his essay, "Shakspeare, Ford, and Jonson" (*ante* To EM, 18 Jan.; *post* To EM, 25 Feb.) and informed him, in answer to a query (*ante* To EM, 29 Jan.), that the bookseller who had mentioned paying £1,000 for rights to the *Life* was George Robinson (Journ. 20 Feb.).

To Malone,
Thursday 10 February 1791

MS. Hyde Collection.
ADDRESS: To Edmond Malone Esq. at the Right Honble. Lord Sunderlin's, Sackville Street, Dublin, Single Sheet.
POSTMARKS: [London] FE 10 91 [Dublin] FE 14.

London, 10 Febry. 1791

MY DEAR MALONE: Yours of the 5th reached me yesterday. I instantly went to the Don who purchased for you at the office of Hazard and Co. a half stamped by Government and warranted undrawn of No. 43m152 in the English State Lottery. I have marked on the back of it Edmond Henrietta and Catharine Malone, and if Fortune will not favour those three united, I shall blame her. This half shall lye in my Bureau with my one whole

[7] The State Lottery was run by contractors and licensed dealers, but there were many unlicensed dealers and fraud was common. The Treasury stamp was intended to reduce forgery (Ewen, p. 252).

one, till you desire it to be placed elsewhere. The cost with registration is £8. 12. 6. A half is always proportionally dearer than a whole. I bought my ticket at Nicholson's[1] the day before and paid £16. 8 for it. I did not look at the number but sealed it up. In the evening a handbill was circulated by Nicholson that a ticket the day before sold at his office for £16. 8 was drawn a prize of £5000. The number was mentioned in the handbill. I had resolved not to *know* what mine was, till after the drawing of the Lottery was finished, that I might not receive a *sudden* shock of blank. But this unexpected circumstance which elated me by calculating that mine must certainly be one of 100 or at most 200 sold by Nicholson the day before, made me look at the two *last figures* of it which alas were 48, whereas those of the fortunate one were 33. I have remanded my ticket to its secresy. O could I but get a few thousands, what a difference would it make upon my state of mind, which is harrassed by thinking of my debts. I am anxious to hear your determination as to my *Magnum Opus*. I am very very unwilling to part with the property of it, and certainly would not if I could but [get] credit for £1000 for three or four years. Could you not assist me in that way, on the security of the Book and of an Assignment to one half of my rents £700 which upon my honour are always due, and would be forthcoming in case of my decease. I *will* not sell, till I have your answer as to this.[2]

On tuesday we had a Club of eleven. Lords Lucan (in the chair), Ossory, Macarteney, Eliot, Bishop of Clonfert,[3] Young Burke, myself, Courtenay, Windham, Sir Joshua, and Charles Fox, who takes to us exceedingly, and asked to have dinner a little later; so it is now to be at ½ past five. Burke had made great interest for his Drum Major,[4] and would you believe it? had not

[1] William Nicholson, stockbroker and dealer in lottery tickets, Bank St., Cornhill (*Univ. Brit. Directory* i. 239).

[2] *Post* From EM, 24 Feb.

[3] Charles Bingham (1735–99), first Baron Lucan of Castlebar and later (1795) first Earl of Lucan, member since 1782. George Macartney (1737–1806), first Baron Macartney and later (1794) first Earl Macartney, member since 1786; for a biographical account, see Fifer, pp. lxxvi–lxxvii, 105 n. 19. Edward Craggs-Eliot (1727–1804), first Baron Eliot of St. Germans, member since 1782; see Fifer, pp. xlvii–xlviii. Richard Marlay (c. 1728–1802), D.D., Bishop of Clonfert, member since 1777; see Fifer, pp. lxxvii–lxxviii.

[4] French Laurence, called EB's "Drum Major" because of his position as counsel for the managers in the impeachment of Warren Hastings, had the distinction of being blackballed three times before his election to The Club in 1802 (Minute Book).

Courtenay and I been there, he would have been chosen. Banks was quite indignant; but had company at home. Lord Ossory ventured to put up the Bishop of Peterborough, and I really hope he will get in.[5] Courtenay and I will not be there, and probably not again till you come. It was poor work last day. The *whelp*[6] would not let us hear Fox.

I have been with Arnold again, who called his Wife to declare that she herself had the first day of month before last put both Month. Rev. and Gent. Mag. into the Post Office. She was told that as they were directed to the General Post Office Dublin there was no occasion to put a penny with each as is done with Newspapers for Ireland. Whether the *want* of that has occasioned their being stopped I know not. He is to inquire more and let me know. Perry the former editor of the Gazeteer has now the whole of the Morning Chronicle, as he told me.[7] The first gleam of spirits I have, I shall animadvert on your erroneous *history* in the P. A. I am strangely ill, and doubt if even you could dispel the Demonic influence.[8]

I have now before me p. 488[9] in print, yet the 923 page of the Copy only is exhausted; and there remain 80, besides the Death, as to which I shall be concise though solemn—Also many letters.

Pray how shall I wind up. Shall I give the Character in my Tour, somewhat enlarged?

I must have a cancelled leaf in Vol. II of that passage where there is a conversation as to conjugal infidelity on the husband's side, and his wife saying she did not care how many women he went to if he *loved* her alone; with my proposing to mark in a pocket book every time a wife *refuses* etc. etc. I wonder how you and I

[5] John Hinchliffe (1731–94), formerly Master of Trinity College, Cambridge and Vice-Chancellor, became Bishop of Peterborough in 1769. He was noted for his liberal views and his eloquence in the House of Lords. He was not elected to The Club in 1791 (*post* To EM, 25 Feb.) but, proposed again by Lord Ossory and seconded by JB, he was elected in 1792.

[6] Richard Burke, Jr.

[7] James Perry (1756–1821), founder of *Eur. Mag.*, had edited *Gazetteer* from 1783 until Mar. 1789, when he assumed control of *Morn. Chron.* and turned it from a Government to an Opposition paper. He retained nominal control of *Gazetteer* until Nov. 1790, but left the task of producing it to others, and from 1789 on the paper began to decline. Towards the end of 1790, Perry and James Gray, who also had worked at *Gazetteer*, were negotiating the purchase of *Morn. Chron.* (Lucyle Werkmeister, *The London Daily Press, 1772–1792*, 1963, pp. 74, 283, 317, 336–37).

[8] JB believed, at times anyway, that evil spirits could cause madness (Bailey ii. 239 and n. 14; *Life* iii. 176 n. 1).

[9] *Life* iv. 270–72.

[10] The cancelled passage is printed, *Life* iii. 406 n.†.

admitted this to the publick eye for Windham etc. were struck with its *indelicacy* and it might hurt the Book much. It is however mighty good stuff.[10] No room for compliments. Ever most warmly yours,

J. B.

From Malone,
Thursday 24 February 1791

MS. Yale (C 1924).
ADDRESS: James Boswell, Esqre., Great Portland Street, Portland Chapel, London, Single Sheet.
POSTMARKS: [Dublin] FE 2<4> [London] MR 1 91.

Dublin, Feb. 24, 1791

MY DEAR BOSWELL, Having written to you a few days before I received your last letter, I have delayed answering it for some time, and perhaps should have postponed taking up the pen to another day, but that I have this moment observed you request a speedy answer as to the business you mention. I am really sorry that I cannot comply with your wishes; but the payment of 624£ for a relation for whom I became security some years ago, under which I am now smarting,[1] and the loss of 130£ by my poor friend Dr. Jephson, part of which I furnished him with, or rather borrowed, to assist his son at the Temple, have made me resolve to engage in no securities again of any kind; and I am sure when you consider that my little fortune is but just sufficient to live even on my contracted scale and that it will by no means bear any further diminution, you will think that I have abundant reason for this determination. I hope and trust you will still be able by the means of your book to combat with your present difficulties, and that either Dilly or Baldwin may be induced to furnish you with a good sum on the strength of it.[2]

I have nothing new to send you, and indeed how should it be otherwise? We all here look up to your *great city*, as the source of every thing brilliant and extraordinary, and when ever five or six

[1] Nothing more of this business has been reported.

[2] Dilly and Baldwin each advanced JB £200 (*post* To EM, 9 Mar. and n. 2).

mails are due, as has frequently been the case lately, we suffer a literary and a political famine. What is Steevens doing? has he yet gone to press? By his delay, it should seem, that I have furnished him with some tough morsels.—I have received the Monthly Review and the Gent. Magazine for Jany. but they were not sent on the 1st of this month as they ought to have been. Pray be so good as to tell Arnold so, and at the same time to tell him to send me no more of the *Gazeteers*; but the *Oracle* to Lord Sunderlin as usual. On the 1st of next month, if I am reviewed either in the Critical or the Monthly,[3] I should be glad of either or both; but not otherwise. I have not yet received the Analytical for Jany. but suppose I shall have it from you in a few days. If you can gather any intelligence for me at Payne's, Egerton's and White's,[4] as[5] to the present state of my book, I mean whether they have nearly disposed of their stores, I shall thank you for it; and also for Payne's and Egerton's catalogue, each under cover to John Lees, Esqr., Post Office, Dublin. You will probably find both those catalogues at my house—I dined with your friend *Thomas*[6] at Sir Michl. Cromie's[7] last Sunday, and am to dine with him at his own house in a few days. The Bishop of Dromore's wife[8] is so ill with a stone in the Gall bladder, that he cannot see his friends at home; but I have dined with him elsewhere; and always delight him by a little English News. Another of our Clubmates, poor Lord Charlemont, is by no means well. He has had a very disagreable nervous complaint, accompanied with a heavy cough and great languor, these ten days past. I am just come from him. He is in tolerable spirits; but the great feebleness of his pulse which for

[3] For the review in *Crit. Rev.* (Dec. 1791), see *ante* From EM, 23 Dec. 1790, n. 11. The *Monthly Rev.* did not review EM's edition of Shakespeare until Sept. 1793, n.s. xii. 56–72 and Mar. 1794, n.s. xiii. 241–68; its review was by Thomas Pearne, a Fellow of Peterhouse, Cambridge (B. C. Nangle, *The Monthly Review, Second Series, 1790–1815*, 1955).

[4] For Thomas Payne, bookseller, see *ante* From EM, 24 Oct. 1785, n. 4. John and Thomas Egerton were booksellers in Charing Cross, opposite the Admiralty; Benjamin White (d. 1794) was bookseller with his son Benjamin at No. 63 Horace's Head, Fleet St. (Maxted).

[5] MS. "?how" before "as"

[6] Thomas Barnard, Bishop of Killaloe. He signed himself, in episcopal style, "Thos. Killaloe".

[7] Sir Michael Cromie (c. 1745–c. 1824), Bt., merchant and banker, later fled the country to avoid bankruptcy proceedings and perhaps imprisonment for debt, and died in exile. JB had dined with him at Lord Sunderlin's on 16 July 1785 and at EM's on 5 Nov. 1789 (Journ.).

[8] Thomas Percy had in 1759 married Anne (d. 1806), daughter of Barton Gutteridge of Desborough, Northamptonshire.

several days have beat but 40 times in a minute, (little more than half the healthy pulsation) is a very alarming symptom. I have got through my 12 dinners without breaking a blood vessel, and shall live at home quietly this week—Pray tell C. that I have received his letter,[9] and will write to him very soon—I have literally only room to add that I am, my Dear B., most faithfully and Affectionately yours,

E. MALONE

To Malone,
Friday 25 February 1791

MS. Hyde Collection.

ADDRESS: To Edmond Malone Esq., Sackville Street, Dublin, Single Sheet.

POSTMARKS: [London] FE 26 91 [Dublin] MR 2.

London, 25 Febry. 1791

MY DEAR MALONE: I have been day after day anxiously waiting for a letter from you, for you must have received one from me since yours enclosing the bill which I have discounted and with the contents paid your and Courtenays shares of the duty on the Madeira at the same time with my own, and applied the remainder to your half Lottery Ticket on which N.B. you are some shillings in my debt. I have not seen Sir Joshua I think for a forthnight.[1] I have been worse than you can possibly imagine, or I hope ever shall be able to imagine, which no man can do without experiencing the malady. It has been for some time painful to me to be in company.[2] I however am a little better, and to meet Sir

[9] Not reported.

[1] JB wrote in his journal for this day, "It was not pleasing to find that Sir Joshua had all this time known that I was in sad spirits, and never once called or sent to inquire about me.—We must take our friends as they are."

[2] Apparently others found it painful to be in company with JB during his attack of hypochondria, as Courtenay's letter to EM of 22 Feb. attests: "Poor Boswell is very low—and dispirited—and almos[t] melancholly mad—feels no spring—no pleasure in existence—and is so perceptibly alter'd for the worse—that it is remark'd

Joshua today at dinner at Mr. Dance's,[3] and shall tell him that he is to have good irish claret. My brother is to get me accurate information whether the Bishop of Clonfert's wine may be sent to our *Maitre d'Hotel*, as you call Thomas,[4] and I shall acquaint you.[5] By the way Mr. Dundas has strictly kept his word to me, and given him the first vacant place in his Navy Office. It is not quite £100 a year; but the profit is *something* to so attentive a man, and though he is obliged to attend four or five hours every day, he has time to manage his own business as formerly; and I have no doubt that his attention and accuracy will recommend him so as that he shall obtain much better promotion.[6]

every where—. I try all I can to rouze him—but he recurs so tiresomely and tediously—for the same cursed trite Commonplace topics—about death etc.—that we grow old—and when we are old—we are not young—that I despair of effecting a Cure—Doctr. Warren and Devaynes very kindly interest themselves about him—but you would be of more service to him than Any body is—. I'll write to you at large in a day or two—. Seward gave B. a supper 'tother night (a french pye)—the Company—an opera singer—and a young french Architect—but it did not do:—. He complains like Soloman—that all is Vanity—" (MS. Yale).

[3] Nathaniel Dance (1735–1811), painter, whom JB had met in Rome in 1765. JB wrote about the dinner, "I enjoyed the good things, and the *english conversation* of today a great deal better than I expected to do" (Journ.).

[4] Presumably Tycho Thomas, "hotel-keeper of Dover St." (*Survey of London*, ed. C. R. Ashbee *et al.*, 1900—, xl. 65). The Club was now meeting at Thomas's Tavern in Dover St. (*post* From EM, 5 Mar.), which had previously been called Le Telier's (or Tellier's) and then Baxter's. The last dinner at Thomas's took place on 17 May 1791; The Club then moved to Parsloe's in St. James's St. (*Life* i. 479 and n. 2; *Annals of The Club*, 1914, pp. 31–36). The Club notes state, "recd. of Mr. Thomas 6 dozen of Madeira" on 17 Jan. 1792, but its claret at that point was coming from Reynolds's cellar (*Annals*, p. 36). Reynolds died on 23 Feb. 1792. "Thomas's Dover Street Piccadilly" is said to have flourished 1792–1807; it was succeeded by Thomas's Hotel in Berkeley Square, 1809–27 (Bryant Lillywhite, *London Signs*, 1972, p. 553).

[5] Irish import duties on French wines had been considerably lower than English throughout much of the eighteenth century, and though in 1786 Pitt lowered the English import duty, the established re-export wine business from Ireland to England continued to flourish (*Bordeaux au XVIIIe siècle*, ed. François-Georges Pariset, 1968, pp. 261–68). According to the Act of 18 George III, ch. 27, French wines could not be imported in any vessel or cask smaller than a hogshead (to discourage smuggling of the more easily concealed containers) except "for private Use, and not by way of Merchandize" (*Statutes at Large*, 1780, xiii. 205–06).

The Club had obtained Irish claret in the past: Thomas Barnard presented it with a cask (*Life* iii. 238), and EM was asked to provide a hogshead for which Lord Eliot was to pay (*Annals*, p. 31). See *post* From EM, 5 Mar.; To EM, 9 Mar.

[6] Henry Dundas had promised Lord Auchinleck on his deathbed that he would obtain a position for T. D. Boswell (Journ. 12 Dec. 1784), and, as Treasurer of the Navy, finally made him a clerk in the Navy Pay-Office (Journ. 5 Feb.); in 1792 T. D. was promoted to the position of clerk in the Inspector's Branch at £162. 3*s*. a year (*Roy. Kal.* 1792, p. 132).

I am in a distressing perplexity how to decide as to the property of my Book. You must know that I am *certainly* informed that a certain person who delights in mischief has been *depreciating* it,[7] so that I fear the sale of it may be very dubious. *Two Quartos* and *Two Guineas* sound in an alarming manner. I believe in my present frame I should accept even of £500, for I suspect that were I now to talk to Robinson I should find him not disposed to give £1000. Did he absolutely *offer* it, or did he only express himself so as that you *concluded* he would give it? The pressing circumstance is that I *must* lay down £1000 by the first of May, on account of the purchase of land, which my old family enthusiasm urged me to make.[8] You I doubt not have full confidence in my honesty. May I then ask you if you could venture to join with me in a bond for that sum, as then I would take my chance, and as Sir Joshua says *game* with my Book.[9] Upon my honour your telling me that you cannot comply with what I propose will not in the least surprise me or make any manner of difference as to my opinion of your friendship. I mean to ask Sir Joshua if he will join,[10] for, indeed I should be vexed to sell my *Magnum Opus* for a great deal less than its intrinsick value. I meant to publish on Shrove Tuesday.[11] But if I can get out within the month of March, I shall be satisfied. I have now I think *four* or *five* sheets to print which will make my second volume about 575 pages. But I shall have more cancels. That *nervous* mortal W[illiam] G[erard] H[amilton] is not satisfied with my report of some particulars *which I wrote down from his own mouth*, and is so much agitated, that Courtenay has persuaded me to allow a *new edition* of them by H. himself to be made at H.'s expence.[12]

[7] "I met my friend Dilly, and took a walk with him into Lincolns Inn Fields, being in great despondency as to Life of Johnson. He told me that Stockdale told him it had been depreciated and on being pressed, owned that Steevens had talked against it. It vexed me to think that this malicious man had I feared access to it at the Printing House" (Journ. 20 Feb.).

[8] *Ante* To EM, 29 Jan. and n. 2.

[9] *Ante* From EM, 24 Feb., which JB had not yet received.

[10] There is no record of JB's having made such a request of Reynolds.

[11] 8 Mar.

[12] Hamilton's anecdotes of SJ are preserved in a MS. in JB's hand, which Waingrow prints (pp. 263–65) and dates 6 Feb. 1788 on the basis of a journal entry for that date. This MS. provided four anecdotes for the *Life*, revised proofs of which (Hyde Collection) show that JB originally used two of them anonymously (*Life* ii. 317, iv. 420–21) and two with attributions to Hamilton (*Life* ii. 139, iv. 48–49). In addition, Hamilton provided two anecdotes, which appear on the same page of the revises, with attributions: in one he commented on SJ's talent for "maintaining the wrong side of an argument" (*Life* iv. 111), and in the other SJ told him, "we have now been several hours together; and you

Besides, it has occurred to me that where I mention "a *literary fraud*" by Rolt the Historian in going to Dublin and publishing Akenside's Pleasures of the Imagination with his own name, I may not be able to authenticate it, as Johnson is dead, and he may have relations who may take it up as an offence, perhaps a *Libel*. Courtenay suggests that you may perhaps get intelligence whether it was *true*. The Bishop of Dromore can probably tell, as he knows a great deal about Rolt. In case of doubt, should I not cancel the leaf, and either omit the curious anecdote or give it as a story which Johnson laughingly told as having circulated?[13] There is a glaring mistake into which you and I fell where we agreed, that in No. 39 of the Adventurer on Sleep "a translation from Statius marked C. B. is *certainly* the performance of Dr. Charles Bathurst," for unluckily I find that Bathurst's name was *Richard*. I think I may set that right in my Errata.[14]

have said but one thing for which I envied you" (*Life* iv. 112). Hamilton insisted on revision of the passages in *Life* iv. 48–49, 111–12. The cancelled page that contains the earlier passage is now at Yale; it originally read, "Mr. William Gerard Hamilton informs me that Warburton said of Johnson, 'I admire him, but I cannot bear his style:' and that Johnson being told this, said, 'That is exactly my case as to him.' He expressed in conversation with Mr. Hamilton his admiration of Warburton thus" (P 103). The revisions on the cancel, in Courtenay's hand, substitute "I am well informed" for "Mr. William . . . informs me" and "The manner in which he expressed his admiration of the fertility of Warburton's genius, and of the variety of his materials was" for "He expressed . . . thus". The original versions of the passages in *Life* iv. 111–12 are described by Powell, *Life* iv. 557. Courtenay negotiated with Hamilton on JB's behalf, and the three met on 3 Mar. to revise the offending passages (Journ.). The cost of cancelling the pages was £2. 16*s*., which JB later billed to Hamilton (To Hamilton, 25 Feb. 1793; From Hamilton, 26 Feb. 1793).

[13] EM discussed this note with Bishop Percy, who wrote to JB that he knew of no edition of *Pleasures of the Imagination* with Richard Rolt's (c. 1725–70) name on the title-page, and so recommended that the anecdote be omitted from the *Life* (From Percy, 6 Apr.). JB did not cancel the passage, but in the 2nd ed. he inserted a note citing authorities that supported SJ's accusation and quoting EM's opinion "that the truth probably is, not that an edition was published with Rolt's name in the title-page, but, that the poem being then anonymous, Rolt acquiesced in its being attributed to him in conversation" (*Life* i. 359 and n. 2). No edition of *Pleasures of the Imagination* bearing Rolt's name is known; Akenside's name appeared on the title-page of the 3rd ed. (1744).

[14] JB's "Corrections and Additions" read: "P. 136, l. 6, *for* is certainly the performance of Dr. Charles Bathurst, *read* has been erroneously ascribed to Dr. Bathurst, whose christian name was Richard." The correction was incorporated in later editions (*Life* i. 252). A further mistake, which JB did not correct, is that the translation was not of Statius, but of Cowley's *Sex Libri Plantarum* IV, "Papaver", 49–60 (see Waingrow, p. 391 n. 4). The latest editors of the *Adventurer* state that "the identity of the translator has not been discovered" (*Works SJ*, ii. 349 n. 5). As JB notes in the *Life* (i. 252), SJ wrote all of *Adventurer* no. 39 but the translation.

You have satisfied me that the *Fordian* pamphlet could not be of the date ascribed to it. Yet still Macklin I think may have had it, and mistaken the date of the ingenious fabrication. Be that as it may, I shall take care to have your admirable Detection brought into view in some of the Papers.[15] You may depend on my sending you whatever Reviews mention you, besides the Monthly which Arnold sends. The Annalytical promised their account in a *future* number.[16]

I was not at the Club last tuesday; but there was one black ball which excluded the Bishop of Peterborough. Courtenay engaged to eat hodge podge with me; but sent a note that I should not wait, as he was to be late at the house. His son and my brother dined with me; and went away. Courtenay did not come till about ten, and took his mess which had been kept for him. Poor fellow. His firmness of mind is amazing. Is there no hope of a remittance to him from Ireland? Pray don't hint my inquiring! It is hard that his party cannot do any thing essential for him.[17]

I have thus worked out a Letter. Your chance in the Lottery is still afloat. I shall acquaint you the very moment I hear its fate.

Your account of Dublin Luxury is picturesque. The *four silver tubs* convey a great deal to my imagination.[18] Pray present my best compliments to Lord Sunderlin and the Ladies. My daughters return yours and I ever am most affectionately and sincerely yours,

JAMES BOSWELL

Pray write directly.[19]

[15] *Ante* From EM, 23 Dec. 1790, n. 6. JB noticed EM's essay in his animadversions on Lord Mountmorres's biographical sketch of EM (*ante* To EM, 16 Dec. 1790, n. 3; Appendix 3, pp. 437–38).

[16] The first part of the *Analytical Review* notice of EM's edition of Shakespeare promised to give an account of EM's annotation "in a future number" (Dec. 1790, viii. 454; see also *ante* From EM, 23 Jan. n. 2).

[17] This dinner took place on 22 Feb. Courtenay was born in Ireland and had held various official appointments there, but what possible "remittance" JB had in mind is unknown.

[18] JB had written, "Pray give me some particulars of your irish life" (*ante* To EM, 29 Jan.); he refers here to EM's missing answer of 7 or 8 Feb.

[19] The postscript is written upside down at the top of p. 1, with a box drawn around it.

FROM MALONE, 5 MARCH 1791

From Malone,
Saturday 5 March 1791
MS. Yale (C 1925).
ADDRESS: James Boswell, Esqre., Great Portland Street, Portland Chapel, London, Single Sheet.
POSTMARKS: IRELAND [Dublin] MR 5 [London] MR 9 91.

Dublin, March 5, 1791

MY DEAR BOSWELL, You have some days since received a *volunteer* letter from me. The most material part of yours of the 25th of Feb. is that which relates to Robinson. I really forget what words he used, when he talked to me about your book; but the import, I think, was, that he was willing to give 1000£ for the copy. As it was then to be in one volume, I conceive he could not now offer for two less than 1200£.—Whenever you fix on your title-page, if you will enclose it to me in Ms., I will examine it very carefully, and perhaps may be able to suggest somewhat.—With respect to the Character in your Journal, if you retain it, it certainly should be amplified, and his uniform piety and virtue enlarged upon. Pray omit your *Canterbury Organ* and your *bow wough* entirely.[1]—It will be impossible, I fear, to gain any intelligence of Rolt for you here, unless there was an edition of the Pleasures of Imagination published here with *his name*, in which case I might be able to trace it in Faulkner's Dublin Journal of which there is a complete set at his successor's, from 1730.[2] Let me know how this is. Dublin is very far from being literary even now, but in 1745 was in complete darkness.

Your account of yourself for some time past is very deplorable, but is not your depression entirely owing to yourself, I mean to your own almost uniform intemperance in wine? Without being a very strict moralist, one may say that it is surely *unwise* to indulge

[1] In introducing his block character sketch of SJ at the end of the *Life* (iv. 424–30), JB wrote, "As I do not see any reason to give a different character of my illustrious friend now, from what I formerly gave, the greatest part of the sketch of him in my 'Journal of a Tour to the Hebrides,' is here adopted" (iv. 425 n. 1). JB did omit his comparison of SJ's voice to the Canterbury organ, and Lord Pembroke's observation that "Dr. Johnson's sayings would not appear so extraordinary, were it not for his *bow-wow way*" (*Life* v. 18), which he had already included in a footnote (*Life* ii. 326 n. 5). But he expanded the *Tour* character sketch (v. 16–19) by more than a third.

[2] The *Dublin Journal* was founded by George Faulkner (c. 1699–1775), a prominent Dublin bookseller. His successor at the *Dublin Journal* was his nephew Thomas Todd, who assumed the name of Faulkner upon inheriting his uncle's property.

in such excesses *habitually*, and that the sure consequence of wild and intemperate riot for one half the year, must be the lowest depression during the other. Besides, to talk more seriously; what do the name and all the forms and ceremonies of religion signify, if they have not some[3] relation to our *actions*; and if a sense of duty, which[4] is better than all the forms and ceremonies in the world, does not, *in general* at least, restrain us from these extravagant excesses, which obscure our faculties, make us troublesome, instead of pleasing, companions, and lead directly to disease and death?—But, I see, I am beginning to sermonize, so will only add in the usual form, "consider what has been said."[5]

Pray did you say any thing to Nichols about his fobbing me off with such a lame and brief account of my Shakspeare? I suppose it is not yet too late for him to give something more full and accurate.[6] He garbelled the little character I sent of my poor friend, leaving out all the appropriate and discriminative praise, and inserting only general panegyrick, which Dr. J. justly used to say was good for nothing.[7]—

With respect to the Bishop of Clonfert's wine, it entirely depends on this: whether the act made about 10 years ago admitting wine in bottles, confines that liberty to *gentlemen* only, importing for *their private use*. If it does, I will send the Hogshead at once to Thomas's, for which no licence is necessary.[8] I am still astonished at[9] your judgment concerning Macklin's pamphlet, but one might talk forever in *letters* on such a subject: when I have you at a table, I think I shall convince you.

Charles Bathurst, the *bookseller*, led us into the mistake about the translation from Statius.[10]—I am very glad to find that your brother has obtained something, and make no doubt his diligence

[3] MS. "even" deleted before "some"

[4] MS. "which" superimposed upon erased "does not"

[5] The exhortation to "consider" is frequent in the Book of Common Prayer and in the Bible; see in particular II Timothy 2: 7, "Consider what I say; and the Lord give thee understanding in all things."

[6] The review of EM's edition of Shakespeare in *Gent. Mag.* (Dec. 1790) lx. 1124–25 takes up little more than a column of type; it explains briefly the principles of the edition and enumerates the contents of the two volumes of prolegomena. See *post* To EM, 9 Mar. and n. 12.

[7] *Ante* From EM, 23 Dec. 1790, n. 1. In the *Life of Pope*, SJ wrote, "The difficulty in writing epitaphs is to give a particular and appropriate praise" (*Lives of the Poets*, ed. G. B. Hill, 1905, iii. 263).

[8] *Ante* To EM, 25 Feb. and n. 5; *post* To EM, 9 Mar.

[9] MS. "about" deleted before "at"

[10] *Ante* To EM, 25 Feb. and n. 14. Charles Bathurst (c. 1709–86) had been a bookseller in Fleet St., 1737–86 (Maxted).

and accuracy will soon promote him. Pray remember me very kindly to Courteney etc. and believe me, my dear B., very faithfully and affectionately yours,

EDM. MALONE

To Malone,
Wednesday 9 March 1791

MS. Hyde Collection.
ADDRESS: To Edmond Malone Esq. at Lord Sunderlin's, Sackville Street, Dublin, Double Letter.
POSTMARKS: [London] MR 10 91, MR 10 91 [Dublin] MR 14.

London, 9[1] March 1791

MY DEAR MALONE: I have before me your *volunteer* letter of Feb. 24 and one of *5th current* which if you have dated it right has come with wonderful expedition. You may be perfectly sure that I have not the smallest fault to find with your disinclination to come again under any pecuniary engagements for others, after having suffered so much. Dilly proposes that he and Baldwin should each advance £200 on the credit of my Book; and if they do so I shall manage well enough; for I now find that I can have £600 in Scotland on the credit of my rents; and thus I shall get the £1000 paid in May.[2]

Arnold insists that he did send you the Review and Magazine on the first of the month. I have stopped your Gazeteer. You would observe some stupid lines on Mr. Burke in the Oracle *by*

[1] MS. "8"; JB could not have received EM's letter of 5 Mar. before 9 Mar., the date of the London postmark. The present letter must have been written on the 9th or 10th (the date of the postmark). It is dated by JB's reference to a supper at the London Tavern "the day before yesterday"; the journal shows that this supper took place on 7 Mar. But JB's "8" is not a mere slip of the pen: his statement in this letter, "I hope to have published today", shows that he thought he was writing on Shrove Tuesday, 8 Mar. (*ante* To EM, 16 Dec. 1790). His mistaking the day explains why he thought, as he says below, that EM's letter of 5 Mar. had "come with wonderful expedition": the postmarks on the letters of Dec. 1790 and early 1791 show that a letter might easily go between Dublin and London in four days, but three days would have been unusually quick.

[2] JB repaid Dilly and Baldwin on 24 Nov. 1792. His profit on the 1st edition of the *Life* was £1,555. 18*s*. 2*d*. (Journ.). The other £600 he borrowed from the bank of James Hunter and Co., Ayr. The bond, now at Yale, records that he repaid the principal and remaining interest, £620. 12*s*. 7*d*., on 30 Dec. 1794 (A 55).

Mr. Boswell. I instantly wrote to Mr. Burke expressing my indignation at such impertinence; and had next morning a most obliging answer. Sir William Scott told me I could have no legal redress. So I went *civilly* to Bell,[3] and he promised to mention *handsomely* that *James Boswell Esq.* was not the Authour of the lines. The *note* however on the subject was a second impertinence.[4] But I can do nothing. I wish Fox in his Bill upon *Libels* would make a heavy penalty the consequence of forging any person's name to any composition, which in reality such a trick amounts to.[5]

My brother's accurate information which may be relied on as from the best authority, is as follows.

"*French wine only* may be imported into London in bottles, and dealers must receive it directly from France. If it comes from Ireland in bottles, it must be for the use of private individuals in packages of no less than three dozen of bottles, and it pays a duty of 4 shillings <per> gallon, concerning which duty and the interpretation of the act of Parliament relative to it, there is now a difference of opinion between the Computer of wine duties, and the Solicitor of the Customs, which is to be referred to the Attorney and Solicitor General; so that it is not improbable but what it may soon pay a higher duty. Care must be taken that the wine be in bottles evidently of British Manufactory, as there is an enormous duty on glass bottles not made in Great Britain of 5 shillings per dozen, being about twice their value.

[3] John Bell (1745–1831), "the very Puck of booksellers", was one of the most innovative and successful practitioners of his trade. His speciality was cheap editions in small formats; his 109-volume edition of *The Poets of Great Britain*, 1777–82, provoked a consortium of London booksellers to print the edition for which SJ wrote his *Lives of the Poets*. He had helped found *Morn. Post* (1772), was the first printer of *World* (1787), and had founded *Oracle* (1789) (Maxted).

[4] *Ante* To EB, 5 Mar., From EB, 7 Mar. (pp. 157–59), and, for an account of JB's controversy with Bell, *Lit. Car.* p. 300.

[5] JB had been writing squibs and epigrams for the newspapers since his youth, and by now his journalistic propensities were well known. On 10 Dec. 1790 the following appeared in *Morn. Chron.* p. [3]: "Mr. Boswell has just reclaimed one of the little escapes of his fancy, which has been strolling from newspaper to newspaper, unowned and unprotected for more than twenty years; and to secure the dear offspring of his wit from such vagabondism in future, we understand it is his intention to enter all his *ballads* and *good things* at Stationers' Hall!" And in *Gazetteer*, 9 Dec. 1790, p. [3]: "Bozzy, since the publication of his London *Grocer*, is become the favourite bard of the itinerant warblers. There is not a ballad-singer that does not announce his madrigals to have been written by 'the celebrated and *humoursome* Jemmy Boswell, Esq.' "—Fox's Bill on Libels did not pass until 1792. It sought to increase the discretionary powers of juries, which had hitherto been restricted to matters of fact.

"*No other but French wine* can be imported into London in bottles either from Ireland or any other place."

I believe I mentioned to you that the Bishop of Peterborough was blackballed. Worthy man, I was very sorry for it, and felt uneasy when I met him at Lady Lucan's, where I have been three evenings this winter.[6]

Whom did I find standing at the door of a house in Great Titchfield Street today, but your late Cook Mrs. Hacket who informed me that she was married to the master of the house Mr. Turnpenny a Painter. Shall I forget her new name, as I used to do the old?[7] She begged to have her respects presented to her Master and the Ladies.

In the night between the last of February and first of this month, I had a sudden relief from the inexplicable disorder which occasionally clouds my mind and makes me miserable, and it is amazing how well I have been since. Your friendly admonition as to excess in wine *has* been often too applicable; but upon this late occasion I erred on the other side.[8] However as I am now free from my restriction to Courtenay I shall be much upon my guard; for to tell the truth I did go too deep the day before yesterday; having dined with Michael Angelo Taylor,[9] and then supt at the London Tavern with the Stewards of the Humane Society and continued till—I know not what hour in the morning.[10] John Nichols was joyous to a pitch of bachanalian vivacity. I am to dine with him next monday, an excellent City Party Alderman Curtis, Deputy Birch etc. etc.[11]—I rated him gently on his saying so little of your

[6] Margaret Bingham (d. 1814), daughter of James Smith, M.P., of Canons Leigh, Devon, and wife of the first Baron Lucan. JB spent the evenings of 1, 13, and 27 Feb. at Lady Lucan's (Journ.).

[7] *Ante* To EM, 30 Oct. 1785; From EM, 5 Nov. 1785. Turnpenny has not been further identified. JB doubtless met Mrs. Turnpenny while on the way to visit his brother in Titchfield St. (*ante* To EM, 18 Jan. n. 2).

[8] On 27 Feb. JB wrote, "Dr. Warren felt my hand cold, and said, 'you have not taken a bottle of wine today.' . . . He told me that some people had a power of inspiring cheerfulness instantaneously; that when I was myself, I was one of those, and that for some time, he had missed the effect which I used to have upon him; that I *must* drink more wine; for having been used to it, I required it, especially when low. When my spirits were better, I might take less" (Journ.).

[9] Taylor (c. 1757–1834), son of Sir Robert Taylor the architect, was M.P. for Poole. JB was amused by his "purse-pompousness" (Journ. 7 Mar.).

[10] The Royal Humane Society was founded in 1774 as the Society for the Recovery of Persons Apparently Drowned. JB's journal records that he drank with the stewards until after two in the morning.

[11] William Curtis (1752–1829), Alderman for Tower Ward since 1785 and M.P. for the City of London since 1790, later

Shakspeare. He is ready to receive more ample notice.[12] You may depend on your having whatever Reviews that mention you sent directly. Have I told you that Murphy has written "An Essay on the Life and Writings of Dr. Johnson" to be prefixed to the new edition of his Works. He wrote it in a month, and has received £200 for it.[13] I am quite resolved now to keep the property of my MAGNUM OPUS; and I flatter myself I shall not repent it.

The charge against Rolt is that he published "The pleasures of Imagination" with *his name* to it. I should think the Bishop of Dromore who once shewed me some letters to Rolt.[14] I would wish to avoid all cause of quarrel or even ill will. The Bishop can probably tell what Rolt was, and what became of him. My Title as we settled it is ["]The Life of Samuel Johnson LL.D. comprehending an account of his studies and various works in chronological order his conversations with many eminent persons a series of letters from him[15] to celebrated men and several original pieces of his composition. The whole exhibiting a view of Literature and Literary men in Great Britain for near half a century during which he flourished.["] I think *incidents* should be also introduced. It will be very kind if you will suggest what yet occurs.[16] I hope to have published today. But it will be about a month yet before I launch. I have now before me in print 560 pages of Vol. 2 and I fear I shall have 20 more.

I have made inquiries at White's Payne's and Egerton's about your Shakspeare, and had good accounts. Young Payne who did not know me said "It has sold exceedingly well", which is a good

(1796) Lord Mayor of London and (1802) Baronet. For JB's relations with him, see *Pol. Car.* pp. 172–73 and n. 7. This "hearty City dinner" took place as scheduled on 14 Mar. (Journ.). Samuel Birch (1757–1841), dramatist and pastry cook, had been deputy alderman for Cornhill Ward since 1789. In 1814 he became Lord Mayor of London.

[12] EM's edition of Shakespeare was not reviewed again in *Gent. Mag.*; however, two long letters on the work appeared in 1791 and 1792. The first, by William Stanley, was a tongue-in-cheek defence of EM's practice of rejecting emendations that tended to modernize Shakespeare's language or render it more genteel (Dec. 1791, lxi. 1098–1101). The second, signed "Philalethes", was a defence of EM's copious annotation (Jan. 1792, lxii. 41–43). "Philalethes" was perhaps JB (*Lit. Car.* p. 233; *NCBEL* ii. 1220).

[13] *Ante* To EM, 17 Nov. 1788, n. 11. According to John Nichols, Arthur Murphy received £300 for his "Essay" (*Lit. Anec.* ix. 159).

[14] JB lost track of this sentence in turning the page after the word "some". We should perhaps complete the sentence with "would know".

[15] MS. alternatively "of his letters"

[16] Several changes were made in the title before publication; see *post* To EM, 12 Mar.; From EM, 14 Apr. and nn. 3. 4.

sign—White was the coolest but said *well*. Egerton's sold all theirs long ago and have had more—*ten* at one time. Steevens begins next week. His specimen which is *stately* is left at the Booksellers shops. I have opened Sir Joshua's letter to you to make it *pack* better; but upon my honour have not read one word of it.[17]

I send you tonight Payne's[18] Catalogue and Sir Joshua's Discourse.[19] Tomorrow shall come several Discourses, and Egertons and Robson's[20] Catalogues, the last of which was left at your house. I delivered your message to Hardinge.[21] Ever most sincerely yours,

J. B.

Pray send me correctly Mr. F.'s No need of latin etc. pay the immortality he gave.[22]

To Malone,
Saturday 12 March 1791

MS. Hyde Collection.

ADDRESS: To Edmond Malone Esq., Sackville Street, Dublin, Single Sheet.

POSTMARK: [Dublin] MR 15.

London, 12 March 1791

MY DEAR MALONE: Being the depositary of your chance in the

[17] Reynolds to EM, 8 Mar. (*Letters Reynolds*, pp. 210–11).

[18] MS. "Payne's" written above deleted "Egertons"

[19] Reynolds's fifteenth *Discourse*, which he asked EM in his letter of 8 Mar. (n. 17 above) to distribute complimentary copies of.

[20] James Robson (d. 1806), bookseller at No. 27, the Feathers, New Bond St. (Maxted).

[21] EM's "message to Hardinge" has not been reported; presumably it was contained in his missing letter of 7 or 8 Feb. "Hardinge" may be George Hardinge (1743–1816), M.P. for Old Sarum, Solicitor-General to the Queen, and Senior Justice of the counties of Brecon, Glamorgan, and Radnor. He later published *The Essence of Malone, or, the "Beauties" of that Fascinating Writer*, 1800, followed by *Another Essence of Malone, or, the "Beauties" of Shakspeare's Editor*, 1801. Or perhaps the message was for Silvester Harding (1745–1809), artist and publisher, who with his younger brother Edward was now issuing a series of illustrations of Shakespeare.

[22] For the "sepulchral verses" by Henry Flood (*ante* From EM, 7 Apr. 1786, n. 7) and the note with which he transmitted them to EM, see *Life* iv. 424, 470. The MS. of the verses is now in the Osborn Collection. EM's footnote on these verses (*Life* iv. 424 n. 2) was not added until the second edition. See *post* From EM, between 14 Mar. and c. 1 Apr.

Lottery I am under the disagreable necessity of communicating the bad news that it has been drawn a *Blank*. I am very sorry, both on your account and that of your sisters, and my own, for had your share of good fortune been £3166. 13. 4 I should have hoped for a loan to accomodate me. As it is, I shall as I wrote to you, be enabled to weather my difficulties for some time. But I am still in great anxiety about the sale of my Book, I find so many people shake their heads at the *two quartos* and *two guineas*. Courtenay is clear that I should sound Robinson and accept of a thousand guineas, if he will give that sum. Meantime the Title Page must be made as good as may be. It appears to me that mentioning his studies Works conversations and letters is not sufficient; and I would suggest [“]comprehending an Account in chronological order of his studies works friendships acquaintance and other[1] particulars his[2] conversations with eminent men,[3] a series of his letters to various persons. Also several original pieces of his composition never before published. The Whole[”] etc. You will probably be able to assist me in expressing my idea, and arranging the parts. In the Advertisement I intend to mention the letter to Lord Chesterfield and perhaps the Interview with the King and the names of the correspondents in alphabetical order.[4] How should *in chronological order* stand in the order of the members of my Title. I had at first *celebrated correspondents* which I don't like. How would it do to say “his conversations and epistolary correspondence with eminent (or celebrated) persons”? Shall it be *different* works, and *various* particulars? In short it is difficult to decide.

Courtenay was with me this morning. What a mystery is his going on at all! Yet he looks well, talks well, dresses well, keeps his mare, in short is in all respects like a Parliament Man.[5]

I sent you one of Sir Joshua's Discourses for yourself singly, and next day four for Lord Charlemont Lord Sunderlin and the Jephsons. These all under cover of Mr. Lees. Four I sent under

[1] MS. “other” written above deleted “various”

[2] MS. “and anecdotes” deleted before “his”

[3] MS. “men” written above deleted “persons”

[4] This was not done.

[5] On 21 Feb. JB wrote, “Courtenay was truly fr[i]endly and shewed me much kindness. He now lodged within a few doors of me. I was very ill today. The embarrassed state of my affairs overwhelmed my spirits. Yet here was Courtenay with a wife and seven children, and not a shilling” (Journ.).

cover of the Provost[6] for the ArchBishop of Tuam,[7] the Lord Chancellor[8] and the Bishops of Killaloe and Dromore. Sir Joshua had sent one to the Provost himself.

I am truly sorry for Lord Charlemont's illness, and most sincerely wish he may soon <be> restored to his friends and country.[9]

Do you know, that my bad spirits are returned upon me to a certain degree; and such is the sickly fondness for change of place, and imagination of relief, that I sometimes think you are happier by being in Dublin, than one is in this great metropolis, where hardly any man cares for another. I am persuaded I should relish your irish dinners very much.

I have at last got chambers in the Temple, in the very Staircase where Johnson lived, and when my *Magnum Opus* is fairly launched, there shall I make a trial.[10] God bless you my dear friend. I am ever most warmly yours,

James Boswell

Holding myself bound to notify to you the fate of your ticket, I have taken that opportunity to write. I know not what is become of my own, as it is not registered. I dined at Dilly's on thursday with Cumberland, Sharp,[11] steady Reed etc. His steadiness said that I must not conclude that there are not many of your edition still in the hands of the trade, and will be for some time, and yet the sale be good.

Pray could not you be of some service to my Work, by inquiring whether some of the Irish Booksellers would not take some. I trust to be out on the 15 of April. When are we to see you?

[6] John Hely-Hutchinson (1724–94), Provost of Trinity College, Dublin, since 1774.

[7] Joseph Deane Bourke (1736–94), Archbishop of Tuam since 1782, succeeded his brother as third Earl of Mayo in 1792. JB had met him at Reynolds' on 6 Aug. 1787 (Journ.).

[8] John Fitzgibbon (1748–1802), first Baron Fitzgibbon, Lord Chancellor of Ireland since 1789, was created Earl of Clare in 1795. Reynolds wished to persuade him and Hely-Hutchinson to contribute to the subscription for SJ's monument (*Letters Reynolds*, p. 215).

[9] Lord Charlemont lived until 1799.

[10] JB had been interested in securing chambers in the Temple since at least 21 Mar. 1787 (Journ.). The present rental agreement, dated 15 Jan. 1791, shows that he had taken "two front rooms two pair of stairs No. 1 Inner Temple Lane belonging to Sir Henry Fletcher as his Chambers for one year from the tenth of this month at the rent of eighteen guineas he paying his proportion of taxes" (M 124). Two years later he gave them up as "an ineffectual expence" (Journ. 5 Nov. 1792).

[11] Richard Cumberland (1732–1811), dramatist, many of whose plays Dilly published between 1778 and 1797. Richard Sharp (1759–1835), merchant, because of his social talents came to be known as "Conversation Sharp".

From Malone,
between Monday 14 March and c. Friday 1 April 1791

Not reported. EM sent JB Henry Flood's verses on SJ (*ante* To EM, 9 Mar. and n. 22), which were inserted in the penultimate sheet of the *Life* (E4, ii. 582). JB apparently had a proof of this sheet before 9 Apr. (*post* From EM, 14 Apr.). The *terminus a quo* for this letter is established by the Dublin postmark of JB's letter of 9 Mar.

To Malone,
Saturday 9 April 1791

Not reported. See *post* From EM, 14 Apr.: "Your letter of the 9th reached me yesterday"; also Reynolds to EM, 9 Apr.: "Boswell has been just sealing a letter to you. I begged before the wafer was dry that he would insert a paragraph; he says there is not room for a single word" (*Letters Reynolds*, p. 214). JB's letter apparently contained as an enclosure a copy of the first proof of the title-page of the *Life* (*post* From EM, 14 Apr. and nn. 3, 4).

From Malone,
Thursday 14 April 1791
MS. Yale (C 1926).
ADDRESS: James Boswell, Esqre., Great Portland Street, London, Single Sheet.
POSTMARKS: [Dublin] AP 14 [London] AP 19 91.

Dublin, April 14, 1791

MY DEAR BOSWELL, Your letter of the 9th reached me yesterday. I congratulate you on your drawing so near a conclusion. The proof of your last sheet must, I think, have been before you, when you were writing to me. I wish you had enclosed it. The Advertisement in the cover of the G. M. makes a very handsome figure: but I hope you will not admit into your title-page that heavy word *also*;—("also various" etc.) I suppose it was introduced to avoid ambiguity in consequence of the notice of his Majesty and Lord Chesterfield; but in the title will not be requisite:[1] there it should surely run[2]— "with many eminent persons; *and* various" etc.[3] Your motto will look better if OMNIS stands over *tabella*, with a black line at the beginning:

——————— Quo fit ut OMNIS
Votiva etc. . . . . tabella—[4]

Many thanks for your rectification, which comes out rather late, but better late than never.[5]—I have not seen the Letter to Lord Chesterfield advertised. I suppose you will publish it a day or two only before the *opus magnum*.[6] It is singular enough that I

[1] The editors have not seen a copy of this cover; presumably the advertisement was similar to the notice JB had sent to *Lond. Chron.* (17–19 Mar.) lxix. 268: "*Next Month will be published*, In Two Volumes large Quarto, Price Two Guineas in boards, (Dedicated to Sir JOSHUA REYNOLDS,) THE LIFE of SAMUEL JOHNSON, LL.D. Comprehending an Account of his Studies and numerous Works in Chronological Order; a Series of his Conversations and epistolary Correspondence with many eminent Persons; including his celebrated Letter to the Earl of CHESTERFIELD. Also various Pieces of his Composition, never before published. The Whole exhibiting a VIEW of LITERATURE and LITERARY MEN in Great Britain, for near half a Century, during which he flourished. By JAMES BOSWELL, Esq. London: Printed for Charles Dilly, in the Poultry. *¶* The extraordinary Zeal which has been shown by distinguished Persons in all Parts of the Kingdom, in supplying additional Information, authentic Manuscripts, and singular Anecdotes of Dr. Johnson, has occasioned such an Enlargement of this Work, that it has been unavoidably delayed much longer than was intended."

[2] MS. "shd" deleted before "run"

[3] The first proof of the title-page (Hyde Collection) reads, "conversations with many eminent persons; also, various original pieces of his composition". In the revise (Hyde Collection), "also" was changed to "and".

[4] "Quo fit, ut omnis / votiva pateat veluti descripta tabella / vita senis," Horace, *Satires* II. i. 32–34: "So it comes that the old poet's whole life is open to view, as if painted on a votive tablet" (trans. H. R. Fairclough, Loeb ed.). In the first proof, the motto was printed entirely in italics; in the second, OMNIS and VITA SENIS were in small capitals; in the final version, OMNIS was aligned over *tabella*. The proofs of the title-page are reproduced in *Adam Cat.* ii. between pp. 36 and 37.

[5] JB's "rectification" of Lord Mountmorres's biographical sketch of EM (*ante* To EM, 16 Dec. 1790 and n. 3) appeared in *Pub. Adv.* 24 Mar. p. [1]. For both sketches, see Appendix 3 below, pp. 437–38).

[6] In early 1790 the letter to Chesterfield and the conversation with George III (*Life* i. 261–63, ii. 33–40) were printed separately from the type set for the *Life* and entered at Stationers' Hall on 29 Apr. 1791. A clipping now at Yale (P 100:11) of an advertisement for these pamphlets, from *Pub. Adv.* 30 Apr. p. [1], gives the date of publication as 12 May (the *Life* was published on 16 May), and the price as a half-guinea each; it pointedly mentions that the pamphlets "are separately entered in Stationer's Hall". Few copies of the pamphlets were printed, and the high price probably ensured that few were bought; separate publication was intended only to

should not be in London either at the publication of your work or my own, after all the time that we have passed together while both were going on. If by any chance you should be delayed till the 11th or 12th of next month, I may yet be present at the launch, for I hope to see you by that time. I suspect I have not left my ladies of the household quite enough to sustain them till that time; and request you will call in Queen Anne Street, and ask which ever of them you find, whether they want money for board wages, and supply them with a couple of guineas (not apiece but in the whole) if necessary. I am already in your debt some small matter on the score of the Lottery ticket etc. and this will be another addition to it. I am really sorry to find that the advocates for St. Paul's have prevailed. Sir Joseph Banks wrote to me on the subject, and I was strongly for having the monument in the Abbey. A cenotaph in one church, and Johnson's body in another, *in the same town*, is surely a monumental solecism. Besides five centuries will not give St. Pauls the venerable grandeur and respectability that belongs to the old Cathedral.[7]

I was very sorry to hear of poor Courteney's illness. If he were but as well and as rich as I wish him, he would soon triumph over all his difficulties.

I will take care to collect all the subscriptions.[8] Your friend "Thomas" talks of going to England the beginning of next month.[9] I had a good deal of talk the other day with the Bishop of Dromore about Grainger; I am glad you have satisfied him, for he

protect JB's copyright. See Waingrow, p. 402 n. 4 and *Lit. Car.* pp. 134–41.

[7] For an account of the controversy over SJ's monument, see *Life* iv. 423, 464–72. The members of the committee entrusted with the collection of subscriptions for the monument were Banks (chairman), JB, EB, EM, Metcalfe, Reynolds, Sir William Scott, and Windham. It was Reynolds's idea to place the monument in St. Paul's rather than Westminster Abbey, as originally planned. On 27 Mar. Banks wrote to EM outlining the arguments for and against St. Paul's (*Life* iv. 468); EM, replying on 5 Apr., strongly favoured Westminster Abbey (*Catalogue of the Collection of Autograph Letters and Historical Documents Formed . . . by Alfred Morrison*, 1890, iv. 120). The committee met on 9 Apr. and resolved to refer the matter to the subscribers (Journ.); Reynolds, however, confident of victory, wrote to EM on the same day that the monument would be in St. Paul's (*Letters Reynolds*, pp. 214–15), and the subscribers agreed at a meeting on 16 Apr. (*Life* iv. 468).

[8] Reynolds had asked EM to collect subscriptions in Ireland for SJ's monument (*Letters Reynolds*, pp. 214–15).

[9] Thomas Barnard (*ante* To EM, 13 Oct. 1785, n. 47) did visit England, returning to Ireland in late July or early August (From Barnard, 9 Aug.).

was very earnest about it.[10] He has handed over the materials for Goldsmith's Life to Dr. Campbell, the writer upon Ireland.[11]

The booksellers here have never *advertised* my Shakspeare, though they have sold a large number of them. They make it a rule never to advertise an English Work when they mean to reprint, in order to prevent as much [as] possible the sale of the English edition; and never place it in their windows or on their shop board. To counteract them and by way of punishment for not following my scheme for the Irish edition I have advertised it myself; and would counsel you to employ some person here to do the same—with a "London printed for C. Dilly and sold by—— Dublin."[12] I would do it if I knew to whom Robinson (for he is their chief factor) had orders to consign it.—Farewell, and believe me ever, my dear B., most truly and affectionately yours,

EDM. MALONE

To Malone,
Sunday 16 September 1792

MS. Yale (L 943).

ADDRESS in Lord Eliot's hand: To Edmund Malone Esqe. [Queen Anne Street East, London *deleted*; *added in unidentified hand*] Oxford.[1]

FRANK: Plymouth September the sixteenth 1792. Craggs free Eliot.

POSTMARKS: PLYMOUTH [London] FREE SE 19 92 P, FREE SE 19 92 P, SE 19 92 B.[2]

[10] Thomas Percy had written to JB on 12 or 24 Mar. urging him to soften SJ's ridicule of James Grainger (c. 1721–66), the physician and poet to whom Percy owed his acquaintance with SJ, and JB did so (*Fifer* p. 331 n. 2).

[11] Rev. Thomas Campbell (1733–95) LL.D., had written *A Philosophical Survey of the South of Ireland*, 1778, *A Remedy for the Distilleries of Ireland*, 1783, and *Strictures on the Ecclesiastical and Literary History of Ireland*, 1789. Campbell wrote under Percy's direction, mainly because Percy did not wish to put his own name on the title-page. The biography was all but complete and being delayed only by problems with the publishers when Campbell died. Thereafter it passed through the hands of two more editors (the Rev. Henry Boyd and Samuel Rose) before it finally appeared prefixed to *The Miscellaneous Works of Oliver Goldsmith*, 1801 (K. C. Balderston, *The History and Sources of Percy's Memoir of Goldsmith*, 1926, pp. 29–49).

[12] There is no record that JB took this advice. A pirated Dublin edition appeared in 1792 (*Lit. Car* pp. 156–57; see also p. 167).

[1] EM was now in Oxford transcribing John Aubrey's *Brief Lives* from the MSS. in the Ashmolean Museum (Prior, *Malone*, p. 234).

[2] The letter "P" in the "FREE" postmarks identifies the inspector of franks; the letter "B" in the third London postmark

TO MALONE, 16 SEPTEMBER 1792

Port Eliot, 16 Septr. 1792

MY DEAR MALONE: I have had a wonderful tour in Cornwall. At Gwatkin's there is the strongest likeness of Sir Joshua by himself that ever was painted, and Gwatkin will most readily send it to be copied for THE CLUB. So pray do not *engage* the Streatham Picture.[3]

When I say *wonderful* I am not boasting of *happiness*. Would to GOD I were safe in London! which I hope to be on Saturday the 29th as I must be at Chelmsford for the Essex Sessions, the Monday thereafter viz. 1 Octr.[4]

My Dear Friend I am ever most affectionately your's,

JAMES BOSWELL

P. S. I am to have something for you about King Arthur, the whole of the Song of which Falstaff quotes a line.[5]

identifies the worker who stamped the letter (R. C. Alcock and F. C. Holland, *Postmarks of Great Britain and Ireland* [1940] pp. 20–21, 188).

[3] The Club's book of minutes for 28 Feb., the first dinner after Reynolds's death on 23 Feb., records, "Resolved unanimously that a bust or picture of our late excellent founder and great ornament of this Clubb Sir Joshua Reynolds be set up at the expence of this Clubb in the Club Room" (Minute Book). The portrait belonged to Theophila Palmer Gwatkin, whom JB visited at Killiow, Cornwall, on 1 Sept. JB described it as "the last picture Sir Joshua Reynolds did of himself. It has a sort of *pulled up* look, and not the placid gentleness of his smiling manner; but the features though rather too largely and strongly limned are most exactly pourtrayed, and the dress in every respect being such as he usually wore, I think it the best representation of my celebrated friend" (Journ. 1 Sept.). This portrait, painted in 1789 and reproduced in Derek Hudson, *Sir Joshua Reynolds: A Personal Study*, 1958, plate XVa, now is privately owned. The "Streatham Picture" (undated) was sold in May 1816 (see Mary Hyde, *The Thrales of Streatham Park*, 1977, pp. 299–300); it now hangs in the Tate Gallery. The editors have found no record that either the Gwatkin or the Streatham portrait was copied for The Club. In 1801 the Marchioness of Thomond presented a copy of Reynolds's self-portrait of 1788 to The Club (Minute Book). This portrait was engraved for the *Life*; in 1812 Lady Thomond presented the original to George IV, and the copy still belongs to The Club. The information about the 1788 and 1789 portraits was very kindly supplied by Dr. John Edgcumbe and by Mr. Edward Halliday.

[4] MS. "Augus" deleted before "Octr." JB left London for Cornwall on 17 Aug. (Journ.) and on his return "only *passed through* London" on his way to Chelmsford, where he spent 1–4 Oct. (To Andrew Gibb, 2 Oct.–*Letters JB* ii. 488; A 48). JB's spirits were good throughout the tour, but he complained of "the want of variety of objects to engage and agitate, and a certain unfortunate association of melancholy with the Country, especially about the fall of the leaf" (Journ. 10 Sept.).

[5] JB refers to *2 Henry IV*, II. iv. 33–35, where Falstaff enters singing, " 'When Arthur first in court'—Empty the jordan.—'And was a worthy king.' " As Percy had pointed out in his *Reliques of Ancient English Poetry*, 1765, i. 181–86, these lines are from the ballad "Sir Lancelot du Lake".

To Malone,
Wednesday 20 March 1793
MS. Yale (L 944).
ADDRESS: To Edmond Malone Esq.

Auchinleck, 20 March 1793

MY DEAR MALONE: I return the last part of Vol. Second.[1] I am sorry that seeing it reminded you of *both* books and swains *alone*, as I differ so sturdily from you. Remember you defied me, and said I might add what I pleased in answer. Nevertheless I submit, great Commentator! to your revision of my retort, which please to correct if[2] it require correction[3] though I think it is very well.[4] If the Sheet and half can be delayed till I get to *Town* which *must* be at farthest on the 4th of April we may discuss the matter or rather the *manner* over good Oporto.[5] I have been wonderfully active, and in health and spirits almost incredible; and never once drunk. I think of going for four days to Edinburgh.[6] I congratulate you on *our* glorious Jemappes.[7] My best compliments to all our friends even to the best good man etc. Courtenay.[8] Ever most affectionately yours,

JAMES BOSWELL

[1] Proofs of the 2nd ed. of the *Life*.

[2] MS. "if if"

[3] MS. "corection"

[4] JB refers to some lines from Thomas Parnell's *Hermit*, which he and SJ thought contained a contradiction (see *Life* iii. 220, 392–93). EM maintained in a note for the 2nd ed. (ii. 611) that there was no contradiction, and JB appended a "retort" to EM's note. In the 3rd ed. of 1799 (iii. 419) EM replied to JB's "retort"; this reply is omitted from the Hill-Powell edition of the *Life*.

[5] JB had gone to Auchinleck in Feb. to select a parish minister (*Later Years*, p. 472). He was back in London by 8 Apr. when Dilly paid 10*s*. for his coach fare to Chelmsford, and on 9 Apr. he records a half-guinea fee at the Essex Easter Sessions (Lg 70). See also next note.

[6] JB left Auchinleck for Edinburgh, which he had not visited since his removal to the English bar in Feb. 1786, on 23 Mar. (Book of Company), writing to his Auchinleck overseer, Andrew Gibb, from Glasgow on the same day (*Letters JB* ii. 496). He spent ten days in Edinburgh (To Sir William Forbes, 11 May—MS. Somervell, NLS).

[7] At Jemappes the French Republican army on 6 Nov. 1792 won its first impressive victory over the Austrians. JB uses the name figuratively to mean "victory", but we are unable to explain his reference.

[8] A reference to John Wilmot, Earl of Rochester's *Allusion to Horace, the Tenth Satyr of the First Book*: "For poynted Satyrs, I wou'd Buckhurst choose, / The best good Man, with the worst Natur'd Muse" (*Poems*, ed. Keith Walker, 1984, p. 101). Courtenay's *Poetical and Philosophical Essay on the French Revolution Addressed to the Right Hon. Edmund Burke* was first advertised as "this day . . . published" in *Morn. Chron.* for 8 Jan. p. [1]. It is reviewed in *Crit. Rev.* new arr. vii. (Mar. 1793). 315–17; and in *Monthly Rev.* 2nd ser. x. (Mar. 1793). 343–44).

FROM MALONE, 13 MAY 1793

From Malone,
Monday 13 May 1793
MS. Yale (C 1927).
ADDRESS: James Boswell, Esqre.
ENDORSEMENT: Edmond Malone Esq. May 13, 1793. A strange letter. Answer Within.

Monday, May 13, 1793

DEAR BOSWELL: You have an undoubted right over your own reputation, and to expose yourself in any way you think proper; but you certainly have no right whatsoever over the reputation of others. If therefore you should persevere in printing the wild Rhodomontade which by accident I yesterday saw at the press, as an addition to your new Advertisement,[1] I entreat, not as a favour, but a *right*, that you would cancel whatever relates to me in the former Advertisement:[2] for *noscitur a socio*[3] is a very true[4] adage, and you cannot degrade yourself without injuring at the same time the characters of those whom you mention as your friends. Poor Sir Joshua is in his grave, and *nothing can touch him further*;[5] otherwise he could not but blush, that his name should appear at the head of a dedication, followed by such an Advertisement as the compositor has now in his hands. Yours always very sincerely in *private*, but by no means wishing to be *pilloried* with you in *publick*,

E. M.

[1] At EM's request, and with his help, JB already had extensively revised the Advertisement to the 2nd ed. of the *Life*, which was to have ended with the word "propagators" (*Life* i. 12, line 5; EM to Sir William Forbes, 5 July 1798—MS. Somervell, NLS). But now JB, having got, as EM wrote to Forbes, "into a higher flight of spirits", had tacked on probably five boastful paragraphs: the last four of the Advertisement as printed (*Life* i. 12–13) and one more, an offprint of which is preserved at Yale (P 102): "It is impossible for me an enthusiastic *Tory*, not to tell the world what I feel, and shall express with that reverential fondness which characterises a true royalist. Soon after the death of my illustrious friend, HIS MAJESTY one day at the levee, after observing that he believed Dr. Johnson was as good a man as ever lived; was graciously pleased to say to me, 'There will be many lives of Dr. Johnson: do you give the best.'—I flatter myself that I have obeyed my SOVEREIGN's commands." JB's conversation with the King is related more fully in Journ. 20 May 1785.

[2] The Advertisement to the 1st ed. of the *Life* contained a highly complimentary acknowledgement of EM's help (*Life* i. 7–8).

[3] "One is known by the company he keeps."

[4] MS. "true" written above deleted "wise"

[5] *Macbeth* III. ii. 25–26.

To Malone,
Friday 17 May 1793
MS. Yale (L 945). JB's copy.

17 May 1793

DEAR MALONE: I knew that Steevy's stabs had hurt you;[1] but I did not apprehend to that degree of irritation which your *hyper*critical letter indicated. I could make no answer to it; but just let it cool.

Jack Courtenay however came yesterday and talked with calm and kind earnestness on the subject. I assured him as I do yourself, that I was fully satisfied you acted with real friendship towards me,—but I could not help thinking very erroneously; for surely every man is at liberty to put himself forward in the style he likes best and his praise of his friends in a very different style must not be confounded with his own personal Rhodomontade. But since mine for my second edition has struck you so strongly I am to submit the proof to John of Sarum and let him decide.[2]

I depend on your dining with me tomorrow with some good men and true,[3] who will be disappointed if they do not meet the Commentator on Shakspeare, as I should exceedingly be, for I ever am "blow high blow low"[4] with true regard very faithfully yours.

[1] For Steevens's annoyance over EM's edition of Shakespeare, see *ante* To EM, 4 Dec. 1790, n. 23, 16 Dec. 1790, n. 13. The fourth edition of the Johnson-Steevens Shakespeare, a copy of which EM received on 2 Apr. (EM to Steevens, 2 Apr.—Folger Shakespeare Library), though its text was based on EM's, treated EM's text and notes with scorn. Steevens maintained the superiority of the second folio over the first, freely introduced metrical emendations, and, as EM later wrote, "endeavoured to carp at and depretiate *all* my notes, on which any sarcasm or cavil could be fastned" (*Percy Corres.* p. 93).

[2] No record of JB's consultation with John Douglas, now Bishop of Salisbury, has been reported, but presumably he ruled that JB's paragraph concerning the King should be struck out. EM's letter to Forbes of 5 July 1798 (*ante* From EM, 13 May, n. 1) shows that he wanted JB to delete the other four paragraphs of "Rhodomontade". "I expressed myself so strongly, that for the only time I think in the whole course of our acquaintance, he lost his good humour.—Of course I gave the matter up." The date assigned to the Advertisement to the 2nd ed. as reprinted by EM in the 3rd is 1 July 1793; but EM's memory is not so reliable that his dating is to be trusted completely.

[3] *Much Ado about Nothing* III. iii. 1: "Are you good men and true?" Nothing more concerning this dinner has been reported.

[4] Proverbial phrase, meaning "whatever may happen" (Burton Stevenson, *The Home Book of Proverbs, Maxims, and Familiar Phrases*, 1948, p. 204).

TO MALONE, 22 AUGUST 1793

To Malone,
Thursday 22 August 1793
MS. Yale (L 946).

London, 22 August 1793

MY DEAR MALONE: You would be proud, and with good reason too, were you to know what a blank your absence makes.[1] It is *felt* much and often I can assure you. The feebleness of body and languor of spirits consequent upon my being knocked down, have made me delay from time to time my expedition to the Combined armies;[2] and now I think I have no heart to go; for my good friend and relation Colonel Bosville has fallen.[3] You will probably not see by this post the London Gazette which is to come out;[4] and therefore it is worth while to inform you, that the Dutch were ordered to attack the village of Leinsells in which the French to the number it is said of five thousand were strongly posted. The Brigade of Guards was ordered to follow and support them. When the Guards got up, they found the Dutch had been driven off, and had made off, by a different route. As there were two forts, General Lake[5] saw at once that if the Guards retreated, they would be destroyed. He therefore determined on a vigorous attack, and the Guards behaved with such animated valour, that they carried the place, killed a great number of the french, and took fifty prisoners, and eleven piece of cannon. But our loss has been heavy. Poor Bosville was shot through the head and instantly expired. Colonel De Peyster of the Artillery is also

[1] After being awarded an honorary D.C.L. at Oxford on 5 July, EM visited Lord Sunderlin and his sisters at Harrogate. Then, after a two-year rest from Shakespeare, he returned to work among the records at Worcester and Stratford-upon-Avon (Prior, *Malone*, p. 205; *Percy Corres*. p. 60).

[2] JB had planned an expedition to Holland and Flanders to observe the siege of Condé and Valenciennes by the combined British and Austrian forces, but on 5 June, when walking home drunk, he was robbed and badly injured by a footpad (To Andrew Gibb, 31 May—*Letters JB* ii. 496–97; To Gibb, 18 June; To Temple, 21 June—MS. Pierpont Morgan; see BP xviii. 194–95).

[3] JB had this morning read in his newspaper that Lt.-Col. Thomas Bosville had been killed in action on 18 Aug. (Journ. 22 Aug.).

[4] An "extraordinary" issue of the *London Gazette*, issued 22 Aug., contained a dispatch from Col. Sir James Murray describing the battle at Lincelles in Flanders on 18 Aug. and numbering the wounded and slain.

[5] Major-Gen. Gerard Lake (1744–1808), Lt.-Col. of the 1st Regiment of Footguards, M.P. for Aylesbury since 1790, and later (1807) first Viscount Lake.

killed.[6] Eight or nine of the Officers are wounded, some of them severely; killed 35 noncommissioned officers and privates; Wounded 135. Perhaps I am not quite exact as to the numbers.[7] It was however an action of signal bravery, and highly to the honour of the Guards.

London has been very thin of our friends. Windham you know has returned from Valenciennes full of military enthusiasm.[8] Courtenay who is come from Margate with his family dined with him as I did on thursday last: on Saturday they dined with me; and yesterday Courtenay insisted on our eating a trout with him, which he had bought in the City *cheap*.[9] We did so. He seems quite sick of the french. No wonder.[10]

My second edition goes off *as well as could be expected*. More than 500 are sold.[11]

I beg you may present my respects to Lord Sunderlin and the Ladies. Pray come soon. I ever am most sincerely yours,

JAMES BOSWELL

From Malone,
Sunday 1 September 1793

MS. Yale (C 1928).

ADDRESS: James Boswell Esqre., Great Portland Street, London.

POSTMARKS: STRATFORD ON AVON [London] SE 2 93 E.

Stratford upon Avon, Sepr. 1, 1793

Many thanks, my dear Boswell, for your letter which I found on

[6] Actually Lt. James de Peyster of the Royal Regiment of Artillery (*Army List*, 1793; *Gent. Mag.* 1793, lxiii. 774–75).

[7] According to the *London Gazette* of 22 Aug., 2 officers were killed and 10 wounded, while 38 sergeants and rank and file were killed and 137 wounded.

[8] Windham was an ardent supporter of the war with France, declared in Feb. On 10 July he left for Valenciennes, where he observed the siege so closely that he came under fire himself (*Windham Papers* i. 138–40).

[9] JB's journal records these dinners on 15, 17, and 21 Aug.

[10] Fox, who opposed the war with France, by this time had lost the support of much of his own party. Courtenay, though his "republican frenzy" had lessened (Prior, *Malone*, p. 201), still remained loyal to Fox and the French; EM wondered "that a man in no other respect hard-hearted, should still adhere to these cut-throats" (*Windham Papers* i. 164).

[11] The 2nd ed. of the *Life* was published on 17 July; by 24 July, 400 copies had already been sold (Waingrow, p. lxxvii; To Bennet Langton, 24 July—MS. Hyde Collection).

my arrival here this day sennight, and which brought me the agreable intelligence of your being in town, a circumstance that I scarcely hoped for, as I took it for granted you had gone on your *wandering* scheme to the Continent. Here have I been up to my elbows every day this week past in old papers and parchments, and by the favour of the Corporation have picked up several little particulars for my life of Shakspeare. I worked every day from ten till it was nearly dark, which prevented me from writing to you before this time. In such a cause you will not wonder at my ardour and perseverance. I met with one letter to Shakspeare, but after the most diligent search I could not find his answer,[1] which would have been an ευρηκα[2] indeed; nor with a single scrap of his handwriting. I think however that through a channel which these papers have opened to me, I shall be able to get at it.

I mean to bring the great bard to town with me in the Chaise, I mean the best part of him, his head; of which I have got an admirable mould, for the purpose of making a cast.[3] By my friend Dr. Davenports permission,[4] I have done infinite service to his bust in the church, by doing away the absurdity of which some strolling players were guilty about 40 years ago, who painted him in colours. He is now a very good uniform stone-colour; and the bust appears quite a different thing.[5] There is much character in it, and from[6] many minute circumstances I am clear that it was copied from a mask taken from his face after death.[7] By being placed at least three feet too high, it is never seen rightly, nor did I

[1] The letter from Shakespeare's Stratford friend Richard Quyney (d. 1602), dated 25 Oct. 1598, asks for a loan of £30. Because EM found the letter among Quyney's papers, it may be that it was not sent; in any case no reply has been found. The letter was first printed by James Boswell the younger in EM's third variorum edition of Shakespeare, 1821, ii. 485. See E. I. Fripp, *Master Richard Quyney*, 1924.

[2] "I have found it."

[3] No such cast has been found; however, an engraving of Shakespeare's bust is prefixed to volume two of EM's third variorum Shakespeare.

[4] Rev. James Davenport (c. 1751–1841) had been vicar of Stratford-upon-Avon since 1787 (*Alum. Oxon.*; *Gent. Mag.* 1787, lvii. 1034). EM's correspondence with Davenport from 1788 to 1793 was issued in a limited edition by J. O. Halliwell-Phillipps in 1864.

[5] EM's attempt to transform Shakespeare's painted bust into a piece of neoclassical statuary—one of his rare lapses of judgement—is notorious among Shakespearians. The bust had originally been painted, and what EM saw as vandalism had been in reality restoration undertaken in 1748. See Samuel Schoenbaum, *Shakespeare's Lives*, 1970, p. 187.

[6] MS. "from" superimposed upon erased "it has"

[7] On this improbable conjecture, see Samuel Schoenbaum, *William Shakespeare: Records and Images*, 1981, p. 158.

ever form a just conception of it till I mounted a ladder and was nearly on a level with it.

The subject of monuments reminds me of our friend Johnson, to whom I found a very neat one erected in Lichfield cathedral, as I passed through that town about ten days ago. It is very like him, but like Shakspeare's, much too high. The Inscription is, I think, tame enough. As well as I recollect, it runs thus: "The friends of Samuel Johnson, L.L.D. a native of Lichfield, erected[8] this monument, as a tribute of respect to the memory of a man of extensive learning, a distinguished moral writer, and a sincere christian. He died Decr. 13, 1784." A colder word than *distinguished*, could not easily have been found. I imagine, it is the production of Dr. Vyse.[9] As a companion to Dr. Johnson, Mrs. Garrick has erected a monument[10] exactly in the same style, to her husband, with but a sorry inscription, concluding with Johnson's words, awkwardly enough introduced—"who diminished the stock of harmless pleasure" etc.[11]—I hope to be in town on thursday or friday, and then shall sit down *doggedly* to arrange all my materials and finish the Life.[12] I hope Windham and Courtenay are still with you. Remember me most kindly to them both, and believe me ever, my dear B., most faithfully and affectionately yours,

EDMOND MALONE

[8] MS. "have" deleted before "erected"

[9] The monument is described briefly in Thomas Harwood, *The History and Antiquities of the Church and City of Lichfield*, 1806, pp. 85–86. See also *Life* iv. 472 and Waingrow, p. 400, n. 2. Dr. William Vyse (1742–1816), Rector of Lambeth and a native of Lichfield, had conducted the subscription for the monument (Waingrow, p. 103 n. 37; From Edmund Hector, 8 Apr. 1791). He was the son of the William Vyse who left a pair of new shoes outside SJ's door at Oxford (*Life* i. 77; From John Taylor, 6 May 1785). EM has misquoted the last line of the inscription, which reads, "He died the 13th of December, 1784, aged 75 years" (*Life* iv. 472).

[10] MS. "a monument" written above deleted "one"

[11] For a description of the Garrick monument, see Harwood, p. 86. SJ wrote that DG's death "eclipsed the gaiety of nations and impoverished the publick stock of harmless pleasure" (*Lives of the Poets*, ed. G. B. Hill, 1905, ii. 21).

[12] EM returned to London on 5 Sept. (Journ. 6 Sept.). Although he worked on his biography of Shakespeare, among other projects, for the rest of his life, he left it unfinished; James Boswell the younger finished it and printed it in EM's third variorum edition of Shakespeare, ii. 1–287. For "doggedly", see *Life* v. 40.

From Malone,
Thursday 5 September 1793

Not reported. See Journ. 6 Sept.: "Malone had come to town the day before, and sent me a note, which I found on my return from Dilly's."

From Malone,
c. Wednesday 11 December 1793

Not reported. See Journ. 11 Dec.: "I drank tea at Malone's by a note of invitation."

To Malone,
Tuesday 18 November 1794
MS. Yale (L 947).
ADDRESS: To Edmond Malone Esq., London.

Auchinleck, 18 Novr. 1794

MY DEAR MALONE: If I have been of consequence enough to you in my absence to make you think of me, you will possibly have wondered that you have not heard from me. The truth is that accursed constitutional disease of the spirits seised upon me in such a degree, that I could write of nothing but my own unhappiness; and I recollect my old friend Sir John Pringle censuring a witty but melancholy gentleman for troubling his friends with his complaints. "He was (said Sir John) always resting his burthen on his friends' shoulders."[1] Having a glimpse of cheerfulness, I on the first of this month sat down and wrote letters to you and Courtenay and expressed myself pretty heartily. So All hail Malone and Courtenay, Courtenay and Malone All hail![2] But upon reading those letters next day, I found they were wretched Lamentations. So I would not send them.

[1] This anecdote is not reported elsewhere.

[2] A parody of *Macbeth* I. iii. 68–69.

I have been uncommonly moderate in wine; so cannot blame myself. I have done some good to my Estate, my tenants and the neighbourhood: But my existence has been not only negatively dull, but positively uneasy. I must do my daughters the justice to say, that they have conducted themselves very well.[3] So it is *myself alone* that must answer.

I yesterday dined at Kilmarnock one of our Country Towns, with[4] the Officers of Lord Howard of Walden's (the 4th) Dragoons; and their English language and manners revived me. Tomorrow they are to be here with me.[5] Feeling myself a good deal better, I now write again to you and Courtenay, what I hope may be sent without offence.[6]

How have you been? enviable man! What a number of events have happened since I left you, that would have agitated me, had I been in London.[7] Pray write to me. As the foolish virgins in the Parable, said to the wise "Give us of your oyl, for our lamp is gone out."[8] I have little more business to transact here. But why go to London? What have I to do there? I can see no prospect in life but a thick fog. Could I but recover those pleasing delusions which braced my nerves when I first entered Westminster Hall! In short could I have any object!—But I grow querulous. So, no more.

My Dear Malone, in whatever state I am I never forget your kindness to me, and the innumerable moments of happiness which I owe to you, and I ever am with unalterable regard your obliged, affectionate, and faithful friend,

JAMES BOSWELL

To Malone,
Monday 13 April 1795

MS. British Library (Add. 22549, fol. 12).
ADDRESS: To Edmond Malone Esq.

[3] JB and his two eldest daughters, Veronica and Euphemia, had been at Auchinleck since 1 July (Book of Company).

[4] MS. "with" superimposed upon "at"

[5] JB dined with the officers of the 4th, or "Queen's Own", Regiment of Dragoons on 17, 19, and 20 Nov. and again on 15 and 16 Dec. (Book of Company). Their Colonel (a general in the army) was John Griffin Griffin (1719–97), fourth Baron Howard de Walden.

[6] The letter to Courtenay has not been reported.

[7] For example, the course of the war with France and events in Corsica, to judge by his letters at this time to James Boswell the younger.

[8] Matthew 25: 8.

TO MALONE, 13 APRIL 1795

Great Portland Street, 13 April 1795

Dear Sir:[1] Whatever respect you and I and all who take a concern in erecting a monument to Dr. Johnson may have for the learning and abilities of Dr. Parr, I am clear that we could not be justified in adopting implicitly without so much as having seen it, the inscription which that Gentleman has written. We are answerable to the memory of our illustrious Friend, to the present age, and to Posterity. Let me add—We are answerable to another tribunal, without whose approbation of the epitaph the monument cannot be admitted into St. Paul's Church: I mean the Dean and Chapter of that Cathedral.

When Sir Joshua Reynolds asked Dr. Parr to furnish an Epitaph, I cannot suppose that he meant to preclude even himself from all consideration, and all power of objection; far less that he could entertain a notion that the other gentlemen with whom he had not conferred on the subject, would be so tied up. He certainly understood that this Epitaph, as in all similar cases, was to be subject to revision. He had before him the example of Dr. Johnson himself, who was requested to write Dr. Goldsmith's Epitaph; and how did that great man conduct himself? You will find in my Octavo Edition of his *Life* Vol. 2. p. 448 a letter from him to Sir Joshua in which he says "I send you the poor dear Doctor's epitaph. Read it first yourself; and if you then think it right, shew it to the Club. I am you know willing to be corrected."[2]

I trust that when Dr. Parr reconsiders his unusual proposition, he will be satisfied that, without any offence to him, it must receive a negative.[3] I am with much regard, Dear Sir, your faithful, humble servant,

James Boswell[4]

[1] The formality of this letter ("Dear Sir" rather than "My Dear Malone") contrasts sharply with the warm ease of the other letters in this correspondence. As F. A. Pottle has pointed out, the present letter was "an 'ostensible letter'; i.e. it was really written at Malone's request" (BP xviii. 276) to be shown to Parr and others.

[2] *Life* iii. 81.

[3] The story of the controversy over SJ's epitaph is told in *Life* iv. 469–72. Sir Joshua Reynolds and William Seward had asked Samuel Parr to compose SJ's epitaph; now Parr balked at submitting it for the approval of The Club.

[4] This is the last surviving letter written entirely in JB's own hand. He collapsed while dining with The Club the next day, and died on 19 May.

APPENDIX 1

Garrick's and Boswell's Verses on Strasbourg Cathedral

EIGHT lines of verse "Upon Seeing Strasbourg Cathedral", were composed by DG in 1764 in Strasbourg, where he was much in the company of Gayot (see *ante* To DG, 25 Nov. 1767, n. 13), and published in *St. James's Chron.* 1–3 Oct. 1765 (Knapp no. 243). JB was shown a copy of the verses by Gayot on 22 Nov. 1764, and wrote a rejoinder of sixteen lines. He sent it, with a copy of DG's verses, to the Margrave of Baden-Durlach in a letter of 25 Nov. 1764 (a copy of JB's letter is at Yale—L 21). The episode is covered in Journ. 21–22 Nov. 1764. The text of DG's verses is from a photostat of the copy in JB's hand which is now in the Baden Archives in Karlsruhe. A second copy at Yale (C 1335), also in JB's hand, shows one substantive change: "rapture" for "wonder" (l. 2). The text of JB's reply is taken from a photostat of the original in the Baden Archives. A copy that he made for himself is at Yale (M 284): it lacks a heading but shows no other substantive changes.

Upon seeing Strasbourg Cathedral
Extempore by a Stranger
(By Mr. Garrick.)

That hallow'd Spire which rises to the Skies,
Fills ev'ry heart with wonder and surprise.
Approach the Temple.—Round it's rev'rend base
Vile traffic Shops God's Edifice disgrace.
Are there still Goths in this enlighten'd age,
Who dare oppose and scorn the sacred Page?
Who by one Impious Act at once Express
Their want of Virtue, Taste and Righteousness?

Boswell's reply reads:

APPENDIX 1

Answer of The
Shop-keepers round Strasbourg Cathedral
(By Mr. Boswell.)

Stranger, why storm so fierce, because arround
This grand Cathedral our poor Shops are found?
Why call us Goths? Why rank us among those
Who would the Sacred Oracles oppose?
    In times of old, the greedy Sons of gain
Their Booths set up in Judah's lofty Fane,
The Place of Prayer most impiously made
A crowded Scene of bustling, babling Trade,
Till the Messiah came with awfull rod
And drove the Thieves from out the House of God.
    But we the Temple would not dare defile;
We hold in honour this majestic Pile:
With humble rev'rence by it's Walls we stay,
In honest Bus'ness to employ the day;
And, while thus cover'd by the holy shade
Say, to do wrong who would not be affraid?

APPENDIX 2

The Cause of Cuninghame v. Cuninghame

In the lawsuit alluded to in *ante* To EM, 25 Mar. 1786, JB's clients were postponed creditors on the estate of Lainshaw; Henry Cuninghame was a younger son of Elizabeth Montgomerie (d. 1776), JB's sister-in-law, who had inherited Lainshaw from her brother James Montgomerie (1730–66). After her death, the estate passed to her eldest son, Sir Walter Montgomerie-Cuninghame, who in 1779 was forced to sell it to William Cuninghame.[1] The estate was encumbered with an annuity of £200 for James Montgomerie's widow, Jean, who was still alive at the time of this lawsuit, and in addition Elizabeth Montgomerie had settled an annuity of £300 on her second husband, John Beaumont. In case sufficient money should not be available to set up Beaumont's annuity fund, she also granted him an overlease of a considerable portion of the estate; that is, he would pay a fixed rent of £382.10*s.* to Lainshaw's owner and sublet the land for however much more he could get. When William Cuninghame bought the estate, the purchase price went, by ranking of the Court of Session, first to set up an annuity fund of £4,000 for Jean Montgomerie and next to the heritable creditors on the estate, after which there was not enough left over to set up a fund sufficient to yield Beaumont £300 in yearly interest, or to pay the group of creditors ranked after Beaumont. Thus Beaumont was thrown back upon the profits from his overlease and, after Jean Montgomerie's death, was to have drawn the arrears of his annuity from her fund of £4,000. But Beaumont later sold his right to the annuity to William Cuninghame, who also claimed the right to the profits from the overlease.

The postponed creditors, who were still owed above £10,000 after the purchase price had been divided between Jean Montgomerie's annuity fund and the first group of creditors, could hope for payment only out of the annuity fund, which would be freed after Jean Montgomerie's death. They argued that the overlease

[1] James Paterson, *History of the Counties of Ayr and Wigton*, 1863–66, iii. 587–88, 598; *Ayrshire*, p. 304; *Ominous Years*, p. 379.

was intended only as security for, not as an addition to, Beaumont's (now William Cuninghame's) annuity, and that if William Cuninghame could realize a profit of £300 a year from the overlease he could have no claim on Jean Montgomerie's fund, which should go to them after her death. To find out what was due them, they demanded that Cuninghame give an accounting of the profits from the overlease and be prohibited from granting any more subleases without their knowledge and consent. William Cuninghame claimed that he was entitled both to the full amount of Beaumont's annuity and to the profits from the overlease, which, he maintained, were inconsiderable.

On 27 July and 11 Dec. 1784 the Lord Ordinary ruled in favour of William Cuninghame. JB appealed to the Court of Session in a printed *Petition* dated 23 Dec. 1784; the *Answers for William Cuninghame*, 4 Jan. 1785, are by William Craig.[2] In two interlocutors, dated 17 June and 5 July 1785, the Lords of Session found for the creditors, and on 13 July 1785 William Cuninghame appealed to the House of Lords.[3] He was represented by Alexander Abercromby and William Craig; the creditors were represented by JB and Ilay Campbell.[4] The Lords heard the case on 24 Apr., and on 25 Apr. they rejected William Cuninghame's appeal.[5]

[2] Both documents are in the Murray Collection, Signet Library.

[3] "Appeal of William Cuninghame", MS. House of Lords.

[4] *The Appellant's Case, The Respondents Case*, 12 Apr. 1786, House of Lords.

[5] "Cunninghame against Cunninghame et al.: Judgment", MS. House of Lords; *Journals of the House of Lords*, xxxvii. 448–49.

APPENDIX 3
Two Character Sketches of Edmond Malone

The two following newspaper articles are mentioned in *ante* To EM, 16 Dec. 1790 and n. 3 and From EM, 14 Apr. 1791 and n. 5. The first, presumably by the Viscount Mountmorres, appeared in *Pub. Adv.* 14 Dec. 1790, p. [1]; the second, by JB, appeared in *Pub. Adv.* 24 Mar. 1791, p. [1].

CHARACTER *of Mr.* MALONE, *by a* PARTICULAR FRIEND.

Mr. Malone was called to the Irish Bar, where the abilities of his uncle, the Right Hon. Anthony Malone, had shone with such unrivalled lustre, and he had early given hopes of his being the successor to his character and reputation.

Common accidents often give habits and dispositions which pervade our lives. From his youth he had a turn for theatrical compositions and representations. Some plays had been acted at a private school where he was educated, previous to his admission in the University of Dublin. Jephson, the author of Braganza, as well as Malone, acted in those representations, which were superintended by Macklin.

Whether his diffidence did not him allow to think himself qualified for a situation where so much was expected, or whether forensick labour and exertion were not adapted to a mind devoted to the Belles Lettres he soon quitted the Bar. Possibly a competent fortune left him by his father induced him to follow his own inclination, and to devote himself to science.

Of his edition of SHAKSPEAR, of his labour, minute accuracy, and subtle investigation, too much can scarcely be said. Mr. Malone has that happy combination of good qualities, so concisely, but happily, expressed in Dr. Barrow's epitaph, Summa Eruditio, Par Modestia.

Upon the merits of the various editors of *Shakspear* who can confidently decide, while the names of Pope, Johnson, and Steevens stand in competition? Perhaps it may be said with truth, that Mr. Malone is the best biographer of our immortal bard.

Johnson's Lives of the Poets, and Sheridan's Life of Swift, which are now detached from their respective editions, are universally read and approved. If Mr. Malone's History of the

Drama were printed separately, in a fair, practicable character, it would be a valuable present to the learned world; and if it were continued to the present time, it would be still more acceptable.

Mr. Malone would then appear as an original author, and as *Shakspear*'s best biographer. The labours of the editor do not always attain that praise, nor meet with that compensation which they deserve. While originality claims admiration, the genius of Pope employed in editing Shakspear appears like the skill and mastery of a Raphael, occupied in cleaning a portrait.

Edmund Malone Esq.

Some time ago there appeared in this paper an imperfect, and in some degree erroneous, however friendly, account of that gentleman to whose critical labours, literature, and talents the lovers of Shakespeare are so much indebted. The account is *imperfect*, as it has said nothing of Mr. Malone's ancient and respectable family, from which all his other excellent qualities derive a lustre; nothing of the reputation with which he passed through both school and college at Dublin; nothing of the advantage he had in being educated under the eye of his father, one of the Judges of Ireland. It is *erroneous*, inasmuch as it conveys a notion that Mr. Malone was so fond of acting, from having himself performed at a private theatre, that it gave a colour to the whole of his future life: whereas the real fact is, that he never performed more than a trifling part in a school play; and this has no more relation to his publishing Shakespeare, than any other fact in the world.—Mr. Malone's high admiration of our immortal Bard, and his love of curious research, as well as of correctness and elegance, have induced him to devote a large portion of his time to an edition, which, whether we consider what, as is mostly observed by the writer of the short account, are original works by Mr. Malone himself, or the number, variety, and perfection of his notes, will ever be held in respectful estimation. Had that gentleman persevered in his profession as a lawyer, we cannot doubt that he must, like his father, have been raised to the Bench. Indeed he has given us a remarkable specimen of his ability as a *Judge*, in his Essay entitled "Shakespeare, Jonson, and Ford;" in which there is such a clear arrangement of evidence and argument as does great honour both to his talents and application.

INDEX

Material dealing with Boswell's and Johnson's relationships with others is ordinarily indexed under the other person. Discussions concerned solely with rephrasings in Boswell's *Journal of a Tour to the Hebrides* are ordinarily not indexed; neither are the Introductions to each section, nor sources and authorities.

The following abbreviations are used: D. (Duke), M. (Marquess), E. (Earl), V. (Viscount), B. (Baron), Bt. (Baronet), EB (Edmund Burke), JB (James Boswell), DG (David Garrick), SJ (Samuel Johnson), EM (Edmond Malone), MM (Margaret Montgomerie Boswell), CG (Covent Garden Theatre), DL (Drury Lane Theatre). *Life* refers to Boswell's *Life of Johnson*; *Tour* to his *Journal of a Tour to the Hebrides*.

The index was compiled mainly by Rachel McClellan, with the assistance of Anne Badger, Ian Duncan, Elizabeth Gregory, Judith Hickey, and Steven Meyer.

Ariosto, Ludovico (*cont.*): 48, 52, 56; Hoole's trans. of, 294
Aristippus (c. 435–356 B.C.), philosopher, 305
Aristotle (384–322 B.C.), 323
Armadale, Skye, 254
Arnold, George (fl. 1790), bookseller, 387, 392, 397, 400, 402, 410
Arnot, Hugo (1749–86), advocate and antiquarian, letters to and from JB, 74; *ment.*, 64, 75; *History of Edinburgh*, 74, 115
Arran, Isle of, 226
Artois, Comte d'. *See* Bourbon, Charles-Philippe de
Ashbourne, Derbyshire, 71
Ashburton, 1st B. *See* Dunning, John
Astle, Rev. Daniel (c. 1743–1826), 333
Atkinson, Joseph (fl. 1790), apothecary, 381
Attorney-General. *See* Wedderburn, Alexander (1778–80)
Aubrey, John (1626–97), *Brief Lives*, 420
Auchinleck, Lady. *See* Boswell, Elizabeth (Boswell), 2nd Lady
Auchinleck, Lord. *See* Boswell, Alexander
Auchinleck (house and estate), JB at, 21, 132, 207, 220, 246, 329, 333, 343, 365, 394, 422, 430, describes, 105, 132, 146, invites EB to, 132, 139, 143, 146, as Laird of, 132, 207, 365, 422, 430; Paoli visits, 38; SJ admires, 132–3; mail between London and, 266; postal address of, 324, 333, 355; MM returns to, from London, 343; encumbrances, debts, 358, 394; *ment.*, 220, 246, 329, 427
Ayr (Ayrshire), JB at Quarter Sessions in, 246; by-election in (1788), 344, 352–3, and "State Coalition", 344, 352–3

Bacon, Francis (1561–1616), B. Verulam and V. St Albans, 183; *Essays*, 372–3
Badcock, Samuel (1747–88), dissenting clergyman, 284
Bagnal, Robert, Scots potter, 109
Baker, Sir George (1722–1809), M.D., 366
Baker, John (1712–79), *Diaries*, 47
Baldwin, Henry (c. 1734–1813), printer, 180, 193, 227, 254, 267–8, 358, 377, 401, 410
Baliol, John (1249–1315), King of Scotland, 206
Ballantyne, William, merchant (fl. 1772–73), 52, 57
Balmuto, Fife, 220–1
Banks, Sir Joseph (1743–1820), Bt., 381, 390, 400, 419
Barber, Francis (c. 1742–1801), SJ's servant, 233, 282, 348
Barclay, James (c. 1747–c. 1770), Oxford student, 240, 252
Baretti, Giuseppe Marc' Antonio (1719–1789), critic and writer, 181, 316, 339–40, 350
Barnard, Sir Frederick Augusta (1743–1830), 360
Barnard, Thomas (1726–1806), D.D., Bp. of Killaloe, 213, 325, 377, 380, 402, 415–6, 419
Baronston, Ireland, 383, 392
Barré, Isaac (1726–1802), M.P., 129
Barrington, Hon. Daines (1727–1800), barrister, 378

INDEX

Burney, Charles (1726–1814), Mus. Doc., 288, 300, 323, 349, 381, 390
Burney, Frances (Mme. d'Arblay) (1752–1840), 162, 311
Burzynski, Tadeusz, Count (d. 1773), Polish Envoy, 38
Bushey Park, Middlesex, 196
Butler, Samuel (1612–80), satirist, *Remains*, 189
Bute, 4th E. and 1st M. of. *See* Stuart, John, Lord Mountstuart

Cadell, Thomas (1742–1802), bookseller, 217, 360–61
Cadell, Thomas (1773–1836), bookseller, son of preceding, 361
Caldwell, Sir James (c. 1732–84), 360
Caldwell, Sir John (1750–1830), 360
Calgacus (or Galgacus), Caledonian chieftain, 108
Calonne, Charles-Alexandre de (1734–1802), French Controller-General of Finance, 162
Cambridge, Richard Owen (1717–1802), poet, 288, 376
Cambridge University, Gray and Temple meet at, 37; EM visits, 329–31; voting rights at, 374; colleges: Emmanuel, 239, 330, 374, Trinity, 263, 400, King's, 386, Peterhouse, 402
Camoëns, Luis Vaz de (1524–80), *Lusiad*, Mickle's trans. of, 29, 33
Campbell, Rev. Archibald (1668–1744), *Doctrines of a Middle State*, 240, 251–2
Campbell, George (1719–96), D.D., Principal of Marischal College, Aberdeen, 237
Campbell, Ilay (1734–1823), *later* Lord President and Bt., 135, 436
Campbell, John, (1705–82), 4th E. of Loudoun, 224
Campbell, John (1723–1806), 5th D. of Argyll, 285
Campbell, John (d. 1789), M.D., 334, 363
Campbell, Mary (Montgomerie) (d. 1777), 2nd wife of James Campbell of Treesbank, 73, 128
Campbell, Thomas (1733–95), D.D., 62, 420
Canning, George (d. 1771), lawyer and minor poet, 310, 313
Canterbury, Archbp. of. *See* Tillotson, John (1691–94)
Capell, Edward (1713–81), ed. of Shakespeare, 382
Carlisle, Cumberland, 1786 election in, 344; JB as Recorder of, 344–5, 353, 357–8, 363, 367–70; and Corporation cause, 363
Carlyle, Rev. Joseph Dacre (1759–1804), Arabic scholar, 368
Carter, Elizabeth (1717–1806), trans. of Crousaz's *Examen*, 219
Cassillis, 10th E. of. *See* Kennedy, David
Catiline (c. 108–62 B.C.), 127
Catalogue of Five Hundred Celebrated Authors, 351–2
Cator, John (1730–1806), timber merchant, 396
Caulfeild, James (1728–99), 1st E. of Charlemont, 374, 395–6, 402–3, 415–6

Colman, George (1732–94), the elder, dramatist and theatre manager, 42, 50, 52, 193
Colville, Alexander (1717–70), 7th Lord Colville of Culross, 285
Colville, Elizabeth (Erskine) (c. 1735–94), Lady Colville, 285
Congreve, William (1670–1729), trans. of Ovid, 245; *Way of the World*, 339
Conway, Hon. Henry Seymour (1719–95), Commander-in-Chief, 120–3
Cooke, Thomas (1703–56), translator, 201
Cooke, William (d. 1824), barrister ("Conversation Cooke"), 327; *Conversation*, *Life of Samuel Johnson, LL.D.*, 327
Cooper, Sir Grey (?1726–1801), M.P., 33
Cornwall, 421
Cornwallis, Charles (1738–1805), 2nd E. Cornwallis, 115
Corsica and the Corsicans, 22, 25, 29, 78, 430
Courtenay, John (1738–1816), M.P.: and EB: dines with, 156–7, and note on his wit, 230, 267, *Poetical Essay* addressed to, 422; politics: on committee for impeachment of Hastings, 155, 336, Whig, 347, 362, supports French republican cause, 355, 380, 426, retains Commons seat, 357, 390–1, and Regency, 362; personal characteristics: kindly, cheerful, 200, appearance, 285–6, absent-minded, 309, firmness of mind, 407, "best good man", 422; and JB: friendship with, 200, 415, franks letter for, 200, JB's "ingenious friend", 249, dines with, 296, 339, 376, 407, 426, Courtenay on medical treatment for, 310, approves his wine-drinking, 356, 375–6, 412, buys madeira with, 390, 397–8, 403, on JB's hypochondria, 403–4, and *Tour*: regrets Veronica in, 200, 208, advises, on quarrels with Lord Macdonald, 200, 281, 294–5, 297–8, with Tytler, 274, on treatment of Mrs Piozzi, 249, 318, 321–2, helps with revisions of, 230, 249, 258, 267, 269–70; and *Life*, helps with revisions of, 405–6, 424, advises, to sell copyright of, 415, and Mrs. Rudd, 297; letter to, from Cobham, 355–6, *see also*, Poetical Review *below*; at Bath, 200, 328–9, 356–7, 374, 390–1, in London, 329, 393; and "the Gang", 200, 328, 335; and EM: franks letters for, 200, 226, 246, 253, 281, 286–7, 301, 308–9, 325, 347, 355, EM helps, with verses, 282, Courtenay dines with, 294, 296, 301, 326–7, 339, 348, visits, at Cobham, 362, 355–8, buys madeira with, 390, 397–8, 403, on EM's ed. of Shakespeare, 382; family, 263, 366, 407; Peter Pindar lampoons, in *Bozzy and Piozzi*, 302, Courtenay proposes action against, 304–5; at Club, 381, 399–400; born in Ireland, 407; with Reynolds, 326–7; finances, 351, 357, 390–1, 407; health, 351, 357; *A Poetical Review of the Literary and Moral Character of the Late Samuel*

Johnson, LL.D., quoted or mentioned, 200, 286–8, 302–3, JB and: Courtenay's elogium on, 292, 296, JB proposes extra couplet for, 300, comments on, 303; EM helps, with revisions, 287–8, 301–3, dislikes criticism of SJ's faults in, 322, SJ and: figures influenced by, 300, his poetry, 301–3, 313, attitude towards death, 372; Sir W. Jones in, 301–3; published, 309, 313, 321; *Ode "To Edmond Malone, Esq."*, 282, 285–6, 345; *Poetical and Philosophical Essay on the French Revolution*, 422; *ment.*, 282, 356, 366, 393, 403

Courtenay, John, son of preceding, 407

Courtenay, Kenneth (c. 1769–1838), bro. of preceding, 263

Courtier, John, wig-maker, 43

Cowley, Abraham (1618–67), 78, *Sex Libri Planatarum*, 406

Craggs-Eliot, Edward (1727–1804), 1st B. Eliot of St. Germans, 399, 404, 420

Craig, William (1745–1813), advocate, *later* Lord Craig, 436

Crawford, Lady. *See* Lindsay-Crawford, Jean (Hamilton)

Creech, William (d. 1815), Edinburgh bookseller, 286, 291

Crespin, Daniel (1640–1716), ed. of Ovid, 249

Crisp, Henry. *See* Crisp, Samuel

Crisp, Samuel (c. 1708–83), *Virginia*, 50

Croft, Rev. Herbert (1751–1816), *later* Bt., *Life of Young*, 300

Cromie, Sir Michael (c. 1745–c. 1824), Bt., merchant and banker, 402

Cromwell, Oliver (1599–1658), 294

Crousaz, Jean-Pierre de (1663–1750), Swiss theologian, 299

Cullen, Robert (1742–1810), advocate, *later* Lord Cullen, son of following, 145, 232

Cullen, William (1710–90), M.D., 145

Culloden, battle of, 256

Cumberland, Richard (1732–1811), dramatist, 416; *West Indian*, 49, 239; *Choleric Man*, 63; *Fashionable Lover*, 239, 251

Cuninghame, Annie (d. 1779), niece of MM, 128

Cuninghame, Lt. David (d. 1814), nephew of MM, 87

Cuninghame, Elizabeth. *See* Beaumont, Elizabeth

Cuninghame, Henry Drumlanrig, (d. 1790), nephew of MM, 307, 435

Cuninghame, William (1731–99), 307, 435–6

Cuninghame *v.* Cuninghame, 300, 307, 319, 435–6

Cuninghame, Ayrshire, 226

Cunningham, James (1749–91), 13th E. of Glencairn, 344

Currie, Charles Douglas (fl. 1786–91), London attorney, 343

Curtis, William (1752–1829), M.P., *later* Lord Mayor of London and Bt., 412

D. H., reviewer for *Gent. Mag.*, 283–4

Dalby, John (fl. 1790), goldsmith, 386

Dalrymple, Sir David (1726–92), Bt., Lord Hailes, Scottish judge, 201

Dalrymple, John (1720–89), 5th E. of Stair, 273

Dodsley, James (1724–97), bookseller, 113
Dodsley, Robert (1703–64), poet and bookseller, *Collection of Poems by Several Hands*, 74
Donaldson, Alexander (fl. 1750–94), bookseller and publisher, 30, 39, 41, 47
Douglas, John (1721–1807), D.D., Bp. of Salisbury, 160, 381, 390, 424
Douglas, Sylvester (1743–1823), M.P., *later* 1st B. Glenbervie, 47, 366
Downpatrick (*pseud.*). *See* Rudd, Margaret Caroline
Downpatrick, N. Ireland, 302
Dreghorn, Lord. *See* Maclaurin, John
Drummond, Robert Hay (1711–76), Archbp. of York, 44
Dryden, John (1631–1700), SJ working on "Life of", 78; "Lines on Milton", 192, 241; and translations: used in *Tour*, 217, *Aeneid*, 245, Juvenal, 270; *Oedipus*, 40; *Conquest of Granada*, 291; *Tyrannick Love*, 375
Dublin, EM describes, 381, 401, 407–8, 410, 420
Dublin, University of, 356, 437, confers diploma on SJ, 395; Trinity College, 167, 395–6
Dulwich College, 374
Dumfries, 5th E. of. *See* Macdowall-Crichton, Patrick
Dun, Rev. John (c. 1724–92), minister at Auchinleck, 275
Dunbar, Sir James (d. 1782), of Mochrum, Bt., 120, 122
Dundas, Henry (1742–1811), Lord Advocate, *later* 1st V. Melville, and relief for Scottish Catholics, 106, 108–10; his career, 120, 127, 131, 133, 135; political influence of, 120, 131, 136, 140, 352–3, 404; supports American war, 120, 133; and Indian affairs, 133; dismissed as Lord Advocate, 135; JB on friendly terms with, 131, 145, EB's characterization of JB told to, 140, JB attacks, in *LPS 85*, 293; attempts to help Scottish schoolmasters, 141; helps T. D. Boswell, 404; *ment.*, 123, 136, 344
Dundas, Sir Lawrence (c. 1710–81), Bt., M.P., 109, 134
Dundas, Robert (1737–87), Lord President of the Court of Session, 293
Dundas, Sir Thomas (1741–1820), of Kerse, Bt., M.P., 132, 134, 139
Dundonald Castle, Ayrshire, 226
Dunning, John (1731–83), 1st B. Ashburton, 75

Earl of Chesterfield, ship, 289
Earle, James (1755–1817), surgeon, 369, 371
East India Company, 376, 389
Edial, Staffordshire, 54
EDINBURGH: theatre in, 31–2, 63–4; SJ and JB finish tour to Hebrides in, 54; Robin Hood games in, 74; anti-Catholic riots in, 107–11; narrowness of, 116
Buildings and Institutions: Advocates' Library, 182–3, 285; Bank of Scotland, 358; Castle, 110–1; Court of Session, 174, 274, 292–3, 435; Register House, 185; Theatre Royal, 25, 31, 51, 63; Town Council, 109

INDEX

Frederick William II (1712–86), King of Prussia, 29, 51, 330
French, Mary Cecilia (1766–1816), EB's niece, 379
Fürst, Elisabeth ("Liserl") (1766–1840), 79

"Gang, The", 200, 328, 335
Garden, Francis, (1721–93), Lord Gardenstone, Scottish judge, 135
Garrick, Arabella (1753–1819), niece of DG, 65
Garrick, Carrington (1753–87), nephew of DG, 48
Garrick, Catherine (b. 1756), niece of DG, 65
Garrick, Christopher Philip, great-nephew of DG, 48
GARRICK, DAVID (1717–79)
General. Ill-health: general, 21, 36, gout, 28, 34, 58, 66, 76, kidney stone, 41, 64, 76; country-house, 21; at Court, 22; Continental tour, 22–3; lawsuits, 27–8; and Paoli, 29, 38; and Mickle, 29–30, 33, 37–8, 42, 45–6, 51–2, 56–7; on Edinburgh theatre, 35, 66; acquaintance with Gray, 37, Burzynski, 38, Hugo Arnot, 75, William Robertson, 76; and retirement: thinks about, 34, 36, last season, 68, in retirement, 65, 71–3, 76; collection of early English plays, 39, 45, 74–5; puts Donaldson on "free list" of DL, 39; friendship with John Home, 40, 77, Hannah More, 79; and SJ, misunderstanding over DG's old plays, 45, and SJ's *Drury Lane Prologue*, 49, SJ will discharge DG's debt for books, 56, defends DG's classical knowledge, 61, praises his Prologues, 63, DG on SJ and Ossian controversy, 65–6, curious about Scots reaction to SJ's *Journey*, 66, SJ's words on DG's death, 428; invited to visit Lord Chatham, 51; elected to The Club, 56; on Becket and Ossian controversy, 62, 66; funeral, 65, 264; and Lord Kames, 68, 70; mentioned as "first-rate wit", 193; Mrs Montagu praises, 234; in Cooke's *Conversation*, 327; Lichfield monument to, 428, *ment.*, 314
Relations with JB. JB opens correspondence with, 21, exchanges between DG and: on Continental exploits, Strasbourg, 21–3, Corsica, 24–5, 29, JB's profession, 23, Mickle, 29–30, 33, 37–8, 42, 45–6, 51–2, 54–7, JB's marriage, 30, 35, 42, his family, 52, 69, visiting Scotland, 32, 64, 68, 75, Percy's catalogue of SJ's writings, 44–6, 49, 55, 58, requests for, and purchases of, books, 45–6, 48–9, 52, 56, 60, exchange of letters during *Tour*, 53–5, 59; DG: praises *Account of Corsica*, 24–6, 29, JB's *Prologue* for Edinburgh Theatre Royal, 25; asks JB, about Mrs. Hartley, 42, to subscribe to Morrell's trans., 58, 60, recommends wigmaker to, 43; JB: writes dedication of Shakespeare ed. to, 30–1, 41, asks DG, about his *Matrimonial Thought*, 34, for Johnsoniana,

INDEX

Jephson, William (b. 1767), son of preceding, 385–6
Jephson, "young". *See* Jephson, Richard Mounteney
Jervais, Thomas ("Mr Jarvois") (d. 1799), glass-painter, 254
Jewell *or* Jewel, Ann (Edwards) (d. 1798), actress, wife of following, 31–2, 35
Jewell, William (d. 1828), treasurer of Haymarket Theatre, 32
Johnny Armstrong's Last Good Night, 250, 338
Johnson, Sarah (1669–1759), mother of SJ, 213
JOHNSON, SAMUEL, LL.D. (1709–84)
General. On Ossian, 62, 65, 242, 326, on French, 70, on London, 117–8, on Univ. of St. Andrews, 201–2, on a "good table", 278, on second sight, 326, on panegyric, 409; and Scots, 62; visits Paris, 69; birthplace of, 69; vocabulary, 189, 237, spelling, 216, 221; gesticulations, 206, 208, 227–8, 241–2, 246; supposed brother of, 216; periodicals on, 194, 201–2, 216, 243, 276, 326, 334; forgetfulness, 277; admired (disliked), 38, 284–45, 291, 322–4, 333, 379; love of truth, 315, 333; school of, 322; watch, 373; monuments to, 419, 428, 431; epitaph for, 431
Relations with JB. JB wishes to see in Parliament, 37, SJ to tour (tours) Scotland with, 38–9, 45, 53–6, 59, 62 (*see also under* Tour *in entry* Boswell, James); letters to JB, 38–9, 45, 52, 69, 304; JB sends books to, 52; JB impatient to be with, 132; JB on death of, 146; mentions to EB, 151–2; on JB as his biographer, 304; praises JB, 189–90, 304; records SJ's conversation in public, 314; *in vino veritas*, 310–1, 314–5; sups with JB, 314–5; calls "Bozzy", 360; JB offends, 372
Writings. Catalogue of, 44, 46, 49; political, 112; letters, 285, 292, 322–3, *see also under* Thrale, Hester; imitators of, 299–300; *Dictionary*, 238, 301, 321, *Drury Lane Prologue*, 46, 49; epigram on Cibber's odes, 44, 55; epitaphs: on Philips, 44, 55, 58, on C. Maclaurin, 261, 266–7, 277, on T. Smollett, 261, 266–7, 276–7, on Goldsmith, 431; *False Alarm*, 33, 373–4; *Idler*, 59; *Journey to the Western Islands*, 61–6, 132, 141, 190, 214, 216–7; Latin poems (poetry), 201–2, 208, 261, 289–90, 301, 303, 313, 317; *Lives of the Poets*, 78, 300, 311, 437; *Prayers and Meditations*, 243, 273, 288, 323; *Sermons*, 348; Shakespeare ed., 45, 291, 437; *Taxation No Tyranny*, 65; *Thoughts on Falkland's Islands*, 33; trans. of Dryden, 192, 241, of Crousaz, 299
Johnston, Alexander (fl. 1765–75), box-book keeper at DL, 67, 70
Johnston, John (?1729–86), of Grange, "writer", 35–6, 109, 132, 146
Johnston, Peter (1749–1837), of Carnsalloch, M.P., 315
Johnstone, Gov. George (1730–87), M.P., 45–6, 57

Macpherson, James (1736–96), 62, 65–6, 242, 253, 274, 287, 326; *Fingal*, 62; *History of Great Britain and Ireland*, 65–6
Macpherson, John (1713–65), D.D., 217
Macqueen, Rev. Donald (c. 1716–85), of Kilmuir, Skye, 205
Macqueen, Robert (1722–99), Lord Braxfield, 119
M'Sweyn, Mr. (fl. 1773), of Grissipol, Coll, 225
Maecenas, Gaius Cilnius (c. 73–8 B.C.), 372
Maitland, James (1759–1839), *styled* Viscount Maitland, M.P., 144–5
Malagrida, Gabriel (1689–1761), S.J., 130
Malden, Dr., 48
Mallet, David (c. 1705–65), poet, *William and Margaret*, 306
Mallet, Paul-Henri (1730–1807), historian, 117
Malone, Anthony (1700–76), of Baronston, Irish M.P., uncle of EM, 437
Malone, Catharine (c. 1748–1831), sis. of EM, 196, 321, 342, 335–6, 349–50, 353, 359, 383, 391
MALONE, EDMOND (1741–1812)
General. Residence, 226, house painted, 348, 354, 357, country house, 339, 345, 348, 351, 354–7; low spirits, 287, 292, 368, unhappy love life, 187, 372, allowance for S. Spencer, 386; aids Courtenay with *Poetical Review*, 287–8, 301–3, 309, 322; at Cambridge, 329–31, in Ireland, 365, 367, 369–70, 374–420, at Oxford, 300, 327, 420, in Harrogate, in Worcester, 425, in Stratford, 425–8, intends visiting Brighthelmstone, 366; dines with Agar, 272, Reynolds, 288, 322–4, 327–9, 339, 356, 375, Brocklesby, 327, Windham, 328, Cromie, 402, at Club, 340, goes to twelve dinners, 403; on Mrs. Piozzi, 310–2, 332–3, 340, 350; on Monboddo, 322–3; on W. Jephson, 381, 383–6, 388, 409; at Hastings's trial, 336–9, 341–2; as electioneer, 347–8, 352; active spirit, 368–9; cites Bacon, 372–3; newspaper characters of, 380–1, 392–3, 400, 407, 418, 437–8; early life, 392–3, 437–8; lottery ticket, 397–400, 403, 407, 414–6, 419; finances, 401; reputation, 424, 437–8; D.C.L., 425; and bust of Shakespeare, 427–8
Relations with JB. Excursions together, 196; monthly breakfast, 334; the "hairs" problem, 243, 262, 271–2; advises JB, 271, 276, 291, 297–8, 306, 309–10, 325, 330, 345, 364, 371–2, 374, 408–9; helps JB with house, 292–4, 307, helps JB with poems, 296, 298–9, 302, 339–40, 346, helps JB with reply to Mrs. Piozzi, 318–9, 321–2; does errands for JB, 355, 358, 364, 366, 380; sends JB Mrs. Piozzi's *Anecdotes*, 307, 309; JB sends Mrs. Piozzi's *Letters*, 331–2, returned, 333; JB asks encouragement (advice) from, 219, 291, 305, 354, 368–71, 393–5, 410, 413–5, 419, gets

Mason, John Monck (1726–1809), Irish M.P., 382, 391; *Comments on the Last Edition of Shakespeare's Plays*, 382
Mason, Rev. William (1724–97), poet and scholar, 37, 72, 282; *Poems of Mr. Gray*, 37, 72; *Satirical Poems*, 47
Mauchline, Ayrshire, 336, 341, 355, 365
Maty, Matthew (1718–76), M.D., librarian, *Memoirs of Chesterfield*, 73
Maxwell, William (1732–1818), D.D., 361, 373
Mecci, Francisco (fl. 1783–88), informer, 350
Metastasio, Pietro (1698–1782), Hoole's trans. of, 294
Metcalfe, Christopher (1732–94), bro. of Philip, 360
Metcalfe, Christopher-Barton (1759–1801), nephew of following, 360
Metcalfe, Philip (1733–1818), M.P., 200, 348, 360, 375, 396, 419
Metcalfe, Sophia (Andrews), wife of C.-B. Metcalfe, 360
Michel, M. (d. 1788), French tutor, 349–50
Mickle, William Julius (1735–88), Scottish poet and playwright, corrector to the Clarendon Press, 29; his play, "Chateaubriant", later *Siege of Marseilles*: JB recommends, to DG, 29, 41, 45, acts as intermediary between DG and, for, 29–30, JB warns, not to resent DG's decision about, 51, DG rejects, 29, 33, 38, 42, 45–6, 51, recommends "new-Modelling", 30–3, alterations made in, by T. Warton, 30, 32–3, 38, by J. Home, 46, DG suggests Mickle try CG, 42, Mickle intends to print, 56; and trans. of *Lusiad*, DG's subscriptions for, 33, 51–2, 57; and Gov. Johnstone, 46; will attack DG's theatrical taste, 57; "Prospects of Liberty and of Slavery", 33; *Concubine*, later *Sir Martyn*, 33
Millar, Rev. Alexander (d. 1804), 262
Miller, Thomas (1717–89), Lord Justice Clerk, *later* Lord President *and* Bt., 107
Mills, Sir Thomas (d. 1793), 47
Milton, John (1608–74) SJ's "Life" of, 78; *Paradise Lost*, 229; *Paradise Regained*, 229
Molière (1622–73), *Le Mariage Forcé*, 46
Monaco, Prince of. *See* Grimaldi
Monboddo, Lord. *See* Burnett, James
Monboddo House, Kincardineshire, 215, 285
Monsey, Messenger (1693–1788), M.D., 328
Montagu, Elizabeth (Robinson) (1720–1800), 318, 328; *Essay on Shakespear*, 234, 309, 312, 314–18, 320, 322
Montaigne, Michel de (1533–92), 288, 292
Montgomerie, Alexander (1723–69), 10th E. of Eglinton, 22
Montgomerie, Archibald (1726-96), 11th E. of Eglinton, 282, 292, 344, 352–3
Montgomerie, David (d. before 1752), of Lainshaw, father of MM, 207
Montgomerie, Hugh (1739–1819), of Skelmorlie, *later* 12th E. of Eglinton, 344, 352

O'Brien, Murrough, (1726–1808), 5th E. of Inchiquin, *later* 1st M. of Thomond, 345, 396
O'Brien, William (d. 1815), actor and dramatist, *The Duel*, 46–7, 49; *Cross Purposes*, 49–50
O'Bryen, Dennis (1755–1832), surgeon, dramatist, pamphleteer, 347–8
Oglethorpe, Gen. James Edward (1696–1785), 221
O'Hara, James (?1682–1773), 2nd B. Tyrawley, Field Marshal, 381
Oliphant, Mr. (fl. 1772), tutor, 314–5
Osborne, Francis (1751–99), *styled* M. of Carmarthen, *later* 5th D. of Leeds, 305
Ossory. *See* Upper Ossory
Ovid (43 B.C.–?17 A.D.) *Metamorphoses*, 48, 245, 292; *Amores*, 210, 244; *Epistles*, 233, 249; *Tristia*, 292; "Delphin Classics" edition, 249; trans. of, in *Tour*, 245, 270; *ment.*, 301
Owen, John (?1560–1622), *Epigrammatum*, 30
Oxford, 39–40
Oxford, University of, JB and EM visit, 300, 327; degrees and voting qualifications at, 374; EM awarded honorary D.C.L. by, 425; Ashmolean Museum, 420; Balliol College, 240; Christ Church College, 396; New College, 254–5; Pembroke College, 300, Radcliffe Library, 248; Trinity College, 295; University College, 300

Palmer, Rev. John (c. 1729–90), Unitarian minister, 316
Palmer, Rev. Joseph (1749–1829), *Zaphira*, 316
Palmer, Mary (1750–1820), *later* Countess of Inchiquin *and* Marchioness of Thomond, 345, 360, 396, 421
Palmer, Richard (c. 1714–1805), D.D., 297, 299
Palmer, Wingfield, actor, 60
Paoli, Gen. Pasquale (1725–1807), leads Corsican struggle for independence, 21–2, defeated by French, 29; arrives in London, 29; visits Scotland, 38; and DG, 38; at Wilton, 71; his London address, 29, 148; characterizes EB, 160; is told of MM's death, 363; JB mounts propaganda campaign for, 21–2, visits, in Corsica, 24–5, dines with, 29, converses with King about, 118, lodges with, in London, 148, 152, 154, 197, 243, 276; *ment.*, 109, 120, 126, 243
Parkes, Joseph (fl. 1785), EM's servant, 242
Parliament: *House of Commons*. SJ proposed for, 33; Acts and Bills concerning: Edinburgh slaughter-houses, 114–6, relief for Roman Catholics, 106–7, 109–11, Civil List reforms, 121, 126, 131, Court of Session, 141, 271, Scottish schoolmasters' salaries, 141–2, East India Company, 142–4, Quebec, 162, fortification of dockyards, 296, constitutionality of Hastings's trial, 377, importation of claret, 404, 411, libels, 411; and the American war, 103–5, 114–5, 222–3; and the Regency crisis, 347, 361, 379;

Administrations: North, 115–6, first Rockingham (1765–66), 103–5, second Rockingham (1782), 116–7, 121–2, and aftermath of Rockingham's death, 126–8, Shelburne (1782–83), 130–1, and role of Cabinet in, 130, Fox-North Coalition (1783) assumes power, 134–5, Dundas dismissed by, 135, unpopular in Scotland, 136, Ayrshire support for, 344, 353, Pitt (1783–1801), 271, 347; elections: Lancaster by-election, 306, Ayrshire by-election, 344, 352–3, Carlisle election, 370, General Election (1784), 343, Westminster by-election, 347, 353. *House of Lords*. Decisions, in Donaldson *v.* Becket, 131, Cuninghame *v.* Cuninghame, 300, 307, 319, 435–6; and Hastings trial, 337–8

Parnell, Thomas (1679–1718), *The Hermit*, 422

Parr, Samuel (1747–1825), LL.D., 323, 431

Parsons, William, (fl. 1785–1807), barrister, 396

Payne, Thomas, Sr. (1719–99), bookseller, 244, 402, 413

Payne, Thomas, Jr. (1752–1831), bookseller, 244, 402, 413

Pearne, Thomas (c. 1734–1827), Fellow of Peterhouse, Cambridge, 402

Pembroke, 10th E. of. *See* Herbert, Henry

Penn, Richard (c. 1734–1811), M.P., 370

Pennant, Thomas (1726–98), traveller and naturalist, 308

Pepys, William Weller (1740–1825), Master in Chancery, *later* Bt., 311

Percy, Anne (Gutteridge) (d. 1806), wife of following, 402

Percy, Thomas (1729–1811), D.D., Bp. of Dromore, his catalogue of SJ's writings, 44, 46; and JB: Percy advises, on Rolt and Akenside, 406, 413, asks, to soften treatment of Grainger in *Life*, 419–20; and The Club, 56, 195; EM writes to, 195, dines with, 402; wife's illness, 402; receives copy of Reynolds's *Discourse*, 425–6; acquaintance with SJ, 420; and biography of Goldsmith, 420; *Reliques of Ancient English Poetry*, 74, 306, 421; *ment.*, 382

Perry, James (1756–1821), editor of *Gazetteer*, 234, 387, 400

Perth, 47, 136

Persius, Aulus Flaccus (34–62 A.D.), *Satires*, 208

Peterborough, Bp. of. *See* Hinchliffe, John

Petty, William (1737–1805), 2nd E. of Shelburne, *later* 1st M. of Lansdowne, 115, 121, 123–4, 126–7, 130–1

Peyster, Lt. James de (d. 1793), artillery officer, 425–6

"Phemie". *See* Boswell, Euphemia

Philip II (1527–98), King of Spain, 109

Philips, Claudius Charles (d. 1732), violinist, 44, 55, 58

Piers, Sir Pigott William (1742–1798), Bt., of Tristernagh, 385–6

Pindar, Peter. *See* Wolcot, John

Pinkerton, John (1758–1826), *Ancient Scottish Poems*, 291; *Letters of Literature,* 291
Piozzi, Mrs. *See* Thrale, Hester Lynch (Salusbury)
Piozzi, Gabriel Mario (1740–1809), Italian musician, 2nd husband of Hester Thrale, 311, 340, 333, 350
Pitt, Christopher (1699–1748), translator, 245
Pitt, William (1708–78), 1st E. of Chatham, 51, 222–3, 247
Pitt, William (1759–1806), the younger, 242, 305, 344, 347, 362, 404
Plymouth, Devon, 296, 299
Plymsell, John (fl. 1790–99), compositor and printer, 372, 395
Pomfret, 2nd E. of. *See* Fermor, George
Ponte Nuovo, Corsica, battle of, 29
Pope, Alexander (1688–1744), parodies Addison, 66; grotto at Twickenham, 196; and Warburton, 297; *Epilogue to the Satires*, 33, 132; *Elegy to an Unfortunate Lady*, 36; edition of Shakespeare, 54, 357, 382, 437; *Dunciad*, 56, 66; *Lines on Curll*, 66; *Spring*, 71; *Essay on Man*, 118, 146, 291, 299; *Imitations of Horace*, 104, 126, 292; *Rape of the Lock*, 231; trans. of Homer, 242; trans. of Ovid, 245; *Verses on a Grotto*, 219, 241
Portland, 2nd D. of. *See* Bentinck, William
Portland, 3rd D. of. *See* Bentinck, William Henry
Portsmouth, Hants., 27, 296, 299
Pottinger, Richard (d. 1794), Clerk of the Privy Seal, 312
Postal Service, franks and franking, 355, 375, 420–1; post days, 325; post-route for Auchinleck, 253, 324–5, 333, 341, 346, 355, 365
Presto (fl. 1770s), dog, 316
Preston, Sir George (1702–79), of Valleyfield, Bt., 70
Preston, Robert (1740–1834), M.P., 358
Prestongrange, Lord. *See* Grant, William
Prince of Wales. *See* George Augustus Frederick
Pringle, Sir John (1707–82), Bt., M.D., 22, 117, 429
Pringle, John (1716–92), M.P., 123
Pringle, John (1741–1811), professor, 274
Pringle, Mark (1754–1812), M.P., 123
Pritchard, Hannah (Vaughan) (1711–68), actress, 53
Provence, Comte de. *See* Bourbon, Louis-Stanislaus-Xavier de
Puget, John (d. 1805), merchant, 386

Quevedo y Villegas, Francisco Gomez de (1580–1645), 376
Quyney, Richard (d. 1602), 427

Raasay, Isle of, 214
Ramus, Nicholas (d. 1779), page in King's Household, 22
Raphael (Raffaello da Urbino) (1483–1520), 438
Rattakin (Rattachan), Inverness-shire, 156
Reed, Isaac (1742–1807), editor, 57, 239, 251, 330, 350, 360, 378, 382, 392, 416

Shackleton, Richard (1726–92), Quaker, 153
Shakespeare, William (1564–1616), spelling of his name, 54; editions of works: Blair-Warburton ed. (1753), 30–1, early editions of, 45, 54, 382, Johnson-Steevens (1778), 291, 357, 378, 381–2, 386–7, 414, 424, 437, *see also* Malone, Edmond, writings; Jubilee at Stratford, 57, 69; EM researches life of, 425, whitewashes bust of, 427; *Hamlet*, 39, 66, 68, 76, 342, 350, 357, 386, *Macbeth*, 53–4, 68, 278, 287, 313, 381, 423, 429, *Much Ado about Nothing*, 43, 68, 288, 424, *Richard II*, 65, *1 Henry IV*, 111, *2 Henry IV*, 299, 421, *Midsummer Night's Dream*, 117, *Measure for Measure*, 137, *All's Well That Ends Well*, 229, *King Lear*, 229, *Othello*, 241, 357, *Twelfth Night*, 234, *Romeo and Juliet*, 357, *Titus Andronicus*, 357, sonnets and poems, 357, *1, 2, 3 Henry VI*, 379
Sharp, Richard (1759–1835) ("Conversation Sharp"), 282, 416
Shelburne, 2nd E. of. *See* Petty, William
Sheffield, Yorks., 103, 108
Sheridan, Richard Brinsley (1751–1816), son of following, dramatist and M.P., 57, 75, 100, 296, 336–8
Sheridan, Thomas (1719–88), actor, lecturer, and author, *Life of Swift*, 437
Siddons, Sarah (Kemble) (1755–1831), actress, 70
Simpson, Joseph (1721–c. 1773), friend of SJ's, 333
Sixtus V (1521–90), Pope, 109
Skye, Isle of, 54, 56, 222–3
Smith, Adam (1723–90), 144–5, 313, 352
Smith, James (c. 1681–c. 1734), M.P., 412
Smollett, James (d. 1775), Commissary of Edinburgh, cousin of following, 277
Smollett, Tobias (1721–71), 57, 266, 277
Solicitor-General (Scotland). *See* Haldane, Patrick and Home, Alexander (1746–55); Montgomery, James and Garden, Francis (1760–64); Campbell, Ilay (Feb.–Aug. 1783); Wight, Alexander (Oct. 1783–84)
Sollacarò, Corsica, 21
Spencer, Lady. *See* Spencer, Margaret
Spencer, Margaret Georgiana (Poyntz) (1736–1814), Countess, 38
Spencer, Susanna (fl. 1769–1801), 386
Spottiswoode, John (d. 1805), of Spottiswoode, solicitor, 307
Staindrop, Co. Durham, 207, 219
Stalker, Charles (fl. 1788–93), bookseller, 355
Stanhope, Philip Dormer (1694–1773), 4th E. of Chesterfield, 73, 415, 418, *Memoirs and Letters*, 73
Steevens, George (1736–1800) editor, DG sends a Mickle proof sheet to, 57; and JB: praises JB's projected *Life* of SJ, 194, supplies, with Johnsoniana for, 361,

Steevens, George (*cont.*): discourages, about, 394–5, 405; owns SJ's watch, 373; writes pseudonymous attacks on friends, 283; and EM: considers EM his editorial heir, 378, "dryness" between, 378, brings out new ed. of Shakespeare to rival EM's, 381–2, 387, 414, comments on EM- Macklin controversy, 389; and The Club, 381, 389; associated with *European Magazine*, 392; Johnson-Steevens ed. of Shakespeare, 291, 357, 378, 381–2, 386–7, 391, 414, 424, 437; *ment.*, 193–5, 244, 300, 323
Stepney, George (1663–1707), trans. of Juvenal, 270
Sterne, Laurence (1713–68), *Tristram Shandy*, 306
Stevenson, Mrs. (fl. 1775–90), headmistress, 340, 351
Stewart, Dugald (1753–1828), philosopher, 274
Stockdale, John (c. 1749–1814), bookseller, 405
Stourbridge Fair, Cambridge, 239
Strahan, William (1715–85), King's Printer, 33, 62, 217, 360
Strasbourg, 22–3, 433–4
Stratford-upon-Avon, 36, 57, 69, 425–8
Strawberry Hill, Twickenham, 196
Streatham, Middlesex, 198, 273, 421
Strutt, Joseph (1749–1802), author, antiquary, 199, 268
Stuart, Lt.-Col. the Hon. James Archibald (1747–1818), 117, 144–5
Stuart, John (1744–1814), *styled* Lord Mountstuart, *later* 4th E. *and* 1st M. of Bute, 116–7
Stuart, Margaret (Cunyinghame) (d. 1808), wife of Lt.-Col. James Stuart, 117
Stuart, House of, 206, 223
Sturz, Helfrich Peter (1736–1779), German diplomat and writer, 22
Suetonius Tranquillus, Gaius (c. 69–c. 140 A.D.), *Lives of the Twelve Caesars*, 233
Sumner, Robert Carey (1729–71), D.D., Headmaster of Harrow, 322–3
Sunderlin, B. *See* Malone, Richard
Sutton, Lt.-Col. John (fl. 1786–90), 376
Swift, Jonathan (1667–1745), 255, 291; *Battle of the Books*, 45; *Gulliver's Travels*, 355
Sydenham, Thomas (1624–89), M.D., *Methodus Curandi Febres*, 248

Tacitus, Caius Cornelius (55–120 A.D.), 338
Tasso, Torquato (1544–95), Hoole's trans. of, 294
Taylor, Rev. John (1711–88), LL.D., 71, 348
Taylor, Michael Angelo (c. 1757–1834), M.P., 412
Taylor, Sir Robert (1714–88), architect, 412
Temple, Anne (b. 1772), eldest dau. of W. J. Temple, 369
Temple, Henry (1739–1802), 2nd V. Palmerston, 377, 379
Temple, Rev. William Johnson (1739–96), 25–6, 37, 146, 358, 369; "Sketch of Mr Gray", 37,

72; *Moral and Historical Memoirs*, 113–4

Terence (Publius Terentius Afer) (?195–?159 B.C.), *Eunuch*, 61, 371; *Andria*, 371; *Heautontimorumenos*, 371

Thornton, Bonnell (1724–68), writer, 193

Thrale, Henry (c. 1728–81), M.P., brewer, 69, 311, 335, 350, 396

Thrale, Hester Lynch (Salusbury) (1741–1821), *later* Mrs. Piozzi, wife of preceding, and SJ: Mrs. Thrale tours France with, 69, hears from, about *Lives of Poets*, 78, SJ's terms of endearment for, 307, SJ on her inattention to truth, 315, Mrs. Thrale gathers his letters for publication, 329, *see also* Anecdotes *and* Letters *below*; lets Streatham house while in Italy, 273; and JB: JB reports dispute over Mrs. Montagu in *Tour*, 234, 249, 317–21, taxes her with forgetfulness, 315, Mrs. Thrale reads his Hebridean journal, 318, 322, JB publishes his *Ode by SJ to Mrs. T.*, 335, satirical poems about, 339–40, *see also* Anecdotes *and* Letters *below*; lampooned by Peter Pindar, 302; and EM: EM comments on her Johnsoniana, 308–12, 122–3, resents and abuses, 333–40, 350, *see also* Anecdotes *and* Letters *below*; and Mrs. Montagu, 308–9, 312, 314–8, 320, 322; her marriage to Gabriel Piozzi, 311, 315, 339–40, 350; Baretti abuses, in his "Strictures", 340, 350–1 *Anecdotes of SJ*: published, 307–8, EM's reaction to, 308–12, Mrs. Thrale and SJ in: her stories differing from JB's versions in *Tour*, 308, 310–2, 316, on recording SJ's conversation, 314, SJ on her *littleness*, 314; JB: represented in, 308–10, 314–5, vows to "trim", 314, 318, compares, to cherries in brandy, 317, replies to her Postscript, 321–2, 326; "elucidations and corrections" of, by Reynolds and Seward, 324; *Letters to and from SJ*: published, 332, JB disappointed with, 322, EM's reaction to, 322–3, SJ's condemnation of her marriage omitted from, 338; *ment.*, 150, 217

Thrale, Hester Maria ("Queeney") (1764–1857), dau. of preceding, *later* Viscountess Keith, 69, 333, 340

Thurlow, Edward (1731–1806), 1st B. Thurlow, Lord Chancellor, 292, 305, 343–4

Thynne, Thomas (1734–96), 3rd V. Weymouth, *later* 1st M. of Bath, 107

Tillotson, John (1630–94), D.D., Archbp. of Canterbury, 42

Tighe, Edward (fl. 1753–97), Irish M.P., 364, 392

Tighe, George William (1776–1837), son of preceding, 364, 366

Titian (Tiziano Vecellio) (1570–1650), 302

Tomlins, Thomas Edlyne (1762–1841), corrector at Baldwin's, 395

Vyse, William (1742–1816), D.D., son of preceding, 428
Waller, Edmund (1606–87), 78, 371
Waller, Edmund (d. 1771), M.P., great-grandson of preceding, 225
Walpole, Horace (1717–97), *later* 4th E. of Orford, 26, 47, 60, 312; Epilogue for *Braganza*, 364
Walsingham, Capt. Robert Boyle, R.N., 74
Warburton, William (1698–1779), D.D., Bp. of Gloucester, 212, 220, 297, 360, 406; ed. of Shakespeare, 31, 54, 382; *Doctrine of Grace*, 213
Warren, Richard (1731–97), M.D., 288, 366, 377, 380, 388–9, 403–4, 412
Warton, Joseph (1722–1800), D.D., 37–8, 75, 195, 360, 390, 396
Warton, Rev. Thomas (1728–90), Poet Laureate, 30, 32–3, 37–8, 45, 195, 282–3, 295, 319
Warwick, Sir Philip (1609–83), M.P., *Memoires of the Reigne of King Charles I*, 294
Watson, Prof. Robert (c. 1730–81), Principal of St. Salvator's College, Univ. of St. Andrews, 204
Watson-Wentworth, Charles (1730–82), 2nd M. of Rockingham, 103, 121, 123, 126–7, 130–1, 379
Wedderburn, Alexander (1733–1805), Attorney-General *later* 1st B. Loughborough, 109
Wentworth Woodhouse, Yorks., 130
Westmeath, Ireland, 166
Wetherell, Nathan (1726–1807), D.D., Master of University College, Oxford, 300
Weymouth, 3rd V. *See* Thynne, Thomas
Wharton, Charles Henry (1748–1833), *A Poetical Epistle to George Washington*, 113
Wheeler, Thomas (fl. 1769–76), post-receiver in London, 29
Wherlings, Jeremiah (c. 1720–1811), Mayor of Carlisle, 368
Whitaker, Rev. John (1735–1808), 65–6; *Genuine History of the Britons*, 65; *History of Manchester*, 65
White, Benjamin (d. 1794), bookseller, 402
White, Benjamin (fl. 1785–98), son of preceding, bookseller, 402, 413
Whitefield, Rev. George (1715–70), Methodist preacher, 31
Whitehead, William (1715–85), Poet Laureate, "To Mr. Garrick", 74
Wight, Alexander (d. 1793), Solicitor-General, 135
Wilhelmina Carolina (1743–87), Princess of Orange, 330
Wilkes, John (1727–97), M.P., and JB: friendship with, 206, receives *LPS 85* from, 236, dines with, 376, comments on *Tour*, 217, 257–8, 265, 272, 299, ridicules JB's feudal pretensions, 236, 319; EB makes Latin pun about, 206–8; satirizes SJ's biographers, 217, 235, 320; and *North Briton*, 239, 304; *ment.*, 198–9
Wilkes, Richard (1691–1760), M.D., "Epitaph on Philips", 58

Williams, Anna (1706–83), *Miscellanies in Prose and Verse*, 44
Wilmot, John (1647–80), 2nd E. of Rochester, *Allusion to Horace*, 422
Wilton House, Wiltshire, 77
Windham, William (1750–1810), M.P., and SJ: and Scottish response to *Journey*, 62, correspondence with, 329, friendship with, 200, on committee for monument to, 419; and JB: Windham invited to dine with, 155, comments on *Tour*, 200, 230, advises, in Macdonald dispute, 294–5; and EM: friendship with, 200, comments on his Shakespeare ed., 377; at The Club, 200, 390, 399; manager at Hastings's trial, 337; dines at Reynolds's, 328, 379; and French Revolution, 366, 426; *ment.*, 196, 244, 399
Windsor Castle, 160
Wittenberg, Albrecht (1728–1807), German writer, translates *Tour*, 218–9
Woburn Abbey, Beds., 391
Woffington, Margaret ("Peg") (c. 1714–60), actress, 375
Woffington, Mary. *See* Cholmondeley, Mary
Wolcot, Rev. John (1738–1819) ("Peter Pindar"), M.D., 289, 318; *Poetical Epistle*, 295–6, 304; *Bozzy and Piozzi*, 302
Woodward, Henry (1714–77), actor, 24–5, 32
Worcester, 425
Wraxall, Sir Nathaniel William (1751–1831), Bt., M.P., 285–6

Yates, Mary Ann (Graham) (1728–87), wife of following, actress, 50, 64
Yates, Richard (?1706–96), actor, 50
York, Archbp. of. *See* Drummond, Robert Hay (1761–76); Markham, William (1777–1807)
York, 279, 282, 341
Young, Arthur (1741–1820), *Farmer's Tour through the East of England*, 132
Young, Charles, clerk, 67–8, 70
Young, Edward (1683–1765), D.C.L., biographies of, 300; *Night Thoughts*, 60; *Love of Fame*, 61, 116
Young, Thomas (fl. 1767), actor, 67